MENTAL
ILLNESS

Richard John Kosciejew

ARPress
ILLUMINATING IDEAS
EMPOWERING VOICES

ARPress
45 Dan Road Suite 36
Canton MA 02021

Hotline: 1(800) 220-7660
Fax: 1(855) 752-6001

Ordering Information:
Quantity Sales. Special discounts are available on quantity purchases by corporations, associations, and others. For details, contact the publisher at the address above.

Printed in the United States of America.
Library of Congress Control Number
ISBN-13   Softcover   979-8-89389-186-7
           eBook   979-8-89389-185-0
Library of Congress Control Number: 2024914541

Perhaps there are other avenues taken as forwarding through MENTAL ILLNESS, rather than the development on which MENTAL ILLNESS bases itself on mere generalization. Deriving among such comparative methods as representational conceptuality, as in the mind, a thought, or notion, containing the best of all possible explanations, and to a better understanding for what really should, Be, however, in the finding of only to the bodily things, of bodily things only, and only of bodily things.

To whatever conclusions can be drawn from this, it is as much ado about its own obviousness. But, nonetheless, it is an important part in the belief of a phenomenal world, a world beset on prenominal experience. Such an assemblage of information, must first take issue to derive from their categorical presentations for the existing sense of control, the effect or affect of underlying displacement or discouraging accounts of estrangement depend upon a better understanding and the best of possible explanations for which is not to be expected, even to expect of expectation. What is more important, is to leave of open to a closed condition?

AN INTRODUCTION

Neurophysiology is the study of how nerve cells, or neurons, receives and transmits information. Two types of phenomena are involved in processing nerve signals - electrical and chemical. Electrical events propagate a signal within a neuron, and chemical processes transmit the signal from one neuron to another neuron or to a muscle cell.

A neuron is a long cell that has a thick central area containing the nucleus, it also has one long process called an axon and one or more short, bushy processes called dendrites. Any of the impulse-conducting cells that constitute the brain, spinal column, and nerves, consisting of a nucleated cell body with one or more dendrites and a single axon, also called a nerve cell. As the axon is usually a long process of nerve fibre that generally conducts impulses away from the body of the nerve cell.

Dendrites receive impulses from other neurons. (The exceptions are sensory neurons, such as those that transmit information about temperature or touch, in which the signal is generated by specialized receptors in the skin.) These impulses are propagated electrically along the cell membrane to the end of the axon. At the tip of the axon the signal is chemically transmitted to an adjacent neuron or muscle cell. The dendrite is a mineral crystallizing in another mineral in the form of branching or treelike marks. A

1

branching protoplasmic extension of a nerve cell that conducts impulses from adjacent cells inward toward the cell body, as a single nerve cell posses many dendrites, and also called a dendron.

Like all other cells, neurons contain charged ions: Potassium and sodium (positively charged) and chlorine (negatively charged). Neurons differ from other cells in that they are able to produce a nerve impulse. A neuron is polarized - that is, it has an overall negative charge inside the cell membrane because of the high concentration of chlorine ions and low concentration of potassium and sodium ions. The concentration of these same ions is exactly reversed outside the cell. This charge differential represents stored electrical energy, sometimes referred to as membrane potential or resting potential. The negative charge inside the cell is maintained by two features. The first is the selective permeability of the cell membrane, which is more permeable to potassium than sodium. The second feature is sodium pumps within the cell membrane that actively pump sodium out of the cell. When depolarization occurs, this charge differential across the membrane is reversed, and a nerve impulse is produced.

Depolarization is a rapid change in the permeability of the cell membrane, depolarizing to remove the outlook from a particular influence or control of a partial or completely eliminating counter-interacting polarity, or condition of polarity, as a condition of polarization as a process or state of opposing attributes or principles that partially or complete separation of positive and negative electric charge in a nuclear, atomic, molecular or chemical system.

When sensory input or any other kind of stimulating current is received by the neuron, the membrane permeability is changed, allowing a sudden influx of sodium ions into the cell. The high concentration of sodium, or action potential, changes, on the whole, from that which of one end to another intention of something, especially the charges from that within the cell from its negative to the positive, as the local changes in ion concentration triggers similar reactions along the membrane, by its propagating of the nerve impulse. An impelling force for bearing an interactive surge in bettering the electric current or voltage, in one direction, the electrochemical transmission of a signal along a nerve fibre produces an excitatory or inhibitory response at a target tissue or acting upon an impulse.

Subsequently, it was announced that the refractory period, during which the ionic concentration for reserving to the resting potential, the neuron can repeat this process. Nerve impulses travel at different speeds, depending on the cellular composition of a neuron. Where the acceleration of impulse is important, as in the nervous system, axons are insulated with a membranous substance called myelin. The insulation provided by myelin maintains the ionic charge over long distances. Nerve impulses are propagated at specific points along the myelin sheath; These points are called the Nodes of Ranvier. Examples of myelinated axons are those in sensory nerve fibres and nerves connected to skeletal muscles. In non-myelinated cells, the nerve impulse is propagated more diffusely.

When the electrical signal reaches the tip of an axon, it stimulates small presynaptic situations in front of or occurring before a synapse called neurotransmitter vesicles, is released into the microscopic space between neurons (the synaptic cleft). The neurotransmitter connects and attaches upon the surface of the adjacent neuron. This stimulus causes the adjacent cell to depolarize and propagate an action potential of its own. The duration of a stimulus from a neurotransmitter is limited by the breakdown of the chemicals in the synaptic cleft and the reuptake by the neuron that produced them. Formerly, each neuron was thought to make only one transmitter, but recent studies have shown that an unspecified number or quantity as inferring that a determinant amount in which the significance to believe or progress in the use of some acceptation that cells that can or in the probability of affecting the possibility as having two or more.

During the early 1900s, in examining the workings of the nervous system, physiologists were beginning to explore the idea that the transmission of nerve impulses takes place, in part, via chemical means. Loewi decided to explore this idea. During a stay in London in 1903, he met Sir Dale, who was also interested in the chemical transmission of nerve impulses. However, for Loewi, Dale, and all the other researchers pursuing a chemical transmitter of nerve impulses, years of effort produced no solid evidence. In 1921 Loewi suspended two frogs' hearts in solution, one with a major nerve removed. Removing fluid from the heart that still contained the nerve, and injecting the fluid into the nerveless heart, Loewi observed that the second heart behaved as if the missing nerve were present. The nerves, he concluded, that nerves do not act directly on the heart - it is the action of chemicals, freed by the stimulation of nerves, that causes increases in heart rate and other functional changes. In 1926 Loewi and his colleagues identified one of the chemicals in his experiment as acetylcholine. This was indisputably a neurotransmitter - a chemical that serves to transmit nerve impulses in the involuntary nervous system.

We acknowledge the neurotransmitters are inherently made by chemically induced neurons, or nerve cells. Neurons send out neurotransmitters as chemical signals to activate or inhibit the function of neighbouring cells.

Within the central nervous system, which consists of the brain and the spinal cord, neurotransmitters pass from neuron to neuron. In the peripheral nervous system, which is made up of the nerves that run from the central nervous system to the rest of the body, the chemical signals pass between a neuron and an adjacent muscle or gland cells.

Chemical compounds - belonging to three chemical families - are widely recognized as neurotransmitters. In addition, certain other body chemicals, including adenosine, histamine, enkephalins, endorphins, and epinephrine, have neurotransmitterlike properties. Experts believe that there are many more neurotransmitters as yet undiscovered.

The first of the three families is composed of amines, a group of compounds containing molecules of carbon, hydrogen, and nitrogen. Among the amines neurotransmitters are acetylcholine, norepinephrine, dopamine, and serotonin. Acetylcholine is the most widely used neurotransmitter in the body, and neurons that leave the central nervous system (for example, those running to skeletal muscle) use acetylcholine as their neurotransmitter; neurons that run to the heart, blood vessels, and other organs may use acetylcholine or norepinephrine. Dopamine is involved in the movement of muscles, and it controls the secretion of the pituitary hormone prolactin, which triggers milk production in nursing mothers.

The second neurotransmitter family is composed of amino acids, organic compounds containing both an amino group (NH2) and a carboxylic acid group (COOH). Amino acids that serve as neurotransmitters include glycine, glutamic and aspartic acids, and gamma-amino butyric acid (GABA). Glutamic acid and GABA are the most abundant neurotransmitters within the central nervous system, and especially in the cerebral cortex, which is largely responsible for such higher brain functions as thought and interpreting sensations.

The third neurotransmitter family is composed of peptides, which are compounds that contain at least two, and sometimes as many as 100 amino acids. Peptide neurotransmitters are poorly understood, but scientists know that the peptide neurotransmitter called substance P influences the sensation of pain.

In general, each neuron uses only a single compound as its neurotransmitter. However, some neurons outside the central nervous system are able to release both an amine and a peptide neurotransmitter.

Neurotransmitters are manufactured from precursor compounds like amino acids, glucose, and the dietary amine-called choline. Neurons modify the structure of these precursor compounds in a series of reactions with enzymes. Neurotransmitters that comes from amino acids include serotonin, for which it is derived from tryptophan. Dopamine and norepinephrine, are derived from tyrosine, and glycine, which is derived from threonine, norepinephrine, maintains the substance, both a hormone and a neurotransmitter, secreted by the adrenal medulla and the nerve endings of the sympathetic nervous system to cause vasoconstriction and increase in heart rat e, blood pressure, and the sugar level of th e blood. Among the neurotransmitters made from glucose are glutamate, aspartate, and GABA, choline serves as the precursor for acetylcholine

Neurotransmitters, are kept from weakening by maintaining of a chemical substance, such as acetylcholine or dopamine that transmits nerve impulses across a synapse. These, of the supporting substances undergo the synapsis, for which a side-by-side connection of homologous paternal and material chromosomes during the proper phasing of meiosis, are, nonetheless, the junction across which a nerve impulse passes from an axon terminal to a neuron, muscle or gland cells, such that of pointing directly for being the synapse.

The neurotransmission is significantly relevant in the information for with a reinforcing subsequent in driving a response for an introduction by which a response to the varying transmissions, by some unconditional stimulus along with such meaning, is open to a given impulse, like that in which the reinforcing condition or original occurs, the state or quality for being implied at meaning. If a word by singularity . . . signifying of such indications to indicate of one's linguistic unit or pattern, for being as a succession of speech sounds, can be written or by the gesturing, for which of the conveying linguistic signs. Having or likely to have an effectual cause to occur or the quality of significance to an observer or occurrences that are too closely correlated to be attributed to chance, and in this way, is to start transmissions for being a structure of instances that affect the amounting of products to progress, as already established to rules of conduct, in that to ensure the compliance within the biochemical reaction or process was enacted by a reactionary impulse or the response for which the retributive composition for any the detrimental agreeing as that which a compromise of that which is mutually agreeing, a difference from which each side makes concessions among the resulting integrations as to combine qualities or elements of the different things.

All and all, correlated to a linguistic form or construction that a singularized process, is, nonetheless, to rehabilitate, from a disability and restore the advocacy upon the biochemistry of a sustainable and vital process for occurring in living organisms. Biological chemistry, psychological chemistry being the chemical composition of a particular living system or biological substance, along the lines as the principal chemical compound, whose position takes of the fact upon which the transmitted intent or given to an impulsive force that releases into a microscopic gap, the minute space between the cell membrane of an axon terminal and that of the target cell with which it has the synapsis. Separating the transmitting neuron from the cell receiving the chemical signal, which generates the signal is called the presynaptic cell, while the receiving cell is termed the postsynaptic cell.

After their release into the synapse, neurotransmitters combine chemically with highly specific protein molecules, termed receptors, that are embedded in the surface membranes of the postsynaptic cell. When this combination occurs, the voltage, or electrical force, of the postsynaptic cell is either increased (excited) or decreased (inhibited).

When a neuron is in its resting state, its voltage is about -70 millivolts. An excitatory neurotransmitter alters the membrane of the postsynaptic neuron, making it possible for ions (electrically charged molecules) to move back and forth, as if oscillating across the neuron's membranes. This flow of ions makes the neuron's voltage rise toward zero. If enough excitatory receptors have been activated, the postsynaptic neuron responds by firing, generating a nerve impulse that causes its own neurotransmitter to be released into the next synapse. An inhibitory neurotransmitter causes differentiations that allow for the passing of oscillation across the postsynaptic neuron's membrane, lowering the nerve cell's voltage to -80 or -90 millivolts. The drop in voltage makes it less likely that the postsynaptic cell will fire.

If the postsynaptic cell is a muscle cell rather than a neuron, an excitatory neurotransmitter will give to cause the muscle to contract. If the postsynaptic cell is a gland cell, an excitatory neurotransmitter will cause the cell to secrete its collective contents.

While most neurotransmitters interact with their receptors creating new electrical nerve impulses that energize or inhibit the bordering cell, some neurotransmitter interactions, but not to generate or suppress nerve impulses. Instead, they interact with a second type of receptor, containing a specialized cell or group of nerve endings that responds to sensory stimuli, yet maintains a molecular structure or on the surface or interior of a cell that binds with substances such as hormones, antigens, drugs, or neurotransmitters. Nevertheless, having to change her internal chemistry of the postsynaptic cell by either causing or blocking the formation of chemicals called second messenger molecules. These second messengers regulate the postsynaptic cell's biochemical processes and enable it to conduct the maintenance necessary to continue synthesizing neurotransmitters and conducting nerve impulses. Examples of second messengers, which are formed and entirely contained within the postsynaptic cell, include cyclic adenosine monophosphate, diacylglycerol, and inositol phosphates.

Once neurotransmitters have been secreted into synapses and have passed on their chemical signals, the presynaptic neuron clears the synapse of neurotransmitter molecules. For example, acetylcholine is broken down by the enzyme acetylcholinesterase into choline and acetate. Neurotransmitters like dopamine, serotonin, and GABA is removed by a physical process called reuptake. In reuptake, the suppling of a protein in the presynaptic membrane acts as a sort of sponge, giving to cause the neurotransmitters to

9

reenter the presynaptic neuron, where they can be broken down by enzymes or repackaged for reuse.

Neurotransmitters are known to be involved in a number of conditions that act of a substance for modifying instances of disorders, including Alzheimer's disease. Victims of Alzheimer's disease suffer from loss of intellectual capacity, disintegration of personality, mental confusion, hallucinations, and aggressive - even violent - behaviour. These symptoms are the result of progressive degeneration in many types of neurons in the brain. Forgetfulness, one of the earliest symptoms of Alzheimer's disease, is partly caused by the destruction of neurons that normally release the neurotransmitter acetylcholine. Medications that increase brain levels of acetylcholine have helped restore short-term memory and reduce mood swings in some Alzheimer's patients.

Neurotransmitters also play a role in Parkinson disease, which slowly attacks the nervous system, giving to cause symptoms that worsen over time. Fatigue, mental confusion, a masklike facial expression, stooping posture, shuffling gait, and problems with eating and speaking are among the difficulties suffered by Parkinson victims. These symptoms have been partly linked to the deterioration and eventual death of neurons that run from the base of the brain to the basal ganglia, a collection of nerve cells that manufacture the neurotransmitter dopamine. The reasons why such neurons die or simple decay is yet to be understood, but the related symptoms can be alleviated. L-dopa, or levodopa, widely used to treat Parkinson's disease, acts as a supplementary precursor for dopamine. It causes the surviving neurons in the basal ganglia to increase their production of dopamine, thereby compensating to some extent for the disabled neurons.

Many other effective drugs have been shown to act by influencing neurotransmitter behaviour. Some drugs work by interfering with the interactions between neurotransmitters and intestinal receptors. For example, belladonna decreases intestinal cramps in such disorders as irritable bowel syndrome by blocking acetylcholine from combining with receptors. This process reduces nerve signals to the bowel wall, which prevents painful spasms.

Other drugs block the reuptake process. One explanation is the drug Fluoxetine (Prozac), of which blocks the reuptake of serotonin. Serotonin then remains in the synapse for a longer time, and its ability to act as a signal is also prolonged, with which this contributes to the relief of depression and the control of obsessive-compulsive behaviours.

Serotonin gives to an organic compound, forming tryptophan and found in animal and human tissue, especially the brain, blood serum, and gastric mucous membrane, and active as a neurotransmitter and in vasoconstriction, stimulation of the smooth muscle, and regulation of cyclic body processes.

Dopamine, is a chemical known to be a neurotransmitter which is essential to the functioning of the central nervous system. In the process of neurotransmission, dopamine is transferred from one nerve cell, or neuron, to another, playing a key role in brain function and human behaviour. A neuron is that of any of the impulse-conducting cells that constitute the brain with one or more dendrites and a single axon, also called a nerve cell. Dendrites are given of a material as for crystalizing in another mineral and the form of branching or treelike marks. A branching of protoplasmic extensions of a nerve cell that conducts impulses from surrounding cells forcing them toward the centre of the body cell, from which a single nerve may process several dendrites,

Dopamine forms from a precursor molecule called Dopa, which is manufactured in the liver from the amino acid tyrosine. The unrelenting of Dopa as an amino acid, formed in the liver from tyrosine, which consist s of a white crystalline amino acid that is obtained from the hydrolysis of proteins, such as a casein, which is the basis of cheese and used to mask e plastics, adherents, paints, and foods, including the precursor of epinephrine, thyroxine, and melanin, the forming and which is converted to dopamine in the brain.

The arranging resultant from changes in its particular course of action to be carried from one place to another, as this integration is improved by the condition from the circulatory system, the interchanging being transposed of neurons in the brain, where the conversion to dopamine takes place.

Dopamine is capable of doing many things, mutually agreeing or serving many functions, but, nonetheless, its versatility that suggests the presence or existence of a fact, condition, or quality. The act or gesture used to convey an idea, a desire, information, or of a command that gave to display of a chemical structure, bearing upon or operations of the neurotransmitter, as manifested to approve or ratify by agreeing to the obtainable provisions of another or oneself, if to start transmissions with the departure of another or oneself by one's enlisting associations within the standing representation, and for immortal life. Among its many functions, it plays a major role in two activities of the central nervous system: One that helps control movement, and a second, that are strongly associated with emotionally-based behaviours.

The pathway involved in movement control is called the nigrostriatal pathway. Dopamine is released by neurons that originate from an area of the brain called the substantia nigra and connect to the part of the brain known as the corpora striata, an area known to be important in controlling the musculoskeletal system.

The second brain pathway in which dopamine plays a major role is called the mesocorticolimbic pathway, as neurons in an area of the brain called, the ventral tegmentalarea transmits dopamine to other neurons connected to various parts of the limbic system, which is responsible for regulating emotion, motivation, behaviour, the sense of smell, and variously autonomic, or involuntary, functions like heartbeat and breathing. A growing body of evidence suggests that dopamine is involved in several major brain disorders. Narcolepsy, a disorder characterized of brief, recurring episodes of sudden, deep sleep, is associated with abnormally high levels of both dopamine and a second neurotransmitter, as acetylcholine. As chorea, an inherited, fatal illness in which neurons in the base of the brain are progressively destroyed, is also linked to an excess of dopamine and any of various disorders of the nervous system marked by involuntary, jerky movements, especially of the arms, legs, and face, and by incoordination.

Commonly known as shaking palsy, Parkinson's disease is another brain disorder in which dopamine is involved. Besides tremors of the limbs, Parkinson patients suffer from muscular rigidity, which leads to difficulties in walking, writing, and speaking. This disorder results from the degeneration and death of neurons in the nigrostriatal pathway, resulting in low levels of dopamine. The symptoms of Parkinson disease can be minimized by treatment with a drug called levodopa, or L-dopa, of that which is an amino acid that is the metabolic precursor of dopamine and is converted in the brain into dopamine and used in synthetic form to treat Parkinson's disease.

Schizophrenia is a psychiatric disorder characterized by loss of contact with reality and major changes in personality. Schizophrenics have normal levels of dopamine in the brain, but because they are highly sensitive to this neurotransmitter, these normal levels of dopamine triggers unusual behaviours. Drugs such as thorazine that blocks the action of dopamine have been found to decrease the symptoms of schizophrenia.

Of, relating to, or having a personality disorders marked by extreme shyness, flatten effect, reclusiveness, discomfort with others, and an inability to form close relationships of, or relating to, or suggestive of schizophrenia . . . that schizoid is no-longer used in the scientific terminological phrasing but is characterized by the coexistence of disparate or antagonistic elements.

Studies indicate that people who are addicted to alcohol and other drugs like, cocaine and nicotine, have less amounts or a degree over which the valuation of dopamine is expended by a lower count of potential as gathered in the extent of dopamine in the mesocorticolimbic pathway. These drugs appear to increase dopamine levels, resulting in the pleasurable feelings associated with the drugs.

A serotonin, neurotransmitter, or chemical that transmits messages across the synapses, or gap, between adjacent cells, among its many functions, serotonin is released from blood cells called platelets to activate blood vessel constriction and blood clotting. In the gastrointestinal tract, serotonin inhibits gastric acid production and stimulates muscle contraction in the intestinal wall. Its functions in the central nervous system and effects on human behaviour - including mood, memory, and appetite control - have been the subject of a great deal of research. This intensive study of serotonin has revealed important knowledge about the serotonin-related cause and treatment of many illnesses.

Serotonin is produced in the brain from the amino acid tryptophan, which is derived from foods high in protein, such as meat and dairy products. Tryptophan is transported to the brain, where it is broken down by enzymes to produce serotonin. In the process of neurotransmission, serotonin is transferred from one nerve cell, or neuron, to another, triggering an electrical impulse that stimulates or inhibits cell activity as needed. Serotonin is then reabsorbed by the first neuron, in a process known as reuptake, where it is recycled and used again or converted into an inactive chemical form and excreted.

While the complete picture of serotonin's function in the body is still being investigated, many disorders are known to be associated with an imbalance of serotonin in the brain. Drugs that manipulate serotonin levels have been used to alleviate the symptoms of serotonin imbalances. Some of these drugs, known as selective serotonin reuptake inhibitors (SSRIs), block or inhibit the reuptake of serotonin into neurons, enabling serotonin to remain active in the synapses for a longer period of time. These medications are used to treat such psychiatric disorders as depression; Obsessive-compulsive disorder, in which repetitive and disturbing thoughts trigger bizarre, ritualistic behaviours, and impulsive aggressive behaviours. Fluoxetine (more commonly known by the brand name Prozac), is a widely prescribed SSRI used to treat depression, and more recently, obsessive-compulsive disorder.

Drugs that affect serotonin levels may prove beneficial in the treatment of nonpsychiatric disorders as well, including diabetic neuropathy (degeneration of nerves outside the central nervous system in diabetics) and premenstrual syndrome. Recently the serotonin-releasing agent dexfenfluramine has been approved for patients who are 30 percent or, moreover, their ideal body weight. By preventing serotonin reuptake, dexfenfluramine promotes satiety, or fullness, after eating less food.

Other drugs serve as agonists that react with neurons to produce effects similar to those of serotonin. Serotonin agonists have been used to treat migraine headaches, in which low levels of serotonin cause arteries in the brain to swell, resulting in a headache. Sumatriptan is an agonist drug that mimics the effects of serotonin in the brain, constricting blood vessels and alleviating pain. In that which pain is an unpleasant sensation occurring in varying degrees of severity as a consequence, or injury, or emotional influence.

Drugs known as antagonists bind with neurons to prevent serotonin neurotransmission. Some antagonists have been found effective in treating the nausea that typically accompanies radiation and chemotherapy in cancer treatment. Antagonists are also being tested to treat high blood pressure and other cardiovascular disorders by blocking serotonin's ability to constrict blood vessels. Other antagonists may produce an effect on learning and memory in age-associated memory impairment.

The synapse, for giving to signals conveying everything that human beings sense and think, and every motion they make, follows nerve pathways in the human body as waves of ions (atoms or groups of atoms that carries electric charges). Australian physiologist Sir John Eccles discovered many of the intricacies of this electrochemical signalling process, particularly the pivotal step in which a signal is conveyed from one nerve cell to another. He shared the 1963 Nobel Prize in Physiology or medicine for this work, which he described in a 1965 Scientific American article.

How does one nerve cell transmit the nerve impulse to another cell? Electron microscopy and other methods show that it does so by means of special extensions that deliver a squirt of transmitter substance

The human brain is the most highly organized form of matter known, and in plexuities the brains of the other higher animals are not greatly inferior. For certain purposes it is expedient to regard the brain for being analogous to a machine. Even if it is so regarded, however, it is a machine of a totally different kind from those made by man. In trying to understand the workings of his own brain man meets his highest challenge. Nothing is given; There are no operating diagrams, no maker's instructions.

The first step in trying to better understand the brain by describing to what is the best of explanations, as to examine its structure in order to discover the components from which it is built and how they are related to each another. After which time, that one can attempt to understand the mode of operation of the simplest components. These two modes of investigation - the morphological and the physiological - have now become complementary. In studying the nervous system with today's sensitive electrical device, however, it is all too easy to find physiological events that cannot be correlated with any known anatomical structure. Conversely, the electron microscope reveals many structural details whose physiological significance is obscure or unknown.

At the close of the past century the Spanish anatomist Santiago Ramón Cajal showed how all parts of the nervous system are built up of individual nerve cells of many different shapes and sizes. Like other cells, each nerve cell has a nucleus and the surrounding cytoplasm. Its outer surface consists of numerous fine branches - the dendrites - that receive nerve impulses from other nerve cells, and one relatively long branch - the axon - that transmits nerve impulses. Near its end the axon divides into branches that terminate at the dendrites or bodies of other nerve cells. The axon can be as short as a fraction of a millimetre or as long as a metre, depending on its place and function. It has many of the properties of an electric cable and is uniquely specialized to conduct the brief electrical waves called nerve impulses. In very thin axons these impulses travel at less than one metre per second; In others, for example in the large axons of the nerve cells that activate muscles, they travel as fast as 100 metres per second.

The electrical impulse that travels along the axon ceases abruptly when it comes to the point or the gathering junction, in that which the axon's terminal fibres make contact with another nerve cell, the grouping junction was given the name "synapses" by Sir Charles Sherrington, who laid the foundations of what is sometimes called synaptology. If the nerve impulse is to continue beyond the synapse, it must be regenerated afresh on the other side. As recently as 15 years ago some physiologists held that transmission at the synapse was predominantly, if not exclusively, an electrical phenomenon. Now, however, there is abundant evidence that transmission is effectuated by the release of specific chemical substances that trigger a regeneration of the impulse. In fact, the first strong evidence showing that some transmitter substances act across the synapse was announced more than 40 years ago by Sir Henry Dale and Otto Loewi.

It has been estimated that the human central nervous system, which of course includes the spinal cord as well as the brain itself, consists of about 10 billion (1010) nerve cells. With rare exceptions each nerve cell receives information directly in the form of impulses from many other nerve cells - often hundreds - and transmits information to a like number. Depending on its threshold of response, a given nerve cell may fire an impulse when stimulated by only a few incoming fibres or it may not fire until stimulated by many incoming fibres. It has long been known that this threshold can be raised or lowered by various factors. Moreover, it was conjectured some 60 years ago that some of the incoming fibres must inhibit the firing of the receiving cell rather than excite it. The conjecture was subsequently confirmed, and the mechanism of the inhibitory effect has now been clarified. This mechanism and its equally fundamental counterpart - nerve-cell excitation - are of its topic.

At the level of anatomy there are some clues to indicate how the fine axon terminals impinging on a nerve cell can make the cell regenerate a nerve impulse of its own nerve cell and its dendrites are covered by fine branches of nerve fibres that terminate in knoblike structures. These structures are the synapses.

The electron microscope has revealed structural details of synapses that fit in nicely with the view that a chemical transmitter is involved in nerve transmission. Enclosed in the synaptic knob are many vesicles, or tiny sacs, which appear to contain the transmitter substances that induce synaptic transmission. Between the synaptic knob and the synaptic membrane of the adjoining nerve cell is a remarkably uniform space of about 20 millimicrons that is termed the synaptic cleft. Many of the synaptic vesicles are concentrated adjacent to this cleft; It seems plausible that the transmitter substance is discharged from the nearest vesicles into the cleft, where it can act on the adjacent cell membrane. This hypothesis is supported by the discovery that the transmitter is released in packets of a few thousand molecules.

The study of synaptic transmission was revolutionized in 1951 by the introduction of delicate techniques for recording electrically from the interior of single nerve cells. This is done by inserting into the nerve cell an extremely fine glass pipette with a diameter of .5 microns - about a fifty-thousandth of an inch. The pipette is filled with an electrically conducting salt solution such as concentrated potassium chloride. If the pipette is carefully inserted and held rigidly in place, the cell membrane appears to seal quickly around the glass, thus preventing the flow of a short-circuiting current through the puncture in the cell membrane. Impaled in this fashion, nerve cells can function normally for hours. Although there is no way of observing the cells during the insertion of the pipette, the insertion can be guided by using as clues the electric signals that the pipette picks up when close to active nerve cells.

At the John Curtin School of Medical Research in Canberra first employed this technique, choosing to study the large nerve cells called motoneurons, which lie in the spinal cord and whose function is to activate muscles. This was a fortunate choice: Intracellular investigations with motoneurons have proved to be easier and more rewarding than those with any other kind of mammalian nerve cell.

Finding that the nerve cell responds to the chemical synaptic transmitter, the response depends, in part, on characteristic features of ionic compositions, that are also concerned with the transmission of impulses in the cell along its axon, when the nerve cell is at rest, its physiological makeup resembles that of most other cells in that the water solution inside the cell is quite different in composition from the solution in which the cell is bathed. The nerve cell is able to exploit this difference between external and internal composition and its uses are quite different in ways for generating an electrical impulse and synaptic transmissions.

The composition of the external solution is well grounded because the solution is essentially the same as blood from which cells and proteins have been removed. The composition of the internal solution is known only approximately. Indirect evidence indicates that the concentrations of sodium and chloride ions outside the cell are respectively some 10 and 14 times higher than the concentrations inside the cell. In contrast, the concentration of potassium ions inside the cell is about 30 times higher than the concentration outside.

How can one account for this remarkable state of affairs? Part of the explanation is that inside of the cell is negatively charged with the respect of the cell by about 70 millivolts. Since like charges repel each other, this internal negative charge tends to drive chloride ions (Cl-) outward through the cell membrane and, at the same time, to impede their inward movement. In fact, a potential difference of 70 millivolts is just sufficient to maintain the observed disparity in the concentration of chloride ions inside the cell and outside it; Chloride ions diffuse inward and outward at equal rates. A drop of 70 millivolts across the membrane therefore defines the "equilibrium potential" for chloride ions.

To obtain a concentration of potassium ions (K) that is 30 times higher inside the cell than outside would require that the interior of the cell membrane be about 90 millivolts negative with respect to the exterior. Since the actual interior is only 70 negative millivolts, it falls short of the equilibrium potential for potassium ions by 20 millivolts. Evidently the thirtyfold concentration can be achieved and maintained only if there is some auxiliary mechanism for "pumping" potassium ions into the cell at a rate equal to their spontaneous net outward diffusion.

The pumping mechanisms are applicably fewer but some more difficult tasks of pumping sodium ions (Na) out of the cell against a potential gradient of 130 millivolts. This figure is obtained by adding the 70 millivolts of internal negative charge to the equilibrium potential for sodium ions, which is 60 millivolts of internal positive charge. If it were not for this postulated pump, the concentration of sodium ions inside and outside the cell would be almost the reverse of what is observed.

In their classic studies of nerve-impulse transmission in the giant axon of the squid, A. L. Hodgkin, A. F. Huxley and Bernhard Katz of Britain demonstrated that the propagation of the impulse coincides with abrupt changes in the permeability of the axon membrane. When a nerve impulse has been triggered in some way, what can be described as a gate opens and lets sodium ions pour into the axon during the advance of the impulse, making the interior of the axon locally positive. The process is self-reinforcing in that the flow of some sodium ions through the membrane opens the gate further and makes it easier for others to follow. The sharp reversal of the internal polarity of the membrane constitutes the nerve impulse, which moves like a wave until it has travelled the length of the axon. In the wake of the impulse the sodium gate closes and a potassium gate opens, thereby restoring the normal polarity of the membrane within a millisecond or less.

With this understanding of the nerve impulse in hand, one is ready to follow the electrical events at the excitatory synapse. One might guess that if the nerve impulse results from an abrupt inflow of sodium ions and a rapid change in the electrical polarity of the axon's interior, something similar must happen at the body and dendrites of the nerve cell in order to generate the impulse in the first place. Indeed, the function of the excitatory synaptic terminals on the cell body and its dendrites is to depolarize the interior of the cell membrane essentially by permitting an inflow of sodium ions. When the depolarization reaches a threshold value, a nerve impulse is triggered.

As a simple instance of this phenomenon we have recorded the depolarization that occurs in a single motoneuron activated directly by the large nerve fibres that enter the spinal cord from special stretch-receptors known as annulospiral endings. These receptors in turn are located in the same muscle that is activated by the motoneuron under study. Thus the whole system forms a typical reflex arc, such as the arc responsible for the patellar reflex, or "knee jerk."

To conduct the experiment we anaesthetized an animal (most often a cat) and free by dissection a muscle nerves that contains these large nerve fibres. By applying a mild electric shock to the exposed nerve one can produce a single impulse in each of the fibres; Since the impulses travel to the spinal cord almost synchronously, they are referred to collectively as a volley. The number of impulses contained in the volley can be reduced by reducing the stimulation applied to the nerve. The volley strength is measured at a point just outside the spinal cord and is displayed on an oscilloscope. About half a millisecond after detection of a volley there is a wavelike change in the voltage inside the motoneuron that has received the volley. The change is detected by a microelectrode inserted in the motoneuron and is displayed on another oscilloscope.

What we find is that the negative voltage inside the cell becomes progressively fewer negative as more of the fibres impinging on the cell are stimulated to fire. This observed depolarization is in fact a simple summation of the depolarization produced by each individual synapse. When the depolarization of the interior of the motoneurons reaches a critical point, a "spike" suddenly appears on the second oscilloscope, showing that a nerve impulse has been generated. During the spike the voltage inside the cell changes from about 70 millivolts negative to as much as 30 positive millivolts. The spike regularly appears when the depolarization, or reduction of membrane potential, reaches a critical level, which is usually between 10 and 18 millivolts. The only effect of a further strengthening of the synaptic stimulus is to shorten the time needed for the motoneuron to reach the firing threshold. The depolarizing potentials produced in the cell membrane by excitatory synapses are called excitatory postsynaptic potentials, or EPSP's.

Through one barrel of a double-barrelled microelectrode (a small electrode often used to study electric characteristics of living cells and tissue) one can apply a background current to change the resting potential of the interior of the cell membrane, either increasing it or decreasing it. When the potential is made more negative, the EPSP rises more steeply to an earlier peak. When the potential is made less negative, the EPSP rises more slowly to a lower peak. Finally, when the charge inside the cell is reversed so as to be positive with respect to the exterior, the excitatory synapses give rise to an EPSP that is actually the reverse of the normal one.

These observations support the hypothesis that excitatory synapses produce what amounts virtually to a short circuit in the synaptic membrane potential. When this occurs, the membrane no longer acts as a barrier to the passage of ions but lets them flow through in response to the differing electric potential on the two sides of the membrane. In other words, the ions are momentarily allowed to travel freely down their electrochemical gradients, which means that the sodium ions flow into the cell and, to a lesser degree, potassium ions flow out. It is this net flow of positive ions that creates the excitatory postsynaptic potential. The flow of negative ions, such as the chloride ions, is apparently not involved. By artificially altering the potential inside the cell one can establish that there is no flow of ions, and therefore no EPSP, when the voltage drop across the membrane is zero.

How is the synaptic membrane converted from a strong ionic barrier into an ion-permeable state? It is currently accepted that the agency of conversion is the chemical transmitter substance contained in the vesicles inside the synaptic knob. When a nerve impulse reaches the synaptic knob, some of the vesicles are caused to eject the transmitter substance into the synaptic cleft. The molecules of the substance would take only a few microseconds to diffuse across the cleft and become attached to specific receptor sites on the surface membrane of the adjacent nerve cell.

Presumably the receptor sites are associated with fine channels in the membrane that are opened in some way by the attachment of the transmitter-substance molecules to the receptor sites. With the channels thus opened, sodium and potassium ions flow through the membrane thousands of times more readily than they normally do, thereby producing the intense ionic flux that depolarizes the cell membrane and produces the EPSP. In many synapses the current flows strongly for only about a millisecond before the transmitter substance is eliminated from the synaptic cleft, either by diffusion into the surrounding regions or as a result of being destroyed by enzymes. The latter process is known to occur when the transmitter substance is acetylcholine, which is destroyed by the enzyme acetylcholinesterase.

The substantiation of this general picture of synaptic transmission requires the solution of many fundamental problems. Since we do not know the specific transmitter substance for the vast majority of synapses in the nervous system we do not know if there are many different substances or only a few. The only one identified with reasonable certainty in the mammalian central nervous system is acetylcholine. We know practically nothing about the mechanism by which a presynaptic nerve impulse causes the transmitter substance to be injected into the synaptic cleft. Nor do we know how the synaptic vesicles not immediately adjacent to the synaptic cleft ensue to moved up to the firing line to replace the emptied vesicles. It is conjectured that the vesicles contain the enzyme systems needed to recharge themselves. The entire process must be swift and efficient: the total amount of transmitter substance in synaptic terminals is enough for only a few minutes of synaptic activity at normal operating rates. There are also knotty problems to be solved on the other side of the synaptic cleft. What, for example, is the nature of the receptor sites? How are the ionic channels in the membrane opened up?

The second type of synapse that has been identified in the nervous system, in the synapse that can inhibit the firing of a nerve cell even though it may be receiving a volley of excitatory impulses? When inhibitory synapses are examined in the electron microscope, they look very much like excitatory synapses. (There are probably some subtle differences, but they need not concern us here.) The insertion of a microelectrode, the recordings of the activity of single motoneurons and other nerve cells have now shown that the inhibitory postsynaptic potential (IPSP) is virtually a mirror image of the EPSP. Moreover, individual inhibitory synapses, like

26

excitatory synapses, have a cumulative effect. The chief difference is simply that the IPSP makes the cell's internal voltage more negative than it is normally, which is in a direction opposite to that needed for generating a spike discharge.

By driving the internal voltage of a nerve cell in the negative direction inhibitory synapses oppose the action of excitatory synapses, which of course drive it in the positive direction. Hence if the potential inside a resting cell is 70 negative millivolts, a strong volley of inhibitory impulses can drive the potential to 75 or 80 millivolts depreciating count. One can easily see that if the potential is made more negative in this way the excitatory synapses find it more difficult to raise the internal voltage to the threshold point for the generation of a spike. Thus, the nerve cell responds to the algebraic sum of the internal voltage changes produced by excitatory and inhibitory synapses.

If, as in the experiment described earlier, the internal membrane potential is altered by the flow of an electric current through one barrel of a double-barrelled microelectrode, one can observe the effect of such changes on the inhibitory postsynaptic potential. When the internal potential is made less negative, the inhibitory postsynaptic potential is deepened. Conversely, when the potential is made more negative, the IPSP diminishes; it finally reverses when the internal potential is driven below minus 80 millivolts.

One can be assured that inhibitory synapses share with excitatory synapses the ability to change the ionic permeability of the synaptic membrane. The difference is that inhibitory synapses enable ions to flow freely down an electrochemical gradient that has an equilibrium point at minus 80 millivolts rather than at zero, as is the case for excitatory synapses. This effect could be achieved by the outward flow of positively charged ions such as potassium or the inward flow of negatively charged ions such as chloride, or by a combination of negative and positive ionic flows such that the interior reaches equilibrium at minus 80 millivolts.

If the concentration of chloride ions within the cell is increased as much as three times, the inhibitory postsynaptic potential reverses and acts as a depolarizing current; that is, it resembles excitatory potential. On the other hand, if the cell is heavily injected with sulfate ions, which are also negatively charged, there is no such reversal. This simple test shows that under the influence of the inhibitory transmitter substance, which is still unidentified, the subsynaptic membrane becomes permeable momentarily to chloride ions but not to sulfate ions. During the generation of the IPSP the outflow of chloride ions is so rapid that it more than outweighs the flow of other ions that generate the normal inhibitory potential.

Apart from the formate ion all the ions to which the membrane is permeable have a diameter not greater than 1.14 times the diameter of the potassium ion; That is, they are less than 2.9 angstrom units in diameter. Comparable investigations in other laboratories have found the same permeability effects, including the exceptional behaviour of the formate ion, in fishes, toads and snails. It may well be that the ionic mechanism responsible for synaptic inhibition is the same throughout the animal kingdom.

The significance of these and other meaningful studies is that they strongly indicate that the inhibitory transmitter substance opens the membrane to the flow of potassium ions but not to sodium ions. It is known that the sodium ion is somewhat larger than any of the negatively charged ions, including the formate ion, that are able to pass through the membrane during synaptic inhibition. It is not possible, however, to test the effectiveness of potassium ions by injecting excess amounts into the cell because the excess is immediately diluted by an osmotic flow of water into the cell.

The concentration of potassium ions inside the nerve cell is about 30 times greater than the concentration outside, and to maintain this large difference in concentration without the help of some metabolic pumps inside of the membrane would have to be charged 90 negative millivolts with respect to the exterior. This implies that if the membrane were suddenly made porous to potassium ions, the resulting outflow of ions would make the interiorized potential of the membrane, is, that, to the greater extent for being more negative than it is in the resting state, and that is just what happens during synaptic inhibition. The membrane must not simultaneously become porous to sodium ions, because they exist in much higher concentration outside the cell than inside and their rapid inflow would more than compensate for the potassium outflow. In fact, the fundamental difference between synaptic excitation and synaptic inhibition is that the membrane freely passes sodium ions in response to the former and largely excludes the passage of sodium ions in response to the latter.

This fine discrimination between ions that are not very different in size must be explained by any hypothesis of synaptic action. It is most unlikely that the channels through the membrane are created afresh and accurately maintained for a thousandth of a second every time a burst of transmitter substance is released into the synaptic cleft. It is more likely that channels of at least two different sizes are built directly into the membrane structure. In some way the excitatory transmitter substance would selectively unplug the larger channels and permit the free inflow of sodium ions. Potassium ions would simultaneously flow out and thus would tend to counteract the large potential change that would be produced by the massive sodium inflow. The inhibitory transmitter substance would selectively unplug the smaller channels that are large enough to pass potassium and chloride ions but not sodium ions.

To explain certain types of inhibition other features must be added to this hypothesis of synaptic transmission. In a simple hypothesis chloride and potassium ions can flow freely through pores of all inhibitory synapses. It has been shown, that, nonetheless, the inhibition of the contraction of heart muscle by the vagus nerve is due almost exclusively to potassium-ion flow. On the other hand, in the muscles of crustaceans and in nerve cells in the snail's brain synaptic inhibition is due largely to the flow of chloride ions. This selective permeability could be explained if there were fixed charges along the walls of the channels. If such charges were negative, they would repel negatively charged ions and prevent their passage; if they were positive, they would similarly prevent the passage of positively charged ions. One can now suggest that the channels opened by the excitatory transmitter are negatively charged and so do not permit the passage of the negatively charged chloride ion, even though it is small enough to move through the channel freely.

One might wonder if a given nerve cell can have excitatory synaptic action at some of its axon terminals and inhibitory action at others. The answer is no. Two different kinds of nerve cells are needed, one for each type of transmission and synaptic transmitter substance. This can readily be demonstrated by the effect of strychnine and tetanus toxins in the spinal cord; They specifically prevent inhibitory synaptic action and leave excitatory action unaltered. As a result the synaptic excitation of nerve cells is uncontrolled and convulsions result. The special types of cells responsible for inhibitory synaptic action are now being recognized in many parts of the central nervous system.

This account of communication between nerve cells is necessarily oversimplified, yet it shows that some significant advances are being made at the level of individual components of the nervous system. By selecting the most favourable situations we have been able to throw light on some details of nerve-cell behaviour. We can be encouraged by these limited successes. But the task to a better understanding are the ways that are comprehensively staggering among the operative imaginations that the human brain, is least to travel.

Our brain begins with its portion of the central nervous system contained within the skull. The brain is the control centre for movement, sleep, hunger, thirst, and virtually every other vital activity necessary to survival. All human emotions - including love, hate, fear, anger, elation, and sadness - are controlled by the brain. It also receives and interprets the countless signals that are sent to it from other parts of the body and from the external environment. The brain makes us conscious, emotional, and intelligent

The human brain has three major structural components: the large dome-shaped cerebrum, the smaller somewhat spherical cerebellum, and the brainstem. Prominent in the brainstem are the medulla oblongata and the thalamus, between the medulla and the cerebrum. The cerebrum is responsible for intelligence and reasoning. The cerebellum helps to maintain balance and posture. The medulla is involved in maintaining involuntary functions such as respiration, and the thalamus act as a relay centre for electrical impulses travelling to and from the cerebral cortex.

The adult human brain is a 1.3kg. (3-lb.) Mass of pinkish-gray jellylike tissue made up of approximately 100 billion nerve cells or neurons: The Neuroglia (supporting-tissue) cells, and vascular (blood-carrying) and other tissues.

Between the brain and the cranium - the part of the skull that directly covers the brain - are three protective membranes, or meninges. The outermost membrane, the dura mater, is the toughest and thickest. Below the dura mater is a middle membrane, called the arachnoid layer. The innermost membrane, the pia mater, consists mainly of small blood vessels and follows the contours of the surface of the brain.

A clear liquid, the cerebrospinal fluid, bathes the entire brain and fills a series of four cavities, called ventricles, near the centre of the brain. The cerebrospinal fluid protects the internal portion of the brain from varying pressures and transports chemical substances within the nervous system.

From the exterior, the brain appears as having three associatively distinctly but connected parts, the cerebrum (the Latin word for brain) - two large, almost symmetrical hemispheres; the cerebellum ('little brain') - two smaller hemispheres located at the back of the cerebrum: And the brain stem - a central core that gradually becomes the spinal cord, exiting the skull through an opening at its base called the foramen magnum. Two other major parts of the brain, the thalamus and the hypothalamus, lie in the midline above the brain stem underneath the cerebellum.

The brain and the spinal cord together make up the central nervous system, which communicates with the rest of the body through the peripheral nervous system. The peripheral nervous system consists of 12 pairs of cranial nerves extending from the cerebrum and brain stem; a system of other nerves branching throughout the body from the spinal cord, and the autonomic nervous system, which regulates vital functions that are under conscious control, such as the activity of the heart muscle, smooth muscle (involuntary muscle found in the skin, blood vessels, and internal organs), and glands.

Many motor and sensory functions have been "mapped" to specific areas of the cerebral cortex, some of which are indicated here. In general, these areas exist in both hemispheres of the cerebrum, each serving the opposite side of the body. Fewer defined are the areas of association, located mainly in the frontal cortex, operatives in functions of thought and emotion and responsible for linking input from different senses. The areas of language are an exception: Both Wernicke's area, concerned with the comprehension of spoken language, and Broca's area, governing the production of speech, have been pinpointed on the cortex.

Most high-level brain functions take place in the cerebrum. Its two large hemispheres make up approximately 85 percent of the brain's weight. The exterior surface of the cerebrum, the cerebral cortex, is a convoluted, or folded, grayish layer of cell bodies known as the gray matter. The gray matter covers an underlying mass of fibres called the white matter. The convolutions are made up of ridgelike bulges, known as gyri, separated by small grooves called sulci and larger grooves called fissures. Approximately two-thirds of the cortical surface is hidden in the folds of the sulci. The extensive convolutions enable a very large surface area of brain cortices - as roughly as, 1.5m2 (16 ft2) in an adult - to fit within the cranium. The pattern of these convolutions is similar, although not identical, in all humans.

The two cerebral hemispheres are partially separated from each other by a deep fold known as the longitudinal fissure. Communication between the two hemispheres is through several concentrated bundles of axons, called commissures, the largest of which is the corpus callosum.

Several major sulci divides the cortex into distinguishable regions. The central sulcus, or Rolandic fissure, runs from the middle of the top of each hemisphere downward, forwards, and toward another major sulcus, the lateral (side), or Sylvian, sulcus. These and other sulci and gyri divide the cerebrum into five lobes: The frontal, parietal, temporal, and occipital lobes and the insula.

Although the cerebrum is symmetrical in structure, with two lobes emerging from the brain stem and matching motor and sensory areas in each, certain intellectual functions are restricted to one hemisphere. A person's dominant hemisphere is usually occupied with language and logical operations, while the in other hemisphere (whether it is the left or the right hemisphere) controls emotion and artistic and spatial skills. In nearly all right-handed and many left-handed people, the left hemisphere is dominant.

The frontal lobe is the largest of the five and consists of all the cortices in front of the central sulcus. Broca's area, a part of the cortex related to speech, is located in the frontal lobe. The parietal lobe consists of the cortex behind the central sulcus to some sulcus near the back of the cerebrum known as the parieto-occipital sulcus. The parieto-occipital sulcus, in turn, form the front border of the occipital lobe, which is, otherwise, the rearmost part of the cerebrum. The temporal lobe is to the side of and below the lateral sulcus. Wernicke's area, a part of the cortex related to the understanding of language, is located in the temporal lobe. The insula lies deep within the folds of the lateral sulcus.

The cerebrum receives information from all the sense organs and sends motor commands (signals that results in activity in the muscles or glands) to other parts of the brain and the rest of the body. Motor commands are transmitted by the motor cortex, a strip of cerebral cortex extending from side to side across the top of the cerebrum just in front of the central sulcus. The sensory cortex, parallel strips of cerebral cortex just in back of the central sulcus, receives input from the sense organs.

Many other areas of the cerebral cortex have also been mapped according to their specific functions, such as vision, hearing, speech, emotions, language, and other aspects of perceiving, thinking, and remembering. Cortical regions known as associative cortices are responsible for integrating multiple inputs, processing the information, and carrying out complex responses.

The cerebellum coordinates body movements. Located at the lower back of the brain beneath the occipital lobes, the cerebellum is divided into two lateral (side-by-side) lobes connected by a fingerlike bundle of white fibres called the vermis. The outer layer, or cortex, of the cerebellum consists of fine folds called folia. As in the cerebrum, the outer layer of cortical gray matter surrounds a deeper layer of white matter and nuclei (groups of nerve cells). Three fibre bundles called cerebellar peduncle, giving to connect the cerebellum to the three parts of the brain stem - the midbrain, the pons, and the medulla oblongata.

The cerebellum coordinates voluntary movements by fine-tuning commands from the motor cortex in the cerebrum. The cerebellum also maintains posture and balance by controlling muscle tone and sensing the position of the limbs. All motor activity, from hitting a baseball to fingering a violin, depends on the cerebellum.

The limbic system is a group of brain structures that play a role in emotion, memory, and motivation. For example, electrical stimulation of the amygdala in laboratory animals can provoke fear, anger, and aggression. The hypothalamus regulates hunger, thirst, sleep, body temperature, sexual drive, and other functions.

The thalamus and the hypothalamus lie underneath the cerebrum and connect it to the brain stem. The thalamus consist of two rounded masses of gray tissue lying within the middle of the brain, between the two cerebral hemispheres. The thalamus are the main relay station for incoming sensory signals to the cerebral cortex and for outgoing motor signals from it. All sensory input to the brain, except that of the sense of smell, connects to individual nuclei of the thalamus.

The hypothalamus lies beneath the thalamus on the midline at the base of the brain. It regulates or is involved directly in the control of many of the body's vital drives and activities, such as eating, drinking, temperature regulation, sleep, emotional behaviour, and sexual activity. It also controls the function of internal body organs by means of the autonomic nervous system, interacts closely with the pituitary gland, and helps coordinate activities of the brain stem.

The brain stem, shown here in coloured cross section, is the lowest part of the brain. It serves as the path for messages travelling between the upper brain and spinal cord but is also the seat of basic and vital functions such as breathing, blood pressure, and heart rates, as well as reflexes like eye movement and vomiting. The brain stem has three main parts: The medulla, pons, and midbrain. A canal runs longitudinally through these structures carrying cerebrospinal fluid. Also distributed along its length is a network of cells, referred to as the reticular formation, that governs the state of alertness.

The brain stem is revolutionarily the most primitive part of the brain and is responsible for sustaining the basic functions of life, such as breathing and blood pressure. It includes three main structures lying between and below the two cerebral hemispheres - the midbrain, pons, and medulla oblongata.

The topmost structure of the brain stem is the midbrain. It contains major relay stations for neurons transmitting signals to the cerebral cortex, as well as many reflex centres - pathways carrying sensory (input) information and motor (output) command. Relays and reflex centres for visual and auditory (hearing) functions are located in the top portion of the midbrain. A pair of nuclei called the superior colliculus control reflex actions of the eye, such as blinking, opening and closing the pupil, and focussing the lens. A second pair of nuclei, called the inferior colliculus, controls auditory reflexes, such as adjusting the ear to the volume of sound. At the bottom of the midbrain are reflex and relay centres relating to pain, temperature, and touch, as well as several regions associated with the control of movement, such as the red nucleus and the substantia nigra.

Continuous with and below the midbrain and directly in front of the cerebellum is a prominent bulge in the brain stem called the pons. The pons consists of large bundles of nerve fibres that connect the two halves of the cerebellum and also connect each side of the cerebellum with the opposite-side cerebral hemisphere. The pons serves mainly as a relay station linking the cerebral cortex and the medulla oblongata.

The long, stalklike lowermost portion of the brain stem is called the medulla oblongata. At the top, it is continuous with the pons and the midbrain; at the bottom, it makes a gradual transition into the spinal cord at the foramen magnum. Sensory and motor nerve fibres connecting the brain and the rest of the body cross over to the opposite side as they pass through the medulla. Thus, the left half of the brain communicates with the right half of the body, and the right half of the brain with the left half of the body.

Running up the brain stem from the medulla oblongata through the pons and the midbrain is a netlike formation of nuclei known as the reticular formation. The reticular formation controls respiration, cardiovascular function, digestion, levels of alertness, and patterns of sleep. It also determines which parts of the constant flow of sensory information into the body are received by the cerebrum.

There are two main types of brain cells, neurons and neuroglia. Neurons are responsible for the transmission and analysis of all electrochemical communication within the brain and other parts of the nervous system. Each neuron is composed of a cell body called a soma, which is exclusive of the entire body of an organism especially to include that of the germ cells, also of an organism and the major fibre called an axon, is usually a long process of a nerve fibre that generally conducts impulses away from the body of the nerve cell. A finally, a system and a system of branches called dendrites. Dendrites are a composition where a mineral crystallizing in another mineral in the form of branching or treelike marks, a branch protoplasmic extension of a nerve cell that conducts impulses from adjacent cells inward toward the cell body, manifesting the essential life functions of a cell and composed of proteins, fats, and other molecules suspended in water.

A single nerve may possess many dendrites, and is also called dendron, as a nerve impulse is contained by a wave of physical and chemical excitation along a nerve fibre in response to a stimulus, accompanied by a transient change in electric potential in the membrane of the fibre, that is, a threadlike process of a neuron, especially the prolonged axon that conducts nerve impulses. However, a neuron of the impulse-conducting cells that constitute the brain, spinal column, and nerves, consists of a nucleated cell body with one or more dendrites of a single axon.

Briefly, an axon, also called nerve fibres that convey electrical signals away from the nerve fibres that can measure in length to (3.3 ft.) measurably. Most axons are covered with a protective sheath of myelin, in that of a substance made of fats and protein of which is composed of one or more chains of amino acids, that insulate the axon. Myelinated axons have a myelin sheath that surrounds the core of a nerve fibre or axon and facilitates the transmission of nerve impulses, in the peripheral nervous system, the sheath is formed from the cell membrane of the Schwann cell and, in the central nervous system, from oligodendrocytes, that is, one of the cells comprising the oligodendroglia. In that which a neuroglia consisting of cells similar to but smaller than astrocytes, found in the central nervous system and is associated with the formation of myelin.

The transmission exerted by the nerve impulse or the neuronal signals travels faster than do the unmyelinated axons. Dendrites convey electrical signals toward the soma, are shorter than axons, and are usually multiple and branching.

Neuroglia is the delicate network of branched cells and fibre that support the tissue of the central nervous system. These cells are twice as numerous as neurons and account for half of the brain's weight. Neuroglia (from glia, Greek for 'glue') that provide structural support to the neurons, neuroglial cells, also form myelin, guide developing neurons, takes up chemicals involved in cell-to-cell communication, and contributes to the maintenance of the environmental surroundings of the neurons.

Twelve pairs of cranial nerves arise symmetrically from the base of the brain, these of several nerves that arise in pairs from the brainstem and reach the peripheral through openings in the skull. There are 12 such pairs in mammals, birds, and reptile, and usually 10 pairs in amphibians and fish. Conveying information from the sense organs and others contain fibres, of both sensory and motor impulses. The first and second pairs of cranial nerves - the olfactory (smell) nerves and the optic (vision) nerve - carry sensory information from the nose and eyes, respectively, to the undersurface of the cerebral hemispheres. The other ten pairs of cranial nerves originate in or end in the brain stem.

The brain functions by complex neuronal, or nerve cell, circuits. Communication between neurons is both electrical and chemical and always travels from the dendrites of a neuron, through its soma, and out its axon to the dendrites of another neuron.

Dendrites of one neuron receive signals from the axons of other neurons through chemicals known as neurotransmitters. The neurotransmitters set off electrical charges in the dendrites, which then carry the signals electrochemically to the soma. The soma integrates the information, which is then transmitted electrochemically down the axon to its tip.

At the tip of the axon, small, bubble-like structures called vesicles' release neurotransmitters that carries the signal across the synapse, or gap, between two neurons. There are many types of neurotransmitters, including norepinephrine, dopamine, and serotonin. Neurotransmitters can be excitatory (that is, they excite an electrochemical response in the dendrite receptors) or inhibitory (they block the response of the dendrite receptors).

One neuron may communicate with thousands of other neurons, and many thousands of neurons are involved with even the simplest behaviour. It is believed that these connections and their efficiency can be modified, or altered, by experience.

Scientists have used two primary approaches for studying how the brain works. One approach is to study brain function after parts of the brain have been damaged. Functions that disappear or that is no longer normal after injury to specific regions of the brain can often be associated with the damaged areas. The second approach is to study the response of the brain to direct stimulation or to stimulation of various sense organs.

Neurons are grouped by function into collections of cells called nuclei. These nuclei are connected to form sensory, motor, and other systems. Scientists can study the function of somatosensory (pain and touch), motor, olfactory, visual, auditory, language, and other systems by measuring the physiological (physical and chemical) change that occur in the brain when these senses are activated. For example, electroencephalography (EEG) measures the electrical activity of specific groups of neurons through electrodes attached to the surface of the skull. Electrodes incorporate directly into the brain can give readings of individual neurons. Changes in blood flow, glucose (sugar), or oxygen consumption in groups of active cells can also be mapped.

Although the brain appears symmetrical, how it functions is not. Each hemisphere is specializing and dominates the other in certain functions. Research has shown that hemispheric dominance is related to whether a person is predominantly right-handed or left-handed. In most right-handed people, the left hemisphere processes arithmetic, language, and speech. The right hemisphere interprets music, complex imagery, and spatial relationships and recognizes and expresses emotion. In left-handed people, the pattern of brain organization is more variable.

Hemispheric specialization has traditionally been studied in people as having sustained damage to the connections between the two hemispheres, may occur with a stroke, an interruption of blood flow to an area of the brain that causes a death of nerve cells in that area or region of mishap. The division of functions between the two hemispheres has also been studied in people having had the connection between the two hemispheres surgically cut in order to control severe epilepsy, a neurological disease characterized by convulsions and loss of consciousness.

The visual system of humans is one of the most advanced sensory systems in the body. More information is conveyed visually than by any other means. In addition to the structures of the eye itself, several cortical regions - collectively called a primary visual and visual associative cortex - as well as the midbrain are involved in the visual system. Conscious processing of visual input occurs in the primary visual cortex, but reflexive - that is, immediate and unconscious - responses occur at the superior colliculus in the midbrain. Associative cortical regions - specializing regions that can associate, or integrate, multiple inputs - in the parietal and frontal lobes along with parts of the temporal lobe are also involved in the processing of visual information and the establishment of visual memories.

Language involves specialized cortical regions in a complex interaction that allows the brain to comprehend and communicate abstract ideas. The motor cortex initiates impulses that travel through the brain stem to produce audible sounds. Neighbouring regions of motor cortices, called the supplemental motor cortex, are involved in sequencing and coordinating sounds. Broca's area of the frontal lobe is responsible for the sequencing of language elements for output. The comprehension of language is dependent upon Wernicke's area of the temporal lobe. Other cortical circuits connect these areas.

Memory is usually considered a diffusely stored associative process - that is, it puts together information from many different sources. Although research has failed to identify specific sites in the brain as locations of individual memories, certain brain areas are critical for memory to function. Immediate recall - the ability to repeat short series of words or numbers immediately after hearing them - is thought to be located in the auditory associative cortex. Short-term memory - the ability to retain a limited amount of information for up to an hour - is located in the deep temporal lobe. Long-term memory probably involves exchanges between the medial temporal lobe, various cortical regions, and the midbrain.

The autonomic nervous system regulates the life support systems of the body reflexively - that is, without conscious direction. It automatically controls the muscles of the heart, digestive system, and lungs; Certain glands, and homeostasis - that is, the equilibrium of the internal environment of the body. The autonomic nervous system itself is controlled by nerve centres in the spinal cord and brain stem and is fine-tuned by regions higher in the brain, such as the midbrain and cortex. Reactions such as blushing indicate that cognitive, or thinking, centres of the brain are also involved in autonomic responses.

The brain is guarded by several highly developed protective mechanisms. The bony cranium, the surrounding meninges, and the cerebrospinal fluid all contribute to the mechanical protection of the brain. In addition, a filtration system called the blood-brain barrier protects the brain from exposure to potentially harmful substances carried in the bloodstream.

Brain disorders have a wide range of causes, including head injury, stroke, bacterial diseases, complex chemical imbalances, and changes associated with aging.

Head injury can initiate a cascade of damaging events. After a blow to the head, a person may be stunned or may become unconscious for a moment. This injury, called - concussion, - usually leaves no permanent damage. If the blow is more severe and haemorrhage (excessive bleeding) and swelling occurs, however, severe headache, dizziness, paralysis, a convulsion, or temporary blindness may result, depending on the area of the brain affected. Damage to the cerebrum can also result in profound personality changes.

Damage to Broca's area in the frontal lobe causes difficulty in speaking and writing, a problem known as Broca's aphasia. Injury to Wernicke's area in the left temporal lobe results in an inability to comprehend spoken language, called Wernicke's aphasia.

An injury or disturbance to a part of the hypothalamus may cause a variety of different symptoms, such as loss of appetite with an extreme drop in body weight, increase in appetite leading to obesity; Extraordinary thirst with excessive urination (diabetes insipidus), failure in body-temperature control, resulting in either low temperature (hypothermia) or high temperature (fever), excessive emotionality, and uncontrolled anger or aggression. If the relationship between the hypothalamus and the pituitary gland is damaged, other vital bodily functions may be disturbed, such as sexual function, metabolism, and cardiovascular activity.

Injury to the brain stem is even more serious because it houses the nerve centres that control breathing and heart action. Damage to the medulla oblongata usually results in immediate death.

A stroke is a particular damage to the brain due to an interruption in blood flow. The interruption may be caused by a blood clot, constriction of a blood vessel, or rupture of a vessel accompanied by bleeding. A pouchlike expansion of the wall of a blood vessel, called an aneurysm, may weaken and burst, for example, because of high blood pressure.

Sufficient quantities of glucose and oxygen, transported through the bloodstream, are needed to keep nerve cells alive. When the blood supply to a small part of the brain is interrupted, the cells in that area die and the function of the area is lost. A massive stroke can cause a one-sided paralysis (hemiplegia) and sensory loss on the side of the body opposite the hemisphere damaged by the stroke.

Some brain diseases, such as multiple sclerosis and Parkinson disease, are progressive, becoming worse over time. Multiple sclerosis damages the myelin sheath around axons in the brain and spinal cord. As a result, the affected axons cannot transmit nerve impulses properly. Parkinson disease destroys the cells of the substantia nigra in the midbrain, resulting in a deficiency in the neurotransmitter dopamine that affects motor functions.

Cerebral palsy is a broad term for brain damage sustained close to birth that permanently affects motor function. The damage may take place either in the developing fetus, during birth, or just after birth and is the result of the faulty development or breaking down of motor pathways. Cerebral palsy is nonprogressive - that is, it does not worsen with time.

A bacterial infection in the cerebrum or in the coverings of the brain, swelling of the brain, or an abnormal growth of healthy brain tissue can all cause an increase in intracranial pressure and result in serious damage to the brain.

Scientists are finding that certain brain chemical imbalances are associated with mental disorders such as schizophrenia and depression. Such findings have changed scientific understanding of mental health and have resulted in new treatments that chemically correct these imbalances.

During childhood development, the brain is particularly susceptible to damage because of the rapid growth and reorganization of nerve connections. Problems that originate in the immature brain can appear as epilepsy or other brain-function problems in adulthood.

Several neurological problems are common in aging. Alzheimer's disease damages many areas of the brain, including the frontal, temporal, and parietal lobes. The brain tissue of people with Alzheimer's disease shows characteristic patterns of damaged neurons, known as plaques and tangles. Alzheimer's disease produces progressive dementia, characterized by symptoms such as failing attention and memory, loss of mathematical ability, irritability, and poor orientation in space and time.

A magnetic resonance imaging (MRI) scan of the human brain reveals the contours of one of the brain's hemispheres. The gyri, or ridges, appear in red, while the sulci, or valleys, are shown in blue. Each person has slightly different patterns of gyri and sulci, which reflect individual differences in brain development.

Several commonly used diagnostic methods give images of the brain without invading the skull. Some portray anatomy - that is, the structure of the brain - whereas others measure brain function. Two or more methods may be used to complement each other, together providing a more complete picture than would be possible by one method alone.

Magnetic resonance imaging (MRI), introduced in the early 1980s, beams high-frequency radio waves into the brain in a highly magnetized field that causes the protons that form the nuclei of hydrogen atoms in the brain to remit the radio waves. The remitted radio waves are analyzed by computer to create thin cross-sectional images of the brain. MRI provides the most detailed images of the brain and is safer than imaging methods that use X-rays. However, MRI is a lengthy process and also cannot be used with people who have pacemakers or metal implants, both of which are adversely affected by the magnetic field.

Computed tomography (CT), also known as CT scans, developed in the early 1970's. This imaging method X-rays the brain from many different angles, feeding the information into a computer that produces a series of cross-sectional images, as the CT scan is particularly useful for diagnosing blood clots and brain tumours. It is a much quicker process than magnetic resonance imaging and is therefore advantageous in certain situations - for example, with people that are extremely ill.

This positron emission tomography (PET) scans of the brain shows the activity of brain cells in the resting state and during three types of auditory stimulation. PET uses radioactive substances introduced within the brain to measure such brain functions as cerebral metabolism, blood flow and volume, oxygen use, and the formation of neurotransmitters. This imaging method collects data from many different angles, feeding the information into a computer that produces a series of cross-sectional images.

Changes in brain function due to brain disorders can be visualized in several ways. Magnetic resonance spectroscopy measures the concentration of specific chemical compounds in the brain that may change during specific behaviours. Functional magnetic resonance imaging (fMRI) maps changes in oxygen concentration that correspond to nerve cell activity.

Positron emission tomography (PET), developed in the mid-1970s, uses computed tomography to visualize radioactive tracers, radioactive substances are introduced into the brain intravenously or by inhalation. PET can measure such brain functions as cerebral metabolism, blood flow and volume, oxygen use, and the formation of neurotransmitters. Single photon emission computed tomography (SPECT), developed in the 1950's through until the 1960's, used radioactive tracers to visualize the circulation and volume of blood in the brain.

Brain-imaging studies have provided new insights into sensory, motor, language, and memory processes, as well as brain disorders such as epilepsy, cerebrovascular disease; Alzheimer's, Parkinson, and Huntington's diseases, and various mental disorders, such as schizophrenia.

Although all vertebrate brains share the same basic three-part structure, the development of their constituent parts varies across the evolutionary scale. In fish, the cerebrum is dwarfed by the rest of the brain and serves mostly to process input from the senses.

In reptiles and amphibians, the cerebrum is proportionally larger and begins to connect and form conclusions about this input. Birds have well-developed optic lobes, making the cerebrum even larger. Among mammals, the cerebrum dominates the brain. It is most developed among primates, in whom cognitive ability is the highest.

In lower vertebrates, such as fish and reptiles, the brain is often tubular and bears a striking resemblance to the early embryonic stages of the brains of more highly evolved animals. In all vertebrates, the brain is divided into three regions: the forebrain (prosencephalon), the midbrain (mesencephalon), and the hindbrain (rhombencephalon). These three regions further the references that subdivide into different structures, systems, nuclei, and layers.

The more highly evolved the animal, the more complex is the brain structure. Human beings have the most complex brains of all animals. Evolutionary forces have also resulted in a progressive increase in the size of the brain. In vertebrates lower than mammals, the brain is small. In meat-eating animals, particularly primates, the brain increases dramatically in size.

The cerebrum and cerebellum of higher mammals are highly convoluted in order to fit the most gray matter surface within the confines of the cranium. Such highly convoluted brains are called gyrencephalic. Many lower mammals have a smooth, or lissencephalic (smooth head), cortical surfaces.

There is also evidence of evolutionary adaption of the brain. For example, many birds depend on an advanced visual system to identify food at great distances while in flight. Consequently, their optic lobes and cerebellum are well developed, giving them keen sight and outstanding motor coordination in flight. Rodents, on the other hand, as nocturnal animals, do not have a well-developed visual system. Instead, they rely more heavily on other sensory systems, such as a highly-developed sense of smell and facial whiskers.

Recent research in brain function suggests that there may be sexual differences in both brain anatomy and brain function. One study indicated that men and women may use their brains differently while thinking. Researchers used functional magnetic resonance imaging to observe which parts of the brain were activated as groups of men and women tried to determine whether sets of nonsense words rhymed. Men used only Broca's area in this task, whereas women used Broca's area plus an area on the right side of the brain.

The Cell, in [biology] is the most basic unit of life. Cells are the smallest structures capable of basic life processes, such as taking in nutrients, expelling waste, and reproducing. All living things are composed of cells. Some microscopic organisms, such as bacteria and protozoa, are unicellular, meaning they consist of a single cell. Plants, animals, and fungi are multicellular; that is, they are composed of a great many cells working in concert. But whether it makes up an entire bacterium or is just one of the trillions in a human being, the cell is a marvel of design and efficiency. Cells carry out thousands of biochemical reactions each minute and reproduce new cells that perpetuate life.

The word cell refers to several types of organisms. Cells such as paramecia, dinoflagellates, diatoms, and spirochetes are self-maintaining organisms; cells such as lymphocytes, erythrocytes, muscle cells, nerve cells, cardiac muscle, and chromoplasts are more specializing cells that are a part of higher multicellular organisms. Nonetheless, of its size or whether the cell is a complete organism or just part of an organism, all cells have certain structural components in common, as do of all cells that have some type of outer cell boundary that permits some materials to leave and enter the cell and a cell interior composed of a water-rich, fluid material called cytoplasm that contains hereditary material in the form of deoxyribonucleic acid (DNA).

Cells vary considerably in size, in that of the smallest cell is a type of bacterium-known as a mycoplasma, measuring 0.0001mm. (0.000004 in) in measure of length. The process of events involving the growth, replication, and division of a eukaryotic cell, is that, of a celled or multicellular organism that is capable of independent functioning, consisting of one or more nuclei, cytoplasm, and various organelles, all surrounded by a semipermeable cell membrane: That of a thin, pliable layer of tissue converting surfaces or separating or connecting regions, structures, or organs of an animal or a plant

The mycoplasma of any numerous parasitic pathogenic microorganisms of the genus Mycoplasma, but lacking a true cell wall, but gram-negative, and need of steroids, such as cholesterol for growth. In humans, one species is a primary cause of nonbacterial pneumonia, and is also called pleuropneumonia-like organisms, that being, of an individual form of life, such as a plant, animal, bacterium, protest, or fungus, a body made up of organs, organelles, or other parts that work together to carry on the various processes of life. A system considered as analogous in its structure or function to a living body, in organizing the social organism. The concept that society or the universe is analogous to a biological organism, as in development or organization. The doctrine that the total organization of an organism, rather than the functioning of individual organs, is the principal or exclusive determinant of every life process, however, the theory that all disease is associated with structural alternations of organs. Something that has been organized or the act or process of organization is made into an ordered whole. Something made up of elements with varied functions that contribute to the whole and to collective functions, just for being the called-for of an organism.

That, to a greater extent, there is about 10,000 of nonbacterial mycoplasma' of any number of parasitic pathogenic microorganisms of the genus Mycoplasma, that lack a free cell wall, are gram-negative, and need sterols such as cholesterol for growth. In humans, one species is a primary cause of nonbacterial pneumonia, also called Pleuropneumonia, for which of the inflammation of the pleura and lungs, the pneumonia aggravated by pleurisy, as an infectious febrile disease of cattle, caused by a mycoplasma and is characterized by inflammation of the pleura and lungs.

That in having to a wider diameter, its width is identical to a human hair, that among the largest cells are the nerve cells that run down a giraffe's neck; these cells, to a greater extent, can measure beyond or outside of 3m. (9.7 ft.) in length. Human cells also display a variety of sizes, from small red blood cells that measure 0.00076mm. (0.00003 in.) to liver cells that may, in at least, are ten times as great. About 10,000 average-sized human cells can fit on the head of a pin.

Along with their differences in size, cells present an array of shapes. Some, such as the bacterium Escherichia coli, resemble rods. The paramecium, a type of protozoan, is a slipper shaped and the amoeba, another protozoan, has an irregular form that changes shape as it moves around. Plant cells typically resemble boxes or cubes. In humans, the outermost layers of skin cells are flat, while muscle cells are long and thin. Some nerve cells, with their elongated, tentacle-like extensions, suggest an octopus.

In multicellular organisms, shape is typically tailored to the cell's job. For example, flat skin cells pack tightly into a layer that protects the underlying tissues from invasions by bacteria. Long, thin muscle cells' contract readily to move bones. The numerous extensions from a nerve cell enable it to connect to several other nerve cells in order to send and receive messages rapidly and efficiently.

By itself, each cell is a model of independence and self-containment. Like some miniature, walled city in perpetual rush hour, the cell constantly bustles with traffic, shuttling essential molecules from place to place to carry out the business of living. Despite their individuality, however, cells also display a remarkable ability to join, communicate in the manner from which they coordinate with other cells. The human body, for example, consists of an estimated 20 to 30 trillion cells. Dozens of different kinds of cells are organized into specialized groups called tissues. Tendons and bones, for example, are composed of connective tissue, whereas skin and mucous membranes are built from epithelial tissue. Different tissue types are assembled into organs, which are structures specialized to perform particular functions. Examples of organs include the heart, stomach, and brain. Organs, in turn, are organized into systems such as the circulatory, digestive, or nervous systems. All together, these assembled organ systems form the human body.

The components of cells are molecules, nonliving structures formed by the union of atoms. Small molecules serve as building blocks for larger molecules. Proteins, nucleic acids, carbohydrates, and lipids, which include fats and oils, are the four major molecules that underlie cell structure and also participate in cell functions. For example, a tightly organized arrangement of lipids, proteins, and protein-sugar compounds forms the plasma membrane, or outer boundary, of certain cells. The organelles, membrane-bound compartments in cells, are built largely from proteins. Biochemical reactions in cells are guided by enzymes, specialized proteins that speed up chemical reactions. The nucleic acid deoxyribonucleic acid (DNA) contains the hereditary or ancestral information for cells, and another nucleic acid, ribonucleic acid (RNA), works with DNA to build the thousands of proteins the cell needs.

Cells fall into one of two categories of Prokaryotic organelles, in that of the kingdom Monera (or prokaryotes), comprising the bacteria and cyanobacterial, characterized by the absence of a distinct membrane-bound nucleus or membrane-bound organelles, and by DNA that is not organized into chromosomes, also called moeran. This category pronounced by another bacterium. For that which has given by any of the unicellular prokaryotic microorganisms of the class Schizomycetes, which varies in terms of morphology, oxygen and nutritional requirements, and motility, that may be identical to free-living saprophytic organisms, especially a fungus or bacterium, that grows and derives its nourishment from dead or decaying organic matter.

For the eukaryotic, in a prokaryotic cell, is found that is only found in bacteria and archaebacteria, all the components, including the DNA, mingling freely in the cell's interior, a single compartment. Eukaryotic cells, of any single celled or multicellular organism whose cells contain a distinct membrane-bound nucleus, which make up plants, animals, fungi, and all other life forms, and contain numerous compartments, or organelles, within each cell. The DNA in eukaryotic cells is enclosed in a special organelle called the nucleus, which serves as the cell's command centre and information library. The term prokaryote comes from Greek words that mean "before the nucleus" or "prenucleus," while eukaryote means "a true nucleus."

Bacteria's cells typically are surrounded by a rigid, protective cell wall. The cell membrane, also called the plasma membrane, regulates passage of materials into and out of the cytoplasm, the semifluids that fill the cell. The DNA, located in the nucleoid region, contains the genetic information for the cell. Ribosomes carry out protein synthesis. Many bacteria contain some pilus (plural pili), a structure that extends out of the cell to transfer DNA to another bacterium. The flagellum, finds of a long threadlike appendage, especially of a whipcord extension of certain cells or unicellular organisms that function as an organ of a self-propelling locomotion, as for some bacteria contain a plasmid, a small chromosomes with extra genes. Others have a capsule, a sticky substance external to the cell wall that protects bacteria from attack by white blood cells, as the function as an organ of which certain cells or organisms are extensions beyond which of certain or specific cells. Mesosomes were formerly thought to be structures with unknown functions, but now are known to be artifacts created when cells are prepared for viewing with electron microscopes.

Prokaryotic cells are among the tiniest of all cells, ranging in size from 0.0001 to 0.003mm. (0.000004 to 0.0001 in.) in a pointed diameter. About a hundred typical prokaryotic cells lined up in a row would match the thickness of a book page. These cells, which can be rod-like, spherical, or spiral in shape, are surrounded by a protective cell wall. Like most cells, prokaryotic cells live in a watery environment, whether it is soil moisture, a pond, or the fluid surrounding cells in the human body. Tiny porous or interstices in the cell wall enable water and the substances dissolved in it, such as oxygen, to flow into the cell; these pores also allow wastes to flow out. As an organism, the prokaryote also procaryote, composing the bacteria and cyanobacteria and characterised by the absence of an indistinct membrane -bound organelles, and by DNA that is not organized into chromosomes.

Pushed up against the inner surface of the prokaryotic cell wall is a thin membrane called the plasma membrane. The plasma membrane, composed of two layers of flexible lipid molecules and interspersed with durable proteins, is both supple and strong. Unlike the cell wall, whose open pores allow the unregulated traffic of materials in and out of the cell, the plasma membrane is selectively permeable, meaning it allows only certain substances to pass through. Thus, the plasma membrane actively separates the cell's contents from its surrounding fluids.

While small molecules such as water, oxygen, and carbon dioxide diffuse freely across the plasma membrane, the passage of many larger molecules, including amino acids (the building blocks' of proteins) and sugars, is carefully regulated. Specialized transport proteins accomplish this task. The transport proteins span the plasma membrane, forming an intricate system of pumps and channels through which traffic is conducted. Some substances swirling in the fluid around the cell can enter it only if they bind to and are escorted in by specific transport proteins. In this way, the cell fine-tunes its internal environment.

The plasma membrane encloses the cytoplasm, the semifluids that fill the cell. Composed of about 65 percent of water, the cytoplasm, of which the protoplasm outside the nucleus of the cell is packed within or about a billion molecules per cell, a rich storehouse that includes enzymes and dissolved nutrients, such as sugars and amino acids. The water provides a favourable environment for the thousands of biochemical reactions that take place in the cell.

Within the cytoplasm of all prokaryote is deoxyribonucleic acid (DNA), a complex molecule in the form of a double helix, a shape similar to a spiral staircase. The DNA is about 1,000 times the length of the cell, and to fit inside, it repeatedly twists and folds to form a compact structure called a chromosome. The chromosome in prokaryote is circular, and is located in a region of the cell called the nucleoid. Often, smaller chromosomes called Plasmid, which of any circular double-stranded unit of DNA that replicates within a cell independently of the chromosomal DNA. Plasmids are most often found in bacteria, which replicates within a cell independently of the chromosomal DNA and used in recombinant DNA in the transfer of gens between cells. The DNA is divided into units called genes, just like a long train is divided into separate cars. Depending on the species, the DNA contains several hundred or even thousands of genes. Such that the hereditary unit consisting of a sequence of DNA that occupies a specific location on a chromosome and determines a particular characteristic in an organism. Genes undergo mutation when their DNA sequence changes as of hereditary factors in the frequence of occurrence as contained by the descent of a person, family, or group from ancestry or ancestors, in that which of study or investigation of ancestry and family histories. In that of great age, a person from whom one is descended, especially if more remote that a grandparent, a forerunner or predecessor with an actual or hypothetical organism or stock is from which later kinds is to evolve.

Chromosomes are threadlike linear strands of DNA and associated proteins in the nucleus of eukaryotic cells that carry the gene and functions in the transmission of hereditary information. As a circular strand of DNA in bacteria that contains the hereditary information necessary for cell life.

Typically, one gene contains encoded instructions for building all or part of a single protein. Hereditary and consisting of a sequence of DNA that occupies a specific location on a chromosome and determines a particular characteristic or organism. Genes undergo mutation when their DNA sequence changes. As drug resistance in cancer cells are linked to amplification of the gene that prevents absorption of the chemotherapeutic agent by the cell.

Nonetheless, enzymes, which are specialized proteins, determine virtually all the biochemical reactions that support and sustain the cell. Th e sequence of nucleotides in DNA o r RNA that determines the specific amino acid sequence in the synthesis of proteins. It is the biochemical base of heredity and nearly universal in all organisms and functioning as some catysts

Also immersed in the body or located, dwelling or residing within the cytoplasm, the protoplasm outside the nucleus of a cell that only the organelles in prokaryotic cells, and tiny beadlike structures called ribosomes. These are the cell's protein factories. Following the instructions encoded in the DNA, ribosomes expel proteins by the hundreds every minute, providing needed enzymes, that is to say, enzymes induced by living organisms and functioning as biochemical catalysts. The replacement for worn-out transport proteins, or other proteins that are required by the cells, such that the Procaryote, as characterize by the absence of some distinct membrane-bound nucleus membrane-bound organelles, and by DNA that is not organised into chromosomes.

While relatively simple in construction, prokaryotic cells display extremely complicating and complex activity. They have a greater range of biochemical reactions than those found in their larger relatives, the eukaryotic cells. The extraordinary biochemical diversity of prokaryotic cells is manifested in the wide-ranging lifestyles of the archaebacteria and the bacteria, whose habitats include polar ice, deserts, and hydrothermal vents - deep regions of the ocean under great pressure where hot water geysers erupt from cracks in the ocean floor.

In whatever manner, in that of a nucleic acid that carries the genetic information in the cell and is capable of self-replication and synthesis of RNA. DNA consisted of two long chains of nucleotides twisted into a double strand d helix and joined by hydrogen bonds between the complementary-based adenine and thymine or cytosine and guacin. The sequence of some nucleides determines an individual's inherent characteristics.

An animal cell characteristically contains several types of membrane-bound organs, or organelles. The nucleus directs activities of the cell and carries genetic information from generation to generation. The mitochondrion generates energy for the cell. In containing of a spherical or elongated organelle in the cytoplasm of nearly all eukaryotic cells, containing genetic material and many enzymes, that which is important for cell metabolisms, including the significant relevance under which are responsible for the conversion of food to usable energy.

Protein is manufactured by ribosomes and composed of RNA and found in the cytoplasm of living cells serving as the junction for polypeptide as encoded by messenger RNA. In which the rough endoplasmic reticulum of a membrane network within the cytoplasm of cells involved in the synthesis that cells involved in, modification, and transport of cellular materials for which the protoplasm manifests the essential life functions of a cell. That outside the nucleus of a cell that the protoplasm consisting of one or more nuclei, cytoplasm, and various organelles surrounded by a semipermeable cell membrane of a single cell. Protein, of any a group of complex organic macromolecules that contain carbon hydrogen, oxygen, nitrogen, and usually sulfur and are composed of one or more chains of amino acids. Proteins are fundamental components of all living cells and include many substances, such as enzymes, hormones, and antibodies, that is necessary for the proper functioning of an organism. They are essential in the diet of animals for the growth and repair of tissue and can be obtained from foods, such as meat, fish, eggs, milk, and legumes. The Golgi apparatus has to a network of stacked membranous vesicles present in most living cells that function in the formation of secretions within the cell. Similarly, protein modifies protein functioning as packages, and distributes protein while lysosomes collectively store enzymes for digesting food. A membrane-bound organelle in the cytoplasm of most cells containing various hydrolytic enzyme s that function in intracellular digestion, of which the entire cell is wrapped in a lipid membrane that selectively permits materials to pass in and out of the cytoplasm.

The lipid and also, lipide in that of any a group of organs compounds, including the fats, oils, waves, sterols, and triglyrides, in which of a water insoluble but soluble in polar organic solvents. Triglyceride as a naturally occurring ester of three fatty acids and glycerol that is the chief constituent of fats and oils.

The glycerol compounded composition of the lipid category occurring of three fatty acids and glycerol, which is the chief constituent of fats and oils, as a byproduct of saponification, in that which a reaction in which ester is heated with an alkali, such as sodium hydroxides, producing a free alcohol and an acid salt, especially an alkaline hydrolysis of a fatty oil to make soap. The using of a solvent, as antifreeze, a plasticizer, and a sweetener and in the manufacture of dynamite, cosmetics, liquid soaps, inks, and lubricant. Glycerol is a containment of a syrup, sweet colourless, or yellowish liquid, and manufactured of a solvent, such as antifreeze, plastics, and sweetener, and in the manufactured as dynamite, cosmetics, liquids, inks, liquid soaps, and as a lubricant.

Eukaryotic cells are typically about ten times larger than prokaryotic bacteria and cyanobacteria, characterized by the absence of a distinct membrane-bound nucleus or membrane-bound structure within a cell as a mitochondrion, vacuole, or chloroplast, that performs a specific function. In animal cells, the plasma membrane, rather than a cell wall, forms the cell's outer boundary. With a design similar to the plasma membrane of prokaryotic cells, it separates the cell from its surroundings and regulates the traffic across the membrane. Maintained by a single-celled or multicellular organism whose cells contain a distinct membrane -bound nucleuses.   This, in the finding of cells hereditary material and controlling its metabolism, growth, and reproduction, for what is to be said, of a biological theory stating that all species or organisms and develop through the natural diversity of small inherent variations that increase t he individuals' ability to complete survival and reproduce, whereas, the prokaryotic cells are characterized by the absence of a distinct membrane-bound nucleus or membrane-bound organelles, and by DNA that is not organized into chromosomes.

The eukaryotic cell cytoplasm is similar to that of the prokaryote cell except for one major difference: Eukaryotic cells house a nucleus and numerous other membrane-enclosed organelles. Like separate rooms of a house, these organelles enable specialized functions to be carried out efficiently. The building of proteins and lipids, for example, takes place in separate organelles where specialized enzymes geared for each job are located.

The plasma membrane that surrounds eukaryotic cells is a dynamic structure composed of two layers of phospholipid molecules interspersed with cholesterol and proteins. As a thin pliable layer of tissue covering surfaces or separating or connecting regional strictures or organs of an animal or a plant, as when the cell membranes orchestrate a piece of parchment, that by saying, that this thin sheet of natural or synthetic material that can be permeated or penetrated, especially by liquid or gases, and to substances in solution

Phospholipids are of any various phosphorus containing lipids, such as lecithin that is composed mainly of fatty acids, a phosphate group, and a simple organic molecule. The composition is composed of a hydrophilic, or water, having to a head and two tails which are hydrophobic, or water-hating. The two phospholipid layers face each other in the membrane, with the heads directed outward and the tails pointing inward. The water-attracting heads anchor the membrane to the cytoplasm, the watery fluid inside the cell, and also to the water surrounding the cell. The water-hating tails block large water-soluble molecules from passing through the membrane while permitting fat-soluble molecules, including medications such as tranquillizers and sleeping pills, to freely cross the membrane. Proteins embedded in the plasma membrane carry out a variety of functions, including transport of large water soluble molecules such as sugars and certain amino acids. Glycoproteins, proteins bonded to carbohydrates, serve in part to identify the cell as belonging to a unique organism, enabling the immune system to detect foreign cells, such as invading bacteria, which carry different glycoprotein, that is said, that of any a group of conjugated protein that contains a carbohydrate at the nonprotein components. Cholesterol molecules in the plasma membrane act as stabilizers that limit the movement of the two slippery phospholipid layers, which slide back and forth in the membrane. Tiny gaps in the membrane enable small molecules such as oxygen to diffuse readily into and out of the cell. Since cells constantly use up oxygen, decreasing its concentration within the cell, the higher concentration of oxygen outside the cell causes a net-flow of oxygen into the cell. The steady stream of oxygen into the cell enables it to carry out aerobic respiration continually, a process that provides the cell with the energy needed to carry out its functions. Nevertheless, is that of a white crystalline substance, found in animal tissue and various foods that it normally systemized by the liver and is important as a constituent of cell membranes and a precursor to steroid hormones. It s level in the bloodstream can influence the pathogenesis of certain conditions, such as the development of atherosclerotic plaque and coronary artery disease.

The nucleus is the largest organelle in an animal cell. It contains numerous strands of DNA, the length of each strand being many times the diameter of the cell. Unlike the circular prokaryotic DNA, long sectors of eukaryotic DNA pack into the nucleus by wrapping around proteins. As a cell begins to divide, each DNA strand folds over onto itself several times, forming a rod-shaped chromosome.

The nucleus is surrounded by a double-layered membrane that protects the DNA from potentially damaging chemical reactions that occur in the cytoplasm. Messages pass between the cytoplasm and the nucleus through nuclear pores, which are holes in the membrane of the nucleus. In each nuclear pore, molecular signals flash back and forth as often as ten times per second. For example, a signal to activate a specific gene comes into the nucleus and instructions for production of the necessary protein go out to the cytoplasm.

The nucleus, present in eukaryotic cells, is a discrete structure containing chromosomes, which hold the genetic information for the cell. Separated from the cytoplasm of the cell by a double-layered membrane called the nuclear envelope, and the nucleus contains a cellular material called nucleoplasm. Nuclear pores, present around the circumference of the nuclear membrane, allow the exchange of cellular materials between the nucleoplasm and the cytoplasm.

Attached to the nuclear membrane is an elongated membranous sac called the Endoplasmic reticulum. This organelle structure within the cell that performs a specific function tunnels through the cytoplasm, folds back and forth to form a series of membranous stacks. Relating to, made of, or similar to a membrane. The membranous stacks are the fluid-filled membranous sacs of the associated pathologically manifested characterizations by which information of a membrane of a layer similar to a membrane. The membrane [biologically] is a thin, pliable layer of tissue covering surfaces or separating or connecting region for being structures or organs of an animal or a plant, as a membrane of a thin sheet of natural or synthetic material that is permeable to substances in solution. The Endoplasmic reticulums, of any membrane network within the cytoplasm of cells is involved in the synthesis, modification, and transport of cellular materials.

Thousands of ribosomes particles of RNA and protein that are found in the cytoplasm of living cells and serves as the site of assembly for polypeptide encoded by messenger RNA.

In that of any minute round particle composed of RNA and protein that is found in the cytoplasm of living cells and serves as the junction for which is assembly of polypeptide. Ribosomes attached to the membrane's surface, the ribosomes in eukaryotic cells have the same function as those in prokaryotic and protein synthesis - but they differ slightly in structure. Eukaryote-ribosomes are composed of RNA and proteins and bound to the endoplasmic reticulum, a membrane network within the cytoplasm, that are distinguishable by certain cells. Generally, helping in the assembly of proteins that typically are exported from the cell. The ribosomes work with other molecules to link amino acids to partially completed proteins. The incomplete component s of one or more chains of amino acids and other necessary functioning organism find that any substance as enzymes, hormones, and antibodies, that is essential for the growth and repair of tissue and can be obtained from a variety of first quality essencities.

Protein's travels to the inner chamber of the endoplasmic reticulum, placing of chemical modifications, such as the addition of a sugar, are carried out. Chemical modification of lipids, as a group of organic compounds including the fats, oils, waxes, steroids, and triglycerides, that are insoluble in water but soluble in nonpolar organic solvents, and together with carbohydrases and protein constitute the principal structural material of living cells. Even so, are carried out in the endoplasmic reticulum. The ribosome is a minute round particle composed of RNA and protein that is found in the cytoplasm of living cells and serves as the junction site of assembly for polypeptide encoded or to specified genetic code for a protein molecule, for example.

In that which a polymeric constituent of all living cells and many verses, consisting of a long, usually single-strand chain of alternating phospohate and ribose units with the base adenine, guanine, cytosine, and uracil bonded to ribose, the structure and base sequence of RNA are determinants of protein synthesis and the transmission of genetic information. Ribose, a pentose sugar, occurring as a component of riboflavin muclotides, and nucleic acids. The principal growth promoting factor in the vitamin B complex, naturally occurring in milk, leafy vegetables, fresh meat, and egg yolks, the nucleotide of various compounds consisting of a nucleoside combine with a phosphate group and forming th e basic constitution of DNA and RNA.

The act or process of transmitting, something as a message, that is transmitted. These transmissible signals or other information to impart or convey to others by heredity or inheritance, the evolving hand-me-downs from one part of a mechanism to another. An electronic device that generates and amplifies a carrier wave, -modulate within a meaningful signal derived from speech or other sources, and radiates the resulting signal from an antenna. Impulses that are conveyed to a remote receiver. However, a neurotransmitter maintaining of a chemical substance, such as acetylcholine or dopamine, that transmits nerve impulses across a synapse, resulting in the signal required within the communications of the mind. This signalling of th e impulse -conducting the cell as that consists of a nucleated cell body with one or more dendrites and a single axon.

The endoplasmic reticulum and its bounded ribosomes, are particularly dense in cells that produce many proteins for export, such as the white blood cells of the immune system, which produce and secrete antibodies. Some ribosomes that manufacture proteins that are found in the cytoplasm and serves as the junction site of assembly for polypeptide (molecules of amino acids, typically between 10 and 100). But, are not attached to the endoplasmic reticulum, otherwise, these so-called Free-ribosomes disperse in the cytoplasm and typically cause proteins in the enzymes to remain in the cell. Ribosomes are a minute round particles composed of RNA and proteins that are found in the cytoplasm of living cells and serve as the junction site assembly for polypeptide encoded by messenger RNA.

RNA is a polymeric constituent of all living cells and many viruses, consisting of a living, usually a single stranded chain of alternating phosphate and occurring as a component of riboflavin, nucleotides, and nucleic acids, these ribose units with the bases of adenine, guanine, cytosine, and uracil boded to the ribose. Holding of a pyrimidine base. Uracil is an essential constituent of RNA. Its structure and base, the structure and base sequence of RNA are determinants of protein synthesis and the transmission of genetic information.

The second form of a membrane network within the cytoplasm of cells is involved in the synthesis, modification, and transport of cellular materials (an Endoplasmic reticulum), the smooth endoplasmic reticulum (SER) as a membrane network within the cytoplasm of cells involved in the synthesis, modification and transport of cellular materials, yet lacking the minute round particles composed of RNA and protein that are found in the cytoplasm of living cells and serves as the site of assembly for polypeptide being encoded by massager RNA. Within the winding channels of the smooth endoplasmic reticulum are the enzymes needed for the construction of molecules such as carbohydrates and lipids, which of a group of organic compounds, include the fats, oils, waxes, sterols and triglycerides, that is insoluble in water but soluble in nonpolar organic solvents, is oily to the touch and together with carbohydrates and proteins constitute the principal structural material of living cells.

The smooth endoplasmic reticulum is prominent in liver cells, where it also serves to detoxify substances such as alcohol, drugs, and other poisons.

Any of a group of complex organic macromolecules that contains, hydrogen, oxygen, nitrogen and usually sulfur and are composed of one or more chains of amino acids. Proteins are fundamental compounds of all living cells and include man y substances, such as enzymes, hormones, and antibodies, that is necessary for the proper functioning of an organism. They are essential in the diet of animals for the growth and repair of tissue, which can be obtained in food foods such as meat, fish, eggs, milk and legumes.

Proteins are transported from free and bound ribosomes to the Golgi apparatus, as a differentiated structure within a cell, such as a mitochondrion, vacuole, or chloroplast, that perform a specific function, that of an organelle that resembles a stack of deflated balloons. It is packed with enzymes that complete the processing of proteins. These enzymes add sulfur or phosphorus atoms to certain junctions of the protein, for example, or chop off tiny pieces from the ends of the proteins. The completed protein then leaves the Golgi apparatus for its final destination inside or outside the cell. During its assembly on the ribosome, each protein has acquired a group of from 4 to 100 amino acids called a signal. The signal works as a molecular shipping label to direct the protein to its proper location.

To assume the existence of protein, that is, the containment for which of the plexuity or organic, macromolecules that contain carbon, hydrogen, oxygen, nitrogen, and usually sulfur and are composed of one or more chains of amino acids. Proteins, are fundamental components of all living cells and include many substances, such as, enzymes, hormones, and antibodies, that are necessary for the proper functioning of an organism. They are essential in the diet of animals for the growth and repair of tissue and can be obtained from foods, as of, meat, fish, eggs, milk, and that of the pea family.

Lysosomes are small, often spherical organelles that function as the cell's recycling centre and garbage disposal. Powerful digestive enzymes concentrated in the lysosome breaks down worn-out organelles, such as a mitochondrion, vacuole or chloroplast that perform a specific function. Lysosome is a membrane-bound organelle in the cytoplasm of most cells containing various hydrolytic enzyme's function in intracellular digestion, such as mitochondrion, vacuole, or chloroplast, cells containing various hydrolytic enzymes, functioning as biochemical catalysts.

These of the building blocks to the cytoplasm where they are used to construct new organelles within the cell, such as a mitochondrion, vacuole, or chloroplast, that preform specific functions. Lysosomes also dismantle and recycle proteins, lipids, and other molecules. A membrane-bound organelle in the cytoplasm of most cells containing various hydrolytic enzymes that function in intracellular digestion.

The mitochondria is the powerhouse of the cell. Within the long, slender organelles, which can appear oval or bean shaped under the electron microscope, enzymes convert the sugar glucose and other nutrients into adenosine triphosphate (ATP). This molecule, in turn, serves as an energy battery for countless cellular processes, including the shuttling of substances across the plasma membrane, the building and transport of proteins and lipids, the recycling of molecules and organelles, and the dividing of cells. Muscle and liver cells are particularly active and require dozens and sometimes up to hundreds mitochondria per cell to meet their energy needs. Mitochondria, as any spherical or elongated organelles in the cytoplasm of nearly all eukaryotic cells, containing genetic material and many enzymes important for a cell metabolism, included are the metabolic processes responsible for the conversion of food into usable energy.

Unlike the tiny prokaryotic cell, which contains the bacteria and cyanobacteria, characterized by the absence of a distinct membrane-bound nucleus or membrane-bound organelle, and by DNA that is not organized into chromosomes. The relatively large eukaryotic cell requires structural support. The cytoskeleton, a dynamic network of protein tubes, filaments, and fibres, crisscrosses the cytoplasm, anchoring the organelles in place and providing shape and structure to the cell. Many components of the cytoskeleton are assembled and disassembled by the cell as needed. During cell division, for example, a special structure called a spindle is built to move chromosomes around. Prokaryotic cells consist of the bacteria and cyanobacteria, characterized by the absence of a distinct membrane-bound nucleus or membrane-bound organelles, and by DNA that is not organized into chromosomes, also called moneran.

After cell division, the spindle, no longer needed, is dismantled. Some components of the cytoskeleton serve as microscopic tracks along which proteins and other molecules travel like miniature trains. Recent research suggests that the cytoskeleton also may be a mechanical communication structure that converse with the nucleus to help organize events in the cell.

Plant cells have all the components of animal cells and boast several added features, including chloroplasts, the chlorophyll of any a group of green-pigments or group of green pigments that are found in the chloroplasts plants and in other photosynthetic organisms such as cyanobacteria. Plastids are found in algal and green plant cells, with a central vacuole, of a small cavity in the cytoplasm of a cell-bound by a single membrane and containing water, food, or metabolic waste. Chloroplasts, containing plastid finds in algal and green plant cells. Chloroplasts, like mitochondria, possess a circular chromosome and prokaryote-like ribosomes, which manufacture the proteins that the chloroplasts typically need.

The central vacuole of a mature plant cell typically takes up most of the room in the cell. The vacuole, a membranous bag, crowds the cytoplasm and organelles into the edges of the cell. The central vacuole stores water, salts, sugars, proteins, and other nutrients. In addition, it stores the blue, red, and purple pigments that give certain flowers their colours. The central vacuole also contains plant wastes that taste bitter to certain insects, thus discouraging the insects from feasting on the plant.

Contained in plant cells, is a sturdy cell wall surround and protects the plasma membrane. Its pores enable materials to pass freely into and out of the cell. The strength of the wall also enables a cell to absorb water into the central vacuole and swell without bursting. The resulting pressure in the cells provides plants with rigidity and support for stems, leaves, and flowers. Without sufficient water pressure, the cells collapse and the plant wilts.

To stay alive, cells must be able to carry out a variety of functions. Some cells must be able to move, and most cells must be able to divide. All cells must maintain the right concentration of chemicals in their cytoplasm, ingest food and use it for energy, recycle molecules, expel wastes, and construct proteins. Cells must also be able to respond to changes in their environment.

Although many forms of bacteria are not capable of independent movement, species such as the Salmonella bacterium pictured here can move by means of fine threadlike projections called flagella. The arrangement of flagella across the surface of the bacterium differs from species to species; they can be present at the ends of the bacterium or all across the body surface. Forward movement is accomplished either by a tumbling motion or in a forward manner without tumbling.

Many unicellular organisms swim, glide, thrash, or crawl to search for food and escape enemies. Swimming organisms often move by means of a flagellum, a long tail-like structure made of protein. Many bacteria, for example, have one, two, or many flagella that rotate like propellers to drive the organism along. Some single-celled eukaryotic organisms, such as the euglena, which of any various minute single-celled fresh-water organism of the genus Euglena, charactered by the presence of chlorophyll, a reddish eyespot, and a single anterior flagellum, also, having to a longer and thicker than the prokaryotic flagellum. The eukaryotic flagellum works by waving up and down, similar to the like, as the same operation of oscillation. In higher animals, the sperm cell uses a flagellum to swim toward the female egg for fertilization.

Movement in eukaryotes is also accomplished with cilia, short, hairlike proteins built by centrioles, which are barrel-shaped structures located in the cytoplasm that assemble and break down protein filaments. Typically, thousands of cilia extend through the plasma membrane and cover the surface of the cell, giving it a dense, hairy appearance. By beating its cilia as if they were oars, an organism such as the paramecium propels itself through its watery environment. In cells that do not move, cilia are used for other purposes. In the respiratory tract of humans, for example, millions of ciliated cells prevent inhaled dust, smog, and microorganisms from entering the lungs by sweeping them up on a current of mucus into the throat, where they are swallowed. Eukaryotic flagella and cilia are formed from basal bodies, small protein structures located just inside the plasma membrane. Basal bodies also help to anchor flagella and cilia.

Still other eukaryotic cells, such as amoebas and white blood cells, move by amoeboid motion, or crawling. They extrude their cytoplasm to form temporary pseudopodia, or false feet, which actually are placed in front of the cell, rather like extended arms. They then drag the trailing end of their cytoplasm up to the pseudopodia. A cell using amoeboid motion would lose a race to a euglena or paramecium. But while it is slow, amoeboid motion is strong enough to move cells against a current, enabling water-dwelling organisms to pursue and devour prey, for example, or white blood cells roaming the blood stream to stalk and engulf a bacterium or virus.

An amoeba, a single-celled organism lacking internal organs, approaching a much smaller paramecium, which it begins to engulf with large outflowing of its cytoplasm, called pseudopodia. Once the paramecium is completely engulfed, a primitive digestive cavity, called a vacuole, forms around it. In the vacuole, acids break the paramecium down into chemicals that the amoeba can diffuse back into its cytoplasm for nourishment.

All cells require nutrients for energy, and they display a variety of methods for ingesting them. Simple nutrients dissolved in pond water, for example, can be carried through the plasma membrane of pond-dwelling organisms via a series of molecular pumps. In humans, the cavity of the small intestine contains the nutrients from digested food, and cells that form the walls of the intestine use similar pumps to pull amino acids and other nutrients from the cavity into the bloodstream. Certain unicellular organisms, such as amoebas, are also capable of reaching out and grabbing food. They used a process known as endocytosis, in which the plasma membrane surrounds and engulfed the food particle, enclosing it in a sac, called a vesicle, that is within the amoeba's interior.

Cells require energy for a variety of functions, including moving, building up and breaking down molecules, and transporting substances across the plasma membrane. Nutrients contain energy, but cells must convert the energy locked in nutrients to another form - specifically, the ATP molecule, the cell's energy battery - before it is useful. In single-celled eukaryotic organisms, such as the paramecium, and in multicellular eukaryotic organisms, such as plants, animals, and fungi, mitochondria is responsible for this task. The interior of each mitochondrion consists of an inner membrane that is folded into a mazelike arrangement of separate compartments called cristae. Within the cristae, enzymes form an assembly line where the energy in glucose and other energy-rich nutrients is harnessed to build ATP; thousands of ATP molecules are constructed each second in a typical cell. In most eukaryotic cells, this process requires oxygen and is known as aerobic respiration.

Some prokaryotic organisms also carry out aerobic respiration. They lack mitochondria, however, and carry out aerobic respiration in the cytoplasm with the help of enzymes sequestered there. Many prokaryote species live in environments where there is little or no oxygen, environments such as mud, stagnant ponds, or within the intestines of animals. Some of these organisms produce ATP without oxygen in a process known as anaerobic respiration, where sulfur or other substances take the place of oxygen. Still other prokaryotes, and yeast, a single-celled eukaryote, build ATP without oxygen in a process known as fermentation.

Almost all organisms rely on the sugar glucose to produce ATP. Glucose is made by the process of photosynthesis, in which light energy is transformed to the chemical energy of glucose. Animals and fungi cannot carry out photosynthesis and depend on plants and other photosynthetic organisms for this task. In plants, as we have seen, photosynthesis takes place in organelles called chloroplastid. Chloroplasts contain numerous internal compartments called thylakoids where enzymes aid in the energy conversion process. A single leaf cell contains 40 to 50 chloroplasts, with sufficient sunlight, one large tree is capable of producing upwards of two tons of sugar in a single day. Photosynthesis in prokaryotic organisms - typically aquatic bacteria - is carried out with enzymes clustered in plasma membrane folds called chromatophores. Aquatic bacteria produce the food consumed by tiny organisms living in ponds, rivers, lakes, and seas.

A typical cell must have on hand, about 30,000 proteins at any given time. Many of these proteins are enzymes needed to construct the major molecules used by cells - carbohydrates, lipids, proteins, and nucleic acids - nor to aid in the breakdown of such molecules after they have worn out. Other proteins are part of the cell's structure - the plasma membrane and ribosomes, for example. In animals, proteins also function as hormones and antibodies, and they function like delivery trucks to transport other molecules around the body. Haemoglobin, for example, is a protein that transports oxygen in red blood cells. The cell's demand for proteins never ceases.

Before a protein can be made, however, the molecular directions to build, it must be extracted from one or more genes. In humans, for example, one gene holds the information for the protein insulin, the hormone that cells need to import glucose from the bloodstream, while at least two genes hold the information for collagen, the protein that imparts strength to skin, tendons, and ligaments. The process of building proteins begins when enzymes, in response to a signal from the cell, bind to the gene that carries the code for the required protein, or part of the protein. The enzymes transfer the code to a new molecule called messenger RNA, which carries the code from the nucleus to the cytoplasm. This enables the original genetic code to remain safe in the nucleus, with messenger RNA delivering small bits and pieces of information from the DNA to the cytoplasm as needed. Depending on the cell type, hundreds or even thousands of molecules of messenger RNA are produced each minute.

Once in the cytoplasm, the messenger RNA molecule links up with a ribosome. The ribosome moves along the messenger RNA like a monorail car along a track, stimulating another form of RNA - transfer RNA - to gather and link the necessary amino acids, pooled in the cytoplasm, to form the specific protein, or section of protein. The protein is modified as necessary by the endoplasmic reticulum within the cytoplasm of the cell and Golgi apparatus of a network of stacked membrane vesicles presented in most living cells that function in the formation of secretion within the cell, of which occurs before embarking upon the forming of specific proteins, or a section of the protein. Cells teem with activity as they forge the numerous, diverse proteins that are indispensable for life. When there are a hundred or more cells, they formed a hollow ball of cells, called a blastula, surrounding a fluid-filled cavity. Later divisions produce three layers of cells - endoderm (inner), mesoderm (middle), and ectoderm (outer) - from which the principal features of the animal will differentiate.

Most cells divide at some time during their life cycle, and some divide dozens of times before they die. Organisms rely on cell division for reproduction, growth, and repair and replacement of damaged or worn out cells. Three types of cell division occur: Binary fission, mitosis, and meiosis. Binary fissions, maintains the method used by prokaryotes, of these, an organism of the kingdom Monera (or, prokaryotes) accompanied the bacteria and cyanobacteria, characterized by the absence of a distinct membrane-bound nucleus or membrane-bound organelle, and by DNA t hat is not organized into chromosomes.

The more complex process of mitosis, which also produces two genetically identical cells from a single cell, is used by many unicellular eukaryotic organisms for reproduction. Multicellular organisms use mitosis for growth, cell repair, and cell replacement. In the human body, for example, of an approximate quantity division that equal to about 25 million mitotic cell divisions that every second in order to replace cells that have completed their normal life cycles. Cells of the liver, intestine, and skin may be replaced every few days. Recent research indicates that even brain cell, once thought to be incapable of mitosis, undergo cell division in the part of the brain associated with memory.

In a landmark intersection of science and fiction, cloning leapt from the world's imagination to its front page in February 1997. It arrived in the innocent body of a sheep named Dolly: The first exact genetic duplicate of an adult mammal due to genetic engineering. Scottish scientists had created Dolly from deoxyribonucleic acid (DNA) - the basic unit of heredity - taken from a single adult sheep cell. The accomplishment threw open the door too profound ethical as well as scientific controversy over the potential uses and abuses of cloning. "However the debate is resolved," wrote Los Angeles Times science reporter Thomas H. Maugh II, "the genie is irretrievably out of the bottle."

The type of cell division required for sexual reproduction is meiosis. That sexual procreation forwarded among organisms includes seaweeds, fungi, plants, and animals - including, of course, human beings. Meiosis differs from mitosis in that cell division begins with a cell that has a full complement of chromosomes and ends with gamete cells, such as sperm and eggs, that have only half the complement of chromosomes. When a sperm and egg unite during fertilization, the cell resulting from the union, called a zygote, the cell formed by the union of two gametes, specially a fertilized ovum before cleavage, the organism that develops from a fertilized cell.

The story of how cells evolved remains under an open and actively investigated question in science. The combined expertise of physicists, geologists, chemists, and evolutionary biologists has been required to shed light on the evolution of cells from the nonliving matter of early Earth. The planet formed about 4.5 to 5.0 billion years ago, and for millions of years, violent volcanic eruptions blasted substances such as carbon dioxide, nitrogen, water, and other small molecules into the air. These small molecules, bombarded by ultraviolet radiation and lightning from intense storms, collided to form the stable chemical bonds of larger molecules, such as amino acids and nucleotides - are the building blocks of proteins and nucleic acids. Experiments indicate that these larger molecules form spontaneously under laboratory conditions that simulate the probable early environment of Earth.

Proteins are any of a group of complex organic compounds that are essential for life. A complex organic macromolecules that contain carbon, hydrogen, oxy gen, nitrogen, and usually sulphur and are composed of one or more chains of amino acids. Proteins are fundamental components of all living cells and include many substances, such as enzymes, hormones, and antibodies, that is necessary for the proper functioning of an organism. They are essential in the life of animals for the growth and repair of tissue and can be obtained from foods, such as meat, fish, eggs, milk, and legumes.

Scientists have speculated that rain may have carried these molecules into lakes to create a primordial soup - the breeding ground for the assembly of proteins, the nucleic acid RNA, and lipids. Some scientists postulate that these more complex molecules formed in hydrothermal vents rather than in lakes. Other scientists propose that these key substances may have reached Earth on meteorites from outer space. Regardless of the origin or environment, however, scientists do agree that proteins, nucleic acids, and lipids provided the raw materials for the first cells. In the laboratory, scientists have observed lipid molecules joining to form spheres that resemble a cell's plasma membrane. As a result of these observations, scientists postulate that millions of years of molecular collisions resulted in lipid spheres enclosing RNA, the simplest molecule capable of self-replication. These primitive aggregations would have been the ancestors of the first prokaryotic cells.

Fossil studies indicate that cyanobacteria, bacteria capable of photosynthesis, were among the earliest bacteria to evolve, an estimated 3.4 billion to 3.5 billion years ago. In the environment of the early Earth, there were no oxygen, and cyanobacteria probably used fermentation to produce ATP. Over the eons, cyanobacteria performed photosynthesis, which produces oxygen as a byproduct; The result was the gradual accumulation of oxygen in the atmosphere. The presence of oxygen set the stage for the evolution of bacteria that used oxygen in aerobic respiration, a more efficient ATP-producing process than fermentation. Some molecular studies of the evolution of genes in archaebacteria suggest that these organisms may have evolved in the hot waters of hydrothermal vents or hot springs slightly earlier than cyanobacteria, around 3.5 billion years ago. Like cyanobacteria, archaebacteria probably relied on fermentation to synthesize ATP.

Eukaryotic cells of a single celled or multicellular organism whose cells contain a distinct membrane-bound nucleus, which may have evolved from the governing evolutionary principles of primitivity, as the prokaryotes in about 2 billion years ago. One hypothesis suggests that some prokaryotic cells lost their cell walls, permitting the cell's plasma membrane to expand and fold. These folds, ultimately, may have given rise to separate compartments within the cell - the forerunners of the nucleus and other organelles now found in eukaryotic cells. Another key hypothesis is known as endosymbiosis. Molecular studies of the bacteria-like DNA and ribosomes in mitochondria and Chloroplasts indicate that mitochondrion and chloroplast ancestors were once free-living bacteria. Scientists propose that these free-living bacteria were engulfed and maintained by other prokaryotic cells for their ability to produce ATP efficiently and to provide a steady supply of glucose. Over generations, eukaryotic cells have been taken on the appearance, form or making of a physical system or particular situation as to create a representation or model with which an image is vaguely in the likeness as the simulation of the mechanisms of operation or features of such that use of another.

That being the situation with which mitochondrial organelles in the cytoplasm of nearly all eukaryotic cells, carrying genetic material and many enzymes important for cell metabolisms, including the genetic mitochondrial and cell metabolisms responsible for the conversion of food to usable energy. A single eukaryote cell has a possibility for a multicellular-organism whose cells contain a distinct membrane-bound nucleus. As a nucleus, is that of a group of specialized nerve cells or a localized mass of gray matter in the brain or spinal cord. In that which of a large membrane-bound, usually spherical protoplasmic structure within a living cell, containing the cell materials and the controlling of its metabolism, growth and reproduction.

The first observations of cells were made in 1665 by English scientist Robert Hooke, who used a crude microscope of his own invention to examine a variety of objects, including a thin piece of cork. Noting the rows of tiny boxes that made up the dead wood's tissue, Hooke coined the term cell because the boxes reminded him of the small cells occupied by monks in a monastery. While Hooke was the first to observe and describe cells, he did not comprehend their significance. At about the same time, the Dutch maker of microscopes Antoni van Leeuwenhoek pioneered the invention of one of the best microscopes of the time. Using his invention, Leeuwenhoek was the first to observe, draw, and describe a variety of living organisms, including bacteria gliding in saliva, one-celled organisms cavorting in pond water, and sperm swimming in semen. Two centuries passed, however, before scientists grasped the true importance of cells.

Many advances have been made in microscope technology. An article from the 1994 Collier's Year Book begins with the microscope most young students are familiar with and tracks the breakthroughs in the development of new types of microscopes - including those that use ultrasonic imaging and those that "feel" an object's surface.

Modern ideas about cells appeared in the 1800s, when improved light microscopes enabled scientists to observe more details of cells. Working together, German botanist Matthias Jakob Schleiden and German zoologist Theodor Schwann recognized the fundamental similarities between plant and animal cells. In 1839 they proposed the revolutionary idea that all living things are made up of cells. Their theory gave rise to modern biology: a whole new way of seeing and investigating the natural world.

By the late 1800s, as light microscopes improved still further, scientists were able to observe chromosomes within the cell. Their research was aided by new techniques for staining parts of the cell, which made possible the first detailed observations of cell division, including observations of the differences between mitosis and meiosis in the 1880s. In the first few decades of the 20th century, many scientists focussed on the behaviour of chromosomes during cell division. At that time, it was generally held that mitochondria transmitted the hereditary information. By 1920, however, scientists determined that chromosomes carry genes and that genes transmit hereditary information from generation to generation.

During this period, scientists began to understand some of the chemical processes in cells. In the 1920s, the ultracentrifuge was developed. The ultracentrifuge is an instrument that spins cells or other substances in test tubes at high speeds, which causes the heavier parts of the substance to fall to the bottom of the test tube. This instrument enabled scientists to separate the relatively abundant and heavy mitochondria from the rest of the cell and study their chemical reactions. By the late 1940s, scientists were able to explain the role of mitochondria in the cell. Using refined techniques with the ultracentrifuge, scientists subsequently isolated the smaller organelles and gained an understanding of their functions.

The deoxyribonucleic acid (DNA) molecule is the genetic blueprint for each cell and ultimately the blueprint that determines every characteristic of a living organism. In 1953 American biochemist James Watson, left, and British biophysicist Francis Crick, described the structure of the DNA molecule for being a double-stranded helix, somewhat like a spiral staircase with many individual steps. Their work was aided by X-ray diffraction pictures of the DNA molecule taken by British biophysicist Maurice Wilkins and British physical chemist Rosalind Franklin. In 1962 Crick, Watson, and Wilkins received the Nobel Prize for their pioneering work on the structure of the DNA molecule.

While some scientists were studying the functions of cells, others were examining details of their structure. They were aided by a crucial technological development in the 1940s, the invention of the electron microscope, which uses high energy electrons instead of light waves to view specimens. New generations of electron microscopes have provided resolution, or the differentiation of separate objects, thousands of times more powerful than that available in light microscopes. The state or quality of being to separate into its optically active constituents into visible and distinct reductions as a purposive resolution, might that the act or process of separating or reducing something into its constituent parts, to reveal as the fineness of detail that can be distinguished in an image, as complications are resolved or simplified.

The Lysosome is a membrane bound organelle in the cytoplasm of most cells, containing various hydrolytic enzymes that function in intracellular digestion, the Golgi apparatuses, in that of a network of membranous vesicles presented in most living cells that function in the formation of secretions within the cell, also called Golgi complex, and the cytoskeleton, in which of an internal framework of a cell, composed largely of actin filaments and microtubules. The scientific fields of cell structure and function continue to complement each other as scientists explore the enormous plexuity of cells.

The discovery of the structure of DNA in 1953 by the American biochemist James D. Watson and British biophysicist Francis Crick ushered in the era of molecular biology. Today, investigation inside the world of cells - of genes and proteins at the molecular level - constitutes one of the largest and fastest moving areas in all of science. One particularly active field in recent years has been the investigation of cell signalling, the process by which molecular messages find their way into the cell through a series of plexuities as protein pathways in the cell.

Another busy area in cell biology concerns programmed cell death, or bounded particle apoptosis, which of the disintegration of cells into membrane-bound particles that are then eliminated by phagocytosis, that ingest bacteria or other foreign bodies by phagocytes or by shedding, by phagocytosis, or phagocytotic by the engulfing and ingestion of bacteria or other foreign bodies.

Millions of times per second in the human body, cells commit suicide as an essential part of the normal cycle of cellular replacement. This also seems to be a check against disease: When mutations build up within a cell, the cell will usually self-destruct. If this fails to occur, the cell may divide and give rise to mutated daughter cells, which continue to divide and spread, gradually forming a growth called a tumour. This unregulated growth by rogue cells can be benign, or harmless, or cancerous, which may threaten healthy tissue. The study of apoptosis is one avenue that scientists explore in an effort to understand how cells become cancerous.

Scientists are also discovering exciting aspects of the physical forces within cells. Cells employ a form of architecture called Tensegrity, which enables them to withstand battering by a variety of mechanical stresses, such as the pressure of blood circulating about the cells, or the particular movement of organelles within the cell. As a structure within the cell, such as a mitochondrion, vacuole, or chloroplast, a chlorophyll-containing plastid, that is found in alga and green plant cells, mitochondrion is a spherical or elongated organelle in the cytoplasm of nearly all eukaryotic cells, containing genetic material and many enzymes important for cell metabolisms, including any of the responsible for the conversion of food to usable energy, also called chondriosomes. This insurgence is held in the stability of the Tensegrity cells, by evenly distributing mechanical stresses to the cytoskeleton and other cell components. Tensegrity may also explain how a change in the cytoskeleton, of which the internal framework of a cell, is composed largely of a fine or thinly spun fibre, of likes a series of cells, as in many algae, that certain enzymes are anchored and initiate biochemical reactions within the cell, and can even influence the action of genes. The mechanical rules of Tensegrity may also account for the assembly of molecules into the first cells. Such new insights - made some 300 years after the tiny universe of cells was first glimpsed - show that cells continue to yield fascinating new worlds of discovery.

The Nervous System signifies the elements within the animal organism that are concerned with the reception of stimuli, the transmission of nerve impulses, or the activation of muscle mechanisms.

The reception of stimuli is the function of special sensory cells. The conducting elements of the nervous system are cells called neurons; these may be capable of only slow and generalized activity, or they may be highly efficient and rapidly conducting units. The specific response of the neuron—the nerve impulse - and the capacity of the cell to be stimulated makes this cell a receiving and transmitting unit capable of transferring information from one part of the body to another.

Each nerve cell consists of a central portion containing the nucleus, known as the cell body, of which one or more structures are inferred as axons and dendrites. The dendrites are rather short extensions of the cell body and are involved in the reception of stimuli. The axon, by contrast, is usually a single elongated extension, it is especially important in the transmission of nerve impulses from the region of the cell body to other cells.

Although all many-celled animals have some kind of nervous system, the plexuity of its organization varies considerably among different animal types. In simple animals such as jellyfish, the nerve cells form a network capable of mediating only a relatively stereotyped response. In more complex animals, such as shellfish, insects, and spiders, the nervous system is more complicated. The cell bodies of neurons are organized in clusters called ganglia. These clusters are interconnected by the neuronal processes to form a ganglionated chain, for having a group of nerve cells forming a nerve centre, especially one loathed outside the brain or spinal cord. A centre of power, activity, or energy, however, a pathological beneign cystic lesion resembling a tumour, occurring in a tendon sheath or joint capsule for being a group of nerve cells forming in one location outside the brain seems to occur as a gangliatic surface membrane of nerve cells.

Such chains are found in all vertebrates, in which they represent a special part of the nervous system, related especially to the regulation of the activities of the heart, the glands, and the involuntary Vertebrate animals have a bony spine and skull in which the central part of the nervous system is housed; The peripheral part extends throughout the remainder of the body.

That part of the nervous system located in the skull is referred to as the brain, which is found in the spine and called the spinal cord. The brain and the spinal cord are continuous through an opening in the base of the skull; Both are also in contact with other parts of the body through the nerves. The distinction made between the central nervous system and the peripheral nervous system is based on the different locations of the two intimately related parts of a single system. Some of the processes of the cell bodies conduct sense impressions and others conduct muscle responses, called reflexes, such as those caused by pain. All and all, pain is an unpleasant sensation occurring in varying degrees of severity as a consequence of injury, disease, or emotional disorder.

In the skin are cells of several types called receptors; each is especially sensitive to particular stimuli. Free nerve endings are sensitive to pain and are directly activated. The neurons so activated send impulses into the central nervous system and have junctions with other cells that have axons extending back into the periphery. Impulses are carried from processes of these cells to motor endings within the muscles. These neuromuscular endings excite the muscles, resulting in muscular contraction and appropriate movement. The pathway taken by the nerve impulse in mediating this simple response is in the form of a two-neuron arc that begins and ends in the periphery. Many of the actions of the nervous system can be explained on the basis of such reflex arcs, which are chains of interconnected nerve cells, stimulated at one end and capable of bringing about movement or glandular secretion at the other.

The cranial nerves connect to the brain by passing through openings in the skull, or cranium. Nerves associated with the spinal cord pass through openings in the vertebral column and are called spinal nerves. Both cranial and spinal nerves consist of large numbers of processes that convey impulses to the central nervous system and also carry messages outward; the former processes are called afferent, and the latter are called efferent. Afferent impulses are referred to as sensory deferent impulses, referred to as either somatic or visceral motor, according to what part of the body they reach. Most nerves are mixed nerves made up of both sensory and motor elements.

The cranial and spinal nerves are paired; The number in humans are 12 and 31, respectively. Cranial nerves are distributed to the head and neck regions of the body, with one conspicuous exception: The tenth cranial nerve, called the vagus. In addition to supplying structures in the neck, the vagus is distributed to structures located in the chest and abdomen. Vision, auditory and vestibular sensation, and taste is mediated by the second, eighth, and seventh cranial nerves, respectively. Cranial nerves also mediate motor functions of the head, the eyes, the face, the tongue, and the larynx, as well as the muscles that function in chewing and swallowing. Spinal nerves, after they exit from the vertebrae, are distributed in a band-like fashion to regions of the trunk and to the limbs. They interconnect extensively, thereby forming the brachial plexus, which runs to the upper extremities, and the lumbar plexus, which passes to the lower limbs.

Among the motor fibres is found groups that carry impulses to viscera, which are the soft internal organs of the body, especially those contained within the abdominal and thoracic cavities. These fibres are designated by the special name of autonomic nervous system. That system consists of two divisions, more or less antagonistic in function, that emerge from the central nervous system at different points of origin. One division, the sympathetic, arises from the middle portion of the spinal cord, joins the sympathetic ganglionated chain, courses through the spinal nerves, and is widely distributed throughout the body. The other division, the parasympathetic, arises both above and below the sympathetic, that is, from the brain and from the lower part of the spinal cord. These two divisions control the functions of the respiratory, circulatory, digestive, and urogenital systems.

Consideration of disorders of the nervous system is the province of neurology. Psychiatry deals with behavioural disturbances of a functional nature. The division between these two medical specialties cannot be sharply defined, because neurological disorders often manifest both organic and mental symptoms.

Diseases of the nervous system include genetic malformations, poisonings, metabolic defects, vascular disorders, inflammations, degeneration, and tumours, and they involve either nerve cells or their supporting elements. Vascular disorders, such as cerebral haemorrhage or other forms of a stroke, are among the most common causes of paralysis and other neurologic plexuity. Some diseases exhibit peculiar geographic and age distribution. In temperate zones, multiple sclerosis is a common degenerative disease of the nervous system, but it is rare in the Tropics.

The nervous system is subject to infection by a great variety of bacteria, parasites, and viruses. For example, meningitis, or infection of the meninges investing the brain and spinal cord, can be caused by many different agents. On the other hand, one specific virus causes rabies. Some viruses causing neurological ills can change or result by affecting certain or accessible parts of the nervous system. For example, the virus causing poliomyelitis commonly affects the spinal cord, as viruses that manufacture encephalitis that attack the brain.

Inflammations of the nervous system are named according to the part affected. Myelitis is an inflammation of the spinal cord; Neuritis is an inflammation of a nerve. It may be caused not only by infection but also by poisoning, alcoholism, or injury. Tumours originating in the nervous system usually are composed of meningeal tissue or neuroglia (supporting tissue) cells, depending on the specific part of the nervous system affected, but other types of tumours may metastasize to or invade the nervous system. In certain disorders of the nervous system, such as neuralgia, migraine, and epilepsy, no evidence may exist of organic damage. Another disorder, cerebral palsy, is associated with birth defects.

Pain, an unpleasant sensory and emotional experience caused by real or potential injury or damage to the body or described in terms of such damage. Scientists believe that pain evolved in the animal kingdom as a valuable three-part warning system. First, it warns of injury. Secondly, pain tends to protect against further injury by causing a reflexive withdrawal from the source of injury. Pain leads to a period of reduced activity, enabling injuries to heal more efficiently.

Pain is difficult to measure in humans because it has an emotional, or psychological component as well as a physical component. Some people express extreme discomfort from relatively small injuries, while others show little or no pain even after suffering severe injury. Sometimes pain is present even though no injury is apparent at all, or pain lingers long after an injury appears to have healed.

The signals that warn the body of tissue damage are transmitted through the nervous system. In this system, the basic unit is the nerve cell or neuron. A nerve cell is composed of three parts: a central cell body, a single major branching fibre called an axon, and a series of smaller branching fibres known as dendrites. Each nerve cell meets other nerve cells at certain points on the axons and dendrites, forming a dense network of interconnected nerve fibres that transmit sensory information about touch, pressure, or warmth, as well as pain.

Sensory information is transmitted from the different parts of the body to the brain through the spinal cord, which is a complex set of nerves that extend from the brain down along the back, protected by the bones of the spine. About as wide as a finger, the spinal cord is like a cable packed with many bundles of wires. The bundles are nerve pathways for transmitting information. But the spinal cord is more than just a message transmitter, it is also an extension of the brain. It contains neurons that process incoming sensory information, and generate messages to be carried to other parts of the body.

In the nervous system, a message-carrying impulse travels from one end of a nerve cell to the other by means of an electrical impulse. When it reaches the terminal end of a nerve cell, the impulse trigger's tiny sacs called presynaptic vesicles to release their contents, chemical messengers called neurotransmitters. The neurotransmitters float across the synapse, or gap between adjacent nerve cells. When they reach the neighbouring nerve cell, the neurotransmitters fit into specialized receptor sites much as a key fits into a lock, causing that nerve cell to "firing," or generate an electric message-carrying impulse. As the message continues through the nervous system, the presynaptic cell absorbs the excess neurotransmitters, and repackages them in presynaptic versicles in a process called neurotransmitter reuptake.

Information being transmitted between and within the brain and spinal cord travels through the nervous system using both chemical and electrical mechanisms. A message-carrying impulse travels from one end of a nerve cell to another by means of an electric signal. When the electric signal reaches the terminal end of a nerve cell, a gap called a synapse prevents the electric signal from crossing to the next cell. The electric signal triggers the cell to release chemicals called neurotransmitters, which float across the synapse to the neighbouring nerve cell. These neurotransmitters fit into specialized receptors found on the adjacent nerve cell, much as a key fits into a lock, generating an electric impulse in the neighbouring cell. This new impulse travels to the end of the long cell, in turn triggering the release of neurotransmitters to carry the message across the next synapse. Not all neurotransmitters initiate a message in a neighbouring nerve cell. Some specialize in preventing neighbouring cells from generating an electrical signal, while others function as helpers, facilitating the message's journey to the brain.

While most of the sensory nerves in the skin and other body tissues have special structures covering their nerve endings, those nerves that signal injury have free nerve endings. These simple nerve endings specialize in detecting noxious stimuli - a catchall term for injury-causing stimuli such as intense heat, extreme pressure, or sharp pricks or cuts. The nerve endings that detect pain are called nociceptors, and the process of transmitting pain signals when harmful stimulation occurs is called nociception. Causing of pain, as used of a stimulus caused by or responding to a painful stimulus as a nociceptive spinal reflex. Several million nociceptors are interlaced through the tissues and organs of the body. To encroach upon an inhabiting and an unpleasant sensation for occurring to a varying degree of severity, from that of an effect of injury, disease, or emotional disorder pain is itself the accumulation of unjust comfort.

When a person experiences an injury, such as a stubbed toe, specialized cells called nociceptors sense potential tissue damage (1) and send an electric signal, called an impulse, to the spinal cord via a sensory nerve (2). A specialized region of the spinal cord known as the dorsal horn (3) processes the pain signal, immediately sending another impulse back down the leg via a motor nerve (4). This causes the muscles in the leg to contract and pull the toe away from the source of injury (6). At the same time, the dorsal horn sends another impulse up the spinal cord to the brain. During this trip, the impulse travels between nerve cells. When the impulse reaches a nerve ending, (7) the nerve released chemical messengers, called neurotransmitters, which carry the message to the adjacent nerve. When the impulse reaches the brain (8), it is analyzed and processed as an unpleasant physical and emotional sensation.

An injury triggers pain signals in two types of nociceptors, one with large, insulated axons known as A-delta fibres and one with small, uninsulated axons known as C fibres. The large A-delta fibres conduct signals quickly, and the smaller C fibres transmit information slowly. The difference in the functions of these two fibres becomes obvious to a person that stubs a toe. At first the injured person is aware of a sharp, flashing pain at the point of injury. Generated by the A-delta fibres, this short-lived pain intrudes upon the thoughts and perceptions occurring in the brain. Just as this first pain subsides, a second pain begins that is vague, throbbing, and persistent. This sensation is derived from the C fibres.

Pain information from the A-delta and C fibres travels through the spinal cord to the brain. When it receives the pain message, the spinal cord generates impulses that travel back down to muscles, which lead to a reflexive contraction that pulls the body away from the source of injury. Other reflexes may affect skin temperature, blood flow, sweating, and other changes.

While this reflex action is underway, the pain message continues up the spinal cord to relay centres in the brain. The sensory information is routed to many other parts of the brain, including the cortex, where thinking processes occur

The Adrenal Gland is the vital endocrine gland that secretes hormones into the bloodstream, situated, in humans, on top of the upper end of each kidney. The two parts of the gland - the inner portion, or medulla, and the outer portion, or the cortex - are like separate organs: They are composed of different types of tissue and perform different functions. The adrenal medulla, composed of chromaffin as readily stained with chromium salts, as to be derived of the adrenal medulla, these cells secrete the hormone epinephrine, also called adrenaline, in response to stimulation of the sympathetic nervous system at times of stress. Epinephrine is a hormone secreted by the adrenal medulla that is released into the bloodstream in response to physical or mental stress, as from fear or injury. It initiates many bodily responses, including the stimulation of heart action concentration. Also, called adrenaline. Comprising a white too brownish crystalline compound, isolated from the adrenal gland of certain mammals or synthesized and used in medicine as a heart simulator, vasoconstrictors, and bronchial relaxant.

The medulla also secretes the hormone norepinephrine, which plays a role in maintaining normal blood circulation. The hormones of the medulla are called catecholamines. Unlike the adrenal cortex, the medulla can be removed without endangering the life of an individual.

The adrenal outer layer, or cortex, secretes about 30 steroid hormones, but only a few are secreted in significant amounts. Aldosterone, one of the most important hormones, regulates the balance of salt and water in the body. Cortisone and hydrocortisone are necessary to regulate fat, carbohydrate, and protein metabolism. Adrenal sex steroids have a minor influence on the reproductive system. Modified steroids, now produced synthetically, are superior to naturally secreted steroids for treatment of Addison's disease and other disorders.

Adrenocorticotropic Hormone is also known as corticotropin, hormones secreted by the anterior part of the pituitary gland. The specific function of ACTH is to stimulate the growth and secretions of the cortex (outer layers) of the adrenal gland. One of these secretions is cortisone, a hormone involved in carbohydrate and protein metabolisms. ACTH is used medically for its anti-inflammatory action to alleviate symptoms of allergies and arthritis. ACTH is a complex protein molecule containing 39 amino acids. The biological activity of the ACTH of various animal species is similar to that of humans, but the sequence of amino acids has been found to vary somewhat among species. ACTH production is controlled in part by the hypothalamus and in part by the existing levels of adrenal gland hormones. ACTH levels increased in response to stress, disease, and decreased blood pressure.

The Pituitary Gland is the master endocrine gland in vertebrate animals. The hormones secreted by the pituitary stimulate and control the functioning of almost all the other endocrine glands in the body. Pituitary hormones also promote growth and control the water balance of the body.

The pituitary is a small bean-shaped, reddish-gray organ located in the saddle-shaped depression (sella turcica) in the floor of the skull (the sphenoid bone) and attached to the base of the brain by a stalk; it is located near the hypothalamus. The pituitary has two lobes - the anterior lobe, or adenohypophysis, and the posterior lobe, or neurohypophysis - which differ in structure and function. The anterior lobe is derived embryologically from the roof of the pharynx and is composed of groups of epithelial cells separated by blood channels; the posterior lobe is derived from the base of the brain and is composed of nervous connective tissue and nerve-like secreting cells. The area between the anterior and posterior lobes of the pituitary is called the intermediate lobe; it has the same embryological origin as the anterior lobe.

Concentrated chemical substances, or hormones, which control 10 to 12 functions in the body, have been obtained as extracts from the anterior pituitary glands of cattle, sheep, and swine. Eight hormones have been isolated, purified, and identified; All of them are peptides, that is, they are composed of amino acids. A growth hormone (GH), or the somatotropic hormone (STH), is essential for normal skeletal growth and is neutralized during adolescence by the gonadal sex hormones. Thyroid-stimulating hormones (TSH) control the normal functioning of the thyroid gland, and the adrenocorticotropic hormone (ACTH) controls the activity of the cortex of the adrenal glands and takes part in the stress reaction. Prolactin, also called lactogenic, luteotropic, or mammotropic hormones, it initiates milk secretion in the mammary gland after the mammary tissues have been prepared during pregnancy by the secretion of other pituitary and sex hormones, from which a substance, usually a peptide or steroid produced by one tissue and conveyed by the bloodstream to another to affect physiological activity, such as growth or metabolism. As a substance, usually a peptide or steroid, produced by one tissue and conveyed by th e bloodstream to another to affect physiological activity, such as growth or metabolism, a synthetic compound that acts like a hormone in the body, any of the various similar substances can be found in plants and insects that regulate development.

The gonadotropin releasing hormone produced by the hypothalamus that signals the anterior pituitary gland to begin secreting luteinizing hormone and follicle stimulating hormones, and called luteinizing hormone-releasing hormones.

The luteinizing hormone stimulates the formation of ovarian hormones after ovulation and initiates lactation in the female, in the male, it stimulates the tissues of the testes to elaborate testosterone. In 1975 scientists identified the pituitary peptide endorphin, which acts in experimental animals as a natural pain reliever in times of stress. Endorphin and ACTH are made as parts of a single large protein, which subsequently splits. This may be the body's mechanism for coordinating the physiological activities of two stress-induced hormones. The same large prohormone that contains ACTH and endorphin also contains short peptides called melanocyte-stimulating hormones. These substances are analogous to the hormone that regulates pigmentation in fish and amphibians, but in humans they have no known function.

Research has shown that the hormonal activity of the anterior lobe is controlled by chemical messengers sent from the hypothalamus through tiny blood vessels to the anterior lobe. In the 1950s, the British neurologist Geoffrey Harris discovered that cutting the blood supply from the hypothalamus to the pituitary impaired the function of the pituitary. In 1964, chemical agents called releasing factors were found in the hypothalamus; These substances, it was learned, affect the secretion of growth hormones, a thyroid-stimulating hormone called thyrotropin, and the gonadotropic hormones involving the testes and ovaries.

In 1969 the American endocrinologist Roger Guillemin and colleagues isolated and characterized thyrotropin-releasing factors, which stimulates the secretion of thyroid-stimulating hormones from the pituitary. In the next few years his group and that of the American physiologist Andrew Victor Schally isolated the luteinizing hormone-releasing factor, which stimulates secretion of both LH and FSH, and somatostatin, which inhibits release of growth hormones. For this work, which proved that the brain and the endocrine system are linked, they shared the Nobel Prize in physiology or medicine in 1977. Human somatostatin was one of the first substances to be grown in bacteria by recombinant DNA.

The presence of the releasing factors in the hypothalamus helped to explain the action of the female sex hormones, estrogen and progesterone, and their synthetic versions contained in oral contraceptives, or birth-control pills. During a woman's normal monthly cycle, several hormonal changes are needed for the ovary to produce an egg cell for possible fertilization. When the estrogen level in the body declines, the follicle-releasing factor (FRF) flows to the pituitary and stimulates the secretion of the follicle-stimulating hormone. Through a similar feedback principle, the declining level of progesterone causes a release of luteal-releasing factors (LRF), which stimulates secretion of the luteinizing hormone. The ripening follicle in the ovary then produces estrogen, and the high level of that hormone influence the hypothalamus, as the part of the brain that lies below the thalamus, forming the major portion of the ventral region of the diencephalon and functioning to regular bodily temperature, certain metabolic processes, and other autonomic activities: These influence the temporary shut down in the production of the FSH. Increased progesterone, which is a steroid hormone that acts to prepare the uterus for implantation of the fertilized ovum, it is prepared from natural or synthetic progesterone, used in the prevention of a miscarriage, in the treatment of menstrual disorders and as a constituent of some oral contraceptives, delivering feedback to the hypothalamus shut down of the LH production by the pituitary. The daily doses of synthetic estrogen and progesterone in oral contraceptives, or injections of the actual hormones, inhibit the normal reproductive activity of the ovaries by mimicking the effect of these hormones on the hypothalamus.

In lower vertebrates this part of the pituitary secretes melanocyte-stimulating hormones, which brings about skin-colour changes. In humans, it is present only for a short time early in life and during pregnancy, and is not known to have any function.

Two hormones are secreted by the posterior lobe. One of these is the antidiuretic hormone (ADH), vasopressin. Vasopressin stimulates the kidney tubules to absorb water from the filtered plasma that passes through the kidneys and thus controls the amount of urine secreted by the kidneys. The other posterior pituitary hormone is oxytocin, which causes the contraction of the smooth muscles in the uterus, intestines, and blood arterioles. Oxytocin stimulates the contractions of the uterine muscles during the final stage of pregnancy to stimulate the expulsion of the fetus, and it also stimulates the ejection, or letdown, of milk from the mammary gland following pregnancy. Synthesized in 1953, oxytocin was the first pituitary hormone to be produced artificially. Vasopressin was synthesized in 1956.

The pituitary gland of or secreting phlegm or mucus of phlegm, which is a thick, sticky, stringy mucus secreted by the pituitary phlemy. Of or relating to the pituitary gland as secreting phlegm or mucus, from the early belief that it produced mucus, nonetheless, the pituitary gland as a small oval endocrine gland attached to the base of the vertebrate brain, and consisting of an anterior and a posterior lobe, its secretions of which control the other endocrine glands and influence growth, metabolism and maturation.

Pituitary functioning may be disturbed by such conditions as tumours, blood poisoning, blood clots, and certain infectious diseases. Conditions resulting from a decrease in anterior-lobe secretion include dwarfism, acromicria, Simmonds's disease, and Fröhlich's syndrome. The dwarfism occurs when anterior pituitary deficiencies occur during childhood; acromicria, in which the bones of the extremities are small and delicate, results when the deficiency occurs after puberty. Simmonds's disease, which is caused by extensive damage to the anterior pituitary, is characterized by premature aging, loss of hair and teeth, anaemia, and emaciation; it can be fatal. Fröhlich's syndrome, also called adiposogenital dystrophy, is caused by both anterior pituitary deficiency and a lesion of the posterior lobe or hypothalamus. The result is obesity, dwarfism, and retarded sexual development. Glands under the influence of anterior pituitary hormones are also affected by anterior pituitary deficiency.

Over secretion of one of the anterior pituitary hormones, somatotropin, results in a progressive chronic disease called acromegaly, which is characterized by enlargement of some parts of the body. Posterior-lobe deficiency results in diabetes insipidus.

Tissue, the aggregation of morphologically similar cells and associated intercellular matter acting together to perform one or more specific functions in the body. There are four basic types of tissue: muscle, nerve, epidermal, and connective.

Animal tissues, to which this article is limited, take their first form when the blastula cells, arising from the fertilized ovum, differentiate into three germ layers: they are ectoderm, mesoderm, and endoderm. Through further cell differentiation, or histogenesis, groups of cells grow into more specialized units to form organs made up, usually, of several tissues of similarly performing cells. Animal tissues are classified into four main groups.

These tissues include the skin and the inner surfaces of the body, such as those of the lungs, stomach, intestines, and blood vessels. Because its primary function is to protect the body from injury and infection, epitheliums are made up of tightly packed cells with little intercellular substance between them.

About 12 kinds of epithelial tissue occur. One kind is stratified squamous tissue found in the skin and the linings of the esophagus and vagina. It is made up of thin layers of flat, scalelike cells that form rapidly above the blood capillaries and is pushed toward the tissue surface, where they die and are shed. Another is a simple columnar epithelium, which lines the digestive system from the stomach to the anus; Simple columnar epithelium cells stand upright and not only control the absorption of nutrients but also secrete mucus through individual goblet cells. Glands are formed by the inward growth of epithelium-for examples, the sweat glands of the skin and the gastric glands of the stomach. Outward growth results in hair, nails, and other structures.

These tissues, which support and hold parts of the body together, comprises the fibrous and elastic connective tissues, the adipose (fatty) tissues, and cartilage and bone. In contrast to an epithelium, the cells of these tissues are widely separated from one another, with a large amount of intercellular substance between them. The cells of fibrous tissue, found throughout the body, connect to one another by an irregular network of strands, forming a soft, cushiony layer that also supports blood vessels, nerves, and other organs. Adipose tissue has a similar function, except that its fibroblasts also contain store fat. Elastic tissue, found in ligaments, the trachea, and the arterial walls, stretches and contracts again with each pulse beat. In the human embryo, the fibroblast cells that originally secreted collagen for the formation of fibrous tissue later change to secrete a different form of protein called chondrion, for the formation of cartilage, some cartilage later becomes calcified by the action of osteoblast to form bones. Blood and lymph are also often considered connective tissues.

Tissues, which contract and relax, comprise the striated, smooth, and cardiac muscles. Striated muscles, also called skeletal or voluntary muscles, include those that are activated by the somatic, or voluntary, nervous system. They are joined together without cell walls and have several nuclei. The smooth, or involuntary muscles, which are activated by the autonomic nervous system, are found in the internal organs and consist of simple sheets of cells. Cardiac muscles, which have characteristics of both striated and smooth muscles, are joined together in a vast network. These highly complex groups of cells, called ganglia, transfer information from one part of the body to another. Each neuron, or nerve cell, consists of a cell body with branching dendrites and one long fibre, or axons. The dendrites connect one neuron to another; The axon transmits impulses to an organ or collects impulses from a sensory organ.

Once, again, in the nervous system, a message-carrying impulse travels from one end of a nerve cell to the other by means of an electrical impulse. When it reaches the terminal end of a nerve cell, the impulse trigger's tiny sacs called presynaptic vesicles to release their contents, chemical messengers called neurotransmitters. The neurotransmitters float across the synapse, or gap between adjacent nerve cells. When they reach the neighbouring nerve cell, the neurotransmitters fit into specialized receptor sites much as a key fits into a lock, causing that nerve cell to fire or generate an electric message-carrying impulse. As the message continues through the nervous system, the presynaptic cell absorbs the excess neurotransmitters, and repackages them in presynaptic versicles in a process called neurotransmitter reuptake.

Reflex, in physiology, is the involuntary response to a stimulus by the animal organism. In its simplest form, it consisted of the stimulation of an afferent nerve through a sense organ, or receptor, followed by transmission of the stimulus, usually through a nerve centre, to an efferent motor nerve, resulting in action of a muscle or gland, called the effector. In most reflex action, however, the stimulus passes through one or more intermediate nerve cells, which modify and direct its action, sometimes to the extent of involving the muscular activity of the entire organism. For example, a painful stimulus applied to the hand causes a reflex withdrawal of the hand, which involves contraction of the flexor group of muscles and reflexation of the opposing extensor group; if the stimulus is strong, the coordinating nerve cells pass it to the arm muscles and also to the muscles of the trunk and legs, the result being a jump that removes not only the arm, but the entire person from the vicinity of the painful stimulus.

The system of coordinating nerve cells is such that several different kinds of stimuli may produce the same result. For example, the stimulus produced by the sight of food and that caused by the smell of food travel different afferent pathways, but both have a common final path that stimulates the salivary glands to secretion. The final common path may also be activated through associated nerve tracts by a stimulus that ordinarily is not directly connected with the response. This type of reflex was named for a conditioned reflex by its discoverer, the Russian physiologist Ivan Pavlov, about 1904. Pavlov found that sounding a bell every time a dog was about to be given food eventually caused a reflex flow of saliva, which later persisted even when no food was produced. Elaborations of this habituative type of reflex are regarded by some physiologists and psychologists as an important basis for many behaviours, both voluntary and involuntary.

The normal pathways of many reflexes are generally known, and the presence, absence, or exaggerations of the normal physical responses to certain stimuli are symptoms used by neurologists to determine the condition of the neural pathways involved. A familiar reflex commonly tested by physicians is the patellar reflex, in which an involuntary jerk of the knee is evoked by lightly striking the tendon of the patella, or kneecap, indicating the efficiency of certain nerve tracts in the spinal cord.

Like all other cells, neurons contain charged ions: Potassium and sodium (positively charged) and chlorine (negatively charged). Neurons differ from other cells in that they are able to produce a nerve impulse. A neuron is polarized - that is, it has an overall negative charge inside the cell membrane because of the high concentration of chlorine ions and low concentration of potassium and sodium ions. The concentration of these same ions is exactly reversed outside the cell. This charge differential represents stored electrical energy, sometimes referred to as membrane potential or resting potential. The negative charge inside the cell is maintained by two features. The first is the selective permeability of the cell membrane, which is more permeable to potassium than sodium. The second feature is sodium pumps within the cell membrane that actively pump sodium out of the cell. When depolarization occurs, this charge differential across the membrane is reversed, and a nerve impulse is produced.

Depolarization is a rapid change in the permeability of the cell membrane. When sensory input or any other kind of stimulating current is received by the neuron, the membrane permeability is changed, allowing a sudden influx of sodium ions into the cell. The high concentration of sodium, or action potential, changes the intrinsic property of matter responsible for all electric phenomena, in particular for the force of the electromagnetic interaction, occurring in this property, however, is that the permeability of charges within the cell from negative too positive. The local changes in ion concentration triggers similar reactions along the membrane, propagating the nerve impulse. After a brief period called the refractory period, during which the ionic concentration returned to resting potential, the neuron can repeat this process.

Nerve impulses travel at different speeds, depending on the cellular composition of a neuron. Where speed of impulse is important, as in the nervous system, axons are insulated with a membranous substance called myelin. The insulation provided by myelin maintains the ionic charge over long distances. Nerve impulses are propagated at specific points along the myelin sheath; These points are called the Nodes of Ranvier. Examples of myelinated axons are those in sensory nerve fibres and nerves connected to skeletal muscles. In non-militated cells, the nerve impulse is propagated more diffusely.

The nervous system has two divisions: The somatic, which allow voluntary control over skeletal muscle, and the autonomic, which is involuntary and controls cardiac and smooth muscle and glands. The autonomic nervous system has two divisions: The sympathetic and the parasympathetic. Many, but not all, of the muscles and glands that distribute nerve impulses to the larger interior organs possess a double nerve supply; in such cases the two divisions may exert opposing effects.

Thus, the sympathetic system increases heartbeat, and the parasympathetic system decreases heartbeat. The two nervous systems are not always antagonistic, however. For example, both nerve supplies to the salivary glands excite the cells of secretion. Furthermore, a single division of the autonomic nervous system may both excite and inhibit a single effector, as in the sympathetic supply to the blood vessels of skeletal muscle. Finally, the sweat glands, the muscles that cause involuntary erection or bristling of the hair, the smooth muscle of the spleen, and the blood vessels of the skin and skeletal muscle are actuated only by the sympathetic division.

Voluntary movement of head, limbs, and body is caused by nerve impulses arising in the motor area of the cortex of the brain and carried by cranial nerves or by nerves that emerge from the spinal cord to connect with skeletal muscles. The reaction involves both excitation of nerve cells stimulating the muscles involved and inhibition of the cells that stimulate opposing muscles. A nerve impulse is an electrical change within a nerve cell or fibre; Measured in millivolts, it lasts a few milliseconds and can be recorded by electrodes.

The human brain has three major structural components: The large dome-shaped cerebrums, the smaller somewhat spherical cerebellum, and the brainstem. Prominent in the brainstem is the medulla oblongata (the egg-shaped enlargement at the centre) and the thalamus (between the medulla and the cerebrum). The cerebrum is responsible for intelligence and reasoning. The cerebellum helps to maintain balance and posture. The medulla is involved in maintaining involuntary functions such as respiration, and the thalamus act as a relay centre for electrical impulses travelling to and from the cerebral cortex. Lack of blood flow to any part of the brain results in a stroke, permanent damage that interferes with the functions of the affected part of the brain.

Movement may occur also in direct response to an outside stimulus, thus, a tap on the knee causes a jerk, and a light shone into the eye makes the pupil contract. These involuntary responses are called reflexes. Various nerve terminals called receptors constantly send impulses into the central nervous system. These are of three classes: exteroceptors, which are sensitive to pain, temperature, touch, and pressure, interceptors react to changes in the internal environment, and proprioceptors, which respond to variations in movement, position, and tension. These impulses terminate in special areas of the brain, as do of those special receptors concerned with sight, hearing, smell, and taste.

Whereas most major nerves emerge from the spinal cord, the 12 pairs of cranial nerves project directly from the brain, with the exception of one pair, that relay motor or sensory information (or both); The tenth, or vagus nerve, affects visceral functions such as heart rate, vasoconstriction, and contraction of the smooth muscle found in the walls of the trachea, stomach, and intestine.

Muscular contractions do not always cause actual movement. A small fraction of the total number of fibres in most muscles is usually contracting. This serves to maintain the posture of a limb and enables the limb to resist passive elongation or stretch. This slight continuous contraction is called muscle tone.

In 1946 Axelrod joined the laboratory of American pharmacologist Bernard Brodie at Goldwater Memorial Hospital in New York. The pair conducted research on pain-relieving drugs called analgesics. They identified a pain-relieving chemical known as acetaminophen. This drug was later developed and marketed by the drug company Johnson & Johnson under the brand-name Tylenol.

In 1949 Axelrod took a position at the National Heart Institute, a branch of the National Institutes of Health (NIH). Where Axelrod studied how the body processes certain drugs that cause behavioural changes, including amphetamines, ephedrine, and mescaline. He identified a group of enzymes that help these drugs break down in the body. These enzymes, called cytochrome-P450 monoxygenases, have been studied extensively by other scientists, particularly in cancer research.

Realizing that career advancement in the sciences requires a doctoral degree, in 1954 Axelrod took a leave of absence from his job at the National Heart Institute to attend The George Washington University. He earned his doctorate in pharmacology in 1955. That same year he was named chief of pharmacology at the National Institute of Mental Health (NIMH) another branch of NIH.

At NIMH, Joseph Axelrod began research on neurotransmitters. A nerve cell releases a neurotransmitter to spur a neighbouring cell into action. In the 1950s most scientists believed that a neurotransmitter became inactive once it stimulated a neighbouring cell. But Axelrod's research found that the neurotransmitter returns to the first nerve cell, in a process known as reuptake, where it is broken down by enzymes or repackaged for reuse. This research led to the creation of a number of drugs that prevent the reuptake process, enabling a neurotransmitter to remain active for a longer period of time.

Axelrod's research revolutionized the understanding of many mental-health disorders, including depression, anxiety, and schizophrenia. Prior to his research, psychiatry focussed on the relationship of life experiences to mental health problems. But Axelrod's research proved that mental-health disorders were often the result of complicated brain chemistry. His research spurred the development of new drugs that advanced the treatment of mental-health conditions. Among these are selective serotonin reuptake inhibitors, including the antidepressant called Fluoxetine (Prozac), sertraline (Zoloft) and paroxetine (Paxil), as oral antidepressants of the SSRI class of drugs.

The study of the biochemistry of memory is another exciting scientific enterprise, but one that can only be touched upon here. Scientists estimate that an adult human brain contains about 100 billion neurons. Each of these is connected to hundreds or thousands of other neurons, forming trillions of neural connections. Neurons communicate by chemical messengers called neurotransmitters. An electrical signal travels along the neuron, triggering the release of neurotransmitters at the synapse, the small gap between neurons. The neurotransmitters travel across the synapse and act on the next neuron by binding with protein molecules called receptors. Most scientists believe that memories are somehow stored among the brain's trillions of synapses, rather than in the neurons themselves.

Scientists who study the biochemistry of learning and memory often focus on the marine snail Aplysia because its simple nervous system allows them to study the effects of various stimuli on specific synapses. A change in the snail's behaviour due to learning can be correlated with a change at the level of the synapse. One exciting scientific frontier is discovering the changes in neurotransmitters that occur at the level of the synapse.

Other researchers have implicated glucose, a sugar and insulin(a hormone secreted by the pancreas) as important to learning and memory. Humans and other animals given these substances show an improved capacity to learn and remember. Typically, when animals or humans ingest glucose, the pancreas responds by increasing insulin production, so it is difficult to determine which substance contributes to improved performance. Some studies in humans that have systematically varied the amount of glucose and insulin in the blood have shown that insulin may be the more important of the two substances for learning.

Scientists also have examined the influence of genes on learning and memory. In one study, scientists bred strains of mice with extra copies of a gene that helps build a protein called N-methyl-D-aspartate, or NMDA. This protein acts as a receptor for certain neurotransmitters. The genetically altered mice outperformed normal mice on a variety of tests of learning and memory. In addition, other studies have found that chemically blocking NMDA receptor impairs learning in laboratory rats. Future discoveries from genetic and biochemical studies may lead to treatments for memory deficits from Alzheimer's disease and other conditions that affect memory.

Alzheimer's Disease, is a progressive brain disorder that causes a gradual and irreversible decline in memory, language skills, perception of time and space, and, eventually, the inability to care for oneself and one's future. This was first described by German psychiatrist Alois Alzheimer in 1906, Alzheimer's disease was initially thought to be a rare condition affecting only young people, and was referred to as prehensile dementia. Today late-onset Alzheimer's disease is recognized as the most common cause of the loss of mental function in those aged 65 and over. Alzheimer's in people in their 30s, 40s, and 50s, called early-onset Alzheimer's disease, occurring to a lesser extent, for an accounting of less than 10 percent of the knowing 4 million cases of Alzheimer's in the United States.

Although Alzheimer's disease is not a normal part of the aging process, the risk of developing the disease increases as people grow older. About 10 percent of the United States population over the age of 65 is affected by Alzheimer's disease, and nearly 50 percent of those over age 85 may have the disease.

Alzheimer's disease takes a devastating toll, not only on the patients, but also on those who love and care for them. Some patients experience immense fear and frustration as they struggle with once commonplace tasks and slowly lose their independence. Family, friends, and especially those who provide daily care suffer immeasurable pain and stress as they witness Alzheimer's disease slowly dehumanize as or as if one's own slips away from them.

The onset of Alzheimer's disease is usually very gradual. In the early stages, Alzheimer's patients have relatively mild problems learning new information and remembering where they have left common objects, such as keys or a wallet. In time, they begin to have trouble recollecting recent events and finding the right words to express themselves. As the disease progresses, patients may have difficulty remembering what day or month it is, or finding their way around familiar surroundings. They may develop a tendency to wander off and then be unable to find their way back. Patients often become irritable or withdrawn as they struggle with fear and frustration when once commonplace tasks become unfamiliar and intimidating. Behavioural changes may become more pronounced as patients become paranoid or delusional and unable to engage in normal conversation.

Eventually Alzheimer's patients become completely incapacitated and unable to take care of their most basic life functions, such as eating and using the bathroom. Alzheimer's patients may live many years with the disease, usually dying from other disorders that may develop, such as pneumonia. Typically the time from initial diagnosis until death is seven to ten years, but this is quite variable and can range from three to twenty years, depending on the age of the onset, other medical conditions present, and the care patients receive.

The brains of patients with Alzheimer's have distinctive formations - abnormally shaped proteins called tangles and plaques - that are recognized as the hallmark of the disease. Not all brain regions show these characteristic formations. The areas most prominently affected are those related to memory.

Tangles are long, slender tendrils found inside nerve cells, or neurons. Scientists have learned that when a protein-called tau becomes altered, it may cause the characteristic tangles in the brain of the Alzheimer's patient. In healthy brains, provides structural support for neurons, but in Alzheimer's patients this structural support collapses.

Plaques, or clumps of fibres, form outside the neurons in the adjacent brain tissue. Scientists found that a type of protein, called amyloid precursor protein, forms toxic plaques when it is cut in two places. Researchers have isolated the enzyme beta-secretes, which is believed to make one of the cuts in the amyloid precursor protein. Researchers also identified another enzyme-called gamma, secreted and, made the second cut in the amyloid precursor protein. These two enzymes snip the amyloid precursor protein into fragments that then accumulate to form plaques that are toxic to neurons.

Scientists have found that tangles and plaques cause neurons in the brains of Alzheimer's patients to shrink and eventually die, first in the memory and language centres and finally throughout the brain. This widespread neuron degeneration leaves gaps in the brain's messaging network that may interfere with communication between cells, causing some of the symptoms of Alzheimer's disease.

Alzheimer's patients have lower levels of neurotransmitters, chemicals that carry complex messages back and forth between the nerve cells. For instance, Alzheimer's disease seems to decrease the level of the neurotransmitter acetylcholine, which is known to influence memory. A deficiency in other neurotransmitters, including somatostatin and corticotropin-releasing factor, and, particularly in younger patients, serotonin and norepinephrine, are of a substance, both a hormone and neurotransmitter, secreted by the adrenal medulla and the nerve endings of the sympathetic nervous system to cause vasoconstriction and increases in heart rate, blood pressure, and the sugar level of the blood, and also called noradrenaline. There is also interference with normal communication between brain cells.

The causes of Alzheimer's disease remain a mystery, but researchers have found that particular groups of people have risk factors that make them more likely to develop the disease than the general population. For example, people with a family history of Alzheimer's are more likely to develop Alzheimer's disease.

Some of the most promising Alzheimer's research is being conducted in the field of genetics to learn the role a family history of the disease has in its development. Scientists have learned that people who are carriers of a specific version of the apolipoprotein E gene (apoE genes), found on chromosome 19, are several times more likely to develop Alzheimer's than carriers of other versions of the apoE gene. The most common version of this gene in the general population is apoE3. Nearly half of all late-onset Alzheimer's patients have the fewer in common apoE4 versions, however, and research has shown that this gene plays a role in Alzheimer's disease. Scientists have also found evidence that variations in one or more genes located on chromosomes 1.10, and 14 may increase a person's risk for Alzheimer's disease. Scientists have identified the gene variations on chromosomes 1 and 14 and learned that these genes produce mutations in proteins called presenilins. These mutated proteins apparently trigger the activity of the enzyme gamma secretase, which splices the amyloid precursor protein. Amyloid is a starchlike substance of which a hard waxy deposit consisting of protein and polysaccharides results from the degeneration of tissue.

Researchers have made similar strides in the investigation of early-onset Alzheimer's disease. A series of genetic mutations in patients with an early-onset of Alzheimer's has been linked to the production of the amyloid precursor protein, a starchlike substance for which is a hard waxy deposit consisting of protein and polysaccharides that result from the degeneration of tissue.

The proteins are fundamental components of all living cells and include many substances, such as enzymes, hormones, and antibodies, that is necessary for the proper functioning of an organism. As protein, which is a carrier of carbon, hydrogen, oxygen, nitrogen, and usually sulfur and is composed of one or more chains of amino acids. However, being that of a small disk-shaped formation or growth deposits of fatty material on the inner lining off an arterial wall, characteristic of atherosclerosis, a film of mucus and bacteria, often a clear round patch of lysed cells in an otherwise opaque layer of a bacterium or cell culture is found to situate in plaques that may be implicated in the destruction of neurons. One mutation is particularly interesting among the geneticists, because it occurs on a gene involved in the genetic disorder Down syndrome. People with Down syndrome usually develop plaques and tangles in their brains as they get older, and researchers believe that learning more about the similarities between Down syndrome and Alzheimer's may further our understanding of the genetic elements of the disease.

Some studies suggest that one or more factors other than heredity may determine whether people develop the disease. One study published in February 2001 compared residents of Ibadan, Nigeria, who eat a mostly low-fat vegetarian diet, with African Americans living in Indianapolis, Indiana, whose diet included a variety of high-fat foods. The Nigerians were less likely to develop Alzheimer's disease compared to their US counterparts. Some researchers suspect that health imposes on high blood pressure, atherosclerosis (arteries clogged by fatty deposits), high cholesterol levels, or other cardiovascular problems may play a role in the development of the disease.

Other studies have suggested that environmental agents may be a possible cause of Alzheimer's disease; for example, one study suggested that high levels of aluminum in the brain may be a risk factor. Several scientists initiated research projects to further investigate this connection, but no conclusive evidence has been found linking aluminum with Alzheimer's disease. Similarly, investigations into other potential environmental causes, such as zinc exposure, viral agents, and food-borne poisons, while initially promising, have generally turned up inconclusive results.

Some studies indicate that brain trauma can trigger a degenerative process that results in Alzheimer's disease. In one study, an analysis of the medical records scribed upon veterans of World War II (1939-1945) linked serious head injury in early adulthood with Alzheimer's disease in later life. The study also looked at other factors that could possibly influence the development of the disease among the veterans, such as the presence of the apoE gene, but no other factors were identified.

Alzheimer's disease is only positively diagnosed by examining brain tissue under a microscope to see the hallmark plaques and tangles, and this is only possible after a patient dies. As a result, physicians rely on a series of other techniques to diagnose probable Alzheimer's disease in living patients. Diagnosis begins by ruling out other problems that cause memory loss, such as stroke, depression, alcoholism, and the use of certain prescription drugs. The patient undergoes a thorough examination, including specialized brain scans, to eliminate other disorders. The patient may be given a detailed evaluation called a neuropsychological examination, which is designed to evaluate a patient's ability to perform specific mental tasks. This helps the physician determine whether the patient is showing the characteristic symptoms of Alzheimer's disease - progressively worsening memory problems, language difficulties, and trouble with spatial direction and time. The physician also asks about the patient's family medical history to learn about any past serious illnesses, which may give a hint about the patient's current symptoms.

Evidence shows that there is inflammation in the brains of Alzheimer's patients, which may be associated with the production of amyloid precursor protein. Studies are underway to find drugs that prevent this inflammation, to possibly slow or even halt the progress of the disease. Other promising approaches centre on mechanisms that manipulate amyloid precursor protein production or accumulation. Drugs are in development that may block the activity of the enzymes that cut the amyloid precursor protein, halting amyloid production. Other studies in mice suggest those vaccinating animals with amyloid precursor protein can produce a reaction that clears amyloid precursor protein from the brain. Physicians have started vaccination studies in humans to determine if the same potentially beneficial effects can be obtained. There is still much to be learned, but as scientists better understand the genetic components of Alzheimer's, the roles of the amyloid precursor protein and the tau protein in the disease, and the mechanisms of nerve cell degeneration, the possibility that a treatment will be developed is more likely.

The responsibility for caring for Alzheimer's patients generally falls on their spouses and children. Care givers must constantly be on guard for the possibility of Alzheimer's patients wandering away or becoming agitated or confused in a manner that jeopardizes the patient or others. Coping with a loved one's decline and inability to recognize familiar face causes enormous pain.

The increased burden faced by families is intense, and the life of the Alzheimer's care giver is often called a 36-hour day. Not surprisingly, care givers often develop health and psychological problems of their own as a result of this stress. The Alzheimer's Association, a national organization with local chapters throughout the United States, was formed in 1980 in large measure to provide support for Alzheimer's care givers. Today, national and local chapters are a valuable source for information, referral, and advice.

Neurophysiology is the study of how nerve cells, or neurons, receives and transmits information. Two types of phenomena are involved in processing nerve signals - Electrical and chemical. Electrical events propagate a signal within a neuron, and chemical processes transmit the signal from one neuron to another neuron or to a muscle cell.

A neuron is a long cell that has a thick central area containing the nucleus, it also has one long process called an axon and one or more short, bushy processes called dendrites. Dendrites receive impulses from other neurons. (The exceptions are sensory neurons, such as those that transmit information about temperature or touch, in which the signal is generated by specialized receptors in the skin.) These impulses are propagated electrically along the cell membrane to the end of the axon. At the tip of the axon the signal is chemically transmitted to an adjacent neuron or muscle cell.

Like all other cells, neurons contain charged ions: Potassium and sodium (positively charged) and chlorine (negatively charged). Neurons differ from other cells in that they are able to produce a nerve impulse. A neuron is polarized - that is, it has an overall negative charge inside the cell membrane because of the high concentration of chlorine ions and low concentration of potassium and sodium ions. The concentration of these same ions is exactly reversed outside the cell. This charge differential represents stored electrical energy, sometimes referred to as membrane potential or resting potential. The negative charge inside the cell is maintained by two features. The first is the selective permeability of the cell membrane, which is more permeable to potassium than sodium. The second feature is sodium pumps within the cell membrane that actively pump sodium out of the cell. When depolarization occurs, this charge differential across the membrane is reversed, and a nerve impulse is produced.

Depolarization is a rapid change in the permeability of the cell membrane. When sensory input or any other kind of stimulating current is received by the neuron, the membrane permeability is changed, allowing a sudden influx of sodium ions into the cell. The high concentration of sodium, or action potential, changing the effective regularity in operations which the overall electric charges in the cell leaves open to emit off its negative into its positive charge of energy, as local changes in the action or process of ion concentration triggers similar reactions along the membrane by propagating the nerve impulse. After a brief period called the refractory period, during which the state or condition in ionic concentration returning to resting potential, the neuron can repeat this process. Nerve impulses travel at different speeds, depending on the cellular composition of a neuron. Where speed of impulse is important, as in the nervous system, axons are insulated with a membranous substance called myelin. The insulation provided by myelin maintains the ionic charge over long distances. Nerve impulses are propagated at specific points along the myelin sheath; These points are called the nodes of Ranvier. Examples of myelinated axons are those in sensory nerve fibres and nerves connected to skeletal muscles. In non-myelinated cells, the nerve impulse is propagated more diffusely.

When the electrical signal reaches the tip of an axon, it stimulates small presynaptic vesicles in the cell. These vesicles contain chemicals called neurotransmitters, which are released into the microscopic space between neurons (the synaptic cleft). The neurotransmitter fastens its chemical substances onto the surface of the adjacent neuron. This stimulus causes the adjacent cell to depolarize and propagate an action potential of its own. The duration of a stimulus from a neurotransmitter is limited by the breakdown of the chemicals in the synaptic cleft and the reuptake by the neuron that produced them. Formerly, each neuron was thought to make only one transmitter, but recent studies have shown that some cells of the physiological activity of a value that such behaviour of a chemical compound resulting of a specific functional application that develops of two or more.

During the early 1900s, in examining the workings of the nervous system, physiologists were beginning to explore the idea that the transmission of nerve impulses takes place, in part, via chemical means. Loewi decided to explore this idea. During a stay in London in 1903, he met Sir Dale, who was also interested in the chemical transmission of nerve impulses. However, for Loewi, Dale, and all the other researchers pursuing a chemical transmitter of nerve impulses, years of effort produced no solid evidence. In 1921 Loewi suspended two frogs' hearts in solution, one with a major nerve removed. Removing fluid from the heart that still contained the nerve, and injecting the fluid into the nerveless heart, Loewi observed that the second heart behaved as if the missing nerve were present. The nerves, he concluded, do not act directly on the heart - it is the action of chemicals, freed by the stimulation of nerves, that causes increases in heart rate and other functional changes. In 1926 Loewi and his colleagues identified one of the chemicals in his experiment as acetylcholine. This was indisputably a neurotransmitter - a chemical that serves to transmit nerve impulses in the involuntary nervous system.

We acknowledge the neurotransmitters are inherently made by chemically induced neurons, or nerve cells. Neurons send out neurotransmitters as chemical signals to activate or inhibit the function of neighbouring cells.

Within the central nervous system, which consists of the brain and the spinal cord, neurotransmitters pass from neuron to neuron. In the peripheral nervous system, which is made up of the nerves that run from the central nervous system to the rest of the body, the chemical signals pass between a neuron and an adjacent muscle or gland cells.

Chemical compounds - belonging to three chemical families - are widely recognized as neurotransmitters. In addition, certain other body chemicals, including adenosine, histamine, enkephalins, endorphins, and epinephrine, have the neurotransmitter like properties. Experts believe that there are many more neurotransmitters as yet undiscovered.

The first of the three families is composed of amines, a group of compounds containing molecules of carbon, hydrogen, and nitrogen. Among the amines neurotransmitters are acetylcholine, norepinephrine, dopamine, and serotonin. Acetylcholine is the most widely used neurotransmitter in the body, and neurons that leave the central nervous system (for example, those running to skeletal muscle) use acetylcholine as their neurotransmitter; neurons that run to the heart, blood vessels, and other organs may use acetylcholine or norepinephrine. Dopamine is involved in the movement of muscles, and it controls the secretion of the pituitary hormone Prolactin, which triggers milk production in nursing mothers.

The second neurotransmitter family is composed of amino acids, organic compounds containing both an amino group (NH2) and a carboxylic acid group (COOH). Amino acids that serve as neurotransmitters include glycine, glutamic and aspartic acids, and gamma-amino butyric acid (GABA). Glutamic acid and GABA are the most abundant neurotransmitters within the central nervous system, and especially in the cerebral cortex, which is largely responsible for such higher brain functions as thought and interpreting sensations.

The third neurotransmitter family is composed of peptides, which are compounds that contain at least two, and sometimes as many as 100 amino acids. Peptide neurotransmitters are poorly understood, but scientists know that the peptide neurotransmitter called substance P influences the sensation of pain.

In general, each neuron uses only a single compound as its neurotransmitter. However, some neurons outside the central nervous system are able to release both an amine and a peptide neurotransmitter.

Neurotransmitters are manufactured from precursor compounds like amino acids, glucose, and the dietary amine-called choline. Neurons modify the structure of these precursor compounds in a series of reactions with enzymes. Neurotransmitters that comes from amino acids include serotonin, for which it is derived from tryptophan. Dopamine and norepinephrine, under which are derived from tyrosine, of a white crystalline amino acid that is obtained from the hydrolysis of proteins and glycine, which is derived from threonine, of which is a colourless crystalline amino acid that is obtained from the hydrolysis of proteins and is an essential component of human nutrition. The hydrolysis is a decomposition of a chemical compound by reaction with water, such as the dissociation of a dissolved salt or the catalytic conversion of starch to glucose.

Among the neurotransmitters made from glucose are glutamate, aspartate, and GABA (gamma-aminobutyric), the natural amine, choline, is often classed in the vitamin B complex and a constituent of many other biologically important molecules, such as acetylcholine and lecithin, serving as the precursor for acetylcholine. Once, again, glucose functions as a monosaccharide sugar, as occurring widely in most plant and animal tissue. It is the principal circulating sugar in the blood and the major energy source of the body. This, colourless to yellowish syrupy mixture of dextrose, maltose, and any of the various soluble polysaccharides obtained from starch and the obtained from starch by application of heat or acids and used mainly as adhesives and thickening agents. In which, of containing in about 20 percent water, and used in confectionery, alcoholic fermentation, tanning, and treating tobacco, also called, starch syrup.

Lecithin being a group of any of various phosphorous-containing lipids, such as lecithin and cephalin, that are composed mainly of fatty acids, a phosphate group and a simple organic molecule, whereas, Lecithin, in that of a group of Phospholipids are found in egg yolks and the plasm membrane of plants and animal cells and used as an emulsifier in a wide range of commercial products, including foods, cosmetics, paints and plastics, also called phosphatidylcholine.

Neurotransmitters are chemical substances, such as acetylcholine or dopamine, that transmits nerve impulses across a synapse, which of a function that joins or act of a condition of being joined, in the transition or, mode of transition from one to another. This junction to which point or terminal to the neuron, of the impulse-conducting cells that constitute the brain, spinal column, and nerves consisting of a nucleated cell body with one or mor e dendrites and a single axon, also called a nerve cell. The junction across nerve impulse passes from an axon terminal to a neuron muscle cell. By joining together in the quest to journey across the synapse and cell into a synapse, joining to infringe upon contacting the emitted internal representation of a side-by-side associations with the homologous paternal and the threadlike linear strands of chromosomes during the first prophase of mitosis, even so, in that, of, or relating to the synapse or a synapse for which of symptomatic nerve endings, the synaptic phase in mitosis, as the minute space between the cell membrane of an axon terminal and the target cell with which it synapses. The process in cell division by which the nucleus divides, typically consisting of four stages, prophase, metaphase, anaphase, and telophase, and normally resulting in two new nuclei, each, of which contain a compl te copy of th e parental chromosomes, wherefore, the entire process of cell division including the division of the nucleus and the cytoplasm.

A synapsis junction site of a synapse is given by inducing their interconnection and to release neurotransmitters, as chemical factors with highly specific protein molecules, termed receptors, that are embedded in the surface membranes of the postsynaptic cell. When this combination occurs, the voltage, or electrical force, of the postsynaptic cell is either increased (excited) or decreased (inhibited).

When a neuron is in its resting potential is voltage is about -70 millivolts. An excitatory neurotransmitter alters the membrane of the postsynaptic neuron, making it possible for ions (electrically charged molecules) to move back and forth across the neuron's membranes. This flow of ions makes the neuron's voltage rise toward zero. If enough excitatory receptors have been activated, the postsynaptic neuron responds by firing, generating a nerve impulse that causes its own neurotransmitter to be released into the next synapse. An inhibitory neurotransmitter causes different ions to pass back and forth across the postsynaptic neuron's membrane, lowering the nerve cell's voltage to -80 or -90 millivolts. The drop in voltage makes it less likely that the postsynaptic cell will fire.

If the postsynaptic cell is a muscle cell rather than a neuron, an excitatory neurotransmitter will cause the muscle to contract. If the postsynaptic cell is a gland cell, an excitatory neurotransmitter will cause the cell to secrete its contents.

While most neurotransmitters interact with their receptors to create new electrical nerve impulses that energize or inhibit the adjoining cell, some neurotransmitter interactions do not generate or suppress nerve impulses. Instead, they interact with a second type of receptor that changes the internal chemistry of the postsynaptic cell by either causing or blocking the formation of chemicals called second messenger molecules. These second messengers regulate the postsynaptic cell's biochemical processes and enable it to conduct the maintenance necessary to continue synthesizing neurotransmitters and conducting nerve impulses. Examples of second messengers, which are formed and entirely contained within the postsynaptic cell, include cyclic adenosine monophosphate, diacylglycerol, and inositol phosphates. In which of a salt or ester of phosphoric acid, contributed of a fertilizer containing phosphorus compounds, its use as a soda foundation drink made by blending carbonated water with flavoured syrup.

It is, that, nevertheless, that once neurotransmitters have been secreted into synapses and have passed on their chemical signals, the presynaptic neuron clears the synapse of neurotransmitter molecules. For example, acetylcholine is broken down by the enzyme acetylcholinesterase into choline and acetate. Neurotransmitters like dopamine, serotonin, and GABA is removed by a physical process called reuptake. In reuptake, a protein in the presynaptic membrane acts as a sort of sponge, causing the neurotransmitters to reenter the presynaptic neuron, where they can be broken down by enzymes or repackaged for reuse.

Neurotransmitters are known to be involved in a number of disorders, including Alzheimer's disease. Victims of Alzheimer's disease suffer from loss of intellectual capacity, disintegration of personality, mental confusion, hallucinations, and aggressive - even violent - behaviour. These symptoms are the result of a progressive degeneration in many types of neurons in the brain. Forgetfulness, one of the earliest symptoms of Alzheimer's disease, is partly caused by the destruction of neurons that normally release the neurotransmitter acetylcholine. Medications that increase brain levels of acetylcholine have helped restore short-term memory and reduce mood swings in some Alzheimer's patients.

Neurotransmitters also play a role in Parkinson's disease, which slowly attacks the nervous system, causing symptoms that worsen over time. Fatigue, mental confusion, a mastlike facial expression, stooping posture, shuffling gait, and problems with eating and speaking are among the difficulties suffered by Parkinson victims. These symptoms have been partly linked to the deterioration and eventual death of neurons that run from the base of the brain to the basal ganglia, a collection of nerve cells that manufacture the neurotransmitter dopamine. The reasons why such neurons die are yet to be understood, but the related symptoms can be alleviated. L-dopa, or levodopa, widely used to treat Parkinson disease, acts as a supplementary precursor for dopamine. It causes the surviving neurons in the basal ganglia to increase their production of dopamine, thereby compensating to some extent for the disabled neurons.

Many other effective drugs have been shown to act by influencing neurotransmitter behaviour. Some drugs work by interfering with the interactions between neurotransmitters and intestinal receptors. For example, belladonna decreases intestinal cramps in such disorders as irritable bowel syndrome by blocking acetylcholine from combining with receptors. This process reduces nerve signals to the bowel wall, which prevents painful spasms.

Other drugs block the reuptake process. One well-known example is the drug Fluoxetine hydrochloride which enhances the activity of serotonin by inhibiting the uptake by neurons of the central nervous system, meaning that the act of uptake would by taking in or absorbing, especially neurons that are involved by taking or aborting energies of both chemical or electrical neurotransmitters across the synapse into living organisms, travelling into the living ritual which blocks the reuptake of serotonin. The Fluoxetine hydrochloride is an oral antidepressant that enhances the activity of serotonin by inhibiting its uptake by neurons of the central nervous system. Serotonin, which remains in the synapse for a longer interval as an ability to act as a signal is prolonged, which contribute the relief of depression and the control of obsessive-compulsive behaviours. Serotonin is an organic compound which is formed from trypropahan and found in animal and human tissue, especially, specially the brain, blood scrum and gastric mucous membranes and the activity as a neurotransmitter and in vasoconstriction (constriction of a blood vessel, as by a nerve or drug), stimulations of the smooth muscles, and regulation of cyclic body processes.

In that which forms of an essential amino acid in forming from of proteins during digestion by the action of proteolytic that of, or relating to, and characterized by or promoting proteolysis, such that the hydrolytic breakdown of protein into simpler, soluble substances such as peptides and amino acids, as occurs during digestion.

Peptide substances are variously of a natural or synthetic compound containing of two or more organic compounds, an amino group carboxylic acid group and any of a various group, of the 20 compounds that have linked together by peptide bonds to form protein or that function as chemical messengers and as intermediate in metabolisms. Peptides of various natural or synthetic compounds for containing two or more amino acids linked by the carboxyl of one amino acid to the amino group of another.

Nonetheless, proteolytic enzymes of numerous or conjugated proteins produced by living organisms and functioning as a biochemical catalyst, which is to say, that chemical substances and vital processes occurring in living organisms, biological and physiological chemistry are the composition of particular living systems or biological substances caused by, or affecting life or living organisms. This having to do with biology related by blood or genetic lineage, for which an internal mechanism in the organism that control the periodicity of various functions or activities. That the metabolic change in sleep cycles or photosynthesis is found in the progression or time periods from puberty to menopause, making abilities to bear upon the science that deals with the application of physics too biological processing, with an appreciation of life and the world. The studies of the relationships between the geochemistry of a region and the animal and plant life in that region, such that the bio-geochemical principles, in that living organisms develop only from other living organisms and not from nonliving matter. That the supposed recurrence of the evolutionary stages of a species during the embryonic development and differentiation of a member of that species. The study of flow and the information about energy in and between living organisms and between living organisms and the environment, as of or relating to the effects of electrical energy on the living tissue as some components of a given substance have in differing formulation of a drug or chemical components. Of which the genesis is derived, as to furnish information regarding an autonomic bodily function, such as heart rate or blood pressure, in an attempt to gain some voluntary control over that function.

Any of a group of naturally occurring, biologically active amines, such as norepinephrine, histarmine, and serotonin, that act primarily as neurotransmitters and capable of affecting mental functioning and regulating blood pressure and body temperature, and different bodily processes. It can be found related in the processes characterized in the structure, function, growth, origin, evolution, and the distribution that deal with the ability of humans to tolerate environmental stresses and variations, as in space travel. The applicable principles of the natural sciences, are especially accredited to biology and physiology, to mood mechanisms.

Dopamine, its chemical known as a neurotransmitter is essential to the functioning of the central nervous system. In the process of neurotransmission, dopamine is transferred from one nerve cell, or neuron, to another, playing a key role in brain function and human behaviour.

Dopamine forms from a precursor molecule called Dopa, which is manufactured in the liver from the amino acid tyrosine, that is obtained from the hydrolysis of proteins such as casein and is a precursor of epinephrine, thyroxine, and melanin. Casein is a whit e, tasteless, odourless protein precipitated from milk by rennin, it is the basis of cheese and is used to make plastics, adhesives, paints and foods. As an enzyme that catalyses the coagulation of milk, rennin is found in the gastric juice of the fourth stomach of young ruminants and used in making cheese and junkets and is also called, chymosin, rennet.

Dopa is an amino acid, formed in the liver from tyrosine, a white crystalline amino acids that are obtained from the hydrolysis of proteins such as casein and is a precursor of epinephrine, thyroxine, and melanin, of these are naturally occurring dark pigments, especially the pigment found in skin, hair, fur, and feathers. That dopamine, as an essential, normal functioning within the brain. Dopamine is a monoamine neurotransmitter formed in the brain by th e decarboxylation of dopa and essential to the functioning of the central nervous system. A production in its concentration within the brain in its association with Parkinson's disease. In that of an amine compound containing one amino group, especially a compound that functions as a neurotransmitter, which is formed in the brain by the decarboxylation of Dopa and essential to the normal functioning of the central nervous system. A reduction in its concentration within the brain is associated with Parkinson's disease. Dopamine is a versatile neurotransmitter. Among its many functions, it plays a major role in two activities of the central nervous system: One that helps control movement, and a second that are strongly associated with emotion-based behaviours. As a monoamine neurotransmitter containing one amino group, especially a compound that functions as a chemical composition of monoamine transitions, for which an active neurotransmitter and in vasoconstriction, stimulation of the smooth muscles, and regulation on cyclicbody processes.

Chemical compositions formed in the brain, for which decarboxylation has brought the removal in a carboxyl group from a chemical compound, usually with hydrogen placing it as dopa, within the normal functioning in the central nervous system. Reduction in its concentration within the brain is associated with Parkinson's disease. Dopa, nonetheless, is an amino acid formed in the liver from tyrosine, a white crystalline amino acid that is obtained from the hydrolysis of proteins such as casein; which is a white, tasteless, odourless protein precipitated from milk by rennin. It is the basis of cheese and is used to make plastics, adhesives, paints, and foods. Rennin, as an enzyme that catalyze the coagulation of milk, found in the gastric juice of the fourth stomach of young ruminants and used in making cheese and junkets, but, nonetheless, the hydrolysis of protein and is a precursor of epinephrine, in that of a hormone secreted by the adrenal medulla, that is released into the bloodstream in response to physical or mental stress, as in fear or injury. It initiates many bodily responses, including the stimulation of heart action and an increase in blood pressure, metabolic rate, and blood glucose concentration. An isolated compound of certain mammals or synthesized and used in medicine as a heart stimulant, vasoconstriction, and bronchial relaxant. Thyroxine, an iodine containing hormone that is produced by the thyroid gland, that increases the rate of cell metabolism and regulates growth and that is made synthetically in the treatment of thyroid disorders.

All and all, Parkinson's disease is a progressive nervous disease occurring most often after the age of 50, associated with the destruction of brain cells that produce dopamine and characterized by muscular tremor, the slowing of apparent movement, partial facial paralysis, peculiarity of gait and posture, and weakness.

The pathway involved in movement control is called the nigrostriatal pathway. Dopamine is released by neurons that originate from an area of the brain called the substantia nigra and connects to the part of the brain known as the corpora striata, an area known to be important in controlling the musculoskeletal system.

The second brain pathway in which dopamine plays a major role is called the mesocorticolimbic pathway, such that-when neurons in an area of the brain called the ventral tegmentalarea transmits dopamine to other neurons connected to various parts of the limbic system, which is responsible for regulating emotion, motivation, behaviour, the sense of smell, and variously autonomic, or involuntary, functions like heartbeat and breathing. A growing body of evidence suggests that dopamine is involved in several major brain disorders. Narcolepsy, a disorder characterized by brief, recurring episodes of sudden deep sleep, is associated with abnormally high levels of both dopamine and a second neurotransmitter, acetylcholine. Huntington's chorea, an inherited fatal illness in which neurons in the base of the brain are progressively destroyed or decayed, and is also linked to an excess of dopamine.

Commonly known as shaking palsy, Parkinson disease is another brain disorder in which dopamine is involved. Besides tremors of the limbs, Parkinson patients suffer from muscular rigidity, which leads to difficulties in walking, writing, and speaking. This disorder results from the degeneration and death of neurons in the nigrostriatal pathway, resulting in low levels of dopamine. The symptoms of Parkinson disease can be minimized by treatment with a drug called levodopa, or L-dopa, which converts to dopamine in the brain.

Schizophrenia is a psychiatric disorder characterized by loss of contact with reality and major changes in personality. Schizophrenics have normal levels of dopamine in the brain, but because they are highly sensitive to this neurotransmitter, these normal levels of dopamine triggers unusual behaviours. Drugs such as thorazine that blocks the action of dopamine have been found to decrease the symptoms of schizophrenia.

Studies indicate that people who are addicted to alcohol and other drugs like, cocaine and nicotine have less dopamine in the mesocorticolimbic pathway. These drugs appear to increase dopamine levels, resulting in the pleasurable feelings associated with the drugs.

Serotonin, is a chemical neurotransmitter, or chemical that transmits messages across the synapses, or gaps, between adjacent cells. Among its many functions, serotonin is released from blood cells called platelets to activate blood vessel constriction and blood clotting. In the gastrointestinal tract, serotonin inhibits gastric acid production and stimulates muscle contraction in the intestinal wall. Its functions in the central nervous system and effects on human behaviour - including mood, memory, and appetite control - have been the subject of a great deal of research. This intensive study of serotonin has revealed important knowledge about the serotonin-related cause and treatment of many illnesses.

Serotonin is produced in the brain from the amino acid tryptophan, which is derived from foods high in protein, such as meat and dairy products. Tryptophan is transported to the brain, where it is broken down by enzymes to produce serotonin. In the process of neurotransmission, serotonin is transferred from one nerve cell, or neuron, to another, triggering an electrical impulse that stimulates or inhibits cell activity as needed. Serotonin is then reabsorbed by the first neuron, in a process known as reuptake, where it is recycled and used again or converted into an inactive chemical form and excreted.

As an organic compound, serotonin is formed from tryptophan and found in animal and human tissue, especially the brain, blood serum, and gastric mucous membranes, and active as a transmitter and in vasoconstriction, stimulation of the smooth muscles, and regulation of cyclic body processes. Tryptophan, as a crystalline substance that formed in plant and animal tissues from tryptophan and is an intermediate in various metabolic processes. As an essential amino acid, serotonin is formed from proteins during digestion by the action of proteolytic enzymes. It is necessary for normal growth and development and is the precursor of several substance s, including serotonin and niacin, which of a whit e crystalline acid that of a component of the vitamin B complex found in meat, wheat germ, dairy products, and yeast and is used to treat and prevent pellagra, it is also called nicotinic acid. Pellagra is a disease caused by a deficiency of niacin and protein in the diet and characterized by skin eruptions, digestive and nervous system distributions, and eventually deterioration.

While the complete picture of serotonin's function in the body is still being investigated, many disorders are known to be associated with an imbalance of serotonin in the brain. Drugs that manipulate serotonin levels have been used to alleviate the symptoms of serotonin imbalances. Some of these drugs, known as selective serotonin reuptake inhibitors (SSRIs), block or inhibit the reuptake of serotonin into neurons, enabling serotonin to remain active in the synapses for a longer period of time. These medications are used to treat such psychiatric disorders as depression; Obsessive-compulsive disorder, in which repetitive and disturbing thoughts trigger bizarre, ritualistic behaviours, and impulsive aggressive behaviours. Fluoxetine (more commonly known by the brand name Prozac), is a widely prescribed SSRIs used to treat depression, and more recently is the Obsessive-compulsive disorder. The Fluoxetine hydrochloride is an antidepressant taken through the mouth, the same as oral vaccine would be taken, enhancing the activity of serotonin by inhibiting its uptake by neurons of the central nervous system.

Drugs that affect serotonin levels may prove beneficial in the treatment of nonpsychiatric disorders, as well, including diabetic neuropathy (degeneration of nerves outside the central nervous system in diabetics) and premenstrual syndrome. Recently the serotonin-releasing agent dexfenfluramine has been approved for patients who are 30 percent or more over their ideal body weight. By preventing serotonin reuptake, dexfenfluramine promotes satiety, or fullness, after eating less food.

Other drugs serve as agonists that react with neurons to produce effects similar to those of serotonin. Serotonin agonists have been used to treat migraine headaches, in which low levels of serotonin cause arteries in the brain to swell, resulting in a headache. Sumatriptan is an agonist drug that mimics the effects of serotonin in the brain, constricting blood vessels and alleviating pain.

Drugs known as antagonists bind with neurons to prevent serotonin neurotransmission. Some antagonists have been found effective in treating the nausea that typically accompanies radiation and chemotherapy in cancer treatment. Antagonists are also being tested to treat high blood pressure and other cardiovascular disorders by blocking serotonin's ability to constrict blood vessels. Other antagonists may produce an effect on learning and memory in age-associated memory impairment.

The Synapse is the signal conveying everything that human beings sense and think, and every motion they make, follows nerve pathways in the human body as waves of ions (atoms or groups of atoms that carries electric charges). Australian physiologist Sir John Eccles discovered many of the intricacies of this electrochemical signalling process, particularly the pivotal step in which a signal is conveyed from one nerve cell to another. He shared the 1963 Nobel Prize in physiology or medicine for this work, which he described in a 1965 Scientific American article.

How does one nerve cell transmit the nerve impulse to another cell? Electron microscopy and other methods show that it does so by means of special extensions that deliver a squirt of transmitter material and particular in character, a kind practical to substance.

The human brain is the most highly organized form of matter known, and in complexity the brains of the other higher animals are not greatly inferior. For certain purposes it is expedient to regard the brain for being analogous to a machine. Even if it is so regarded, however, it is a machine of a totally different kind from those made by man. In trying to understand the workings of his own brain man meets his highest challenge. Nothing is given; There are no operating diagrams, no maker's instructions.

The first step in trying to understand the brain is to examine its structure in order to discover the components from which it is built and how they are related to each another. After which one can attempt to understand the mode of operations in the simplest of components, as these two modes of investigation - the morphological and the physiological - have now become complementary. In studying the nervous system with today's sensitive electrical device, however, it is all too easy to find physiological events that cannot be correlated with any known anatomical structure. Conversely, the electron microscope reveals many structural details whose physiological significance is obscured or unknown.

At the close of the past century the Spanish anatomist Santiago Ramón Cajal showed how all parts of the nervous system are built up of individual nerve cells of many different shapes and sizes. Like other cells, each nerve cell has a nucleus and the surrounding cytoplasm. Its outer surface consists of numerous fine branches - the dendrites - that receive nerve impulses from other nerve cells, and one relatively long branch - the axon - that transmits nerve impulses. Near its end the axon divides into branches that terminate at the dendrites or bodies of other nerve cells. The axon can be as short as a fraction of a millimetre or as long as a metre, depending on its place and function. It has many of the properties of an electric cable and is uniquely specialized to conduct the brief electrical waves called nerve impulses. In very thin axons these impulses travel at less than one metre per second; In others, for example in the large axons of the nerve cells that activate muscles, they travel as fast as 100 metres per second.

The electrical impulse that travels along the axon ceases abruptly when it comes to the point where the axon's terminal fibres make contact with another nerve cell upon which these points were the name "synapses" by Sir Charles Sherrington, who laid the foundations of what is sometimes called synaptology. If the nerve impulse is to continue beyond the synapse, it must be regenerated afresh on the other side. As recently as 15 years ago some physiologists held that transmission at the synapse was predominantly, if not exclusively, an electrical phenomenon. Now, however, there is abundant evidence that transmission is effectuated by the release of specific chemical substances that trigger a regeneration of the impulse. In fact, the first strong evidence showing that some transmitter substance act across the synapse, on which, this insight was confirmed 40 years ago by Sir Henry Dale and Otto Loewi.

It has been positively confirmed that the human central nervous system, which, of course includes the spinal cord as well as the brain itself, consisting of about 10 billion (1010) nerve cells. With rare exceptions each nerve cell receives information directly in the form of impulses from many other nerve cells - often hundreds - and transmits information to a like number. Depending on its threshold of response, a given nerve cell may fire an impulse when stimulated by only a few incoming fibres or it may not fire until stimulated by many incoming fibres. It has long been known that this threshold can be raised or lowered by various factors. Moreover, it was conjectured some 60 years ago that some of the incoming fibres must inhibit the firing of the receiving cell rather than excite it. The conjecture was subsequently confirmed, and the mechanism of the inhibitory effect has now been clarified. This mechanism and its equally fundamental counterpart - nerve-cell excitation - are of its topic.

At the level of anatomy there are some clues to indicate how the fine axon terminals impinging on a nerve cell can make the cell regenerate a nerve impulse of its own nerve cell and its dendrites are covered by fine branches of nerve fibres that terminate in knoblike structures. These structures are the synapses.

The electron microscope has revealed structural details of synapses that fit in nicely with the view that a chemical transmitter is involved in nerve transmission. Enclosed in the synaptic knob are many vesicles, or tiny sacs, which appear to contain the transmitter substances that induce synaptic transmission. Between the synaptic knob and the synaptic membrane of the adjoining nerve cell is a remarkably uniform space of about 20 millimicrons that is termed the synaptic cleft. Many of the synaptic vesicles are concentrated adjacent to this cleft; It seems plausible that the transmitter substance is discharged from the nearest vesicles into the cleft, where it can act on the adjacent cell membrane. This hypothesis is supported by the discovery that the transmitter is released in packets of a few thousand molecules.

The study of synaptic transmission was revolutionized in 1951 by the introduction of delicate techniques for recording electrically from the interior of single nerve cells. This is done by inserting into the nerve cell an extremely fine glass pipette with a diameter of .5 microns - about a fifty-thousandth of an inch. The pipette is filled with an electrically conducting salt solution such as concentrated potassium chloride. If the pipette is carefully inserted and held rigidly in place, the cell membrane appears to seal quickly around the glass, thus preventing the flow of a short-circuiting current through the puncture in the cell membrane. Impaled in this fashion, nerve cells can function normally for hours. Although there is no way of observing the cells during the insertion of the pipette, the insertion can be guided by using as clues the electric signals that the pipette picks up when close to active nerve cells.

At the John Curtin School of Medical Research in Canberra first employed this technique, choosing to study the large nerve cells called motoneurons, which lie in the spinal cord and whose function is to activate muscles. This was a fortunate choice: Intracellular investigations with motoneurons have proved to be easier and more rewarding than those with any other kind of mammalian nerve cell.

Finding that once the nerve cell responds to the chemical synaptic transmitter, the response depends in part on characteristic features of ionic composition, such is the concern with which the transmission of impulses in the cell and along its axon, the axon is the usually long process of a nerve fibre that generally conducts impulses away from the body of the nerve cell, is that of a threadlike process of a neuron, especially the prolonged axon that conducts neve impulses. Plainly, the nerve cell is the body of a neuron without its axon and dendrites, as an impulse is the electrochemical transmission of a signal along a nerve fibre that produces an excitatory or inhibitory response at a target tissue, such as a muscle or another nerve. When the nerve cell is at rest, its physiological makeup resembles that of most other cells in that the water solution inside the cell is quite different in composition from the solution in which the cell is bathed. The nerve cell is able to exploit this difference between external and internal compositions and use it in quite different ways for generating an electrical impulse and for synaptic transmission.

The composition of the external solution is well established because the solution is essentially the same as blood from which cells and proteins have been removed. The composition of the internal solution is known only approximately. Indirect evidence indicates that the concentrations of sodium and chloride ions outside the cell are respectively some 10 and 14 times higher than the concentrations inside the cell. In contrast, the concentration of potassium ions inside the cell is about 30 times higher than the concentration outside.

How can one account for this remarkable state of affairs? Part of the explanation is that inside of the cell is negatively charged with the respect of the cell by about 70 millivolts. Since like charges repel each other, this internal negative charge tends to drive chloride ions (Cl-) outward through the cell membrane and, at the same time, to impede their inward movement. In fact, a potential difference of 70 millivolts is just sufficient to maintain the observed disparity in the concentration of chloride ions inside the cell and outside it; Chloride ions diffuse inward and outward at equal rates. A drop of 70 millivolts across the membrane therefore defines the "equilibrium potential" for chloride ions.

To obtain a concentration of potassium ions (K) that is 30 times higher inside the cell than outside would require that the interior of the cell membrane be about 90 millivolts negative with respect to the exterior. Since the actual interior is only 70 negative millivolts, it falls short of the equilibrium potential for potassium ions by 20 millivolts. Evidently the thirty-fold concentration can be achieved and maintained only if there is some auxiliary mechanism for "pumping" potassium ions into the cell at a rate equal to their spontaneous net outward diffusion.

The pumping mechanism has the action for which fewer or more the difficult tasks of pumping sodium ions (Na) out of the cell against a potential gradient of 130 millivolts. This figure is obtained by adding the 70 millivolts of internal negative charge to the equilibrium potential for sodium ions, which is 60 millivolts of internal positive charge. If it were not for this postulated pump, the concentration of sodium ions inside and outside the cell would be almost the reverse of what is observed.

In their classic studies of nerve-impulse transmission in the giant axon of the squid, A. L. Hodgkin, A. F. Huxley and Bernhard Katz of Britain demonstrated that the propagation of the impulse coincides with abrupt changes in the permeability of the axon membrane. When a nerve impulse has been triggered in some way, what can be described as a gate opens and lets sodium ions pour into the axon during the advance of the impulse, making the interior of the axon locally positive. The process is self-reinforcing in that the flow of some sodium ions through the membrane opens the gate further and makes it easier for others to follow. The sharp reversal of the internal polarity of the membrane constitutes the nerve impulse, which moves like a wave until it has travelled the length of the axon. In the wake of the impulse the sodium gate closes and a potassium gate opens, thereby restoring the normal polarity of the membrane within a millisecond or less.

With this understanding of the nerve impulse in hand, one is ready to follow the electrical events at the excitatory synapse. One might guess that if the nerve impulse results from an abrupt inflow of sodium ions and a rapid change in the electrical polarity of the axon's interior, something similar must happen at the body and dendrites of the nerve cell in order to generate the impulse in the first place. Indeed, the function of the excitatory synaptic terminals on the cell body and its dendrites is to depolarize the interior of the cell membrane essentially by permitting an inflow of sodium ions. When the depolarization reaches a threshold value, a nerve impulse is triggered.

As a simple instance of this phenomenon we have recorded the depolarization that occurs in some single motoneurons activated directly by the large nerve fibres that enter the spinal cord from special stretch-receptors known as annulospiral endings. These receptors in turn are located in the same muscle that is activated by the motoneurons under study. Thus the whole system forms a typical reflex arc, such as the arc responsible for the patellar reflex, or "knee jerk."

To conduct the experiment we anaesthetize an animal (most often a cat) and free by dissection a muscle nerves that contains these large nerve fibres. By applying a mild electric shock to the exposed nerve one can produce a single impulse in each of the fibres; Since the impulses travel to the spinal cord almost synchronously, they are referred to collectively as a volley. The number of impulses contained in the volley can be reduced by reducing the stimulation applied to the nerve. The volley strength is measured at a point just outside the spinal cord and is displayed on an oscilloscope. About half a millisecond after detection of a volley there is a wavelike change in the voltage inside the motoneurons that has received the volley. The change is detected by a microelectrode inserted in the motoneurons and is displayed on another oscilloscope.

What we find is that the negative voltage inside the cell becomes progressively fewer negative as more of the fibres impinging on the cell are stimulated to fire. This observed depolarization is in fact a simple summation of the depolarization, produced by each individual synapse. When the depolarization of the interior of the motoneurons reaches a critical point, a "spike" suddenly appears on the second oscilloscope, showing that a nerve impulse has been generated. During the spike the voltage inside the cell changes from about 70 millivolts negative to as much as 30 positive millivolts. The spike regularly appears when the depolarization, or reduction of membrane potential, reaches a critical level, which is usually between 10 and 18 millivolts. The only effect of a further strengthening of the synaptic stimulus is to shorten the time needed for the motoneurons to reach the firing threshold. The depolarizing potentials produced in the cell membrane by excitatory synapses are called excitatory postsynaptic potentials, or EPSP's.

Through one barrel of a double-barrelled microelectrode one can apply a background current to change the resting potential of the interior of the cell membrane, either increasing it or decreasing it. When the potential is made more negative, the EPSP rises more steeply to an earlier peak. When the potential is made less negative, the EPSP rises more slowly to a lower peak. Finally, when the charge inside the cell is reversed so as to be positive with respect to the exterior, the excitatory synapses give rise to an EPSP that is actually the reverse of the normal one.

These observations support the hypothesis that excitatory synapses produce what amounts virtually to a short circuit in the synaptic membrane potential. When this occurs, the membrane no longer acts as a barrier to the passage of ions but lets them flow through in response to the differing electric potential on the two sides of the membrane. In other words, the ions are momentarily allowed to travel freely down their electrochemical gradients, which means that the sodium ions flow into the cell and, to a lesser degree, potassium ions flow out. It is this net flow of positive ions that creates the excitatory postsynaptic potential. The flow of negative ions, such as the chloride ion, is apparently not involved. By artificially altering the potential inside the cell one can establish that there is no flow of ions, and therefore no EPSP, when the voltage drop across the membrane is zero.

How is the synaptic membrane converted from a strong ionic barrier into an ion-permeable state? It is currently accepted that the agency of conversion is the chemical transmitter substance contained in the vesicles inside the synaptic knob. When a nerve impulse reaches the synaptic knob, some of the vesicles are caused to eject the transmitter substance into the synaptic cleft. The molecules of the substance would take only a few microseconds to diffuse across the cleft and become attached to specific receptor sites on the surface membrane of the adjacent nerve cell.

Presumably the receptor sites are associated with fine channels in the membrane that are opened in some way by the attachment of the transmitter-substance molecules to the receptor sites. With the channels thus opened, sodium and potassium ions flow through the membrane thousands of times more readily than they normally do, thereby producing the intense ionic flux that depolarizes the cell membrane and produces the EPSP. In many synapses the current flows strongly for only about a millisecond before the transmitter substance is eliminated from the synaptic cleft, either by diffusion into the surrounding regions or as a result of being destroyed by enzymes. The latter process is known to occur when the transmitter substance is acetylcholine, which is destroyed by the enzyme acetylcholinesterase.

The substantiation of this general picture of synaptic transmission requires the solution of many fundamental problems. Since we do not know the specific transmitter substance for the vast majority of synapses in the nervous system we do not know if there are many different substances or only a few. The only one identified with reasonable certainty in the mammalian central nervous system is acetylcholine. We know practically nothing about the mechanism by which a presynaptic nerve impulse causes the transmitter substance to be injected into the synaptic cleft. Nor do we know how the synaptic vesicles not immediately adjacent to the synaptic cleft ensue to moved up to the firing line to replace the emptied vesicles. It is conjectured that the vesicles contain the enzyme systems needed to recharge themselves. The entire process must be swift and efficient: the total amount of transmitter substance in synaptic terminals is enough for only a few minutes of synaptic activity at normal operating rates. There are also knotty problems to be solved on the other side of the synaptic cleft. What, for example, is the nature of the receptor sites? How are the ionic channels in the membrane opened up?

The second type of synapse that has been identified in the nervous system is the synapse that can inhibit the firing of a nerve cell even though it may be receiving a volley of excitatory impulses. When inhibitory synapses are examined in the electron microscope, they look very much like excitatory synapses. The insertion of a microelectrode allows the recordings of the activity of single motoneurons and other nerve cells have now shown that the inhibitory postsynaptic potential (IPSP) is virtually a mirror image of the EPSP. Moreover, individual inhibitory synapses, like excitatory synapses, have a cumulative effect. The chief difference is simply that the IPSP makes the cell's internal voltage more negative than it is normally, which is in a direction opposite to that needed for generating a spike discharge.

By driving the internal voltage of a nerve cell in the negative direction inhibitory synapses oppose the action of excitatory synapses, which of course drive it in the positive direction. Hence if the potential of an inside positive potential of a strong resting cell is 70 negative millivolts depreciating count, a strong volley of inhibitory impulses can drive the potential to 75 or 80 millivolts depreciating count. One can easily see that if the potential is made more negative in this way, the excitatory synapses find it more difficult to raise the internal voltage to the threshold point for the generation of a spike. Thus, the nerve cell responds to the algebraic sum of the internal voltage changes produced by excitatory and inhibitory synapses.

In the experiment, the internal membrane potential is altered by the flow of an electric current through one barrel of a double-barrelled microelectrode. One can observe the effect of such changes on the inhibitory postsynaptic potential. When the internal potential is made less negative, the inhibitory postsynaptic potential is deepened. Conversely, when the potential is made more negative, the IPSP diminishes; it finally reverses when the internal potential is driven below minus 80 millivolts.

One can assume, that inhibitory synapse's share with excitatory synapses the ability to change the ionic permeability of the synaptic membrane. The difference is that inhibitory synapses enable ions to flow freely down an electrochemical gradient that has an equilibrium point at minus 80 millivolts rather than at zero, as is the case for excitatory synapses. This effect could be achieved by the outward flow of positively charged ions such as potassium or the inward flow of negatively charged ions such as chloride, or by a combination of negative and positive ionic flows such that the interior reaches equilibrium at minus 80 millivolts.

If the concentration of chloride ions within the cell is increased as much as three times, the inhibitory postsynaptic potential reverses and acts as a depolarizing current; such that it has a strong resemblance of the excitatory potential. Nonetheless, if the cell is heavily injected with sulfate ions, which act of a negative value, and no such instance of reversing. This simple test shows that under the influence of the inhibitory transmitter substance, which is still unidentified, the subsynaptic layer covering surfaces or structures of the membrane become permeable momentarily to chloride ions but not to sulfate ions. During the generation of the IPSP the outflow of chloride ions is so rapid that it more than outweighs the flow of other ions that generate the normal inhibitory potential.

The effect of injecting motoneurons with more than 30 kinds of negative lung ions, with one exception the hydrated ions (ions bound to water) to which the cell membrane is permeable under the influence of the inhibitory transmitter substance are smaller than the hydrated ions to which the membrane is impermeable. The exception is the formate ion (HCO_2-), which may have an ellipsoidal shape and so be able to pass through membrane pores that block smaller spherical ions.

Apart from the formate ion all the ions to which the membrane is permeable have a diameter not greater than 1.14 times the diameter of the potassium ion; That is, they are less than 2.9 angstrom units in diameter. Comparable investigations in other laboratories have found the same permeability effects, including the exceptional behaviour of the formate ion, in fishes, toads and snails. It may well be that the ionic mechanism responsible for synaptic inhibition is the same throughout the animal kingdom.

The significance of these and other studies is that they strongly indicate that the inhibitory transmitter substance opens the membrane to the flow of potassium ions but not to sodium ions. It is known that the sodium ion is somewhat larger than any of the negatively charged ions, including the formate ion, that are able to pass through the membrane during synaptic inhibition. It is not possible, however, to test the effectiveness of potassium ions by injecting excess amounts into the cell because the excess is immediately diluted by an osmotic flow of water into the cell.

The concentration of potassium ions inside the nerve cell is about 30 times greater than the concentration outside, and to maintain this large difference in concentration without the help of some metabolic pumps inside of the membrane would have to be charged 90 millivolts negative with respect to the exterior. This implies that if the membrane were suddenly made porous to potassium ions, the resulting outflow of ions would make the inside potential of the membrane more negative than it is in the resting state, and that is just what happens during synaptic inhibition. The membranes, as having a thin, pliable layer of tissue covering surfaces or separating or connecting regions, structures or organs of an animal or a plant, are found of natural or synthetic material that is permeable to substances in solution. As a member of the body, as its existing in much higher concentrations outside the cell than inside have a rapid inflow, such that, to compensate for more of the potassium outflow, that the fundamental difference between synaptic excitation and synaptic inhibition is that the membrane freely passes sodium ions in response to the former and largely excludes the passage of sodium ions in response to the latter.

This fine discrimination between ions that are not very different in size must be explained by any hypothesis of synaptic action. It is most unlikely that the channels through the membrane are created afresh and accurately maintained for a thousandth of a second every time a burst of transmitter substance is released into the synaptic cleft. It is more likely that channels of at least two different sizes are built directly into the membrane structure. In some way the excitatory transmitter substance would selectively unplug the larger channels and permit the free inflow of sodium ions. Potassium ions would simultaneously flow out and thus would tend to counteract the large potential change that would be produced by the massive sodium inflow. The inhibitory transmitter substance would selectively unplug the smaller channels that are large enough to pass potassium and chloride ions but not sodium ions.

To explain certain types of inhibition other features must be added to this hypothesis of synaptic transmission. In the simple hypothesis chloride and potassium ions can flow freely through pores of all inhibitory synapses. It has been shown, however, that the inhibition of the contraction of heart muscle by the vagus nerve is due almost exclusively to potassium-ion flow. On the other hand, in the muscles of crustaceans and in nerve cells in the snail's brain synaptic inhibition is due largely to the flow of chloride ions. This selective permeability could be explained if there were fixed charges along the walls of the channels. If such charges were negative, they would repel negatively charged ions and prevent their passage; if they were positive, they would similarly prevent the passage of positively charged ions. One can now suggest that the channels opened by the excitatory transmitter are negatively charged and so do not permit the passage of the negatively charged chloride ion, even though it is small enough to move through the channel freely.

One might wonder if a given nerve cell can have excitatory synaptic action at some of its axon terminals and inhibitory action at others. The answer is no. Two different kinds of nerve cells are needed, one for each type of transmission and synaptic transmitter substance. This can readily be demonstrated by the effect of strychnine and tetanus toxins in the spinal cord; They specifically prevent inhibitory synaptic action and leave excitatory action unaltered. As a result the synaptic excitation of nerve cells is uncontrolled and convulsions result. The special types of cells responsible for inhibitory synaptic action are now being recognized in many parts of the central nervous system.

This account of communication between nerve cells is necessarily oversimplified, yet it shows that some significant advances are being made at the level of individual components of the nervous system. By selecting the most favourable situations we have been able to throw light on some details of nerve-cell behaviour. We are encouraged by these limited successes, but the task of a better understanding would be questioned of how the human brain operates, if only staggering its own imagination.

Our brain begins with its portion of the central nervous system contained within the skull. The brain is the control centre for movement, sleep, hunger, thirst, and virtually every other vital activity necessary to survival. All human emotions - including love, hate, fear, anger, elation, and sadness - are controlled by the brain. It also receives and interprets the countless signals that are sent to it from other parts of the body and from the external environment. The brain makes us conscious, emotional, and intelligent.

The human brain has three major structural components: the large dome-shaped cerebrum, the smaller somewhat spherical cerebellum, and the brainstem. Prominent in the brainstem are the medulla oblongata and the thalamus - between the medulla and the cerebrum. The cerebrum is responsible for intelligence and reasoning. The cerebellum helps to maintain balance and posture. The medulla is involved in maintaining involuntary functions such as respiration, and the thalamus act as a relay centre for electrical impulses travelling to and from the cerebral cortex.

The adult human brain is a 1.3-kg. (3-lb.) Mass of pinkish-gray jellylike tissue made up of approximately 100 billion nerve cells or neurons: The Neuroglia (supporting-tissue) cells, and vascular (blood-carrying) and other tissues.

Between the brain and the cranium - the part of the skull that directly covers the brain - are three protective membranes, or meninges. The outermost membrane, the dura mater, is the toughest and thickest. Below the dura mater is a middle membrane, called the arachnoid layer. The innermost membrane, the pia mater, consists mainly of small blood vessels and follows the contours of the surface of the brain.

A clear liquid, the cerebrospinal fluid, bathes the entire brain and fills a series of four cavities, called ventricles, near the centre of the brain. The cerebrospinal fluid protects the internal portion of the brain from varying pressures and transports chemical substances within the nervous system.

From the exterior, the brain appears as having three distinct but associatively connected parts, the cerebrum (the Latin word for brain) - two large, almost symmetrical hemispheres; the cerebellum ('little brain') - two smaller hemispheres located at the back of the cerebrum, and the brain stem - a central core that gradually becomes the spinal cord, exiting the skull through an opening at its base called the foramen magnum. Two other major parts of the brain, the thalamus and the hypothalamus, lie in the midline above the brain stem underneath the cerebellum.

The brain and the spinal cord together make up the central nervous system, which communicates with the rest of the body through the peripheral nervous system. The peripheral nervous system consists of 12 pairs of cranial nerves extending from the cerebrum and brain stem; a system of other nerves branching throughout the body from the spinal cord, and the autonomic nervous system, which regulates vital functions that have no conscious control, such as the activity of the heart muscle, smooth muscle (involuntary muscle found in the skin, blood vessels, and internal organs), and glands.

Many motor and sensory functions have been "mapped" to specific areas of the cerebral cortex, some of which are indicated here. In general, these areas exist in both hemispheres of the cerebrum, each serving the opposite side of the body. Fewer defined are the areas of association, located mainly in the frontal cortex, operatives in functions of thought and emotion and responsible for linking input from different senses. The areas of language are an exception: Both Wernicke's area, concerned with the comprehension of spoken language, and Broca's area, governing the production of speech, have been pinpointed on the cortex.

Most high-level brain functions take place in the cerebrum. Its two large hemispheres make up approximately 85 percent of the brain's weight. The exterior surface of the cerebrum, the cerebral cortex, is a convoluted, or folded, grayish layer of cell bodies known as the gray matter. The gray matter covers an underlying mass of fibres called the white matter. The convolutions are made up of ridgelike bulges, known as gyri, separated by small grooves called sulci and larger grooves called fissures. Approximately two-thirds of the cortical surface is hidden in the folds of the sulci. The extensive convolutions enable a very large surface area of brain cortices - roughly, 1.5m2 (16 ft2) in an adult - that fits the cranium. The pattern of these convolutions is similar, although not identical, in all humans.

The two cerebral hemispheres are partially separated from each other by a deep fold known as the longitudinal fissure. Communication between the two hemispheres is through several concentrated bundles of axons, called commissures, the largest of which is the corpus callosum.

Several major sulci divides the cortex into distinguishable regions. The central sulcus, or Rolandic fissure, runs from the middle of the top of each hemisphere downward, forwards, and toward another major sulcus, the lateral (side), or Sylvian, sulcus. These and other sulci and gyri divide the cerebrum into five lobes: The frontal, parietal, temporal, and occipital lobes and the insula.

Although the cerebrum is symmetrical in structure, with two lobes emerging from the brain stem and matching motor and sensory areas in each, certain intellectual functions are restricted to one hemisphere. A person's dominant hemisphere is usually occupied with language and logical operations, while the other hemisphere controls emotion and artistic and spatial skills. In nearly all right-handed and many left-handed people, the left hemisphere is dominant.

The frontal lobe is the largest of the five and consists of all the cortices in front of the central sulcus. Broca's area, a part of the cortex related to speech, is located in the frontal lobe. The parietal lobe consists of the cortex behind the central sulcus to some sulcus near the back of the cerebrum known as the parieto-occipital sulcus. The parieto-occipital sulcus, in turn, form the front border of the occipital lobe, which is the rearmost part of the cerebrum: the temporal lobe is to the side of and below the lateral sulcus. Wernicke's area, a part of the cortex related to the understanding of language, is located in the temporal lobe. The insula lies deep within the folds of the lateral sulcus.

The cerebrum receives information from all the sense organs and sends motor commands (signals that results in activity in the muscles or glands) to other parts of the brain and the rest of the body. Motor commands are transmitted by the motor cortex, a strip of cerebral cortex extending from side to side across the top of the cerebrum just in front of the central sulcus. The sensory cortex, parallel strips of cerebral cortex just in back of the central sulcus, receives input from the sense organs.

Many other areas of the cerebral cortex have also been mapped according to their specific functions, such as vision, hearing, speech, emotions, language, and other aspects of perceiving, thinking, and remembering. Cortical regions known as associative cortices are responsible for integrating multiple inputs, processing the information, and carrying out complex responses.

The cerebellum coordinates body movements. Located at the lower back of the brain beneath the occipital lobes, the cerebellum is divided into two lateral (side-by-side) lobes connected by a fingerlike bundle of white fibres called the vermis. The outer layer, or cortex, of the cerebellum consists of fine folds called folia. As in the cerebrum, the outer layer of cortical gray matter surrounds a deeper layer of white matter and nuclei (groups of nerve cells). Three fibre bundles called cerebellar peduncle, connecting the cerebellum to the three parts of the brain stem - the midbrain, the pons, and the medulla oblongata.

The cerebellum coordinates voluntary movements by fine-tuning commands from the motor cortex in the cerebrum. The cerebellum also maintains posture and balance by controlling muscle tone and sensing the position of the limbs. All motor activity, from hitting a baseball to fingering a violin, depends on the cerebellum.

The limbic system is a group of brain structures that play a role in emotion, memory, and motivation. For example, electrical stimulation of the amygdala in laboratory animals can provoke fear, anger, and aggression. The hypothalamus regulates hunger, thirst, sleep, body temperature, sexual drive, and other functions.

The thalamus and the hypothalamus lie underneath the cerebrum and connect it to the brain stem. The thalamus consist of two rounded masses of gray tissue lying within the middle of the brain, between the two cerebral hemispheres. The thalamus are the main relay station for incoming sensory signals to the cerebral cortex and for outgoing motor signals from it. All sensory input to the brain, except that of the sense of smell, connects to the individual nuclei of the thalamus.

The hypothalamus lies beneath the thalamus on the midline at the base of the brain. It regulates or is involved directly in the control of many of the body's vital drives and activities, such as eating, drinking, temperature regulation, sleep, emotional behaviour, and sexual activity. It also controls the function of internal body organs by means of the autonomic nervous system, interacts closely with the pituitary gland, and helps coordinate activities of the brain stem.

The brain stem, is the lowest part of the brain. It serves as the path for messages travelling between the upper brain and spinal cord but is also the seat of basic and vital functions such as breathing, blood pressure, and heart rates, as well as reflexes like eye movement and vomiting. The brain stem has three main parts: the medulla, pons, and midbrain. A canal runs longitudinally through these structures carrying cerebrospinal fluid. Also distributed along its length is a network of cells, referred to as the reticular formation, that governs the state of alertness.

The brain stem is revolutionarily the most primitive part of the brain and is responsible for sustaining the basic functions of life, such as breathing and blood pressure. It includes three main structures lying between and below the two cerebral hemispheres - the midbrain, pons, and medulla oblongata.

The topmost structure of the brain stem is the midbrain. It contains major relay stations for neurons transmitting signals to the cerebral cortex, as well as many reflex centres - pathways carrying sensory (input) information and motor (output) command. Relays and reflex centres for visual and auditory (hearing) functions are located in the top portion of the midbrain. A pair of nuclei called the superior colliculus control reflex actions of the eye, such as blinking, opening and closing the pupil, and focussing the lens. A second pair of nuclei, called the inferior colliculus, controls auditory reflexes, such as adjusting the ear to the volume of sound. At the bottom of the midbrain are reflex and relay centres relating to pain, temperature, and touch, as well as several regions associated with the control of movement, such as the red nucleus and the substantia nigra.

Continuous with and below the midbrain and directly in front of the cerebellum is a prominent bulge in the brain stem called the pons. The pons consists of large bundles of nerve fibres that connect the two halves of the cerebellum and also connect each side of the cerebellum with the opposite-side cerebral hemisphere. The pons serves mainly as a relay station linking the cerebral cortex and the medulla oblongata.

The long, stalklike lowermost portion of the brain stem is called the medulla oblongata. At the top, it is continuous with the pons and the midbrain; at the bottom, it makes a gradual transition into the spinal cord at the foramen magnum. Sensory and motor nerve fibres connecting the brain and the rest of the body cross over to the opposite side as they pass through the medulla. Thus, the left half of the brain communicates with the right half of the body, and the right half of the brain with the left half of the body.

Running up the brain stem from the medulla oblongata through the pons and the midbrain is a netlike formation of nuclei known as the reticular formation. The reticular formation controls respiration, cardiovascular function, digestion, levels of alertness, and patterns of sleep. It also determines which parts of the constant flow of sensory information into the body are received by the cerebrum.

There are two main types of brain cells, neurons and neuroglia. Neurons are responsible for the transmission and analysis of all electrochemical communication within the brain and other parts of the nervous system. Each neuron is composed of a cell body called a soma, and a major fibre called an axon, and a system of branches called dendrites. Axons, also called nerve fibres, conveying electrical signals away from the soma and can be up to 1m. or 3.3 ft. in length. Most axons are covered with a protective sheath of myelin, a substance made of fats and protein, which insulates the axon. Myelinated axons conduct neuronal signals faster than do unmyelinated axons. Dendrites convey electrical signals toward the soma, are shorter than axons, and are usually multiple and branching.

Neuroglial cells are twice as numerous as neurons and account for half of the brain's weight. Neuroglia (from glia, Greek for 'glue') provides structural support to the neurons. Neuroglial cells also form myelin, guide developing neurons, take up chemicals involved in cell-to-cell communication, and contribute to the maintenance of the environment around neurons.

Twelve pairs of cranial nerves arise symmetrically from the base of the brain and are numbered, from front to back, in the order in which they arise. They connect mainly with structures of the head and neck, such as the eyes, ears, nose, mouth, tongue, and throat. Some are motor nerves, controlling muscle movement; some are sensory nerves, conveying information from the sense organs; and others contain fibres for both sensory and motor impulses. The first and second pairs of cranial nerves - the olfactory (smell) nerves and the optic (vision) nerve - carry sensory information from the nose and eyes, respectively, to the undersurface of the cerebral hemispheres. The other ten pairs of cranial nerves originate in or end in the brain stem.

The brain functions by complex neuronal, or nerve cell, circuits. Communication between neurons is both electrical and chemical and always travels from the dendrites of a neuron, through its soma, and out its axon to the dendrites of another neuron.

Dendrites of one neuron receive signals from the axons of other neurons through chemicals known as neurotransmitters. The neurotransmitters set off electrical charges in the dendrites, which then carry the signals electrochemically to the soma. The soma integrates the information, which is then transmitted electrochemically down the axon to its tip.

At the tip of the axon, small, bubble-like structures called vesicles' release neurotransmitters that carries the signal across the synapse, or gap, between two neurons. There are many types of neurotransmitters, including norepinephrine, dopamine, and serotonin. Neurotransmitters can be excitatory (that is, they excite an electrochemical response in the dendrite receptors) or inhibitory (they block the response of the dendrite receptors).

One neuron may communicate with thousands of other neurons, and many thousands of neurons are involved with even the simplest behaviour. It is believed that these connections and their efficiency can be modified, or altered, by experience.

Scientists have used two primary approaches to studying how the brain works. One approach is to study brain function after parts of the brain have been damaged. Functions that disappear or that is no longer normal after injury to specific regions of the brain can often be associated with the damaged areas. The second approach is to study the response of the brain to direct stimulation or to stimulation of various sense organs.

Neurons are grouped by function into collections of cells called nuclei. These nuclei are connected to form sensory, motor, and other systems. Scientists can study the function of somatosensory (pain and touch), motor, olfactory, visual, auditory, language, and other systems by measuring the physiological (physical and chemical) change that occur in the brain when these senses are activated. For example, electroencephalography (EEG) measures the electrical activity of specific groups of neurons through electrodes attached to the surface of the skull. Electrodes incorporate directly into the brain can give readings of individual neurons. Changes in blood flow, glucose (sugar), or oxygen consumption in groups of active cells can also be mapped.

Although the brain appears symmetrical, how it functions is not. Each hemisphere is specializing and dominates the other in certain functions. Research has shown that hemispheric dominance is related to whether a person is predominantly right-handed or left-handed. In most right-handed people, the left hemisphere processes arithmetic, language, and speech. The right hemisphere interprets music, complex imagery, and spatial relationships and recognizes and expresses emotion. In left-handed people, the pattern of brain organization is more variable.

Hemispheric specialization has traditionally been studied in people which have sustained damage to the connections between the two hemispheres, as may occur with a stroke, an interruption of blood flow to an area of the brain that causes the death of nerve cells in that area. The division of functions between the two hemispheres has also been studied in people who have had to have the connection between the two hemispheres surgically cut in order to control severe epilepsy, a neurological disease characterized by convulsions and loss of consciousness.

The visual system of humans is one of the most advanced sensory systems in the body. More information is conveyed visually than by any other means. In addition to the structures of the eye itself, several cortical regions - collectively called a primary visual and visual associative cortex - as well as the midbrain are involved in the visual system. Conscious processing of visual input occurs in the primary visual cortex, but reflexive - that is, immediate and unconscious - responses occur at the superior colliculus in the midbrain. Associative cortical regions - specialized regions that can associate, or integrate, multiple inputs - in the parietal and frontal lobes along with parts of the temporal lobe are also involved in the processing of visual information and the establishment of visual memories.

Language involves specialized cortical regions in a complex interaction that allows the brain to comprehend and communicate abstract ideas. The motor cortex initiates impulses that travel through the brain stem to produce audible sounds. Neighbouring regions of motor cortices, called the supplemental motor cortex, are involved in sequencing and coordinating sounds. Broca's area of the frontal lobe is responsible for the sequencing of language elements for output. The comprehension of language is dependent upon Wernicke's area of the temporal lobe. Other cortical circuits connect these areas.

Memory is usually considered a diffusely stored associative process - that is, it puts together information from many different sources. Although research has failed to identify specific sites in the brain as locations of individual memories, certain brain areas are critical for memory to function. Immediate recall - the ability to repeat short series of words or numbers immediately after hearing them - is thought to be located in the auditory associative cortex. Short-term memory - the ability to retain a limited amount of information for up to an hour - is located in the deep temporal lobe. Long-term memory probably involves exchanges between the medial temporal lobe, various cortical regions, and the midbrain.

The autonomic nervous system regulates the life support systems of the body reflexively - that is, without conscious direction. It automatically controls the muscles of the heart, digestive system, and lungs; Certain glands, and homeostasis - that is, the equilibrium of the internal environment of the body. The autonomic nervous system itself is controlled by nerve centres in the spinal cord and brain stem and is fine-tuned by regions higher in the brain, such as the midbrain and cortex. Reactions such as blushing indicate that cognitive, or thinking, centres of the brain are also involved in autonomic responses.

The brain is guarded by several highly developed protective mechanisms. The bony cranium, the surrounding meninges, and the cerebrospinal fluid all contribute to the mechanical protection of the brain. In addition, a filtration system called the blood-brain barrier protects the brain from exposure to potentially harmful substances carried in the bloodstream.

Brain disorders have a wide range of causes, including head injury, stroke, bacterial diseases, complex chemical imbalances, and changes associated with aging.

Head injury can initiate a cascade of damaging events. After a blow to the head, a person may be stunned or may become unconscious for a moment. This injury, called - concussion, - usually leaves no permanent damage. If the blow is more severe and haemorrhage (excessive bleeding) and swelling occurs, however, severe headache, dizziness, paralysis, a convulsion, or temporary blindness may result, depending on the area of the brain affected. Damage to the cerebrum can also result in profound personality changes.

Damage to Broca's area in the frontal lobe causes difficulty in speaking and writing, a problem known as Broca's aphasia. Injury to Wernicke's area in the left temporal lobe results in an inability to comprehend spoken language, called Wernicke's aphasia.

An injury or disturbance to a part of the hypothalamus may cause a variety of different symptoms, such as loss of appetite with an extreme drop in body weight, increase in appetite leading to obesity; Extraordinary thirst with excessive urination (diabetes insipidus), failure in body-temperature control, resulting in either low temperature (hypothermia) or high temperature (fever), excessive emotionality, and uncontrolled anger or aggression. If the relationship between the hypothalamus and the pituitary gland is damaged, other vital bodily functions may be disturbed, such as sexual function, metabolism, and cardiovascular activity.

Injury to the brain stem is even more serious because it houses the nerve centres that control breathing and heart action. Damage to the medulla oblongata usually results in immediate death.

A stroke is damage to the brain due to an interruption in blood flow. The interruption may be caused by a blood clot, constriction of a blood vessel, or rupture of a vessel accompanied by bleeding. A pouchlike expansion of the wall of a blood vessel, called an aneurysm, may weaken and burst, for example, because of high blood pressure.

Sufficient quantities of glucose and oxygen, transported through the bloodstream, are needed to keep nerve cells alive. When the blood supply to a small part of the brain is interrupted, the cells in that area die and the function of the area is lost. A massive stroke can cause a one-sided paralysis (hemiplegia) and sensory loss on the side of the body opposite the hemisphere damaged by the stroke.

Some brain diseases, such as multiple sclerosis and Parkinson disease, are progressive, becoming worse over time. Multiple sclerosis damages the myelin sheath around axons in the brain and spinal cord. As a result, the affected axons cannot transmit nerve impulses properly. Parkinson disease destroys the cells of the substantia nigra in the midbrain, resulting in a deficiency in the neurotransmitter dopamine that affects motor functions.

Cerebral palsy is a broad term for brain damage sustained close to birth that permanently affects motor function. The damage may take place either in the developing fetus, during birth, or just after birth and is the result of the faulty development or breaking down of motor pathways. Cerebral palsy is nonprogressive - that is, it does not worsen with time.

A bacterial infection in the cerebrum or in the coverings of the brain, swelling of the brain, or an abnormal growth of healthy brain tissue can all cause an increase in intracranial pressure and result in serious damage to the brain.

Scientists are finding that certain brain chemical imbalances are associated with mental disorders such as schizophrenia and depression. Such findings have changed scientific understanding of mental health and have resulted in new treatments that chemically correct these imbalances.

During childhood development, the brain is particularly susceptible to damage because of the rapid growth and reorganization of nerve connections. Problems that originate in the immature brain can appear as epilepsy or other brain-function problems in adulthood.

Several neurological problems are common in aging. Alzheimer's disease damages many areas of the brain, including the frontal, temporal, and parietal lobes. The brain tissue of people with Alzheimer's disease shows characteristic patterns of damaged neurons, known as plaques and tangles. Alzheimer's disease produces progressive dementia, characterized by symptoms such as failing attention and memory, loss of mathematical ability, irritability, and poor orientation in space and time.

A magnetic resonance imaging (MRI) scan of the human brain reveals the contours of one of the brain's hemispheres. The gyri, or ridges, appear in red, while the sulci, or valleys, are shown in blue. Each person has slightly different patterns of gyri and sulci, which reflect individual differences in brain development.

Several commonly used diagnostic methods give images of the brain without invading the skull. Some portray anatomy - that is, the structure of the brain - whereas others measure brain function. Two or more methods may be used to complement each other, together providing a more complete picture than would be possible by one method alone.

Magnetic resonance imaging (MRI), introduced in the early 1980s, beams high-frequency radio waves into the brain in a highly magnetized field that causes the protons that form the nuclei of hydrogen atoms in the brain to remit the radio waves. The remitted radio waves are analyzed by computer to create thin cross-sectional images of the brain. MRI provides the most detailed images of the brain and is safer than imaging methods that use X-rays. However, MRI is a lengthy process and also cannot be used with people who have pacemakers or metal implants, both of which are adversely affected by the magnetic field.

Computed tomography (CT), also known as CT scans, developed in the early 1970's. This imaging procedure of the X-ray, gives to a simple picture imaging sequence for applying interiorized images of the brain. The CT, is particularly useful for diagnosing blood clots and brain tumours. It is much quicker of a process than magnetic resonance imaging and is therefore advantageous in certain situations - for example, with people who are severely ill.

This positron emission tomography (PET) scans of the brain shows the activity of brain cells in the resting state and during three types of auditory stimulation. PET uses radioactive substances introduced within the brain to measure such brain functions as cerebral metabolism, blood flow and volume, oxygen use, and the formation of neurotransmitters. This imaging method collects data from many different angles, feeding the information into a computer that produces a series of cross-sectional images.

Changes in brain function due to brain disorders can be visualized in several ways. Magnetic resonance spectroscopy measures the concentration of specific chemical compounds in the brain that may change during specific behaviours. Functional magnetic resonance imaging (fMRI) maps changes in oxygen concentration that correspond to nerve cell activity.

Positron emission tomography (PET), developed in the mid-1970s, uses computed tomography to visualize radioactive tracers, radioactive substances are introduced into the brain intravenously or by inhalation. PET can measure such brain functions as cerebral metabolism, blood flow and volume, oxygen use, and the formation of neurotransmitters. Single photon emission computed tomography (SPECT), developed in the 1950s and 1960s, using radioactive tracers to visualize the circulation and volume of blood in the brain.

Brain-imaging studies have provided new insights into sensory, motor, language, and memory processes, as well as brain disorders such as epilepsy, cerebrovascular disease; Alzheimer's, Parkinson, and Huntington's diseases, and various mental disorders, such as schizophrenia.

Although all vertebrate brains share the same basic three-part structure, the development of their constituent parts varies across the evolutionary scale. In fish, the cerebrum is dwarfed by the rest of the brain and serves mostly to process input from the senses. In reptiles and amphibians, the cerebrum is proportionally larger and begins to connect and form conclusions about this input. Birds have well-developed optic lobes, making the cerebrum even larger. Among mammals, the cerebrum dominates the brain. It is most developed among primates, in whom cognitive ability is the highest.

In lower vertebrates, such as fish and reptiles, the brain is often tubular and bears a striking resemblance to the early embryonic stages of the brains of more highly evolved animals. In all vertebrates, the brain is divided into three regions: the forebrain (prosencephalon), the midbrain (mesencephalon), and the hindbrain (rhombencephalon). These three regions, to a considerable degree are placed or located partitions of three subdivided structures, or, systems, nuclei, and layers.

The more highly evolved the animal, the more complex is the brain structure. Human beings have the most complex brains of all animals. Evolutionary forces have also resulted in a progressive increase in the size of the brain. In vertebrates lower than mammals, the brain is small. In meat-eating animals, particularly primates, the brain increases dramatically in size.

The cerebrum and cerebellum of higher mammals are highly convoluted in order to fit the most gray matter surface within the confines of the cranium. Such highly convoluted brains are called gyrencephalic. Many lower mammals have a smooth, or lissencephalic (smooth head), cortical surfaces.

There is also evidence of evolutionary adaption of the brain. For example, many birds depend on an advanced visual system to identify food at great distances while in flight. Consequently, their optic lobes and cerebellum are well developed, giving them keen sight and outstanding motor coordination in flight. Rodents, on the other hand, as nocturnal animals, do not have a well-developed visual system. Instead, they rely more heavily on other sensory systems, such as a highly-developed sense of smell and facial whiskers.

Recent research in brain function suggests that there may be sexual differences in both brain anatomy and brain function. One study indicated that men and women may use their brains differently while thinking. Researchers used functional magnetic resonance imaging to observe which parts of the brain were activated as groups of men and women tried to determine whether sets of nonsense words rhymed. Men used only Broca's area in this task, whereas women used Broca's area plus an area on the right side of the brain.

The Cell, is the most basic unit of life. Cells are the smallest structures capable of basic life processes, such as taking in nutrients, expelling waste, and reproducing. All living things are composed of cells. Some microscopic organisms, such as bacteria and protozoa, are unicellular, meaning they consist of a single cell. Plants, animals, and fungi are multicellular; that is, they are composed of a great many cells working in concert. But whether it makes up an entire bacterium or is just one of the trillions in a human being, the cell is a marvel of design and efficiency. Cells carry out thousands of biochemical reactions each minute and reproduce new cells that perpetuate life.

The word cell refers to several types of organisms. Cells such as paramecia, dinoflagellates, diatoms, and spirochetes are self-maintaining organisms; cells such as lymphocytes, erythrocytes, muscle cells, nerve cells, cardiac muscle, and chromoplasts are more specializing of cells that are a part of higher multicellular organisms. Nonetheless, of its size or whether the cell is a complete organism or just part of an organism, in that of all cells have certain structural components in common, all cells have some type of exterior cell boundary, as territorially imperative that permits some materials to leave and enter the cell as the interior composition of a water-rich, fluid material called cytoplasm that contains hereditary material in the form of deoxyribonucleic acid (DNA).

Cells vary considerably in size. The smallest cell, a type of bacterium known as a mycoplasma, measures 0.0001mm. or (0.000004 in.) in diameter, being that 10,000 are contained in a row of mycoplasma, which is only as wide as the diameter of a human hair, by comparison, the largest cells are the nerve cells that run down a giraffe's neck, these cells can exceed over 3m. (9.7 ft.) in length. Human cells also display a variety of sizes, from small red blood cells that measure 0.00076mm. (0.00003 in.), as liver cells can measure for being ten times as large. About 10,000 average-sized human cells can fit on the head of a pin.

Along with their differences in size, cells present an array of shapes. Some, such as the bacterium Escherichia coli, resemble rods. The paramecium, a type of protozoan, is a slipper shaped. The amoeba, another protozoan, has an irregular form that changes shape as it moves around. Plant cells typically resemble boxes or cubes. In humans, the outermost layers of skin cells are flat, while muscle cells are long and thin. Some nerve cells, with their elongated, tentacle-like extensions, suggest an octopus.

In multicellular organisms, shape is typically tailored to the cell's job. For example, flat skin cells pack tightly into a layer that protects the underlying tissues from invasions by bacteria. Long, thin muscle cells' contract readily to move bones. The numerous extensions from a nerve cell enable it to connect to several other nerve cells in order to send and receive messages rapidly and efficiently.

By itself, each cell is a model of independence and self-containment. Like some miniature, walled city in perpetual rush hour, the cell constantly bustles with traffic, shuttling essential molecules from place to place to carry out the business of living. Despite their individuality, however, cells also display a remarkable ability to join, communicate, and coordinate with other cells. The human body, for example, consists of an estimated 20 to 30 trillion cells. Dozens of different kinds of cells are organized into specialized groups called tissues. Tendons and bones, for example, are composed of connective tissue, whereas skin and mucous membranes are built from epithelial tissue. Different tissue types are assembled into organs, which are structures specialized to perform particular functions. Examples of organs include the heart, stomach, and brain. Organs, in turn, are organized into systems such as the circulatory, digestive, or nervous systems. All together, these assembled organ systems form the human body.

The components of cells are molecules, nonliving structures formed by the union of atoms. Small molecules serve as building blocks for larger molecules. Proteins, nucleic acids, carbohydrates, and lipids, which include fats and oils, are the four major molecules that underlie cell structure and also participate in cell functions. For example, a tightly organized arrangement of lipids, proteins, and protein-sugar compounds forms the plasma membrane, or outer boundary, of certain cells. The organelles, membrane-bound compartments in cells, are built largely from proteins. Biochemical reactions in cells are guided by enzymes, specialized proteins that speed up chemical reactions. The nucleic acid deoxyribonucleic acid (DNA) contains the hereditary information for cells, and another nucleic acid, ribonucleic acid (RNA), works with DNA to build the thousands of proteins the cell needs.

Cells fall into one of two categories: Prokaryotic or eukaryotic, in a prokaryotic cell, found only in bacteria and archaebacteria, all the components, including the DNA, mingle freely in the cell's interior, a single compartment. Eukaryotic cells, which make up plants, animals, fungi, and all other life forms, contain numerous compartments, or organelles, within each cell. The DNA in eukaryotic cells is enclosed in a special organelle called the nucleus, which serves as the cell's command centre and information library. The term prokaryote comes from Greek words that mean "before the nucleus" or "prenucleus," while eukaryote means "a true nucleus."

Bacteria's cells typically are surrounded by a rigid, protective cell wall. The cell membrane, also called the plasma membrane, regulates passage of materials into and out of the cytoplasm, the semifluids that fill the cell. The DNA, located in the nucleoid region, contains the genetic information for the cell. Ribosomes carry out protein synthesis. Many bacteria contain some pilus (plural pili), a structure that extends out of the cell to transfer DNA to another bacterium. The flagellum, found in numerous species, is used for the locomotion. Some bacteria contain a phasmid, a small chromosomes with extra genes. Others have a capsule, a sticky substance external to the cell wall that protects bacteria from attack by white blood cells. Mesosomes were formerly thought to be structures with unknown functions, but now are known to be artifacts created when cells are prepared for viewing with electron microscopes.

Prokaryotic cells are among the tiniest of all cells, ranging in size from 0.0001 to 0.003 mm. (0.000004 to 0.0001 in.) in diameter. About a hundred typical prokaryotic cells lined up in a row would match the thickness of a book page. These cells, which can be rod-like, spherical, or spiral in shape, are surrounded by a protective cell wall. Like most cells, prokaryotic cells live in a watery environment, whether it is soil moisture, a pond, or the fluid surrounding cells in the human body. Tiny pores in the cell wall enable water and the substances dissolved in it, such as oxygen, to flow into the cell; these pores also allow wastes to flow out.

Pushed up against the inner surface of the prokaryotic cell wall is a thin membrane called the plasma membrane. The plasma membrane, composed of two layers of flexible lipid molecules and interspersed with durable proteins, is both supple and strong. Unlike the cell wall, whose open pores allow the unregulated traffic of materials in and out of the cell, the plasma membrane is selectively permeable, meaning it allows only certain substances to pass through. Thus, the plasma membrane actively separates the cell's contents from its surrounding fluids.

While small molecules such as water, oxygen, and carbon dioxide diffuse freely across the plasma membrane, the passage of many larger molecules, including amino acids (the building blocks' of proteins) and sugars, is carefully regulated. Specialized transport proteins accomplish this task. The transport proteins span the plasma membrane, forming an intricate system of pumps and channels through which traffic is conducted. Some substances swirling in the fluid around the cell can enter it only if they bind to and are escorted in by specific transport proteins. In this way, the cell fine-tunes its internal environment.

The plasma membrane encloses the cytoplasm, the semifluid that fill the cell. Composed of about 65 percent waters, the cytoplasm is packed with up to a billion molecules per cell, a rich storehouse that includes enzymes and dissolved nutrients, such as sugars and amino acids. The water provides a favourable environment for the thousands of biochemical reactions that take place in the cell.

Within the cytoplasm of all prokaryote is deoxyribonucleic acid (DNA), a complex molecule in the form of a double helix, a shape similar to a spiral staircase. The DNA is about 1,000 times the length of the cell, and to fit inside, it repeatedly twists and folds to form a compact structure called a chromosome. The chromosome in prokaryote is circular, and is located in a region of the cell called the nucleoid. Often, smaller chromosomes called Plasmids are located in the cytoplasm. The DNA is divided into units called genes, just like a long train is divided into separate cars. Depending on the species, the DNA contains several hundred or even thousands of genes. Typically, one gene contains coded instructions for building all or part of a single protein.

Enzymes, which are specialized proteins, determine virtually all the biochemical reactions that support and sustain the cell.

Also immersed in the cytoplasm are the only organelles in prokaryotic cells, and tiny beadlike structures called ribosomes. These are the cell's protein factories. Following the instructions encoded in the DNA, ribosomes churn out proteins by the hundreds every minute, providing needed enzymes, the replacements for worn-out transport proteins, or other proteins required by the cell.

While relatively simple in construction, prokaryotic cells display extremely complex activity. They have a greater range of biochemical reactions than those found in their larger relatives, the eukaryotic cells. The extraordinary biochemical diversity of prokaryotic cells is manifested in the wide-ranging lifestyles of the archaebacteria and the bacteria, whose habitats include polar ice, deserts, and hydrothermal vents - deep regions of the ocean under great pressure where hot water geysers erupt from cracks in the ocean floor.

An animal cell typically contains several types of membrane-bound organs, or organelles. The nucleus directs activities of the cell and carries genetic information from generation to generation. The mitochondria generates energy for the cell. Proteins are manufactured by ribosomes, composing of RNA and protein that are found in the cytoplasm and serves as the junction for which of the polypeptide encoded by messenger RNA. The protein-ribosomes compounds are bound to the rough endoplasmic reticulum or float-free in the cytoplasm. The Golgi apparatus modifies, packages, and distributes proteins while lysosomes stores enzymes for digesting food. The entire cell is wrapped in a lipid membrane that selectively permits materials to pass in and out of the cytoplasm.

Eukaryotic cells are typically about ten times larger than prokaryotic cells. In animal cells, the plasma membrane, rather than a cell wall, forms the cell's outer boundary. With a design similar to the plasma membrane of prokaryotic cells, it separates the cell from its surroundings and regulates the traffic across the membrane.

The eukaryotic cell cytoplasm is similar to that of the prokaryote cell except for one major difference: Eukaryotic cells house a nucleus and numerous other membrane-enclosed organelles. Like separate rooms of a house, these organelles enable specialized functions to be carried out efficiently. The building of proteins and lipids, for example, takes place in separate organelles where specialized enzymes geared for each job are located.

The plasma membrane that surrounds eukaryotic cells is a dynamic structure composed of two layers of phospholipid molecules interspersed with cholesterol and proteins. Phospholipids are composed of a hydrophilic, or water-loving, head and two tails, which are hydrophobic, or water-hating. The two phospholipid layers face each other in the membrane, with the heads directed outward and the tails pointing inward. The water-attracting heads anchor the membrane to the cytoplasm, the watery fluid inside the cell, and also to the water surrounding the cell. The water-hating tails block large water-soluble molecules from passing through the membrane while permitting fat-soluble molecules, including medications such as tranquillizers and sleeping pills, to freely cross the membrane. Proteins embedded in the plasma membrane carry out a variety of functions, including transport of large water soluble molecules such as sugars and certain amino acids.

Glycoprotein, proteins bonded to carbohydrates, serves in part to identify the cell as belonging to a unique organism, enabling the immune system to detect foreign cells, such as invading bacteria, which carry different glycoprotein. Cholesterol molecules in the plasma membrane act as stabilizers that limit the movement of the two slippery Phospholipids layers, which slide back and forth in the membrane. As any of various phosphorous-containing lipids, such as lecithin and cephalin, that are composed mainly of fatty acids, the phosphate groups, and a simple organic molecule, that is also called phosphatide, are the various phosphorous-containing lipids, such as lecithin and cephalin, that are composed, mainly of fatty acids, a phosphate group and a simple organic molecule.

Tiny gaps in the membrane enable small molecules such as oxygen to diffuse readily into and out of the cell. Since cells constantly use up oxygen, decreasing its concentration within the cell, the higher concentration of oxygen outside the cell causes a net flow of oxygen into the cell. The steady stream of oxygen into the cell enables it to carry out aerobic respiration continually, a process that provides the cell with the energy needed to carry out its functions.

The nucleus is the largest organelle in an animal cell. It contains numerous strands of DNA, the length of each strand being many times the diameter of the cell. Unlike the circular prokaryotic DNA, long sectors of eukaryotic DNA pack into the nucleus by wrapping around proteins. As a cell begins to divide, each DNA strand folds over onto itself several times, forming a rod-shaped chromosome.

The nucleus is surrounded by a double-layered membrane that protects the DNA from potentially damaging chemical reactions that occur in the cytoplasm. Messages pass between the cytoplasm and the nucleus through nuclear pores, which are holes in the membrane of the nucleus. In each nuclear pore, molecular signals flash back and forth as often as ten times per second. For example, a signal to activate a specific gene comes into the nucleus and instructions for production of the necessary protein go out to the cytoplasm.

The nucleus, present in eukaryotic cells, is a discrete structure containing chromosomes, which hold the genetic information for the cell. Separated from the cytoplasm of the cell by a double-layered membrane called the nuclear envelope. The nucleus contains a cellular material called nucleoplasm. Nuclear pores, present around the circumference of the nuclear membrane, allow the exchange of cellular materials between the nucleoplasm and the cytoplasm.

Attached to the nuclear membrane is an elongated membranous sac called the endoplasmic reticulum, as an organelle, is differentiated by structure within the cell, such as a mitochondrion, vacuole, or chloroplast, that performs a specific function, which tunnels through the cytoplasm of the protoplasm til outside the nucleus of a cell? The back and forth oscillations form a series of membranous stacks. An endoplasmic reticulum performs as a membrane network within the cytoplasm of cells involved in the synthesis, modification, and transport of cellular materials. Having two forms, as rough and smooth, its rough endoplasmic reticulum (RER) is so called because it appears bumpy under a microscope. The bumps are actually thousands of ribosomes attached to the membrane's surface. The ribosomes in eukaryotic cells have the same function as those in prokaryotic cells - protein synthesis - but they differ slightly in structure. Eukaryote is a single-celled or multicellular organism whose cells contain a distinct membrane-bound nucleus, whereas, ribosomes are minute round particle compound of RNA and protein that is found in the cytoplasm of living cells and serves as the site of assembly for polypeptide encoded by messenger RNA. Ribosomes bound to the endoplasmic reticulum help assemble proteins that typically are exported from the cell. The ribosomes work with other molecules to link amino acids to partially completed proteins. These incomplete proteins then travel to the inner chamber of the endoplasmic reticulum, where chemical modifications, such as the addition of a sugar, are carried out. Chemical modifications of lipids are also carried out in the endoplasmic reticulum.

The endoplasmic reticulum and its bound-ribosomes are particularly dense in cells that produce many proteins for export, such as the white blood cells of the immune system, which produce and secrete antibodies. Some ribosomes that manufacture proteins are not attached to the endoplasmic reticulum. These so-called free ribosomes are dispersed in the cytoplasm and typically make proteins - many of them enzymes - that remain in the cell.

The second form of endoplasmic reticulums, the smooth endoplasmic reticulum (SER), lacking ribosomes and has an even surface. Within the winding channels of the smooth endoplasmic reticulum are the enzymes needed for the construction of molecules such as carbohydrates and lipids. The smooth endoplasmic reticulum is prominent in liver cells, where it also serves to detoxify substances such as alcohol, drugs, and other poisons.

Proteins are transported from free and bound ribosomes to the Golgi apparatus, an organelle that resembles a stack of deflated balloons. It is packed with enzymes that complete the processing of proteins. These enzymes add sulfur or phosphorus atoms to certain regions of the protein, for example, or chop off tiny pieces from the ends of the proteins. The completed protein then leaves the Golgi apparatus for its final destination inside or outside the cell. During its assembly on the ribosome, each protein has acquired a group of from 4 to 100 amino acids called a signal. The signal works as a molecular shipping label to direct the protein to its proper location.

Lysosomes are small and often spherical organelles that function as the cell's recycling centre and garbage disposal. Powerful digestive enzymes concentrated in the lysosome breaks down worn-out organelles and transfers or by movement to their building blocks to the cytoplasm, where they are used to construct new organelles, this is a differentiated structure within a cell, such as mitochondrion, vacuole, or chloroplast, that performs a specific function. Of which a small cavity in the cytoplasm of a cell, bound by a single membrane and containing water, or metabolic waste, as the mitochondrion is a spherical or elongated organelle in the cytoplasm of nearly all eukaryotic cells, containing genetic material and many enzymes important for a cell metabolism, including those of an action or of the discharge as based on or characterized by them for that which of a response is the conversion of food to unable energy, also called a chondriosome.

Lysosome is the membrane-bound organelle in the cytoplasm of most cells containing various hydrolytic enzymes that function in intracellular digestion, which of any of the many proteins or conjugated proteins produced by living organisms and functioning as biochemical catalysts. Yet, a differentiated structure within a cell, such as a mitochondrion, vacuole, or chloroplast, that preform a specific function, usually used in small amounts relative to the reactant, that modifies and increases the rate of a reaction without being consumed in the process.

Lysosomes also dismantle and recycle proteins, lipids, and other molecules. Lysosome is a membrane-bound structure within a cell such as mitochondria. Vacuole, or chloroplast, that performs a specific function called as an organelle, positioned of the cytoplasm, as the protoplasm outside the nucleus of a cell. As most cells are contained by various hydrolytic enzymes that function in intracellular digestion.

The mitochondria is the powerhouse of the cell. Within these long, slender organelles, which can appear oval or bean shaped under the electron microscope, enzymes convert the sugar glucose and other nutrients into adenosine triphosphate (ATP). This molecule, in turn, serves as an energy battery for countless cellular processes, including the shuttling of substances across the plasma membrane, the building and transport of proteins and lipids, the recycling of molecules and organelles, and the dividing of cells. Muscle and liver cells are particularly active and require dozens and sometimes up to hundreds mitochondria per cell to meet their energy needs. Mitochondria is unusual in that they contain their own DNA in the form of a prokaryote-like circular chromosome; Have their own ribosomes, which resemble prokaryotic ribosomes, and divide independently of the cell.

Unlike the tiny prokaryotic cell, the relatively large eukaryotic cell requires structural support. The cytoskeleton, a dynamic network of protein tubes, filaments, and fibres, crisscrosses the cytoplasm, anchoring the organelles in place and providing shape and structure to the cell. Many components of the cytoskeleton are assembled and disassembled by the cell as needed. During cell division, for example, a special structure called a spindle is built to move chromosomes around. After cell division, the spindle, no longer needed, is dismantled. Some components of the cytoskeleton serve as microscopic tracks along which proteins and other molecules travel like miniature trains. Recent research suggests that the cytoskeleton also may be a mechanical communication structure that converses with the nucleus to help organize events in the cell.

Plant cells have all the components of animal cells and boast several added features, including the chloroplast, a central vacuole, and a cell wall. Chloroplasts convert light energy - typically from the Sun - into the sugar glucose, a form of chemical energy, in a process known as photosynthesis. Chloroplasts, like mitochondria, possess a circular chromosome and prokaryote-like ribosomes, which manufacture the proteins that the Chloroplasts typically need.

The central vacuole of a mature plant cell typically takes up most of the room in the cell. The vacuole, presented by a small cavity in the cytoplasm of a cell, bound by a single membrane and containing water, food, or metabolic waste. A membrane bags, crowding the membranous bag, herding together the cytoplasm and organelles into the edge of the cell. The central vacuole stores water, salts, sugars, proteins, and other nutrients. In addition, it stores the blue, red, and purple pigments that give certain flowers their colours. The central vacuole also contains plant wastes that taste bitter to certain insects, thus discouraging the insects from feasting on the plant.

In plant cells, has a sturdy cell wall that surrounds and protects the plasma membrane. Its pores enable materials to pass freely into and out of the cell. The strength of the wall also enables a cell to absorb water into the central vacuole and swell without bursting. The resulting pressure in the cells provides plants with rigidity and support for stems, leaves, and flowers. Without sufficient water pressure, the cells collapse and the plant wilts.

To stay alive, cells must be able to carry out a variety of functions. Some cells must be able to move, and most cells must be able to divide. All cells must maintain the right concentration of chemicals in their cytoplasm, ingest food and use it for energy, recycle molecules, expel wastes, and construct proteins. Cells must also be able to respond to changes in their environment.

Although many forms of bacteria are not capable of independent movement, species such as the Salmonella bacterium and can move by means of fine threadlike projections called flagella. The arrangement of flagella across the surface of the bacterium differs from species to species; they can be present at the ends of the bacterium or all across the body surface. Forward movement is accomplished either by a tumbling motion or in a forward manner without tumbling.

Many unicellular organisms swim, glide, thrash, or crawl to search for food and escape enemies. Swimming organisms often move by means of a flagellum, a long tail-like structure made of protein. Many bacteria, for example, have one, two, or many flagella that rotate like propellers to drive the organism along. Some single-celled eukaryotic organisms, such as the euglena, also have a flagellum, but it is longer and thicker than the prokaryotic flagellum. The eukaryotic flagellums work by waving up and down like a whip. In higher animals, the sperm cell uses a flagellum to swim toward the female egg for fertilization.

Movement in eukaryotes is also accomplished with cilia, short, hairlike proteins built by centrioles, which are barrel-shaped structures located in the cytoplasm that assemble and break down protein filaments. Typically, thousands of cilia extend through the plasma membrane and cover the surface of the cell, giving it a dense, hairy appearance. By beating its cilia as if they were oars, an organism such as the paramecium propels itself through its watery environment. In cells that do not move, cilia are used for other purposes. In the respiratory tract of humans, for example, millions of ciliated cells prevent inhaled dust, smog, and microorganisms from entering the lungs by sweeping them up on a current of mucus into the throat, where they are swallowed. Eukaryotic flagella and cilia are formed from basal bodies, small protein structures located just inside the plasma membrane. Basal bodies also help to anchor flagella and cilia.

Still other eukaryotic cells, such as amoebas and white blood cells, move by amoeboid motion, or crawling. They extrude their cytoplasm to form temporary pseudopodia, or false feet, which actually are placed in front of the cell, rather like extended arms. They then drag the trailing end of their cytoplasm up to the pseudopodia. A cell using amoeboid motion would lose a race to a euglena or paramecium. But while it is slow, amoeboid motion is strong enough to move cells against a current, enabling water-dwelling organisms to pursue and devour prey, for example, or white blood cells roaming the blood stream to stalk and engulf a bacterium or virus.

An amoeba, a single-celled organism lacking internal organs, is shown approaching a much smaller paramecium, which it begins to engulf with large outflowing of its cytoplasm, called pseudopodia. Once the paramecium is completely engulfed, a primitive digestive cavity, called a vacuole, forms around it. In the vacuole, acids break the paramecium down into chemicals that the amoeba can diffuse back into its cytoplasm for nourishment.

All cells require nutrients for energy, and they display a variety of methods for ingesting them. Simple nutrients dissolved in pond water, for example, can be carried through the plasma membrane of pond-dwelling organisms via a series of molecular pumps. In humans, the cavity of the small intestine contains the nutrients from digested food, and cells that form the walls of the intestine use similar pumps to pull amino acids and other nutrients from the cavity into the bloodstream. Certain unicellular organisms, such as amoebas, are also capable of reaching out and grabbing food. They used a process known as endocytosis, in which the plasma membrane surrounds and engulfed the food particle, enclosing it in a sac, called a vesicle, that is within the amoeba's interior.

Cells require energy for a variety of functions, including moving, building up and breaking down molecules, and transporting substances across the plasma membrane. Nutrients contain energy, but cells must convert the energy locked in nutrients to another form - specifically, the ATP molecule, the cell's energy battery - before it is useful. In single-celled eukaryotic organisms, such as the paramecium, and in multicellular eukaryotic organisms, such as plants, animals, and fungi, mitochondria is responsible for this task. The interior of each mitochondrion consists of an inner membrane that is folded into a mazelike arrangement of separate compartments called cristae. Within the cristae, enzymes form an assembly line where the energy in glucose and other energy-rich nutrients is harnessed to build ATP; thousands of ATP molecules are constructed each second in a typical cell. In most eukaryotic cells, this process requires oxygen and is known as aerobic respiration.

Some prokaryotic organisms also carry out aerobic respiration. They lack mitochondria, however, and carry out aerobic respiration in the cytoplasm with the help of enzymes sequestered there. Many prokaryote species live in environments where there is little or no oxygen, environments such as mud, stagnant ponds, or within the intestines of animals. Some of these organisms produce ATP without oxygen in a process known as anaerobic respiration, where sulfur or other substances take the place of oxygen. Still other prokaryotes, and yeast, a single-celled eukaryote, build ATP without oxygen in a process known as fermentation.

Almost all organisms rely on the sugar glucose to produce ATP. Glucose is made by the process of photosynthesis, in which light energy is transformed to the chemical energy of glucose. Animals and fungi cannot carry out photosynthesis and depend on plants and other photosynthetic organisms for this task. In plants, as we have seen, photosynthesis takes place in organelles called Chloroplasts. The differentiated structure within a cell, as a mitochondrion, vacuole, or chloroplast, that performs a specific function or the body of an organelle orgasm or the body becoming implemental to a chlorophyll-containing plastid, as found in algal and green plant cells.

To a greater extent, is the amount of the internal compartments, called thylakoids, which are saclike membranes, that the structural units of the Chloroplasts of plant cells as that of enzymes aid in the energy conversion process. A single leaf cell contains 40 to 50 Chloroplasts. With sufficient sunlight, one large tree is capable of producing upwards of two tons of sugar in a single day. Photosynthesis in prokaryotic organisms - typically aquatic bacteria - is carried out with enzymes clustered in plasma membrane folds called chromatophores. Aquatic bacteria produce the food consumed by tiny organisms living in ponds, rivers, lakes, and seas.

A typical cell must have on hand, about 30,000 proteins at one given time. Many of these proteins are enzymes needed to construct the major molecules used by cells - carbohydrates, lipids, proteins, and nucleic acids - nor to aid in the breakdown of such molecules after they have worn out. Other proteins are part of the cell's structure - the plasma membrane and ribosomes, for example. In animals, proteins also function as hormones and antibodies, and they function like delivery trucks to transport other molecules around the body. Haemoglobin, for example, is a protein that transports oxygen in red blood cells. The cell's demand for proteins never ceases.

Before a protein can be made, however, the molecular directions to build, it must be extracted from one or more genes. In humans, for example, one gene holds the information for the protein insulin, the hormone that cells need to import glucose from the bloodstream, while at least two genes hold the information for collagen, the protein that imparts strength to skin, tendons, and ligaments. The process of building proteins begins when enzymes, in response to a signal from the cell, bind to the gene that carries the code for the required protein, or part of the protein. The enzymes transfer the code to a new molecule called messenger RNA, which carries the code from the nucleus to the cytoplasm. This enables the original genetic code to remain safe in the nucleus, with messenger RNA delivering small bits and pieces of information from the DNA to the cytoplasm as needed. Depending on the cell type, hundreds or even thousands of molecules of messenger RNA are produced each minute.

Once in the cytoplasm, the messenger RNA molecule links up with a ribosome. The ribosome moves along the messenger RNA like a monorail car along a track, stimulating another form of RNA - transfer RNA - to gather and link the necessary amino acids, pooled in the cytoplasm, to form the specific protein, or section of protein. The protein is modified as necessary by the endoplasmic reticulum and Golgi apparatus before embarking on its mission. Cells teem with activity as they forge the numerous, diverse proteins that are indispensable for life. For a more detailed discussion about protein synthesis, When there are a hundred or more cells, they formed a hollow ball of cells, called a blastula, surrounding a fluid-filled cavity. Later divisions produce three layers of cells - endoderm (inner), mesoderm (middle), and ectoderm (outer) - from which the principal features of the animal will differentiate.

Most cells divide at some time during their life cycle, and some divide dozens of times before they die. Organisms rely on cell division for reproduction, growth, and repair and replacement of damaged or worn out cells. Three types of cell division occur: Binary fission, mitosis, and meiosis, as binary fission is, the method used by prokaryotes, producing two identical cells from one cell. The more complex process of mitosis, which also produces two genetically identical cells from a single cell, is used by many unicellular eukaryotic organisms for reproduction. Multicellular organisms use mitosis for growth, cell repair, and cell replacement. In the human body, for example, of about 25 million mitotic cells divide every second in order to replace cells that have completed their normal life cycles. Cells of the liver, intestine, and skin may be replaced every few days. Recent research indicates that even brain cell, once thought to be incapable of mitosis, undergo cell division in the part of the brain associated with memory.

In a landmark intersection of science and fiction, cloning leapt from the world's imagination to its front page in February 1997. It arrived in the innocent form of a sheep named Dolly: The first exact genetic duplicate of an adult mammal due to genetic engineering. Scottish scientists had created Dolly from deoxyribonucleic acid (DNA) - the basic unit of heredity - taken from a single adult sheep cell. The accomplishment threw open the door too profound ethical as well as scientific controversy over the potential uses and the abusive treatments as do of cloning. "However the debate is resolved," wrote Los Angeles Times science reporter Thomas H. Maugh II, "the genie is irretrievably out of the bottle."

The type of cell division required for sexual reproduction is meiosis. Sexually reproducing organisms include seaweeds, fungi, plants, and animals - including, of course, human beings. Meiosis differs from mitosis in that cell division begins with a cell that has a full complement of chromosomes and ends with gamete cells, such as sperm and eggs, that have only half the complement of chromosomes. When a sperm and egg unite during fertilization, the cell resulting from the union, called a zygote, contains the full number of chromosomes.

The story of how cells evolved remains an open and actively investigated question in science. The combined expertise of physicists, geologists, chemists, and evolutionary biologists has been required to shed light on the evolution of cells from the nonliving matter of early Earth. The planet had formed in or around 4.0 to 5.0 billion years ago, and for millions of years, violent volcanic eruptions blasted substances such as carbon dioxide, nitrogen, water, and other small molecules into the air, including the instability of gravitation. These small molecules, and waves of gravity were bombarded by ultraviolet radiation and lightning from intense storms, molecules collided, sticking or fusing together, as if glued to the touch, to form the stable chemical bonds of larger molecules, such as amino acids and nucleotides, least of mention, other plants in our solar system, and nucleated acids. Experiments indicate that these larger molecules form spontaneously under laboratory conditions that simulate the probable early environment of Earth.

Scientists speculate that rain may have carried these molecules into lakes to create a primordial soup - the breeding ground for the assembly of proteins, the nucleic acid RNA, and lipids. Some scientists postulate that these more complex molecules formed in hydrothermal vents rather than in lakes. Other scientists propose that these key substances may have reached Earth on meteorites from outer space. Regardless of the origin or environment, however, scientists do agree that proteins, nucleic acids, and lipids provided the raw materials for the first cells. In the laboratory, scientists have observed lipid molecules joining to form spheres that resemble a cell's plasma membrane. As a result of these observations, scientists postulate that millions of years of molecular collisions resulted in lipid spheres enclosing RNA, the simplest molecule capable of self-replication. These primitive aggregations would have been the ancestors of the first prokaryotic cells.

Fossil studies indicate that Cyanobacteria, bacteria capable of photosynthesis, were among the earliest bacteria to evolve, an estimated 3.4 billion to 3.5 billion years ago. In the environment of the early Earth, there were no oxygen, and cyanobacteria probably used fermentation to produce ATP. Over the eons, cyanobacteria performed photosynthesis, which produces oxygen as a byproduct; The result was the gradual accumulation of oxygen in the atmosphere. The presence of oxygen set the stage for the evolution of bacteria that used oxygen in aerobic respiration, a more efficient ATP-producing process than fermentation. Some molecular studies of the evolution of genes in archaebacteria suggest that these organisms may have evolved in the hot waters of hydrothermal vents or hot springs slightly earlier than cyanobacteria, around 3.5 billion years ago. Like cyanobacteria, archaebacteria probably relied on fermentation to synthesize ATP.

Eukaryotic cells may have evolved from primitive prokaryotes about 2 billion evolutionary years ago. The hypothesis suggests that some prokaryotic cells lost their cell walls, permitting the cell's plasma membrane to expand and fold. These folds, ultimately, may have given rise to separate compartments within the cell - the forerunners of the nucleus and other organelles now found in eukaryotic cells. Another key hypothesis is known as endosymbiosis, of which the inward flow of a fluid through a permeable membrane toward fluid of greater concentration.

Molecular studies of the bacteria-like DNA and ribosomes in mitochondria and Chloroplasts are implicated for the containing of plastid, which are found in alga and green plant cells, but, mitochondrion and chloroplast ancestors were once free-living bacteria. Scientists propose that these free-living bacteria were engulfed and maintained by other prokaryotic cells for their ability to produce ATP efficiently and to provide a steady supply of glucose. Over generations, eukaryotic cells situated with mitochondria, of which are the ancestors of animals - or with both mitochondria, which is a spherical and elongated organelle in the cytoplasm of nearly all eukaryotic cells, containing genetic material and many enzymes important for cell metabolisms. Also, Chloroplasts, of which the chlorophyll-containing plastid can be found in algal and green plant cells that have evolved.

The first observations of cells were made in 1665 by English scientist Robert Hooke, who used a crude microscope of his own invention to examine a variety of objects, including a thin piece of cork. Noting the rows of tiny boxes that made up the dead wood's tissue, Hooke coined the term cell because the boxes reminded him of the small cells occupied by monks in a monastery. While Hooke was the first to observe and describe cells, he did not comprehend their significance. At about the same time, the Dutch maker of microscopes Antoni van Leeuwenhoek pioneered the invention of one of the best microscopes of the time. Using his invention, Leeuwenhoek was the first to observe, draw, and describe a variety of living organisms, including bacteria gliding in saliva, one-celled organisms cavorting in pond water, and sperm swimming in semen. Two centuries passed, however, before scientists grasped the true importance of cells.

Many advances have been made in microscope technology. An article from the 1994 Collier's Year Book begins with the microscope most young students are familiar with and tracks the breakthroughs in the development of new types of microscopes - including those that use ultrasonic imaging and those that "feel" an object's surface.

Modern ideas about cells appeared in the 1800s, when improved light microscopes enabled scientists to observe more details of cells. Working together, German botanist Matthias Jakob Schleiden and German zoologist Theodor Schwann recognized the fundamental similarities between plant and animal cells. In 1839 they proposed the revolutionary idea that all living things are made up of cells. Their theory gave rise to modern biology: a whole new way of seeing and investigating the natural world.

By the late 1800s, as light microscopes improved still further, scientists were able to observe chromosomes within the cell. Their research was aided by new techniques for staining parts of the cell, which made possible the first detailed observations of cell division, including observations of the differences between mitosis and meiosis in the 1880s. In the first few decades of the 20th century, many scientists focussed on the behaviour of chromosomes during cell division. At that time, it was generally held that mitochondria transmitted the hereditary information.

By 1920, however, scientists determined that chromosomes carry genes and that genes transmit hereditary information from generation to generation.

During this period, scientists began to understand some of the chemical processes in cells. In the 1920s, the ultracentrifuge was developed. The ultracentrifuge is an instrument that spins cells or other substances in test tubes at high speeds, which causes the heavier parts of the substance to fall to the bottom of the test tube. This instrument enabled scientists to separate the relatively abundant and heavy mitochondria from the rest of the cell and study their chemical reactions. By the late 1940s, scientists were able to explain the role of mitochondria in the cell. Using refined techniques with the ultracentrifuge, scientists subsequently isolated the smaller organelles and gained of some understanding.

Diagnostic and Statistical Manual of Mental Disorders (DSM), is the medical reference book published by the American Psychiatric Association (APA) that describes and classifies all known mental illnesses and emotional disorders. The fourth edition, referred to as DSM-IV, was issued in 1994 and lists more than 300 psychiatric disorders.

Most American psychiatrists, psychologists, researchers, and other mental health professionals use the Diagnostic Statistical Manual (DSM). It provides an objective, standardized way to determine if a person has a mental illness. There are no blood tests or other laboratory procedures to diagnose most mental illnesses. Instead, mental health professionals must use their own judgment to determine if a person is mentally ill. Diagnosis requires careful observation of the person's symptoms and behaviours and evaluation of the person's personal and medical history. Diagnostic Statistical Manual helps to assure an accurate diagnosis by providing a common reference for therapists and researchers to use in communicating about mental illness. In addition, health insurance companies use DSM in determining payment for mental health services. A psychiatrist must list an official DSM code number on each health insurance claim form submitted for a patient.

DSM-IV, all in which, are groups of psychiatric disorders into which 16 major diagnostic classes are categorized, such as mood disorders, anxiety disorders, and substance-abuse disorders. The entry for each disorder includes a definition and a list of signs and symptoms that can be used as diagnostic criteria.

Psychiatrists and psychologists use the list of symptoms as a general guideline for making a diagnosis, rather than as a checklist. They combine DSM information with their own findings from an examination of the patient. If applicable, a DSM entry cites physical or laboratory tests that can help in reaching a diagnosis. Each entry also includes information on the typical age at which the disease occurs, how it changes over time, the number of people in the general population, and whether the effect occurs more frequently in members of the same family. The book also lists factors that psychiatrists and others can use in determining the severity of a patient's condition.

DSM originated from a 1917 project in which the American Psychiatric Association (then called the American Medico-Psychological Association) and the United States Bureau of the Census developed a classification system of 59 mental illnesses to collect uniform data on hospitalized mental patients. The APA expanded the system with publication of the first DSM in 1952, listing 106 mental illnesses. Updated versions followed: DSM-II was published in 1968, DSM-III in 1980, and DSM-III-R (a revision of DSM-III) in 1987. A special, 27-member task force of experts worked for five years to develop DSM-IV, published in 1994. More than 1000 psychiatrists and other experts helped decide what diseases and other information should be included in the book.

Critics of DSM believe that the book regards too many normal human traits and behaviours as possible psychiatric illnesses.

They are concerned that DSM authors sometimes use personal and social values, rather than scientific evidence, to judge whether behaviour is abnormal. For example, homosexuality was classified as a disorder until 1973, when the APA acknowledged that many gay and lesbian people showed no signs of any dysfunction and were satisfied with their sexual orientation.

Many mental health professionals in Western Europe and other parts of the world use a different classification system, the International Classification of Diseases (ICD), published by the World Health Organization, an agency of the United Nations. Developers of the two systems work together to ensure compatible terminology about mental illness.

Mental Illness, are disorders characterized by disturbances in a person's thoughts, emotions, or behaviour, the term mental illness can be regarded for being a wide variety of disorders, ranging from those that cause mild distress to those that severely impair a person's ability to function. Mental health professionals sometimes use the term's psychiatric disorder or psychopathology to refer to mental illness.

Severe mental illness almost always alters a person's life dramatically. People with severe mental illnesses experience disturbing symptoms that can make it difficult to hold down a job, going to school, relate to others, or cope with ordinary life demands. Some individuals require hospitalization because they become unable to care for themselves or because they are at risk of committing suicide.

The symptoms of mental illness can be very distressing. People who develop schizophrenia may hear voices inside their head that say nasty things about them or command them to act in strange or unpredictable ways. Or they may be paralyzed by paranoia—the deep conviction that everyone, including their closest family members, wants to injure or destroy them. People with major depression may feel that nothing brings pleasure and that life is so dreary and unhappy that it is better to be dead. People with panic disorder may experience heart palpitations, rapid breathing, or extreme anxiety. People whom experience episodes of mania may engage in reckless sexual behaviour or may spend money indiscriminately, acts that later cause them to feel guilt, shame, and desperation.

Other mental illnesses, while not always debilitating, create certain problems in living. People with personality disorders may experience loneliness and isolation because their personality style interferes with social relations. People with an eating disorder may become so preoccupied with their weight and appearance that they force themselves to vomit or refuse to eat. Individuals who develop post-traumatic stress disorder may become angry easily, experience disturbing memories, and have trouble concentrating.

Experiences of mental illness often depend upon the differing of culture or social groups, sometimes, to a greater extent, for example, in most of the non-Western world, people with depression complain principally of physical ailments, such as lack of energy, poor sleep, loss of appetite, and various kinds of physical pain. Indeed, even in North America these complaints are commonplace. But in the United States and other Western societies, depressed people and mental health professionals who treat them tend to emphasize psychological problems, such as feelings of sadness, worthlessness, and despair. The experience of schizophrenia also differs by culture. In India, one-third of the new cases of schizophrenia involve catatonia, a behavioural condition in which a person maintains a bizarre statuelike pose for hours or days. This condition is rare in Europe and North America.

With appropriate treatment, most people can recover from mental illness and return to normal life. Even those with persistent, long-term mental illnesses can usually learn to manage their symptoms and live productive lives.

In most societies mental illness carries a substantial stigma, or mark of shame. The mentally ill had often been blamed for bringing on their own illnesses, and others may see them as victims of bad fate, religious and moral transgression, or witchcraft.   S u c h stigmas may keep families from acknowledging that a family member is ill. Some families may hide or overprotect a member with mentally illness—keeping the person from receiving potentially effective care—or they may reject the person from the family. When magnified from individuals to a whole society, such attitudes lead to under-funding of mental health services and terribly inadequate care. In much of the world, even today, the mentally ill, are chained, caged, or hospitalized in filthy, brutal institutions. Yet attitudes toward mental illness have improved in many areas, especially owing to health education and advocacy for the mentally ill.

Mental illness creates enormous social and economic costs. Depression, for example, affects some 500 million people in the world and results in more time lost to disability than such chronic diseases as diabetes mellitus and arthritis. Estimating the economic cost of mental illness is complex because there are direct costs (actual medical expenditures), indirect costs (the cost to individuals and society due to reduced or lost productivity, for example), and support costs (time lost to care of family members with mental illnesses). One study estimated that in 1985 the economic costs of mental illness in the United States totalled $103.7 billion. Of this, treatment and support costs totalled $42.5 billion, which represented 11.5 percent of the total cost of care for all illnesses.

Another method of estimating the cost of mental illness to society measures the impact of premature deaths and disablements. Research by the World Health Organization and the World Bank estimated that in 1990, among the world's population aged 15 to 44 years, depression accounted for more than 10 percent of the total burden attributable to all diseases. Two other illnesses, bipolar disorder and schizophrenia, accounted for another 6 percent of the burden. This research has helped governments recognize that mental illnesses constitute a far greater challenge to public health systems than previously realized.

No universally accepted definition of mental illness exists. Overall, the definition of mental illness depends on a society's norms, or rules of behaviour. Behaviours that violate these norms are considered signs of deviance or, in some cases, of mental illness.

Because norms vary between cultures, behaviours considered signs of mental illness in one culture may be considered normal in other cultures. For example, in the United States, a person who experiences trance and possession states (altered states of consciousness) is usually diagnosed as suffering from a mental illness. Yet, in many non-Western countries, people consider such states an essential part of human experience. In Native American culture, it is common for people to hear the voices of recently deceased loved ones. In contrast, most mental health professionals in Western cultures would consider such behaviour a possible symptom of schizophrenia or psychosis.

The variation in behavioural norms does not mean, however, that definitions of mental illness are necessarily incompatible across cultures. Many behaviours are recognized throughout the world for being indicative of mental illness. These include extreme social withdrawal, violence to oneself, hallucinations (false sensory perceptions), and delusions (fixed, false ideas).

Another way of defining mental illness is based on whether a person's behaviours are maladaptive—that is, whether they cause a person to experience problems in coping with common life demands. For example, people with social phobia may avoid interacting with other people and experience problems at work as a result. Critics note that under this definition, political dissidents could be considered mentally ill for refusing to accept the dictates of their government.

Mental illness affects people of all ages, races, cultures, and socioeconomic classes. The prevalence of mental illness refers, especially how people experience a mental illness during any specific time.

In the United States, researchers estimate that about 24 percent of people 18 or older, or about 44 million adults, experience a mental illness or substance-related disorder during the course of any given year. The most common of these disorders is depression, alcohol dependence, and various phobias (irrational fears of things or situations). An estimated 2.6 percent of adults in the United States, or about 4.8 million people, suffer from a severe and persistent mental illness—such as schizophrenia, bipolar disorder, or a severe form of depression or panic disorder—in any given year. An additional 2.8 percent of adults, or about 5.2 million people, experience a mental illness that seriously interferes with one or more aspects of their daily life, such as their ability to work or relate to other people. All of these figures exclude people who are homeless and those living in prisons, nursing homes, or other institutions—populations that have high rates of mental illness.

International surveys have demonstrated that from 30 to 40 percent of people in a given population experience a mental illness during their lives. These surveys also reveal that anxiety disorders are usually even more common than depression, for making it remeadially difficult in the treatment of medical care. Its victims starve themselves, in some cases, to death. An increasingly common illness among adolescent and young adult women, having anorexia makes it difficult to succeeding their medical care, as person or thing it successfully a difficult matter. A 1998 article from Scientific American Presents explores the factors that contribute to the prevalence of anorexia nervosa and some promising new options for treatment.

Young people can suffer from mental illnesses and psychological problems just as adults can. Prevalence estimates in industrialized countries indicate that from 14 to 20 percent of individuals under age 18 suffer from a diagnosable mental disorder. In the United States, an estimated 9 to 13 percent of children between the ages of 9 and 17 suffer from a serious emotional disturbance—that is, a disorder that severely disrupts a child's daily functioning in the family, school, or community.

Anxiety disorders are the most common childhood mental disorders, affecting an estimated 8 to 10 percent of children and adolescents in the United States. Children with these disorders experience persistent, unrealistic worry or uneasiness that interferes with their ability to function normally. About 4 percent of children and young adolescents experience severe separation anxiety and worry excessively about becoming separated from their parents. Depression is another common childhood mental disorder, affecting up to 2.5 percent of children (under age 13) and up to 8.3 percent of adolescents in the United States. Depression in children can lead to failure in school, poor self-image, troubled social relations, and even suicide.

A number of mental disorders are usually first diagnosed in infancy, childhood, or adolescence. Autism is a relatively rare disorder that appears before the age of three and severely impairs a child's ability to interact socially and to communicate with others. Attention-deficit hyperactivity disorder begins before the age of seven. Its symptoms include an inability to sit still, focus attention, or control impulses. Eating disorders, such as anorexia nervosa and bulimia nervosa most often affect adolescent young women.

With a greater percentage of people living beyond the age of 65—both in the industrialized nations of the West and the developing countries of Asia, Africa, and Latin America—the problem of mental illness among the elderly has grown significantly. Researchers estimate that from 15 to 25 percent of elderly people in the United States suffer from significant symptoms of mental illness. Dementia, characterized by confusion, memory loss, and disorientation, occurs mostly among the elderly. A study of residents of Boston, Massachusetts, revealed that about 10 percent of people over the age of 65 suffer from Alzheimer's disease, the most common form of dementia, and research on residents of Shanghai, China found that 4.6 percent of people more than 65 suffer from this condition.

Major depression, the most severe form of depression, affects from 1 to 2 percent of people aged 65 or older who are living in the community (rather than in nursing homes or other institutions). The prevalence of depression and other mental illnesses is much higher among elderly residents of nursing homes. Although most older people with depression respond to treatment, many cases of depression among the elderly go undetected or untreated. Research indicates that depression is a major risk factor for suicide among the elderly in the United States. People over age 65 in the United States have the highest suicide rate of any age group.

Like physical diseases, the highest rates of mental illness occur among people in the lower socioeconomic classes, especially those living in severe poverty. Rates of almost all mental illnesses decline as levels of income and education increase. A national survey published in 1994 indicated that people who earned $19,000 or less annually in the United States were twice as likely to have experienced an anxiety disorder as people who earned $70,000 or more. The hardships associated with poverty seem to contribute to the development of some mental illnesses, particularly anxiety disorders and depression. In addition, debilitating mental illnesses, such as schizophrenia, may cause individuals to drift to lower socioeconomic classes.

Generally, the overall prevalence rates of mental illnesses between men and women are similar. However, men have much higher rates of antisocial personality disorder and substance abuse. In the United States, women suffer from depression and anxiety disorders at about twice the rate of men. The gender gap is even wider in some countries. For example, in China, women suffer from depression at nine times the rate of men.

Mental illness is becoming an increasing problem for two reasons. First, increases in life expectancy have brought increased numbers of certain chronic mental illnesses. For example, because more people are living into old age, more people are suffering from dementia. Second, a number of studies provide evidence that rates of depression are rising throughout the world. The reasons may be related to such factors as economic change, political and social violence, and cultural disruptions. While some have questioned these findings, dramatic increases in the numbers of refugees and people dislocated from their homes by economic forces or civil strife are associated with great increases in a variety of mental illnesses for those populations. According to the United Nations High Commissioner for Refugees, the number of refugees worldwide increased from 2.5 million in 1971 to 13.2 million in 1996, peaking at 17 million in 1991.

A number of mental illnesses—such as depression, anxiety disorders, schizophrenia, and bipolar disorder—occur worldwide, but seem to occur only in particular cultures, for example, eating disorders, such as anorexia nervosa (compulsive dieting associated with unrealistic fears of fatness), occur mostly between young women and women in Europe, North America, and Westernized areas of Asia, whose cultural views of thinness are an essential proponents of female beauty. In Latin America, people who go through some sorted overwhelming fright after some dangerous or traumatic events are said to have susto (fright), an illness in which their soul has been frightened away. In some societies of West Africa and elsewhere, brain disruption describes individuals (usually students) who experience difficulties in concentrating and thinking, as well as physical symptoms of pain and fatigue.

Most mental health professionals in the United States use the Diagnostic and Statistical Manual of Mental Disorders(DSM), a reference book published by the American Psychiatric Association, as a guide to the different kinds of mental illnesses. The fourth edition, known as DSM-IV, describes more than 300 mental disorders, behavioural disorders, addictive disorders, and other psychological problems and groups them into broad categories, including anxiety disorders, mood disorders, schizophrenia and other psychotic disorders, personality disorders, cognitive disorders, Dissociative disorders, Somatoform disorders, factitious disorders, substance-related disorders, eating disorders, and impulse-control disorders. Mental health professionals in many other parts of the world use a different classification system, the International Classification of Diseases (ICD), published by the World Health Organization.

The DSM and ICD are both categorical systems of classification, in which each mental illness is defined by its own unique set of symptoms and characteristics. In theory, each disorder should possess diagnostic criteria that are independent of each other, just as tuberculosis and lung cancer are discrete diseases. Yet symptoms of many mental disorders overlap, and many people, such as those who experience both depression and severe anxiety, in that of showing symptoms of more than one disorder at the same time. For these reasons, some mental health professionals advocate a dimensional system of classification. In contrast to the categorical approach, which sees mental disorders as qualitatively distinct from normal behaviour, a dimensional system views behaviour as falling along a continuum of normality, with some behaviours considered more abnormally than others. In a dimensional system, diagnoses do not describe discrete diseases but rather portray the relative importance of an array of symptoms.

Definitions and classifications of mental illnesses change as research improves understanding of them. For example, DSM-IV allows a diagnosis of schizophrenia only when characteristic symptoms have lasted at least one month, whereas the previous edition of DSM required a duration of only one week.

Anxiety disorders involve excessive apprehension, worry, and fear. People with generalized anxiety disorder experience constant anxiety about routine events in their lives. Phobias are fears of specific objects, situations, or activities. Panic disorder is an anxiety disorder in which people experience sudden, intense terror and such physical symptoms as rapid heartbeat and shortness of breath. People with obsessive-compulsive disorder experience intrusive thoughts or images (obsessions) or feel compelled to enact upon certain behaviours (compulsions). People with post-traumatic stress disorder relive traumatic events from their past and feel extreme anxiety and distress about the event.

American psychiatrist Kay Redfield Jamison is regarded as one of the world's leading authorities on bipolar disorder, also known as manic-depressive illness. In her book, An Unquiet Mind: A Memoir of Moods and Madness (1995), Jamison reveals her own struggle against the illness, which caused her to experience violent mood swings. She describes her initial resistance to taking medication that, while necessary to prevent debilitating depression, extinguished the exhilarating highs of mania.

Mood disorders, also called affective disorders, create disturbances in a person's emotional life. Depression, mania, and bipolar disorder are examples of mood disorders. Symptoms of depression may include feelings of sadness, hopelessness, and worthlessness, as well as complaints of physical pain and changes in appetite, sleep patterns, and energy level. In mania, on the other hand, an individual experiences an abnormally elevated mood, often marked by exaggerated self-importance, irritability, agitation, and a decreased need for sleep. In bipolar disorder, also called manic-depressive illness, a person's mood alternates between extremes of mania and depression.

Bipolar disorder is a mental illness that causes mood swings. In the manic phase, a person might feel ecstatic, self-important, and energetic. But when the person becomes depressed, the mood shifts to extreme sadness, negative thinking, and apathy. Some studies indicate that the disease occurs at unusually high rates in creative people, such as artists, writers, and musicians. But some researchers contend that the methodology of these studies was flawed and their results were misleading. In the October 1996 Discover magazine article, anthropologist Jo Ann C. Gutin presents the results of several studies that explore the link between creativity and mental illness.

Some people with schizophrenia experience delusions of persecution—false beliefs that other people are plotting against them. This interview between a patient with schizophrenia and his therapist illustrates the paranoia that can affect people with this illness.

People with schizophrenia and other psychotic disorders lose contact with reality. Symptoms may include delusions and hallucinations, disorganized thinking and speech, bizarre behaviour, a diminished range of emotional responsiveness, and social withdrawal. In addition, people who suffer from these illnesses, experience and the inabilities demanded for certain functions, in that of one or more important areas of life, such as, social relations, holding down a job, or school.

Personality disorders are mental illnesses in which one's personality results in personal distress or a significant impairment in social or work functioning. Usually, people with personality disorders have poor perceptions of themselves or others. They may have low self-esteem or overwhelming narcissism, poor impulse control, troubled social relationships, and inappropriate emotional responses. Considerable controversy exists over where to draw the distinction between a normal personality and a personality disorder.

Cognitive disorders, such as delirium and dementia, involve a significant loss of mental functioning. Dementia, for example, is characterized by impaired memory and difficulties in such functions as speaking, abstract thinking, and the ability to identify familiar objects. The conditions in this category usually result from a medical condition, substance abuse, or adverse reactions to medication or poisonous substances.

Dissociative disorders involve disturbances in a person's consciousness, memories, identity, and perception of the environment. Dissociative disorders include amnesia, which has no physical cause; A Dissociative identity disorder happens when a person having, in at least, more than two distinct personalities that alternate in their control over the person's behaviour: Depersonalization or Demolecularization disorder is characterized by the chronic feeling for being forced apart from one's own body or mental processes. As Dissociative fugue amplifies the episodic or sudden departure from ones secured refuge with an accompanying loss of memory. In some parts of the world people experience Dissociative states as "possession" by a god or ghost instead of separate personalities. In many societies, trance and possession states are normal parts of cultural and religious practices and are not considered Dissociative disorders.

Somatoform disorders are characterized by the presence of physical symptoms that cannot be explained by a medical condition or another mental illness. Thus, physicians often judge that such symptoms result from psychological conflicts or distress. For example, in conversion disorder, also called hysteria, a person may experience blindness, deafness, or seizures, but a physician cannot find anything wrong with the person. People with another Somatoform disorder, hypochondriasis, constantly fear that they will develop a serious disease and misinterpret minor physical symptoms as evidence of illness. The term Somatoform comes from the Greek word soma, meaning "body."

In contrast to people with Somatoform disorders, people with factitious disorders intentionally produce or fake physical or psychological symptoms in order to receive medical attention and care. For example, an individual might falsely report shortness of breath to gain admittance to a hospital, report thoughts of suicide to solicit attention, or fabricate blood in the urine or the symptoms of rash so as to appear ill. Munchausen syndrome represents the most extreme and chronic variants of the factitious disorders.

Munchausen Syndrome, a mental illness in which a person intentionally deceives health care professionals into believing he or she is ill. People with this disorder migrate from hospital to hospital, attempting to get admitted by continually faking or producing symptoms of illness. They embellish their medical histories with dramatic stories to attract attention, and they willingly undergo tests and treatments—even surgery—for contrived physical or psychological ailments.

The term "Munchausen's syndrome" was coined in 1951 by the British physician Richard Asher, who adapted it from the surname of Baron Munchausen. The baron, a German cavalry officer in the 18th century, had acquired an erroneous reputation as a pathological liar who greatly exaggerated his adventures.

People with Munchausen syndrome intentionally mislead others about their health and assume the sick role typically because they wanted to be cared for and nurtured. In contrast, patients with hypochondriasis are preoccupied with illness because they misinterpret bodily sensations as evidence of serious disease. In malingering, people fabricate medical symptoms or illnesses in pursuit of specific external goals, such as qualification for disability payments or evasion of military service.

Munchausen syndrome represents the most extreme and chronic variation, that the state or fact of becoming varied or variable as having or exhibiting in the differences for engaging in an act contrary to usual rule. The variance of a group of similar mental ailments called factitious disorders, Doctors diagnose factitious disorders in approximately 1 percent of hospital patients who receive psychiatric evaluations. Individuals with Munchausen syndrome tend to be men who are unmarried, unemployed, and estranged from their families.

People with Munchausen syndrome or other factitious disorders may claim medical symptoms in a variety of ways. These include (1) total fabrication, such for its delusive falsification. (2) Complaints that are exacerbated such as the manipulation of a wound so it will not heal. (3) An illness of inductance, such as injecting oneself with bacteria to cause infection. The maladies may be either relatively common, or so esoteric that most physicians would have only a passing familiarity with them. The most frequently fabricated physical signs include anaemia, rash, fever, and bleeding. Factitious psychological disorders, in which people fabricate emotional symptoms such as depression, are much less common.

In Munchausen syndrome by proxy, also called factitious disorder by proxy, one person (usually a parent) produces symptoms in another (usually his or her child) to experience the sick role vicariously. For example, a mother may induce vomiting or diarrhea in her child with over-the-counter drugs, then present the child for treatment while denying knowledge of the origin of the problem. The parent also may falsely report symptoms and alter laboratory data. Ailments commonly falsified or induced in Munchausen syndrome by proxy include seizures, apnea (cessation of breathing), vomiting, and fever.

Many psychiatrists believe that Munchausen patients have suffered emotional neglect or deprivation in their past and that their "disease forgery" becomes a way of receiving attention and support. At the same time, people with this disorder combat a poor sense of a self-identity by assuming the well-defined role of a sick person. Duping medical professionals also helps stifle feelings of weakness and vulnerability. A hypothesis that brain abnormalities cause Munchausen syndrome remains unprovedly.

Patients diagnosed with Munchausen syndrome rarely consent to treatment of their disorder. Instead, when confronted with their ruse, they generally flee and continue their deceptions elsewhere. Nonconfrontational strategies, such as behaviour modification, have been effective in selected cases. For motivated patients, psychotherapy can both enhance insight and provide the nutrients once obtained through falsified illness. Medications such as antidepressants may be effective when the patients have additional mental illnesses. When addressing Munchausen syndrome by proxy, doctors focus on ensuring the ongoing safety of the child.

Substances-Related disorders result from the abuse of drugs, side effects of medications, or exposure to toxic substances. Many mental health professionals regard these disorders as behavioural or addictive disorders rather than as mental illnesses, although substance-related disorders commonly occur in people with mental illnesses. Common substance-related disorders include alcoholism and other forms of drug dependence. In addition, drug use can contribute to symptoms of other mental disorders, such as depression, anxiety, and psychosis. Drugs associated with substance-related disorders include alcohol, caffeine, nicotine, cocaine, heroin, as well as, amphetamines, hallucinogens, and sedatives.

Osteoporosis, breast cancer, and eating disorders are sometimes considered women's diseases, but doctors have found that men may also suffer from these same medical problems. Because men have these conditions so rarely, detection and treatment are often quite slow. To help with early diagnosis, this article from FDA Consumer describes some of the symptoms and possible causes of these serious diseases.

Eating disorders are conditions in which an individual experience's severe disturbances in eating behaviours. People with anorexia nervosa have an intense fear about gaining weight and refuse to eat adequately or maintain a normal body weight. People with bulimia nervosa, repeatedly engage in episodes of binge eating, usually followed by self-induced vomiting or the use of laxatives, diuretics, or other medications to prevent weight gain. Eating disorders occur mostly among young women in Western societies and certain parts of Asia.

People with impulse-control disorders cannot control an impulse to engage in harmful behaviours, such as explosive anger, stealing (kleptomania), setting fires (pyromania), gambling, or pulling out their own hair (trichotillomania). Some mental illnesses—such as mania, schizophrenia, and antisocial personality disorder—may include symptoms of impulsive behaviour.

People have tried to understand the causes of mental illness for thousands of years. The modern era of psychiatry, which began in the late 19th and early 20th centuries, has witnessed a sharp debate between biological and psychological perspectives of mental illness. The biological perspective views mental illness in terms of bodily processes, whereas psychological perspectives emphasize the roles of a person's upbringing and environment.

These two perspectives are exemplified in the work of German psychiatrist Emil Kraepelin and Austrian psychoanalyst Sigmund Freud. Kraepelin, influenced by the work in the mid-1800s of German psychiatrist Wilhelm Griesinger, believed that psychiatric disorders were disease entities that could be classified like physical illnesses. That is, Kraepelin believed that the fundamental causes of mental illness lay in the physiology and biochemistry of the human brain. His classification system of mental disorders, first published in 1883, formed the basis for later diagnostic systems. Freud, on the other hand, argued that the source of mental illness lay in unconscious conflicts originating in early childhood experiences. Freud found evidence for this idea through the analysis of dreams, free association, and slips of speech.

This debate has continued into the late 20th century. Beginning in the 1960s, the biological perspective became dominant, supported by numerous breakthroughs in psychopharmacology, genetics, neurophysiology, and brain research. For example, scientists discovered many medications that helped to relieve symptoms of certain mental illnesses and demonstrated that people can inherit a vulnerability to some mental illnesses. Psychological perspectives also remain influential, including the psychodynamics used with mental or emotional processes, especially as they influence personalty, behaviour, and attitudes. The study of personality and behaviour in terms of such processes, given to the technique for representing a mental outlook, the humanistic and existential view, the behavioural appearance of objects to a whole, the cognitive ability to normal dimensional surfaces, and the sociocultural evaluation of relative significance.

Many mental health professionals today favour a combination of perspectives, acknowledging that both biology and a person of specified character that forms any of the different forms or inflections as demanded by his environmental surroundings that represent an important role in mental illness. This approach, although individualistic, are not only products of the inherent genes from their parents, but products of the families and social worlds into which they are born. In this view, environments shape how biological factors will be manifested. For example, an infant may inherit genes that could enable her to become a tall adult, but if she is malnourished as a child, she will never achieve that potential. Likewise, an individual who does not possess a biological vulnerability for depression may nevertheless become severely depressed following the death of a loved one or after experiencing an act of torture.

Psychiatry has increasingly emphasized a biological basis for the causes of mental illness. Studies suggest a genetic influence in some mental illnesses, such as schizophrenia and bipolar disorder, although the evidence is not conclusive.

Clinical depression is one of the most common forms of mental illness. Although depression can be treated with psychotherapy, many scientists believe there are biological causes for the disease. In this June 1998 Scientific American article, neurobiologist Charles B. Nemeroff discusses the connection between biochemical changes in the brain and depression.

Scientists have identified a number of neurotransmitters, or chemical substances that enable brain cells to communicate with each other, that appear important in regulating a person's emotions and behaviour. These include dopamine, serotonin, norepinephrine, gamma-amino butyric acid (GABA), and acetylcholine. Excesses and deficiencies in levels of these neurotransmitters have been associated with depression, anxiety, and schizophrenia, but scientists have yet to determine the exact mechanisms involved.

Within the central nervous system, which consists of the brain and the spinal cord, neurotransmitters pass from neuron to neuron. In the peripheral nervous system, which is made up of the nerves that run from the central nervous system to the rest of the body, the chemical signals pass between a neuron and an adjacent muscle or a gland cell.

Nine of or relating to the properties or actions of a chemical belonging among the three families, these are widely recognized as neurotransmitters. For which a chemical substance, such as acetylcholine or dopamine, that transmits nerve impulses across a synapse. In addition, certain other body chemicals, including adenosine, histamine, enkephalins, endorphins, and epinephrine, have neurotransmitter-like properties. Experts believe that there are many more neurotransmitters as yet undiscovered.

The first of the three families is composed of amines, a group of compounds containing molecules of carbon, hydrogen, and nitrogen. Among the amines neurotransmitters are acetylcholine, norepinephrine, dopamine, and serotonin. Acetylcholine is the most widely used neurotransmitter in the body, and neurons that leave the central nervous system (for example, those running to skeletal muscle) use acetylcholine as their neurotransmitter;

neurons that run to the heart, blood vessels, and other organs may use acetylcholine or norepinephrine. Dopamine is involved in the movement of muscles, and it controls the secretion of the pituitary hormone Prolactin, which triggers milk production in nursing mothers.

The second neurotransmitter family is composed of amino acids, organic compounds containing both an amino group (NH2) and a carboxylic acid group (COOH). Amino acids that serve as neurotransmitters include glycine, glutamic and aspartic acids, and gamma-amino butyric acid (GABA). Glutamic acid and GABA are the most abundant neurotransmitters within the central nervous system, and especially in the cerebral cortex, which is largely responsible for such higher brain functions as thought and interpreting sensations.

The third neurotransmitter family is composed of peptides, which are compounds that contain at least 2, and sometimes as many as 100 amino acids. Peptide neurotransmitters are poorly understood, but scientists know that the peptide neurotransmitter called substance P influences the sensation of pain.

Overall, each neuron uses only a single compound as its neurotransmitter. However, some neurons outside the central nervous system are able to release both an amine and a peptide neurotransmitter.

Neurotransmitters are manufactured from precursor compounds like amino acids, glucose, and the dietary amine-called choline. Neurons modify the structure of these precursor compounds in a series of reactions with enzymes. Neurotransmitters that comes from amino acids include serotonin, which is derived from tryptophan; dopamine and norepinephrine, which are derived from tyrosine; and glycine, which is derived from threonine. Among the neurotransmitters made from glucose are glutamate, aspartate, and GABA. Choline, a natural amine that often is classed as the vitamin B complex and a constituent of many other biologically important molecules, such as acetylcholine and lecithin.

The nervous system, a message-carrying impulse travels from one end of a nerve cell to the other by means of an electrical impulse. When it reaches the terminal end of a nerve cell, the impulse trigger's tiny sacs called presynaptic vesicles to release their contents, chemical messengers called neurotransmitters. The neurotransmitters float across the synapse, or gap between adjacent nerve cells. When they reach the neighbouring nerve cell, the neurotransmitters fit into specialized receptor sites much as a key fits into a lock, causing that nerve cell to "fire," or generate an electric message-carrying impulse. As the message continues through the nervous system, the presynaptic cell absorbs the excess neurotransmitters, and repackages them in presynaptic vesicles in a process called neurotransmitter reuptake.

Neurotransmitters are released into a microscopic gap, called a synapse, that separates the transmitting neuron from the cell receiving the chemical signal. The cell that generates the signal is called the presynaptic cell, while the receiving cell is termed the postsynaptic cell.

After their release into the synapse, neurotransmitters combine chemically with highly specific protein molecules, termed receptors, that are embedded in the surface membranes of the postsynaptic cell. When this combination occurs, the voltage, or electrical force, of the postsynaptic cell is either increased (excited) or decreased (inhibited).

When a neuron is in its resting state, its voltage is about -70 millivolts. An excitatory neurotransmitter alters the membrane of the postsynaptic neuron, making it possible for ions (electrically charged molecules) to move back and forth across the neuron's membranes. This flow of ions makes the neuron's voltage rise toward zero. If enough excitatory receptors have been activated, the postsynaptic neuron responds by firing, generating a nerve impulse that causes its own neurotransmitter to be released into the next synapse. An inhibitory neurotransmitter causes different ions to pass back and forth across the postsynaptic neuron's membrane, lowering the nerve cell's voltage to -80 or -90 millivolts. The drop in voltage makes it less likely that the postsynaptic cell will fire.

If the postsynaptic cell is a muscle cell rather than a neuron, an excitatory neurotransmitter will cause the muscle to contract. If the postsynaptic cell is a gland cell, an excitatory neurotransmitter will cause the cell to secrete its contents.

While most neurotransmitters interact with their receptors to create new electrical nerve impulses that energize or inhibit the adjoining cell, some neurotransmitter interactions do not generate or suppress nerve impulses. Instead, they interact with a second type of receptor that changes the internal chemistry of the postsynaptic cell by either causing or blocking the formation of chemicals called second messenger molecules. These second messengers regulate the postsynaptic cell's biochemical processes and enable it to conduct the maintenance necessary to continue synthesizing neurotransmitters and conducting nerve impulses. Examples of second messengers, which are formed and entirely contained within the postsynaptic cell, include cyclic adenosine monophosphate, diacylglycerol, and inositol phosphates.

Once neurotransmitters have been secreted into synapses and have passed on their chemical signals, the presynaptic neuron clears the synapse of neurotransmitter molecules. For example, acetylcholine is broken down by the enzyme acetylcholinesterase into choline and acetate. Neurotransmitters like dopamine, serotonin, and GABA is removed by a physical process called reuptake. In reuptake, a protein in the presynaptic membrane acts as a sort of sponge, causing the neurotransmitters to reenter the presynaptic neuron, where they can be broken down by enzymes or repackaged for reuse.

Neurotransmitters are known to be involved in a number of disorders, including Alzheimer's disease. Victims of Alzheimer's disease suffer from loss of intellectual capacity, disintegration of personality, mental confusion, hallucinations, and aggressive—even violent—behaviour. These symptoms are the result of progressive degeneration in many types of neurons in the brain. Forgetfulness, one of the earliest symptoms of Alzheimer's disease, is partly caused by the destruction of neurons that normally release the neurotransmitter acetylcholine. Medications that increase brain levels of acetylcholine have helped restore short-term memory and reduce mood swings in some Alzheimer's patients.

Neurotransmitters also play a role in Parkinson disease, which slowly attacks the nervous system, causing symptoms that worsen over time. Fatigue, mental confusion, a masklike facial expression, stooping posture, shuffling gait, and problems with eating and speaking are among the difficulties suffered by Parkinson victims. These symptoms have been partly linked to the deterioration and eventual death of neurons that run from the base of the brain to the basal ganglia, a collection of nerve cells that manufacture the neurotransmitter dopamine. The reasons why such neurons die are yet to be understood, but the related symptoms can be alleviated. L-dopa, or levodopa, widely used to treat Parkinson disease, acts as a supplementary precursor for dopamine. It causes the surviving neurons in the basal ganglia to increase their production of dopamine, thereby compensating to some extent for the disabled neurons.

Many other effective drugs have been shown to act by influencing neurotransmitter behaviour. Some drugs work by interfering with the interactions between neurotransmitters and intestinal receptors. For example, belladonna decreases intestinal cramps in such disorders as irritable bowel syndrome by blocking acetylcholine from combining with receptors. This process reduces nerve signals to the bowel wall, which prevents painful spasms.

Other drugs block the reuptake process. One well-known example is the drug Fluoxetine (Prozac), which blocks the reuptake of serotonin. Serotonin then remains in the synapse for a longer time, and its ability to act as a signal is prolonged, which contributes to the relief of depression and the control of obsessive-compulsive behaviours.

Alzheimer's Disease, a progressive brain disorders that causes a gradual and irreversible decline in memory, language skills, perception of time and space, and, eventually, the inability to care for himself. A disease marked by the loss of cognitive ability, and generally over a period of 10 to 15 years, and associated with the development of abnormal tissues and protein deposits in the cerebral cortex.

First described by German psychiatrist Alois Alzheimer in 1906, Alzheimer's disease was initially thought to be a rare condition affecting only young people, and was referred to as presenile dementia. Today late-onset Alzheimer's disease is recognized as the most common cause of the loss of mental function in those aged 65 and over. Alzheimer's in people in their 30s, 40s, and 50s, called early-onset Alzheimer's disease, occurs less in amount or frequency, not less than 10 percent of the 4 million cases as were reviewed for Alzheimer's bearing in the United States.

Former United States President Ronald Reagan announced in early November 1994 that he had been diagnosed with Alzheimer's disease. Reagan wished to increase awareness of Alzheimer's, a degenerative disease of the brain that is characterized by confusion, loss of memory, and other symptoms. Committed to finding a cure for the disease, Reagan and his wife, Nancy, along with the national Alzheimer's Foundation, started the Ronald and Nancy Reagan Research Institute in 1995.

Although Alzheimer's disease is not a normal part of the aging process, the risk of developing the disease increases as people grow older. About 10 percent of the United States population over the age of 65 is affected by Alzheimer's disease, and nearly 50 percent of those over age 85 may have the disease.

Alzheimer's disease takes a devastating toll, not only on the patients, but also on those who love and care for them. Some patients experience immense fear and frustration as they struggle with once commonplace tasks and slowly lose their independence. Family, friends, and especially those who provide daily care suffer immeasurable pain and stress as they witness Alzheimer's disease for taking to a particularly different and direct submission.

The onset of Alzheimer's disease is usually very gradual. In the early stages, Alzheimer's patients have relatively mild problems learning new information and remembering where they have left common objects, such as keys or a wallet. In time, they begin to have trouble recollecting recent events and finding the right words to express themselves. As the disease progresses, patients may have difficulty remembering what day or month it is, or finding their way around familiar surroundings. They may develop a tendency to wander off and then be unable to find their way back. Patients often become irritable or withdrawn as they struggle with fear and frustration when once commonplace tasks become unfamiliar and intimidating. Behavioural changes may become more pronounced as patients become paranoid or delusional and unable to engage in normal conversation.

Eventually Alzheimer's patients become completely incapacitated and unable to take care of their most basic life functions, such as eating and using the bathroom. Alzheimer's patients may live many years with the disease, usually dying from other disorders that may develop, such as pneumonia. Typically the time from initial diagnosis until death is seven to ten years, but this is quite variable and can range from three to twenty years, depending upon the age of the onset, and other medical conditions presented and the care that the patient receives.

The brains of patients with Alzheimer's have distinctive formations—abnormally shaped proteins called tangles and plaques—that is recognized as the hallmark of the disease. Not all brain regions show these characteristic formations. The areas most prominently affected are those related to memory.

Tangles are long, slender tendrils found inside nerve cells, or neurons. Scientists have learned that when a protein-called tau becomes altered, it may cause the characteristic tangles in the brains of Alzheimer's patients. In healthy brains, tau provides structural support for neurons, but in Alzheimer's patients this structural support collapses.

Plaques, or clumps of fibres, form outside the neurons in the adjacent brain tissue. Scientists found that a type of protein, called amyloid precursor protein, forms toxic plaques when it is cut in two places. Researchers have isolated the enzyme beta-secretase, which is believed to make one of the cuts in the amyloid precursor protein. Researchers also identified another enzyme, called gamma secretase, that makes the second cut in the amyloid precursor protein. These two enzymes snip the amyloid precursor protein into fragments that then accumulate to form plaques that are toxic to neurons.

Scientists have found that tangles and plaques cause neurons in the brains of Alzheimer's patients to shrink and eventually die, first in the memory and language centres and finally throughout the brain. This widespread neuron degeneration leaves gaps in the brain's messaging network that may interfere with communication between cells, causing some of the symptoms of Alzheimer's disease.

Alzheimer's patients have lower levels of neurotransmitters, chemicals that carry complex messages back and forth between the nerve cells. For instance, Alzheimer's disease seems to decrease the level of the neurotransmitter acetylcholine, which is known to influence memory. A deficiency in other neurotransmitters, including somatostatin and corticotropin-releasing factor, and, particularly in younger patients, serotonin and norepinephrine, also interferes with normal communication between brain cells.

The causes of Alzheimer's disease remain a mystery, but researchers have found that particular groups of people have risk factors that make them more likely to develop the disease than the general population. For example, people with a family history of Alzheimer's are more likely to develop Alzheimer's disease.

Some of the most promising Alzheimer's research is being conducted in the field of genetics to learn the role a family history of the disease has in its development. Scientists have learned that people who are carriers of a specific version of the apolipoprotein E gene (apoE Gene), found on chromosome 19, are several times more likely to develop Alzheimer's than carriers of other versions of the apoE gene. The most common version of this gene in the general population is apoE3. Nearly half of all late-onset Alzheimer's patients for having the less common of the apoE4 version, however, and research has shown that this gene plays a role in Alzheimer's disease. Scientists have also found evidence that variations in one or more genes located on chromosomes 1, 10, and 14 may increase a person's risk for Alzheimer's disease. Scientists have identified the gene variations on chromosomes 1 and 14 and learned that these genes produce mutations in proteins called presenilins. These mutated proteins apparently trigger the activity of the enzyme gamma secretase, which splices the amyloid precursor protein.

Researchers have made similar strides in the investigation of early-onset Alzheimer's disease. A series of genetic mutations in patients with early-onset Alzheimer's has been linked to the production of amyloid precursor protein, the protein in plaques that may be implicated in the destruction of neurons. One mutation is particularly interesting among geneticists because it occurs on a gene involved in the genetic disorder Down syndrome. People with Down syndrome usually develop plaques and tangles in their brains as they get older, and researchers believe that learning more about the similarities between Down syndrome and Alzheimer's may further our understanding of the genetic elements of the disease.

Some studies suggest that one or more factors other than heredity may determine whether people develop the disease. One study published in February 2001 compared residents of Ibadan, Nigeria, who eat a mostly low-fat vegetarian diet, with African Americans living in Indianapolis, Indiana, whose diet included a variety of high-fat foods. The Nigerians were less likely to develop Alzheimer's disease compared to their US counterparts. Some researchers suspect that certain health problems such as high blood pressure, atherosclerosis (arteries clogged by fatty deposits), high cholesterol levels, or other cardiovascular problems may play a role in the development of the disease.

Other studies have suggested that environmental agents may be a possible cause of Alzheimer's disease; for example, one study suggested that high levels of aluminum in the brain may be a risk factor. Several scientists initiated research projects to further investigate this connection, but no conclusive evidence has been found linking aluminum with Alzheimer's disease. Similarly, investigations into other potential environmental causes, such as zinc exposure, viral agents, and food-borne poisons, while initially promising, have generally turned up inconclusive results.

Some studies indicate that brain trauma can trigger a degenerative process that results in Alzheimer's disease. In one study, an analysis of the medical records of Veterans involved in World War II (1939-1945), linked serious head injury in early adulthood with Alzheimer's disease in later life. The study also looked at other factors that could possibly influence the development of the disease among the veterans, such as the presence of the apoE gene, but no other factors were identified.

Alzheimer's disease is only positively diagnosed by examining brain tissue under a microscope to see the hallmark plaques and tangles, and this is only possible after a patient dies. As a result, physicians rely on a series of other techniques to diagnose probable Alzheimer's disease in living patients. Diagnosis begins by ruling out other problems that cause memory loss, such as stroke, depression, alcoholism, and the use of certain prescription drugs. The patient undergoes a thorough examination, including specialized brain scans, to eliminate other disorders. The patient may be given a detailed evaluation called a neuropsychological examination, which is designed to evaluate a patient's ability to perform specific mental tasks. This helps the physician determine whether the patient is showing the characteristic symptoms of Alzheimer's disease—progressively worsening memory problems, language difficulties, and trouble with spatial direction and time. The physician also asks about the patient's family medical history to learn about any past serious illnesses, which may give a hint about the patient's current symptoms.

There is no known cure for Alzheimer's disease, and treatment focuses on lessening symptoms and attempting to slow the course of the disease. Drugs that increase or improve the function of brain acetylcholine, the neurotransmitter that affects memory, have been approved by the United States Food and Drug Administration (FDA) for the treatment of Alzheimer's disease. Called acetylcholinesterase inhibitors, these drugs have had modest or moderate extent of measure, but clearly positive effects on the symptoms of the disease. These drugs can benefit patients at all stages of illness, but they are particularly effective in the middle stage. This finding corresponds with new evidence that low acetylcholine levels in patients with Alzheimer's disease may not be present in the earliest stage of the illness.

Evidence shows that there is inflammation in the brains of Alzheimer's patients, which may be associated with the production of amyloid precursor protein. Studies are underway to find drugs that prevent this inflammation, to possibly slow or even halt the progress of the disease. Other promising approaches centre on mechanisms that manipulate amyloid precursor protein production or accumulation. Drugs are in development that may block the activity of the enzymes that cut the amyloid precursor protein, halting amyloid production. Other studies related in mice are to suggest for vaccinating animals with amyloid precursor protein can produce a reaction that clears amyloid precursor protein from the brain. Physicians have started vaccination studies in humans to determine if the same potentially beneficial effects can be obtained. There is still much to be learned, but as scientists better understand the genetic components of Alzheimer's, the roles of the amyloid precursor protein and the tau protein in the disease, and the mechanisms of nerve cell degeneration, the possibility that a treatment will be developed is more likely.

The responsibility for caring for Alzheimer's patients generally falls on their spouses and children. Caregivers must constantly be on guard for the possibility of Alzheimer's patients wandering away or becoming agitated or confused in a manner that jeopardizes the patient or others. Coping with a loved one's decline and inability to recognize the quality or conditions with familiarity that cause enormous pain.

The increased burden faced by families is intense, and the life of the Alzheimer's caregiver is often called a 36-hour day. Not surprisingly, caregivers often develop health and psychological problems of their own as a result of this stress. The Alzheimer's Association, a national organization with local chapters throughout the United States, was formed in 1980 in large measure to provide support for Alzheimer's caregivers. Today, national and local chapters are a valuable source for information, referral, and advice.

Tramadol, is a prescription drug used to treat moderate to severe pain including pain following surgery or dental procedures, back or joint pain, or pain associated with cancer. Tramadol is classified as an analgesic. It produces a pain killing effect by interfering with the action of chemicals called neurotransmitters that are vital for nerve transmission.

The sensation of pain results from communication between nerve cells in the brain, spinal cord, and elsewhere in the body. The process begins when certain nerve cell endings, known as pain receptors or nociceptors, is stimulated. Pain receptors are located in the skin, joints, muscles, the linings of the body cavities, and elsewhere in the body. Nerve impulses travel from pain receptors along nerve fibres to the spinal cord and then to the brain. Pain impulses are relayed through a brain structure known as the thalamus and then to the cerebral cortex, the area of the brain that interprets messages and generates the conscious sensation of pain. At several points along their journey from pain-receptor to cerebral-cortex, pain impulses can be modified. For example, chemicals known as endorphins, the body's natural painkillers, interact with nerve cells in the brain and spinal cord to dampen the sensation of pain.

Anticholinergic, be that of any drug that blocks the passage of certain nerve impulses in the central nervous system by inhibiting the production of acetylcholine, a neurotransmitter (a substance that carries signals between nerves and muscles). An anticholinergic's wide range of effects makes it effective as medication before surgery. It may be put in the eyes before examination or treatment to dilate the pupil and paralyzed the muscles of accommodation (the muscles that helps focus the eye), or it may be inhaled to relieve constriction of the airways in bronchitis. An anticholinergic can reduce tremor and rigidity (stiffness) in mild Parkinson disease. In the treatment of urinary frequency, it may improve bladder muscle tone. Its usefulness in relieving or preventing spasms is limited by side effects, such as dry mouth, visual disturbances, and urinary retention.

Clonazepam or Klonopin is part of the anticonvulsant drug, family used to treat epilepsy. It is also sometimes used for panic disorders, Tourette's syndrome (a movement disorder), and the unusual reality of depression. The action for which another thing and dependent on it for its existence, value, or significance, there is a unique element in the set factor as assigned to each element as having the physiological activity of an organ or body part. The characteristic behaviour of a chemical compound, resulting from the presence of a specific functional group. In that or relating to a function or indicating a mathematical function or functions. In a designed or adapted particularity for that which of a probable operative function. As the pathology involving functions rather than a physiological or sectoral function on vectors whose values are scalars. They function of an object that should determine its designated materials. The doctrine stressing purpose, practicality, and utility classified of a group of drugs known as benzodiazepines, of which any of a group of chemical compounds with a common molecular structure and similar pharmacological effects, used as antianxiety agents, muscle relaxants, sedatives, hypnotics, and sometimes as an anticonvulsant.

The drug called Clonazepam must be prescribed by a doctor. Available in tablet form, Clonazepam is taken orally three times a day, with or without food. Starting adult doses' range from 0.5 to 1.5mg, which may be increased, as needed, under a doctor's supervision. The maximum daily dosage is 20mg. Children may safely take this drug, although dosages are determined by body weight. Effectiveness of this drug may not be seen for several weeks, and dosage adjustments for optimum effectiveness may require several months. Clonazepam is a benzodiazepine and used as an anticonvulsant for epilepsy and as a sedative for sleep disorders.

But, side effects may include drowsiness, behaviour changes, or lack of coordination. Also seen, is anaemia, constipation, diarrhea, double vision, hair loss, fever, insomnia, appetite changes, memory loss, confusion, difficult urination, skin rash, twitching, or weight gain. If treatment with this drug is stopped suddenly (which is not recommended), withdrawal symptoms may include muscle cramps, restlessness, tremors, convulsions, or hallucinations.

Patients with severe liver disease or with acute narrow-angle glaucoma, an eye disorder, should not take this drug. Its safety for use during pregnancy has not been adequately studied, but it is known to appear in breast milk. Patients who experience drowsiness with this drug should not drive, operate dangerous machinery, or engage in other risk-related behaviour. Clonazepam should not be combined with alcohol. It may also interact adversely with various kinds of drugs, including antidepressants, tranquillizers, sedatives, narcotic pain relievers, barbiturates, antianxiety drugs, and other anticonvulsants. In addition, it may become habit-forming and may lose its effectiveness over time

Amitriptyline, a tricyclic antidepressant drug, which of a drug used to prevent or treat clinical depression. Amitriptyline may also be used to treat chronic pain, bulimia, migraine headaches, and certain symptoms of multiple sclerosis. It works by restoring levels of neurotransmitters, chemicals in the brain that help transmits nerve impulses. Its wave of physical and chemical excitation along a nerve fibre in response to a stimulus, accompanied by a transient change in electric potential in the membrane, that being a thin pliable layer of tissue covering surfaces or separation connecting regions structures or organs of the animal or a species, of the cell membrane.

Amitriptyline is available only by prescription, as taken orally in tablet form, often once a day at bedtime. Dosages generally begin at 50 or 75mg and are then gradually increased to 150 or 200mg, the maximum daily dosage for adults. Children over age 12 generally take about 30mg per day. Children under age 12 should not take this drug. Benefits from amitriptyline may not be seen for several weeks after first starting the medication. Nonetheless, amitriptyline as a tricyclic antidepressant drug of a group of antidepressant drugs, such as amitriptyline, as functioning as a tricyclic antidepressant drug that contains three fused benzene rings and that block the reuptake of the neurotransmitters norepinephrine, a substance, of both a hormone and neurotransmitter, secreted by the adrenal medulla and the nerve endings of the sympathetic nervous system to cause vasoconstriction and increases in heart rate, blood pressure, and the sugar level of the blood, and also called noradrenaline. Serotonin in the central nervous system that is derived from tryptophan, and found in animal and human tissue, especially the brain, blood serum, and gastric mucous membranes and active as a neurotransmitter and in vasoconstriction, stimulation of the smooth muscles, and regulation of cyclic body processes. Tryptophan, is an essential amino acid formed from protein during digestion by the action or proteolytic enzyme. It is necessary for normal growth and development and is the precursor of several substances, including serotonin and niacin, that niacin maintains of a white crystalline acid, that is a component of the vitamin B complex found in meat, wheat germ, dairy products, and yeast and is used to treat and prevent pellagra, and also called nicotinic acid. Pellagra, a disease caused by a deficiency of niacin and protein in the diet and characterized by skin erupt ion, digestive and nervous system disturbances, and eventually mental deterioration.

Antidepressant medication is used to treat depression, a mood disorder characterized by such symptoms as sadness, decreased appetite, difficulty sleeping, fatigue, and a lack of enjoyment of activities previously found pleasurable. While everyone experiences episodes of sadness at some point in their lives, depression is distinguished from this sadness when symptoms are present most days for a period of at least two weeks. Antidepressants are often the first choice of treatment for depression.

Although the cause of depression is unknown, researchers have found that some depressed people have altered levels of chemicals called neurotransmitters, chemicals made and released by nerve cells, or neurons. One neuron, referred to as the presynaptic neuron, releases a neurotransmitter into the synapse, or space, between the neuron and a neighbouring cell. The neurotransmitter then attaches, or binds, to a neighbouring cell—the postsynaptic cell—to trigger a specific activity. Antidepressants work by interacting with neurotransmitters at three different points: they can change the rate at which the neurotransmitters are either created or broken down by the body; they can block the process in which a spent neurotransmitter is recycled by a presynaptic neuron and used again, called reuptake; or they can interfere with the binding of a neurotransmitter to neighbouring cells.

The first antidepressants, developed in the 1950s, are the tricyclic antidepressants (TCA) and the monoamine oxidase inhibitor enzymes as any of a class of antidepressant drugs that block the action of monoamine oxidase in the brain, thereby allowing the accumulation of monoamines such as norepinephrine. Also, having one that of an inhibitor as a substance that retards or stops the action within a chemical reaction. For example, the reuptake of neurotransmitters into the presynaptic neurons, keeping the neurotransmitter in the synapse longer, and making more of the neurotransmitters available to the postsynaptic cell. TCAs are made up of those that usually reside of, amitriptyline, doxepin, imipramine is a tricyclic compound, used to treat depression and enuresis, in that which is the uncontrolled or involuntary discharge of urine.

Monoamine oxidase inhibitors, of any class of antidepressants that block the action of monoamine oxidase, in that of an enzyme in the cell of an antidepressant drug that blocks the action of monoamine oxidase in th brain, thereby allowing the accumulation of monoamines such as norepinephrine and desipramine, which of a tricyclic antidepressant used in the treatment of psychological depression.

MAO inhibitors decrease the rate at which neurotransmitters are broken down by the body so they are more available to interact with neurons. MAO inhibitors' are currently available in the United States included Phenelzine -a monoamine oxidase inhibitor, and used especially in the form of its sulfate as an antidepressant, as well as tranylcypromine. Phenelzine, is a monoamine oxidase inhibitor, and used in the form of its sulfate as used to prevent or treat clinical depression.

Another group of antidepressants, known as selective serotonin reuptake inhibitors (SSRIs), became available in 1987. SSRIs block the reuptake of the neurotransmitter serotonin into presynaptic neurons, thereby prolonging its activity. There are currently four SSRIs available for use in the United States: Fluoxetine, sertraline, paroxetine, and fluvoxamine. Of this group, the best known is Fluoxetine, commonly known by its brand name, Prozac.

Another antidepressant is venlafaxine, which is an oral antidepressant and once thought to inhibit neuronal uptake of serotonin, norepinephrine and dopamine in the central nervous system. It is structurally unrelated to other antidepressants, The antidepressant nefazodone, a an oral antidepressant with a chemical structure unrelated to SSRI, tricyclics, or monoamine oxidase inhibitors, thought to inhibit neuronal uptake of serotonin and norepinephrine in the cranial nervous system

Tricyclic antidepressants of a group of antidepressant drugs, such as amitriptyline, that contain three fuse benznerings and that block the reuptake of th e neurotransmitters, norepinephrine and serotonin in the central nervous system.

All antidepressants decrease symptoms of depression in about 70 percent of depressed people who take them. Most antidepressants take about two to three weeks of treatment before beneficial effects occur. Because no antidepressant is more effective than the others, doctors determine which antidepressant to prescribe according to the type of side effects an individual can tolerate. For instance, a person who takes TCAs and MAO inhibitors may notice dizziness and fainting when standing up, mouth dryness, difficulty urinating, constipation, and drowsiness. If people who take MAO inhibitors eat certain foods, such as aged cheese or some aged meats, they can experience severe headaches and raised blood pressure. SSRIs can cause side effects such as restlessness, difficulty sleeping, and interference with sexual function.

Nonetheless, amitriptyline is an antidepressant drug. Typically used to treat mental depression, amitriptyline may also be used to treat chronic pain, bulimia, migraine headaches, and certain symptoms of multiple sclerosis. It works by restoring levels of neurotransmitters, chemicals in the brain that help transmits nerve impulses.

The amitriptyline is available only by prescription, and is to be taken in the tablet form, often once a day at bedtime. Dosages generally begin at 50 or 75mg and are then gradually increased to 150 or 200mg, the maximum daily dosage for adults. Children over age 12 generally take about 30mg per day. Children under age 12 should not take this drug. Benefits from amitriptyline mabe seen for several weeks after first starting the medication.

Patients recovering from a heart attack should not take this drug, nor should people who are taking monoamine oxidase inhibitors such as phenelzine, a monoamine oxidase inhibitor, used especially in the form of its sulfate as an antidepressant, also known to appear in breast milk and patients with certain medical conditions avoid amitriptyline unless advised by a doctor, these include seizures, heart or circulatory disorders, liver ailments, and eye disorders such as glaucoma: Amitriptyline is a tricyclic antidepressant drug. In addition, patients undergoing medical or dental procedures should be aware that amitriptyline can react adversely with anaesthetics and other drugs used during these procedures.

Possible side effects of amitriptyline include a wide variety of ailments, including dry mouth, dizziness, drowsiness, blurred vision, breast enlargement, headache, disorientation, diarrhea, constipation, vomiting, fatigue, anxiety, high fever, heart attack, impotence, insomnia, seizures, or stroke. This drug may also increase the skin's sensitivity to sunlight. These side effects are more likely to appear when the drug is first used and usually disappear after a few days. Lowering the dosage or eliminating the drug can produce side effects as well; these may include headache, nausea, irritability, or sleep disturbances. An overdose of amitriptyline can be fatal.

This drug may interact adversely with a broad variety of drugs, including but not limited to allergy and cold medications, barbiturates, antihistamines, tranquillizers, muscle relaxants, oral contraceptives, painkillers, seizure medications, sleep medications, thyroid hormones, and large doses of vitamin C. It should not be combined with alcohol.

This drug may interact adversely with a broad variety of drugs, including but not limited to allergy and cold medications, barbiturates, antihistamines, tranquillizers, muscle relaxants, oral contraceptives, painkillers, seizure medications, sleep medications, thyroid hormones, and large doses of vitamin C. It should not be combined with alcohol.

Although the cause of depression is unknown, researchers have found that some depressed people have altered levels of chemicals called neurotransmitters, chemicals made and released by nerve cells, or neurons. One neuron, referred to as the presynaptic neuron, releases a neurotransmitter into the synapse, or space, between the neuron and a neighbouring cell. The neurotransmitter then attaches, or binds, to a neighbouring cell—the postsynaptic cell—to trigger a specific activity. Antidepressants work by interacting with neurotransmitters at three different points: they can change the rate at which the neurotransmitters are either created or broken down by the body; they can block the process in which a spent neurotransmitter is recycled by a presynaptic neuron and used again, called reuptake; or they can interfere with the binding of a neurotransmitter to neighbouring cells.

As Fluoxetine, is the type of drug-prescribed antidepressant, for the treatment of depression, particularly depression lasting longer than two weeks and interfering with daily functioning. Fluoxetine works by regulating serotonin levels in the brain. Serotonin is a neurotransmitter, a chemical in the body's nervous system associated with maintaining a general sense of well-being. An insufficient amount of serotonin in the brain may contribute to depression. Fluoxetine may also be prescribed for treatment of other conditions related to insufficient levels of serotonin including eating disorders (obesity and bulimia), obsessive-compulsive disorder, and premenstrual syndrome.

Nortriptyline, the drug used to treat major mental depression. It is also used to treat chronic, severe pain and attention-deficit hyperactivity disorder (ADHD) in adolescents. Nortriptyline relieves depression by regulating production of the brain's neurotransmitters, chemicals crucial to the transmission of nerve impulses.

This drug is available by prescription only in capsules and as a liquid. The capsule is taken orally in doses of 10 mg, 25 mg, 50 mg, and 75 mg. The initial adult dosage is 25 mg three to four times a day. The usual maintenance dosage ranges from 50 to 100 mg per day. A reduced dosage of 30 to 50 mg per day is recommended for adolescents and the elderly. It may take two to three weeks for this drug to produce results.

This drug, named Nortriptyline, should not be used by persons who have had a previous allergic reaction to it or pregnant, or breast-feeding women and persons recovering from a recent heart attack or with narrow-angle glaucoma. Also persons who have taken a monoamine oxidase (MAO) inhibitor drug within the past 14 days. Nortriptyline is a tricyclic antidepressant and should be used with caution by persons with liver damage or problems with urination. Its safety and effectiveness for children have not been established. Exposure to excessive heat or cold should be avoided. Driving and other risk-related activities should not be undertaken if drowsiness occurs. This drug should be discontinued gradually rather than abruptly.

Nortriptyline, which is a tricyclic antidepressant drug that side-effects should disappear as the body adjusts to the drug, that include anxiety, drowsiness, blurred vision, confusion, constipation, a dry mouth, fatigue, headache, insomnia, lightheadedness, memory problems, nausea, peculiar tastes in the mouth, decreased urination, and weight gain or loss. More serious but fewer common side effects include aggravation of paranoid psychoses and schizophrenia, hallucinations, irregular heart rhythm, nightmares, seizures and uncoordinated movements or balance problems. Nortriptyline may cause sensitivity to sunlight and may activate latent diabetes, epilepsy, or glaucoma.

Alcoholic beverages should be completely avoided while using this drug. Nortriptyline may also interact adversely with other drugs including antiseizure medications, birth control pills and antihistamines, including, barbiturates, tranquillizers, narcotics, or sleeping medications, as well for, carbamazepine, cimetidine, epinephrine, fluconazole, fluoxetine, and monoamine oxidase (MAO) inhibitor. The monoamine oxidase (MAO) has been given by any of a class of antidepressant drugs that block the action of monoamine oxidase in the brain, thereby allowing the accumulation of monoamines such as norepinephrine. Inhibitors, present of one of a substance that retards or stops a chemical reaction.

The Phenelzine medication, used as a monoamine oxidase inhibitor, and used, especially in the form of its sulfates as an antidepressant, and is used to treat depression, anxiety, or phobias. Phenelzine is known as a MAO inhibitor, and it works by blocking the action of the enzyme, monoamine oxidase (MAO), which normally breaks down certain chemicals known as neurotransmitters in the brain. Blocking the breakdown of neurotransmitters permits these chemicals to become more highly concentrated, producing a more stable emotional state in the patient.

Available by prescription only, Phenelzine tablets are taken orally, with or without food, usually three times a day. Total daily dosages may range from 15 to 90 mg. The benefits of taking phenelzine, which of a monoamine oxidase inhibitor used especially in the form of its sulfate as an antidepressant, and its gainful effectiveness is usually apparent after three to four weeks of treatment, and long-term usage (months to years) may be prescribed.

Patients with a history of congestive heart failure, liver disease, or an adrenal gland tumour should not take phenelzine. It should be used with caution by patients with diabetes, heart disease, or epilepsy. In general, it is safe for children under the age of 16 or for pregnant or nursing women. The use of phenelzine may complicate other medical treatment and all patients should notify their physicians and dentists that they are using this drug. Patients should also carry a medic-alert card or wear a bracelet that will alert medical personnel to the patient's use of the drug in an emergency. The phenelzine as a monoamine oxidase inhibitor, of a class of antidepressant drugs that block the action of monoamine oxidase in the brain, thereby allowing the accumulation of monoamine such as norepinephrine, which is a substance, both a hormone and neurotransmitter, secreted by the adrenal medulla and nerve endings of the sympathetic nervous system to cause vasoconstriction and increases in heart rate, blood pressure, and sugar level of the blood. Side effects of phenelzine may include constipation, dizziness, drowsiness or fatigue, headache, fluid retention, dry mouth, muscle weakness, twitching or tremors, weight gain, or insomnia. It may detract from sexual performance in males. Abruptly ending treatment can cause agitation, nightmares, or convulsions.

Phenelzine, being a monoamine oxidase inhibitor, used especially in the form of its sulfate as an antidepressant, however, it can cause serious reactions, including death, if combined with certain foods or drugs, so it is important that patients taking phenelzine must understand the dietary and medical restrictions that the uses of this drug demands. Among the foods that should be avoided are those containing tyramine, an amino acid contained in aged cheeses and meats, products that contain yeast, alcoholic beverages, and bananas. Examples of drugs to avoid include cold and cough remedies, sinus and hay-fever medications, nasal decongestants, appetite suppressants, bronchodilators inhalants, amphetamines, and other antidepressants. Serious complications can occur up to two weeks after phenelzine treatment ends.

Venlafaxine, a prescription drug used to treat mental depression. Classified as an antidepressant, it works by interfering with the action of serotonin and dopamine, chemicals associated with nerve impulse transmission in the central nervous system.

Tablets are taken orally, with or without food, in dosages starting at 75mg per day, usually divided into several small doses. If necessary, a doctor may prescribe a dosage as high as 225mg per day. Effectiveness is usually apparent within two weeks of beginning treatment.

Patients with impaired liver or kidney function, high blood pressure, heart disease, or a history of seizures should use this drug with caution. Children under the age of 18 should not use venlafaxine. Its safety for pregnant or breast-feeding women is not known, but as an oral antidepressant and once thought to inhibit neuronal uptake of serotonin, norepinephrine and dopamine in the central nervous system. It is structurally unrelatd to other antidepressants. Norepinephrine is a substance with both a hormone and neurotransmitter, secreted by th e adrenal medulla and the nerve endings of the sympathetic nervous system to cause vasoconstriction and increase in heart rate, blood pressure, and the sugar level of the blood.

A variety of possible side effects are associated with venlafaxine, including nausea, diarrhea, dry mouth, sweating, dizziness, blurred vision, weight loss, sleepiness, or increased blood pressure.

In whatever manner, this may have serious or sometimes fatal interactions with another group of antidepressants known as monoamine oxidase (MAO) inhibitors. This drugs, as phenelzine which is used especially in the form of its sulfate as an antidepressant and tranylcypromine, should be discontinued, at least two weeks before starting treatments with venlafaxine, an oral antidepressant, thought to inhibit neuronal uptake of serotonin, norepinephrine, and dopamine in the central nervous system. It is structurally unrelated to other antidepressants. Other drug groups that may have adverse interactions with Venlafaxine include tranquillizers, narcotic pain relievers, sleep aids, and cimetidine. Tranquillizers, such as that are serves to tranquillize, as any various drugs used to reduce tension or anxiety, an antianxiety drug and used to treat psychotic states; an antipsychotic drug, yet is not scientific.

Buspirone, is a milder form of tranquillizing drugs, used to treat the various forms of anxiety and nervous tension. It works by interacting with the neurotransmitter serotonin to produce a calming effect.

Tablets are taken orally, usually three times per day, with or without food. Total daily dosages range from 15mg to 60mg, depending on the patient's condition. Buspirone's effectiveness may not be evident until one to two weeks after beginning treatment.

Patients with impaired kidney or liver function should not take this drug. Its safety for use by pregnant women and children under age 18 has not been determined, and it is not known whether it appears in breast milk. Alcohol should be avoided during treatment with Buspirone, and certain drugs may interact adversely with it. These include antidepressants that act as a monoamine oxidase (MAO) inhibitors such as phenelzine, narcotics, haloperidol, trazodone, warfarin, and fluoxetine.

Unlike many tranquillizers, Buspirone has minimal sedative effects. It is not addictive and does not usually cause withdrawal symptoms when treatment is stopped. Possible side effects include dizziness, dry mouth, headache, fatigue, nausea, or nervousness. Also, possible is blurred vision, bone or muscle pain, constipation, diarrhea, rapid heartbeat, skin rash, upset stomach, sweating, or vomiting. Patients taking buspirone should not drive, operate dangerous machinery, or engage in other risk-related activities.

In the nervous system, a message-carrying impulse travels from one end of a nerve cell to the other by means of an electrical impulse. When it reaches the terminal end of a nerve cell, the impulse trigger's tiny sacs called presynaptic vesicles to release their contents, chemical messengers called neurotransmitters. The neurotransmitters float across the synapse, or 'gap' between adjacent nerve cells. When they reach the neighbouring nerve cell, the neurotransmitters fit into specialized receptor sites much as a key fits into a lock, causing that nerve cell to "fire," or generate an electric message-carrying impulse. As the message continues through the nervous system, the presynaptic cell absorbs the excess neurotransmitters, and repackages them in presynaptic vessicles in a process called neurotransmitter reuptake.

Anxiety also appears to be related to certain brain functions. Chemicals in the brain called neurotransmitters enable neurons, or brain cells, to communicate with each other. One neurotransmitter, gamma-amino butyric acid (GABA), appears to play a role in regulating one's level of anxiety. Lower levels of GABA are associated with higher levels of anxiety. Some studies suggest that the neurotransmitter's norepinephrine and serotonin play a role in panic disorder.

The brain functions by complex neuronal, or nerve cell, circuits. Communication between neurons is both electrical and chemical and always travels from the dendrites of a neuron, through its soma, and out its axon to the dendrites of another neuron.

Dendrites of one neuron receive signals from the axons of other neurons through chemicals known as neurotransmitters. The neurotransmitters set off electrical charges in the dendrites, which then carry the signals electrochemically to the soma. The soma integrates the information, which is then transmitted electrochemically down the axon to its tip.

At the tip of the axon, small, bubble like structures called vesicle's release neurotransmitters that carry the signal across the synapse, or gap, between two neurons. There are many types of neurotransmitters, including norepinephrine, dopamine, and serotonin. Neurotransmitters can be excitatory (that is, they excite an electrochemical response in the dendrite receptors) or inhibitory (they block the response of the dendrite receptors).

One neuron may communicate with thousands of other neurons, and many thousands of neurons are involved with even the simplest behaviour. It is believed that these connections and their efficiency can be modified, or altered, by experience.

Scientists have used two primary approaches to studying how the brain works. One approach is to study brain function after parts of the brain have been damaged. Functions that disappear or that is no longer normal after injury to specific regions of the brain can often be associated with the damaged areas. The second approach is to study the response of the brain to direct stimulation or to stimulation of various sense organs.

Neurons are grouped by function into collections of cells called nuclei. These nuclei are connected to form sensory, motor, and other systems. Scientists can study the function of somatosensory (pain and touch), motor, olfactory, visual, auditory, language, and other systems by measuring the physiological (physical and chemical) change that occur in the brain when these senses are activated. For example, electroencephalography (EEG) measures the electrical activity of specific groups of neurons through electrodes attached to the surface of the skull. Electrodes that have been inserted directly into the brain can give readings of individual neurons. Changes in blood flow, glucose (sugar), or oxygen consumption in groups of active cells can also be mapped.

Although the brain appears symmetrical, how it functions is not. Each hemisphere is specific or specialized and dominates the other in certain functions. Research has shown that hemispheric dominance is related to whether a person is predominantly right-handed or left-handed. In most right-handed people, the left hemisphere processes arithmetic, language, and speech. The right hemisphere interprets music, complex imagery, and spatial relationships and recognizes and expresses emotion. In left-handed people, the pattern of brain organization is more variable.

Hemispheric specialization has traditionally been studied in people who have sustained damage to the connections between the two hemispheres, as may occur with a stroke, an interruption of blood flow to an area of the brain that causes the death of nerve cells in that area. The division of functions between the two hemispheres has also been studied in people who have had to have the connection between the two hemispheres surgically cut in order to control severe epilepsy, a neurological disease characterized by convulsions and loss of consciousness.

Other mechanisms reduce pain sensation by blocking, or inhibiting, the transmission of the pain message to the brain. To alter the pain sensation, the brain and spinal cord release specialized, neurotransmitters called endorphins and enkephalins. These chemicals interfere with pain impulse transmission by occupying the nerve cell receptors required to send the impulse across the synapse. By making the pain impulse carries on with less efficiency, endorphins and enkephalins can significantly lessen the perception of pain. In extreme circumstances, they can even make severe injuries nearly painless. If an athlete is injured during the height of competition, or a soldier injured during combat, they may not realize they have been injured until after the stressful situation has ended. This happens because the brain produces abnormally high levels of endorphins or enkephalins in periods of intense stress or excitement.

When a person experiences an injury, such as a stubbed toe, specialized cells called nociceptors sense potential tissue damage (1) and send an electric signal, called an impulse, to the spinal cord via a sensory nerve (2). A specialized region of the spinal cord known as the dorsal horn (3) processes the pain signal, immediately sending another impulse back down the leg via a motor nerve (4). This causes the muscles in the leg to contract and pull the toe away from the source of injury (6). At the same time, the dorsal horn sends another impulse up the spinal cord to the brain. During this trip, the impulse travels between nerve cells. When the impulse reaches a nerve ending (7), the nerve released chemical messengers, called neurotransmitters, which carry the message to the adjacent nerve. When the impulse reaches the brain (8), it is analyzed and processed as an unpleasant physical and emotional sensation.

Anxiety also appears to be related to certain brain functions. Chemicals in the brain called neurotransmitters enable neurons, or brain cells, to communicate with each other. One neurotransmitter, gamma-amino butyric acid (GABA), appears to play a role in regulating one's level of anxiety. Lower levels of GABA are associated with higher levels of anxiety. Some studies suggest that the neurotransmitter's norepinephrine and serotonin play a role in panic disorder.

The adrenal gland also secretes a substance chemically related to epinephrine, called norepinephrine, noradrenaline, or levoarterenol. In general, the function of norepinephrine seems to be the maintenance of normal blood circulation. It is also the chemical agent responsible for transmission of nerve impulses in the autonomic nervous system. Large amounts of epinephrine and norepinephrine are produced by some tumours of the adrenal glands, resulting in a great increase in blood pressure.

Serotonin, neurotransmitter, or chemical that transmits messages across the synapses, or gaps, between adjacent cells. Among its many functions, serotonin is released from blood cells called platelets to activate blood vessel constriction and blood clotting. In the gastrointestinal tract, serotonin inhibits gastric acid production and stimulates muscle contraction in the intestinal wall. Its functions in the central nervous system and effects on human behaviour—including mood, memory, and appetite control—have been the subject of a great deal of research. This intensive study of serotonin has revealed important knowledge about the serotonin-related cause and treatment of many illnesses.

Serotonin is produced in the brain from the amino acid tryptophan, which is derived from foods high in protein, such as meat and dairy products. Tryptophan is transported to the brain, where it is broken down by enzymes to produce serotonin. In the process of neurotransmission, serotonin is transferred from one nerve cell, or neuron, to another, triggering an electrical impulse that stimulates or inhibits cell activity as needed. Serotonin is then reabsorbed by the first neuron, in a process known as reuptake, where it is recycled and used again or converted into an inactive chemical form and excreted.

While the complete picture of serotonin's function in the body is still being investigated, many disorders are known to be associated with an imbalance of serotonin in the brain. Drugs that manipulate serotonin levels have been used to alleviate the symptoms of serotonin imbalances. Some of these drugs, known as selective serotonin reuptake inhibitors (SSRIs), block or inhibit the reuptake of serotonin into neurons, enabling serotonin to remain active in the synapses for a longer period of time. These medications are used to treat such psychiatric disorders as depression; obsessive-compulsive disorder, in which repetitive and disturbing thoughts trigger bizarre, ritualistic behaviours; and impulsive aggressive behaviours. Fluoxetine (more commonly known by the brand name Prozac), is a widely prescribed SSRIs used to treat depression, and more recently, obsessive-compulsive disorder.

Drugs that affect serotonin levels may prove beneficial in the treatment of nonpsychiatric disorders as well, including diabetic neuropathy (degeneration of nerves outside the central nervous system in diabetics) and premenstrual syndrome. Recently the serotonin-releasing agent dexfenfluramine has been approved for patients who are 30 percent or more over their ideal body weight. By preventing serotonin reuptake, dexfenfluramine promotes satiety, or fullness, after eating less food.

Other drugs serve as agonists that react with neurons to produce effects similar to those of serotonin. Serotonin agonists have been used to treat migraine headaches, in which low levels of serotonin cause arteries in the brain to swell, resulting in a headache. Sumatriptan is an agonist drug that mimics the effects of serotonin in the brain, constricting blood vessels and alleviating pain.

Drugs known as antagonists bind with neurons to prevent serotonin neurotransmission. Some antagonists have been found effective in treating the nausea that typically accompanies radiation and chemotherapy in cancer treatment. Antagonists are also being tested to treat high blood pressure and other cardiovascular disorders by blocking serotonin's ability to constrict blood vessels. Other antagonists may produce an effect on learning and memory in age-associated memory impairment.

Research shows that the more genetically related a person is to someone with schizophrenia, the greater the risk that person has of developing the illness. For example, children of one parent with schizophrenia have a 13 percent chance of developing the illness, whereas children of two parents with schizophrenia have a 46 percent chance of developing the disorder.

Advances in brain imaging techniques, such as magnetic resonance imaging (MRI) and positron emission tomography (PET), have enabled scientists to study the role of brain structure in mental illness. Some studies have revealed structural brain abnormalities in certain mental illnesses. For example, some people with schizophrenia have enlarged brain ventricles (cavities in the brain that contains cerebrospinal fluid). However, this may be a result of schizophrenia rather than a cause, and not all people with schizophrenia show this abnormality.

A variety of medical conditions can cause mental illness. Brain damage and strokes can cause loss of memory, impaired concentration and speech, and unusual changes in behaviour. In addition, brain tumours, if left to grow, can cause psychosis and personality changes. Other possible biological factors in mental illness include an imbalance of hormones, deficiencies in diet, and infections from viruses.

In the late 19th century Viennese neurologist Sigmund Freud developed a theory of personality and a system of psychotherapy known as psychoanalysis. According to this theory, people are strongly influenced by unconscious forces, including innate sexual and aggressive drives. In this 1938 British Broadcasting Corporation interview, Freud recounts the early resistance to his ideas and later acceptance of his work. Freud's speech is slurred because he was suffering from cancer of the jaw. He died the following year.

The interaction of various conscious and unconscious mental or emotional processes, especially as they influence personality, behaviour and attitudes, as the study o f personality, behaviour in terms of such processes.

The psychodynamic position as drawn upon whether mental illness is caused by unconscious and unresolved conflicts created in the mind. As stated by Freud, these conflicts arise in early childhood and may cause mental illness by impeding the balanced development of the three systems that constitute the human psyche: the id, which comprises innate sexual and aggressive drives: The ego, in that of the conscious portion of the mind, in that, it mediates between the unconscious and reality and the superego, which controls the primitive impulses of the id and represents moral ideals. In this view, generalized anxiety disorder stems from a signal of unconscious danger whose source can only be identified through a thorough analysis of the person's personality and life experiences. Modern psychodynamic theorists tend to emphasize sexuality less than the state or fact of being derived upon or source for making something which is the historical origin and development of a word by changing the base or by adding an affixed change to the generative linguistic description of the possessive word information. In general, a formal representation or description of the series of ordered linguistic rules and the operations that generate a surface structure from a deep structure, as a conclusive fact, as one is to trace the origin or developments of a word by chemical reactions.

Of or relating to the issue from a source to produce or obtain a compounding substance by chemically reenforced reactions, included is a sequence that generates a surface structure from a resulting statement as the theorem or a formula necessarily followed from the initial assumptions as derivational as Freud focussed more on problems in the individual's relationships with others.

Both the humanistic and existential perspectives view abnormal behaviour as resulting from a person's failure to find meaning in life and fulfill his or her potential. The humanistic school of psychology, as represented in the work of American psychologist Carl Rogers, views mental health and personal growth as the natural conditions of human life. In Rogers's view, every person possesses a drive toward Self-actualization, of which the fulfilment of one's greatest potential. Mental illness develops when prevailing circumstances as one's environment, blocking this condition of such a mechanism. The existential perspective sees emotional disturbances as the result of a person's failure to act authentically—that is, to behave in accordance with one's own goals and values, rather than the goals and values of others.

The pioneers of behaviourism, American psychologist's John B. Watson and B. F. Skinner, maintained that psychology should confine itself to the study of observable behaviour, rather than explore a person's unconscious feelings. The behavioural perspective explains mental illness, as well as all of human behaviour, as a learned response to stimuli. In this view, rewards and punishments in a person's environment shape that person's behaviour. For example, a person involved in a serious car accident may develop a phobia of cars or generalize the fear to all forms of transportation.

The cognitive perspective holds that mental illness result from problems in cognition, that is, problems in how a person reasons, perceives events, and solves problems. American psychiatrist Aaron Beck proposed that some mental illnesses, such as depression, anxiety disorders, and personality disorders—result from a way of thinking learned in childhood that is not consistent with reality. For example, people with depression tend to see themselves in a negative light, exaggerate the importance of minor flaws or failures, and misinterpret the behaviour of others in negative ways. It remains unclear, however, whether these kinds of cognitive problems actually cause mental illness or merely represent symptoms of the illnesses themselves.

The sociocultural perspective regards mental illness as the result of social, economic, and cultural factors. Evidence for this view comes from research that has demonstrated an increased risk of mental illness among people living in poverty. In addition, the incidence of mental illness rises in times of high unemployment. The shift in the world population from rural areas to cities—with their crowding, noise, pollution, decay, and social isolation has also been implicated in causing relatively high rates of mental illness. Furthermore, rapid social change, which has particularly affected indigenous peoples throughout the world, brings about high rates of suicide and alcoholism. Refugees and victims of social disasters—warfare, displacement, genocide, violence— have a higher risk of mental illness, especially depression, anxiety, and post-traumatic stress disorder.

Social scientists emphasize that the link between social ills and mental illness is correlational rather than causal. For example, although societies undergoing rapid social change often have high rates of suicide the specific causes have not been identified. Social and cultural factors may create relative risks for a population or class of people, but it is unclear how such factors raise the risk of mental illness for an individual.

There are no blood tests, imaging techniques, or other laboratory procedures that can reliably diagnose a mental illness. Thus, the diagnosis of mental illness is always a judgment or an interpretation by an observer based on the speech, ideas, behaviours, and experiences of the patient.

For the most part, mental health professionals determine the presence of mental illness in an individual by conducting an interview intended to reveal symptoms of abnormal behaviour. That is, the professional asks the patient questions about his or her mental state: "Do you hear voices of people who are not with you?" "Have you felt depressed or lost interest in most activities?" "Have you experienced a marked increase or decrease in your appetite?" "Have you been sleeping less than normal?" "Are you easily distracted?" The answers to these questions will suggest other questions. Eventually, the clinician will feel that he or she has enough information to determine whether the patient is suffering from a mental illness and, if so, to make a diagnosis.

The process of diagnosis is not as simple as it might seem. Patients often have difficulty remembering symptoms or feel reluctant to talk about their fantasies, sex life, or use of drugs and alcohol. Many patients that suffer, in at least, from more than one disorder at a time—for example, depression and anxiety, or schizophrenia and depression—and determining which symptoms constitute the primary problem are complex. In addition, symptoms may not be specific to mental illnesses. For example, brain tumours, malaria, and infections of the central nervous system can produce symptoms that mimic those of the psychotic disorders.

Another problem in diagnosis is that mental health professionals may interpret symptoms differently based on their personal or cultural biases. One study examined this effect by showing 300 American and British psychiatrists videotaped interviews of eight patients with mental illnesses. Although the psychiatrists' diagnoses substantially agreed for patients with "textbook" cases of schizophrenia, their diagnoses varied widely for patients who had symptoms of both schizophrenia and other disorders, depending on whether the psychiatrist was American or British. The risk of misdiagnosis is even greater when the mental health professional and the patient come from different cultural groups.

Mental health professionals use a number of methods to treat people with mental illnesses. The two most common treatments by far are drug therapy and psychotherapy. In drug therapy, a person takes regular doses of a prescription medication intended to reduce symptoms of mental illness. Psychotherapy is the treatment of mental illness through verbal and nonverbal communication between the patient and a trained professional. A person can receive psychotherapy individually or in a group setting.

The type of treatment administered depends on the type and severity of the disorder. For example, doctors usually treat schizophrenia primarily with drugs, but specialized forms of psychotherapy may more effectively relieve phobias. For some mental illnesses, such as depression, the most effective treatment seems to be a combination of drug therapy and psychotherapy. Although some people with severe mental illnesses may never fully recover, most people with mental illnesses improve with treatment and can resume normal lives. Despite the availability of effective treatments, only about 40 percent of people with mental illnesses ever seek professional help.

A variety of mental health professionals offer treatment for mental illness. These include psychiatrists, psychologists, psychotherapists, psychiatric social workers, and psychiatric nurses.

Drugs introduced in the mid-1950s enabled many people who otherwise would have spent years in mental institutions to return to the community and live productive lives. Since then, advances in psychopharmacology have led to the development of drugs of even greater effectiveness. These drugs often relieve symptoms of schizophrenia, depression, anxiety, and other disorders. However, they may produce undesirable and sometimes serious side effects. In addition, relapses may occur when they are discontinued, so long-term use may be required. Drugs that control the symptoms of mental illness are called psychotherapeutic, as the major categories of psychotherapeutic drugs including or contains antipsychotic drugs, antianxiety drugs, antidepressants, and antimanic drugs.

Psychotic episodes of, or relating to, or affected by psychosis, as a person affected by psychosis. A severe mental disorder, with or without organic damage, and characterized by derangement of personality and loss of contact with reality, causing deterioration by derangement of personality and loss of contact with reality and social functioning. All the same, by any of a group of drugs, such as the phenothiazine, which is a yellow organic compound, used in insecticides, livestock and anthemintics, and dyes. Any of a group of drugs derived from this compound and used in the treatment of psychiatric disorders, such as schizophrenia. Butyrophenone, as of any group of neuroleptic drugs, such as haloperidol-a tranquillizer that is used especially in the treatment of psychosis disorders, including schizophrenia and also in the management of Tourette's syndrome, which of a severe neurological disorder characterized by multiple facial and other body tics, usually beginning in childhood or adolescence and often accompanied by grunts and compulsive utterances, as of interjection, rejection and obscenities, it is also called Gilles de la Tour et e syndrome after George Gilles de la Tourette (1857-1904). As these drugs administered in the treatment of acute psychotic episodes, schizophrenia, and other psychiatric disorders.

Antipsychotic drugs, also called neuroleptics or major tranquillizers, control symptoms of psychoses, such as hallucinations and delusions, which characterize schizophrenia and related disorders. They can also prevent such symptoms from returning. Antipsychotic drugs may produce side effects ranging from dry mouth and blurred vision to tardive dyskinesia, a permanent condition that produces involuntary movements of the lips, mouth, and tongue.

Antianxiety drugs, also called minor tranquillizers, reduce high levels of anxiety. Composed of a group of drugs, such as the benzodiazepines, that are used to treat anxiety without causing excessive sedation. That of any of a group of chemical compounds with a common molecular structure and similar pharmacological effects, used as an antianxiety agent, muscle relaxant, sedatives, hypnotics, and sometimes as anticonvulsant.

They may help people with generalized anxiety disorder, panic disorder, and other anxiety disorders. Benzodiazepines, a class of drugs that includes diazepam (Valium), are the most widely prescribed antianxiety drugs. Benzodiazepines can be addictive and may cause drowsiness and impaired coordination during the day. Benzodiazepine, is that of any group of chemical compounds with a common molecular structure and similar pharmacological effects, and used as an anticonvulsant.

Antidepressant drugs help relieve symptoms of depression. Some antidepressant drugs can relieve symptoms of other disorders as well, such as panic disorder and obsessive-compulsive disorder. Antidepressant drugs comprise three major classes: Tricyclics, monoamine oxidase inhibitors (MAO inhibitors), and selective serotonin reuptake inhibitors (SSRIs). A monoamine oxidase (MAO inhibitor) is of an amine compound containing one amino group, especially a compound that functions as a neurotransmitter. Of which that of a given process of transmission in sending of a signal, or other information from a transmitter, by conveying through by hereditary or inheritance as to pass along (news or information) to communicate through a medium from one part of a mechanism t o another.

Nonetheless, people taking the monoamine oxidase (MAO inhibitors) may experience some of the same effects, and must follow a special diet that excludes certain foods. SSRIs generally produce fewer side effects, although these may include anxiety, drowsiness, and sexual dysfunction. One type of SSRI, fluoxetine (Prozac), is the most widely prescribed antidepressant drug. As the SSRI is a class of drugs, such as fluoxetine hydrochloride, an oral antidepressant that stops the activity of serotonin by inhibiting its uptake by neurons of the central nervous system.

Sertraline, an oral antidepressant that enhances serotonin activity by inhibiting its uptake by neurons of the central nervous system, and primarily used in the treatment of depression and obsessive e compulsive disorder.

Antimanic drugs help control the mania that occurs as part of bipolar disorder. One of the most effective antimanic drugs that is most popular is lithium carbonate, having to a white granular powder and used in the treatment of depression and bipolar disorder, as common side effects are those of nausea, stomach upset, vertigo, and increased thirst and urination. In addition, long-term use of lithium can damage the kidneys.

Bipolar disorder as of, relating to having two poles or change. As relating to a major affective disorder that is characterized by episodes of mania and depression.

A psychiatric disorder by alternating episodes of mania and depression. Its an excessively intense enthusiasm, interest, or desire, the craze of mania. A manifestation of bipolar disorder, characterized by profuse and rapidly changing ideas, exaggerated sexuality, gaiety, or irritability and decreased sleep. For depression that posits the act of depression, as a psychiatric disorder characterized by an inability to concentrate. Ins omnia, loss of appetite, the absence of pleasure or the inability to experience it, feeling of extreme sadness, guilt, helplessness and hopelessness, and thoughts of death.

Psychotherapy can be an effective treatment for many mental illnesses. Unlike drug therapy, psychotherapy produces no physical side effects, although it can cause psychological damage when improperly administered. On the other hand, psychotherapy may take longer than drugs to produce benefits. In addition, sessions may be expensive and time-consuming. In response to this complaint and demands from insurance companies to reduce the costs of mental health treatment, many therapists have started providing therapy of shorter duration.

Psychotherapy encompasses a wide range of techniques and practices. Some forms of psychotherapy, such as psychodynamic and humanistic therapy, focus on helping people understand the internal motivations for their problematic behaviour. Other forms of therapy, such as behavioural therapy and cognitive therapy, focus on behaviour itself and teach people skills to correct it. The majority of therapists today incorporate treatment techniques from a number of theoretical perspectives. For example, cognitive-behavioural therapy combines aspects of cognitive therapy and behavioural therapy.

Psychodynamic therapy is one of the most common forms of psychotherapy. The therapist focuses on a person's past experiences as a source of internal, unconscious conflicts and tries to help the person resolve those conflicts. Some therapists may use hypnosis to uncover repressed memories. Psychoanalysis, a technique developed by Freud, is one kind of psychodynamic therapy. In psychoanalysis, the person lies on a couch and says whatever comes to mind, a process called free association. The therapist interprets these thoughts along with the person's dreams and memories. For that psychoanalysis to which requires years of intensive treatment is not as widely practised today as in previous years.

Both humanistic therapy and existential therapy treat mental illnesses by helping people achieve personal growth and attain meaning in life. The best-known humanistic therapy is client-centred therapy, developed by Carl Rogers in the 1950s. In this technique, the therapist provides no advice but restates the observations and insights of the client (the person in treatment) in nonjudgmental terms. In addition, the therapist offers the person unconditional empathy and acceptance. Existential therapists help people confront basic questions about the meaning of their lives and guide them toward discovery of their own uniqueness.

Psychotherapists whom practice behavioural therapy does not focus on a person's past experiences or inner life. Instead, they help the person to change patterns of abnormal behaviour by applying established principles of conditioning and learning. Behavioural therapy has proven effective in the treatment of phobias, obsessive-compulsive disorder, and other disorders.

The goal of cognitive therapy is to identify patterns of irrational thinking that cause a person to behave abnormally. The therapist teaches skills that enable the person to recognize the irrationality of the thoughts. The person eventually learns to perceive people, situations, and himself or herself in a more realistic way and develops improved problem-solving and coping skills. Psychotherapists use cognitive therapy to treat depression, panic disorder, and some personality disorders.

Rehabilitation programs assist people with severe mental illnesses in learning independent living skills and in obtaining community services. Counsellors may teach them personal hygiene skills, home cleaning and maintenance, meal preparation, social skills, and employment skills. In addition, case managers or social workers may help people with mental illnesses obtain employment, medical care, housing, education, and social services. Some intensive rehabilitation programs strive to provide active follow-up and social support to prevent hospitalization.

Therapists often use play therapy to treat young children with depression, anxiety disorders, and problems stemming from child abuse and neglect. The therapist spends time with the child in a playroom filled with dolls, puppets, and drawing materials, which the child may use to act out personal and family conflicts. The therapist helps the child recognize and confront his or her feelings.

In group therapy, a number of people gather together to discuss problems under the guidance of a therapist. By sharing their feelings and experiences with others, group members learn their problems are not unique, receive emotional support, and learn ways to cope with their problems. Psychodrama is a type of group therapy in which participants act out emotional conflicts, often on a stage, with the goals of increasing their understanding of their behaviours and resolving conflicts. Group therapy generally costs less per person than individual psychotherapy.

Family intervention programs help families learn to cope with and manage a family member's chronic mental illness, such as schizophrenia. Family members learn to monitor the illness, help with daily life problems, ensure adherence to medication, and cope with stigma.

Electroconvulsive therapy (ECT) is a treatment for severe depression in which an electrical current is passed through the patient's brain for one or two seconds to induce a controlled seizure. The treatments are repeated over a period of several weeks. For unknown reasons, ECT often relieves severe depression even when drug therapy and psychotherapy have failed. The treatment has created controversy because its side effects may include confusion and memory loss. Both of these effects, however, are usually temporary.

Seeking a treatment for extreme cases of mental illness, Portuguese neurologist António Egas Moniz invented the lobotomy, a surgical technique that destroys tissue in the frontal lobe of the brain. The procedures, widely performed in the 1940s and 1950s, often leaving people in a vegetative state or caused drastic changes in personality and behaviour.

Even more controversial than ECT is psychosurgery, the surgical removal or destruction of sections of the brain in order to reduce severe and chronic psychiatric symptoms. The best-known example of psychosurgery is the lobotomy, a procedure developed by Portuguese neurologist António Egas Moniz that was widely performed in the 1940s through until the early 1950s. Psychosurgery is now rarely performed because no research has proven it effective and because it can produce drastic changes in personality and behaviour.

A significant portion of the homeless population in the United States suffers from a chronic mental illness, such as schizophrenia. The shortage of mental health treatment centres in many cities may partly account for the large number of mentally ill people who are homeless or in jail.

Treatment for mental illness takes places in a number of settings. Mental hospitals or psychiatric wards in general hospitals are used to treat patients in acute phases of their illnesses and when the severity of their symptoms requires constant supervision. Most individuals who suffer from severe mental illness, however, do not require such close attention, and they can usually receive treatment in community settings.

Often, patients who have just completed a period of hospitalization go to group homes or halfway houses before returning to independent living. These facilities offer patients the opportunity to take part in group activities and to receive training in social and job skills. In supportive housing, mentally ill individuals can live independently in an environment that offers an array of mental health and social services. Some people with chronic and severe mental illnesses require care in long-term facilities, such as nursing homes, where they can receive close supervision.

Unfortunately, many areas have a shortage of treatment centres, especially community mental health centres and supportive housing environments. This shortage may partly account for the large number of mentally ill people who are homeless or in jail.

Most non-Western countries still lack adequate treatment facilities and services for the mentally ill. In China, with its 1.2 billion people, there are 4.5 million patients with schizophrenia, but only about 100,000 beds for the mentally ill and fewer than 10,000 psychiatrists. On the other hand, there are hundreds of thousands of traditional healers, many of whom treat mentally ill patients. Other people with mental illnesses receive treatment from general physicians. In most countries of sub-Saharan Africa, psychiatric services are so limited that most people with mental illnesses receive little if any professional care. Some developing countries, however, have begun substantial reform and expansion of mental health services.

Trepanning, the procedure of cutting a hole in the skull, is the earliest known medical operation. Some anthropologists believe that Trepanning was performed on people with mental illnesses to drive out evil spirits from their heads. This skull dates from the Inca civilization.

Evidence for Trepanning, the surgical procedure of cutting a hole in the skull, dates back 4,000 to 5,000 years. Some anthropologists speculate that Stone Age societies performed Trepanning on people with mental illnesses to release evil spirits or demons from their heads. In the absence of written records, however, it is impossible to know why the operation was performed.

The Greek physician Hippocrates was one of the first scholars to challenge the notion that disease was punishment sent from the gods. He believed that all illnesses, including mental illnesses, had natural origins.

The literature of ancient Greece and Rome contains evidence of the belief that spirits or demons cause mental illness. In the 5th century Bc the Greek historian Herodotus wrote an account of a king who was driven beyond his limitations by evil spirits. The legend of Hercules describes how, driven insane by a curse, he killed his own children. The Roman poets Virgil and Ovid repeated these themes in their works. The early Babylonian, Chinese, and Egyptian civilizations also viewed mental illness as possession, and used exorcism—which sometimes involved beatings, restraint, and starvation—to drive the evil spirits from their victim.

Not all ancient scholars agreed with this theory of mental illness. The Greek physician Hippocrates believed that all illnesses, including mental illnesses, had natural origins. For example, he rejected the prevailing notion that epilepsy had its origins in the divine or sacred, viewing it as a disease of the brain. Hippocrates classifications of mental illnesses into categories that included mania, melancholia (depression) and phrenitis (brain fever), and he advocated humane treatment that included rest, bathing, exercise, and dieting. The Greek philosopher Plato, although adhering to a somewhat supernatural view of mental illness, believed that childhood experiences shaped adult behaviours, anticipating modern psychodynamic theories by more than 2000 years.

The Middle Ages in Europe, from the fall of the Roman empire in the 5th century ad too about the 15th century, was a period in which religious beliefs, specifically Christianity, dominated concepts of mental illness. Much of the society believed that mentally ill people were possessed by the devil or demons, or accused them of being witches and infecting others with madness. Thus, instead of receiving care from physicians, the mentally ill became objects of religious inquisition and barbaric treatment. On the other hand, some historians of medicine cite evidence that in the Middle Ages, many people believed mental illness to have its basis in physical and psychological disturbances, such as imbalances in the four bodily humours (blood, black bile, yellow bile, and phlegm), poor diet, and grief.

The Islamic world of North Africa, Spain, and the Middle East generally held far more humane attitudes toward people with mental illnesses. Following the belief that God loved insane people, communities began establishing asylums beginning in the 8th century ad, first in Baghdd and later in Cairo, Damascus, and Fez. The asylums offered patients special diets, baths, drugs, music, and pleasant surroundings.

The Renaissance, which began in Italy in the 14th century and spread throughout Europe in the 16th and 17th centuries, brought both deterioration and progress in perceptions of mental illness. On the one hand, witch-hunts and executions escalated throughout Europe, for which of the mentally ill were among those persecuted. The infamous Malleus Maleficarum, which served as a handbook for inquisitors, claimed that witches could be identified by delusions, hallucinations, or other peculiar behaviour. To make matters worse, many of the most eminent physicians of the time fervently advocated these beliefs.

On the other hand, some scholars vigorously protested these supernatural views and called renewed attention to more rational explanations of behaviour. In the early 16th century, for example, the Swiss physician Paracelsus returned to the views of Hippocrates, asserting that mental illnesses were due to natural causes. Later in the century, German physician Johann Weyer argued that witches were actually mentally disturbed people in need of humane medical treatment.

French physician Philippe Pinel supervised the unchaining of mentally ill patients in 1794 at La Salpêtrière, a large hospital in Paris. Pinel believed in treating mentally ill people with compassion and patience, rather than with cruelty and violence. This painting, Pinel Frees the Insane from Their Chains, was completed by French artist Tony Robert-Fleury in 1876.

Physicians in the 18th and 19th centuries used crude devices to treat mental illness, none of which offered any real relief. The circulating swing, top left, was used to spin depressed patients at high speed. American physician Benjamin Rush devised the tranquillizing chair, top right, to calm people with mania. The crib, bottom, was widely used to restrain violent patients.

During the Age of Enlightenment, in the 18th and early 19th centuries, people with mental illnesses continued to suffer from poor treatment. For the most part, they were left to wander the countryside or committed to institutions. In either case, conditions were generally wretched. One mental hospital, the Hospital of Saint Mary of Bethlehem in London, England, became notorious for its noisy, chaotic conditions and cruel treatment of patients.

The Hospital of Saint Mary of Bethlehem, a London mental hospital commonly known as Bedlam, sold admission tickets to the public in the 18th century, becoming a popular tourist attraction. In this engraving by English artist William Hogarth, part of his series A Rake's Progress (1735), two women tour the hospital, watching the mentally ill patients for their amusement. The hospital became notorious for its miserable conditions and cruel treatment of patients.

Yet as the public's awareness of such conditions grew, improvements in care and treatment began to appear. In 1789 Vincenzo Chiarugi, superintendent of a mental hospital in Florence, Italy, introduced hospital regulations that provided patients with high standards of hygiene, recreation and work opportunities, and minimal restraint. At nearly the same time, Jean-Baptiste Pussin, superintendent of a ward for "incurable" mental patients at La Bicêtre hospital in Paris, France, forbade staff to beat patients and released patients from shackles. Philippe Pinel continued these reforms upon becoming chief physician of La Bicêtre's ward for the mentally ill in 1793. Pinel began to keep case histories of patients and developed the concept of "moral treatment," which involved treating patients with kindness and sensitivity, and without cruelty or violence. In 1796 a Quaker named William Tuke founded the York Retreat in rural England, which became a model of compassionate care. The retreat enabled people with mental illnesses to rest peacefully, talk about their problems, and work. Eventually these humane techniques became widespread in Europe.

In 1908, after his release from the mental asylum, Clifford Whittingham Beers wrote A Mind That Found Itself, which exposed the poor conditions he had suffered while confined. He went on to establish several organizations dedicated to the promotion of mental health reforms in the United States.

People living in the colonies of North America in the 17th and 18th centuries generally explained bizarre or deviant behaviour as God's will or the work of the devil. Some people with mental illnesses received care from their families, but most were jailed or confined in almshouses with the poor and infirm. By the mid-18th century, however, American physicians came to view mental illnesses as diseases of the brain, and advocated specialized facilities to treat the mentally ill. The Pennsylvania Hospital in Philadelphia, which opened in 1752, became the first hospital in the American colonies to admit people with mental illnesses, housing them in a separate ward. However, in the hospital's early years, mentally ill patients were chained to the walls of dark, cold cells.

In the 1780s American physician Benjamin Rush instituted changes at the Pennsylvania Hospital that greatly improved conditions for mentally ill patients. Although he endorsed the continued use of restraints, punishment, and bleeding, he also arranged for heat and better ventilation in the wards, separation of violent patients from other patients, and programs that offered work, exercise, and recreation to patients. Between 1817 and 1828, following the examples of Tuke and Pinel, a number of institutions opened that devoted themselves exclusively to the care of mentally ill people. The first private mental hospital in the United States was the Asylum for the Relief of Persons Deprived of the Use of Their Reason (now Friends Hospital), opened by Quakers in 1817 in what is now Philadelphia. Other privately established institutions soon followed, and state-sponsored hospitals—in Kentucky, New York, Virginia, and South Carolina-opened beginning in 1824.

Nevertheless, circumstances for most mentally ill people in the United States, especially those who were poor, remained dreadful. In 1841 Dorothea Dix, a Boston schoolteacher, began a campaign to make the public aware of the plight of mentally ill people. By 1880, as a direct result of her efforts, 32 psychiatric hospitals for the poor had opened. Increasingly, society viewed psychiatric institutions as the most appropriate form of care for people with mental illnesses. However, by the late 19th century, conditions in these institutions had deteriorated. Overcrowded and understaffed, psychiatric hospitals had shifted their treatment approach from moral therapy to warehousing and punishment. In 1908 Clifford Whittingham Beers aroused new concern for mentally ill individuals with the publication of A Mind That

Found Itself, an account of his experiences as a mental patient. In 1909 Beers founded the National Committee for Mental Hygiene, which worked to prevent mental illness and ensure humane treatment of the mentally ill.

Following World War II (1939-1945), a movement emerged in the United States to reform the system of psychiatric hospitals, in which hundreds of thousands of mentally ill persons lived in isolation for years or decades. Many mental health professionals-seeing that large state institutions caused as much, if not more, harm to patients than mental illnesses themselves—came to believe that only patients with severe symptoms should be hospitalized. In addition, the development in the 1950s of antipsychotic drugs, which helped to control bizarre and violent behaviour, allowed more patients to be treated in the community. In combination, these factors led to the deinstitutionalisation movement: the release, over the next four decades, of hundreds of thousands of patients from state mental hospitals. In 1950, 513,000 patients resided in these institutions. By 1965 there were 475,000, and by 1990 state mental hospitals housed only 92,000 patients on any given night. Many patients who were released returned to their families, although many were transferred to questionable conditions in nursing homes or board-and-care homes. Many patients had no place to go and began to live on the streets.

The National Mental Health Act of 1946 created the National Institute of Mental Health as a centre for research and funding of research on mental illness. In 1955 Congress created a commission to investigate the state of mental health care, treatment, and prevention. In 1963, as a result of the commission's findings, Congress passed the Community Mental Health Centres Act, that had authorized the construction or developmental institutions of mental health centres throughout the country. Implementation of these centres was not as extensive as originally planned, and many people with severe mental illnesses failed to receive care of any kind.

One of the most important developments in the field of mental health in the United States has been the establishment of advocacy and support groups. The National Alliance for the Mentally Ill (NAMI), one of the most influential of these groups, was founded in 1972. NAMI's goal is to improve the lives of people with severe mental illnesses and their families by eliminating discrimination in housing and employment and by improving access to essential treatments and programs.

During the 1980s, all levels of government in the United States cut back on funding for social services. For example, the Social Security Administration discontinued benefits for approximately 300,000 people between 1981 and 1983. Of these, an estimated 100,000 were people with mental illnesses. Although the government eventually restored Social Security benefits to many of these people, the interruption of services caused widespread hardship.

The emergence of managed care in the 1990s as a way to contain health care costs had a tremendous impact on mental health care in the United States. Health insurance companies and health maintenance organizations increasingly scrutinized the effectiveness of various psychotherapies and drug treatments and put stricter limits on mental health care. In response to these restrictions, Congress passed the Mental Health Parity Act of 1996. This law required private medical plans that offer mental health coverage to set equal yearly and lifetime payment limits for coverage of both mental and physical illnesses.

In 1997 the US Equal Employment Opportunity Commission issued new guidelines intended to prevent discrimination against people with mental illnesses in the workplace. The rules, based on the Americans with Disabilities Act of 1990, prohibit employers from asking job applicants if they have a history of mental illness and require employers to provide reasonable accommodations to workers with mental illnesses.

In recent years international agencies, led by the World Health Organization (WHO) of the United Nations (UN) have developed mental health policies that seek to reduce the huge burden of mental illness worldwide. These agencies are working to improve the quality of mental health services in Africa, Asia, Latin America, the Middle East, and elsewhere by educating governments on prevention and treatment of mental illness and on the rights of the mentally ill.

Serotonin is a neurotransmitter chemical that transmits messages across the synapses, or gaps, between adjacent cells. Among its many functions, serotonin is released from blood cells called platelets to activate blood vessel constriction and blood clotting. In the gastrointestinal tract, serotonin inhibits gastric acid production and stimulates muscle contraction in the intestinal wall. Its functions in the central nervous system and effects on human behaviour—including mood, memory, and appetite control—have been the subject of a great deal of research. This intensive study of serotonin has revealed important knowledge about the serotonin-related cause and treatment of many illnesses.

Serotonin is produced in the brain from the amino acid tryptophan, which is derived from foods high in protein, such as meat and dairy products. Tryptophan is transported to the brain, where it is broken down by enzymes to produce serotonin. In the process of neurotransmission, serotonin is transferred from one nerve cell, or neuron, to another, triggering an electrical impulse that stimulates or inhibits cell activity as needed. Serotonin is then reabsorbed by the first neuron, in a process known as reuptake, where it is recycled and used again or converted into an inactive chemical form and excreted.

While the complete picture of serotonin's function in the body is still being investigated, many disorders are known to be associated with an imbalance of serotonin in the brain. Drugs that manipulate serotonin levels have been used to alleviate the symptoms of serotonin imbalances. Some of these drugs, known as selective serotonin reuptake inhibitors (SSRIs), block or inhibit the reuptake of serotonin into neurons, enabling serotonin to remain active in the synapses for a longer period of time. These medications are used to treat such psychiatric disorders as depression; obsessive-compulsive disorder, in which repetitive and disturbing thoughts trigger bizarre, ritualistic behaviours; and impulsive aggressive behaviours. Fluoxetine (more commonly known by the brand name Prozac), is a widely prescribed SSRI used to treat depression, and more recently, obsessive-compulsive disorder.

Drugs that affect serotonin levels may prove beneficial in the treatment of nonpsychiatric disorders as well, including diabetic neuropathy (degeneration of nerves outside the central nervous system in diabetics) and premenstrual syndrome. Recently the serotonin-releasing agent dexfenfluramine has been approved for patients who are 30 percent or more over their ideal body weight. By preventing serotonin reuptake, dexfenfluramine promotes satiety, or fullness, after eating less food.

Other drugs serve as agonists that react with neurons to produce effects similar to those of serotonin. Serotonin agonists have been used to treat migraine headaches, in which low levels of serotonin cause arteries in the brain to swell, resulting in a headache. Sumatriptan is an agonist drug that mimics the effects of serotonin in the brain, constricting blood vessels and alleviating pain.

Drugs known as antagonists bind with neurons to prevent serotonin neurotransmission. Some antagonists have been found effective in treating the nausea that typically accompanies radiation and chemotherapy in cancer treatment. Antagonists are also being tested to treat high blood pressure and other cardiovascular disorders by blocking serotonin's ability to constrict blood vessels. Other antagonists may produce an effect on learning and memory in age-associated memory impairment.

Neurotransmitters are chemically made by neurons, or nerve cells. Neurons send out neurotransmitters as chemical signals to activate or inhibit the function of neighbouring cells.

Synapses' are the signals conveying everything that human beings sense and think, and every motion they make, follows nerve pathways in the human body as waves of ions (atoms or groups of atoms that carries electric charges). Australian physiologist Sir John Eccles discovered many of the intricacies of this electrochemical signalling process, particularly the pivotal step in which a signal is conveyed from one nerve cell to another. He shared the 1963 Nobel Prize in physiology or medicine for this work, which he described in a 1965 Scientific American article.

Within the central nervous system, which consists of the brain and the spinal cord, neurotransmitters pass from neuron to neuron. In the peripheral nervous system, which is made up of the nerves that run from the central nervous system to the rest of the body, the chemical signals pass between a neuron and an adjacent muscle or the gland cell.

Nine chemical components—belonging to three chemical families—are widely recognized as neurotransmitters. In addition, certain other body chemicals, including adenosine, histamine, enkephalins, endorphins, and epinephrine, have neurotransmitter like properties. Experts believe that there are many more neurotransmitters as yet undiscovered.

The first of the three families is composed of amines, a group of compounds containing molecules of carbon, hydrogen, and nitrogen. Among the amines neurotransmitters are acetylcholine, norepinephrine, dopamine, and serotonin. Acetylcholine is the most widely used neurotransmitter in the body, and neurons that leave the central nervous system (for example, those running to skeletal muscle) use acetylcholine as their neurotransmitter; neurons that run to the heart, blood vessels, and other organs may use acetylcholine or norepinephrine. Dopamine is involved in the movement of muscles, and it controls the secretion of the pituitary hormone prolactin, which triggers milk production in nursing mothers.

The second neurotransmitter family is composed of amino acids, organic compounds containing both an amino group (NH2) and a carboxylic acid group (COOH). Amino acids that serve as neurotransmitters include glycine, glutamic and aspartic acids, and gamma-amino butyric acid (GABA). Glutamic acid and GABA are the most abundant neurotransmitters within the central nervous system, and especially in the cerebral cortex, which is largely responsible for such higher brain functions as thought and interpreting sensations.

The third neurotransmitter family is composed of peptides, which are compounds that contain at least 2, and sometimes as many as 100 amino acids. Peptide neurotransmitters are poorly understood, but scientists know that the peptide neurotransmitter called substance P influences the sensation of pain.

In general, each neuron uses only a single compound as its neurotransmitter. However, some neurons outside the central nervous system are able to release both an amine and a peptide neurotransmitter.

Neurotransmitters are manufactured from precursor compounds like amino acids, glucose, and the dietary amines called choline. Neurons modify the structure of these precursor compounds in a series of reactions with enzymes. Neurotransmitters that comes from amino acids include serotonin, which is derived from tryptophan dopamine and norepinephrine, which are produced or obtained from tyrosine and glycine, which obtain or receives from threonine. Among the neurotransmitters made from glucose are glutamate, aspartate, and GABA. Choline serves as the precursor for acetylcholine.

In the nervous system, a message-carrying impulse travels from one end of a nerve cell to the other by means of an electrical impulse. When it reaches the terminal end of a nerve cell, the impulse trigger's tiny sacs called presynaptic vessicles to release their contents, chemical messengers called neurotransmitters. The neurotransmitters float across the synapse, or gap between adjacent nerve cells. When they reach the neighbouring nerve cell, the neurotransmitters fit into specialized receptor sites much as a key fits into a lock, causing that nerve cell to "fire," or generate an electric message-carrying impulse. As the message continues through the nervous system, the presynaptic cell absorbs the excess neurotransmitters, and repackages them in presynaptic vessicles in a process called neurotransmitter reuptake.

Neurotransmitters are released into a microscopic gap, called a synapse, that separates the transmitting neuron from the cell receiving the chemical signal. The cell that generates the signal is called the presynaptic cell, while the receiving cell is termed the postsynaptic cell.

After their release into the synapse, neurotransmitters combine chemically with highly specific protein molecules, termed receptors, that are embedded in the surface membranes of the postsynaptic cell. When this combination occurs, the voltage, or electrical force, of the postsynaptic cell is either increased (excited) or decreased (inhibited).

When a neuron is in its resting state, its voltage is about -70 millivolts. An excitatory neurotransmitter alters the membrane of the postsynaptic neuron, making it possible for ions (electrically charged molecules) to move back and forth across the neuron's membranes. This flow of ions makes the neuron's voltage rise toward zero. If enough excitatory receptors have been activated, the postsynaptic neuron responds by firing, generating a nerve impulse that causes its own neurotransmitter to be released into the next synapse. An inhibitory neurotransmitter causes different ions to pass back and forth across the postsynaptic neuron's membrane, lowering the nerve cell's voltage to -80 or -90 millivolts. The drop in voltage makes it less likely that the postsynaptic cell will fire.

If the postsynaptic cell is a muscle cell rather than a neuron, an excitatory neurotransmitter will cause the muscle to contract. If the postsynaptic cell is a gland cell, an excitatory neurotransmitter will cause the cell to secrete its contents.

While most neurotransmitters interact with their receptors to create new electrical nerve impulses that energize or inhibit the adjoining cell, some neurotransmitter interactions do not generate or suppress nerve impulses. Instead, they interact with a second type of receptor that changes the internal chemistry of the postsynaptic cell by either causing or blocking the formation of chemicals called second messenger molecules. These second messengers regulate the postsynaptic cell's biochemical processes and enable it to conduct the maintenance necessary to continue synthesizing neurotransmitters and conducting nerve impulses. Examples of second messengers, which are formed and entirely contained within the postsynaptic cell, include cyclic adenosine monophosphate, diacylglycerol, and inositol phosphates.

Once neurotransmitters have been secreted into synapses and have passed on their chemical signals, the presynaptic neuron clears the synapse of neurotransmitter molecules. For example, acetylcholine is broken down by the enzyme acetylcholinesterase into choline and acetate. Neurotransmitters like dopamine, serotonin, and GABA is removed by a physical process called reuptake. In reuptake, a protein in the presynaptic membrane acts as a sort of sponge, causing the neurotransmitters to reenter the presynaptic neuron, where they can be broken down by enzymes or repackaged for reuse.

Neurotransmitters are known to be involved in a number of disorders, including Alzheimer's disease. Victims of Alzheimer's disease suffer from loss of intellectual capacity, disintegration of personality, mental confusion, hallucinations, and aggressive—even violent—behaviour. These symptoms are the result of progressive degeneration in many types of neurons in the brain. Forgetfulness, one of the earliest symptoms of Alzheimer's disease, is partly caused by the destruction of neurons that normally release the neurotransmitter acetylcholine. Medications that increase brain levels of acetylcholine have helped restore short-term memory and reduce mood swings in some Alzheimer's patients.

Neurotransmitters also play a role in Parkinson disease, which slowly attacks the nervous system, causing symptoms that worsen over time. Fatigue, mental confusion, a masklike facial expression, stooping posture, shuffling gait, and problems with eating and speaking are among the difficulties suffered by Parkinson victims. These symptoms have been partly linked to the deterioration and eventual death of neurons that run from the base of the brain to the basal ganglia, a collection of nerve cells that manufacture the neurotransmitter dopamine. The reasons why such neurons die are yet to be understood, but the related symptoms can be alleviated. L-dopa, or levodopa, widely used to treat Parkinson disease, acts as a supplementary precursor for dopamine. It causes the surviving neurons in the basal ganglia to increase their production of dopamine, thereby compensating to some extent for the disabled neurons.

Many other effective drugs have been shown to act by influencing neurotransmitter behaviour. Some drugs work by interfering with the interactions between neurotransmitters and intestinal receptors. For example, belladonna decreases intestinal cramps in such disorders as irritable bowel syndrome by blocking acetylcholine from combining with receptors. This process reduces nerve signals to the bowel wall, which prevents painful spasms.

Other drugs block the reuptake process. One well-known example is the drug Fluoxetine (Prozac), which blocks the reuptake of serotonin. Serotonin then remains in the synapse for a longer time, and its ability to act as a signal is prolonged, which contributes to the relief of depression and the control of obsessive-compulsive behaviours.

The brains of patients with Alzheimer's have distinctive formations—abnormally shaped proteins called tangles and plaques—that is recognized as the hallmark of the disease. Not all brain regions show these characteristic formations. The areas most prominently affected are those related to memory.

Tangles are long, slender tendrils found inside nerve cells, or neurons. Scientists have learned that when a protein-called tau becomes altered, it may cause the characteristic tangles in the brains of an Alzheimer patient. In healthy brains, which provides structural support for neurons, but in Alzheimer's patients this structural support collapses.

Plaques, or clumps of fibres, form outside the neurons in the adjacent brain tissue. Scientists found that a type of protein, called amyloid precursor protein, forms toxic plaques when it is cut in two places. Researchers have isolated the enzyme beta-secretase, which is believed to make one of the cuts in the amyloid precursor protein. Researchers also identified another enzyme, called gamma secretase, that makes the second cut in the amyloid precursor protein. These two enzymes snip the amyloid precursor protein into fragments that then accumulate to form plaques that are toxic to neurons.

Scientists have found that tangles and plaques cause neurons in the brains of Alzheimer's patients to shrink and eventually die, first in the memory and language centres and finally throughout the brain. This widespread neuron degeneration leaves gaps in the brain's messaging network that may interfere with communication between cells, causing some of the symptoms of Alzheimer's disease.

Alzheimer's patients have lower levels of neurotransmitters, chemicals that carry complex messages back and forth between the nerve cells. For instance, Alzheimer's disease seems to decrease the level of the neurotransmitter acetylcholine, which is known to influence memory. A deficiency in other neurotransmitters, including somatostatin and corticotropin-releasing factor, and, particularly in younger patients, serotonin and norepinephrine, also interferes with normal communication between brain cells.

Buspirone is a mild tranquillizer, a drug used to treat various forms of anxiety and nervous tension. It works by interacting with the neurotransmitter serotonin to produce a calming effect.

Tablets are taken orally, usually three times per day, with or without food. Total daily dosages range from 15 mg to 60 mg, depending on the patient's condition. Buspirone's effectiveness may not be evident until one to two weeks after beginning treatment.

Patients with impaired kidney or liver function should not take this drug. Its safety for use by pregnant women and children under age 18 has not been determined, and it is not known whether it appears in breast milk. Alcohol should be avoided during treatment with Buspirone, and certain drugs may interact adversely with it. These include antidepressants that act as monoamine oxidase (MAO) inhibitors such as phenelzine, narcotics, haloperidol, trazodone, warfarin, and fluoxetine.

Unlike many tranquillizers, Buspirone has minimal sedative effects. It is not addictive and does not usually cause withdrawal symptoms when treatment is stopped. Possible side effects include dizziness, dry mouth, headache, fatigue, nausea, or nervousness. Also, possible is blurred vision, bone or muscle pain, constipation, diarrhea, rapid heartbeat, skin rash, upset stomach, sweating, or vomiting. Patients taking Buspirone should not drive, operate dangerous machinery, or engage in other risk-related activities.

Paul Greengard, born in 1925, an American Neuroscientist and Nobel laureate who studied the biochemical steps involved in the way billions of nerve cells, or neurons, in the human brain communicate. In work carried out during the 1970s, Greengard had shown that chemical messengers known as neurotransmitters, such as dopamine and serotonin, caused a complex cascade of events within neurons. This biochemical cascade changes the character of proteins within the neuron, ultimately determining how the neuron behaves as signals are flashed throughout the brain and nervous system. For his groundbreaking work Greengard shared the 2000 Nobel Prize in physiology or medicine with two other scientists: His occasional collaborator, the American Neuroscientist's Eric Kandel, and the Swedish pharmacologist Arvid Carlsson. These scientists forged the new knowledge of molecular mechanisms by which neurons communicate with one another in basic processes such as movement.

Dopamine, a chemical known as a neurotransmitter essential to the functioning of the central nervous system. In the process of neurotransmission, dopamine is transferred from one nerve cell, or neuron, to another, playing a key role in brain function and human behaviour.

Dopamine forms from a precursor molecule called Dopa, which is manufactured in the liver from the amino acid tyrosine. Dopa is then transported by the circulatory system to neurons in the brain, where the conversion to dopamine takes place.

Neurotransmitters also play a role in Parkinson disease, which slowly attacks the nervous system, causing symptoms that worsen over time. Fatigue, mental confusion, a masklike facial expression, stooping posture, shuffling gait, and problems with eating and speaking are among the difficulties suffered by Parkinson victims. These symptoms have been partly linked to the deterioration and eventual death of neurons that run from the base of the brain to the basal ganglia, a collection of nerve cells that manufacture the neurotransmitter dopamine. The reasons why such neurons die are yet to be understood, but the related symptoms can be alleviated. L-dopa, or levodopa, widely used to treat Parkinson disease, acts as a supplementary precursor for dopamine. It causes the surviving neurons in the basal ganglia to increase their production of dopamine, thereby compensating to some extent for the disabled neurons.

Dopamine forms from a precursor molecule called Dopa, which is manufactured in the liver from the amino acid tyrosine. Dopa is then transported by the circulatory system to neurons in the brain, where the conversion to dopamine takes place.

Dopamine is a versatile neurotransmitter. Among its many functions, it plays a major role in two activities of the central nervous system: one that helps control movement, and a second that are strongly associated with emotion-based behaviours.

The pathway involved in movement control is called the nigrostriatal pathway. Dopamine is released by neurons that originate from an area of the brain called the substantia nigra and connect to the part of the brain known as the corpora striata, an area known to be important in controlling the musculoskeletal system.

Dopamine is a versatile neurotransmitter. Among its many functions, it plays a major role in two activities of the central nervous system: one that helps control movement, and a second that are strongly associated with emotion-based behaviours.

The pathway involved in movement control is called the nigrostriatal pathway. Dopamine is released by neurons that originate from an area of the brain called the substantia nigra and connect to the part of the brain known as the corpora striata, an area known to be important in controlling the musculoskeletal system.

The second brain pathway in which dopamine plays a major role is called the mesocorticolimbic pathway. Neurons in an area of the brain called the ventral tegmentalarea, which transmits dopamine to other neurons connected to various parts of the limbic system, which is responsible for regulating emotion, motivation, behaviour, the sense of smell, and variously autonomic, or involuntary, functions like heartbeat and breathing.

A growing body of evidence suggests that dopamine be involved in several major brain disorders. Narcolepsy, a disorder characterized by brief, recurring episodes of sudden, deep sleep, is associated with abnormally high levels of both dopamine and a second neurotransmitter, acetylcholine. Huntington's chorea, an inherited, fatal illness in which neurons in the base of the brain are progressively destroyed, is also linked to an excess of dopamine.

Commonly known as shaking palsy, Parkinson disease is another brain disorder in which dopamine is involved. Besides tremors of the limbs, Parkinson patients suffer from muscular rigidity, which leads to difficulties in walking, writing, and speaking. This disorder results from the degeneration and death of neurons in the nigrostriatal pathways, resulting in low levels of dopamine. The symptoms of Parkinson's disease can be minimized by treatment with a drug called levodopa, or L-dopa, which converts to dopamine in the brain.

Parkinson's disease, disorder of the nervous system that affects muscle control. Marked by trembling of the arms and legs, muscular rigidity, and poor balance, Parkinson disease is slowly progressive, worsening over time. Eventually symptoms may cause problems with walking or talking and, in some people, difficulty thinking. Physicians do not know how to cure Parkinson's disease, but drug therapy or surgery may alleviate some of the most troubling symptoms. The disease is named for British physician James Parkinson, who first described it in 1817. In a report describing six patients, Parkinson called the disorder paralysis agitans, Latin words that means "shaking palsy."

The National Parkinson Foundation based in Miami, Florida, estimated that 1.5 million people in the United States are affected with Parkinson disease, although estimates are difficult to make because symptoms of the disease are often mistaken for the normal effects of aging or are attributed to other diseases. Parkinson disease occurs in people all over the world, with the incidence in men slightly higher than in women. Caucasians have a higher incidence of the disease than people of other races. People most commonly develop Parkinson disease around the age of 60, and the incidence rises with age. However, at least 10 percent of cases occur in people under age 40, and a rare form of the disease affects teenagers.

Parkinson disease may initially be mistaken for one or more of a group of nervous system diseases collectively known as parkinsonism (also known as Parkinson Plus diseases), all of which have certain symptoms in common. Unlike most cases of Parkinson disease, most forms of parkinsonism develop from an identifiable cause, such as exposure to certain chemicals, drugs, or viruses. Often initially diagnosed as Parkinson disease, parkinsonism diseases do not respond to the drug therapies that treat Parkinson's disease symptoms effectively. Physicians have also noted that the changes in the nervous system in people who have parkinsonism differ from those in patients who have Parkinson's disease.

Parkinson's disease is a progressive nervous disease occurring most often after the age of 50, and associated with the destruction of brain cells that produce dopamine and characterized by muscular tremor, slowing of movement, particular facial paralysis and peculiarity of gait and posture, and weakness.

Parkinson's disease develops as a part of the brain known as the substantia nigra degenerates. The substantia nigra is located in the midbrain, halfway between the cerebral cortex and the spinal cord. In healthy people, the substantia nigra contained certain nerve cells, called nigral cells, that produce the chemical dopamine. Dopamine travelled along nerve cell pathways from the substantia nigra to another region of the brain, called the striatum. In the striatum, dopamine activates nerve cells that coordinate normal muscle activity. In people with Parkinson's disease, nigral cells deteriorate and die at an accelerated rate, and the loss of these cells reduces the supply of dopamine to the striatum. Without adequate dopamine, nerve cells of the striatum generated to activate improperly, impairing a person's ability to control movement.

A study published in 2000 found that people with Parkinson's disease have a decreased number of nerve fibres in the heart. These results suggest that the disease affects nerves in organs outside the brain and may explain symptoms common in people with Parkinson's disease, such as a drop in blood pressure when a person stands up, constipation, and difficulty urinating.

Scientists do not understand the mechanisms underlying nerve cell death in Parkinson disease. Most researchers believe that Parkinson disease results from a combination of factors involving genetics, environmental agents, and abnormalities in cellular processes.

Studies suggest that genetic makeup may place a person at higher risk for developing Parkinson disease. Fifteen percent of people with Parkinson disease have one or more family members who also have the disease. In studies of families in which members from at least three generations have been diagnosed with the disease, scientists have identified three genes that, when mutated, may play a role in the development of Parkinson's disease. Genes provide coded instructions for the manufacture of proteins. One of the suspected gene codes for a protein called alpha-synnuclein. A second gene code for a protein called parkin, and a third gene coded for a protein belonging to a family of proteins known as ubiquitin. Researchers still do not understand the function of alpha-synnuclein, but parkin and ubiquitin may play a crucial role of cleaning up abnormal deposits of proteins in the cell. When the genes that produce these proteins are mutated, parkin and ubiquitin are unable to prevent protein deposits from building up. The accumulation of these deposits may play a role in nigral cell degeneration.

A recent study among identical twins also suggests that genetics plays a role in Parkinson's disease. In the study, doctors found that if one twin developed the disease before age 50, the chance was higher that the other twin would develop the disease if the twins were identical than it was if they were fraternal. Identical twins have the same genetic makeup, whereas the genes of fraternal twins are as different as those of any two siblings. This study suggests that the identical twins both have a gene that places them at risk for the disease.

Given the obvious symptoms associated with Parkinson's disease, such as tremor and imbalance, it is odd that the first description of the disease did not appear until 1817. Some researchers propose that the disease may have been uncommon before the Industrial Revolution, the period starting in the 18th century when machinery began replacing manual labour. The increased number of patients diagnosed with the disease today may be related to the presence of an environmental toxin (poisonous chemical) released as a byproduct from machines and other technology. Alternatively, the higher incidence of the disease may be related to increasingly longer life spans that enable people to reach an age when the physical effects of Parkinson's disease become more apparent.

Scientists have yet to identify a particular drug or toxin that causes Parkinson disease, although they have identified a number of drugs, chemicals, and viruses that cause diseases that resemble Parkinson's disease. The chemical MPTP, a byproduct created in the synthesis of certain illicit drugs, is linked to the development of a disease in some drug abusers that closely resembles Parkinson's disease. People who use some common garden pesticides and insecticides also seem to have a higher incidence of Parkinson disease, although a direct link between Parkinson disease and these chemicals has not yet been established. Certain people may develop parkinsonism if they are exposed to other agents, including carbon monoxide, cyanide, manganese, certain tranquillizers, and some rare viruses, or if they suffer head injuries or strokes. These parkinsonism diseases may be initially mistaken for Parkinson's disease.

Some research on Parkinson's disease focuses on the role of free radicals, potentially damaging molecules produced in cells as part of normal cell activity or in response to injury. Certain free radicals can cause cell damage, injuring the lining of cell membranes, destroying mitochondria (the cell's energy-producing organelles), and triggering cell death. Studies show that dopamine-producing cells are particularly vulnerable to free-radical destruction. Healthy people typically have adequate quantities of antioxidants, molecular scavengers that defend cells from free-radical destruction. Further research may identify antioxidants that may be useful in blunting the actions of free radicals.

Parkinson's disease most notably affects motor control (muscle activity). The disease progresses differently for each individual—symptoms develop swiftly in some people and slowly in others. Some Parkinson's patients may develop problems that affect their intellect or ability to reason, or they may suffer from depression or anxiety.

Doctors look for the presence of four principal symptoms in patients they suspect may have Parkinson's disease. A tremor (the involuntary shaking of limbs) is the major symptom for most people who have Parkinson's disease, although at least a third of the people diagnosed with the disease do not develop this symptom. Tremors are typically to begin in one hand but may eventually progress to the other hand, as well as to the arms, legs, and jaw.

Parkinson's disease may also produce stiffness of the joints, similar to arthritis, and rigidity of the limbs, in which muscles are tensed, or contracted. This rigidity makes movement difficult and may contribute to muscle ache and fatigue. Often the rigidity impairs the small muscles of the hand, making everyday tasks such as fastening with buttons on a shirt or writing difficulties.

The most disabling symptom of Parkinson's disease is bradykinesia, which causes slowness in all voluntary movement and speech and contributes to varied problems, such as a distinctive shuffling walk and small, cramped handwriting.

Parkinson's disease also causes postural instability, in which a person has difficulty adjusting to changes in body position. A healthy person who trips and starts to fall are able to quickly move the trunk and limbs to prevent or ease the fall. But people with postural instabilities who trip cannot move fast enough to stop or lessen their fall. This impaired reflex typically appears as unsteadiness or lack of balance.

Several secondary symptoms accompany Parkinson's disease, some of which are caused by one or more of these principal symptoms. For example, many people with Parkinson's disease have difficulty walking, resulting from a combination of bradykinesia and postural instability. Their walking is marked by short, shuffling steps that sometimes inadvertently quicken into a short run. Their balance problems may cause them to stagger forward or backward, giving them a lurching gait. They may have difficulty turning or stopping as they walk, or sometimes may inexplicably come to an abrupt stop. Other secondary symptoms include difficulty speaking or swallowing, an unchanging or masklike facial expression, drooling, dizziness when moving from a sitting position to a standing position, difficulty of urination, and impotence. Many patients find these secondary symptoms more troubling than the principal symptoms.

Around 30 percent of Parkinson's patients develop dementia, a decline in intellect marked by failing memory, short attention span, and personality changes. Sometimes dementia in Parkinson's patients resembles Alzheimer's disease, which has a number of the same symptoms, including certain motor control problems.

Twenty percent of people with Parkinson's disease develop an impairment in which information processing slows. These people may have difficulty completing formerly simple tasks, such as balancing a checkbook. This impairment of information processing may be a forerunner of dementia.

Depression, a condition marked by hopelessness, low self-esteem, sadness, apathy, and pessimism, occurs in 40 percent of people with Parkinson disease. A majority of people with Parkinson's disease experience anxiety, which may produce panic attacks— sudden, overpowering fears, accompanied by breathlessness, sweating, chest pain, choking, and dizziness. Depression or anxiety may appear before motor symptoms develop or they may appear as a reaction to motor symptoms.

Many people with Parkinson's disease also suffer from an inability to sleep at night coupled with daytime drowsiness. This sleep disturbance may be caused by anxiety or depression, or it could be a side effect of drugs used to treat Parkinson symptoms. It may also be a mechanism of the disease—the sleep centres in the brain lie near the substantia nigra and may be altered by the disease.

Some medical conditions initially produce symptoms similar to those of Parkinson's disease, but within two to five years additional symptoms usually develop that enable doctors to distinguish the conditions from Parkinson's disease. For example, a disease called progressive supranuclear palsy (PSP), which produces slowness of movement and difficulty with balance, and very much as similar to Parkinson disease. However, people with PSP also develop eye movement problems that prevent them from looking up, down, or sideways without moving the head, and these symptoms can be used to distinguish this condition from Parkinson's disease. Parkinson's disease-of the nerve cells, called amyotrophic lateral sclerosis. Lateral sclerosis causes to be seen of a chronic progressive disease marked by a gradual degeneration of the nerve cells in the central nervous system of cells in the central nervous system that control voluntary muscle movement. The disorder causes muscle weakness and atrophy and usually results in death., It is also called Lou Gehrig's disease.

Multiple system atrophy (MA), also known as Shy-Drager syndrome, displays symptoms similar to those of Parkinson disease. Of that which (MSA) affects the autonomic nervous system, producing problems with blood pressure regulation, heart rate, and bladder function. Parkinson's disease also affects the autonomic nervous system, but the symptoms of MSA are usually more severe. Another way that these diseases can be distinguished from Parkinson's disease is that they respond poorly to the drugs used to treat Parkinson's disease.

Diagnosing Parkinson disease may be difficult, particularly in the early stages of the disease when symptoms resemble other medical conditions, and misdiagnosis occurs occasionally. No single laboratory test can diagnose the disease. Blood tests are performed to eliminate conditions such as a low thyroid, which may result in slowness of apparent movement.

Brain imaging techniques, such as a magnetic resonance image (MRI), positron emission tomography (PET scans), and single photon emission computed tomography (SPECT), may be used to help doctors exclude other medical conditions, such as stroke or brain tumours, that produce symptoms similar to those of Parkinson's disease. Doctors quiz patients about their exposure to drugs, viruses, and environmental toxins to determine if a particular factor may be causing a Parkinsonism disorder. They document the medical history of the patient's blood relatives to determine the likelihood of a genetic predisposition for Parkinson disease or other disorders. And they carefully observe a patient's muscular activity over a period of time—as the disease progresses, and motions particular to Parkinson's disease become more obvious.

Doctors usually diagnose Parkinson disease if a patient develops, in at least, two or more of the principal symptoms, one of which is tremor or bradykinesia. The diagnosis is usually confirmed if people with suspected Parkinson disease respond well to drug treatment. Those with parkinsonism disorders or other medical conditions with similar symptoms typically do not respond to the drugs used in treating Parkinson's disease.

There is no known cure for Parkinson disease—that is, no treatment that prevents the disease from progressing. But the symptoms of the disease can be controlled by various drugs and, in some cases, by surgery.

Parkinson disease is a progressively disabling disorder of the nervous system that causes a marked tremor of the limbs an increased stiffness of the muscles, and impaired balance among other debilitating symptoms. At present there is no cure for the disease, but a variety of medications, known as antiparkinson drugs, provide dramatic relief from symptoms. Antiparkinson drugs restore the chemical dopamine in the brain or imitate dopamine's actions. That, as a monoamine neurotransmitter forms in the brain by the decarboxylation of Dopa and essential in the normal functioning of the central nervous system. A reduction in its concentration within the brain is associated with Parkinson's disease.

Most symptoms of Parkinson disease arise from a deficiency of dopamine in the brain. But simply giving a patient a dose of dopamine to restore depleted stores is ineffective because dopamine cannot pass from the bloodstream to the brain. Drugs that treat Parkinson disease, known as antiparkinson drugs, use other methods to temporarily restore dopamine in the brain or closely mimic dopamine's actions. In this section, each drug is designated by its generic name, followed by trade name examples in parentheses.

The most effective antiparkinson drug available is levodopa (Laradopa), an oral drug introduced in 1967 that treats bradykinesia, rigidity, tremor, and difficulty walking. Levodopa's structure enables it to enter the brain, where it transforms into dopamine. L-dopa is identified as an amino acid that is the metabolic precursor of dopamine, and converted in the brain into dopamine, and used in synthetic form to treat Parkinson's disease. Also, called levodopa.

When levodopa is taken alone, however, the body breaks down about 95 percent of the drug into dopamine before it reaches the brain. Instead of being used by the brain, the dopamine travels throughout the body, producing side effects, including nausea and vomiting, before it is broken down, or metabolized, by the liver and other tissues. Combining levodopa with a drug such as carbidopa enables more levodopa to enter the brain before it converts into dopamine. Carbidopa/levodopa (Atamet, Sinemet) lessens rigidity and bradykinesia but is less effective in treating tremor or balance problems. A similar drug combining carbidopa and benserazide (Madopar) are available in Canada and Europe.

Carbidopa/levodopa the amino acid and the metabolic precursor of dopamine, and is converted in the brain to dopamine, and use in synthetic form to treat Parkinson's disease, also called levodopa. These chemical ingredients can produce side effects in some people. As many as half of the people who take this drug for two to five years begin to notice fluctuations in the drug's effectiveness, known as an on-off effect. Others develop a dyskinesia, of unconscious movements, as jerking or twitching. Nonetheless, carbidopa/levodopa are liking to L-dopa, and consist of the amino acid that is the metabolic precursor of dopamine, is converted in the brain to dopamine and used in synthetic form to treat Parkinson's disease.

As Parkinson's disease progresses, the effectiveness of carbidopa/levodopa decreases and patients need higher and more frequent doses to control their symptoms. Depending upon the severity of symptoms, most doctors combine carbidopa/levodopa with other drugs to enhance levodopa's effects. In that, of an amino acid that is the metabolic precursor of dopamine, is converted in the brain to dopamine, and used in synthetic form to treat Parkinson's disease.

Dopamine agonists mimic the action of dopamine by activating nerve cells in the striatum. Dopamine agonists are increasingly used alone in the early stages of Parkinson's disease in order to lower a patient's risk of developing the dyskinesia associated with levodopa therapy. Later in the course of the disease they are more likely to be combined with carbidopa/levodopa to alleviate that drug's on-off effects. Side effects range from nausea, headache, and nasal congestion to nightmares and hallucinations. Dopamine agonists include pergolide (Permax), paramipexole (Mirapex), and ropinirole, which is a dopamine agonist used in the treatment of Parkinson's disease.

Levodopa does not permanently restore dopamine in the brain, and the drug may wear off at a certain point after each dose, diminishing dopamine levels. This may produce intermittent or discontinuous symptom relief, which may contribute to the on-off effect experienced by some Parkinson disease patients. A number of drugs are available that can prolong levodopa's effectiveness. A sustained or controlled-release, a form of carbidopa/levodopa releases a smaller amount of levodopa over a longer period, extending the time that levodopa is operatively effective.

Some drugs prolonged relief from symptoms by blocking the enzyme catechol-O-methy transferase, in that of any of various enzymes that catalyze the transfer of a chemical group, such as a phospohate or amine, from one molecule to another, breaking down of levodopa before it reaches the brain. Taken at the same time as levodopa drugs, these inhibitors-including entacapone increasing the time that levodopa is effective in the brain and reduces the on-off effect. Working in a similar manner, drugs that block the action of the enzyme monoamine oxidase-B, called MAO-B inhibitors, prevent this enzyme from breaking down dopamine in the brain. Used alone or in combination with carbidopa/levodopa, MAO-B inhibitors, including selegiline

(Eldepryl), do not prolong the actions of levodopa as well as COMT inhibitors.

When dopamine levels in the brain drop, another neurotransmitter called acetylcholine becomes overactive, and the resulting dopamine and acetylcholine imbalance affects motor skills. Drugs called anticholinergic's block the action of acetylcholine. Typically used in the early stages of the disease when symptoms are mild, anticholinergic drugs such as trihexiphenidyl (Artane) and biperidine (Akineton) may lessen tremors and drooling but, do not work effectively in treating adykinesia or posture instability.

The drug, amantadine (Symmetrel), was originally developed as an antiviral drug, but later was found effective in the treatment for Parkinson disease. Scientists are unsure how amantadine works, however, it may have an anticholinergic effect, and more recent studies show that it also blocks the action of glutamates, for which of a brain chemical that triggers production of free radicals, such that of a salt or ester of glutamine acid, especially on e that functions as a neurotransmitter t hat excite cells of the central nervous system. Amantadine is an antiviral drug, it also is used in the treatment of Parkinson's disease, but in combination with carbidopa/levodopa, is used as an antiviral drug, which is use in the treatment of the dyskinesia, which of an impairment in the ability to control movements, as characterized by spasmodic or repetitive motions or lack of coordination.

In the 1950s and 1960s, brain surgery was a common method for treating tremor and rigidity in Parkinson patients, even though the success rate of surgery varied and life-threatening complications often developed. But surgery fell out of favour with the introduction in 1967 of levodopa, a safer and more effective treatment alternative. In recent years the advent of new brain-imaging techniques has improved surgical precision, and surgery has gained renewed popularity as a treatment for some people with Parkinson disease who no longer respond to drug therapy.

Two similar surgical procedures that have been used to treat Parkinson disease involve destroying part of the brain. To control tremor and rigidity, surgeons perform a thalamotomy to destroy a small region of the thalamus, a part of the brain that relays signals coordinating movement. Pallidotomy targets the globus pallidum, a part of the brain that produces uncontrolled spasmodic movements in Parkinson disease patients. Doctors now prefer to perform a more effective surgical procedure called deep brain stimulation. In this procedure, the patient's head is immobilized in a halo-like device called a stereotaxic frame. Using an MRI, the surgeon locates the thalamus, and the globus pallidum, or a related region called the subthalamic nucleus in the brain. After drilling a small hole in the skull, the surgeon inserts a probe deep into the brain to the target tissue. A short burst of electricity sent through the probe normalizes the electrical activity in the brain region, reversing the symptoms of Parkinson disease. This surgery is reasonably safe, and symptom relief is immediate. But as with any surgery, risks are involved, including the chance that a stroke may develop.

In a surgical procedure still in the experimental stage, doctors transplant dopamine-producing cell tissue into the brain. In this procedure, doctors use different sources of cell tissue that make dopamine, including cells from aborted fetuses and pig embryos. Some studies have shown that these procedures have alleviated symptoms in some Parkinson's patients.

Some doctors are also investigating the use of human stem cells, immature cells that easily manipulated, can become dopamine-producing cells. Stem cells are hardy and eager to reproduce, in that one stem cell can generate billions of copies. The use of stem cells is controversial because some studies have obtained stem cells from aborted human embryos. But other sources of human stem cells are available, including the discarded umbilical cord from healthy babies and the bone marrow of adults. Using stem cells from these sources may make this treatment more acceptable. So far studies on the effectiveness of this procedure have provided conflicting results.

Other doctors are performing animal experiments in which a gene that produces dopamine is inserted into the brain cells of an animal with Parkinson disease. The gene causes brain cells to make dopamine. This procedure, called gene transfer that one day it may help alleviate symptoms or cure Parkinson's disease in humans.

In the nervous system, a message-carrying impulse travels from one end of a nerve cell to the other by means of an electrical impulse. When it reaches the terminal end of a nerve cell, the impulse trigger's tiny sacs called presynaptic vessicles to release their contents, chemical messengers called neurotransmitters. The neurotransmitters float across the synapse, or gap between adjacent nerve cells. When they reach the neighbouring nerve cell, the neurotransmitters fit into specialized receptor sites much as a key fits into a lock, causing that nerve cell to "fire," or generate an electric message-carrying impulse. As the message continues through the nervous system, the presynaptic cell absorbs the excess neurotransmitters, and repackages them in presynaptic vessicles in a process called neurotransmitter reuptake.

The road to the discovery of the prion began with investigations into the cause of TSEs. In 1967 British scientist Tikvah Alper and her colleagues at the Hammersmith Hospital in London extracted brain tissue from scrapie-infected sheep. They chemically treated the tissue to isolate a virus, bacteria, or other agent that might cause the disease. This processed tissue was then injected into healthy sheep to see if the disease would be transmitted. The healthy sheep contracted scrapie, indicating that the infectious agent was in the diseased brain tissue. Further, this experiment showed that the infectious agent could reproduce in healthy animals to cause disease.

Alper then exposed similar scrapie-infected tissue extracts to ultraviolet radiation—a treatment that normally destroys DNA and RNA. She found that the extracts maintained their ability to transmit scrapie. The resistance of the infectious agent to ultraviolet radiation suggested that neither a virus nor bacteria, which reproduce through their nucleic acids, caused the disease. Her discovery indicated that a previously unknown kind of infectious agent was responsible for scrapie. Her findings galvanized debate among scientists about the nature of this infectious particle.

In the early 1980s Prusiner, working at the University of California at San Francisco, found that similar tissue extracts no longer caused disease after they were exposed to treatments that destroy proteins. Prusiner concluded in a study published in 1982 that proteins alone were responsible for TSEs. He suggested that proteins cause these diseases by replicating in tissues of the nervous system.

Prusiner's revolutionary idea has met with great resistance because DNA and RNA are the only substances now known to replicate in body tissues. The concept of a proteinaceous infectious particle capsized the widely accepted convictions about agents of infectious disease.

Prusiner received the 1997 Nobel Prize in physiology or medicine for his work with prions. A prion is a microscopic protein in a particle similar to a virus but lacking nucleic acid, thought to be the infectious agent responsible for scrapie and certain other degenerative disease of the nervous system. Even so, his theory that prions alone produce TSEs and, yet, remain controversial. Some scientists believe that TSEs are caused by an as yet unidentified slow-acting virus. Some believe that a small virus accompanies a prion, and both are needed to produce scrapie, BSE, and other TSEs. Still other scientists think that other proteins, called "chaperones," initiate the improper folding of the normal proteins.

Individual viruses, or virus particles, also called virions, contain genetic material, or genomes, in one of several forms. Unlike cellular organisms, in which the genes always are made up of DNA, viral genes may consist of either DNA or RNA. Like cell DNA, almost all viral DNA is double-stranded, and it can have either a circular or a linear arrangement. Almost all viral RNA is single-stranded; it is usually linear, and it may be either segmented (with different genes on different RNA molecules) or nonsegmented (with all genes on a single piece of RNA).

The viral protective shell, or capsid, can be either helical (spiral-shaped) or icosahedral (having 20 triangular sides). Capsids are composed of repeating units of one or a few different proteins. These units are called protomers or capsomers. The proteins that make up the virus particle are called structural proteins. Viruses also carry genes for making proteins that are never incorporated into the virus particle and are found only in infected cells. These viral proteins are called nonstructural proteins; they include factors required for the replication of the viral genome and the production of the virus particle.

Capsids and the genetic material (DNA or RNA) their containment is referred to as nucleocapsids. Some virus particles consist only of nucleocapsids, while others contain additional structures.

A bacteriophage is a type of virus that destroys bacteria. It consists of a head, containing the genetic material, and a tail, which attaches to the exterior of some bacterium. The genetic material of the bacteriophage passes from its head through its tail into the bacterium. The genetic material then directs the bacterium to create new bacteriophages, which eventually burst from their host and, in the process, destroy the bacterium. The released bacteriophages attack nearby bacteria, and the infection process continues.

Some icosahedral and helical animal viruses are enclosed in a lipid envelope acquired when the virus buds through hosting-cell membranes. Inserted into this envelope are the glycoproteins, in that of any group of conjugated proteins that contain a carbohydrate as the non-proven component. The viral genome directs the cell to make; these molecules bind virus particles to susceptible host cells.

The most expounding of the viruses is the bacteriophages, which use bacteria for their hosts. Some bacteriophages resemble an insect with an icosahedral head attached to a tubular sheath. From the base of the sheath extend several long tail fibres that help the virus attach to the bacterium and inject its DNA to be replicated and to direct capsid production and virus particle assembly inside the cell.

Viroids and prions are smaller than viruses, but they are similarly associated with disease. Viroids are plant pathogens that consist only of a circular, independently replicating RNA molecules.

The single-stranded RNA circle collapses on itself to form a rodlike structure. The only known mammalian pathogens, which resemble plant viroids are the deltavirus (hepatitis D), which require hepatitis B virus proteins to package its RNA into virus particles. Co-infection with hepatitis B and D can produce more severe disease than can infection with hepatitis B alone. Prions are microscopic protein particles, similar to a virus but lacking nucleic acid, and thought to be infectious agents responsible for scrapie and certain of other degenerative diseases of the nervous system. These are the mutated forms of a normal protein found on the surface of certain animal cells. The mutated protein, known as a prion, has been implicated in some neurological diseases such as Creutzfeldt-Jakob disease and Bovine Spongiform Encephalopathy, that by saying, that Bovine Spongiform Encephalopathy has been given as an infectious degenerative brain disease occurring in cattle, it is also called mad cow disease.

There is some evidence that prions resemble viruses in their ability to cause infection. Prions, however, lack the nucleic acid found in viruses. The prion is a minute protein particle, being or appears to be in the finding similarity to a virus is but lacking nucleic acid, and thought to be the infectious agents responsible for scrapie and certain other degenerative diseases of the nervous system. A disease cause by a virus is something that poison's one's spirit of mind. All the same, of any of the variously simple submicroscopic parasites of plants, animals, or bacteria that often cause disease and that consists essentially of a core of RNA or DNA surrounded by a protein coat. Unable to replicate without a host cell, viruses are typically not considered for being living organisms

Viruses are classified according to their type of genetic material, their strategy of replication, and their structure. The International Committee on Nomenclature of Viruses (ICNV), established in 1966, devised a scheme to group viruses into families, subfamilies, genera, and species. The ICNV report published in 1995 assigned more than 4000 viruses into 71 virus families. Hundreds of other viruses remain unclassified or non-categorical because of the lack of sufficient information.

Creutzfeldt-Jakob Disease (CJD) forms of human spongiform encephalopathy caused by an infection of the brain, probably by a particle called a prion. The disease causes fatal degradation of brain tissue and produces a dementia that affects men and women, often between the ages of 50 and 65. Some 90 percent of cases progress to death within one year and sometimes within a month, as symptoms include loss of speech, difficult swallowing, rigid limbs, and contraction of the facial muscles, with death often resulting from a complication following these symptoms. The remaining 10 percent of cases develop dementia and may slowly decline over several years. There is no record of anyone recovering from the disease and there is no known treatment.

Creutzfeldt-Jakob disease is found worldwide but is relatively rare, affecting about 0.9 people per million in the United States. The mean age of death is 67 years. Deaths from Creutzfeldt-Jakob disease are uncommon in people under age 50. In people age 70 to 74 years, the disease causes 5.7 deaths per million people.

In the mid-1980s American neurologist Stanley Prusiner first proposed the existence of infectious agents that contain no genetic material and are made entirely of protein. Prusiner suggested that these particles—which he called prions—were responsible for neurodegenerative diseases, such as bovine spongiform encephalopathy (BSE), or "mad cow disease," in cows and Creutzfeldt-Jakob disease (CJD) in humans. He described his research on prions in the following 1995 Scientific American article. In 1997 Prusiner was the sole recipient of the Nobel Prize in physiology or medicine "for his discovery of Prions-a new biological principle of infection." The award was unusual because it went to a single recipient and because Prusiner's findings still lack a scientific consensus. Some scientists believe a slow-acting virus may cause the spongiform encephalopathy diseases.

Creutzfeldt-Jakob disease is associated with prions, mutated forms of a normal protein produced in nerve cells, white blood cells, muscle cells, and the cells of many other tissues. Just how prions cause the disease symptoms to remain unclear. Still, there are three types of the disease: sporadic, genetic, and iatrogenic.

Sporadic Creutzfeldt-Jakob disease is the most common form and accounts for around 85 percent of all human prion disease. In such cases, the gene coding for the prion protein undergoes a spontaneous mutation. The gene then encodes for the abnormal, or the infectious form of the protein. A small number of mutant cells producing a small amount of prion protein can initiate a progressive infection. Recent research suggests that this occurs because the abnormal protein can transform normal molecules by causing them to change their configuration.

Genetic Creutzfeldt-Jakob disease causes 10 to 15 percent of prion disease cases. It occurs when a mutant prion gene is passed genetically from one generation to another. In families expressing the mutant gene, about half the members die of the disease.

Iatrogenic Creutzfeldt-Jakob disease results from an individual with the disease infecting a healthy individual. This is rare but known cases involve surgery or transfusion procedures such as corneal transplants or human growth hormone injection. The disease has been characterized only recently and it may take up to 20 years to express itself or may not be recognized until the patient dies. For these reasons, many individuals may have been infected inadvertently with Creutzfeldt-Jakob disease in the past and could be at risk of developing the disease. It is estimated that 25,000 such cases exist worldwide.

Creutzfeldt-Jakob disease is similar to bovine spongiform encephalopathy (BSE), a prion-related brain disease of cows discovered in the United Kingdom in 1986 and commonly known as mad cow disease. Mad cow disease can be transmitted from sheep to cows, but until recently there has been no significant evidence that cattle contaminated with BSE can infect humans. Prions are generally species-specific—that is, they tend to affect species closely related to the organism originally producing the protein. For this reason, scientists thought it unlikely that humans could contract the disease from eating infected cattle.

Nevertheless, in late March 1996 the British Ministry of Health announced the discovery of 10 cases of a newly described type of fatal CJD, called variant CJD (vCJD). The victims of vCJD had distinct brain tissue abnormalities, they exhibited unusual behaviour, they were all under the age of 42, and they had no hereditary record of the disease. Despite a lack of scientific evidence proving the cattle-human disease link, the British government admitted that the victims may have contracted the disease through contact with BSE-infected cattle. The announcement represented an about-face in the stance of the government, which had previously denied any possible link between BSE and human disease. Rising concern over the possibility of transmission of

BSE to humans from infected beef resulted in the banning of exported beef from the United Kingdom in 1996.

Although the hypothesis of the cattle-to-human transmission has yet to be verified, it is supported by the results of a number of scientific studies, including two released in 1997. Laboratory mice injected with brain tissue from BSE-infected cows and another group injected with brain tissue from vCJD-infected humans both developed the same symptoms of brain degeneration and the infection was ultimately fatal in both groups. In addition, researchers found the same prion strain in both groups of mice. In one of the studies, researchers injected a third group of mice with tissue from humans who had died of classical CJD; these mice developed no symptoms and survived the trial.

In early 1998 scientists found that prions are found not only in the brain tissue of infected humans but in other organs and the blood as well. The potential public health problems have focussed the attention of the medical community on the various forms of CJD and other prion diseases.

Creutzfeldt-Jakob disease is similar to bovine spongiform encephalopathy (BSE), a prion-related brain disease of cows discovered in the United Kingdom in 1986 and commonly known as mad cow disease. Mad cow disease can be transmitted from sheep to cows, but until recently there has been no significant evidence that cattle contaminated with BSE can infect humans. Prions are generally species-specific—that is, they tend to affect species closely related to the organism originally producing the protein. For this reason, scientists thought it unlikely that humans could contract the disease from eating infected beef.

Prions are extremely tiny protein particles found in the brain, nerve, and muscle cells. A controversial theory states that prions cause disease by changing normal proteins into an abnormal shape. These mutated proteins in turn force other proteins to change shape, leading to destruction of tissue, primarily in the brain. Some researchers have hypothesized that prions cause transmissible spongiform encephalopathies, a group of rare infectious diseases that includes Creutzfeldt-Jakob disease in humans, scrapie in sheep, and bovine spongiform encephalopathy (commonly known as mad cow disease) in cattle. Some evidence suggests that prion-related disease can be transmitted through food infected with mutated proteins.

In 1955, while studying virology at the Hall Institute, Gajdusek learned of an unusual progressive and fatal neurodegenerative disease among the aborigines. For people of New Guinea were at first, assumed that the disease, which the is called kuru, and was genetic in origin, Gajdusek found instead that it was caused by a substance transmitted through a ritual that involved eating the brains of deceased relatives. Autopsy examination of the brains of people who had died of kuru showed nerve damage, but Gajdusek was unable to determine the cause. A researcher studying neurodegenerative disease in animals suggested that kuru was similar to scrapie, a neurodegenerative disease of sheep. Gajdusek showed that kuru was indeed similar to scrapie, as well as to Creutzfeldt-Jakob disease, a neurodegenerative disorder of humans. Gajdusek attributed these diseases to infectious agents, which he called slow-acting viruses. Scientists now believe that these agents are infectious protein particles, known as prions. Prions have since been implicated in bovine spongiform encephalopathy, a disease of cattle and commonly known as mad cow disease.

But, as the nerve cells transmit information from one part of the body to another. Each nerve cell has branching dendrites to connect to other dendrites, and a long axon to transmit or collect impulses.

`These highly complex groups of cells, called ganglia, transfer information from one part of the body to another. Each neuron, or nerve cell, consists of a cell body with branching dendrites and one long fibre, or axon. The dendrites connect one neuron to another; the axon transmits impulses to an organ or collects impulses from a sensory organ

Two types of phenomena are involved in processing nerve signals: electrical and chemical. Electrical events propagate a signal within a neuron, and chemical processes transmit the signal from one neuron to another neuron or to a muscle cell.

The signals conveying everything that human beings sense and think, and every motion that is made, follow a nerve pathway in the human body as waves of ions (atoms or groups of atoms that carries electric charges). Australian physiologist Sir John Eccles discovered many of the intricacies of this electrochemical signalling process, particularly the pivotal step in which a signal is conveyed from one nerve cell to another. He shared in the 1963 Nobel Prize in physiology or medicine for this work, which he described in a 1965 Scientific American article.

A neuron is a long cell that has a thick central area containing the nucleus; it also has one long process called an axon and one or more short, bushy processes called dendrites. Dendrites receive impulses from other neurons. (The exceptions are sensory neurons, such as those that transmit information about temperature or touch, in which the signal is generated by specialized receptors in the skin.) These impulses are propagated electrically along the cell membrane to the end of the axon. At the tip of the axon the signal is chemically transmitted to an adjacent neuron or muscle cell.

Like all other cells, neurons contain charged ions: potassium and sodium (positively charged) and chlorine (negatively charged). Neurons differ from other cells in that they are able to produce a nerve impulse. A neuron is polarized—that is, it has an overall negative charge inside the cell membrane because of the high concentration of chlorine ions and low concentration of potassium and sodium ions. The concentration of these same ions is exactly reversed outside the cell. This charge differential represents stored electrical energy, sometimes referred to as membrane potential or resting potential. The negative charge inside the cell is maintained by two features. The first is the selective permeability of the cell membrane, which is more permeable to potassium than sodium. The second feature is sodium pumps within the cell membrane that actively pump sodium out of the cell. When depolarization occurs, this charge differential across the membrane is reversed, and a nerve impulse is produced.

Depolarization is a rapid change in the permeability of the cell membrane. When sensory input or any other kind of stimulating current is received by the neuron, the membrane permeability is changed, allowing a sudden influx of sodium ions into the cell. The high concentration of sodium, or action potential, changes the overall charges within the cell from negative too positive, as the local charges in ion concentration triggers similar reactions along the membrane, propagating the nerve impulse. After a brief period called the refractory period, during which the ionic concentration returns to resting potential, the neuron can repeat this process.

Nerve impulses travel at different speeds, depending on the cellular composition of a neuron. Where speed of impulse is important, as in the nervous system, axons are insulated with a membranous substance called myelin. The insulation provided by myelin maintains the ionic charge over long distances. Nerve impulses are propagated at specific points along the myelin sheath; these points are called the nodes of Ranvier. Examples of myelinated axons are those in sensory nerve fibres and nerves connected to skeletal muscles. In non-myelinated cells, the nerve impulse is propagated more diffusely.

When the electrical signal reaches the tip of an axon, it stimulates small presynaptic vesicles in the cell. These vesicles contain chemicals called neurotransmitters, which are released into the microscopic space between neurons (the synaptic cleft). The neurotransmitters attach themselves upon specialized receptors, as located on the surface of the adjacent neuron. This stimulus causes the adjacent cell to depolarize and propagate an action potential of its own. The duration of a stimulus from a neurotransmitter is limited by the breakdown of the chemicals in the synaptic cleft and the reuptake by the neuron that produced them. Formerly, each neuron was thought to make only one transmitter, but recent studies have shown that some cells, in production for achieving of two or more.

The brain functions by complex neuronal, or nerve cell, circuits. Communication between neurons is both electrical and chemical and always travels from the dendrites of a neuron, through its soma, and out its axon to the dendrites of another neuron.

Dendrites of one neuron receive signals from the axons of other neurons through chemicals known as neurotransmitters. The neurotransmitters set off electrical charges in the dendrites, which then carry the signals electrochemically to the soma. The soma integrates the information, which is then transmitted electrochemically down the axon to its tip.

At the tip of the axon, small, bubblelike structures called vesicle release neurotransmitters that carries the signal across the synapse, or gap, between two neurons. There are many types of neurotransmitters, including norepinephrine, dopamine, and serotonin. Neurotransmitters can be excitatory (that is, they excite an electrochemical response in the dendrite receptors) or inhibitory (they block the response of the dendrite receptors).

One neuron may communicate with thousands of other neurons, and many thousands of neurons are involved with even the simplest behaviour. It is believed that these connections and their efficiency can be modified, or altered, by experience.

Scientists have used two primary approaches to studying how the brain works. One approach is to study brain function after parts of the brain have been damaged. Functions that disappear or that is no longer normal after injury to specific regions of the brain can often be associated with the damaged areas. The second approach is to study the response of the brain to direct stimulation or to stimulation of various sense organs.

Neurons are grouped by function into collections of cells called nuclei. These nuclei are connected to form sensory, motor, and other systems. Scientists can study the function of somatosensory (pain and touch), motor, olfactory, visual, auditory, language, and other systems by measuring the physiological (physical and chemical) change that occur in the brain when these senses are activated. For example, electroencephalography (EEG) measures the electrical activity of specific groups of neurons through electrodes attached to the surface of the skull. Electrodes that have been directly inserted into the brain can give readings of individual neurons. Changes in blood flow, glucose (sugar), or oxygen consumption in groups of active cells can also be mapped.

Although the brain appears symmetrical, how it functions is not. Each hemisphere is specific and specialized for its dominance in certain other functions. Research has shown that hemispheric dominance is related to whether a person is predominantly right-handed or left-handed. In most right-handed people, the left hemisphere processes arithmetic, language, and speech. The right hemisphere interprets music, complex imagery, and spatial relationships and recognizes and expresses emotion. In left-handed people, the pattern of brain organization is more variable.

Hemispheric specialization has traditionally been studied in people who have sustained damage to the connections between the two hemispheres, as may occur with stroke, an interruption of blood flow to an area of the brain that causes the death of nerve cells in that area. The division of functions between the two hemispheres has also been studied in people who have had to have the connection between the two hemispheres surgically cut in order to control severe epilepsy, a neurological disease characterized by convulsions and loss of consciousness.

Nerve cells transmit information from one part of the body to another. Each nerve cell has branching dendrites to connect to other dendrites, and a long axon to transmit or collect impulses.

These highly complex groups of cells, called ganglia, transfer information from one part of the body to another. Each neuron, or nerve cell, consists of a cell body with branching dendrites and one long fibre, or axon. The dendrites connect one neuron to another; the axon transmits impulses to an organ or collects impulses from a sensory organ.

Schizophrenia is a psychiatric disorder characterized by loss of contact with reality and major changes in personality. Schizophrenics have normal levels of dopamine in the brain, but because they are highly sensitive to this neurotransmitter, these normal levels of dopamine trigger unusual behaviours. Drugs such as thorazine that blocks the action of dopamine have been found to decrease the symptoms of schizophrenia.

Studies indicate that people who are addicted to alcohol and other drugs as cocaine and nicotine have less dopamine in the mesocorticolimbic pathway. These drugs appear to increase dopamine levels, resulting in the pleasurable feelings associated with the drugs.

Schizophrenia, severe mental illness characterized by a variety of symptoms, including loss of contact with reality, bizarre behaviour, disorganized thinking and speech, decreased emotional expressiveness, and social withdrawal. Usually only some of these symptoms occur in any one person. The term schizophrenia comes from Greek words meaning "split mind." However, contrary to common belief, schizophrenia does not refer to a person with a split personality or multiple personality. For a description of a mental illness in which a person has multiple personalities, To observers, schizophrenia may seem like madness or insanity.

People with schizophrenia have disturbed, frightening thoughts and may have trouble telling the difference between real and unreal experiences. Perhaps more than any other mental illness, schizophrenia has a debilitating effect on the lives of the people who suffer from it. A person with schizophrenia may have difficulty telling the difference between real and unreal experiences, logical and illogical thoughts, or fittingly and ill-timed behaviour. Schizophrenia seriously impairs a person's ability to work, go to school, enjoy relationships with others, or take care of oneself. In addition, people with schizophrenia frequently require hospitalization because they pose a danger to themselves. About 10 percent of people with schizophrenia commit suicide, and many others attempt suicide. Once people develop schizophrenia, they usually suffer from the illness for the rest of their lives. Although there is no cure, treatment can help many people with schizophrenia lead productive lives.

Schizophrenia also carries an enormous cost to society. People with schizophrenia occupy about one-third of all beds in psychiatric hospitals in the United States. In addition, people with schizophrenia account for at least 10 percent of the homeless population in the United States. The National Institute of Mental Health has estimated that schizophrenia costs the United States tens of billions of dollars each year in direct treatment, social services, and lost productivity.

Approximately 1 percent of people develop schizophrenia at some time during their lives. Experts estimate that about 1.8 million people in the United States have schizophrenia. The prevalence of schizophrenia is the same, disregarding of sex, race, and culture. Although women are just as likely as men to develop schizophrenia, women tend to experience the illness less severely, with fewer hospitalizations and better social functioning in the community.

Schizophrenia usually develops in late adolescence or early adulthood, between the ages of 15 and 30. Much less common, schizophrenia develops later in life. The illness may begin abruptly, but it usually develops slowly over months or years. Mental health professionals diagnose schizophrenia based on an interview with the patient in which they determine whether the person has experienced specific symptoms of the illness.

Symptoms and functioning in people with schizophrenia tend to vary over time, sometimes worsening and other times improving. For many patients the symptoms gradually become less severe as they grow older. About 25 percent of people with schizophrenia become symptom-free later in their lives.

A variety of symptoms characterize schizophrenia. The most prominent include symptoms of psychosis—such as delusions and hallucinations—as well as bizarre behaviour, strange movements, and disorganized thinking and speech. Many people with schizophrenia do not recognize that their mental functioning is disturbed.

Some people with schizophrenia experience delusions of persecution—false beliefs that other people are plotting against them. This interview between a patient with schizophrenia and his therapist illustrates the paranoia that can affect people with this illness.

Delusions are false beliefs that appear obviously untrue to other people. For example, a person with schizophrenia may believe that he is the king of England when he is not. People with schizophrenia may have delusions that others, such as the police or the FBI, are plotting against them or spying on them. They may believe that aliens are controlling their thoughts or that their own thoughts are being broadcast to the world so that other people can hear them.

People with schizophrenia may also experience hallucinations (false sensory perceptions). People with hallucinations see, hear, smell, feel, or taste things that are not really there. Auditory hallucinations, such as hearing voices when no one else is around, are especially common in schizophrenia. These hallucinations may include at least, two or more voices conversing with each other, voices that continually comment on the person's life, or voices that command the person to do something.

People with schizophrenia often behave bizarrely. They may talk to themselves, walk backward, laugh suddenly without explanation, make funny faces, or masturbate in public. In rare cases, they maintain a rigid, bizarre pose for hours on end. Alternately, they may engage in constant random or repetitive movements.

People with schizophrenia sometimes talk in incoherent or nonsensical ways, which only is to suggest of a confused or disorganized pattern of conversation that of inclining inclinations that the lines of conversation are incoherent and unstable or loosely associated phrases. They may combine words and phrases in meaningless ways or make up new words. In addition, they may show poverty of speech, in which they talk less and more slowly than other people, or fail to answer questions or reply only briefly, or suddenly stop, as if afflicted against the spoken exchange.

Another common characteristic of schizophrenia is social withdrawal. People with schizophrenia may avoid others or act as though others do not exist. They often show decreased emotional expressiveness. For example, they may talk in a low, monotonous voice, avoid eye contact with others, and display a blank facial expression. They may also have difficulties experiencing pleasure and may lack interest in participating in activities.

Other symptoms of schizophrenia include difficulties with memory, attention span, abstract thinking, and planning ahead. People with schizophrenia commonly have problems with anxiety, depression, and suicidal thoughts. In addition, people with schizophrenia are much more likely to abuse or become dependent upon drugs or alcohol than other people. The use of alcohol and drugs often worsens the symptoms of schizophrenia, resulting in relapses and hospitalizations.

Schizophrenia, which of any of a group of psychotic disorders usually characterized by a withdrawal from reality, illogical patterns of thinking, delusions, and hallucinations, and accompanied in varying degrees by other emotional, behavioural, or intellectual disturbances. Schizophrenia is associated with dopamine imbalances in the brain and defects of the frontal lobe and is caused by genetic, and biological, and psychosocial factors. A situation or condition that results from the coexistence of disparate or antagonistic qualities or identity. Schizophrenia appears to result not from a single cause, but from a variety of factors. Most scientists believe that schizophrenia is a biological disease caused by genetic factors, an imbalance of chemicals in the brain, structural brain abnormalities, or abnormalities in the prenatal environment. In addition, stressful life events may contribute to the development of schizophrenia in those who are predisposed to the illness.

Research shows that the more genetically related a person is to someone with schizophrenia, the greater the risk that person has of developing the illness. For example, children of one parent with schizophrenia have a 13 percent chance of developing the illness, whereas children of two parents with schizophrenia have a 46 percent chance of developing the disorder.

Research suggests that the genes' one inheritance strongly influence one's risk of developing schizophrenia. Studies of families have shown that the more close one is related to someone with schizophrenia, the greater the risk one has of developing the illness. For example, the children of one parent with schizophrenia have about a 13 percent chance of developing the illness, and children of two parents with schizophrenia have about a 46 percent chance of eventually developing schizophrenia. This increased risk occurs even when such children are adopted and raised by mentally healthy parents. In comparison, children in the general population have only about a 1 percent chance of developing schizophrenia.

Some evidence suggests that schizophrenia may result from an imbalance of chemicals in the brain called neurotransmitters. These chemicals enable neurons (brain cells) to communicate with each other. Some scientists suggest that schizophrenia result from excess activity of the neurotransmitter dopamine in certain parts of the brain or from an abnormal sensitivity to dopamine. Support for this hypothesis comes from antipsychotic drugs, which reduce psychotic symptoms in schizophrenia by blocking brain receptors for dopamine. In addition, amphetamines, which increase dopamine activity, intensify psychotic symptoms in people with schizophrenia. Despite these findings, many experts believe that excess dopamine activity alone cannot account for schizophrenia. Other neurotransmitters, such as serotonin and norepinephrine, may play important roles as well.

Brain imaging techniques, such as magnetic resonance imaging and positron-emission tomography, have led researchers to discover specific structural abnormalities in the brains of people with schizophrenia. For example, people with chronic schizophrenia tend to have enlarged brain ventricles (cavities in the brain that contains cerebrospinal fluid). They also have a smaller overall volume of brain tissue compared to mentally healthy people. Other people with schizophrenia show abnormally low activity in the frontal lobe of the brain, which governs abstract thought, planning, and judgment. Research has identified possible abnormalities in many other parts of the brain, including the temporal lobes, basal ganglia, thalamus, the Hippocampus and superior temporal gyrus. These defects may partially explain the abnormal thoughts, perceptions, and behaviours that characterize schizophrenia.

Evidence suggests that factor's in the prenatal environment and during birth can increase the risk of a person later developing schizophrenia. These events are believed to affect the brain development of the fetus during a critical period. For example, pregnant women who have been exposed to the influenza virus or who have poor nutrition have a slightly increased chance of giving birth to a child who later develops schizophrenia. Also, an obstetric complication during the birth of a child—for example, birthing a delivery using forceps, slightly increases the chances of the child later developing schizophrenia.

Although scientists favour a biological cause of schizophrenia, stress in the environment may affect the onset and course of the illness. Stressful life circumstances—such as maturation and living in poverty, the death of a loved one, an important change in jobs or relationships, or chronic tension and hostility at home—can increase the chances of schizophrenia in a person biologically predisposed to the disease. In addition, stressful events can trigger a relapse of symptoms in a person who already has the illness. Individuals who have effective skills for managing stress may be less susceptible to its negative effects. Psychological and social rehabilitation can help patients develop more effective skills for dealing with stress.

Although there is no cure for schizophrenia, effective treatment exists that can improve the long-term course of the illness. With many years of treatment and rehabilitation, significant numbers of people with schizophrenia experience partial or full remission of their symptoms.

Treatment of schizophrenia usually involves a combination of medication, rehabilitation, and treatment of other problems the person may have. Antipsychotic drugs are any of a group of drugs, such as the phenothiazine or butyrophenones, that are used to treat psychosis and also called major tranquiller, neuroleptic, and called of the class of neuroleptics. Antipsychotic drugs, are the most frequently used medications for treatment of schizophrenia. Psychological and social rehabilitation programs may help people with schizophrenia function in the community and reduce stress related to their symptoms. Treatment of secondary problems, such as substance abuse and infectious diseases, is also an important part of an overall treatment program.

Antipsychotic medications, developed in the mid-1950s, can dramatically improve the quality of life for people with schizophrenia. The drugs reduce or eliminate psychotic symptoms such as hallucinations and delusions. The medications can also help prevent these symptoms from returning. Common antipsychotic drugs include risperidone (Risperdal), olanzapine (Zyprexa), clozapine (Clozaril), quetiapine (Seroquel), haloperidol (Haldol), thioridazine (Mellaril), chlorpromazine (Thorazine), fluphenazine (Prolixin), and trifluoperazine (Stelazine). Antipsychotic drugs of any group of drugs, such as the phenothiazines or by tyrophenones, that is used to treat psychosis, also called major tranquiller or a neuroleptic.

People with schizophrenia usually must take medication for the rest of their lives to control psychotic symptoms. Antipsychotic medications appear to be less effective at treating other symptoms of schizophrenia, such as social withdrawal and apathy.

Antipsychotic drugs help reduce symptoms in 80 to 90 percent of people with schizophrenia. However, those who benefit often stop taking medication because they do not understand that they are ill or because of unpleasant side effects. Minor side effects include weight gain, dry mouth, blurred vision, restlessness, constipation, dizziness, and drowsiness. Other side effects are more serious and debilitating. These may include muscle spasms or cramps, tremors, and tardive dyskinesia, an irreversible condition marked by uncontrollable movements of the lips, mouth, and tongue. Newer drugs, such as clozapine, olanzapine, risperidone, and quetiapine, tend to produce fewer of these side effects. However, clozapine can cause agranulocytosis, a significant reduction in white blood cells necessary to fight infections. This condition can be fatal if not detected early enough. For this reason, people taking clozapine must have weekly tests to monitor their blood.

Because many patients with schizophrenia continue to experience difficulties despite taking medication, psychological and social rehabilitation is often necessary. A variety of methods can be effective. Social skill training helps people with schizophrenia learn specific behaviours for functioning in society, such as making friends, purchasing items at a store, or initiating conversations. Behavioural training methods can also help them learn self-care skills such as personal hygiene, money management, and proper nutrition. In addition, cognitive-behavioural therapy, a type of psychotherapy, can help reduce persistent symptoms such as hallucinations, delusions, and social withdrawal.

Family intervention programs can also benefit people with schizophrenia. These programs focus on helping family members understand the nature and treatment of schizophrenia, how to monitor the illness, and how to help the patient make progress toward personal goals and greater independence. They can also lower the stress experienced by everyone in the family and help prevent the patient from relapsing or being rehospitalized.

Because many patients have difficulty obtaining or keeping jobs, supported employment programs that help patients find and maintain jobs are a helpful part of rehabilitation. In these programs, the patient works alongside people without disabilities and earns competitive wages. An employment specialist (or vocational specialist) helps the person maintain their job by, for example, training the person in specific skills, helping the employer accommodate the person, arranging transportation, and monitoring performance. These programs are most effective when the supported employment is closely integrated with other aspects of treatment, such as medication and monitoring of symptoms.

Some people with schizophrenia are vulnerable to frequent crises because they do not regularly go to mental health centres to receive the treatment they need. These individuals often relapse and face rehospitalization. To ensure that such patients take their medication and receive appropriate psychological and social rehabilitation, assertive community treatment (ACT) programs have been developed that deliver treatment to patients in natural settings, such as in their homes, in restaurants, or on the street.

People with schizophrenia often have other medical problems, so an effective treatment program must attend to these as well. One of the most commonly associated problems is substance abuse. Successful treatment of substance abuse in patients with schizophrenia requires careful coordination with their mental health care, so that the same clinicians are treating both disorders at the same time.

The high rate of substance abuse in patients with schizophrenia contributes to a high prevalence of infectious diseases, including hepatitis B and C and the human immunodeficiency virus (HIV). Assessment, education, and treatment or management of these illnesses is critical for the long-term health of patients.

Other problems frequently associated with schizophrenia include housing instability and homelessness, legal problems, violence, trauma and post-traumatic stress disorder, anxiety, depression, and suicide attempts. Close monitoring and psychotherapeutic interventions are often helpful in addressing these problems.

Several other psychiatric disorders are closely related to schizophrenia. In schizoaffective disorder, a person shows symptoms of schizophrenia combined with either mania or severe depression. Schizophreniform disorder refers to an illness in which a person experiences schizophrenic symptoms for more than one month but fewer than six months. In schizotypal personality disorder, a person engages in odd thinking, speech, and behaviour, but usually does not lose contact with reality. Sometimes mental health professionals refer to these disorders together as schizophrenia-spectrum disorders.

Anxiety, is an emotional state in which people feel uneasy, apprehensive, or fearful. People usually experience anxiety about events they cannot control or predict, or about events that seem threatening or dangerous. For example, students taking an important test may feel anxious because they cannot predict the test questions or feel certain of a good grade. People often use the words fear and anxiety to describe the same thing. Fear also describes a reaction to immediate danger characterized by a strong desire to escape the situation.

The physical symptoms of anxiety reflect chronic "readiness" to deal with some future threat. These symptoms may include fidgeting, muscle tension, sleeping problems, and headaches. Higher levels of anxiety may produce such symptoms as rapid heartbeat, sweating, increased blood pressure, nausea, and dizziness.

All people experience anxiety to some degree. Most people feel anxious when faced with a new situation, such as a first date, or when trying to do something well, such as give a public speech. A mild to moderate of an amount of anxiety in these situations is normal and even beneficial. Anxiety can motivate people to prepare for an upcoming event and can help keep them focussed on the task at hand.

However, too little anxiety or too much anxiety can cause problems. Individuals who feel no anxiety when faced with an important situation may lack alertness and focus. On the other hand, individuals who experience an abnormally high amount of anxiety often feel overwhelmed, immobilized, and unable to accomplish the task at hand. People with too much anxiety often suffer from one of the anxiety disorders, a group of mental illnesses. In fact, more people experience anxiety disorders than any other type of mental illness. A survey of people aged 15 to 54 in the United States found that about 17 percent of this population suffers from an anxiety disorder during any given year.

The fourth edition of the Diagnostic and Statistical Manual of Mental Disorders, a handbook for mental health professionals, describes a variety of anxiety disorders. These include generalized anxiety disorder, phobias, panic disorder, obsessive-compulsive disorder, and post-traumatic stress disorder.

People with generalized anxiety disorder feel anxious most of the time. They worry excessively about routine events or circumstances in their lives. Their worries often relate to finances, family, personal health, and relationships with others. Although they recognize their anxiety as irrational or out of proportion to actual events, they feel unable to control their worrying. For example, they may worry uncontrollably and intensely about money despite evidence that their financial situation is stable. Children with this disorder typically worry about their performance at school or about catastrophic events, such as tornadoes, earthquakes, and nuclear war.

People with generalized anxiety disorder often find that their worries interfere with their ability to function at work or concentrate on tasks. Physical symptoms, such as disturbed sleep, irritability, muscle aches, and tension, may accompany the anxiety. To receive a diagnosis of this disorder, individuals must have experienced its symptoms for at least six months.

Generalized anxiety disorder affects about 3 percent of people in the general population in any given year. From 55 to 66 percent of people with this disorder are female.

Phobic anxiety is distinguishable from other forms of anxiety only in that it occurs specifically in relation to a certain object or situation. This anxiety is characterized by physiological symptoms such as a rapid, pounding heartbeat, stomach disorders, nausea, diarrhea, frequent urination, choking feelings, flushing of the face, perspiration, tremulousness, and faintness. Some phobic people are able to confront their fears. More commonly, however, they avoid the situation or object that causes the fear—an avoidance that impairs the sufferer's freedom.

Psychiatrists recognize three major types of phobias. Simple phobias are fears of specific objects or situations such as animals, closed spaces, and heights. The second type, agoraphobia, is fear of open, public places and situations (such as public vehicles and crowded shopping centres) from which escape is difficult; agoraphobics tend increasingly to avoid more situations until eventually they become housebound. Social phobias, the third type, are fears of appearing stupid or shameful in social situations. The simple phobias, especially the fear of animals, may begin in childhood and persist into adulthood. Agoraphobia characteristically begins in late adolescence or early adulthood, and social phobias are also associated with adolescence.

Although agoraphobia is more often seen in treatment than the other types of phobia, it is not believed to be as common as simple phobia. Taken together, the phobias are believed to afflict 5 to 10 persons in 100. Agoraphobia and simple phobia are more commonly diagnosed in women than in men; the distribution for social phobia is not known. Agoraphobias, social phobias, and animal phobias tend to run in families.

Behavioural techniques have proved successful in treating phobias, especially simple and social phobias. One technique, systematic desensitization, involves gradually confronting the phobic person with situations or objects that are increasingly close to the feared ones. Exposure therapy, another behavioural method, has recently been shown more operative in effect. In this procedural technique that finds that phobics are repeatedly exposed to the feared situation or object so that they can see that no harm befalls them; the fear gradually fades. Antianxiety is distributed as an antianxiety drug having been used as palliatives. Antidepressant drugs have also proved successful in treating some phobias.

Behaviour Modification can be a prolonged psychological method for treating maladjustment and for changing observable behaviour patterns. In the behaviour modification process, the procedures are monitored so that changes can be made when necessary. Physical and mental coercion, brain surgery, brainwashing, drug use, and psychotherapy are often considered methods of behaviour modification because they try to, and frequently do, change behaviour. None of them, however, is behaviour modification as the term is used in present-day psychology.

Russian physiologist Ivan Pavlov won the 1904 Nobel Prize in physiology or medicine. Pavlov is best known for his work on reflex behaviour.

The foundation for behaviour modification was laid at the beginning of the 20th century in the experimental laboratory of the Russian physiologist Ivan P. Pavlov. A dog was being trained to salivate when a circle was projected on a screen and not to salivate when an ellipse was shown. The shape of the ellipse was gradually modified to resemble the circle. When only a slight difference between the circle and the ellipse could be perceived, the dog became agitated and no longer displayed the conditioned response it had acquired. This type of disturbance was called an "experimentally induced neurosis."

A second landmark event for behaviour modification took place when Pavlov's conditioning principles were extended to humans. In 1920 the American psychologists John B. Watson and Rosalie Rayner reported an experimental study in which a 11-month-old baby who had previously played with a white laboratory rat was conditioned to be fearful of the rat by associating a loud noise with the animal, a process known as pairing. The psychologist Mary Cover Jones later performed experiments designed to reduce already established fears in children. She found two methods particularly effective: (1) associating a feared object with a different stimulus capable of arousing a positive reaction, and (2) placing the child who feared a certain object with other children who did not.

Behaviour modification techniques were used in the 1940s and '50s by psychologists in South Africa, England, and the United States. Joseph P. Wolpe, a South African physician, questioned the effectiveness of psychotherapy for treating disturbed young adults, especially those with disabling fear reactions. To deal with anxiety disturbances, Wolpe devised treatment procedures based on Pavlov's classical-conditioning model. At about the same time, a group of psychologists in London, headed by Hans J. Eysenck and M. B. Shapiro, launched a new program of research on the development of treatment techniques, basing their investigations on the learning theory of the American psychologist's Clark L. Hull and Kenneth W. Spence.

In the US, two kinds of investigations helped to establish the field of behaviour modification. One was a further extension of the classical-conditioning principles to clinical problems such as bed-wetting and alcoholism. The other was the application of the operant-conditioning principles developed by B. F. Skinner to the education and training of disabled children in schools and institutions and to the treatment of adults in psychiatric hospitals.

By the early 1960s, behaviour modification had become a clearly identifiable applied psychology movement with two components: behaviour therapy and applied behaviour analysis.

Some of the treatment techniques used in behaviour therapy became prominent enough to acquire specific names. Among them are systematic desensitization, aversion therapy, and biofeedback.

Systematic desensitization, the most widely used technique, attempts to treat disturbances having identifiable sources, such as a paralysing fear of closed spaces. This method usually involves training the individual to relax in the presence of fear-producing stimuli. The therapist assumes that the anxiety reaction will be replaced gradually with the new relaxation response; this is called reciprocal inhibition.

Aversion therapy is used to break disabling bad habits. An aversive stimulus, such as an electric shock, is given together with the "bad habit," such as an alcoholic drink. Repeated pairings result in changing the values of such stimuli from positive attraction to repulsion.

Biofeedback is most often used in treating disturbed behaviour that has a physical basis. It provides an individual with information about an ongoing physiological process such as blood pressure or heartbeat rates. By the use of a mechanical device, indications of moment-to-moment variations in bodily functioning can be observed and monitored by the individual. The therapist may provide some reward for desirable changes, such as a decrease in blood pressure.

Applied behaviour analysis is used to develop educational and treatment techniques that can be tailored to each individual's requirements while still following a constant format, whether the patients are retarded or disturbing children in a school or residential setting, or adults in a psychiatric hospital or rehabilitation centre. Five essential steps characterize this approach: (1) Deciding what the individual can do to ameliorate the problem; (2) Devising a program to weaken undesirable behaviour and strengthen desirable substitute behaviour; (3) Complete treatment programs according to behavioural principles (4) Keeping careful and objective records. (5) Alternating the program if progress can thereby be improved.

About 2 percent of people in the United States suffer from panic disorder during any given year, and the condition affects more than twice as many women as men. People with panic disorder may experience panic attacks frequently, such as daily or weekly, or more sporadically. Additionally, panic attacks may occur as part of other anxiety disorders, such as phobias—in which a specific object or situation triggers the attack—and, more rarely, post-traumatic stress disorder.

People with panic disorder frequently develop agoraphobia, a fear of being in places or situations from which escape might be difficult if a panic attack occurs. People with agoraphobia typically fear situations such as travelling in a bus, train, car, or aeroplane, shopping at malls, going to theatres, crossing over bridges or through tunnels, and being alone in unfamiliar places. Therefore, they avoid these situations and may eventually become reluctant to leave their home. In addition, people with panic disorder appear to have an increased risk of alcoholism and drug dependence. Some studies indicate they also have a higher risk of depression and suicide.

Panic disorder, in that of both with and without agoraphobia, results from a combination of biological and psychological factors. Some individuals may inherit a vulnerability to stresses or anxiety, having an increased risk of experiencing panic attacks. In addition, certain physiological cues may trigger a panic attack. For example, if a person experiences a racing heart during a panic attack, he or she may begin to associate this sensation with panic attacks. A rapid heartbeat, even if caused by exercise, may then trigger future panic attacks.

Not everyone who experiences a panic attack develops panic disorder. For example, most people experience rapid heartbeats after running but do not perceive the sensation as dangerous. Those who develop panic disorder tend to interpret their physical sensations as more terrible than they really are. Some psychologists believe that early in childhood experiences of separation from important people, such as parents, increases the risk of developing panic disorder.

Mental health professionals usually treat panic disorder with medications, specialized psychotherapy, or a combination of both. Benzodiazepines, a grouping of tranquillizing medication drugs that include, alprazolam (Xanax) and diazepam (Valium), which often reduce anxiety with few physical side effects. However, these medications can be addictive and may impair movement and concentration in some people. Some antidepressant drugs, such as imipramine (Tofranil), also reduce panic symptoms in some people but can produce side effects, such as dizziness or dry mouth. Another class of drug administration, are the selective serotonin reuptake inhibitors (SSRIs), appearing to reduce panic symptoms with fewer side effects. SSRIs used to treat panic disorder includes paroxetine (Paxil) and fluvoxamine (Luvox). Medication eliminates panic symptoms in 50 to 60 percent of patients. For many patients, however, panic attacks return when they stop taking the medication.

Research has shown that cognitive-behavioural therapy, a type of psychotherapy, eliminates panic attacks in 80 to 100 percent of patients. In this method, therapists help patients re-create the physical symptoms of a panic attack, teach them coping skills, and help them to alter their beliefs about the danger of these sensations. Patients with agoraphobia face their feared situations under the therapist's supervision, using coping skills to overcome their strong anxiety. These coping skills may include physical relaxation techniques, such as deep breathing and muscle relaxation, as well as cognitive techniques that help people think rationally about anxiety-provoking situations. About 70 percent of panic disorder are patients who also have moderate to severe agoraphobia benefit from this type of treatment.

Stress as a [psychology] can be an unpleasant state of emotional and physiological arousals, in unspecific situations when people experience, or that of its perception of something perceived as dangerous or life threatening, in of which the situational circumstance or consequent, of either a psychological or emotional succumbing to some unduly influence through which of the inherent perceptions of the world have.

In becoming of either a psychological or emotional situation or event, however the interpretive measure on which prove it to be a pathological situation, as accorded to this information, all of which could be an immediate misinterpretation that gives into false representation, especially a world less interpreted by inherent perceptions as situational or eventful circumstance or the consequent interpretation, given by false or misguided representations.

Defining stress for being eventful or situational that of causing them to feel bodily tensions, pressure, or negative emotions such as anxiety and anger. Others view stress as the response to these situations. This response includes physiological changes, such as increased heart rate and muscle tension, as well as emotional and behavioural changes. However, most psychologists regard stress as a process involving a person's interpretation and response to a threatening event.

Stress is a common experience. We may feel stress when we are very busy, have important deadlines to meet, or have too little time to finish all of our tasks. Often people experience stresses, because of problems at work or in social relationships, such as a poor evaluation by a supervisor or an argument with a friend. Some people may be particularly vulnerable to stress in situations involving the threat of failure or personal humiliation. Others have extreme fears of objects or things associated with physical threats, such as snakes, illness, storms, or flying in an aeroplane- and becoming stressed when they encounter or think about these perceived threats. Major life events, such as the death of a loved one, can cause severe stress.

Stress can have both positive and negative effects. Stress is a normal, adaptive reaction to threat. It signals danger and prepares us to take defensive action. Fear of things that pose realistic threat motivates us to deal with them or avoid them. Stress also motivates us to achieve and fuels creativity. Although stress may hinder performance on difficult tasks, moderate stress seems to improve motivation and performance of fewer complex tasks. In personal relationships, stress often leads to less cooperation and more aggression.

If not managed appropriately, stress can lead to serious problems. Exposure to chronic stress can contribute to both physical illnesses, such as heart disease, and mental illnesses, such as anxiety disorders. The field of health psychology focuses in part on how stress affects bodily functioning and on how people can use stress management techniques to prevent or minimize disease.

The circumstances that cause stress are called stressors. Stressors vary in severity and duration. For example, the responsibility of caring for a sick parent may be an ongoing source of major stress, whereas getting stuck in a traffic jam may cause mild, short-term stress. Some events, such as the death of a loved one, are stressful for everyone. But in other situations, individuals may respond differently to the same event—what is a stressor for one person may not be stressful for another. For example, a student who is unprepared for a chemistry test and anticipates a bad grade may feel stress, whereas a classmate who studies in advance may feel confident of a good grade. For an event or situation to be a stressor for a particular individual, the person must appraise the situation as threatening and lack the coping resources to deal with it effectively.

Stressors can be classified into three general categories: Catastrophic events, major life changes, and daily hassles. In addition, simply thinking about unpleasant past events or anticipating unpleasant future events can cause stress for many people.

Life-threatening disasters, such as earthquakes, cause severe stress and can take a heavy psychological toll on their victims. Pictured here are buildings in Mexico City destroyed by a September 1985 earthquake. The quake left almost 30,000 people homeless and 7000 dead.

A catastrophe is a sudden, often life-threatening calamity or disaster that pushes people to the outer limits of their coping capability. Catastrophes include natural disasters—such as earthquakes, tornadoes, fires, floods, and hurricanes—as well as wars, torture, automobile accidents, violent physical attacks, and sexual assaults. Catastrophes often continue to affect their victims' mental health long after the event has ended. For example, in 1972 a dam burst and flooded the West Virginia mining town of Buffalo Creek, destroying the town. Two years after the disaster, most of the adult survivors continued to show emotional disturbances. Similarly, most of the survivors of concentration camps in World War II (1939-1945) continued to experience nightmares and other symptoms of severe emotional problems long after their release from the camps.

The most stressful events for adults involve major life changes, such as death of a spouse or family member, divorce, imprisonment, losing one's job, and major personal disability or illness. For adolescents, the most stressful events are the death of a parent or a close family member, divorce of their parents, imprisonment of their mother or father, and major personal disability or illness. Sometimes, apparently positive events can have stressful components. For example, a woman who gets a job promotion may receive a higher salary and greater prestige, but she may also feel stress from supervising coworkers who were once peers. Getting married is usually considered a positive experience, but planning the wedding, deciding whom to invite, and dealing with family members may cause couples to feel stressed.

Much of the stress in our lives results from having to deal with daily hassles pertaining to our jobs, personal relationships, and everyday living circumstances. Many people's experience the same and every day hassles. Examples of daily hassles include living in a noisy neighbourhood, commuting to work in heavy traffic, disliking one's fellow workers, worrying about owing money, waiting in a long line, and misplacing or losing things. When taken individually, these hassles may feel like only minor irritants, but cumulatively, over time, they can cause significant stress. The amounting of exposure people has to daily hassles is strongly related to their daily mood. Generally, the greater their exposure is to hassles, the worse is their mood. Studies have found that one's exposure to daily hassles is actually more predictive of illness than is exposure to major life events.

Studies conducted in countries around the world demonstrate that people can actually work themselves to death. Factors such as workplace stress and long hours contribute to the risk of death from overwork. In this article from Scientific American Presents, Harvey B. Simon, a professor at Harvard Medical School, explores recent findings about the dangers of working too hard and suggests ways of developing healthier work habits.

A person who is stressed typically has anxious thoughts and difficulty concentrating or remembering. Stress can also change outward behaviours. Teeth clenching, hand wringing, pacing, nail biting, and heavy breathing are common signs of stress. People also feel physically different when they are stressed. Butterflies in the stomach, cold hands and feet, dry mouth, and increased heart rate are all physiological effects of stress that we associate with the emotion of anxiety.

When a person appraises an event as stressful, the body undergoes a number of changes that heighten physiological and emotional arousal. First, the sympathetic division of the autonomic nervous system is activated. The sympathetic division prepares the body for action by directing the adrenal glands to secrete the hormones epinephrine (adrenaline) and norepinephrine (noradrenaline). In response, the heart begins to beat more rapidly, muscle tension increases, blood pressure rises, and blood flow is diverted from the internal organs and skin to the brain and muscles. Breathing speeds up, the pupils dilate, and perspiration increases. This reaction is sometimes called the fight-or-flight response because it energizes the body to either confront or flee from a threat.

Another part of the stress response involves the hypothalamus and the pituitary gland, parts of the brain that are important in regulating hormones and many other bodily functions. In times of stress, the hypothalamus directs the pituitary gland to secrete an adrenocorticotropic hormone. This hormone, in turn, stimulates the outer layer, or cortex, of the adrenal glands to release glucocorticoid, primarily the stress hormone cortisol. Glucocorticoid, is of any a group of steroid hormones, such as cortisone, that is produced by th e adrenal cortex, is involved in carbohydrate, protein, and fat metabolism, and have anti-inflammatory properties.

Canadian scientist Hans Selye was one of the first people to study the stress response. As a medical student, Selye noticed that patients with quite different illnesses shared many of the same symptoms, such as muscle weakness, weight loss, and apathy. Selye believed these symptoms might be part of a general response by the body to stress. In the 1930s Selye studied the reactions of laboratory rats to a variety of physical stressors, such as heat, cold, poisons, strenuous exercise, and electric shock. He found that the different stressors all produced a similar response: Enlargement of the adrenal glands, shrinkage of the thymus gland (a gland involved in the immune response), and bleeding stomach ulcers.

Selye proposed a three-stage model of the stress response, which he termed the general adaptation syndrome. The three stages in

Selye's model are alarm, resistance, and exhaustion. The alarm stage is a generalized state of arousal during the body's initial response to the stressor. In the resistance stage, the body adapts to the stressor and continues to resist it with a high level of physiological arousal. When the stress persists for a long time, and the body is chronically overactive, resistance fails and the body moves to the exhaustion stage. In this stage, the body is vulnerable to disease and even death.

The stress test, also called an exercise electrocardiogram, measures the heart rate of a person during exercise and identifies any abnormal changes in heart function. Such changes may indicate the presence of coronary or arterial disease.

Physicians increasingly acknowledge that stress is a contributing factor in a wide variety of health problems. These problems include cardiovascular disorders such as hypertension (high blood pressure) coronary heart disease (coronary) atherosclerosis, or narrowing of the heart's arteries, and gastrointestinal disorders, such as ulcers. Stress also appears to be a risk factor in cancer, chronic pain problems, and many other health disorders.

Researchers have clearly identified stress, and specifically a person's characteristic way of responding to stress, as a risk factor for cardiovascular diseases. The release of stress hormones has a cumulative negative effect on the heart and blood vessels. Cortisol, for example, increases blood pressure, which can damage the inside walls of blood vessels. It also increases the free fatty acids in the bloodstream, which in turn leads to plaque buildups on the lining of the blood vessels. As the blood vessels narrow over time, it becomes increasingly difficult for the heart to pump sufficient blood through them.

People with certain personality types seem to be physiologically over responsive to stress and therefore more vulnerable to heart disease. For example, the so-called Type A personality is characterized by competitiveness, impatience, and hostility. When Type A people experience stress, their heart rate and blood pressure climb higher and recovery takes longer than with more easygoing people. The most "toxic" personality traits of Type A people are frequent reactions of hostility and anger. These traits are correlated with an increased risk of coronary heart disease.

Stress also appears to influence the development of cancer, but the relationship is not as well established as it is for cardiovascular diseases. There is a moderate positive correlation between extent of exposure and life stressors and cancer—the more stressors, the greater the likelihood of cancer. In addition, a tendency to cope with unpleasant events in a rigid, unemotional manner is associated with the development and progression of cancer.

Ordinarily the immune system is a marvel of precision. It protects the body from disease by seeking out and destroying foreign invaders, such as viruses and bacteria. But there is substantial evidence that stress suppresses the activity of the immune system, leaving an organism more susceptible to infectious diseases. An organism with a weakened immune system is also less able to control naturally occurring mutant cells that overproduce and lead to cancer.

Numerous studies have linked stress with decreased immune response. For example, when laboratory animals are physically restrained, exposed to inescapable electric shocks, or subjected to overcrowding, loud noises, or maternal separation, they show decreased immune system activity. Researchers have reported similar findings for humans. One study, for example, found weakened immune response in people whose spouses had just died. Other studies have documented weakened immune responses among students taking final examinations; people who are severely deprived of sleep; recently divorced or separated men and women, and generally people of a family member with Alzheimer's disease, and people who have recently lost their jobs.

Stress appears to depress immune function in two main ways. First, when people experience stress, they more often engage in behaviours that have adverse effects on their health: cigarette smoking, using more alcohol or drugs, sleeping less, exercising less, and eating poorly. In addition, stress may alter the immune system directly through hormonal changes. Research indicates that glucocorticoids—hormones that are secreted by the adrenal glands during the stress response—actively suppress the body's immune system.

At one time, scientists believed the immune system functioned more or less as an independent system of the body. They now know that the immune system does not operate by itself, but interacts closely with other bodily systems. The field of psychoneuroimmunology focuses on the relationship between psychological influences (such as stress), the nervous system, and the immune system.

Stress influences mental health as well as physical health. People experiencing a high level of stress, and who cope poorly with this stress—may become irritable, socially withdrawn, and emotionally unstable. They may also have difficulty concentrating and solving problems. Some people under intense and prolonged stress may start to suffer from extreme anxiety, depression, or other severe emotional problems. Anxiety disorders caused by stress may include generalized anxiety disorder, phobias, panic disorder, and obsessive-compulsive disorder. People who survive catastrophes sometimes develop an anxiety disorder called post-traumatic stress disorder. They reexperience the traumatic event again and again in dreams and in disturbing memories or flashbacks during the day. They often seem emotionally numb and may be easily startled or angered.

Coping with stress means using thoughts and actions to deal with stressful situations and lower our stress levels. Many people have a characteristic way of coping with stress based on their personality. People who cope well with stress tend to believe they can personally influence what happens to them. They usually make more positive statements about themselves, resist frustration, remain optimistic, and persevere even under extremely adverse circumstances. Most important, they choose the appropriate strategies to cope with the stressors they confront. Conversely, people who cope poorly with stress tend to have somewhat opposite personality characteristics, such as lower self-esteem and a pessimistic outlook on life.

Psychologists distinguish two broad types of coping strategies: Problems of focussed coping and emotion-focussed coping. The goal of both strategies is to control one's stress level. In problem-focussed coping, people try to short-circuit negative emotions by taking some action to modify, avoid, or minimize the threatening situation. They change their behaviour to deal with the stressful situation. In emotion-focussed coping, people try directly to moderate or eliminate unpleasant emotions. Examples of emotion-focussed coping include rethinking the situation in a positive way, relaxation, denial, and wishful thinking.

To understand these strategies, consider the example of a pre-medical student in college who faces three difficult final examinations in a single week. She knows she must get top grades in order to have a chance at acceptance to medical school. This situation is a potential source of stress. To manage she could organize a study group and master the course materials systematically (problem-focussed coping). Or she could decide that she needs to relax and collect herself for an hour or so (emotion-focussed coping) before proceeding with an action plan (problem-focussed coping). She might also decide to watch television for hours on end to prevent having to think about or study for her exams (emotion-focussed coping).

In general, problem-focussed coping is the most effective coping strategy when people have realistic opportunities to change aspects of their situation and reduce stress. Emotion-focussed coping is most useful as a short-term strategy. It can help reduce one's arousal level before engaging in problem-solving and taking action, and it can help people deal with stressful situations in which there are few problem-focussed coping options.

Support from friends, family members, and others who care for us goes a long way in helping us to get by in times of trouble. Social support systems provide us with emotional sustenance, tangible resources and aid, and information when we are in need. People with social support feel cared about and valued by others and feel a sense of belonging to a larger social network.

A large body of research has linked social support to good health and a superior ability to cope with stress. For example, one long-term study of several thousand California residents found that people with extensive social ties lived longer than those with few close social contacts. Another study had found that in heart-attack victims who lived alone were nearly twice as likely to have another heart attack as those who lived with someone. Even the perception of social support can help people to cope with stress.

Studies have found that people's appraisal of the availability of social support is more closely related to how well they deal with stressors than the actual amount of support they receive or the size of their social network.

Research also suggests that the companionship of animals can help lower stress. For example, one study found that in times of stress, people with pet dogs made fewer visits to the doctor than those without pets.

Biofeedback, is a technique in which people learn voluntary control of stress-related physiological responses, as skin temperature, muscle tension, or blood pressure, and heart rates. Normally, people cannot control these responses voluntarily. In biofeedback training, people are connected to an instrument or machine that measures a particular physiological response, such as heart rate, and feeds that measurement back to them in an understandable way. For example, the machine can beep with for each one heartbeat, or display the number of heartbeats per minute on a digital screen. Next, individuals learn to be sensitive to subtle changes inside their body that affect the response system being measured. Gradually, they learn to produce changes in that response system, for example, to voluntarily lower their heart rate. Typically individuals use different techniques and proceed by trial and error until they discover a way to produce the desired changes.

Scientists do not understand the mechanisms by which biofeedback works. Nonetheless, it has become a widely used and generally accepted technique for producing relaxation and lowering physiological arousal in patients with stress-related disorders. One use with the interplay of the biofeedback is in the treatment of tension headaches. By learning to lower muscle tension in the forehead, scalp, and neck, many tension headache sufferers can find long-term relief.

In addition to a biofeedback, two other major methods of relaxation are progressive muscular relaxation and meditation. Progressive muscular relaxation involves systematically tensing and then relaxing different groups of skeletal (voluntary) muscles, while directing one's attention toward the contrasting sensations produced by the two procedures. After practising progressive muscular relaxation, individuals become increasingly sensitive to rising tension levels and can produce the relaxation response during everyday activities (often by repeating a cue word, such as calm, to themselves).

Meditation, in addition to teaching relaxation, is designed to achieve subjective goals such as contemplation, wisdom, and altered states of consciousness. Some forms have a strong Eastern religious and spiritual heritage, based in Zen Buddhism and yoga. Other varieties emphasize a particular lifestyle for practitioners. In most of instances of meditation, transcendental meditation, involved focussing attention on and repeating a mantra, which is a word, sound, or phrase thought to have particularly calming properties.

Both progressive muscle relaxation and meditation reliably reduce stress-related arousal. They have been used successfully to treat a range of stress-related disorders, including hypertension, migraine and tension headaches, and chronic pain.

Aerobic exercise, such as running, walking, biking, and skiing— can help keep stress levels down. Because aerobic exercise increases the endurance of the heart and lungs, an aerobically fit individual will have a lower heart rate at rest and lower blood pressure, less reactivity to stressors, and quicker recovery from stressors. In addition, studies show that people who exercise regularly have higher self-esteem and suffer less from anxiety and depression than comparable people who are not aerobically fit. The American College of Sports Medicine recommends exercising three to four times a week for at least 20 minutes to reduce the risk of cardiovascular disease.

A number of different aspects of life can influence mental health. In a mid-1970s study of people living in the United States, researchers identified critical areas that influence one's mental health. These areas are working life, family life, and the social role that one occupies in the community. Negative experiences in these areas, such as an unreasonable boss or a turbulent family life, can reduce one's overall sense of well-being.

Another important influence on mental health is stress. In general, people experience stress when the demands placed on them exceeds the resource available to meet those demands. Significant sources of stress include major life events, such as divorce, death of a spouse, loss of a job, and illness in the family. These events can overwhelm a person's ability to cope and function effectively. In addition, one source of stress may lead to another, as when financial hardship follows job loss. People whom experience unusually traumatic events, such as rape and natural disasters, may develop post-traumatic stress disorder.

People may experience chronic stress when confronted with a continuing set of demands that reduce their ability to function. Examples of such demands include working long hours under difficult circumstances and caring for a chronically ill relative. Economic hardship, unemployment, and poverty can also produce chronic stress and undermine mental health.

Some studies suggest that genetic factors may partly determine one's level of happiness and mental health. People seem to display a characteristic level of well-being, with some people usually feeling happy and others typically feeling sad or unhappy. Researchers have found that although people's moods change in response to both positive and negative events, the effect wears off over time. For example, people winning the lottery or receive an unexpected promotion may feel happier at first, but over time they return to their former characteristic level of mental health. Research suggests that one's genetic background—that be, the genes inherited from one's parents—explains more than half of the differences in people's characteristic mood levels. Genes may also partly determine the range of ups and downs that people feel, including whether people have large mood swings or remain stable from day to day.

Post-Traumatic Stress Disorder, a mental illness that some people develop after experiencing traumatic or life-threatening events. Such events include warfare, rape and other sexual assaults, violent physical attacks, torture, child abuse, natural disasters such as earthquakes and floods, and automobile or aeroplane crashes. People who attest to traumatic events may also develop the disorder.

Post-traumatic stress disorder in war veterans is sometimes called shell shock or combat fatigue. In victims of sexual or physical abuse, the disorder has been called rape trauma or battered woman syndrome. The American Psychiatric Association (APA) adopted the current name of the disorder in 1980.

In the late 1960s and early 1970s, mass demonstrations erupted throughout the United States protesting US involvement in the Vietnam War (1959-1975). Thousands of veterans joined together in a national organization, Vietnam Veterans Against the War, that supported and influenced the antiwar movement. In this transcript from an April 22, 1971, hearing before the Senate Committee on Foreign Relations, committee chairman Senator J. William Fulbright exemplified his sympathy for the antiwar movement. Fulbright's comments were followed by the testimony of Vietnam veteran John Kerry, who called for an end to the war. Kerry also detailed what he believed to be the war's negative effect in both Vietnam and the United States. Kerry became a Democratic senator from Massachusetts in 1985.

People with this disorder relive the traumatic event again and again through nightmares and disturbing memories during the day. They sometimes have flashbacks, in which they suddenly lose touch with reality and relive images, sounds, and other sensations from the trauma. Because of their extreme anxiety and distress about the event, they try to avoid anything that reminds them of it. They may seem emotionally numb, detached, irritable, and easily startled. They may feel guilty about surviving a traumatic event that killed other people. Other symptoms include trouble concentrating, depression, and sleep difficulties. Symptoms of the disorder usually begin shortly after the traumatic event, although some people may not show symptoms for several years. If left untreated, the disorder can last for years.

Post-traumatic stress disorder can severely disrupt one's life. Besides the emotional pain of reliving the trauma, the symptoms of the disorder may cause a person to think that he or she is "going crazy." In addition, people with this disorder may have unpredictable, angry outbursts at family members. At other times, they may seem to have no affection for their loved ones. Some people try to mask their symptoms by abusing alcohol or drugs. Others work very long hours to prevent any "down" periods when they might relive the trauma. Such actions may delay the onset of the disorder until these individuals retire or become sober.

Studies have in finding that from 1 to 14 percent of people suffer from post-traumatic stress disorder at some point during their lives. The findings vary widely due to differences in the populations studied and the research methods used. Among people who have survived traumatic events, the prevalence appears to be much higher. The disorder may be particularly prevalent among people who have served in combat. For example, one study of veterans of the Vietnam War (1959-1975) found that veterans exposed to a high level of combat were nine times more likely to have post-traumatic stress disorder than military personnel who did not serve in the war zone of Southeast Asia.

Post-traumatic stress disorder is an extreme reaction to extreme stress. In moments of crisis, people respond in ways that allow them to endure and survive the trauma. Afterward those responses, such as emotional numbing, may persist even though they are no longer necessary.

Not everyone who experiences a traumatic event develops post-traumatic stress disorder. Several factors influence whether people develop the disorder. Those who experience severe and prolonged trauma is more likely to develop the disorder than people who experience less severe trauma. Additionally, those who directly witness or experience death, injury, or attacks are more likely to develop symptoms.

People may also have existed under biological and psychological vulnerabilities that make them more likely to develop the disorder. Those with histories of anxiety disorders in their families may have inherited a genetic predisposition to react more severely toward stress and trauma, than other people. In addition, people's life experiences, especially in childhood, can affect their psychological vulnerability to the disorder. For example, people whose early childhood experiences made them feel that events are unpredictable and uncontrollable have greater likelihood than others of developing the disorder. Individuals with a strong, supportive social network of friends and family members seem somewhat protected from developing post-traumatic stress disorder.

Treatment of post-traumatic stress disorder may involve psychotherapy, psychoactive drugs, or both. Psychotherapists help individuals confront the traumatic experience, work through their strong negative emotions, and overcome their symptoms. Many people with post-traumatic stress disorder benefit from group therapy with other individuals suffering from the disorder. Physicians may prescribe antidepressants or anxiety-reducing drugs to treat the mood disturbances that sometimes accompany the disorder.

Stress-Related Disorders, diseases brought on or worsened by psychological stress. These disorders commonly involve the autonomic nervous system, which controls the body's internal organs. Disorders that can be caused by stress include hypertension (high blood pressure), headaches, back pain, skin disorders, irritable bowel syndrome, and ulcers. Stress is also believed to contribute to coronary heart disease (atherosclerosis, or narrowing of the heart's arteries) and some cases of cancer.

Physicians have long recognized that people are more susceptible to diseases of all kinds when subjected to great stress. Negative events, such as the death of a loved one, seem to cause enough stress to lower the body's resistance to disease. Positive circumstances, however, such as a new job or a new baby in the house, can also upset a person's normal ability to fend off disease. Social scientists have devised a list of life events and rated the relative stressfulness of each. With that, the death of their spouse rates of a 100 on the scale; getting divorced, 73, marital separation 65, going to jail 63, also, the death of a close family member 63, a major personal injury or illness 53, and so forth. People also experience stress from daily hassles, such as living in crowded, noisy conditions, commuting to work, and waiting in line. Although these are minor irritants when experienced individually, the cumulative effect of daily hassles can cause substantial stress.

Studies conducted in countries around the world demonstrate that people can actually work themselves to death. Factors such as workplace stress and long hours contribute to the risk of death from overwork. In an article from Scientific American Presents, Harvey B. Simon, a professor at Harvard Medical School, explores recent findings about the dangers of working too hard and suggests ways of developing healthier work habits.

Stress hampers function of the immune system, leaving people more vulnerable to many diseases. It also affects some disorders directly. When people experience stress, their heart beats faster, blood pressure rises, and other body systems prepare to meet the perceived threat. When a person does something active to cope with a threat, these systems return to normal. Running away or fighting—the so-called flight-or-fight response, are both successful ways of coping with many physical threats. Problems arise, however, when the body is prepared to cope with danger but cannot do so. Being caught in a traffic jam, for example, can cause the body to prepare for a flight-or-fight response, but when no action can be taken, the body's systems remain overly active. Similar repeated experiences of this frustrating nature can lead to conditions such as high blood pressure. Scientists attribute at least part of this effect to evolutionary history. They reason that at one time, people had to live with constant physical threats from wild animals and the elements, as well as from one another, and that the body developed in a way that helped it cope with these physical stresses.

Certain personality traits might lead to stress-related disorders. The so-called Type A personality, characterized by competitive, hard-driving intensity, is common in American society. Although early studies suggested a link between Type A behaviour and coronary heart disease, most studies since the 1980s have failed to find such a relationship. However, research has consistently demonstrated that people who show a high level of hostility, anger, and cynicism—often components of Type A behaviour—have a higher risk of coronary heart disease than people without these traits.

High blood pressure, or hypertension, is one of the most common disorders made worse by stress. About 25 percent of adult Americans have high blood pressure. Although it has no noticeable symptoms, hypertension can damage the kidneys and can lead in having a stoke or heart attack

Gastrointestinal problems are an even more common result of stress. Peptic ulcers are sores in the lining of the stomach or the duodenum (the upper part of the small intestine). Most researchers believe that stress contributes to ulcers by causing excessive secretion of hydrochloric acid. Normally this acid aids digestion by breaking down food in the stomach. But when the stomach produces excessive acid in the absence of food, the acid can eat through the protective mucous lining of the stomach or duodenum. Other stress-related gastrointestinal disorders include irritable bowel syndrome and some inflammatory diseases of the colon and bowel, such as regional enteritis.

Stress can also contribute to some respiratory disorders. For example, stress can trigger an attack of asthma. Asthma attacks are characterized by wheezing, panting, and a feeling of being suffocated. In addition, emotional stress can cause or aggravate many skin disorders, from those that produce itching, tickling, and pain to those that cause rashes and acne.

Major traumatic events such as accidents, catastrophes, or battle experiences may bring on a condition called post-traumatic stress disorder. Once known under war conditions as shell shock or battle fatigue, post-traumatic stress disorder gained its current name after it appeared in many veterans returning from the Vietnam War (1959-1975) as they tried to readjust to civilian life. Symptoms may appear long after the initial trauma. These are to include of re-experiencing the trauma through disturbing nightmares and memories, emotional numbness, nervous irritability, depression, and sleep difficulties.

Treatment of stress-related disorders depends on the specific disorder. In some cases, treatment is limited to relieving the particular physical symptom involved. Psychological treatments are directed at helping the person to relieve the source of stress or else to learn to cope more effectively with it. Physicians often recommend combinations of physical and psychological treatments.

Depression is the mental illness in which a person experiences deep, unshakable sadness and diminished interest in nearly all activities. People also use the term depression to describe the temporary sadness, loneliness, or blues that everyone feels from time to time. In contrast to normal sadness, severe depression, also called major depression, can dramatically impair a person's ability to function in social situations and at work. People with major depression often have feelings of despair, hopelessness, and worthlessness, as well as thoughts of committing suicide.

Depression can take several other forms. In bipolar disorder, sometimes called manic-depressive illness, a person's mood swings back and forth between depression and mania. People with seasonal affective disorder typically suffer from depression only during autumn and winter, when there are fewer hours of daylight. Dysthymia is a mood disorder characterized by mild depression (pronounced dis-THI-mee-uh), people have low self-esteem, and concentrate poorly most of the time-often for a period of years, but their symptoms are milder than in major depression. Some people with dysthymia, as a given mood disorder and is characterized by a mild depression. For those as having experienced this occasional episode of major depression. Mental health professionals use the term clinical depression to refer to any of the above forms of depression.

Bipolar disorder is a mental illness that causes mood swings. In the manic phase, a person might feel ecstatic, self-important, and energetic. But when the person becomes depressed, the mood shifts to extreme sadness, negative thinking, and apathy. Some studies indicate that the disease occurs at unusually high rates in creative people, such as artists, writers, and musicians. But some researchers contend that the methodology of these studies was flawed and their results were misleading. In the October 1996 Discover magazine article, anthropologist Jo Ann C. Gutin presents the results of several studies that explore the link between creativity and mental illness.

Surveys indicate that people commonly view depression as a sign of personal weakness, but psychiatrists and psychologists view it as a real illness. In the United States, the National Institute of Mental Health has estimated that depression costs society many billions of dollars each year, mostly in lost work time.

Abraham Lincoln, 16th president of the United States, suffered from episodes of severe depression throughout his life. In 1841 he wrote: "I am now the most miserable man living. If what I feel were equally distributed to the whole human family, there would not be one cheerful face on the earth. Whether I shall ever be better, I cannot tell."

Depression is one of the most common mental illnesses. At least 8 percent of adults in the United States experience serious depression at some point during their lives, and estimates range as high as 17 percent. The illness affects all people, regardless of sex, race, ethnicity, or socioeconomic standing. However, women are two to three times more likely than men to suffer from depression. Experts disagree on the reason for this difference. Some cite differences in hormones, and others point to the stress caused by society's expectations of women.

Studies indicate that depression is more prevalent among women than it is among men. Genetics and environment seem to be the keys to unlocking this gender-gap mystery, although the complexity of the puzzle makes progress slow. In this article for Scientific American Presents, physician Ellen Leibenluft explores the physiology of depression and explains how scientific research may make it possible to develop better treatments for both sexes.

Depression occurs in all parts of the world, although the pattern of symptoms can vary. The prevalence of depression in other countries varies widely, from 1.5 percent of people in Taiwan to 19 percent of people in Lebanon. Some researchers believe methods of gathering data on depression account for different rates.

A number of large-scale studies indicate that depression rates have increased worldwide over the past several decades. Furthermore, younger generations are experiencing depression at an earlier age than did previous generations. Social scientists have proposed many explanations, including changes in family structure, urbanization, and reduced cultural and religious influences.

Although it may appear anytime from childhood to old age, depression usually begins during a person's 20s or 30s. The illness may come on slowly, then deepen gradually over months or years. On the other hand, it may erupt suddenly in a few weeks or days. A person who develops severe depression may appear confused, frightened, and unbalanced in that observers spoke of a decline into a nervous breakdown. However it begins, and depression causes serious changes in a person's feelings and outlook. A person with major depression feels sad nearly every day and may cry often. People, work, and activities that used to bring them pleasure no longer do.

Symptoms of depression can vary by age. In younger children, depression may include physical complaints, such as stomachaches and headaches, as well as irritability, "moping around," social withdrawal, and changes in eating habits. They may feel unenthusiastic about school and other activities. In adolescents, common symptoms include sad mood, sleep disturbances, and lack of energy. Elderly people with depression usually complain of physical rather than emotional problems, which sometimes leads doctors to misdiagnose the illness.

Symptoms of depression can also vary by culture. In some cultures, depressed people may not experience sadness or guilt but may complain of physical problems. In Mediterranean cultures, for example, depressed people may complain of headaches or nerves. In Asian cultures they may complain of weakness, fatigue, or imbalance.

If left untreated, an episode of major depression typically lasts eight or nine months. About 85 percent of people who experience one bout of depression will experience future episodes.

Depression usually alters a person's appetite, sometimes increasing it, but usually reducing it. Sleeping habits often change as well. People with depression may oversleep or, more commonly, sleep for fewer hours. A depressed person might go to sleep at midnight, sleep restlessly, then wake up at 5:00 a.m. feeling tired and blue. For many depressed people, early morning is the saddest time of the day.

Depression also changes one's energy level. Some depressed people may be restless and agitated, engaging in fidgety movements and pacing. Others may feel sluggish and inactive, experiencing great fatigue, lack of energy, and a feeling of being worn out or carrying a heavy burden. Depressed people may also have difficulty thinking, poor concentration, and problems with memory.

People with depression often experience feelings of worthlessness, helplessness, guilt, and self-blame. They may interpret a minor failing on their part as a sign of incompetence or interpret minor criticism as condemnation. Some depressed people complain of being spiritually or morally dead. The mirror seems to reflect someone ugly and repulsive. Even a competent and decent person may feel deficient, cruel, stupid, phony, or guilty of having deceived others. People with major depression may experience such extreme emotional pain that they consider or attempt suicide. At least 15 percent of seriously depressed people commit suicide, and many more attempt it.

In some cases, people with depression may experience psychotic symptoms, such as delusions (false beliefs) and hallucinations (false sensory perceptions). Psychotic symptoms indicate an especially severe illness. Compared to other depressed people, those with psychotic symptoms have longer hospital stays, and after leaving, they are more likely to be moody and unhappy. They are also more likely to commit suicide.

Some depressions seem to come out of the blue, even when things are going well. Others seem to have an obvious cause: a marital conflict, financial difficulty, or some personal failure. Yet many people with these problems do not become deeply depressed. Most psychologists believe depression results from an interaction between stressful life events and a person's biological and psychological vulnerabilities.

Clinical depression is one of the most common forms of mental illness. Although depression can be treated with psychotherapy, many scientists believe there are biological causes for the disease. In the June 1998 Scientific American article, neurobiologist Charles B. Nemeroff discusses the connection between biochemical changes in the brain and depression.

Depression runs in families. By studying twins, researchers have found evidence of a strong genetic influence in depression. Genetically identical twins raised in the same environment are three times more likely to have depression in common than fraternal twins, who have only about half of their genes in common. In addition, identical twins are five times more likely to have bipolar disorder in common. These findings suggest that vulnerability to depression and bipolar disorder can be inherited. Adoption studies have provided more evidence of a genetic role in depression. These studies show that children of depressed people are vulnerable to depression even when raised by adoptive parents.

Genes may influence depression by causing abnormal activity in the brain. Studies have shown that certain brain chemicals called neurotransmitters play an important role in regulating moods and emotions. Neurotransmitters involved in depression include norepinephrine, dopamine, and serotonin. Research in the 1960s suggested that depression result from lower than normal levels of these neurotransmitters in parts of the brain. Support for this theory came from the effects of antidepressant drugs, which work by increasing the levels of neurotransmitters involved in depression. However, later studies have discredited this simple explanation and have suggested a more complex relationship between neurotransmitter levels and depression.

An imbalance of hormones may also play a role in depression. Many depressed people have higher than normal levels of hydrocortisone (cortisol), a hormone secreted by the adrenal gland in response to stress. In addition, an underactive or overactive thyroid gland can lead to depression.

A variety of medical conditions can cause depression. These include dietary deficiencies in vitamin B6, vitamin B12, and folic acid; generative neurological disorders, such as Alzheimer's disease and Huntington's disease; strokes in the frontal part of the brain; and certain viral infections, such as hepatitis and mononucleosis. Certain medications, such as steroids, may also cause depression.

Psychological theories of depression focuses on the way people think and behave. In a 1917 essay, Austrian psychoanalyst Sigmund Freud explained melancholia, or major depression, as a response to loss—either real loss, such as the death of a spouse, or symbolic loss, such as the failure to achieve an important goal. Freud believed that a person's unconscious anger over loss weakens the ego, resulting in self-hate and self-destructive behaviour.

Cognitive theories of depression emphasize the role of irrational thought processes. American psychiatrist Aaron Beck proposed that depressed people tend to view themselves, their environment, and the future in a negative light because of errors in thinking. These errors include focussing on the negative aspects of any situation, misinterpreting facts in negative ways, and blaming themselves for any misfortune. In Beck's view, people learn these self-defeating ways of looking at the world during early childhood. This negative thinking makes situations seem much worse than they really are and increases the risk of depression, especially in stressful situations.

In support of this cognitive view, people with "depressive" personality traits that appears to be more vulnerable than others to actual depression. Examples of depressive personality traits include gloominess, pessimism, introversion, self-criticism, excessive skepticism and criticism of others, deep feelings of inadequacy, and excessive brooding and worrying. In addition, people who regularly behave in dependent, hostile, and impulsive ways appear at greater risk for depression.

American psychologist Martin Seligman had proposed, that depression stems from "learned helplessness," an acquired belief that one cannot control the outcome of events. In this view, prolonged exposure to uncontrollable and inescapable events leads to apathy, pessimism, and loss of motivation. An adaptation of this theory by American psychologist Lynn Abramson and her colleagues have argued that depression resulted only from helplessness, but also from hopelessness. The hopelessness theory attributes depression to a pattern of negative thinking in which people blame themselves for negative life events, view the causes of those events as permanent, and overgeneralize specific weaknesses as applying to many areas of their life.

Psychologists agree that stressful experiences can trigger depression in people who are predisposed to the illness. For example, the death of a loved one may trigger depression. Psychologists usually distinguish true depression from grief, a normal process of mourning a loved one who has died. Other stressful experiences may include divorce, pregnancy, the loss of a job, and even childbirth. About 20 percent of women experience an episode of depression, known as postpartum depression, after having a baby. In addition, people with serious physical illnesses or disabilities often develop depression.

People who have experienced child abuse appear more vulnerable to depression than others. So, too, do people living under chronically stressful conditions, such as single mothers with many children and little or no support from friends or relatives.

Depression typically cannot be shaken or willed away. An episode must therefore run its course until it weakens either on its own or with treatment. Depression can be treated effectively with antidepressant drugs, psychotherapy, or a combination of both.

Despite the availability of effective treatment, most depressive disorders go untreated and undiagnosed. Studies indicate that general physicians fail to recognize depression in their patients at least half of the time. In addition, many doctors and patients view depression in elderly people as a normal part of aging, even though treatment for depression in older people is usually very effective.

Up to 70 percent of people with depression respond to antidepressant drugs. These medications appear to work by altering the levels of serotonin, norepinephrine, and other neurotransmitters in the brain. They generally take at least two to three weeks to become effective. Doctors cannot predict which type of antidepressant drug will work best for any particular person, so depressed people may need to try several types. Antidepressant drugs are not addictive, but they may produce unwanted side effects. To avoid relapses, people usually must continue taking the medication for several months after their symptoms improve.

Commonly used antidepressant drugs fall into three major classes: Three tricyclics, tricyclics, monoamine oxidase inhibitors (MAO inhibitors), and selective serotonin reuptake inhibitors (SSRIs). Tricyclics, named for their three-ring chemical structure, include amitriptyline (Elavil), imipramine (Tofanil), desipramine (Norpramin), doxepin (Sinequan), and nortriptyline (Pamelor). Side effects of tricyclics may include drowsiness, dizziness upon standing, blurred vision, nausea, insomnia, constipation, and dry mouth.

MAO inhibitors include isocarboxazid (Marplan), phenelzine (Nardil), and tranylcypromine (Parnate). People who take MAO inhibitors must follow a diet that excludes tyramine—a substance found in wine, beer, some cheeses, and many fermented foods— to avoid illness one must rest and eat a balanced diet, to escape from the clutches of some dangerous rise in blood pressure or worse. In addition, MAO inhibitors have many of the same side effects as tricyclics.

Selective serotonin reuptake inhibitors include fluoxetine (Prozac), sertraline (Zoloft), and paroxetine (Paxil). These drugs generally produce fewer and milder side effects than do other types of antidepressants, although SSRIs may cause anxiety, insomnia, drowsiness, headaches, and sexual dysfunction. Some patients have alleged that Prozac causes violent or suicidal behaviour in a small number of cases, but the US Food and Drug Administration has failed to substantiate this claim.

Prozac became the most widely used antidepressant in the world soon after its introduction in the late 1980s by drug manufacturer Eli Lilly and Company. Many people find Prozac extremely effective in lifting depression. In addition, some people have reported that Prozac actually transforms their personality by increasing their self-confidence, optimism, and energy level. However, mental health professionals have expressed serious ethical concerns over Prozac's use as a "personality enhancer," especially among people without clinical depression.

Doctors often prescribe lithium carbonates to standard moods to delay or even prevent subsequent mood swings. Side effects of lithium include nausea, stomach upset, vertigo, and frequent urination.

Studies have shown that short-term psychotherapy can relieve mild to moderate depression as effectively as antidepressant drugs. Unlike medication, psychotherapy produces no physiological side effects. In addition, depressed people treated with psychotherapy appear less likely to experience a relapse than those treated only with antidepressant medication. However, psychotherapy usually takes longer to produce benefits.

There are many kinds of psychotherapy. Cognitive-behavioural therapy is to assume, that depression stems from negative, often irrational thinking about one's misfortunes. In this type of therapy, a person learns to understand and eventually eliminate those habitual negativities by such abstractive thinking. In interpersonal therapy, the therapist helps a person resolve problems in relationships with others that may have caused the depression. The subsequent improvement in social relationships and support helps alleviate the depression. Psychodynamic therapy views depression as the result of internal, unconscious conflicts. Psychodynamic therapists focus on a person's past experiences and the resolution of childhood conflicts. Psychoanalysis is an example of this type of therapy. Critics of long-term psychodynamic therapy will argue that its effectiveness is scientifically unproven.

Hysteria, has become a type of mental illness, stemming of some emotionally laden mental conflicts that appear as physical symptoms, called conversion reactions, or as severe mental dissociation. In modern psychological classification, hysteria is known as solarization disorder or conversion disorder, depending on the specific symptoms displayed. Psychiatric diagnosis of hysteria depends on recognition of a mental conflict and of the unconscious connections between conflict and symptoms. The term mass hysteria is applied to situations in which large groups of people exhibiting the same kinds of physical symptoms with no organic cause. For example, one incident of mass hysteria reported in 1977 involved 57 members of a high school marching band who experienced headache, nausea, dizziness, and fainting after a football game. After a fruitless search for organic causes, researchers concluded that a heat reaction among a few band members had spread by emotional suggestion to other members of the band. The term collective stress reaction is now preferred for these situations.

Psychosomatic Illness, illness that has no basic physical or organic cause but appears to be the result of psychological conditions, such as stress, anxiety, and depression. Such illnesses reflect the general belief that the mind is capable of strongly affecting bodily reactions, and that a person's mental condition can actually cause changes in the chemistry of the body, thereby creating physical illness. In cases of psychosomatic illness, a marked change in the body can often be readily detected.

The most effective treatment for psychosomatic disorders has taken into account of both the physical and the emotional aspects of the disease. The physical symptoms usually cannot be cured until the person's psychological environment has improved. For instance, a business executive working under severe pressure may develop ulcers. Although medicine and a special diet can improve this condition, if the person fails to cut down on work or learn relaxation techniques, he or she will probably continue to suffer from the disease and may even develop additional psychosomatic illnesses. In more serious cases of psychosomatic illness, doctors may recommend that the patient undergo some form of psychotherapy in addition to treatment for the physical aspects of the illness.

Although scientists favour a biological cause of schizophrenia, stress in the environment may affect the onset and course of the illness. Stressful life circumstances, such as growing up and living in poverty, the death of a loved one, an important change in jobs or relationships, or chronic tension and hostility at home, can increase chances of schizophrenia in a person biologically predisposed to the disease. In addition, stressful events can trigger a relapse of symptoms in a person who already has the illness. Individuals who have effective skills for managing stress may be less susceptible to its negative effects. Psychological and social rehabilitation can help patients develop more effective skills for dealing with stress.

Stress-Related Disorders, diseases brought on or worsened by psychological stress. These disorders commonly involve the autonomic nervous system, which controls the body's internal organs. Disorders that can be caused by stress include hypertension (high blood pressure), headaches, back pain, skin disorders, irritable bowel syndrome, and ulcers. Stress is also believed to contribute to coronary heart disease (atherosclerosis, or narrowing of the heart's arteries) and some cases of cancer.

Physicians have long recognized that people are more susceptible to diseases of all kinds when subjected to great stress. Negative events, such as the death of a loved one, seem to cause enough stress to lower the body's resistance to disease. Positive circumstances, however, such as a new job or a new baby in the house, can also upset a person's normal ability to fend off disease. Social scientists have devised a list of life events and rated the relative stressfulness of each. Yet people whom experience stress from daily hassles, such as living in crowded, noisy conditions, commuting to work, and waiting in line. Although these are minor irritants when experienced individually, the cumulative effect of daily hassles can cause substantial stress.

Studies conducted in countries around the world demonstrate that people can actually work themselves to death. Factors such as workplace stress and long hours contribute to the risk of death from overwork. In this article from Scientific American Presents,

Harvey B. Simon, a professor at Harvard Medical School, explores recent findings about the dangers of working too hard and suggests ways of developing healthier work habits.

Stress hampers function of the immune system, leaving people more vulnerable to many diseases. It also affects some disorders directly. When people experience stress, their heart beats faster, blood pressure rises, and other body systems prepare to meet the perceived threat. When a person does something active to cope with a threat, these systems return to normal. Running away or fighting—the so-called flight-or-fight response, are both successful ways of coping with many physical threats. Problems arise, however, when the body is prepared to cope with danger but cannot do so. Being caught in a traffic jam, for example, can cause the body to prepare for a flight-or-fight response, but when no action can be taken, the body's systems remain overly active. Similar repeated experiences of this frustrating nature can lead toward conditions such as high blood pressure. Scientists attribute at least part of this effect to evolutionary history. They reason that at one time, people had to live with constant physical threats from wild animals and the elements, as well as from one another, and that the body developed in a way that helped it cope with these physical stresses.

Certain personality traits may also lead to stress-related disorders. The so-called Type A personality, characterized by competitive, hard-driving intensity, is common in American society. Although early studies suggested a link between Type A behaviour and coronary heart disease, most studies since the 1980s have failed to find such a relationship. However, research has consistently demonstrated that people who show a high level of hostility, anger, and cynicism—often components of Type A behaviour—have a higher risk of coronary heart disease than people without these character traits.

Stress can also contribute to some respiratory disorders. For example, stress can trigger an attack of asthma. Asthma attacks are characterized by wheezing, panting, and a feeling of being suffocated. In addition, emotional stress can cause or aggravate many skin disorders, from those that produce itching, tickling, and pain to those that cause rashes and acne.

Major traumatic events such as accidents, catastrophes, or battle experiences may bring on a condition called post-traumatic stress disorder. Once known under war conditions as shell shock or battle fatigue, post-traumatic stress disorder gained its current name after it appeared in many veterans returning from the Vietnam War (1959-1975) as they tried to readjust to civilian life. Symptoms may appear long after the initial trauma. As these had in concluding the re-experiencing the trauma through disturbing nightmares and memories, emotional numbness, nervous irritability, depression, and sleeping difficulties.

Treatment of stress-related disorders depends on the specific disorder. In some cases, treatment is limited to relieving the particular physical symptom involved. Psychological treatments are directed at helping the person to relieve the source of stress or else to learn to cope more effectively with it. Physicians often recommend combinations of both physical and psychological treatments.

Sedative, any of the drugs used to reduce nervous tension or induce sleep. Often referred to as sedative-hypnotic drugs, these substances generally have a calming and relaxing effect on the central nervous system and muscles when taken in small doses, and a hypnotic, or sleep-producing, affect when taken in larger doses. For centuries alcohol and opium were the only substances known to produce these effects, but in recent decades over 50 other substances have been discovered, each differing slightly in its effect on the user. Among the sedatives prescribed for calming the patient was the tranquillizers, librium (a chlordiazepoxide hydrochloride) and Valium (diazepam), which are commonly used to relieve emotional stress. Drugs administered to produce sleep includes barbiturates such as secobarbital, pentobarbital, and phenobarbital, which produce short, medium, and prolonged durations of sleep, respectively. Chloral hydrate, paraldehyde, antihistamine, and Quaalude (methaqualone) are other sedative-hypnotic drugs.

Sedatives are habit-forming and can cause severe addiction problems. Easily obtainable from physicians, they have become, since the 1960s, among the most abused drugs.

Those individuals in the field of behavioural medicine include specialists in psychology, sociology, anthropology, education, epidemiology, biostatistics, psychiatry, biology, and medicine. Typically, they do research into how stress produces disease, how placebos work, how pain can be regulated, and how patients can be encouraged to comply with medical advice. Among the disorders of greatest concern to scientists in behavioural medicine are high blood pressure, heart disease, obesity, and alcohol and drug abuse.

Stress is pervasive among prison personnel. Stress is a nonspecific physical and emotional response to perceived threats to one's well-being. For correctional officers, stress stems from several sources, including job dissatisfaction, officer-inmate interactions, paperwork and performance pressures, or low self-esteem that precipitates of a somewhat public image, and job risks and liabilities. In the United States, violence by inmates against staff is relatively high. For example, in 1997 officials recorded more than 14,000 assaults by inmates in US prisons. In Canada, one assault by an inmate on a staff member was reported in 1997.

Stress may cause burnout, a syndrome of emotional exhaustion and detachment from one's work. Stress and burnout are especially likely to occur during the first year of a correctional officer's job. Symptoms of burnout may include poorer job performance. Burnout among officers may also result in increased turnover of personnel. Annual turnover rates of prison personnel in the United States range as high as 38 percent, with an average across all prison systems of 14 percent. Canadian correctional officer turnover a registered average for bing 10 percent annually.

The responsibilities of prison wardens include hiring and firing personnel, implementing new correctional policies, insuring the safety of prisoners and staff, and establishing regulations to deal effectively with rule infractions by staff or inmates. However, no single administrative style characterizes the typical prison warden or superintendent. No uniformity exists among the states about how each prison should be managed and what rules should govern the behaviour of correctional officers. In general, fixed and limited correctional budgets impose serious constraints that prevent administrators from being fully effective in the performance of their tasks.

Prison administrators come from diverse backgrounds. Often, former correctional personnel are appointed to warden positions after many years of service in other correctional capacities. Wardens, superintendents, and other prison managers are typically hired or appointed by governors.

The vast majority of prison administrators in the United States are men. Women make up only 20 percent of all administrative prison staff. In a private study of more than 1,500 wardens in the United States, researchers determined that wardens serve an average of about three years. Those with the longest tenure served an average of 13 years. According to this study, about 82 percent of wardens have completed some college and 15 percent possess advanced degrees. Most wardens are between the ages of 39 and 45.

Geneticists have provided some of the oldest proof of a biological component to depression in many people. Depression and manic-depression frequently run in families. Thus, close blood relatives (children, siblings and parents) of patients with severe depressive or bipolar disorder is much more likely to suffer from those or related conditions than are members of the general population. Studies of identical twins (who are genetically indistinguishable) and fraternal twins (whose genes generally are no more alike than those of other pairs of siblings) also support an inherited component. The finding of illness in both members of a pair is much higher for manic-depression in identical twins than in fraternal ones and is somewhat elevated for depression alone.

In the past 20 years, genetic researchers have expended great effort trying to identify the genes at fault. So far, though, those genes have evaded discovery, perhaps because a predisposition to depression involves several genes, each of which makes only a small, hard-to-detect contribution.

Preliminary reports from a study of an Amish population with an extensive history of manic-depression once raised the possibility that chromosome 11 held one or more genes producing vulnerability to bipolar disorder, but the finding did not hold up. A gene somewhere on the X chromosome could play a role in some cases of that condition, but the connection is not evident in most people who have been studied. Most recently, various regions of chromosome 18 and a site on chromosome 21 have been suggested to participate in vulnerability to bipolar illness, but these findings await replication.

As geneticists continue their searches, other investigators are concentrating on neurochemical aspects. Much of that makes to focus on neurotransmitters. In particular, many cases of depression apparently stem at least in part from disturbances in brain circuits that convey signals through certain neurotransmitters of the monoamine class. These biochemicals, all derivatives of amino acids, include serotonin, norepinephrine and dopamine; of these, only evidence relating to norepinephrine and serotonin is abundant.

Monoamines first drew the attention of depression researchers in the 1950s. Early in that decade, physicians discovered that severe depression arose in about 15 percent of patients who were treated for hypertension with the drug reserpine. This agent turned out to deplete the monoamines. At about the same time, doctors found that an agent prescribed against tuberculosis-elevated moods in some users who were depressed. Follow-up investigations revealed that the drug inhibited the neuronal breakdown of monoamines by an enzyme (monoamine oxidase); presumably the agent eased depression by allowing monoamines to avoid degradation and to remain active in brain circuits. Together these findings implied that abnormally low levels of monoamines in the brain could cause depression. This insight led to the development of monoamine oxidase inhibitors as the first class of antidepressants.

But which monoamines were most important in depression? In the 1960s Joseph J. Schildkraut of Harvard University cast his vote with norepinephrine in the now classic "catecholamine" hypothesis of mood disorders. He proposed that the reality of depression stems from a deficiency of norepinephrine (which is also classified as a catecholamine) in certain brain circuits and that mania arises from an overabundance of the substance. The theory has since been refined, acknowledging, for instance, that decreases or elevations in norepinephrine do not alter moods in everyone. Nevertheless, the proposed link between norepinephrine depletion and depression has gained much experimental support. These circuits originate in the brain stem, primarily in the pigmented locus caeruleus, and project to many areas of the brain, including to the limbic system. Of a group of cortical and subcortical areas that play a significant part in regulating emotions.

To understand the recent evidence relating to norepinephrine and other monoamines. It helps to know how those neurotransmitters work. The points of contact between two neurons, or nerve cells, are termed synapses. Monoamines, like all neurotransmitters, travel from one neuron (the presynaptic cell) across a small gap (the synaptic cleft) and attach to receptor molecules on the surface of the second neuron (the postsynaptic cell). Such binding elicits intracellular changes that stimulate or inhibit firing of the postsynaptic cell. The effect of the neurotransmitter depends greatly on the nature and concentration of its receptors on the postsynaptic cells. Serotonin receptors, for instance, come in 13 or more subtypes that can vary in their sensitivity to serotonin and in the effects they produce.

The strength of signalling can also be influenced by the amount of neurotransmitter released and by how long it remains in the synaptic cleft—properties influenced by at least two kinds of molecules on the surface of the releasing cell: autoreceptors and transporters. When an autoreceptor becomes bound by neurotransmitter molecules in the synapse, the receptors signal the cell to reduce its firing rate and thus its release of the transmitter. The transporters physically pump neurotransmitter molecules from the synaptic cleft back into presynaptic cells, a process termed reuptake. Monoamine oxidase inside cells can affect synaptic neurotransmitter levels as well, by degrading monoamines and so reducing the amounting of molecules that find the availability for release.

Among the findings linking impoverished synaptic norepinephrine levels to depression is the discovery in many studies that indirect markers of norepinephrine levels in the brain—levels of its metabolites, or by-products, in more accessible material (urine and cerebrospinal fluid)—are often low in depressed individuals. In addition, postmortem studies have revealed increased densities of certain norepinephrine receptors in the cortex of depressed suicide victims.

Observers unfamiliar with receptor display might assume that elevated numbers of receptors were a sign of more contact between norepinephrine and its receptors and more signal transmission. But this pattern of receptor "up-regulation" is actually one that scientists would expect if norepinephrine concentrations in synapses were abnormally low. When transmitter molecules become unusually scarce in synapses, postsynaptic cells often expand receptor numbers in a compensatory attempt to pick up whatever signals are available.

A recent discovery supporting the norepinephrine hypothesis is that new drugs selectively able to block norepinephrine reuptake, and so increase norepinephrine in synapses, are effective antidepressants in many people. One compound, reboxetine, is available as an antidepressant outside the US and is awaiting approval here.

The data connecting norepinephrine to depression are solid and still growing. Yet research into serotonin has taken a centre stage in the 1990s, thanks to the therapeutic success of Prozac and related antidepressants that manipulate serotonin levels. Serious investigations into serotonin's role in mood disorders, however, have been going on for almost 30 years, ever since Arthur J. Prange, Jr., of the University of North Carolina at Chapel Hill, Alec Coppen of the Medical Research Council in England and their co-workers put forward the so-called permissive hypothesis. This view held that synaptic depletion of serotonin was another cause of depression, one that worked by promoting, or "permitting," a fall in norepinephrine levels.

Defects in serotonin-using circuits could certainly dampen norepinephrine signalling. Serotonin-producing neurons project from the raphae nuclei in the brain stem to neurons in diverse regions of the central nervous system, including those that secrete or control the release of norepinephrine. Norepinephrine, a substance, both a hormone and neurotransmitter, secreted by the adrenal medulla and the nerve endings of th e sympatric nervous system to cause vasoconstriction and increase in heart rate, blood pressure, and the sugar level of the blood, and also called noradrenaline.

Serotonin depletion might contribute to depression by affecting other kinds of neurons as well; serotonin-producing cells extend into many brain regions thought to participate in depressive symptoms—including the amygdala (an area involved in emotions), the some educing amounts (involved in appetite, libido and sleep) and cortical areas that participate in cognition and other higher processes.

Among the findings supporting a link between low synaptic serotonin levels and depression is that cerebrospinal fluid in depressed, and especially in suicidal patients that contain of a reducing amount of serotonin by-products (signifying reduced levels of serotonin in the brain itself). In addition, levels of a surface molecule unique to serotonin-releasing cells in the brain are lower in depressed patients than in healthy subjects, implying that the numbers of serotonergic cells are reduced. Moreover, the density of at least one form of serotonin receptor—type 2—is greater in postmortem brain tissue of depressed patients; as was true in studies of norepinephrine receptors, this up-regulation is suggestive of a compensatory response to too little serotonin in the synaptic cleft.

Further evidence comes from the remarkable therapeutic effectiveness of drugs that block presynaptic reuptake transporters from drawing serotonin out of the synaptic cleft. Tricyclic antidepressants (so-named because they contain three rings of chemical groups) joined monoamine oxidase inhibitors on pharmacy shelves in the late 1950s, although their mechanism of action was not known at the time. Eventually, they were found to produce many effects in the brain, including a decrease in serotonin reuptake and a consequent rise in serotonin levels in synapses. All the same, the tricyclic has or being to have a molecule structures that contain three closed rings, however, tricyclic antidepressants of any a group of antidepressant drugs, such as amitriptyline that contain three fused benzene rings and that block the reuptake of the neurotransmitter's norepinephrine and serotonin in the central nervous system.

Investigators suspected that this last effect accounted for their antidepressant action, but confirmation awaited the introduction in the late 1980s of Prozac and then other drugs (Paxil, Zoloft and Luvox) enabling to block serotonin reuptake transporters without affecting other brain monoamines. These selective serotonin reuptake inhibitors (SSRIs) have now revolutionized the treatment of depression, because they are highly effective and produce in a resulting of lesser amounts of side effects than older drugs do. Today even newer antidepressants, such as Effexor (the trade mark used for the drug venlafaxme) blocking the reuptake of both serotonin and norepinephrine.

Studies of serotonin have also offered new clues to why depressed individuals are more susceptible to heart attack and stroke. Activation and clumping of blood platelets (cell-like structures in blood) contribute to the formation of thrombi that can clog blood vessels and shut off blood flow to the heart and brain, thus damaging those organs. Work in my laboratory and elsewhere has shown that platelets of depressed people are particularly sensitive to activation signals, including, it seems, to those issued by serotonin, which amplifies platelet reactivity too other, stronger chemical stimuli. Further, the platelets of depressed patients bear reduced numbers of serotonin reuptake transporters. In other words, compared with the platelets of healthy people, those in depressed individuals probably are less able to soak up serotonin from their environment and thus to reduce their exposure to platelet-activation signals.

Disturbed functioning of serotonin or norepinephrine circuits, or both, contributes to depression in many people, but compelling work can equally claim that depression often involves the dysregulation of brain circuits that control the activities of certain hormones. Indeed, hormonal alterations in depressed patients have long been evident.

The hypothalamus of the brain lies at the top of the hierarchy regulating hormone secretion. It manufactures and releases peptides (small chains of amino acids) that act on the pituitary, at the base of the brain, stimulating or inhibiting the pituitary's release of various hormones into the blood. These hormones—among them growth hormone, thyroid-stimulating hormone and adrenocorticotropic hormone (ACTH)—control the release of other hormones from target glands. In addition to functioning outside the nervous system, the hormones released in response to pituitary hormones feed back to the pituitary and hypothalamus. There they deliver inhibitory signals that keep hormone manufacture from becoming excessive.

Depressed patients have repeatedly been demonstrated to show a blunted response to a number of substances that normally stimulate the release of developing hormones, but display aberrant responses to the hypothalamic substance that normally induces secretion of the thyroid-stimulating hormones from the pituitary. In addition to a common cause that is non-responsive to antidepressants in the presence of previously undiagnosed thyroid insufficiencies.

All these findings are intriguing, but so far the strongest case has been made for dysregulation of the hypothalamic-pituitary-adrenal (HPA) axis—the system that manages the body's response to stress. When a threat to physical or psychological well-being is detected, the hypothalamus amplifies production of corticotropin-releasing factor (CRF), which induces the pituitary to secrete ACTH. ACTH then instructs the adrenal gland atop each kidney to release a cortisol. Together all the changes prepare the body to fight or flee and cause it to shut down activities that would distract from a self-protection. For instance, a cortisol enhances the delivery of fuel to muscles. At the same time, CRF depresses the appetite for food and sex and heightens alertness. Chronic activation of the HPA axis, however, may lay the ground for illness and, it appears, for depression.

As long ago as the late 1960s and early 1970s, several research groups reported increased activity in the HPA axis in unmedicated depressed patients, as evinced by raised levels of cortisol in urine, blood and cerebrospinal fluid, as well as by other measures. Hundreds, perhaps even thousands, of subsequent studies have in confirming that substantial numbers of depressed patients— particularly those most severely affected—display HPA-axis hyperactivity. Indeed, the finding is surely the most replicated one in all of biological psychiatry.

Deeper investigation of the phenomenon has now revealed alterations at each level of the HPA axis in depressed patients. For instance, both the adrenal gland and the pituitary are enlarged, as the adrenal gland, hypersecretes cortisol, but many researchers, including my colleagues and me at Emory University, has become persuaded that aberrations in CRF-producing neurons of the hypothalamus and elsewhere bear most of the responsibility for HPA-axis hyperactivity and the emergence of depressive symptoms.

Notably, study after study has shown CRF concentrations in cerebrospinal fluid to be elevated in depressed patients, compared with control subjects or individuals with other psychiatric disorders. This magnification of CRF levels is reduced by treatment with antidepressants and by effective electroconvulsive therapy. Further, postmortem brain tissue studies have revealed a marked exaggeration both in the number of CRF-producing neurons in the hypothalamus and in the expression of the CRF gene (resulting in elevated CRF synthesis) in depressed patients as compared with controls. Moreover, delivery of CRF to the brains of laboratory animals produces behavioural effects that are cardinal features of depression in humans, namely, insomnia, decreased appetite, decreased libido and anxiety.

Neurobiologists do not yet know exactly how the genetic, monoamine and hormonal findings piece together, if indeed they always do. The discoveries nonetheless suggest a partial scenario for how people who endure traumatic childhoods become depressed later in life. I call this hypothesis the stress-diathesis model of mood disorders, in recognition of the interaction between experience (stress) and an inborn predisposition (diathesis).

The observation that depression runs in families means that certain genetic traits in the affected families somehow lower the threshold for depression. Conceivably, the genetic features directly or indirectly diminish monoamine levels in synapses or increase reactivity of the HPA axis to stress. The genetically determined threshold is not necessarily low enough to induce depression in the absence of serious stress but may then be pushed still lower by early, adverse life experiences.

If the hyperactivity in the neurons of children persisted through adulthood, these supersensitive cells would react vigorously even to mild stressors. This effect in people already innately predisposed to depression could then produce both the neuroendocrine and behavioural responses characteristic of the disorder.

To test the stress-diathesis hypothesis, we have conducted a series of experiments in which neonatal rats were neglected. We removed them from their mothers for brief periods on about 10 of their first 21 days of life, before allowing them to grow up (after weaning) in a standard rat colony. As adults, these maternally deprived rats showed clear signs of changes in CRF-containing neurons, all in the direction observed in depressed patients, such as rises in stress-induced ACTH secretion and elevations of CRF concentrations in several areas of the brain. Levels of the corticosterone (the rat's cortisol) also rose. These findings suggested that a permanent increase in CRF gene expression and thus in CRF production occurred in the maternally deprived rats, an effect now confirmed by Paul M. Plotsky.

Finding that an increase in CRF-receptor density in certain brain regions of maternally deprived rats. Receptor amplification commonly reflects an attempt to compensate for a decrease in the substance that acts on the receptor. In this case, though, the rise in receptor density evidently occurs not as a balance to decreased CRF but in spite of an increase—the worst of all possibilities. Permanently elevated receptor concentrations would tend to magnify the action of CRF, thereby forever enhancing the depression-inducing effects of CRF and stress.

In an exciting preliminary finding, Plotsky has observed that treatment with one of the selective serotonin reuptake inhibitors (Paxil) returns CRF levels too normal, compensates for any gain in receptor sensitivity or number (as indicated by normal corticosterone production lower down in the axis) and normalizes behaviour (for instance, the rats become less fearful).

We do not know exactly how inhibition of serotonin reuptake would lead to normalization of the HPA axis. Even so, the finding implies that serotonin reuptake inhibitors might be particularly helpful in depressed patients with a history of childhood trauma. Plotsky further reports that all the HPA-axis and CRF abnormalities returned when treatment stopped, a hint that pharmaceutical therapy in analogous human patients might have to be continued indefinitely to block recurrences of depression.

Studies of Bonnet macaque monkeys, which as primates more closely resemble humans, yielded similar results. Newborns and their mothers encountered three foraging conditions for three months after the babies' birth: a plentiful, a scarce and a variable food supply. The variable situation (in which food was available unpredictably) evoked considerable anxiety in monkey mothers, who became so anxious and preoccupied that they basically ignored their offspring. As our model predicts, the neonates in the variable-foraging condition were less active, withdrew from interactions with other monkeys and froze in novel situations. In adulthood, they also exhibited a distinctive feature of elevations in CRF concentrations in spinal fluid.

The rat and monkey data raise profound clinical and public health questions. In the US alone in 1995, more than three million children were reportedly abused or neglected, and at least a million of those reports were verified. If the effects in human beings resemble those of the animals, the findings imply that abuse or neglect may produce permanent changes in the developing brain—changes that chronically boost the output of, and responsiveness to, CRF, and therefore increase the victims' lifelong vulnerability to depression.

If that conclusion is correct, investigators will be eager to determine whether noninvasive techniques able to assess the activity of CRF-producing neurons or the number of CRF receptors could identify abused individuals at risk for later depression. In addition, they will want to evaluate whether antidepressants or other interventions, such as psychotherapy, could help prevent depression in children who are shown to be especially susceptible. Researchers will also need to find out whether depressed adults with a history of abuse need to take antidepressants in perpetuity and whether existing drugs or psychotherapy can restore normal activity in CRF-producing neurons in humans.

The stress-diathesis model does not account for all cases of depression; not everyone who is depressed has been neglected or abused in childhood. But individuals who have both a family history of the condition and a traumatic childhood seem to be unusually prone to the condition. People who have no genetic predisposition to depression (as indicated by no family history of the disorder) could conceivably be relatively protected from serious depression even if they have a bad childhood or severe trauma later in life. Conversely, some people have implicated by underlying vulnerabilities, that even in later life are free of trauma.

More work on the neurobiology of depression is clearly indicated, but the advances achieved so far are already being translated into ideas for new medications. Several pharmaceutical houses are developing blockers of CRF receptors to test the antidepressant value of such agents. Another promising class of drugs activates specific serotonin receptors; such agents can potentially exert powerful antidepressive effects without stimulating serotonin receptors on neurons that play no part in depression.

More therapies based on new understandings of the biology of mood disorders are sure to follow as well. As research into the neurobiological underpinnings progresses, treatment should become ever more effective and less likely to produce unwanted side effects.

A phobia is an excessive, enduring fear of clearly defined objects or situations that interferes with a person's normal functioning. Although they know their fear is irrational, people with phobias always try to avoid the source of their fear. Common phobias include fear of heights (acrophobia), fear of enclosed places (claustrophobia), fear of insects, snakes, or other animals, and fear of air travel. Social phobias involve a fear of performing, of critical evaluation, or of being embarrassed in front of other people.

Panic is an intense, overpowering surge of fear. People with panic disorder experience panic attacks—periods of quickly escalating, intense fear and discomfort accompanied by such physical symptoms as rapid heartbeat, trembling, shortness of breath, dizziness, and nausea. Because people with this disorder cannot predict when these attacks will strike, they develop anxiety about having additional panic attacks and may limit their activities outside the home.

In obsessive-compulsive disorder, people persistently experience certain intrusive thoughts or images (obsessions) or feel compelled to perform certain behaviours (compulsions). Obsessions may include unwanted thoughts about inadvertently poisoning others or injuring a pedestrian while driving. Common compulsions include repetitive hand washing or such mental acts as repeated counting. People with this disorder often perform compulsions to reduce the anxiety produced by their obsessions. The obsessions and compulsions significantly interfere with their ability to function and may consume a great deal of time.

Post-traumatic stress disorder sometimes occurs after people experience traumatic or catastrophic events, such as physical or sexual assaults, natural disasters, accidents, and wars. People with this disorder relive the traumatic event through recurrent dreams or intrusive memories called flashbacks. They avoid things or places associated with the trauma and may feel emotionally detached or estranged from others. Other symptoms may include difficulty sleeping, irritability, and trouble concentrating.

Most anxiety disorders do not have an obvious cause. They result from a combination of biological, psychological, and social factors.

Studies suggest that anxiety disorders run in families. That is, children and close relatives of people with disorders are more likely than most to develop anxiety disorders. Some people may inherit genes that make them particularly vulnerable to anxiety. These genes do not necessarily cause people to be anxious, but the genes may increase the risk of anxiety disorders when certain psychological and social factors are also present.

Anxiety also appears to be related to certain brain functions. Chemicals in the brain called neurotransmitters enable neurons, or brain cells, to communicate with each other. One neurotransmitter, gamma-amino butyric acid (GABA), appears to play a role in regulating one's level of anxiety. Lower levels of GABA are associated with higher levels of anxiety. Some studies suggest that the neurotransmitter's norepinephrine and serotonin play a role in affect with panic disorder.

Psychologists have proposed a variety of models to explain anxiety. Austrian psychoanalyst Sigmund Freud suggested that anxiety result from internal, unconscious conflicts. He believed that a person's mind represses wishes and fantasies about which the person feels uncomfortable. This repression, Freud believed, results in anxiety disorders, which he called neuroses.

In that of any various mental or emotional disorder, such as hypochondria or neurasthenia arising from no apparent organic lesion or change and involving symptoms, such as insecurity, anxiety, depression and irrational fears, but without psychotic symptoms, such as delusion or hallucinations, all, of which are without any scientific use.

More recently, behavioural researchers have challenged Freud's model of anxiety. They believe one's anxiety level relates to how much a person believes events can be predicted or controlled. Children who have little control over events, perhaps because of overprotective parents, may have little confidence in their ability to handle problems as adults. This lack of confidence can lead to increased anxiety.

Behavioural theorists also believe that children may learn anxiety from a role model, such as a parent. By observing their parent's anxious response to difficult situations, the child may learn a similar anxious response. A child may also learn anxiety as a conditioned response. For example, an infant often startled by a loud noise while playing with a toy may become anxious just at the sight of the toy. Some experts suggest that people with a high level of anxiety misinterpret normal events as threatening. For instance, they may believe their rapid heartbeat indicates they are experiencing a panic attack when in reality it may be the result of exercise.

While some people may be biologically and psychologically predisposed to feel anxious, most anxiety is triggered by social factors. Many people feel anxious in response to stress, such as a divorce, starting a new job, or moving. Also, how a person expresses anxiety appears to be shaped by social factors. For example, many cultures accept the expression of anxiety and emotion in women, but expect more reserved emotional displays from men.

Mental health professionals use a variety of methods to help people overcome anxiety disorders. These include psychoactive drugs and psychotherapy, particularly behaviour therapy. Other techniques, such as exercise, hypnosis, meditation, and biofeedback, may also prove helpful.

Psychiatrists often prescribe benzodiazepines, a group of tranquillizing drugs, to reduce anxiety in people with high levels of anxiety. Benzodiazepines help to reduce anxiety by stimulating the GABA neurotransmitter system. Common benzodiazepines include alprazolam (Xanax), clonazepam (Klonopin), and diazepam (Valium). Our classes of antidepressant drugs— tricyclics and selective serotonin reuptake inhibitors (SSRIs) also have proven effective in treating certain anxiety disorders, as apprehension, uncertainty and fear resulting from anticipation of a realistic or fantasied state that even fear, resulting from the anticipation of a threatening and even a situation of impairing physical and psychological functioning. That an uneasy and apprehensive uncertainties, even a matter of some amounting desire from which of torment, arising feelings of anxiousness or uneasiness.

Benzodiazepines can work quickly with few unpleasant side effects, but they can also be addictive. In addition, benzodiazepines can slow down or impair motor behaviour or thinking and must be used with caution, particularly in elderly persons. SSRIs take longer to work than the benzodiazepines but are not addictive. Some people experience anxiety symptoms again when they stop taking the medications.

Therapists who attribute the cause of anxiety to unconscious, internal conflicts may use psychoanalysis to help people to a better understanding and resolve their interiorized conflicts. Other types of psychotherapy, such as cognitive-behavioural therapy, have proven effective in treating anxiety disorders. In cognitive-behavioural therapy, the therapist often educates the person about the nature of his or her particular anxiety disorder. Then, the therapist may help the person, as to encourage the challenge of irrational thought, which leads to anxiety. For example, to treat a person with a snake phobia, a therapist might gradually expose the person to snakes, beginning with pictures of snakes and progressing to rubber snakes and real snakes. The patient can use relaxation techniques acquired in therapy to overcome the fear of snakes.

Research has shown psychotherapy to be as effective or more effective than medications in treating many anxiety disorders. Psychotherapy may also provide more lasting benefits than medications when patients discontinue treatment.

Panic Disorder, a mental illness in which a person experiences repeated, unexpected panic attacks and persistent anxiety about the possibility that the panic attacks will recur. A panic attack is a period of intense fear, apprehension, or discomfort. In panic disorder, the attacks usually occur without warning. Symptoms include a racing heart, shortness of breath, trembling, choking or smothering sensations, and fears of "going crazy," losing control, or dying from a heart attack. Panic attacks may last from a few seconds to several hours. Most peak within 10 minutes and end within 20 or 30 minutes.

About 2 percent of people in the United States suffer from panic disorder during any given year, and the condition affects more than twice as many women as men. People with panic disorder may experience panic attacks frequently, such as daily or weekly, or more sporadically. Additionally, panic attacks may occur as part of other anxiety disorders, such as phobias—in which a specific object or situation triggers the attack—and, more rarely, post-traumatic stress disorder.

People with panic disorder frequently develop agoraphobia, a fear of being in places or situations from which escape might be difficult if a panic attack occurs. People with agoraphobia typically fear situations such as travelling in a bus, train, car, or aeroplane, shopping at malls, going to theatres, crossing over bridges or through tunnels, and being alone in unfamiliar places. Therefore, they avoid these situations and may eventually become reluctant to leave their home. In addition, people with panic disorder appear to have an increased risk of alcoholism and drug dependence. Some studies indicate they also have a higher risk of depression and suicide.

Panic disorder, with or without agoraphobia, results from a combination of biological and psychological factors. Some individuals may inherit a vulnerabilities to stress and anxiety but with an increased risk of experiencing panic attacks. In addition, certain physiological cues may trigger a panic attack. For example, if a person experiences a racing heart during a panic attack, he or she may begin to associate this sensation with panic attacks. Rapid-heart beat, if caused by exercise, may then trigger future panic attacks.

Not everyone who experiences a panic attack develops panic disorder. For example, most people experience rapid heartbeats after running but do not perceive the sensation as dangerous. Those who develop panic disorder tend to interpret their physical sensations as more terrible than they really are. Some psychologists believe that in early childhood experiences of separation from important people, such as parents, increasing the risk of developing panic disorder.

Mental health professionals usually treat panic disorder with medications, specialized psychotherapy, or a combination of both. Benzodiazepines, a grouping of tranquillizing drugs that include alprazolam (Xanax) and diazepam (Valium), often reduce anxiety with few physical side effects. However, these medications can be addictive and may impair movement and concentration in some people. Some antidepressant drugs, such as imipramine (Tofranil), also reduce panic symptoms in some people but can produce side effects such as dizziness or dry mouth. Another class of drugs, selective serotonin reuptake inhibitors (SSRIs), appears to reduce panic symptoms with fewer side effects. SSRIs used to treat panic disorder including paroxetine (Paxil) and fluvoxamine (Luvox). Medication eliminates panic symptoms in 50 to 60 percent of patients. For many patients, however, panic attacks return when they stop taking the medication.

Research has shown that cognitive-behavioural therapy, a type of psychotherapy, eliminates panic attacks in 80 to 100 percent of patients. In this method, therapists help patients re-create the physical symptoms of a panic attack, teach them coping skills, and help them to alter their beliefs about the danger of these sensations. Patients with agoraphobia face their feared situations under the therapist's supervision, using coping skills to overcome their strong anxiety. These coping skills may include physical relaxation techniques, such as deep breathing and muscle relaxation, as well as cognitive techniques that help people think rationally about anxiety-provoking situations. About 70 percent of panic disorders patients who also have moderate to severe agoraphobia benefit from this type of treatment.

Although scientists favour a biological cause of schizophrenia, stress in the environment may affect the onset and course of the illness. Stressful life conditions, as tension, and hostility at home, indicated the chances of schizophrenia in a person biologically predisposed to the disease, that in addition, stressful events or situations can trigger a relapse of symptoms in a person who already has the illness. Individuals who have effective skills for managing stress may be less susceptible to its negative effects. Psychological and social rehabilitation can help patients develop more effective skills for dealing with stress.

Psychosomatic Illness, an illness that has no basic physical or organic cause but appears to be the result of psychological conditions, such as stress, anxiety, and depression. Such illnesses reflect the general belief that the mind is capable of strongly affecting bodily reactions, and that a person's mental condition can actually cause changes in the chemistry of the body, thereby creating physical illness. In cases of psychosomatic illness, a marked change in the body can often be readily detected.

The greatest in extent, amounted to most of the effective treatments for psychosomatic disorder's takes into account both the physical and the emotional aspects of the disease. The physical symptoms usually cannot be cured until the person's psychological environment has improved. For instance, a business executive working under severe pressure may develop ulcers. Although medicine and a special diet can improve this condition, if the person fails to cut down on work or learn relaxation techniques, he or she will probably continue to suffer from the disease and may even develop additional psychosomatic illnesses. In more serious cases of psychosomatic illness, doctors may recommend that the patient undergo some form of psychotherapy in addition to treatment for the physical aspects of the illness.

Psychotherapy, treatment of individuals with emotional problems, behavioural problems, or mental illness primarily through verbal communication. In most types of psychotherapy, a person discusses his or her problems one-on-one with a therapist. The therapist tries to understand the person's problems and to help the individual change distressing thoughts, feelings, or behaviours.

A psychologist listens to her client during a psychotherapy session. Psychotherapy can be an effective treatment for many mental disorders. Some forms of psychotherapy try to help people by resolving their internal, unconscious conflicts, and other forms teach people skills to correct their abnormal behaviour.

People often seek psychotherapy when they have tried other approaches to solving a personal problem. For example, people who are depressed, anxious, or have drug or alcohol problems may find that talking to friends or family members is not enough to resolve their problems. Sometimes people may want to talk to a therapist about problems they would feel uncomfortable discussing with friends or family, such as being sexually abused as a child. Finding a therapist to talk to who is knowledgeable about emotional problems, has patients' best interests at heart, and is relatively objective can be extremely helpful.

Psychotherapy differs in two ways from the informal help or advice that one person may give another. First, psychotherapy is conducted by a trained, certified, or licensed therapists. In addition, treatment methods in psychotherapy are guided by well-developed theories about the sources of personal problems.

At one time the term psychotherapy referred to a form of psychiatric treatment used with severely disturbed individuals, whereas counselling referred to the treatment of people with milder psychological problems or to advise given on vocational and educational matters. Today the distinction between psychotherapy and counselling is quite blurred, and many mental health professionals use the terms interchangeably. Psychotherapists and counsellors often treat the same kinds of problems and use the same set of techniques.

Psychotherapy is an important form of treatment for many kinds of psychological problems. Two of the most common problems for which people seek help from a therapist are depression and persistent anxiety. In the act of depression, the condition of feeling sad or despondent of being depressed. Depression is a psychiatric disorder and characterized by an inability to concentrate, insomnia, loss of appetite, and thoughts of death. It is also called clinical depression, for having a reduction in activity or force, in that which a reduction in psychological vigour or activity.

People with depression may have low self-esteem, and a sense of hopelessness about the future, and a lack of interest in people and activities once found pleasurable. People with anxiety disorders may feel anxious all the time or suffer from phobias, a fear of specific objects or situations. Psychotherapy, by itself or in combination with drug treatment, can often help people overcome or manage these problems.

People experiencing an emotional crisis due to marital problems, family disputes, problems at work, loneliness, or troubled social relationships may benefit from psychotherapy. Other problems often treated with psychotherapy include obsessive-compulsive disorder, personality disorders, alcoholism and other forms of drug dependence, problems stemming from child abuse, and behavioural problems, such as eating disorders and juvenile delinquency.

Mental health professionals do not rely on psychotherapy to treat schizophrenia, a severe mental illness. Drugs are used to treat this disorder. However, some psychotherapeutic techniques may help people with schizophrenia learn appropriate social skills and skills for managing anxiety. Another severe mental illness, bipolar disorder (popularly called manic depression), is treated with drugs or a combination of drugs and psychotherapy.

Before 1950, psychoanalysis was virtually the only form of psychotherapy available. In a traditional psychoanalysis, patients met with a therapist several times a week. Patients would lie on a couch and talk about their childhood, their dreams, or whatever came to mind. The psychoanalyst interpreted these thoughts and helped patients resolve unconscious conflicts. This type of therapy often took years and was very expensive.

Over the next several decades the field of psychotherapy and counselling expanded enormously, both in the number of approaches available and in the number of people choosing to enter the profession. Variants of psychoanalysis emerged that focussed more on the patient's current level of functioning and required less time in therapy. In the 1950s and 1960s therapists began using behavioural and cognitive therapies that focussed less on the inner world of the client and more on the client's problem behaviours or thoughts.

As the number of approaches to therapy grew throughout the 1960s and 1970s, the practice of psychotherapy and counselling spread from hospitals and private psychiatric offices to new settings—elementary schools, high schools, colleges, prisons, mental health clinics, military bases, businesses, and churches and synagogues. With more opportunities for individuals to receive help for their problems, and with more affordable treatments, psychotherapy has become increasingly popular. Although a reliable count of the number of people who receive psychotherapy is difficult to obtain, researchers estimate that 3.5 percent of women and 2.5 percent of men in the United States receive psychotherapy in any given year.

The increased availability and use of psychotherapy have led to more positive attitudes toward mental health care among the general public. Before the 1960s, people often viewed the need for psychotherapy as a sign of personal weakness or a sign that the person was abnormal. Those who received therapy seldom told others about their treatment. Since then the stigma attached to psychotherapy has decreased significantly. It is now common for people to consider seeing a therapist for an emotional problem, and recipients of therapy are more willing to disclose their therapy to friends. Today psychotherapy is a topic of immense public interest. In the scientific community and in the media, people assess methods of therapy and debate which approaches are best for particular problems and disorders.

One of the strongest trends in psychotherapy in recent years has been the shift toward short-term treatment, or brief therapy. Rather than spending years in therapy, clients receive treatment over the course of several weeks or months. Brief therapies usually focus on the client's specific problems and may make use of techniques from a variety of theoretical orientations. Brief approaches to therapy evolved in part from consumer dissatisfaction with the length, scope, and cost of psychoanalysis and similar approaches. With extensive publicity about short-term therapies, many consumers have come to expect faster treatment for mental health problems than in the past.

To provide mental health care at lower costs, managed-care firms, such as health maintenance organizations (HMOs), limit the number of therapy sessions that they will pay for during a year for each insured person. Typical managed-care firms allow up to 20 sessions per year, but some allow as few as 8 sessions per year. Case reviewers for the managed-care company decide how many sessions of therapy each person should receive. Usually a case reviewer will authorize only a small number of sessions at first. If the therapist and client wish to continue beyond this number, the therapist must get approval from the case reviewer for additional sessions. If the client wishes to continue after reaching the maximum, he or she must pay the full cost of therapy.

Other managed-care company's pay therapists a set fee to meet with a client for up to a specified maximum number of sessions depending on the nature of the problem, dissimulated of any interference from case reviewers, for example, a managed-care firm may pay a therapist $200 to hold up to eight sessions with a person. If the client uses all eight sessions, the therapist normally loses money. But if treatment stops after two or three sessions, the therapist makes a profit. This relatively new system is controversial because it creates a financial incentive for the therapist to shorten the length of treatment.

Managed care has affected the practice of psychotherapy in other important ways. Rather than selecting a therapist based on personal referrals, people enrolled in managed-care plans must select from a list of therapists provided by their managed-care organization. Clients cannot be assured of complete confidentiality because therapists must provide case reviewers with treatment plans and details of progress. Increasingly, managed-care companies are reluctant to authorize more than several sessions of psychotherapy, favouring drug treatment instead.

Critics argue that managed-care companies have embraced a "quick fix" mentality that pushes short-term therapy even when long-term therapy may be more appropriate. Others note that managed care has brought greater accountability to the profession of psychotherapy, forcing therapists to justify the effectiveness of their treatment approach. In the late 1990s most Americans with health insurance were enrolled in plans with managed mental health care.

Psychotherapists and counsellors come principally from the fields of psychiatry, psychology, social work, and psychiatric nursing. Their training is quite different, considering that their actual therapeutic techniques may be quite similar.

Psychiatrists are physicians who specialize in the treatment of psychological disorders. They attend medical school for four years to earn an MD. (doctor of medicine) degree. Then they receive training in psychiatry during a residency of three or four years. They differ from other therapists in that they can prescribe medications, such as antidepressants and antianxiety drugs.

Clinical psychologists and counselling psychologists have a PhD (doctor of philosophy) or Psy.D. (doctor of psychology) degree that requires four to six years of graduate study. They work in settings such as businesses, schools, mental health centres, and hospitals. Licensing requirements vary in the United States, but most states require psychologists to have postdoctoral training.

Psychiatric social workers have a master's degree in social work (M.S.W.), usually requiring two years of graduate study. They may work in mental health agencies or medical settings practising individual therapy or family and marital therapy. Psychiatric social workers make up the single largest group of mental health professionals. Licensing requirements vary in the United States.

Psychiatric nurses are registered nurses who usually have a master's degree in psychiatric nursing. They often work in a hospital setting conducting individual or group therapy with patients under the supervision of a psychiatrist.

Psychoanalysts specialize in psychoanalysis. Although anyone may use the title of psychoanalyst, those accredited by the International Psychoanalytic Association are usually psychiatrists, psychologists, or social workers who have completed six to ten years of psychoanalytic training. They are also required to undergo a personal analysis themselves.

All but a few states license professional counsellors, usually under the title of a licensed professional counsellor or licensed mental health counsellor. The National Board for Certified Counsellors offers certification for counsellors who have a minimum of a master's degree and who meet the organization's professional standards.

Members of the clergy—priests, ministers, and rabbis—usually take courses in counselling and psychology as part of their seminary training. Some ministers specialize in pastoral counselling, working with members of a congregation who are in distress.

Any person, even one with no training, can legally use the title of therapist, psychotherapist, or other titles not covered under licensing and certification laws. Therefore, clients should ask therapists who practice under such titles about their academic and professional training.

Psychotherapy encompasses a large number of treatment methods, but each developed from different theories about the causes of psychological problems and mental illnesses. There are more than 250 kinds of psychotherapy, but only a fraction of these has found mainstream acceptance. Many kinds of psychotherapy are offshoots of well-known approaches or build upon the work of earlier theorists.

In individual therapy, a patient or client meets regularly with a therapist, typically over a period of weeks or months. The methods of therapists vary depending on their theory of personality, or way of understanding another individual. Most therapies can be classified as (1) Psychodynamic, (2) humanistic, (3) behavioural, (4) cognitive, or (5) eclectic. In the United States, about 40 percent of therapists consider their approach eclectic, which means they combine techniques from a number of theoretical approaches and often tailor their treatment to the particular psychological problem of a client.

Forms of therapy that treat more than one person at a time includes group therapy, family therapy, and couples therapy. These therapies may use techniques from any theoretical approach. Other forms of therapy specialize in treating children or adolescents with psychological problems.

People seeking help for their problems most often select individual therapy over group therapy and other forms of therapy. People may prefer individual therapy because it allows the therapist to focus exclusively on their problems, without distractions from others.

Also, individuals may desire more privacy and confidentiality than is possible in a group setting. Sometimes people combine individual therapy and group therapy.

In the late 19th century Viennese neurologist Sigmund Freud developed a theory of personality and a system of psychotherapy known as psychoanalysis. According to this theory, people are strongly influenced by unconscious forces, including innate sexual and aggressive drives. In his 1938 British Broadcasting Corporation interview, Freud recounts the early resistance to his ideas and later acceptance of his work. Freud's speech is slurred because he was suffering from cancer of the jaw. He died the following year.

Psychodynamic therapies are those therapies in some way derived from the work of Austrian physician Sigmund Freud, the founder of psychoanalysis. In general, psychodynamic therapists emphasize the importance of discovering and resolving internal, unconscious conflicts, often through an exploration of one's childhood and past experiences. Although psychoanalysis, are a recognized and acknowledged condition of the form of psychodynamic therapy. Theorists have developed many other psychodynamic therapies, some very different from Freud's original techniques.

Sigmund Freud, the founder of psychoanalysis, compared the human mind to an iceberg. The tip above the water represents consciousness, and the vast region below the surface symbolizes the unconscious mind. Of Freud's three basic personality structures— id, ego, and superego—only the id is totally unconscious.

Freud developed the theory and techniques of psychoanalysis in the 1890s. He believed that much of an individual's personality develops before the age of six. He also proposed that children pass through a series of psychosexual stages, during which they express sexual energy in different ways. For example, during the phallic stage, from about age three to age five, children focus on feelings of pleasure in their genital organs. At this time, according to Freud, boys become sexually attracted to their mothers and feel hostility and jealousy toward their fathers. Similarly, girls develop sexual feelings toward their fathers and feel rage toward their mothers. In Freud's view, such innate sexual and aggressive drives cause feelings and thoughts that the person regards as unacceptable. In response, the individual represses these feelings, driving them into the unconscious mind. In the process, three basic personality structures are formed: the id, the ego, and the superego. The id represents unchecked, instinctual drives; the superego is the voice of social conscience; and the ego is the rational thinking that mediates between the id and superego and deals with reality. These three systems function as a whole, not separately. Id forces are unconscious and often emerge without an individual's awareness, causing fear, anxiety, depression, or other distressing symptoms. Freud used the term neurosis to refer to such symptoms.

In psychoanalysis, Freud sought to eliminate neurotic symptoms by bringing the individual's repressed fantasies, memories, and emotions into consciousness. He placed particular emphasis on helping patients uncover memories about early childhood trauma and conflict, which he regarded as the source of emotional problems in adults. At first, he used hypnosis as a way to gain access to a person's unconscious. Later he developed free association, a method in which patients say whatever thoughts come to their minds about dreams, fantasies, and memories. The analyst's interpretations of this material, Freud believed, could provide patients with insight into their unconscious—insight that would help them become less anxious, less depressed, or better in other ways.

Freud also placed great value on what could be learned from transference, the patient's emotional response to the therapist. Freud believed that during therapy, patients transfer repressed feelings toward their family members to their relationship with the therapist. Transference exposes these repressed feelings and allows the patient to work through them. Free association and transference are still central features of Freudian psychoanalysis.

In traditional or classical psychoanalysis the patient lies on a couch and the therapist sits out of sight from the patient. This practice is intended to minimize the presence of the therapist and allow the patient to engage in free association more easily. Classical psychoanalysis requires three to four sessions of therapy each week for several years. At a rate of $100 or more per session, three sessions per week costs more than $15,000 per year. Classical psychoanalysis is not typically covered by insurance plans with managed mental health care. Therefore, relatively few individuals choose this intensive and long-term therapy.

In contemporary forms of psychoanalysis, the duration of therapy is often shorter-between one and four years, meetings may take place one or two times a week. Other psychoanalytically oriented therapists work in a brief format of 30 sessions or less. The patient sits on a chair across from the therapist rather than lying on a couch. Modern psychoanalysts tend to focus more on current functioning and make less use of free association techniques.

American psychoanalyst and social philosopher Erich Fromm stressed the importance of social and economic factors on human behaviour. His focus was a departure from traditional psychoanalysis, which emphasized the role of the subconscious. In this 1969 essay for Collier's Year Book, Fromm presents various explanations for human violence. He argues that violence cannot be controlled by imposing stronger legal penalties, but rather by creating a more just society in which people connect with each other as humans and are able to control their own lives.

Several of Freud's followers developed new theories about the causes of psychological disorders. Three important neo-Freudians were Erich Fromm, Karen Horney, and Erik Erikson, who emphasized the role of social and cultural influences in the formation of personality. All three emigrated from Germany to the United States in the 1930s. Their theories have influenced modern psychodynamic therapists.

Fromm believed that the fundamental problem people had in confronting, in sense of isolation, deriving from their own separability. According to Fromm, the goal of therapy is the orientation for which to establish oneself and redraw the roots as find security by uniting with other people while remaining as separately individualized.

Horney had departed from the Freudian occupation, her belief in the importance of social forces in personality formation. She asserted that people develop anxiety and other psychological problems because of feelings of isolation during childhood and unmet needs for love and respect from their parents. The goal of therapy, in her view, is to help patients overcome anxiety-driven neurotic needs and move toward a more realistic image of themselves.

Erikson extended Freud's emphasis on childhood development to cover the entire lifespan. Referred to as an ego psychologist, he emphasized the importance of the ego in helping individuals develop healthy ways to deal with their environment. Often working with children, Erikson helped individuals develop the basic trust and confidence needed for the development of a healthy ego.

Other psychoanalytic therapists focussed on how relationships develop between the child and others, especially the mother. British pediatrician Donald Winnicott and Austrian-American pediatrician Margaret Mahler were known as object-relations analysts because of their emphasis on the child's love object (such as the mother or father). They and other object-relations therapists, such as Austrian-born British psychoanalyst Melanie Klein, helped patients deal with problems that arose from being separated inappropriately or at too early an age or from their mothers.

Swiss psychiatrist Carl Jung began his studies of human motivation in the early 1900s and created the school of psychoanalysis known as analytical psychology. A contemporary of Austrian psychoanalyst Sigmund Freud, Jung at first collaborated closely with Freud but eventually moved on to pursue his own theories, including the exploration of personality types. According to Jung, there are two basic personality types, extroverted and introverted, which alternate equally in the completely normal individual. Jung also believed that the unconscious mind is formed by the personal unconscious (the repressed feelings and thoughts developed during an individual's life) and the collective unconscious (those inherited feelings, thoughts, and memories shared by all humanity).

Unlike the psychoanalytic therapists, Swiss psychiatrist Carl Jung developed a very different system of therapy. He had worked closely with Freud, but broke away totally from Freud in his own work.

Jung created a school of psychology that he called analytical psychology. He felt that Freud focussed too much on sexual drives and not enough on all of the creative instincts and impulses that motivate individuals. Whereas Freud had described the personal unconscious, which reflected the sum of one person's experience, Jung added the concept of the collective unconscious, which he defined as the reservoir of the experience of the entire human race. The collective unconscious contains images called archetypes that are common to all individuals. They are often expressed in mythological concepts such as good and evil spirits, fairies, dragons, and gods.

In general, Jungian therapists see psychological problems as arising from unconscious conflicts that create disturbances in psychic energy. They treat psychological problems by helping their patients bring material from their personal and collective unconscious into conscious awareness. The therapists do this through a knowledge of symbolism—not only symbols from mythology and folk culture, but also current cultural symbols. By interpreting dreams and other materials, Jungian therapists help their patients become more aware of unconscious processes and become stronger individuals.

Austrian psychologist and psychiatrist Alfred Adler studied under Sigmund Freud, the founder of psychoanalysis, before developing his own theories about human behaviour. Adler's best-known theories stress that individuals are mainly motivated by feelings of inferiority, which he called an inferiority complex.

Like Jung, Austrian physician Alfred Adler believed that Freud overemphasized the importance of sexual and aggressive drives. Adler was particularly interested in sibling relationships, birth order, and relationships with parents. He would ask patients about their early memories and use this information to analyze their attitudes, beliefs, and behaviours. He helped his patients by encouraging them to meet important life goals: love, work, and friendship.

For Adler and modern therapists who draw from his work, interests in others and participation in society are important goals of therapy. Adlerian therapists view therapy in part as educational, and they use a number of innovative action techniques to help patients change mistaken beliefs and interact more fully with family members and others.

Humanistic therapies focus on the client's present rather than past experiences, and on conscious feelings rather than unconscious thoughts. Therapists try to create a caring, supportive atmosphere and to guide clients toward personal realizations and insights. Clients are encouraged to take responsibility for their lives, to accept themselves, and to recognize their own potential for growth and change.

The length of therapy depends on the severity of the problem and on a client's ability to change and try new behaviours. Because humanistic therapies emphasize the relationship between client and therapist and a gradual development of increased responsibility by the client, these therapies come typically in sequential maturation, some taken to be of a year in length or weekly or biweekly sessions.

Three of the most influential forms of humanistic therapy are existential therapy, person-centred therapy, and Gestalt therapy.

Based on a philosophical approach path of people and their existence, existential therapy deals with important life themes. These themes include living and dying, freedom, responsibility to self and others, finding meaning in life, and dealing with a sense of meaninglessness. More than other kinds of therapists, existential therapists examine individuals' awareness of themselves and their ability to look beyond their immediate problems and daily events to problems of human existence.

The first existential therapists were European psychiatrists trained in psychoanalysis who were dissatisfied with Freud's emphasis on biological drives and unconscious processes. Existential therapists help their clients confront and explore anxiety, loneliness, despair, fear of death, and the feeling that life is meaningless. There are few techniques specific to existential therapy. Therapists normally draw on techniques from a variety of therapies. One well-known existential therapy is logotherapy, developed by Austrian psychiatrist Viktor E. Frankl in the 1940s (logo is Greek for 'meaning').

In the 1940s and 1950s American psychologist Carl Rogers developed a form of psychotherapy known as person-centred therapy. This approach emphasizes that each person has the capacity for self-understanding and self-healing. The therapist tries to demonstrate empathy and true caring for clients, allowing them to reveal their true feelings without fear of being judged.

Person-centred therapy, originally called client-centred therapy, is perhaps the best-known form of humanistic therapy. American psychologist Carl Rogers developed this type of therapy in the 1940s and 1950s. Rogers believed that people, like other living organisms, are driven by an innate tendency to maintain and enhance themselves, which in turn moves them toward growth, maturity, and life enrichment. Within each person, Rogers believed, is the capacity for self-understanding and constructive change.

Person-centred therapy emphasizes understanding and caring rather than diagnosis, advice, and persuasion. Rogers strongly believed that the quality of the therapist-client relationship influences the success of therapy. He felt that effective therapists must be genuine, accepting, and empathic. A genuine therapist expresses true interest in the client and is open and honest. An accepting therapist cares for the client unconditionally, even if the therapist does not always agree with him or her. An empathic therapist demonstrates a deep understanding of the client's thoughts, ideas, experiences, and feelings and communicates this empathic understanding to the client. Rogers believed that when clients feel unconditional positive regard from a genuine therapist and feel empathically understood, they will be less anxious and more willing to reveal themselves and their weaknesses. By doing so, clients gain a better understanding of their own lives, move toward self-acceptance, and can make progress in resolving a wide variety of personal problems.

Person-centred therapists use an approach called active listening to demonstrate empathy—letting clients know that they are being fully listened to and understood. First, therapists must show through their body position and facial expression that they are paying attention, for example, by directly facing the client and making good eye contact. During the therapy session, the therapist tries to restate what the client has said and seeks clarification of the client's feelings. The therapist may use such phrases as "What I hear you saying is" and "You're feeling like" The therapist seeks mainly to reflect the client's statements back to the client accurately, and does not try to analyze, judge, or lead the direction of discussion. For example:

> Client: I always felt my husband loved me. I just
> don't understand why this happened.

Therapist: You feel surprised by the fact that he left you, because you thought he loved you. It comes as a real surprise.

Client: M-hm. I guess I haven't really accepted that he could do this to me. A big part of me still loves him.

Therapist: You seem to still be hurting from what he did. The love you have   for him is so strong.

Many therapists, not just those of humanistic orientation, have adopted elements of Rogers's approach.

Gestalt is a German word referring to wholeness and the concept that a whole unit is more than the sum of its parts. Gestalt therapy was developed in the 1940s and 1950s by Frederick (Fritz) Perls, a German-born psychiatrist who immigrated to the United States. Like person-centred therapy, Gestalt therapy tries to make individuals take responsibility for their own lives and personal growth and to recognize their capacity for healing themselves. However, Gestalt therapists are willing to use confrontational questions and techniques to help clients express their true feelings. In the following example, the therapist helps the client become more aware of her own behaviour and her responsibility for it:

Client: You know, you just can't do anything right in today's world.

Therapist: Please repeat that phrase using the word I instead of you.

Client: I can't do anything right, it seems.

Therapist: Would you change the word can't to won't?

Client: I won't do anything right.

Therapist: What won't you do that you want to do?

The general goal of Gestalt therapy is awareness of self, others, and the environment that bring about growth, wholeness, and integration of one's thoughts, feelings, and actions. Gestalt therapists use a wide variety of techniques to make clients more aware of themselves, and they often invent or experiment with techniques that might help to accomplish this goal. One of the best-known Gestalt techniques is the empty-chair technique, in which an empty chair represents another person or another part of the client's self. For example, if a client is angry at herself for not being kinder to her mother, the client may pretend her mother is sitting in an empty chair. The client may then express her feelings by speaking in the direction of the chair. Alternatively, the client might play the role of the understanding daughter while sitting in one chair and the angry daughter while sitting in another. As she talks to different parts of herself, differences may be resolved. The empty-chair technique reflects Gestalt therapy's strong emphasis on dealing with problems in the present.

Behavioural therapies differ dramatically from psychodynamic and humanistic therapies. Behavioural therapists do not explore an individual's thoughts, feelings, dreams, or past experiences. Rather, they focus on the behaviour that is causing distress for their clients. They believe that behaviour of all kinds, both normal and abnormal, is the product of learning. By applying the principles of learning, they help individuals replace distressing behaviours with more appropriate ones. Behavioural therapy is a form of psychotherapy that uses basic learning techniques to modify maladaptive behaviour patterns by substituting new responses to given stimuli for undesirable ones, as behaviour modification is of use in the basic techniques, such as conditioning, biofeedback, reinforcement or aversion therapy, to alter human behaviour.

Typical problems treated with behavioural therapy include alcohol or drug addiction, phobias (such as a fear of heights), and anxiety. Modern behavioural therapists work with other problems, such as depression, by having clients develop specific behavioural goals—such as returning to work, talking with others, or cooking a meal. Because behavioural therapy can work through nonverbal means, it can also help people who would not respond to other forms of therapy. For example, behavioural therapists can teach social and self-care skills to children with severe learning disabilities and to individuals with schizophrenia who are out of touch with reality.

Behavioural therapists begin treatment by finding out as much as they can about the client's problem and the circumstances surrounding it. They do not infer causes or look for hidden meanings, but rather focus on observable and measurable behaviours. Therapists may use a number of specific techniques to alter behaviour. These techniques include relaxation training, systematic desensitization, exposure and response prevention, aversive conditioning, and social skills training.

Relaxation training is a method of helping people with high levels of anxiety and stress. It also serves as an important component of some other behavioural treatments.

In one type of relaxation exercise, people learn to tighten and then relax one muscle group at a time. This method, called progressive relaxation, was developed in the 1930s by American physiologist and psychologist Edmund Jacobson. At first, the therapist gives spoken instructions to the client. Later the client can practice the relaxation exercise at home, using a tape recording of the therapist's voice. The following example, adapted from Jacobson's work, illustrates a brief relaxation procedure:

Just settle back as comfortably as you can, close your eyes, and let yourself relax to the best of your ability . . . but, now both fists tighter and tighter and study the tension as you do so. Keep them clenched and feel the tension in your fists, hands, forearms . . . Now relax. Let the fingers of your hands become loose and observe the contrast in your feelings . . . Now let yourself go and try to become more relaxed all over. Take a deep breath . . . your whole body become more and more relaxed.

Another relaxation technique is meditation. In meditation, people try to relax both the mind and the body. In many forms of meditation, people begin by sitting comfortably on a cushion or chair. Then they gradually relax their body, begin to breathe slowly, and concentrate on a sensation—such as the inhaling and exhaling of breath—or on an image or object. In Transcendental Meditation, a person does not try to concentrate on anything, but merely sits in a quiet atmosphere and repeats a mantra (a specially chosen word) to try to achieve a state of restful alertness.

Systematic desensitization, a procedure developed by South African psychiatrist Joseph Wolpe in the 1950s, gradually teaches people to be relaxed in a situation that would otherwise frighten them. It is often used to treat phobias and other anxiety disorders. The word desensitization refers to making people less sensitive to or frightened of certain situations.

In the first step of desensitization, the therapist and client establish an anxiety hierarchy—a list of fear-provoking situations arranged in order of how much fear they provoke in the client. For a man afraid of spiders, for example, holding a spider may rank at the top of his anxiety hierarchy, whereas seeing a small picture of a spider may rank at the bottom. In the second step, the therapist has the client relax using one of the relaxation techniques described above. Then the therapist asks the client to imagine each situation on the anxiety hierarchy, beginning with the least-feared situation and moving upward. For example, the man may first imagine seeing a picture of a spider, then imagine seeing a real spider from far away, then from a short distance, and so forth. If the client feels anxiety at any stage, he or she is instructed to stop thinking about the situation and to return to a state of deep relaxation. The relaxation and the imagined scene are paired until the client feels no further anxiety. Eventually the client can remain free of anxiety while imagining the most-feared situation.

Asking a client to encounter the feared situation is a technique called in vivo exposure. For the man who is afraid of spiders, a therapist might arrange to go to a park or zoo where visitors can touch large spiders. The therapist would model for the client how to approach a spider and how to handle it. The therapist may also encourage the man to walk gradually closer to the spider, reinforcing his progress with praise and reassurance as he does so. The goal for the therapist and patient would be for the man to pick up the spider.

Problems are rarely as clear and simple as fear of spiders. Therapists may spend considerable time deciding on appropriate goals, which ones to pursue first, and then reevaluating or changing goals as therapy progresses. Systematic desensitization typically takes from 10 to 30 sessions, depending on the severity of the problem. In vivo therapies are more direct and may take less time.

Exposure and response prevention is a behavioural technique often used to treat people with obsessive-compulsive disorder. In this technique, the therapist exposes the client to the situation that causes obsessive thoughts, but then prevents the client from acting on these thoughts. For example, to treat people who compulsively wash their hands because they fear contamination from germs, a therapist might have them handle something dirty and then prevent them from washing their hands. Therapists have also experimented with exposure and response prevention to treat people with bulimia nervosa, an eating disorder in which people engage in binge eating and afterward force themselves to vomit or, more occasionally, take laxatives. The therapist feeds the bulimia patients small amounts of food but prevents them from binging, taking laxatives, or vomiting.

Behavioural therapists occasionally use a technique called aversive conditioning or aversion therapy. In this method, clients receive an unpleasant stimulus, such as an electric shock, whenever they perform an undesirable task or behaviour. For example, therapists treating patients with alcoholism may have them ingest the drug disulfiram (Antabuse). Disulfiram is a drug used in the treatment of alcoholism that interferes with the metabolic degradation of alcohol, producing an unpleasant reaction when even a small quantity of alcohol is consumed.

The drug makes the patients violently sick if they drink alcohol. Many therapists have found that aversive conditioning is not as effective as other behavioural techniques, and as a result, they use this technique very infrequently. For some problems, however, aversive conditioning can work when all other techniques have failed. For example, therapists have found that immediate application of an unpleasant stimulus can eliminate self-mutilation and other self-destructive behaviours in children with autism.

Social skill training is a method of helping people who have problems interacting with others. Clients learn basic social skills such as initiating conversations, making eye contact, standing at the appropriate distance, controlling voice volume and pitch, and responding to questions. The therapist first describes and models the behaviour. Then the patient or client practices the behaviour in skits or role-playing exercises. The therapist watches the exercises and provides constructive criticism and further modelling. Therapists often conduct this kind of training with groups of people with similar problems. Social skills training often can help people with schizophrenia function more easily in public situations and reduce their risk of relapse or rehospitalization.

One popular form of social skills training is assertiveness training, another technique pioneered by Joseph Wolpe. This technique teaches people, often those who are shy, to make appropriate responses when someone does something to them, seems inappropriate or offensive or violates their rights. For example, if a woman has trouble saying no to a coworker who inappropriately asks her to handle some of his job responsibilities, she may benefit from learning how to become more assertive. In this example, the therapist would model assertive behaviour for the client, who would then role-play and rehearse appropriate responses to her coworker.

Cognitive therapies are similar to behavioural therapies in that they focus on specific problems. However, they emphasize changing beliefs and thoughts, rather than observable behaviours. Cognitive therapists believe that irrational beliefs or distorted thinking patterns can cause a variety of serious problems, including depression and chronic anxiety. They try to teach people to think in more rational, constructive ways.

In the mid-1950s American psychologist Albert Ellis developed one of the first cognitive approaches to therapy, rational-emotive therapy, now commonly called rational-emotive behaviour therapy. Trained in psychoanalysis in the 1940s, Ellis quickly became disillusioned with psychoanalytic methods, viewing them as slow and inefficient. Influenced by Alfred Adler's work, Ellis came to regard irrational beliefs and illogical thinking as the major cause of most emotional disturbances. In his view, negative events such as losing a job or breaking up with a lover do not by themselves cause depression or anxiety. Rather, emotional disorders result when a person perceives the events in an irrational way, such as by thinking, "I'm a worthless human being."

Although rational-emotive behaviour therapists use many techniques, the most common technique is that of disputing irrational thoughts. First the therapist identifies irrational beliefs by talking with the client about his or her problems. Examples of irrational beliefs, according to Ellis, include the idea that unhappiness is caused by external events, the idea that one must be accepted and loved by everyone, and the idea that one must always be competent and successful to be a worthwhile person.

To dispute the client's irrational beliefs and longstanding assumptions, rational-emotive behaviour therapists often use confrontational techniques. For example, if a student tells the therapist, "I must get an A on this test or I will be a failure in life," the therapist might say, "Why must you? Do you think your entire career as a student will be through if you get a B?" The therapist helps the client replace irrational thoughts with more reasonable ones, such as "I would like to get an A on the test, but if I don't, I have strategies I can use to do better next time."

Like Ellis before him, American psychiatrist Aaron T. Beck became disenchanted with psychoanalysis, finding that it often did not help relieve depression for his patients. In the 1960s Beck developed his own form of cognitive therapy for treating depression, and later applied it to other disorders. In Beck's view, depressed people tend to have negative views of themselves, interpret their experiences negatively, and feel hopeless about their future. He sees these tendencies as a problem of faulty thinking. Like rational-emotive behaviour therapists, practitioners of Beck's technique challenge the client's absolute, extreme statements. They try to help the client identify distorted thinking, such as thinking about negative events in catastrophic terms, and then suggest ways to change this thinking. The following example illustrates how a cognitive therapist might challenge a client's absolute statement.

Client: Everyone at work is smarter than me.

Therapist: Everyone? Every single person at work is smarter than you?

> Client: Well, maybe not. There are a lot of people at work I don't know well at all. But my boss seems smarter; she seems to really know what's going on.
> Therapist: Notice how we went from everyone at work being smarter than you to just your boss.

Cognitive therapists often give their clients homework assignments designed to help them identify their own irrational patterns of thinking and to reinforce what they learn in therapy. For example, clients often keep a daily log in which they write down distressing emotions, the situation that caused the emotions, their thoughts at the time, whether the thoughts were distorted or not, and alternative ways of thinking about the situation.

Helping individuals change problematic behaviours, thoughts, or feelings is not an easy task. Therapists have tried many creative approaches to help patients, some of which do not fall neatly into the major categories of psychodynamic, humanistic, behavioural, or cognitive. Two such therapies still in use today are transactional analysis and reality therapy.

In the 1950s and 1960s Canadian-American psychiatrist Eric Berne developed a form of therapy he called transactional analysis. Although trained in psychoanalysis, Berne felt that the complexity of psychoanalytic terminology excluded patients from full participation in their own treatment. He developed a theory of personality based on the view that when people interact with each other, they function as either a parent, adult, or tike. For example, he would characterize social interactions between two people as parent-adult, parent-child, adult-child, adult-adult, and so forth depending on the situation. He referred to social interactions as transactions and to analysis of these interactions as transactional analysis.

In therapy, which is often conducted in groups, patients learn to recognize when they are assuming one of these roles and to understand when being an authoritarian parent or an impulsive child is appropriate or inappropriate. In addition to identifying these roles, clients learn how to change roles in order to behave in more desirable ways.

American psychiatrist William Glasser developed reality therapy in the 1960s, after working with teenage girls in a correctional institution and observing work with severely disturbed schizophrenic patients in a mental hospital. He observed that psychoanalysis did not help many of his patients change their behaviour, even when they understood the sources of it. Glasser felt it was important to help individuals take responsibility for their own lives and to blame others less. Largely because of this emphasis on personal responsibility, his approach has found widespread acceptance between drug and alcohol-abuse counsellors, corrections' workers, school counsellors, and those working with clients who may be disruptive to others.

Reality therapy is based on the premise that all human behaviour is motivated by fundamental needs and specific wants. The reality therapist first seeks to establish a friendly, trusting relationship with clients in which they can express their needs and wants. Then the therapist helps clients explore the behaviours that created problems for them. Clients are encouraged to examine the consequences of their behaviour and to evaluate how well their behaviour helped them fulfill their wants. The therapist does not accept excuses from clients. Finally, the therapist helps the client formulate a concrete plan of action to change certain behaviours, based on the client's own goals and ability to make choices.

Currently, many therapists describe their approach as eclectic or integrative, meaning that they use ideas and techniques from a variety of therapies. Many therapists like the opportunity to draw from many theories and not limit themselves to one or two. Most therapists who adopt an eclectic approach have a rationale for which techniques they use with specific clients, rather than just choosing an approach randomly or because it suits them at the time.

One of the most influential eclectic approaches is cognitive-behavioural therapy. Other eclectic approaches use other combinations of therapies.

There are almost no pure cognitive or behavioural therapists. Usually therapists combine cognitive and behavioural techniques in an approach known as cognitive-behavioural therapy. For example, to treat a woman with depression, a therapist may help her identify irrational thinking patterns that cause the distressing feelings and to replace these irrational thoughts with new ways of thinking. The therapist may also train her in relaxation techniques and have her try new behaviours that help her become more active and less depressed. The client then reports the results back to the therapist.

Cognitive-behavioural therapy has rapidly become one of the most popular and influential forms of psychotherapy, in part because it takes a relatively short period of time compared to humanistic and psychoanalytic therapies, and also because of its ability to treat a wide range of problems. Sometimes cognitive-behavioural therapy takes only a few sessions, but more often it extends for 20 or 30 sessions over four to six months. The length of therapy usually depends on the severity and number of the client's problems.

Some therapists have one particular way of understanding clients—that is, they cling upon one theory of personality—but use many techniques from a variety of theories. Other therapists may understand clients using two or three theories of personality and only use techniques to bring about changes that are consistent with those theories. Some therapists have combined psychodynamic and behavioural therapies in ways to help their clients deal with fears and anxieties but also understand their causes.

Therapists may use different approaches to treat different problems. For example, a therapist might find that clients who are grieving over the loss of a spouse may respond best to a humanistic approach, in which they can share their grieving and their hurts with the therapist. However, the same therapist may use a cognitive-behavioural approach with a person who reports being anxious most of the time.

All of the individual therapies can also be used with groups. People may choose group therapy for several reasons. First, group therapy is usually less expensive than individual therapy, because group members share the cost. Group therapy also allows a therapist to provide treatment to more people than would be possible otherwise. Aside from cost and efficiency advantages, group therapy allows people to hear and see how others deal with their problems. In addition, group members receive vital support and encouragement from others in the group. They can try out new ways of behaving in a safe, supportive environment and learn how others perceive them.

Groups also have disadvantages. Individuals spend less time talking about their own problems than they would in one-on-one therapy. Also, certain group members may interact with other group members in hurtful ways, such as by yelling at them or criticizing them harshly. Generally, therapists try to intercede when group members act in destructive ways. Another disadvantage of group therapy involves confidentiality. Although group members usually promise to treat all therapy discussions as confidential, some group members may worry that other members will share their secrets outside of the group. Group members who believe this may be less willing to disclose all of their problems, lessening the effectiveness of therapy for them.

Groups vary widely in how they work. The typical group size is from six to ten people with one or two therapists. Often two therapists prefer to work together in a group so that they can respond not only to one person's issues, but also to discussions between group members that may be occurring quickly. Some groups are open or drop-in groups—new clients may join at any time and members may attend or skip whatever sessions they desire. Other groups are closed and admit new members only when all members agree. Regular attendance is usually required in these groups. In closed groups, both the therapist and group members will ask a member to provide an explanation for missing a meeting.

When forming a group, therapists try to make clear to potential participants the goals of the group and for whom it is appropriate. Therapists will often screen potential participants to learn about their problems and decide whether the group is right for them. Sometimes therapists prefer diversity among group members in terms of age, gender, and problem. In other cases, therapists may limit membership in a group to individuals with similar problems and backgrounds. For example, some groups may form specifically for individuals who are grieving the loss of a loved one, individuals who abuse drugs or alcohol, people with eating disorders, people suffering from depression, or troubled elderly individuals.

The techniques used in group therapy depend largely on the theoretical orientation of the therapist. Humanistic therapists tend to respond to the feelings and experiences of other members. They may also interpret or comment on social interactions between group members. In cognitive-behavioural groups, group members try to change their own thoughts and behaviours and support and encourage other members to do the same. Psychoanalytic groups focus on childhood experiences and their impact on participants' current behaviours, thoughts, and feelings.

Psychodrama, the first form of group therapy, was developed in the 1920s by Jacob L. Moreno, an Austrian psychiatrist. Moreno brought his method to the United States in 1925, and its use spread to other parts of the world. Participants involved in psychodrama acts out their problems—often on a real stage and with props—as a means of heightening their awareness of them. The therapist serves as the director, suggesting how participants might act out problems and assigning roles to other group members. For example, a woman might reenact a scene from her childhood with other group members playing her father, mother, brother, or sister. Groups who use psychodramas may do so weekly or simply as a one-time demonstration.

A self-help group or support groups involve people with a common problem, meet regularly to share their experiences, support each other emotionally and encourage change or recovery. They are usually free of charge to interested participants. Self-help groups are not strictly considered psychotherapy because they are not led by a licensed mental health professional. However, they can serve as an important source of help for people in emotional distress.

There are thousands of self-help and support groups in the United States and Canada. The oldest and best known is Alcoholics Anonymous, which uses a 12-step program to treat alcoholism. Other groups have formed for cancer patients, parents whose children have been murdered, compulsive gamblers, battered women, obese people, and many other types of people.

Family therapy involves the participation of one or more members of the same family who seeks help for troubled family relationships or the problems of individual family members. Typical problems that bring families into family therapy are delinquent behaviour by a child or adolescent, a child's poor performance in school, hostilities between a parent and child or between siblings, and severe psychological disturbance or mental illness in a parent or child.

One of the most influential forms of family therapy, family systems therapy, views the family as a single, complex system or unit. Individual members are interdependent parts of the system. Rather than treating one person's symptoms in isolation, therapists try to understand the symptoms in the larger context of the family. For example, a boy who begins picking fights with classmates might do so to get more attention from his busy parents. Therapists work from the rationale, that current family unit relationships profoundly affect, and are affected by, an individual family member's psychological problems. For this reason, most family therapists prefer to work with the entire family during a session, rather than meeting with family members individually.

In most family therapy sessions, the therapist encourages family members to air their feelings, frustrations, and hostilities. By observing how they interact, the therapist can help them recognize their roles and relationships with each other. The therapist tries to avoid assigning blame to any particular family member. Instead, the therapist makes suggestions about how family members might adjust their roles and prevent future conflict.

Couples therapy, also called marital therapy or marriage counselling, is designed to help intimate partners improve their relationship. Therapists treat married couples as well as unmarried couples of the opposite or same sex. Therapists normally hold sessions with both partners present. At certain times during therapy, however, the therapist may choose to see the partners individually.

Couples may seek therapy for a variety of problems, many of which concern a breakdown of communication or trust between the partners. For example, an extramarital affair by one partner may cause the other partner to feel emotional pain, anger, and distrust. Some partners may feel distant from one another or experience sexual problems. In other cases, one or both partners may have psychological problems or alcohol or drug problems that negatively affect their relationship.

The techniques used in therapy vary depending on the theoretical orientation of the therapist and the nature of the couple's problem. Most often, therapists focus on improving communication between partners and on helping them learn to manage conflict. By observing the partners as they talk to each other, the therapist can learn about their communication patterns and the roles they assume in their relationship. The therapist may then teach the partners new ways of expressing their feelings verbally, how to listen to each other, and how to work together to solve problems. The therapist may also suggest that they try out new roles. For example, if one partner makes all of the decisions in the relationship, the therapist may encourage the couple to try sharing decision-making power.

Because most couple's therapists also have been training in family therapy, they often examine the influence of the couple's relationships with parents, children, and siblings. Psychoanalytically oriented therapists may focus on how the partners' childhood experiences affect their current relationship with each other. For couples who cannot work through their differences or reestablish trust and intimacy, separation or divorce may be the best choice. Therapists can help such partners separate in constructive ways.

Some psychotherapists specialize in working with children. Therapists deal with children who are anxious, depressed, or have difficulty getting along with others at home or school. Some children have psychological problems resulting from family issues such as divorce, new stepparents, single-parent homes, death of a parent or sibling, being homeless, or being raised in an alcoholic family. Other children have emotional problems related to physical disabilities, learning disabilities, or attention-deficit hyperactivity disorder.

Play therapy is a special technique that therapists often use with children aged 2 to 12. For children, play is a natural way of learning and relating to others. Play therapy can help therapists both to understand children's problems and to help children deal with their feelings, behaviours, and thoughts. Therapists may use playhouses, puppets, a toy telephone, dolls, sandboxes, food, finger paints, and other toys or objects to help children express their thoughts and feelings. In addition to projecting a caring and gentle manner, therapists who work with children are trained to understand and interpret children's nonverbal and verbal expressions.

For most people, psychotherapy involves a common sequence of events: finding a therapist, assessing the problem, exploring the problem, resolving the problem, and terminating therapy. Sometimes therapy will end prematurely, before the problem is resolved. For example, the therapist or client may move to a new city.

When someone has a personal problem and seeks help from a therapist, the individual may turn to a variety of people to get a referral—a friend, a pastor or rabbi, or a family physician. Phone books list associations of psychologists, psychiatrists, and social workers that can also provide referrals to therapists. As noted earlier, however, some health insurance plans may restrict a person's choice of therapist.

When prospective clients call a therapist for an appointment, they may discuss several aspects of therapy. One concerns of availability—is the therapist taking on new patients? Are there hours when both patient and therapist can meet? Another issue is fees. Both therapists in private practice and those in community mental health agencies have to negotiate fees depending in part on the client's health insurance plan. Some agencies do not require health insurance and have very low fees or a sliding scale that sets fees depending on the ability of the client to pay.

During the first meeting, clients try to explain their problems to the therapist. The therapist usually asks about the nature of the problems, what may make the problems better or worse, and how long the problems have existed. For many therapists, hearing details, even small ones, helps them to assess the problems and to decide the best form of treatment. Some therapists collaborate with clients in deciding the goals of therapy and what treatment methods will be used. Assessment does not stop with the first session, but continues through therapy. Occasionally, goals of therapy change upon assessment of new issues or problems.

During therapy, the client sits across from the therapist—except in classical psychoanalysis, in which the client lies on a couch. The specific nature of the discussions between therapist and client differs greatly depending on the therapist's theoretical orientation. Some therapists are interested in unconscious forces and the early childhood years of the client (psychodynamic therapy), others in actions of the client (behavioural therapy), others in the client's thinking patterns (cognitive therapy), and yet others in all or some of these aspects. Therapists often take notes during a session or make notes after the session has ended. Sessions typically last from 45 to 50 minutes, although therapists may hold longer sessions during the initial stages of treatment. Clients typically meet weekly with the therapist, although some may meet twice a week or more.

When does therapy end? Clients and therapists discuss this issue together and determine when it is best to stop. Ideally their decision depends on their judgments about the client's degree of progress and improvement. Some clients may find that therapy does not seem to be making progress, and may decide to change therapists. However, the cost of therapy may also factor in the decision to end therapy. Managed-care companies generally limit the number of sessions they will subsidize to between 15 and 20. Some therapists, especially those in private practice, may arrange to go beyond these limits by negotiating a fee that the client will pay for services. In other cases, the therapist may refer the client to other mental health agencies that have lower fees and do not require insurance. At the end of therapy, the therapist may schedule a follow-up session several months later to check the client's progress. Also, the therapist and client agree on what to do if the client's problems recur.

Almost since the inception of psychotherapy, therapists and their clients have asked, "Does it work? Does psychotherapy help person resolve their problems, feel better, and change the way they deal with other people?" Therapists and clients are not the only ones asking these questions. In recent years, the agencies that fund mental health services—health insurance companies, health maintenance organizations, and government organizations—have increased their scrutiny of the effectiveness of various psychotherapies in an effort to contain costs.

Measuring the effectiveness of psychotherapy is an extremely complex task. Asking psychotherapists or their clients, "How helpful has therapy been?" is only a start? The answer does provide some information about how therapists and their clients perceive therapy. However, it does not answer the question of whether psychotherapy is effective because both therapists and clients have vested interests in believing that therapy succeeded. Therapists want to uphold their professional reputation and sense of competence, and clients want to feel that their investment of time and money has been worthwhile. Because of these biases, most studies of effectiveness rely on other evaluations of a client's improvement: psychological tests given before and after treatment, reports from the client's friends and family, and reports from impartial interviewers who do not know the client or whether the client received any therapy.

In 1952 British psychologist Hans Eysenck reviewed the results of 24 studies of psychotherapy and came to a controversial conclusion: Although two-thirds of the patients who received psychotherapy showed improvement, a roughly equal proportion of patients who had been on a waiting list for therapy improved with no treatment. According to Eysenck, the patients on the waiting list showed spontaneous remission—recovery without treatment. Although researchers soon exposed flaws in his analysis and problems with the original studies, Eysenck's findings touched off hundreds of new studies on the effectiveness of psychotherapy.

In 1980 American researchers statistically combined the results of 475 studies on psychotherapy outcomes using a technique known as meta-analysis. Their study found that the average psychotherapy recipient showed more improvement than 80 percent of untreated individuals. Later studies have confirmed, that as a whole, psychotherapy is better than no therapy at all. Furthermore, it appears at least as effective as drug treatment for most psychological problems. However, psychotherapy is not effective for everyone. About 10 percent of people who receive psychotherapy show no improvement or actually get worse.

Researchers have also studied how quickly people improve with psychotherapy. One analysis, which reviewed data from more than 2400 psychotherapy patients, found that 50 percent of people receiving once-a-week psychotherapy showed significant improvement after eight sessions, or two months. After six months, or 26 sessions, about 75 percent of people show improvement. However, most people required about a year of psychotherapy for relief from severe symptoms, such as feelings of worthlessness.

Are some types of psychotherapy more effective than others? This question has been hotly debated for decades, and researchers on this issue present many difficulties. In conducting studies that compare different therapies, researchers seek to make sure that each treatment group is as similar as possible. For example, researchers may limit the groups to people with the same severity of depression. In addition, within each treatment group, researchers try to make sure that therapists are using the same techniques and are trained similarly. However, patients do not come to therapy with simple problems that fit easily into studies. Furthermore, therapists of the same theoretical orientation may vary in their techniques and in the skillfulness with which they apply them.

Because of these problems, there is no conclusive answer about which type of therapy is best. Most studies have failed to demonstrate that at any given approach is superior to another. The meta-analysis of 475 studies mentioned earlier, for example, found that psychodynamic, humanistic, behavioural, and cognitive approaches were all about equally effective. In the 1990s a major study by the National Institute of Mental Health compared the effectiveness of cognitive-behavioural therapy, interpersonal psychotherapy (a form of short-term psychodynamic therapy that focuses on social relations), and drug therapy for people with depression. The study found that all three types of treatment helped individuals become less depressed. Furthermore, no one method was significantly more effective than the others.

Some researchers suggest that all therapies share certain qualities, and that these qualities account for the similar effectiveness of therapies despite quite different techniques. For instance, all therapies offer people hope for recovery. People who begin therapy often expect that therapy will help them, and this expectation alone may lead to some improvement (a phenomenon known as the placebo effect). Also, people in psychotherapy may find that simply being able to talk freely and openly about their problems helps them to feel better. Finally, the support, encouragement, and warmth that clients feel from their therapist lets them know they are cared about and respected, which may positively affect their mental health.

Although different therapeutic approaches may be equally effective on average, mental health researchers agree that some types of therapy are best for particular problems. For panic disorder and phobias, behavioural and cognitive-behavioural therapies seem most effective. Behavioural techniques, often in combination with medication, are also an effective treatment for an obsessive-compulsive disorder, post-traumatic stress disorder, generalized anxiety disorder, and sexual dysfunction. Cognitive-behavioural, psychodynamic, and humanistic approaches all provide moderate relief from depression.

Mental health professionals agree that the effectiveness of therapy depends to a large extent on the quality of the relationship between the client and therapist. In general, the better the rapport is between therapist and client, the better the outcome of therapy. If a person does not trust a therapist enough to describe deeply personal problems, the therapist will have trouble helping the person change and improve. For clients, trusting that the therapist can provide help for their problems is essential for making progress.

The founder of person-centred therapy, Carl Rogers, believed that the most important qualities in a therapist are being genuine, accepting, and empathic. Almost all therapists today would agree that these qualities are important. Being genuine means that therapists care for the client and behave toward the client as they really feel. Being accepting means that therapists should appreciate clients for who they are, despite the things that they may have done. Therapists do not have to agree with clients, but they must accept them. Being empathic means that therapists understand the client's feelings and experiences and convey this understanding back to the client.

In helping their clients, all therapists follow a code of ethics. First, all therapy is confidential. Therapists notify others of a client's disclosures only in exceptional cases, such as when children disclose abuse by parents, parents disclose abuse of children, or clients disclose an intention to harm themselves or others. Also, therapists avoid dual relationships with clients—that is, being friends outside of therapy or maintaining a business relationship. Such relationships may reduce the therapist's objectivity and ability to work with the client. Ethical therapists also do not engage in sexual relationships with clients, and do not accept as clients people with whom they have been sexually intimate.

As more immigrants to the United States and Canada have entered therapy, psychotherapists and counsellors have learned the importance of taking a client's cultural background into account when assessing the problem and determining treatment. Scholars recognize that most psychotherapies are based on

Western systems of psychology, which stress the desirability of individualism and independence. However, cultures of Asia and other regions commonly emphasize different values, such as conformity, dependency on others, and obeying one's parents. Thus, techniques that might be effective for someone from North America, Europe, or Australia might be inappropriate for a recent immigrant from Vietnam, Japan, or India. In order to provide effective treatment, therapists must be aware of their own cultural biases and become familiar with their client's ethnic and cultural background.

Sigmund Freud (1856-1939), Austrian physician, neurologist, and founder of psychoanalysis. Freud was born in Freiberg (now P_íbor, Czech Republic), on May 6, 1856, and educated at Vienna University. When he was three years old his family, fleeing from the anti-Semitic riots then raging in Freiberg, moved to Leipzig. Shortly thereafter, the family settled in Vienna, where Freud remained for most of his life.

Although Freud's ambition from childhood had been a career in law, he decided to become a medical student shortly before he entered Vienna University in 1873. Inspired by the scientific investigations of the German poet Goethe, Freud was driven by an intense desire to study natural science and to solve some of the challenging problems confronting contemporary scientists.

In his third year at the university Freud began research work on the central nervous system in the physiological laboratory under the direction of the German physician Ernst Wilhelm von Brücke. Neurological research was so engrossing that Freud neglected the prescribed courses and as a result remained in medical school three years longer than was required normally to qualify as a physician. In 1881, after completing a year of compulsory, military service, he received his medical degree. Unwilling to give up his experimental work, however, he remained at the university as a demonstrator in the physiological laboratory. In 1883, at Brücke's urging, he reluctantly abandoned theoretical research to gain practical experience.

Freud spent three years at the General Hospital of Vienna, devoting himself successively to psychiatry, dermatology, and nervous diseases. In 1885, following his appointment as a lecturer in neuropathology at Vienna University, he left his post at the hospital. Later the same year he was awarded a government grant enabling him to spend 19 weeks in Paris as a student of the French neurologist Jean Charcot. Charcot, who was the director of the clinic at the mental hospital, the Salpêtrière, was then treating nervous disorders by the use of hypnotic suggestion. Freud's studies under Charcot, which centred largely on hysteria, influenced him greatly in channelling his interests to psychopathology.

In 1886 Freud established a private practice in Vienna specializing in nervous disease. He met with violent opposition from the Viennese medical profession because of his strong support of Charcot's unorthodox views on hysteria and hypnotherapy. The resentment he incurred was to delay any acceptance of his subsequent findings on the origin of neurosis.

Freud's first published work, On Aphasia, appeared in 1891; it was a study of the neurological disorder in which the ability to pronounce words or to name common objects is lost as a result of organic brain disease. His final work in neurology, an article, "Infantile Cerebral Paralysis," was written in 1897 for an encyclopaedia only at the insistence of the editor, since by this time Freud was occupied largely with psychological rather than physiological explanations for mental illnesses. His subsequent writing were devoted entirely to that field, which he had named psychoanalysis in 1896.

Freud's new orientation was heralded by his collaborative work on hysteria with the Viennese physician Josef Breuer. The work was presented in 1893 in a preliminary paper and two years later in an expanded form under the title Studies on Hysteria. In this work the symptoms of hysteria were ascribed to manifestations of undischarged emotional energy associated with forgotten psychic traumas. The therapeutic procedure involved the use of a hypnotic state in which the patient was led to recall and reenact the traumatic experience, thus discharging by catharsis the emotions causing the symptoms. The publication of this work marked the beginning of psychoanalytic theory formulated on the basis of clinical observations.

During the intermittent period from 1895 though until the 1900s, Freud developed many of the concepts that were later incorporated into psychoanalytic practice and doctrine. Soon after publishing the studies on hysteria he abandoned the use of hypnosis as a cathartic procedure and substituted the investigation of the patient's spontaneous flow of thoughts, called free association, to reveal the unconscious mental processes at the root of the neurotic disturbance.

In his clinical observations Freud found evidence for the mental mechanisms of repression and resistance. He described repression as a device operating unconsciously to make the memory of painful or threatening events inaccessible to the conscious mind. Resistance is defined as the unconscious defence against awareness of repressed experiences in order to avoid the resulting anxiety. He traced the operation of unconscious processes, using the free associations of the patient to guide him in the interpretation of dreams and slips of speech. Dream analysis led to his discoveries of infantile sexuality and of the so-called Oedipus complex, which constitutes the erotic attachment of the child for the parent of the opposite sex, together with hostile feelings toward the other parent. In these years he also developed the theory of transference, the processes by which emotional attitudes, are established originally toward parental figures in childhood, are transferred in later life to others. The end of this period was marked by the appearance of Freud's most important work, The Interpretation of Dreams (1899). Here Freud analyzed many of his own dreams recorded in the 3-year period of his self-analysis, begun in 1897. This work expounds all the fundamental concepts underlying psychoanalytic technique and doctrine.

In 1902 Freud was appointed a full professor at Vienna University. This honour was granted not in recognition of his contributions but as a result of the efforts of a highly influential patient. The medical world still regarded his work with hostility, and his next writings, The Psychopathology of Everyday Life (1904) and Three Contributions to the Sexual Theory (1905), only increased this antagonism. As a result Freud continued to work virtually alone in what he termed "splendid isolation."

By 1906, however, a small number of pupils and followers had gathered around Freud, including the Austrian psychiatrists William Stekel and Alfred Adler, the Austrian psychologist Otto Rank, the American psychiatrist Abraham Brill, and the Swiss psychiatrists Eugen Bleuler and Carl Jung. Other notable associates, who joined the circle in 1908, were the Hungarian psychiatrist Sándor Ferenczi and the British psychiatrist Ernest Jones.

Increasing recognition of the psychoanalytic movement made possible the formation in 1910 of a worldwide organization called the International Psychoanalytic Association. As the movement spread, gaining new adherents through Europe and the US, Freud was troubled by the dissension that arose among members of his original circle. Most disturbing were the defections from the group of Adler and Jung, each of whom developed a different theoretical basis for disagreement with Freud's emphasis on the sexual origin of neurosis. Freud met these setbacks by developing further his basic concepts and by elaborating his own views in many publications and lectures.

After the onset of World War I Freud devoted little time to clinical observation and concentrated on the application of his theories to the interpretation of religion, mythology, art, and literature. In 1923 he was stricken with cancer of the jaw, which necessitated constant, painful treatment in addition to many surgical operations. Despite his physical suffering he continued his literary activity for the next 16 years, writing mostly on cultural and philosophical problems.

When the Germans occupied Austria in 1938, Freud, a Jew, was persuaded by friends to escape with his family to England. He died in London on September 23, 1939.

Freud created an entirely new approach to the understanding of human personality by his demonstration of the existence and force of the unconscious. In addition, he founded a new medical discipline and formulated basic therapeutic procedures that in modified form are applied widely in the present-day treatment of neuroses and psychoses. Although never accorded full recognition during his lifetime, Freud is generally acknowledged as one of the great creative minds of modern times.

The Oedipus Complex, in psychoanalysis, a son's largely unconscious sexual attraction toward his mother accompanied by jealousy toward his father. The term Oedipus complex, derived from the Greek legend of Oedipus, was first used in the late 1800s by Austrian psychiatrist Sigmund Freud, the founder of psychoanalysis. Freud thought that the Oedipus complex was the most important event of a boy's childhood and had a great effect on his subsequent adult life. Freud claimed that in nearly all cases the boy represses the desire for his mother and the jealousy toward his father. As a result of this unconscious experience, Freud believed, a boy with an Oedipus complex feels guilt and experiences strong emotional conflicts.

Freud thought that girls go through a similar experience, in which they are attracted to their father and become antagonistic toward their mother. He called this the Electra complex. According to Freud, if a woman remains under the influence of the Electra complex, she is likely to choose a husband with characteristics similar to those of her father.

The Id, in psychoanalytic theory, one of the three basic elements of personality, the others being the ego and the superego. The id can be equated with the unconscious of common usage, which is the reservoir of the instinctual drives of the individual, including biological urges, wishes, and affective motives. The id is dominated by the pleasure principle, through which the individual is pressed for immediate gratification of his or her desires. In strict Freudian theory the energy behind the instinctual drives of the id is known as the libido, a generalized force, basically sexual in nature, through which the sexual and psychosexual nature of the individual finds expression.

The Ego, in psychoanalysis, term denoting the central part of the personality structure that deals with reality and is influenced by social forces. According to the psychoanalytic theories developed by Sigmund Freud, the ego constitutes one of the three basic provinces of the mind, the other two being the id and the superego. Formation of the ego begins at birth in the first encounters with the external world of people and things. The ego learns to modify behaviour by controlling those impulses that are socially unacceptable. Its role is that of mediator between unconscious impulses and acquired social and personal standards.

In philosophy, ego means the conscious self or "I." It was viewed by some philosophers, notably the 17th-century Frenchman René Descartes and the 18th-century German Johann Gottlieb Fichte, as the sole basis of reality; they saw the universe as existing only in the individual's knowledge and experience of it. Other philosophers, such as the 18th-century German Immanuel Kant, proposed two forms of ego, one perceiving and the other thinking.

The Unconscious, in psychology, is the hypothetical region of the mind containing wishes, memories, fears, feelings, and ideas that are prevented from expression in conscious awareness. They manifest themselves, instead, by their influence on conscious processes and, most strikingly, by such anomalous phenomena as dreams and neurotic symptoms. Not all mental activity of which the subject is unaware belongs to the unconscious; for example, thoughts that may be made conscious by a new focussing of attention are termed foreconscious or preconscious.

The concept of the unconscious was first developed in the period from 1895 to 1900 by Sigmund Freud, who theorized that it consists of survivals of feelings experienced during infantile life, including both instinctual drives or libido and their modifications by the development of the superego. According to the Swiss psychoanalyst Carl Jung, the unconscious also consists of a racial unconscious that contains certain inherited, universal, archaic fantasies belonging to what Jung termed the collective unconscious.

The Collective Unconscious, in psychology is a shared pool of memories, ideas, and modes of thought. According to Swiss psychiatrist Carl Jung, it comes from the life experience of one's ancestors and from the entire human race. The collective unconscious coexists with the personal unconscious, which contains the material of individual experience, and may be regarded as an immense depository of ancient wisdom.

Primal experiences are represented in the collective unconscious by archetypes, symbolic pictures, or personifications that appear in dreams and are the common elements in myths, fairy tales, and religious literature. Examples include the serpent, the sphinx, the Great Mother, the anima (representing the nature of woman), and the mandala (representing balanced wholeness, human or divine).

Personality Disorders are specific disorders to which one's personality results in personal distress or significantly impairs social or work functioning. Every person has a personality, that is, a characteristic way of thinking, feeling, behaving, and relating to others. Most people experience at least some difficulties and problems that result from their personality. The specific point at which those problems justify the diagnosis of a personality disorder is controversial. To some extend definition of a personality disorder is arbitrary, only reflecting subjective as well as professional judgment about the person's degree of dysfunction, need for change, and motivation for change.

Personality disorders involve behaviour that deviates from one's expectations or the norms of one's culture. However, people who deviate from cultural norms are not necessarily dysfunctional, nor are people who conform to cultural norms necessarily healthy. Many personality disorders represent extreme variants of behaviour patterns that people usually value and encourage. For example, most people value confidence but not arrogance, agreeableness but not submissiveness, and conscientiousness but not perfectionism.

Because no clear line exists between healthy and unhealthy functioning, critics question the reliability of personality disorder diagnoses. A behaviour that seems deviant to one person may seem normal to another depending on one's gender, ethnicity, and cultural background. The personal and cultural biases of mental health professionals may influence their diagnoses of personality disorders.

An estimated 20 percent of people in the general population have one or more personality disorders. Some people with personality disorders have other mental illnesses as well. About 50 percent of people who are treated for any psychiatric disorder have a personality disorder.

Mental health professionals rarely diagnose personality disorders in children because their manner of thinking, feeling, and relating to others does not usually stabilize until young adulthood. Thereafter, personality traits usually remain stable. Personality disorders often decrease in severity as its person ages.

People with antisocial personality disorder act in a way that disregards the feelings and rights of other people. Antisocial personalities often break the law, and they may use or exploit other people for their own gain. They may lie repeatedly, act impulsively, and get into physical fights. They may mistreat their spouses, neglect or abuse their children, and exploit their employees. They may even kill other people. People with this disorder are also sometimes called sociopaths or psychopaths. Antisocial behaviour in people less than 18 years old is called conduct disorder.

Antisocial personalities usually fail to understand that their behaviour is dysfunctional because their ability to feel guilty, remorseful, and anxious is impaired. Guilt, remorse, shame, and anxiety are unpleasant feelings, but they are also necessary for social functioning and even physical survival. For example, people who lack the ability to feel anxious will often fail to anticipate actual dangers and risks. They may take chances that other people would not take.

Antisocial personality disorder affects about 3 percent of males and 1 percent of females. This is the most heavily researched personality disorder, in part because it costs society the most. People with this disorder are at high risk for premature and violent death, injury, imprisonment, loss of employment, bankruptcy, alcoholism, drug dependence, and failed personal relationships.

People with borderline personality disorder experience intense emotional instability, particularly in relationships with others. They may make frantic efforts to avoid real or imagined abandonment by others. They may experience minor problems as major crises. They may also express their anger, frustration, and dismay through suicidal gestures, self-mutilation, and other self-destructive acts. They tend to have an unstable self-image or sense of self.

As children, most people with this disorder were emotionally unstable, impulsive, and often bitter or angry, although their chaotic impulsiveness and intense emotions may have made them popular at school. At first they may impress people as stimulating and exciting, but their relationships tend to be unstable and explosive.

About 2 percent of all people have borderline personality disorder. About 75 percent of people with this disorder are female. Borderline personalities are at high risk for developing depression, alcoholism, drug dependence, bulimia, dissociative disorders, and post-traumatic stress disorder. As many as 10 percent of people with this disorder commit suicide by the age of 30. People with borderline personality disorder are among the most difficult to treat with psychotherapy, in part because their relationship with their therapist may become as intense and unstable as their other personal relationships.

Avoidant personality disorder is social withdrawal due to intense, anxious shyness. People with Avoidant personalities are reluctant to interact with others unless they feel positive of being liked and accepted. They fear being criticized and rejected. Often they view themselves as socially inept and inferior to others.

Dependent personality disorder involves severe and disabling emotional dependency on others. People with this disorder have difficulty making decisions without a great deal of advice and reassurance from others. They urgently seek out another relationship when a close relationship ends. They feel uncomfortable by themselves.

People with histrionic personality disorder constantly strive to be the centre of attention. They may act overly flirtatious or dress in ways that draw attention. They may also talk in a dramatic or theatrical style and display exaggerated emotional reactions.

People with narcissistic personality disorder have a grandiose sense of the self-importance, which they seek excessive for the admiration from others and fantasize about unlimited success or power. They believe they are special, unique, or superior to others. However, they often have very fragile self-esteem.

Obsessive-compulsive personality disorder is characterized by a preoccupation with details, orderliness, perfection, and control. People with this disorder often devote excessive amounts of time for work and productivity and fail to take time for leisure activities and friendships. They tend to be rigid, formal, stubborn, and serious. This disorder differs from obsessive-compulsive disorder, which often includes more bizarre behaviour and rituals.

People with paranoid personality disorder feel constant suspicion and distrust toward other people. They believe that others are against them and constantly look for evidence to support their suspicions. They are hostile toward others and react angrily to perceived insults.

Schizoid personality disorder involves social isolation and a lack of desire for close personal relationships. People with this disorder prefer to be alone and seem withdrawn and emotionally detached. They seem indifferent to praise or criticism from other people.

People with schizotypal personality disorder engage in odd thinking, speech, and behaviour. They may ramble or use words and phrases in unusual ways, and they may believe they have magical control over others. They feel very uncomfortable with close personal relationships and tend to be suspicious of others. Some research have suggested that this disorder is a less severe form of schizophrenia.

Many psychiatrists and psychologists use two additional diagnoses. Depressive personality disorder is characterized by chronic pessimism, gloominess, and cheerlessness. In passive-aggressive personality disorder, a person passively resists completing tasks and chores, criticizes and scorns authority figures, and seems negative and sullen.

Personality disorders result from a complex interaction of inherited traits and life experience, not from a single cause. For example, some cases of antisocial personality disorder may result from a combination of a genetic predisposition to impulsiveness and violence, very inconsistent or erratic parenting, and a harsh environment that discourage feelings of empathy and warmth but rewards exploitation and aggressiveness. Borderline personality disorder may result from a genetic predisposition to impulsiveness and emotional instability combined with parental neglect, intense marital conflicts between parents, and repeated episodes of severe emotional or sexual abuse. Dependent personality disorder may result from genetically based anxiety, an inhibited temperament, and overly protective, clinging, or neglectful parenting.

The pervasive and chronic nature of personality disorders makes them difficult to treat. People with these disorders often fail to recognize that their personality has contributed to their social, occupational, and personal problems. They may not think they have any real problems despite a history of drug abuse, failed relationships, and irregular employment. Thus, therapists must first focus on helping the person understand and become aware of the significance of their personality traits.

People with personality disorders sometimes feel that they can never change their dysfunctional behaviour because they have always acted the same way. Although personality change is exceedingly difficult, sometimes people can change the most dysfunctional aspects of their feelings and behaviour.

Therapists use a variety of methods to treat personality disorders, depending on the specific disorder. For example, cognitive and behavioural techniques, such as role playing and logical argument, may help alter a person's irrational perceptions and assumptions about himself or herself. Certain psychoactive drugs may help control feelings of anxiety, depression, or severe distortions of thought. Psychotherapy may help people to understand the impact of experiences and relationships during childhood.

Psychotherapy is usually ineffective for people with antisocial personality disorder because these individuals tend to be manipulative, unreliable, and dishonest with the therapist. Therefore, most mental health professionals favour removing people with this disorder from their current living situation and placing them in a residential treatment centre. Such residential programs strictly supervise patients' behaviour and impose rigid, consistent rules and responsibilities. These programs appear to help some people, but it is unclear how long their beneficial effects last.

Therapists treating people with borderline personality disorder sometimes use a technique called dialectical behaviour therapy. In this type of therapy, the therapist initially focuses on reducing suicidal tendencies and other behaviours that disrupt treatment. The therapist then helps the person develop skills to cope with anger and self-destructive impulses. In addition, the person learns to achieve personal strength through an acceptance of the many disappointments and interpersonal conflicts that are a natural part of life.

Personality disorders are mental illnesses in which one's personality results in personal distress or a significant impairment in social or work functioning. In general, people with personality disorders have poor perceptions of themselves or others. They may have low self-esteem or overwhelming narcissism, poor impulse control, troubled social relationships, and inappropriate emotional responses. Considerable controversy exists over where to draw the distinction between a normal personality and a personality disorder.

Dissociative Identity Disorder, often called multiple personality disorder, mental illness in which a person has two or more distinct identities or personality states, which recurrently take control of the person's consciousness and behaviour. The person often gives the alternate identities their own personal names, and these identities may have characteristics that differ sharply from the person's primary identity. In addition, a person with such disorders experiences some degree of amnesia, in that one personality usually will not recall what occurred when another personality controlled the person.

People often act and feel differently in various settings. For example, teenagers may act differently at a party than they do at school. However, people in good mental health maintain continuous awareness of themselves no matter what the situation. Individuals with dissociative identity disorder do not. They experience sudden shifts in consciousness, identity, and memory. They may find themselves in a strange apartment and not remember how they got there, or discover new clothing in their closet without knowing how it was purchased. Their identity is fragmented into pieces with different emotions, memories, and styles of interacting with people.

They may shift from being passive and accepting of advice from others to being hostile and uncooperative. They are often at war with themselves, with certain personalities being quite critical of other personalities. At times one personality may go so far as inflicting physical harm on one of the other personalities. In one case, a woman with dissociative identity disorder carved the words "I hate Joan" on her forearm while in a different personality state.

In 1994 the American Psychiatric Association (APA) changed the name of the disorder from multiple personality disorder to dissociative identity disorder. Psychiatrists wanted to emphasize the fact that the disorder does not really consist of many personalities living in one body, but rather of a failure to integrate various aspects of identity into a unified personality. In a sense, people with this disorder suffer not from having more than one personality but rather from having less than one personality.

Typically the disorder begins in childhood or adolescence, although the symptoms may not become evident to others for many years. In childhood, individuals with dissociative identity disorder often appear moody or irresponsible because they may switch personalities suddenly or deny having done something they no longer remember. Doctors often misdiagnose people with this disorder as having other mental illnesses. Although critics claim the disorder is an invention of therapists, most experts agree it is a real but rare condition.

Most individuals with dissociative identity disorder report histories of severe and repeated physical, sexual, or emotional abuse in childhood. This does not mean that everyone with the disorder was necessarily mistreated. However, most psychiatrists now understand the disorder as a reaction to chronic trauma and stress. People frequently enter altered states of consciousness during traumatic events such as physical or sexual assault, natural disasters, motor vehicle accidents, or combat. They detach or dissociate themselves from their immediate circumstances as a means of protecting themselves from overwhelming mental or physical pain. In dissociative identity disorder this useful ability may become conditioned by repeated trauma, leading to separate personality states that may be triggered by any anxiety or stress.

The best treatment for the disorder is long-term psychotherapy aimed at helping patients to gain insight into each of their personality states, work through the aftermath of traumatic memories, achieve greater self-acceptance, and reduce self-damaging behaviour. Hypnosis may help a person control spontaneous switching of personality states. Many people with this disorder suffer from depression and may benefit from antidepressant medication as well.

Depersonalization Disorder, is a mental illness in which people experience an unwelcome sense of a detachment from their own bodies. They may feel as though they are floating above the ground, outside observers of their own mental or physical processes. Other symptoms may include a feeling that they or other people are mechanical or unreal, a feeling of being in a dream, a feeling that their hands or feet are larger or smaller than usual, and a deadening of emotional responses. These symptoms are chronic and severe enough to impede normal functioning in a social, school, or work environment.

Depersonalization disorder is a relatively rare syndrome thought to result from severe psychological stress. It may occur as part of other mental illnesses, especially anxiety disorders. For example, some people with panic disorder feel nervous, have a sense of doom about their future and health, and have a troubling sense of displacement and loss control over their bodies. Depersonalization disorder may also be a component of more severe mental illness, such as schizophrenia. Treatment may include training in relaxation techniques that enhance body perception and control, hypnosis to modify symptoms, and psychotherapy to explore possible stress-related components of the disorder.

Psychiatrists classify depersonalization disorder as one of the dissociative disorders. Such disorders involve a disruption of consciousness, memory, identity, or perception.

Dissociative Fugue, the mental illness in which a person forgets his or her personal identity and unexpectedly wanders away from home. In many cases, people with this disorder travel to a distant location and adopt a new identity, complete with a new name, personal history, and place of residence. They may wander hundreds of miles, leaving their families mystified about their disappearance. Sometimes they appear in hospital emergency rooms unable to explain who they are. People with this disorder usually appear normal and do not attract public attention.

Dissociative fugues typically occurs after serious psychological stress of some kind, such as the death of a family member, the loss of a job, or a failed relationship. This disorder is quite rare, and psychiatrists must rule out more common causes of memory loss such as alcoholism or drug dependence before making a diagnosis. Dissociative fugue is usually reversible with intensive psychotherapy or hypnosis. In many cases, fugue victims will suddenly "wake up," failing to remember any of the events that occurred while in the fugue state.

Psychiatrists classify dissociative fugue as one of the dissociative disorders. Such disorders involve a disruption of consciousness, memory, identity, or perception.

Under the stress of mental conflict, anyone may react temporarily with physical symptoms. In conversion reactions, mental conflicts are unconsciously converted to symptoms that appear to be physical, but no organic cause is found. Common symptoms of conversion reactions include muscular paralysis, blindness, deafness, and tremors.

Patients with conversion reactions may have periods of intense emotion and defective power of self-observation. In such a mental condition, patients may interact with others in a bizarre way. Extreme symptoms of dissociation are shown in dissociative fugue, in which a person forgets his or her identity and unexpectedly wanders away from home.

The ancient Greeks accounted for the instability and mobility of physical symptoms and of attacks of emotional disturbance in women, when these were otherwise unaccountable, by a theory that the womb somehow became transplanted to different positions. This "wandering of the uterus" theory gave the name hysteria (Greek hystera, "uterus") to disease phenomena characterized by highly emotional behaviour. During the Middle Ages hysteria was attributed to demonic possession and to witchcraft, which led to persecution.

As the sciences of anatomy and physiology developed in the 19th century, a tendency to interpret all mental phenomena in terms of diseased structure of the brain became apparent in medical circles. At the end of the 19th century, however, the French neurologist Jean Martin Charcot demonstrated that morbid ideas could produce physical manifestations. Subsequently his pupil, the French psychologist Pierre Janet, formulated a description of hysteria as a psychological disorder. Later Austrian psychoanalyst Sigmund Freud began to develop the theory that hysterical symptoms are the result of conflict between the social and ethical standards of an individual and an unsuccessfully repressed wish.

Modern treatment of hysteria consists of some form of psychotherapy and, in some cases, prolonged forms of analytic psychotherapy, or of psychoanalysis. For cases of acute hysteria associated with anxiety, tranquillizing medication may also be necessary.

Somatoform disorders are characterized by the presence of physical symptoms that cannot be explained by a medical condition or another mental illness. Thus, physicians often judge that such symptoms result from psychological conflicts or distress. For example, in conversion disorder, also called hysteria, a person may experience blindness, deafness, or seizures, but a physician cannot find anything wrong with the person. People with another Somatoform disorder, hypochondriasis constantly fear that they will develop a serious disease and misinterpret minor physical symptoms as evidence of illness. The term somatoform comes from the Greek word soma, meaning "body."

Mania, abnormal mental state that is characterized by an elevated or irritable mood, exaggerated self-importance, racing thoughts, and hyperactivity. People with mania typically feel intoxicated with themselves and with life. They may display an indiscriminate enthusiasm for manipulating people, spending money, and pursuing sexual adventure. Manic people may also display impatience or hostility toward other people. If frustrated, they may physically abuse their friends, children, or spouse.

Mania has many other characteristics. People with mania often have inflated self-esteem and self-confidence, and assume they have more wit, courage, imagination, and artistry than everyone else. Severe mania may include delusions of grandeur, such as the belief that one is chosen by God for a special mission. Mania typically involves a decreased need for sleep, so manic people often wake up early in a highly energized state. Mania makes people extremely talkative. Their loud, rapid-fire speech sometimes continues unabated without regard for others. Mania also involves a flight of ideas, racing thoughts that cause speech to go off in many different directions. People in a manic state become easily distracted by irrelevant sights, sounds or ideas, which further disrupts thinking and speech.

People with mania may also devise grandiose plans or engage in reckless self-indulgence. For example, they may invest indiscriminately in risky projects, get involved in many different social activities, flirt to the point of indecency, and intrude in other people's private lives to the point of being obnoxious. Manic people display many signs of impaired judgment and self-destructive behaviour. These signs include taking aeroplane trips all over the country, gambling to excess, buying outrageously expensive gifts, engaging in reckless sexual behaviour, and abusing alcohol or other drugs.

Most people who experience episodes of mania also experience spells of severe depression. This pattern of mood swings between mania and depression defined a mental illness known as bipolar disorder, and called manic-depressive illness. In bipolar disorder, episodes of mania usually begin abruptly and last from several weeks to several months. Mild manic episodes can last a year or more. Depression may follow immediately or begin after a period of relatively normal functioning. Manic episodes may require hospitalization because of impaired social behaviour or the presence of psychotic symptoms.

Mania may result from other conditions besides bipolar disorder. Medical conditions, such as a brain tumour or an overactive thyroid gland, can cause manic symptoms. Certain medications, such as steroids and antidepressants, can also cause mania.

Bipolar Disorder, mental illness in which a person's mood alternates between extreme mania and depression. Bipolar disorder is also called manic-depressive illness. When manic, people with bipolar disorder feel intensely elated, self-important, energetic, and irritable. When depressed, they experience painful sadness, negative thinking, and indifference to things that used to bring them happiness.

English novelist Virginia Woolf, who suffered from bipolar disorder, recognized that her extremes of a mood contributed to her creativity. She wrote of her disorder: "As an experience, madness is terrific . . . and in its lava I still find most of the things I write about." In 1941, feeling that she could no longer fight the disease, Woolf drowned herself in the Ouse River.

Bipolar disorder is much less common than depression. In North America and Europe, about 1 percent of people experience bipolar disorder during their lives. Rates of bipolar disorder are similar throughout the world. In comparison, at least 8 percent of people experience serious depression during their lives. Bipolar disorder affects men and women about equally and is somewhat more common in higher socioeconomic classes. At least 15 percent of people with bipolar disorder commit suicide. This rate roughly equals the rate for people with major depression, the most severe form of depression.

Bipolar disorder is a mental illness that causes mood swings. In the manic phase, a person might feel ecstatic, self-important, and energetic. But when the person becomes depressed, the mood shifts to extreme sadness, negative thinking, and apathy. Some studies indicate that the disease occurs at unusually high rates in creative people, such as artists, writers, and musicians. But some researchers contend that the methodology of these studies was flawed and their results were misleading. In the October 1996 Discover magazine article, anthropologist Jo Ann C. Gutin presents the results of several studies that explore the link between creativity and mental illness.

Some research suggests that highly creative people—such as artists, composers, writers, and poets—show unusually high rates of bipolar disorder, and that periods of mania fuel their creativity. Famous artists and writers who probably suffered from bipolar disorder include poets Lord Byron and Anne Sexton, the novelists Virginia Woolf and Ernest Hemingway, composers Peter Ilyich Tchaikovsky and Sergey Rachmaninoff, and painters Amedeo Modigliani and Jackson Pollock. Critics of this research note that many creative people do not suffer from bipolar disorder, and that most people with bipolar disorder are not especially creative.

Bipolar disorder usually begins in a person's late teens or 20s. Men usually experience mania as the first mood episode, whereas women typically experience depression first. Episodes of mania and depression usually last from several weeks to several months. On average, people with untreated bipolar disorder experience four episodes of mania or depression over any ten-year period. Many people with bipolar disorder function normally between episodes. In "rapid-cycling" bipolar disorder, however, which represents 5 to 15 percent of all cases, a person experiences four or more mood episodes within a year and may have little or no normal functioning in between episodes. In rare cases, swings between mania and depression occur over a period of days.

In another type of bipolar disorder, a person experiences major depression and hypomanic episodes, or episodes of milder mania. In a related disorder called cyclothymic disorder, a person's mood alternates between mild depression and mild mania. Some people with cyclothymic disorder later develop full-blown bipolar disorder. Bipolar disorder may also follow a seasonal pattern, with a person typically experiencing depression in the fall and winter and mania in the spring or summer.

People in the depressive phase of bipolar disorder feel intensely sad or profoundly indifferent to work, activities, and people that once brought them pleasure. They think slowly, concentrate poorly, feel tired, and experience changes—usually an increase—in their appetite and sleep. They often feel a sense of worthlessness or helplessness. In addition, they may feel pessimistic or hopeless about the future and may think about or attempt suicide. In some cases of severe depression, people may experience psychotic symptoms, such as delusions (false beliefs) or hallucinations (false sensory perceptions).

In the manic phase of bipolar disorder, people feel intensely and inappropriately happy, self-important, and irritable. In this highly energized state they sleep less, have racing thoughts, and talk in rapid-fire speech that goes off in many directions. They have inflated self-esteem and confidence and may even have delusions of grandeur. Mania may make people impatient and abrasive, and when frustrated, physically abusive. They often behave in socially inappropriate ways, think irrationally, and show impaired judgment. For example, they may take aeroplane trips all over the country, make indecent sexual advances, and formulate grandiose plans involving indiscriminate investments of money. The self-destructive behaviour of mania includes excessive gambling, buying outrageously expensive gifts, abusing alcohol or other drugs, and provoking confrontations with obnoxious or combative behaviour.

Clinical depression is one of the most common forms of mental illness. Although depression can be treated with psychotherapy, many scientists believe there are biological causes for the disease. In this June 1998 Scientific American article, neurobiologist Charles B. Nemeroff discusses the connection between biochemical changes in the brain and depression.

The genes that a person inherits seem to have a strong influence on whether the person will develop bipolar disorder. Studies of twins provide evidence for this genetic influence. Among genetically identical twins where one twin has bipolar disorder, the other twin has the disorder in more than 70 percent of cases. But among pairs of fraternal twins, who have about half their genes in common, both twins have bipolar disorder in less than 15 percent of cases in which one twin has the disorder. The degree of genetic similarity seems to account for the difference between identical and fraternal twins. Further evidence for a genetic influence comes from studies of adopted children with bipolar disorder. These studies show that biological relatives of the children have a higher incidence of bipolar disorder than do people in the general population. Thus, bipolar disorder seems to run in families for genetic reasons.

Personal or work-related stress can trigger a manic episode, but this usually occurs in people with a genetic vulnerability. Other factors—such as prenatal development, childhood experiences, and social conditions—seem to have relatively little influence in causing bipolar disorder. One study examined the children of identical twins in which only one member of each pair of twins had bipolar disorder. The study found that regardless of whether the parent had bipolar disorder or not, all of the children had the same high 10-percent rate of bipolar disorder. This observation clearly suggests that risk for bipolar illness comes from genetic influence, not from exposure to a parent's bipolar illness or from family problems caused by that illness.

Different therapies may shorten, delay, or even prevent the extreme moods caused by bipolar disorder. Lithium carbonates, is a natural mineral salt, can help control both mania and depression in bipolar disorder. The drug generally takes two to three weeks to become effective. People with bipolar disorder may take lithium during periods of relatively normal moods to delay or prevent subsequent episodes of mania or depression. Common side effects of lithium include nausea, increased thirst and urination, vertigo, loss of appetite, and muscle weakness. In addition, long-term use can impair functioning of the kidneys. For this reason, doctors do not prescribe lithium to bipolar patients with kidney disease. Many people find the side effects so unpleasant that they stop taking the medication, which often results in relapse.

From 20 to 40 percent of people do not respond to lithium therapy. For these people, two anticonvulsants drugs may help dampen severe manic episodes: carbamazepine (Tegretol) and valproate (Depakene). The use of traditional antidepressants to treat bipolar disorder carries risks of triggering a manic episode or a rapid-cycling pattern.

Psychosis, mental illness in which a person loses contact with reality and has difficulty functioning in daily life. Psychotic symptoms can indicate severe mental illnesses, such as schizophrenia and bipolar disorder (manic-depressive illness). Unlike people with fewer severe psychological problems, psychotic individuals do not usually recognize that their mental functioning is disturbed.

Mental health professionals generally divide psychotic symptoms into three broad types: Hallucinations, delusions, and bizarre behaviour. Hallucinations refer to hearing, seeing, smelling, feeling, or tasting something when nothing in the environment actually caused that sensation. For example, a person experiencing an auditory hallucination might hear a voice calling her or his name even though no one else is actually present. A delusion is a false belief held by a person that appears obviously untrue to other people in that person's culture. For example, a man may believe that Martians have implanted a microchip in his brain that controls his thoughts. Bizarre behaviour refers to behaviour in a person that is strange or incomprehensible to others who know the person. For example, hoarding unused scraps of tin because of their "magical properties" would be a type of bizarre behaviour.

A psychosis can occur in a number of mental illnesses. These include schizophrenia and schizophrenia-related disorders, bipolar disorder, paranoid personality disorder, and delusional disorder. Less common are psychotic symptoms, which occur in major depression, dissociative disorders, and post-traumatic stress disorder.

Psychotic symptoms can also result from substance abuse. Stimulants, such as cocaine and amphetamines, can cause psychotic symptoms, especially if taken in high doses or over long periods of time. Hallucinogenic substances, such as lysergic acid diethylamide (LSD), mescaline, and phencyclidine (PCP), can cause psychosis. Alcohol and marijuana can occasionally cause psychotic symptoms as well. Individuals with alcoholism may experience psychotic symptoms, especially hallucinations, as they withdraw from alcohol use. Alcohol dependence over a long period of time can result in Korsakoff's psychosis, a syndrome that may include psychotic symptoms and an inability to form new memories. Certain medical conditions can also cause psychosis. Syphilis, especially if untreated for many years, can lead to psychosis. Brain tumours can also lead to psychotic symptoms.

Treatment of psychotic symptoms usually involved taking antipsychotic drugs, and called neuroleptics. Common antipsychotic drugs include chlorpromazine (Thorazine), fluphenazine (Prolixin), thioridazine (Mellaril), trifluoperazine (Stelazine), clozapine (Clozaril), haloperidol (Haldol), olanzapine (Zyprexa), and risperidone (Risperdal). These medications can help reduce psychotic symptoms and prevent symptoms from returning. However, they can also cause severe side effects, such as muscle spasms, tremors, and tardive dyskinesia, a permanent condition marked by uncontrollable lip smacking, grimacing, and tongue movements. Psychotic symptoms in individuals with bipolar disorder may respond to other types of medication, including lithium, carbamazepine (Tegretol), and valproate (Depakene).

Psychotic symptoms that occur as a result of substance abuse usually disappear gradually after the person stops using the substances. Physicians sometimes use antipsychotic medications temporarily to treat these individuals. Physicians have not discovered any effective treatments for Korsakoff's psychosis. Korsakoff's syndrome is a syndrome of severe mental impairment characterized by multiple neuritis, confusion, disorientation, and amnesia in which memory of recent events is especially impaired often causing the patient to attempt to compensate through the confabulation.

Psychotic symptoms resulting from medical conditions often disappear after treatment of the underlying medical problem.

Emil Kraepelin (1856-1926), German Psychiatrist, born in Neustrelitz, who developed the first widely accepted classification of mental illnesses. He also established the categories of manic-depressive psychosis and dementia praecox (now called schizophrenia). Kraepelin, who became director of the Research Institute of Psychiatry in Munich in 1922, stressed the likely physiological causes of such disorders, and the need to study them through the use of well-defined tests and measurements.

Scottish physician William Cullen coined the term neurosis near the end of the 18th century to describe a wide variety of nervous behaviours with no apparent physical cause. Austrian psychoanalyst Sigmund Freud and his followers popularized the word in the late 19th and early 20th centuries. Freud defined neurosis as one class of mental illnesses. In his view, people became neurotic when their conscious mind repressed inappropriate fantasies of the unconscious mind.

Until 1980 neurosis appeared as a specific diagnostic category in the Diagnostic and Statistical Manual of Mental Disorders, a handbook for mental health professionals. Neurosis encompassed a variety of mental illnesses, including dissociative disorders, anxiety disorders, and phobias.

In the psychoanalytic model, neurosis differs from psychosis, another general term used to describe mental illnesses. Individuals with neuroses can function at work and in social situations, whereas people with psychoses find it quite difficult to function adequately. People with neuroses do not grossly distort or misinterpret reality as those with psychoses do. In addition, neurotic individuals recognize that their mental functioning is disturbed while psychotic individuals usually do not. Most mental health professionals now use the term psychosis to refer to symptoms such as hallucinations, delusions, and bizarre behaviour.

Mood disorders, also called affective disorders, create disturbances in a person's emotional life. Depression, mania, and bipolar disorder are examples of mood disorders. Symptoms of depression may include feelings of sadness, hopelessness, and worthlessness, as well as complaints of physical pain and changes in appetite, sleep patterns, and energy level. In mania, on the other hand, an individual experiences an abnormally elevated mood, often marked by exaggerated self-importance, irritability, agitation, and a decreased need for sleep. In bipolar disorder, also called manic-depressive illness, a person's mood alternates between extremes of mania and depression.

Antianemic drugs, as certain vitamins or iron, enhance the formation of red blood cells. Anticoagulants like heparin reduce blood-clot formation and ensure free blood flow through major organs in the body. Thrombolytic drugs dissolve blood clots, which can block blood vessels and deprive the heart or brain of blood and oxygen, possibly leading to heart attack or stroke.

Drugs can be classified in many ways, in ways that are dispensed-over the counter or by prescription, or by the substance from which they are derived—plant, mineral, or animal, by the form as taken in a capsule, liquid, or gas; and by the way they are administered—by mouth, injection, inhalation, or direct application to the skin (absorption). Drugs are also classified by their names. All drugs have three names: a chemical name, which describes the exact structure of the drug; a generic or proprietary name, which is the official medical name assigned by the United States Adopted Name Council (a group composed of pharmacists and other scientists); and a brand or trade name given by the particular manufacturer that sells the drug. If a company holds the patent on a drug—that is, if the company has the exclusive right to make and sell a drug, then the drug is available under one brand name only. After the patent expires, typically after 17 years in the United States, other companies can also manufacture the drug and market it under the generic name, or give it a new brand name.

Another way to categorize drugs is by the way they act against diseases or disorders; chemotherapeutic drugs attack specific organisms that cause a disease without harming the host, while pharmocodynamic drugs alter the function of bodily systems by stimulating or depressing normal cell activity in a given system. The most common way to categorize a drug is by its effect on a particular area of the body or a particular condition.

Endocrine drugs correct the overproduction or underproduction of the body's natural hormones. For example, insulin is a hormone used to treat diabetes. The female sex hormone's estrogen and progesterone are used in birth control pills. To relieve uncomfortable symptoms of menopause, including sweating, hot flashes, and mood swings, as well as to delay some long-term consequences of menopause, including osteoporosis and atherosclerosis, physicians often prescribe the synthetic hormones estrogen, progestin (a synthetic form of progesterone), and sometimes androgens. This therapeutic approach is called hormone replacement therapy (HRT). However, recent studies indicate that HRT may be associated with an increased risk of breast cancer, heart attacks, strokes, and blood clots, and it is unclear if the benefits of HRT outweigh these risks. Each woman and her health care provider should assess her need for menopausal symptom control and her potential risks and benefits before starting HRT.

Anti-infective drugs are classified as antibacterial, antiviral, or antifungal depending on the type of microorganism they combat. Anti-infective drugs interfere selectively with the functioning of a microorganism while leaving the human host unharmed.

Antibacterial drugs, or antibiotics—sulfa drugs, penicillins, cephalosporins, and many others—either kill bacteria directly or prevent them from multiplying so that the body's immune system can destroy invading bacteria. Antibacterial drugs act by interfering with some specific characteristics of bacteria. For example, they may destroy bacterial cell walls or interfere with the synthesis of bacterial proteins or deoxyribonucleic acid (DNA)— the chemical that carries the genetic material of an organism. Antibiotics often cure an infection completely. However, bacteria can spontaneously mutate and produce further strains that are resistant to existing antibiotics.

Antiviral drugs interfere with the life cycle of a virus by preventing its penetration into a host cell or by blocking the synthesis of new viruses. Antiviral drugs may cure, but often only suppress, viral infections; and flare-ups of an infection can occur after symptom-free periods. With some viruses, such as human immunodeficiency viruses (HIV), which causes acquired immunodeficiency syndrome (AIDS), antiviral drugs can only prolong life, not cure the disease.

Vaccines are used as antiviral drugs against diseases such like mumps, measles, smallpox, poliomyelitis, and influenza. Vaccines are made from either live, weakened viruses or killed viruses, both of which are designed to stimulate the immune system to produce antibodies, proteins that attack foreign substances. These antibodies protect the body from future infections by viruses of the same type.

Antifungal drugs selectively destroy fungal cells by altering cell walls. The cells' contents leak out and the cells die. Antifungal drugs can cure, or may only suppress, a fungal infection.

Cardiovascular drugs affect the heart and blood vessels and are divided into categories according to function. Antihypertensive drugs reduce blood pressure by dilating blood vessels and reducing the amount of blood pumped by the heart into the vascular system. Antiarrhythmic drugs normalize irregular heartbeats and prevent cardiac malfunction and arrest.

Antianemic drugs, such as certain vitamins or iron, enhance the formation of red blood cells. Anticoagulants like heparin reduce blood-clot formation and ensure free blood flow through major organs in the body. Thrombolytic drugs dissolve blood clots, which can block blood vessels and deprive the heart or brain of blood and oxygen, possibly leading to heart attack or stroke.

Central nervous system drugs—that is, drugs that affect the spinal cord and the brain—are used to treat several neurological (nervous system) and psychiatric problems. For instance, antiepileptic drugs reduce the activity of overexcited brain areas and reduce or eliminate seizures.

Antipsychotic drugs are used to regulate certain brain chemicals called neurotransmitters, which do not function properly in people with psychoses, major mental disorders often characterized by extreme behaviours and hallucinations, such as in schizophrenia. Antipsychotic drugs can often significantly alleviate hallucinations and other abnormal behaviours. Antipsychotic drugs of a group of drugs, such as th e phenothiazines or butyrophenones, that are used to treat psychosis. Psychotropic drugs, having an altering effect on perception, emotion, or behaviour and used of a group as psychotropic drug or other agent. Psychosis is a severe mental disorder with or without organic damage, characterized by derangement of personality and loss of contact with reality and causing deterioration of normal social functioning.

Antidepressant drugs reduce mental depression. Antimanic drugs reduce excessive mood swings in people with manic-depressive illness, which is characterized by behavioural fluctuations between highs of extreme excitement and activity and lows of lethargy and depression. Both types of drugs act by normalize chemical activity in the emotional centres of the brain. Antianxiety drugs, also referred to as tranquillizers, treat anxiety by decreasing the activity in the anxiety centres of the brain. Of or relating to, or having bipolar disorder, as to manifest trouble, emotionally or mentally upset, for showing signs or symptoms of mental or emotional illness. The disordering to refuse or fail to follow an order or rule or neglect to act in accord with the wishes obeyed by some annoyance or vexation to cause displeasure, is, nonetheless, a lack of order or regular arrangement. That such an ailment that affects the function of mind or body, but, nevertheless, relating to or having two poles or charges, having two opposite or contradictory ideas or natures or extremities that relate to a major affective disorder that is characterized by episodes of mania and depression.

Anaesthesia induces unconsciousness and loss of sensation prior to surgery. During surgery, the anesthesiologist monitors the patient's condition and increases or decreases the dosage of Anaesthesia as needed.

Sedative-hypnotic drugs are used both as sedatives to reduce anxiety and as hypnotics to induce sleep. Sedative-hypnotic drugs act by reducing brain-cell activity. Stimulatory drugs, on the other hand, increase neuronal (nerve cell) activity and reduce fatigue and appetite.

Analgesic drugs reduce pain and are generally categorized as narcotics and non-narcotics. Narcotic analgesics, also known as opioids, include opium and the natural opium derivatives, codeine and morphine; synthetic derivatives of like morphine, such as, heroin and synthetic drugs as meperidine and propoxyphene hydrochloride. Narcotics relieve pain by acting on specific structures, called receptors, located on the nerve cells of the spinal cord or brain. Non-narcotic analgesics such as aspirin, acetaminophen, and ibuprofen reduce pain by inhibiting the formation of nerve impulses at the site of pain. Some of these drugs can also reduce fever and inflammation.

General anaesthetics, used for surgery or painful procedures, depress brain activity, causing a loss of sensation throughout the body and unconsciousness. Local anaesthetics are directly applied to or injected in a specific area of the body, causing a loss of sensation without unconsciousness; they prevent nerves from transmitting impulses signalling pain.

Anticancer drugs eliminate some cancers or reduce rapid growth and spread. These drugs do not affect all cancers but are specific for cancers in certain tissues or organs such as the bladder, brain, liver, or bones. Anticancer drugs interfere with specific cancer-cell components. For example, alkylating agents are cytotoxic (cell-poisoning) drugs that alter the DNA of cancer cells. Vinca alkaloids, chemicals produced by the periwinkle plant, prevent cancer cell division.

Many other categories of drugs also exist, such as anti-inflammatory, antiallergic, antiparkinson, antiworm, diuretic, gastrointestinal, pulmonary, and muscle-relaxant drugs. Often a drug in one category can also be used for problems in other categories. For example, lidocaine can be used as a local anaesthetic or as a cardiac drug.

Certain drugs work by interacting with receptors, special sites on the surface of body cells. Drugs may bind to a specific receptor, possibly preventing naturally occurring chemicals from binding to the receptor. In so doing, if a drug enhances cell activity, it is called an agonist; if it blocks cell activity, it is called an antagonist.

The effect of a drug on the body depends on a number of processes that the drug undergoes as it moves through the body. All these processes together are known as pharmacokinetics (literally, "motion of the drug"). First in these processes is the administration of the drug after which it must be absorbed into the bloodstream. From the bloodstream, the drug is distributed throughout the body to various tissues and organs. As the drug is metabolized, or broken down and used by the body, it goes through chemical changes that produce metabolites, or altered forms of the drug, most of which have no effect on the body. Finally, the drug and its metabolites are eliminated from the body.

Some drugs can be absorbed well into the body through the skin. A transdermal patch allows controlled release of small amounts of a drug over a long period of time. Drugs applied in this way include heart medications for angina pectoris, antinausea drugs for travel sickness, and hormone replacements. One of the more popular uses of drug patches is the nicotine patch, used in stop-smoking programs as a way to gradually decrease the amount of nicotine needed by addicted smokers.

Depending on the drug and its desired effect, there are a variety of administration methods. Most drugs are administered orally—that is, through the mouth. Only drugs that will not be destroyed by the digestive processes of the stomach or intestines can be given orally. Drugs can also be administered by injection into a vein (intravenously), which assures quick distribution through the bloodstream and a rapid effect; under the skin (subcutaneously) into the tissues, which results in localized action at a particular site as with local anaesthetics; or into a muscle (intramuscularly), which enables rapid absorption through the many blood vessels found in muscles. An intramuscular injection may also be given as a depot preparation, in which the drug is combined with other substances so that it is slowly released into the blood.

A syringe is used when drugs need to be administered through a vein or muscle. The syringe consists of a needle attached to a hollow cylinder that is marked with precise measurements so that the exact amount of medication can be given.

Inhaled drugs are designed to act in the nose or lungs. General anaesthetics may be given through inhalation. Some drugs are administered through drug-filled patches that stick to the skin. The drug is slowly released from the patch and enters the body through the skin. Drugs may be administered topically—that is, they can be applied directly to the skin or rectally, in that is absorbed through an enema (or, an injection of liquid into the rectum) or by a rectal suppository (a pellet of medication that melts when inserted in the rectum).

Absorption is the transfer of a drug from its site of administration to the bloodstream. Drugs that are inhaled or injected enter the bloodstream more quickly than drugs taken orally. Oral drugs are absorbed by the stomach or small intestine and then passed through the liver before entering the bloodstream.

Distribution is the transport of a drug from the bloodstream to tissue sites where it will be effective, as well as to sites where the drug may be stored, metabolized, or eliminated from the body. Once a drug reaches its intended destination, the drug molecules move from blood through cellular barriers to various tissues. These barriers include the walls of blood vessels, the walls of the intestines, the walls of the kidneys, and the special barrier between the brain and the bloodstream that act as a filtration system to protect the brain from exposure to potentially harmful substances.

The drug molecules move from an area of high drug concentration—the bloodstream—to an area of low drug concentration—the tissues—until a balance between the two areas is reached. This process is known as diffusion. When a drug reaches its highest concentration in the tissues, the body begins to eliminate the drug and its effect on the body begins to diminish. The time it takes for the level of a drug to fall by 50 percent is known as the drug's half-life. Depending on the drug, this measurement can vary from a few minutes to hours or even days. For example, if a drug's highest concentration level in the blood is 1 mg/ml and this level falls to 0.5 mg/ml after five hours, the half-life of the drug is five hours. A drug's half-life is used to determine frequency of dosage and the amount of drug administered.

Distribution of a drug may be delayed by the binding of the drug to proteins in the blood. Because the proteins are too large to pass through blood vessel walls, the drug remains in the blood for a longer period until it is eventually released from the proteins. While this process may increase the particular amounts of times intermittence in the body, deceasing the amount of the drug's available potential among the tissues.

While circulating through the body, a drug undergoes chemical changes as it is broken down in a process called metabolism, or biotransformation. Most of these changes occur in the liver, but they can take place in other tissues as well. Various enzymes oxidize (add oxygen to), reduce (remove oxygen from), or hydrolyze (add water to) the drug. These changes produce new chemicals or metabolites that may continue to be medically active in the body or may have no activity at all. A drug may be broken down into many different metabolites. Eventually, most drugs or their metabolites circulate through the kidney, where they are discharged, or eliminated, into the urine. Drugs can also be excreted in the body's solid waste products, or evaporated through perspiration or the breath.

The extent of the body's response to a drug depends on the amount administered, called the dose. At a low dose, no response may be apparent. A higher dose, however, may produce the desired effect. An even higher dose may produce an undesirable or harmful response. For example, to relieve a headache most adults require two tablets of aspirin. A half tablet may provide no relief from pain while ten tablets may cause burning pain in the stomach or nausea.

The doses prescribed by physicians are those recommended by each drug's manufacturer to produce the best therapeutic, or medically beneficial, responses in the majority of patients. However, doses may need to be adjusted in certain individuals. For example, a person may be born without the enzyme required to metabolize a particular drug while other individuals may suffer from lung disorders that prevent them from absorbing inhaled drugs. Factors such as alcohol consumption, age, the method of drug administration, and whether or not the individual has taken the drug previously can affect an individual's response to a drug.

Drugs interact with cell receptors, small parts of proteins that control a multitude of chemical reactions and functions in the body. Receptors have a specific, chemical structure compatible only with certain drugs or endogenous compounds—substances that originate within the body such as hormones and neurotransmitters. This relationship can be compared to that of a lock and key: A drug molecule—the "key"—attaches briefly to its specific receptor—the "lock" that only this molecule can open. The lock-and-key combination of the drug and receptor results in a cascade of chemical events. The extent of the response is determined by the number of receptors activated. Stimulation of only a few receptors may not produce a response while stimulation of a certain number of receptors is needed to produce the desired effect.

The same receptors can be found in different tissues and organs in the body, but receptors produce different responses depending on their location. As a result, a specific drug can affect the body in more than one way. Desirable effects are called therapeutic or beneficial responses. Undesirable or harmful effects are called adverse reactions. Some adverse reactions, or side effects, can be predicted. The most common side effects are drowsiness, headache, sleeplessness, nausea, and diarrhea. Other reactions, such as those that occur only in specific individuals for unexpected reasons, called idiosyncratic reactions, and those that occur with the triggering of the body's immune system, called allergic reactions, are less predictable.

Drug toxicity, or poisoning, can occur when drugs are given in too large a dose or when individuals take a particular drug over a long period of time, the drug may build up to dangerous levels in the kidneys and liver and damage these organs. For some drugs, such as those used to treat epilepsy, the difference between therapeutic and toxic concentrations is small. Physicians constantly monitor the precise levels of such drugs in an individual's bloodstream to prevent drug poisoning.

Other drugs, such as those used to treat cancer, are known to have toxic effects; all the same, benefits outweigh the risks—that is, treatment without them may result in death.

When a previously healthy 53-year-old woman died of heart failure in August 1997, doctors were baffled. Eventually, the medical examiner's autopsy report would link her death to complications associated with the use of fenfluramine and phentermine, a diet drug combination popularly known as fen-phen. At the time of the woman's death, doctors were writing about 20 million prescriptions for this drug therapy annually. In September 1997, two months after the United States Food and Drug Administration (FDA) issued this warning, the FDA asked manufacturers to voluntarily withdraw fen-phen from the market.

When taken together, drugs can interact with one another and produce desirable or undesirable results. Some drugs have an additive effect—that is, they increase the effect of other drugs. For example, alcoholic beverages intensify the drowsiness-producing effect of some sedatives. Drugs that displace, or take the place of other drugs present in blood proteins, make the displaced drugs more active in the body, increasing their effect. Other drugs have a reducing effect—that is, they interfere with the action of drugs already present in the body. For example, antacids prevent antibiotics from being absorbed by the stomach. Some drugs combine with other drugs to create a substance that has no medical benefit. In some cases, however, drug interactions can produce desirable results. Doctors have found that using three drugs to fight AIDS is more effective than one drug used alone.

Drugs are most effective when properly prescribed by physicians and taken correctly by patients. Missing doses, taking drugs at the wrong time of the day or with instead of before meals, and stopping drug use too soon can markedly reduce the medical benefits of many drugs.

Drug abuse is characterized by taking more than the recommended dose of prescription drugs such as barbiturates without medical supervision, or using government-controlled substances such as marijuana, cocaine, heroin, or other illegal substances. Legal substances, such as alcohol and nicotine, are also abused by many people. Abuse of drugs and other substances can lead to physical and psychological dependence.

Drug abuse can cause a wide variety of adverse physical reactions. Long-term drug use may damage the heart, liver, and brain. Drug abusers may suffer from malnutrition if they habitually forget to eat, cannot afford to buy food, or eat foods lacking the proper vitamins and minerals. Individuals who abuse injectable drugs risk contracting infections such as hepatitis and HIV from dirty needles or needles shared with other infected abusers. One of the most dangerous effects of illegal drug use is the potential for overdosing—that is, taking too large or too strong a dose for the body's systems to handle. A drug overdose may cause an individual to lose consciousness and to breathe inadequately. Without treatment, an individual may die of a drug overdose.

Drug addiction is marked by a compulsive craving for a substance. Successful treatment methods vary and include psychological counselling, or psychotherapy, and detoxification programs— medically supervised programs that gradually wean an individual from a drug over a period of days or weeks. Detoxification and psychotherapy are often used together.

The illegal use of drugs was once considered a problem unique to residents of poor, urban neighbourhoods. Today, however, people from all economic levels, in both cities and suburbs, abuse drugs. Some people use drugs to relieve stress and to forget about their problems. Genetic factors may predispose other individuals to drug addiction. Environmental factors such as peer pressure, especially in young people, and the availability of drugs, also influence people to abuse drugs.

Humans have always experimented with substances derived from minerals, plants, and animal parts to treat pain, illness, and restore health. In ancient Egypt, physicians prescribed figs, dates, and castor oil as laxatives and used tannic acid to treat burns. The early Chinese and Greek pharmacies included opium, known for its pain-relieving qualities, while Hindus used the cannabis and henbane plants as anaesthetics and the root of the plant Rauwolfia serpentina, which contains reserpine, as a tranquillizer.

A school of pharmacy established in Arabia from 750 to 1258 ad discovered many substances effective against illness, such as burned sponge (which contains iodine) for the treatment of goiters—a noncancerous enlargement of the thyroid gland, visible as a swelling at the front of the neck. In Europe, the 15th century Swiss physician and chemist Philippus Aureolus Paracelsus identified the characteristics of numerous diseases such as syphilis, a chronic infectious disease usually transmitted in sexual intercourse, and used ingredients such as sulfur and mercury compounds to counter the diseases.

During the 17th and 18th centuries, physicians treated malaria, a disease transmitted by the bite of an infected mosquito, with the bark of the cinchona tree (which contains quinine). Heart failure was treated with the leaves of the foxglove plant (which contains digitalis); scurvy, a disease caused by vitamin C deficiency, was treated with citrus fruit (which contains vitamin C); and smallpox was prevented using inoculations of cells infected with a similar viral disease known as cowpox. The therapy developed for smallpox stimulated the body's immune system, which defends against disease-causing agents, to produce cowpox and smallpox-specific antibodies.

In the 19th century scientists continued to discover new drugs including ether, morphine, and a vaccine for rabies, an infectious, often fatal, viral disease of mammals that attacks the central nervous system and is transmitted by the bite of infected animals. These substances, however, were limited to those occurring naturally in plants, minerals, and animals. A growing understanding of chemistry soon changed, the way drugs were developed. Heroin and aspirin, two of the first synthetic drugs created from other elements or compounds using chemical reactions, were produced in the late 1800s. This development, combined with the establishment of a new discipline called pharmacology, the study of drugs and their actions on the body, signalled the birth of the modern drug industry.

Developing a new drug is a time-consuming, expensive process that often requires up to 10 years. The process begins with laboratory experiments resulting in the synthesis and purification of a possible new drug. The compound then goes through a series of tests in animal and human subjects to determine if it is safe and effective against disease. When those studies are completed, the Food and Drug Administration (FDA) decides whether to approve the drug for sale in the United States.

Today most drugs are synthesized by chemists in the laboratory. Synthetic drugs are better controlled than those occurring naturally, which ensures that each dose imparts the same effect. Some new synthetic drugs are developed by modifying the structure of existing substances. These new drugs are called analogues. For example, prednisone is an analogue of the hormone cortisone. Because scientists can selectively alter the drug's structure, analogues may be more effective and cause fewer side effects than the drugs from which they were derived.

The design and synthesis of new molecules is as much a process of human creativity as is the composition of a poem or the production of a sculpture, Polish-born American chemist Roald Hoffmann argues in the following article. Hoffmann, who shared the 1981 Nobel Prize in chemistry, compares and contrasts the artificial synthesis of naturally occurring compounds and the production of new molecules conceived of by chemists. Hoffmann's essay appeared in Scientific American in 1993.

One of the newer methods for developing drugs involves the use of gene splicing, or recombinant DNA. In drug research, this technique joins the DNA of a specific type of human cell to the DNA of a second organism, usually a harmless bacterium, to produce a recombinant (or "recombined") DNA. The altered organism then begins to produce the substance produced by the human cell. This substance is extracted from the bacteria and purified for use as a drug.

The first drug produced in this manner was the hormone insulin in 1982, which was created in large quantities by inserting the human insulin gene in Escherichia coli (E. coli) bacteria. Since 1982 other genetically engineered drugs for humans have been developed, including its tissue plasminogen activator (tPA), an enzyme used to dissolve blood clots in people who have suffered heart attacks, and erythropoetin, a hormone used to stimulate the production of red blood cells in people with severe anaemia.

Because of the great expense and time involved, most new drugs are created by large, well-funded pharmaceutical companies. From idea to production, the development of a new drug can take up to ten years and cost about $200 million. The process usually starts with the idea that an existing chemical substance has therapeutic value or that the structure of an existing drug can be modified for new clinical uses. Out of 10,000 chemicals tested in a laboratory, only one may eventually become a drug.

Once drug researchers have determined that a new substance may have medical value, an elaborate testing program begins. The drug is tested first on small animals such as rats and mice, and then on larger animals such as monkeys and dogs. If these tests indicate that the new drug is effective against its intended target—such as a particular disease—and shows an acceptably low level of toxicity, the drug company requests permission from the Food and Drug Administration (FDA), an agency of the US Department of Health and Human Services, to test the drug in humans.

If the agency approves the request, clinical trials on humans can begin. These experiments are usually divided into three phases, each of which can last from several months to several years. In the first phase, the drug is tested on a small number of healthy individuals to determine its effect on the body. The second phase tests the drug on a small number of people who have the disease or disorder the drug manufacturer hopes the drug will treat. These individuals are divided into two groups: those who receive the drug and those who receive a placebo, or inactive compound. Neither the investigating physicians nor the members of the test group know who is receiving the drug or who is receiving the placebo. This procedural protocol is called a double-blind study, ensures that no one consciously or unconsciously influence the drug's effect. The third phase tests the drug on a much larger group of people and determines specific doses, possible interactions with other drugs, responses related to gender, and other information used for drug labelling. At the end of the third phase, a drug manufacturer compiles the results of the clinical trials and submits them to the FDA in a new product application. If the drug has been proven effective and safe, and its benefits outweigh any risks, the agency approves the drug for marketing. FDA approval of a new drug may take up to 18 months; however, the agency is working to reduce the time to 12 months for most drugs and 6 months for highly effective drugs that treat previously incurable conditions.

Just weeks after United States drug czar General Barry McCaffrey described his Mexican counterpart, General Jesus Gutiérrez Rebollo, as a man of "absolute, unquestioned integrity," Gutiérrez was arrested in Mexico on charges of taking bribes from a drug cartel in exchange for protecting cocaine shipments into the United States.

Because drugs can produce harmful effects when manufactured or taken improperly, most governments control drug development as well as availability. In the United States, the FDA determines how drugs are produced and how they are sold. Drugs that can be sold over the counter (OTC)—that is, without a prescription from a physician—are called proprietary drugs. They are considered safe for unsupervised use by the general population. Drugs that must be prescribed by physicians and dispensed by pharmacists are known as ethical drugs. Their use is monitored closely by medical personnel.

The FDA regulates the sale and manufacture of drugs in the United States as outlined in applicable laws enacted over the past century. Legal standards for composition and preparation of drugs in the United States are found in the publication known as the United States Pharmacopeia (USP). Drugs that can be abused, such as the powerful narcotic heroin, are regulated by the Drug Enforcement Administration (DEA) of the US Department of Justice to ensure that they are not prescribed or sold illegally.

Before 1900 any individual could sell a drug and claim it offered therapeutic benefits without medical proof. This changed after 1906 with the passage of the Pure Food and Drug Act, which required drug manufacturers to state the content, strength, and purity of each drug they produced. The Pure Food and Drug Act ended the practice of including morphine, cocaine, and heroin in drugs without the public's knowledge. In 1914 the US legislature began to strictly regulate the trade of narcotics with the enactment of the Harrison Narcotic Act; in 1937 the government added marijuana to this list of controlled substances (the Marijuana Tax Act).

The Federal Food, Drug, and Cosmetic Act was enacted in 1938 requiring that new drugs be safe for humans; however, it did not require that manufacturers prove their drugs' effectiveness. It would be 24 years before legislation was passed that would require proof of the efficacy of new drugs (the Kefaver-Harris Amendments, 1962). Enforcement of this law was entrusted to the FDA.

Two laws enacted in the 1960s strengthened the FDA's efforts to reduce drug abuse. The Drug Abuse Control Amendments of 1965 provided penalties for the illegal sale or possession of stimulants, sedatives, and hallucinogens, and the Narcotic Addict

Rehabilitation Act of 1966 set up a federal program for addicts that provided them with the option of receiving treatment for their drug problems in place of a prison sentence.

In 1970 the Comprehensive Drug Abuse Prevention and Control Act established rules for manufacturing and prescribing habit-forming drugs. It stipulated that physicians can prescribe all drugs, but a special license is required to prescribe drugs with high abusive potential. This license is issued by the Drug Enforcement Administration.

The Anti-Drug Abuse Acts, signed into law in 1986 and 1988, set up funding for the treatment of drug abuse and for the creation of law-enforcement programs to fight the illegal sale of drugs. These acts also detailed severe punishments for individuals selling and possessing drugs illegally. Harsh penalties for using anabolic steroids (hormones that promote the storage of protein and the growth of tissue that are sometimes abused by competitive athletes) were included in the 1988 act, along with the requirement that all alcoholic beverages be labelled with warnings about alcohol's potentially dangerous effect on the body. The 1988 act also established the Office of National Drug Control Policy to develop an action plan that would involve the public, as well as private agencies, in eliminating the illegal sale of drugs; in helping individuals to discontinue and prevent users from ever starting to use drugs.

The US government and its regulatory agencies continually monitor the development and use of all drugs sold in the United States to ensure that the American public has access only to drugs that are safe and effective. Recently, the FDA introduced legislation requiring warning labels on all over-the-counter medication after research indicated that the nonaspirin pain reliever acetaminophen can cause liver damage when taken in high doses with large quantities of alcohol.

Psychoactive Drugs, chemical substances that alter mood, behaviour, perception, or mental functioning. Throughout history, many cultures have found ways to alter consciousness through the ingestion of substances. In current professional practice, psychoactive substances known as Psychotropic drugs have been developed to treat patients with severe mental illness.

Psychoactive substances exert their effects by modifying biochemical or physiological processes in the brain. The message system of nerve cells, or neurons, relies on both electrical and chemical transmission. Neurons rarely touch each other; the microscopic gap between one neuron and the next, called the synapse, is bridged by chemicals called neuroregulators, or neurotransmitters. Psychoactive drugs act by altering neurotransmitter function. The drugs can be divided into six major pharmacological classes based on their desired behavioural or psychological effect: alcohol, sedative-hypnotics, narcotic analgesics, stimulant-euphoriants, hallucinogens, and Psychotropic agents.

Alcohol has always been the most widely used psychoactive substance. In most countries it is the only psychoactive drug legally available without prescription. Pleasant relaxation is commonly the desired effect, but intoxication impairs judgment and motor performance. When used chronically, alcohol can be toxic to liver and brain cells and can be physiologically addicting, producing dangerous withdrawal syndromes.

Sedative-hypnotics, such as the barbiturates and diazepam (widely known under the brand name Valium), include brain depressants, which are used medically to help people sleep (sleeping pills), and antianxiety agents, which are used to calm people without inducing sleep. Sedative-hypnotics are used illegally to produce relaxation, tranquillity, and euphoria. Overdoses of sedative-hypnotics can be fatal; all can be physiologically addicting, and some can cause a life-threatening withdrawal syndrome.

Narcotic analgesics—opiates, such as morphine and heroin—are prescribed to produce analgesia. Because the relief of pain is one of the primary tasks of medical treatment, opiates have been among the most important and valuable drugs in medicine. Illegal use of narcotic analgesics involves injecting these substances, particularly heroin, into the veins to produce euphoria. Opiates are physiologically addicting and can produce a quite unpleasant withdrawal syndrome.

Stimulant-euphoriants, such as amphetamines, are prescribed by physicians to suppress the appetite and to treat children often diagnosed as hyperactive. Although amphetamines stimulate adults, they have a paradoxically calming effect on certain children who have short attention spans and are hyperactive. Cocaine is used medically as a local anaesthetic. Amphetamines and cocaine are used illegally to produce alertness and euphoria, to prevent drowsiness, and to improve performance in physical and mental tasks such as athletic events and college examinations.

Hallucinogens—psychedelic drugs such as LSD (Lysergic Acid Diethylamide), mescaline, and PCP (Phencyclidine)—thus far have little medical use. They are taken illegally to alter perception and thinking patterns. Marijuana is a weak hallucinogen that may be medically useful in suppressing the nausea caused by cancer treatments and possibly in reducing eye pressure in certain severe glaucomas.

Psychotropic drugs have been in use since the early 1950s. Antipsychotic drugs decrease the symptoms of schizophrenia, allowing many schizophrenic patients to leave the hospital and rejoin community life. Antidepressant drugs help the majority of patients with severe depression recover from their disorder. Lithium salts eliminate or diminish the episodes of mania and depression experienced by manic-depressive patients

Generally, the overall prevalence rates of mental illnesses between men and women are similar. However, men have much higher rates of antisocial personality disorder and substance abuse. In the United States, women suffer from depression and anxiety disorders at about twice the rate of men. The gender gap is even wider in some countries. For example, in China, women suffer from depression at nine times the rate of men.

Mental illness is becoming an increasing problem for two reasons. First, increases in life expectancy have brought increased numbers of certain chronic mental illnesses. For example, because more people are living into old age, more people are suffering from dementia. Second, a number of studies provide evidence that rates of depression are rising throughout the world. The reasons may be related to such factors as economic change, political and social violence, and cultural disruptions. While some have questioned these findings, dramatic increases in the numbers of refugees and people dislocated from their homes by economic forces or civil strife are associated with great increases in a variety of mental illnesses for those populations. According to the United Nations High Commissioner for Refugees, the number of refugees worldwide increased from 2.5 million in 1971 to 13.2 million in 1996, peaking at 17 million in 1991.

A number of mental illnesses—such as depression, anxiety disorders, schizophrenia, and bipolar disorder—occur worldwide. Others seem to occur only in particular cultures. For example, eating disorders, such as anorexia nervosa (compulsive dieting associated with unrealistic fears of fatness), occurs mostly between girls and women in Europe, North America, and Westernized areas of Asia, whose cultures view thinness as an essential component of female beauty. In Latin America, people who experience overwhelming fright after a dangerous or traumatic event are said to have susto (fright), an illness in which their soul has been frightened away. In some societies of West Africa and elsewhere, brain fatigue describes individuals (usually students) who experience difficulties in concentrating and thinking, as well as physical symptoms of pain and fatigue.

Most mental health professionals in the United States use the Diagnostic and Statistical Manual of Mental Disorders(DSM), a reference book published by the American Psychiatric Association, as a guide to the different kinds of mental illnesses. The fourth edition, known as DSM-IV, describes more than 300 mental disorders, behavioural disorders, addictive disorders, and other psychological problems and groups them into broad categories. This article describes some of the major categories, including anxiety disorders, mood disorders, schizophrenia and other psychotic disorders, personality disorders, cognitive disorders, dissociative disorders, somatoform disorders, factitious disorders, substance-related disorders, eating disorders, and impulse-control disorders. Mental health professionals in many other parts of the world use a different classification system, the International Classification of Diseases (ICD), published by the World Health Organization.

The DSM and ICD are both categorical systems of classification, in which each mental illness is defined by its own unique set of symptoms and characteristics. In theory, each disorder should possess diagnostic criteria that are independent of one another, just as tuberculosis and lung cancer are discrete diseases. Yet symptoms of many mental disorders overlap, and many people— such as those who experience both depression and severe anxiety— show symptoms of more than one disorder at the same time. For these reasons, some mental health professionals advocate a dimensional system of classification. In contrast to the categorical approach, which sees mental disorders as qualitatively distinct from normal behaviour, a dimensional system views behaviour as falling along a continuum of normality, with some behaviours considered more abnormal than others. In a dimensional system, diagnoses do not describe discrete diseases but rather portray the relative importance of an array of symptoms.

Definitions and classifications of mental illnesses change as research improves understanding of them. For example, DSM-IV allows a diagnosis of schizophrenia only when characteristic symptoms have lasted at least one month, whereas the previous edition of DSM required a duration of only one week.

Anxiety disorders involve excessive apprehension, worry, and fear. People with generalized anxiety disorder experience constant anxiety about routine events in their lives. Phobias are fears of specific objects, situations, or activities. Panic disorder is an anxiety disorder in which people experience sudden, intense terror and such physical symptoms as rapid heartbeat and shortness of breath. People with obsessive-compulsive disorder experience intrusive thoughts or images (obsessions) or feel compelled to perform certain behaviours (compulsions). People with post-traumatic stress disorder relive traumatic events from their past and feel extreme anxiety and distress about the event.

Mood disorders, also called affective disorders, create disturbances in a person's emotional life. Depression, mania, and bipolar disorder are examples of mood disorders. Symptoms of depression may include feelings of sadness, hopelessness, and worthlessness, as well as complaints of physical pain and changes in appetite, sleep patterns, and energy level. In mania, on the other hand, an individual experiences an abnormally elevated mood, often marked by exaggerated self-importance, irritability, agitation, and a decreased need for sleep. In bipolar disorder, also called manic-depressive illness, a person's mood alternates between extremes of mania and depression.

Bipolar disorder is a mental illness that causes mood swings. In the manic phase, a person might feel ecstatic, self-important, and energetic. But when the person becomes depressed, the mood shifts to extreme sadness, negative thinking, and apathy. Some studies indicate that the disease occurs at unusually high rates in creative people, such as artists, writers, and musicians. But some researchers contend that the methodology of these studies was flawed and their results were misleading. In the October 1996 Discover magazine article, anthropologist Jo Ann C. Gutin presents the results of several studies that explore the link between creativity and mental illness.

Some people with schizophrenia experience delusions of persecution—false beliefs that other people are plotting against them. This interview between a patient with schizophrenia and his therapist illustrates the paranoia that can affect people with this illness.

People with schizophrenia and other psychotic disorders lose contact with reality. Symptoms may include delusions and hallucinations, disorganized thinking and speech, bizarre behaviour, a diminished range of emotional responsiveness, and social withdrawal. In addition, people who suffer from these illnesses experience the inability to function in one or more important areas of life, such as social relations, work, or school.

Personality disorders are mental illnesses in which one's personality results in personal distress or a significant impairment in social or work functioning. In general, people with personality disorders have poor perceptions of themselves or others. They may have low self-esteem or overwhelming narcissism, poor impulse control, troubled social relationships, and inappropriate emotional responses. Considerable controversy exists over where to draw the distinction between a normal personality and a personality disorder.

Cognitive disorders, such as delirium and dementia, involve a significant loss of mental functioning. Dementia, for example, is characterized by impaired memory and difficulties in such functions as speaking, abstract thinking, and the ability to identify familiar objects. The conditions in this category usually result from a medical condition, substance abuse, or adverse reactions to medication or poisonous substances

Senile Dementia, form of general intellectual impairment observed in elderly people. Approximately 10 percent of all people more than 65 years of age have clinically important intellectual impairment. Although about 20 percent of these cases may be due to treatable causes such as toxic drug reactions, most cases are what is known as Alzheimer's disease.

Senile dementia begins with failing attention and memory, loss of mathematical ability, irritability and loss of sense of humour, and poor orientation in space and time. Alzheimer's disease is relentlessly progressive and leads to death in 5 to 15 years. Examinations of the brains of persons who have died of Alzheimer's disease show characteristic twisted fibres, called neurofibrilar tangles, in certain areas of the brain, and cores of abnormal protein, called neuritic plaques, interspersed among nerve cells. No cure is known for Alzheimer's disease. A form of this disease strikes younger persons, in whom it is known as presenile dementia.

Dissociative disorders are involved in a psychological dissociation or the condition of having been dissociated, that the process by which the action of a change in psychological social condition. As the causes a molecule to spin into simpler groups of atoms or ions. The separation of an electrolyte into ions of opposite charge such as a psychological defence mechanism into ions of opposite change, yet a psychological emotion, or physical sensation are s separated from the rest of the psyche. For which a highly disputed psychological disorder in which a person exhibits two or more dissociative personalities, each functioning as a distinct entity.

Also, to involve disturbances in a person's consciousness, memories, identity, and perception of the environment. Dissociative disorders include amnesia that has no physical cause; dissociative identity disorder, in which a person has two or more distinct personalities that alternate in their control of the person's behaviour, depersonalization or demecularization disorders characterized by a chronic feeling of being detached from one's body or mental processes, and dissociative fugue, an episode of sudden departure from home or work with an accompanying loss of memory. In some parts of the world people experience dissociative states as "possession" by a god or ghost instead of separate personalities. In many societies, trance and possession states are normal parts of cultural and religious practices and are not considered dissociative disorders.

Somatoform disorders are characterized by the presence of physical symptoms that cannot be explained by a medical condition or another mental illness. Thus, physicians often judge that such symptoms result from psychological conflicts or distress. For example, in conversion disorder, also called hysteria, a person may experience blindness, deafness, or seizures, but a physician cannot find anything wrong with the person. People with another significantly relevant somatoform disorder, hypochondriasis constantly fears that they will develop a serious disease and misinterpret minor physical symptoms as evidence of that illness. The term somatoform comes from the Greek word soma, meaning "body."

In contrast to people with somatoform disorders, people with factitious disorders intentionally produce or fake physical or psychological symptoms in order to receive medical attention and care. For example, an individual might falsely report shortness of breath to gain admittance to a hospital, report thoughts of suicide to solicit attention, or fabricate blood in the urine or the symptoms of rash so as to appear ill. Munchausen syndrome represents the most extreme and chronic variants of the factitious disorders.

Substance-related disorders result from the abuse of drugs, side effects of medications, or exposure to toxic substances. Many mental health professionals regard these disorders as behavioural or addictive disorders rather than as mental illnesses, although substance-related disorders commonly occur in people with mental illnesses. Common substance-related disorders include alcoholism and other forms of drug dependence. In addition, drug use can contribute to symptoms of other mental disorders, such as depression, anxiety, and psychosis. Drugs associated with substance-related disorders include alcohol, caffeine, nicotine, cocaine, heroin, amphetamines, hallucinogens, and sedatives.

Osteoporosis, breast cancer, and eating disorders are sometimes considered women's diseases, but doctors have found that men may also suffer from these same medical problems. Because men have these conditions so rarely, detection and treatment are often quite slow. To help with early diagnosis, this article from FDA Consumer describes some of the symptoms and possible causes of these serious diseases.

Eating disorders are conditions in which an individual experience severe disturbances in eating behaviours. People with anorexia nervosa have an intense fear about gaining weight and refuse to eat adequately or maintain a normal body weight. People with bulimia nervosa repeatedly engage in episodes of binge eating, usually followed by self-induced vomiting or the use of laxatives, diuretics, or other medications to prevent weight gain. Eating disorders occur mostly among young women in Western societies and certain parts of Asia.

People with impulse-control disorders cannot control an impulse to engage in harmful behaviours, such as explosive anger, stealing (kleptomania), setting fires (pyromania), gambling, or pulling out their own hair (trichotillomania). Some mental illnesses—such as mania, schizophrenia, and antisocial personality disorder—may include symptoms of impulsive behaviour.

People have tried to understand the causes of mental illness for thousands of years. The modern era of psychiatry, which began in the late 19th and early 20th centuries, has witnessed a sharp debate between biological and psychological perspectives of mental illness. The biological perspective views mental illness in terms of bodily processes, whereas psychological perspectives emphasize the roles of a person's upbringing and environment.

These two perspectives are exemplified in the work of German psychiatrist Emil Kraepelin and Austrian psychoanalyst Sigmund Freud. Kraepelin, influenced by the work in the mid-1800s of German psychiatrist Wilhelm Griesinger, believed that psychiatric disorders were disease entities that could be classified like physical illnesses. That is, Kraepelin believed that the fundamental causes of mental illness lay in the physiology and biochemistry of the human brain. His classification system of mental disorders, first published in 1883, formed the basis for later diagnostic systems. Freud, on the other hand, argued that the source of mental illness lay in unconscious conflicts originating in early childhood experiences. Freud found evidence for this idea through the analysis of dreams, free association, and slips of speech.

This debate has continued into the late 20th century. Beginning in the 1960s, the biological perspective became dominant, supported by numerous breakthroughs in psychopharmacology, genetics, neurophysiology, and brain research. For example, scientists discovered many medications that helped to relieve symptoms of certain mental illnesses and demonstrated that people can inherit a vulnerability to some mental illnesses. Psychological perspectives also remain influential, including the psychodynamic perspective, the humanistic and existential perspectives, the behavioural perspective, the cognitive perspective, and the sociocultural perspective.

Many mental health professionals today favour a combination of perspectives, acknowledging that both biology and a person's environment play important roles in mental illness. This approach recognizes that people are not only products of the genes inherited from their parents, but products of the families and social worlds into which they are born. In this view, environments shape how biological factors will be manifested. For example, an infant may inherit genes that could enable her to become a tall adult, but if she is malnourished as a child, she will never achieve that potential. Likewise, an individual who does not possess a biological vulnerability for depression may nevertheless become severely depressed following the death of a loved one or after experiencing an act of torture.

MAO Inhibitor, any of a group of drugs used to treat depression, anxiety, or phobias. Properly known as monoamine oxidase (MAO) inhibitors, these drugs work by inhibiting or preventing the enzyme monoamine oxidase, found in the nervous system, from breaking down neurotransmitters, chemicals in the brain that control nerve impulse transmission and affect mood. MAO inhibitors produce a more balanced emotional state.

MAO inhibitors must be prescribed by a physician. Available in tablet form, these drugs are taken with or without food in one or more doses ranging from 30 to 90 mg per day, depending on the particular drug and the condition being treated. Effectiveness is usually apparent after three to four weeks of treatment, and long-term use for months or even years may be prescribed. MAO inhibitors should not be taken by pregnant women. Their safety for breast-feeding mothers or children under the age of 16 is not known.

These drugs should be used with caution by patients with heart or liver problems, diabetes, or epilepsy. MAO inhibitors can cause serious reactions, including death, if combined with certain foods that contain the chemical substance tyramine. Such foods include beer, wine, cheese, chocolate, sausage, liver, smoked meats or fish, sauerkraut, yogurt, and beverages containing caffeine.

Drugs to avoid while using MAO inhibitors include cold and cough remedies, sinus and hay fever medications, nasal decongestants, appetite suppressants, sleep aids, bronchodilators inhalants, amphetamines, and other antidepressants. Serious interactions can occur up to two weeks after drug treatment ends.

One significant side effect of MAO inhibitor drug use is high blood pressure, which may cause frequent headaches, heart palpitations, and vomiting. Other side effects include constipation, dizziness, fatigue, weakness, sleep disorders, digestive disorders, muscle spasms, problems with male sexual performance, and tremors or twitching. Because of the potential for serious side effects, patients taking MAO inhibitors are usually advised to carry a card or wear a bracelet that alerts medical personnel to their use of a MAO inhibitor in case of an emergence.

Antidepressant drugs help relieve symptoms of depression. Some antidepressant drugs can relieve symptoms of other disorders as well, such as panic disorder and obsessive-compulsive disorder. Antidepressant drugs comprise three major classes: tricyclic, monoamine, oxidase inhibitors (MAO inhibitors, and selective serotonin reuptake inhibitors (SSRIs). Side effects of tricyclics may include dizziness upon standing, blurred vision, dry mouth, difficulty urinating, constipation, and drowsiness. People who take MAO inhibitors may experience some of the same side effects, and must follow a special diet that excludes certain foods. SSRIs generally produce fewer side effects, although these may include anxiety, drowsiness, and sexual dysfunction. One type of SSRI, fluoxetine (Prozac) is the most widely prescribed antidepressant drug.

Antipsychotic drugs are used to regulate certain brain chemicals called neurotransmitters, which do not function properly in people with psychoses, major mental disorders often characterized by extreme behaviours and hallucinations, such as in schizophrenia. Antipsychotic drugs can often significantly alleviate hallucinations and other abnormal behaviours.

Antidepressant drugs reduce mental depression. Antimanic drugs reduce excessive mood swings in people with manic-depressive illness, which is characterized by behavioural fluctuations between highs of extreme excitement and activity and lows of lethargy and depression. Both types of drugs act by normalize chemical activity in the emotional centres of the brain. Antianxiety drugs, also referred to as tranquillizers, treat anxiety by decreasing the activity in the anxiety centres of the brain.

Anaesthesia induces unconsciousness and loss of sensation prior to surgery. During surgery, the anesthesiologist monitors the patient's condition and increases or decreases the dosage of Anaesthesia as needed.

Sedative-hypnotic drugs are used both as sedatives to reduce anxiety and as hypnotics to induce sleep. Sedative-hypnotic drugs act by reducing brain-cell activity. Stimulatory drugs, on the other hand, increase neuronal (nerve cell) activity and reduce fatigue and appetite.

Analgesic drugs reduce pain and are generally categorized as narcotics and non-narcotics. Narcotic analgesics, also known as opioids, include opium and the natural opium derivative's as of codeine and morphine synthetic derivatives of morphia, as in, heroin and synthetic drugs such as a meperidine and propoxyphene hydrochloride. Narcotics relieve pain by acting on specific structures, called receptors, located on the nerve cells of the spinal cord or brain. Non-narcotic analgesics such as aspirin, acetaminophen, and ibuprofen reduce pain by inhibiting the formation of nerve impulses at the site of pain. Some of these drugs can also reduce fever and inflammation.

Many other categories of drugs also exist, such as anti-inflammatory, antiallergic, antiparkinson, antiworm, diuretic, gastrointestinal, pulmonary, and muscle-relaxant drugs. Often a drug in one category can also be used for problems in other categories. For example, lidocaine can be used as a local anaesthetic or as a cardiac drug.

Certain drugs work by interacting with receptors, special sites on the surface of body cells. Drugs may bind to a specific receptor, possibly preventing naturally occurring chemicals from binding to the receptor. In so doing, if a drug enhances cell activity, it is called an agonist; if it blocks cell activity, it is called an antagonist.

The effect of a drug on the body depends on a number of processes that the drug undergoes as it moves through the body. All these processes together are known as pharmacokinetics (literally, "motion of the drug"). First in these processes is the administration of the drug after which it must be absorbed into the bloodstream. From the bloodstream, the drug is distributed throughout the body to various tissues and organs. As the drug is metabolized, or broken down and used by the body, it goes through chemical changes that produce metabolites, or altered forms of the drug, most of which have no effect on the body. Finally, the drug and its metabolites are eliminated from the body.

Depression is a mental illness in which a person experiences deep, unshakable sadness and diminished interest in nearly all activities. People also use the term depression to describe the temporary sadness, loneliness, or blues that everyone feels from time to time. In contrast to normal sadness, severe depression, also called major depression, can dramatically impair a person's ability to function in social situations and at work. People with major depression often have feelings of despair, hopelessness, and worthlessness, as well as thoughts of committing suicide.

Depression can take several other forms. In bipolar disorder, sometimes called manic-depressive illness, a person's mood swings back and forth between depression and mania. People with seasonal affective disorder typically suffer from depression only during autumn and winter, when there are fewer hours of daylight. In dysthymia (pronounced dis-THI-mee-uh), people feel depressed, have low self-esteem, and concentrate poorly most of the time—often for a period of years—but their symptoms are milder than in major depression. Some people with dysthymia experience mood disorders characterized by depression.

Bipolar disorder is a mental illness that causes mood swings. In the manic phase, a person might feel ecstatic, self-important, and energetic. But when the person becomes depressed, the mood shifts to extreme sadness, negative thinking, and apathy. Some studies indicate that the disease occurs at unusually high rates in creative people, such as artists, writers, and musicians. But some researchers contend that the methodology of these studies was flawed and their results were misleading. In the October 1996 Discover magazine article, anthropologist Jo Ann C. Gutin presents the results of several studies that explore the link between creativity and mental illness.

Surveys indicate that people commonly view depression as a sign of personal weakness, but psychiatrists and psychologists view it as a real illness. In the United States, the National Institute of Mental Health has estimated that depression costs society many billions of dollars each year, mostly in lost work time.

The reality of depression is one of the most common mental illnesses. At least 8 percent of adults in the United States experience serious depression at some point during their lives, and estimates range as high as 17 percent. The illness affects all people, regardless of sex, race, ethnicity, or socioeconomic standing. However, women are two to three times more likely than men to suffer from depression. Experts disagree on the reason for this difference. Some cite differences in hormones, and others point to the stress caused by society's expectations of women.

Studies indicate that depression is more prevalent among women than it is among men. Genetics and environment seem to be the keys to unlocking this gender-gap mystery, although the complexity of the puzzle makes progress slow. In this article for Scientific American Presents, physician Ellen Leibenluft explores the physiology of depression and explains how scientific research may make it possible to develop better treatments for both sexes.

Depression occurs in all parts of the world, although the pattern of symptoms can vary. The prevalence of depression in other countries varies widely, from 1.5 percent of people in Taiwan to 19 percent of people in Lebanon. Some researchers believe methods of gathering data on depression account for different rates.

A number of large-scale studies indicate that depression rates have increased worldwide over the past several decades. Furthermore, younger generations are experiencing depression at an earlier age than did previous generations. Social scientists have proposed many explanations, including changes in family structure, urbanization, and reduced cultural and religious influences.

Although it may appear anytime from childhood to old age, depression usually begins during a person's 20s or 30s. The illness may come on slowly, then deepen gradually over months or years. On the other hand, it may erupt suddenly in a few weeks or days. A person who develops severe depression may appear confused, frightened, and unbalanced that observers spoke of a "nervous breakdown." However it begins, that depression causes serious changes in a person's feelings and outlook. A person with major depression feels sad nearly every day and may cry often. People, work, and activities that used to bring them pleasure no longer do.

Symptoms of depression can vary by age. In younger children, depression may include physical complaints, such as stomachaches and headaches, as well as irritability, "moping around," social withdrawal, and changes in eating habits. They may feel unenthusiastic about school and other activities. In adolescents, common symptoms include sad mood, sleep disturbances, and lack of energy. Elderly people with depression usually complain of physical rather than emotional problems, which sometimes leads doctors to misdiagnose the illness.

Symptoms of depression can also vary by culture. In some cultures, depressed people may not experience sadness or guilt but may complain of physical problems. In Mediterranean cultures, for example, depressed people may complain of headaches or nerves. In Asian cultures they may complain of weakness, fatigue, or imbalance.

If left untreated, an episode of major depression typically lasts eight or nine months. About 85 percent of people who experience one bout of depression will experience future episodes.

Depression usually alters a person's appetite, sometimes increasing it, but usually reducing it. Sleeping habits often change as well. People with depression may oversleep or, more commonly, sleep for fewer hours. A depressed person might go to sleep at midnight, sleep restlessly, then wake up at 5:00 a.m. feeling tired and blue. For many depressed people, early morning is the saddest time of the day.

Depression also changes one's energy level. Some depressed people may be restless and agitated, engaging in fidgety movements and pacing. Others may feel sluggish and inactive, experiencing great fatigue, lack of energy, and a feeling of being worn out or carrying a heavy burden. Depressed people may also have difficulty thinking, poor concentration, and problems with memory.

People with depression often experience feelings of worthlessness, helplessness, guilt, and self-blame. They may interpret a minor failing on their part as a sign of incompetence or interpret minor criticism as condemnation. Some depressed people complain of being spiritually or morally dead. The mirror seems to reflect someone ugly and repulsive. Even a competent and decent person may feel deficient, cruel, stupid, phony, or guilty of having deceived others. People with major depression may experience such extreme emotional pain that they consider or attempt suicide. At least 15 percent of seriously depressed people commit suicide, and many more attempt it.

In some cases, people with depression may experience psychotic symptoms, such as delusions (false beliefs) and hallucinations (false sensory perceptions). Psychotic symptoms indicate an especially severe illness. Compared to other depressed people, those with psychotic symptoms have longer hospital stays, and after leaving, they are more likely to be moody and unhappy. They are also more likely to commit suicide.

Some depressions seem to come out of the blue, even when things are going well. Others seem to have an obvious cause: a marital conflict, financial difficulty, or some otherwise personal failure. Yet many people with these problems do not become deeply depressed. Most psychologists believe depression results from an interaction between stressful life events and a person's biological and psychological vulnerabilities.

Clinical depression is one of the most common forms of mental illness. Although depression can be treated with psychotherapy, many scientists believe there are biological causes for the disease. In the June 1998 Scientific American article, neurobiologist Charles B. Nemeroff discusses the connection between biochemical changes in the brain and depression.

Depression runs in families. By studying twins, researchers have found evidence of a strong genetic influence in depression. Genetically identical twins raised in the same environment are three times more likely to have depression in common than fraternal twins, who have only about half of their genes in common. In addition, identical twins are five times more likely to have bipolar disorder in common. These findings suggest that vulnerability to depression and bipolar disorder can be inherited. Adoption studies have provided more evidence of a genetic role in depression. These studies show that children of depressed people are vulnerable to depression even when raised by adoptive parents.

Genes may influence depression by causing abnormal activity in the brain. Studies have shown that certain brain chemicals called neurotransmitters play an important role in regulating moods and emotions. Neurotransmitters involved in depression include norepinephrine, dopamine, and serotonin. Research in the 1960s has suggested, that depression results from lower than normal levels of these neurotransmitters in parts of the brain. Support for this theory came from the effects of antidepressant drugs, which work by increasing the levels of neurotransmitters involved in depression. However, later studies have discredited this simple explanation and have suggested a more complex relationship between neurotransmitter levels and depression.

An imbalance of hormones may also play a role in depression. Many depressed people have higher than normal levels of hydrocortisone (cortisol), a hormone secreted by the adrenal gland in response to stress. In addition, an underactive or overactive thyroid gland can lead to depression.

Psychological theories of depression focus on the way people think and behave. In a 1917 essay, Austrian psychoanalyst Sigmund Freud explained melancholia, or major depression, as a response to loss—either real loss, such as the death of a spouse, or symbolic loss, such as the failure to achieve an important goal. Freud believed that a person's unconscious anger over loss weakens the ego, resulting in self-hate and self-destructive behaviour.

Cognitive theories of depression emphasize the role of irrational thought processes. American psychiatrist Aaron Beck proposed that depressed people tend to view themselves, their environment, and the future in a negative light because of errors in thinking. These errors include focussing on the negative aspects of any situation, misinterpreting facts in negative ways, and blaming themselves for any misfortune. In Beck's view, people learn these self-defeating ways of looking at the world during early childhood. This negative thinking makes situations seem much worse than they really are and increases the risk of depression, especially in stressful situations.

In support of this cognitive view, people with "depressive" personality traits appear to be more vulnerable than others to actual depression. Examples of depressive personality traits include gloominess, pessimism, introversion, self-criticism, excessive skepticism and criticism of others, deep feelings of inadequacy, and excessive brooding and worrying. In addition, people who regularly behave in dependent, hostile, and impulsive ways appear at greater risk for depression.

American psychologist Martin Seligman proposed that depression stem from "learned helplessness," an acquired belief that one cannot control the outcome of events. In this view, prolonged exposure to uncontrollable and inescapable events leads to apathy, pessimism, and loss of motivation. An adaptation of this theory by American psychologist Lynn Abramson and her colleagues argues that depression result not only from helplessness, but also from hopelessness. The hopelessness theory attributes depression to a pattern of negative thinking in which people blame themselves for negative life events, view the causes of those events as permanent, and overgeneralize specific weaknesses as applying to many areas of their life.

Psychologists agree that stressful experiences can trigger depression in people who are predisposed to the illness. For example, the death of a loved one may trigger depression. Psychologists usually distinguish true depression from grief, a normal process of mourning a loved one who has died. Other stressful experiences may include divorce, pregnancy, the loss of a job, and even childbirth. About 20 percent of women experience an episode of depression, known as postpartum depression, after having a baby. In addition, people with serious physical illnesses or disabilities often develop depression.

People having had the experience of child abuse appear more vulnerable to depression than others, so too, that people living under chronically stressful conditions, such as single mothers with many children and little or no support from friends or relatives.

Depression typically cannot be shaken or willed away. An episode must therefore run its course until it weakens either on its own or with treatment. Depression can be treated effectively with antidepressant drugs, psychotherapy, or a combination of both.

Despite the availability of effective treatment, most depressive disorders go untreated and undiagnosed. Studies indicate that general physicians fail to recognize depression in their patients at least half of the time. In addition, many doctors and patients view depression in elderly people as a normal part of aging, even though treatment for depression in older people is usually very effective.

Up to 70 percent of people with depression respond to antidepressant drugs. These medications appear to work by altering the levels of serotonin, norepinephrine, and other neurotransmitters in the brain. They generally take at least two to three weeks to become effective. Doctors cannot predict which type of antidepressant drug will work best for any particular person, so depressed people may need to try several types. Antidepressant drugs are not addictive, but they may produce unwanted side effects. To avoid relapses, people usually must continue taking the medication for several months after their symptoms improve.

Commonly used antidepressant drugs fall into three major classes: tricyclics, monoamine oxidase inhibitors (MAO inhibitors), and selective serotonin reuptake inhibitors (SSRIs). Tricyclics, named for their three-ring chemical structure, include amitriptyline (Elavil), imipramine (Tofanil), desipramine (Norpramin), doxepin (Sinequan), and Nortriptyline (Pamelor). Side effects of tricyclics may include drowsiness, dizziness upon standing, blurred vision, nausea, insomnia, constipation, and dry mouth.

MAO inhibitors include isocarboxazid (Marplan), phenelzine (Nardil), and tranylcypromine (Parnate). People who take MAO inhibitors must follow a diet that excludes tyramine—a substance found in wine, beer, some cheeses, and many fermented foods—avoiding a dangerous rise in blood pressure. In addition, MAO inhibitors have many of the same side effects as tricyclics.

Selective serotonin reuptake inhibitors include fluoxetine (Prozac), sertraline (Zoloft), and paroxetine (Paxil). These drugs generally produce fewer and milder side effects than do other types of antidepressants, although SSRIs may cause anxiety, insomnia, drowsiness, headaches, and sexual dysfunction. Some patients have alleged that Prozac causes violent or suicidal behaviour in a small number of cases, but the US Food and Drug Administration has failed to substantiate this claim.

Prozac became the most widely used antidepressant in the world soon after its introduction in the late 1980s by drug manufacturer Eli Lilly and Company. Many people find Prozac extremely effective in lifting depression. In addition, some people have reported that Prozac actually transforms their personality by increasing their self-confidence, optimism, and energy level. However, mental health professionals have expressed serious ethical concerns over Prozac's use as a "personality enhancer," especially among people without clinical depression.

Doctors often prescribe lithium carbonates, a natural mineral salt, to treat people with bipolar disorder. People often take lithium during periods of relatively normal moods to delay or even prevent subsequent mood swings. Side effects of lithium include nausea, stomach upset, vertigo, and frequent urination.

A psychologist listens to her client during a psychotherapy session. Psychotherapy can be an effective treatment for many mental disorders. Some forms of psychotherapy assist in helping people resolve their internal, unconscious conflicts, and other forms teach people skills to correct their abnormal behaviour.

Studies have shown that short-term psychotherapy can relieve mild to moderate depression as effectively as antidepressant drugs. Unlike medication, psychotherapy produces no physiological side effects. In addition, depressed people treated with psychotherapy appear less likely to experience a relapse than those treated only with antidepressant medication. However, psychotherapy usually takes longer to produce benefits.

There are many kinds of psychotherapy. Cognitive-behavioural therapy recognizes and acknowledges, that depression stems from negative, often irrational think about oneself and one's future. In this type of therapy, a person learns to understand and eventually eliminate those habits of negative thinking. In interpersonal therapy, the therapist helps a person resolve problems in relationships with others that may have caused the depression. The subsequent improvement in social relationships and support helps alleviate the depression. Psychodynamic therapy views depression as the result of internal, unconscious conflicts. Psychodynamic therapists focus on a person's past experiences and the resolution of childhood conflicts. Psychoanalysis is an example of this type of therapy. Critics of long-term psychodynamic therapy argue that its effectiveness is scientifically unproven.

Antidepressant, medication used to treat depression, a mood disorder characterized by such symptoms as sadness, decreased appetite, difficulty sleeping, fatigue, and a lack of enjoyment of activities previously found pleasurable. While everyone experiences episodes of sadness at some point in their lives, depression is distinguished from this sadness when symptoms are present most days for a period of at least two weeks. Antidepressants are often the first choice of treatment for depression.

Although the cause of depression is unknown, researchers have found that some depressed people have altered levels of chemicals called neurotransmitters, chemicals made and released by nerve cells, or neurons. One neuron, referred to as the presynaptic neuron, releases a neurotransmitter into the synapse, or space, between the neuron and a neighbouring cell. The neurotransmitter then attaches, or binds, to a neighbouring cell—the postsynaptic cell—to trigger a specific activity. Antidepressants work by interacting with neurotransmitters at three different points: they can change the rate at which the neurotransmitters are either created or broken down by the body; they can block the process in which a spent neurotransmitter is recycled by a presynaptic neuron and used again, called reuptake; or they can interfere with the binding of a neurotransmitter to neighbouring cells.

The first antidepressants, developed in the 1950s, are the tricyclic antidepressants (TCA) and the monoamine oxidase (MAO) inhibitors. TCAs block the reuptake of neurotransmitters into the presynaptic neurons, keeping the neurotransmitter in the synapse longer, and making more of the neurotransmitter available to the postsynaptic cell. TCAs include amitriptyline also a tricyclic antidepressant, doxepin, and imipramine that of any a tricyclic compound that is used to treat depression and enuresis is that which of the uncontrolled or involuntary discharge of urine happens, and nortriptyline acting as a tricyclic antidepressant, and desipramine of a tricyclic and used in the treatment of psychological depression, which is a tricyclic antidepressant used in the treatment of psychological depressions.

Monoamine oxidase (MAO) inhibitors as an amine compound-containing one amino group especially a compound that functions as a neurotransmitter, which are broken down by the body so they are more available to interact with neurons. MAO inhibitors currently available in the United States include phenelzine as a monoamine oxidase inhibitor, and used especially in the form of its sulfate as an antidepressant, and tranylcypromine.

Another group of antidepressants, known as selective serotonin reuptake inhibitors (SSRI), became available in 1987. SSRIs are a class of drugs, such as fluoxetine or sertraline that inhibit the uptake of serotonin by neurons of the central nervous system and are primarily used in the treatment of depression and obsessive compulsive disorders. There are currently four SSRIs available for use in the United States: fluoxetine, sertraline, paroxetine, and fluvoxamine. Of this group, the best known is fluoxetine as a derivative of enothiazine and used for the treatment of schizophrenia and other psychotic disorders

Another antidepressant is venlafaxine, which works very similar to TCAs but does not share their chemical structure, but also causes different side effects. Venlafaxine is an oral antidepressant and thought to inhibit neuronal uptake of serotonin, norepinephrine and dopamine in the central nervous system. It is structurally unrelatd to other antidepressants. The antidepressant nefazodone prevents serotonin from binding to neighbouring neurons at one specific binding junction (serotonin can bind to neurons on many sites). It weakly b locks the reuptake of serotonin. Nefazodone is an oral antidepressant with a chemical structure unrelated to SSRIs, tricyclics, or serotonin and norepinephrine in the central nervous system.

All antidepressants decrease symptoms of depression in about 70 percent of depressed people who take them. Most antidepressants take about two to three weeks of treatment before beneficial effects occur. Because no antidepressant is more effective than the others, doctors determine which antidepressant to prescribe according to the type of side effects an individual can tolerate. For instance, a person who takes TCAs and MAO inhibitors may notice dizziness and fainting when standing up, mouth dryness, difficulty urinating, constipation, and drowsiness. If people who take MAO inhibitors eat certain foods, such as aged cheese or some aged meats, they can experience severe headaches and raised blood pressure. SSRIs can cause side effects such as restlessness, difficulty sleeping, and interference with sexual function.

Mood disorders, also called affective disorders, create disturbances in a person's emotional life. Depression, mania, and bipolar disorder are examples of mood disorders. Symptoms of depression may include feelings of sadness, hopelessness, and worthlessness, as well as complaints of physical pain and changes in appetite, sleep patterns, and energy level. In mania, on the other hand, an individual experiences an abnormally elevated mood, often marked by exaggerated self-importance, irritability, agitation, and a decreased need for sleep. In bipolar disorder, also called manic-depressive illness, a person's mood alternates between extremes of mania and depression.

Depression, a condition marked by hopelessness, low self-esteem, sadness, apathy, and pessimism, occurs in 40 percent of people with Parkinson disease. A majority of people with Parkinson disease experience anxiety, which may produce panic attacks—sudden, overpowering fears, accompanied by breathlessness, sweating, chest pain, choking, and dizziness. Depression or anxiety may appear before motor symptoms develop or they may appear as a reaction to motor symptoms.

Many people with Parkinson disease also suffer from an inability to sleep at night coupled with daytime drowsiness. This sleep disturbance may be caused by anxiety or depression, or it could be a side effect of drugs used to treat Parkinson symptoms. It may also be a mechanism of the disease—the sleep centres in the brain lie near the substantia nigra and may be altered by the disease.

People who develop anorexia nervosa often share certain personality attributes, such as perfectionism, introversion, low self-esteem, difficulty expressing emotions, and a need for control. As the disorder develops, they may experience depression, irritability, sleep problems, lack of sexual interest, and they may withdraw from friends and family.

Anorexia nervosa is sometimes present with other mental illnesses, particularly depression and anxiety disorder. About 35 percent of people with anorexia nervosa also have obsessive-compulsive disorder. People with this disorder experience recurrent and often irrational thoughts or fears and feels compelled to perform certain behaviours over and over. Some evidence suggests that the psychological symptoms of anorexia nervosa, such as obsessive behaviour, preoccupation with food, and depression, may actually be an effect of food deprivation. In many cases, however, the reality of depression or another mental illness develops before the diagnosis of anorexia nervosa, and some scientists believe these other mental illnesses may make people more vulnerable to developing anorexia nervosa.

People with anorexia nervosa usually deny that they have a problem. They do not see low weight as a health risk or symptom of a psychological problem. They believe that dieting and losing weight is logical because they perceive themselves to be fat. Many feel pride in their ability to adhere to their strict diet. To the outside world, anorexics frequently appear normal. They are often successful in school and other activities, and may be perceived as respectful, obedient, helpful, and compliant—in short, they are seen as model young people.

Amitriptyline, as an antidepressant drug, that is typically used to treat mental depression, amitriptyline may also be used to treat chronic pain, bulimia, migraine headaches, and certain symptoms of multiple sclerosis. It works by restoring levels of neurotransmitters, chemicals in the brain that help transmit nerve impulses.

Amitriptyline is available only by prescription. It is taken orally in tablet form, often once a day at bedtime. Dosages generally begin at 50 or 75mg and are then gradually increased to 150 or 200mg, the maximum daily dosage for adults. Children over age 12 generally take about 30mg per day. Children under age 12 should not take this drug. Benefits from amitriptyline may not be seen for several weeks after first starting the medication.

Patients recovering from a heart attack should not take this drug, nor should people who are taking monoamine oxidase inhibitors such as Phenelzine, a monoamine oxidase inhibitor used especially in the form of its sulfate as another type of another type of antidepressant. Its safety for use during pregnancy has not been adequately studied, but it is known to appear in breast milk. Patients with certain medical conditions should avoid using amitriptyline unless advised by a doctor; these include seizures, heart or circulatory disorders, liver ailments, and eye disorders such as glaucoma. In addition, patients undergoing medical or dental procedures should be aware that amitriptyline can react adversely with anaesthetics and other drugs used during these procedures.

Possible side effects of amitriptyline include a wide variety of ailments, including dry mouth, dizziness, drowsiness, blurred vision, breast enlargement, headache, disorientation, diarrhea, constipation, vomiting, fatigue, anxiety, high fever, heart attack, impotence, insomnia, seizures, or stroke. This drug may also increase the skin's sensitivity to sunlight. These side effects are more likely to appear when the drug is first used and usually disappear after a few days. Lowering the dosage or eliminating the drug can produce side effects as well; these may include headache, nausea, irritability, or sleep disturbances. An overdose of amitriptyline can be fatal.

This drug may interact adversely with a broad variety of drugs, including but not limited to allergy and cold medications, barbiturates, antihistamines, tranquillizers, muscle relaxants, oral contraceptives, painkillers, seizure medications, sleep medications, thyroid hormones, and large doses of vitamin C. It should not be combined with alcohol.

Geneticists have provided some of the oldest proof of a biological component to depression in many people. Depression and manic-depression frequently run in families. Thus, close blood relatives (children, siblings and parents) of patients with severe depressive or bipolar disorders are much more likely to suffer from those or related conditions than are members of the general population. Studies of identical twins (who are genetically indistinguishable) and fraternal twins (whose genes generally are no more alike than those of other pairs of siblings) also support an inherited component. The finding of illness in both members of a pair is much higher for manic-depression in identical twins than in fraternal ones and is somewhat elevated for depression alone.

In the past 20 years, genetic researchers have expended great effort trying to identify the genes at fault. So far, though, those genes have evaded discovery, perhaps because a predisposition to depression involves several genes, each of which makes only a small, hard-to-detect contribution.

Preliminary reports from a study of an Amish population with an extensive history of manic-depression once raised the possibility that chromosome 11 held one or more genes producing vulnerability to bipolar disorder, but the finding did not hold up. A gene somewhere on the X chromosome could play a role in some cases of that condition, but the connection is not evident in most people who have been studied. Most recently, various regions of chromosome 18 and a site on chromosome 21 have been suggested to participate in vulnerability to bipolar illness, but these findings await replication.

As geneticists continue their searches, other investigators are concentrating on neurochemical aspects. Much of that work focuses on neurotransmitters. In particular, many cases of depression apparently stem at least in part from disturbances in brain circuits that convey signals through certain neurotransmitters of the monoamine class. These biochemicals, all derivatives of amino acids, include serotonin, norepinephrine and dopamine; of these, only evidence relating to norepinephrine and serotonin is abundant.

Monoamines first drew the attention of depression researchers in the 1950s. Early in that decade, physicians discovered that severe depression arose in about 15 percent of patients who were treated for hypertension with the drug reserpine. This agent turned out to deplete monoamines. At about the same time doctors found that an agent prescribed against tuberculosis-elevated moods in some users who were depressed. Follow-up investigations revealed that the drug inhibited the neuronal breakdown of monoamines by an enzyme (monoamine oxidase); presumably the agent eased depression by allowing monoamines to avoid degradation and to remain active in brain circuits. Together these findings implied that abnormally low levels of monoamines in the brain could cause depression. This insight led to the development of monoamine oxidase inhibitors as the first class of antidepressants.

But which monoamines were most important in depression? In the 1960s Joseph J. Schildkraut of Harvard University cast his vote with norepinephrine in the now classic "catecholamine" hypothesis of mood disorders. He proposed that depression stem from a deficient supply of norepinephrine (which is also classified as a catecholamine) in certain brain circuits and that mania arises from an overabundance of the substance. The theory has since been refined, acknowledging, for instance, that decreases or elevations in norepinephrine do not alter moods in everyone. Nevertheless, the proposed link between norepinephrine depletion and depression has gained much experimental support. These circuits originate in the brain stem, primarily in the pigmented locus coeruleus, and project to many areas of the brain, including to the limbic system—a group of cortical and subcortical areas that play a significant part in regulating emotions.

To understand the recent evidence relating to norepinephrine and other monoamines, it helps to know how those neurotransmitters work. The points of contact between two neurons, or nerve cells, are termed synapses. Monoamines, like all neurotransmitters, travel from one neuron (the presynaptic cell) across a small gap (the synaptic cleft) and attach to receptor molecules on the surface of the second neuron (the postsynaptic cell). Such binding elicits intracellular changes that stimulate or inhibit firing of the postsynaptic cell. The effect of the neurotransmitter depends greatly on the nature and concentration of its receptors on the postsynaptic cells. Serotonin receptors, for instance, come in 13 or more subtypes that can vary in their sensitivity to serotonin and in the effects they produce.

The strength of signalling can also be influenced by the amount of neurotransmission released and by how long it remains in the synaptic cleft—properties influenced by at least two kinds of molecules on the surface of the releasing cell: autoreceptors and transporters. When an autoreceptor becomes bound by neurotransmitter molecules in the synapse, the receptors signal the cell to reduce its firing rate and thus its release of the transmitter. The transporters physically pump neurotransmitter molecules from the synaptic cleft back into presynaptic cells, a process termed reuptake. Monoamine oxidase inside cells can affect synaptic neurotransmitter levels as well, by degrading monoamines and so reducing the resultant amounts in molecules available for release.

Among the findings linking impoverished synaptic norepinephrine levels to depression is the discovery in many studies that indirect markers of norepinephrine levels in the brain—levels of its metabolites, or by-products, in more accessible material (urine and cerebrospinal fluid)—are often low in depressed individuals. In addition, postmortem studies have revealed increased densities of certain norepinephrine receptors in the cortex of depressed suicide victims.

Observers unfamiliar with receptor display might assume that elevated numbers of receptors were a sign of more contact between norepinephrine and its receptors and more signal transmission. But this pattern of receptor "up-regulation" is actually one that scientists would expect if norepinephrine concentrations in synapses were abnormally low. When transmitter molecules become unusually scarce in synapses, postsynaptic cells often expand receptor numbers in a compensatory attempt to pick up whatever signals are available.

A recent discovery supporting the norepinephrine hypothesis is that new drugs selectively able to block norepinephrine reuptake, and so increase norepinephrine in synapses, are effective antidepressants in many people. One compound, reboxetine, is available as an antidepressant outside the US and is awaiting approval here.

The data connecting norepinephrine to depression are solid and still growing. Yet research into serotonin has taken centre stage in the 1990s, thanks to the therapeutic success of Prozac and related antidepressants that manipulate serotonin levels. Serious investigations into serotonin's role in mood disorders, however, have been going on for almost 30 years, ever since Arthur J. Prange, Jr., of the University of North Carolina at Chapel Hill, Alec

Coppen of the Medical Research Council in England and their co-workers put forward the so-called permissive hypothesis. This view held that synaptic depletion of serotonin was another cause of depression, one that worked by promoting, or "permitting," a fall in norepinephrine levels.

Defects in serotonin-using circuits could certainly dampen norepinephrine signalling. Serotonin-producing neurons project from the raphe nuclei in the brain stem to neurons in diverse regions of the central nervous system, including those that secrete or control the release of norepinephrine. Serotonin depletion might contribute to depression by affecting other kinds of neurons as well; serotonin-producing cells extend into many brain regions thought to participate in depressive symptoms, including the amygdala (an area involved in emotions), the hypothalamus (involved in appetite, libido and sleep) and cortical areas that participate in cognition and other higher processes.

Among the findings supporting a link between low synaptic serotonin levels and depression, is that cerebrospinal fluid in depressed, and especially in suicidal, patients contain a reduced resultant in the amounts of serotonin by-products (signifying reduced levels of serotonin in the brain itself). In addition, levels of a surface molecule unique to serotonin-releasing cells in the brain are lower in depressed patients than in healthy subjects, implying that the numbers of serotonergic cells are reduced. Moreover, the density, is at least, one form of serotonin receptor type 2- in that which is greater in postmortem brain tissue of depressed patients; as being true in studies of norepinephrine receptors, this upper-regulation is suggestive of a compensatory response in the bracketing for to little serotonin in the synaptic cleft.

Further evidence comes from the remarkable therapeutic effectiveness of drugs that block presynaptic reuptake transporters from drawing serotonin out of the synaptic cleft. Tricyclic antidepressants (so-named because they contain three rings of chemical groups) joined monoamine oxidase inhibitors on pharmacy shelves in the late 1950s, although their mechanism of action was not known at the time. Eventually, though, they were found to produce many effects in the brain, including a decrease in serotonin reuptake and a consequent rise in serotonin levels in synapses.

Investigators suspected that this last effect accounted for their antidepressant action, but confirmation awaited the introduction in the late 1980s of Prozac and then other drugs (Paxil, Zoloft and Luvox) able to block serotonin reuptake transporters without affecting other brain monoamines. These selective serotonin reuptake inhibitors (SSRIs) have now revolutionized the treatment of depression, because they are highly effective and produce quite milder side effects than older drugs do. Today even newer antidepressants, such as Effexor, block reuptake of both serotonin and norepinephrine.

Studies of serotonin have also offered new clues to why depressed individuals are more susceptible to heart attack and stroke. Activation and clumping of blood platelets (cell-like structures in blood) contribute to the formation of thrombi that can clog blood vessels and shut off blood flow to the heart and brain, thus damaging those organs. Work in my laboratory and elsewhere has shown that platelets of depressed people are particularly sensitive to activation signals, including, it seems, to those issued by serotonin, which amplifies platelet reactivity to other, stronger chemical stimuli. Further, the platelets of depressed patients bear reduced numbers of serotonin reuptake transporters. In other words, compared with the platelets of healthy people, those in depressed individuals probably are less able to soak up serotonin from their environment and thus to reduce their exposure to platelet-activation signals.

Disturbed functioning of serotonin or norepinephrine circuits, or both, contributes to depression in many people, but compelling work can equally claim that depression often involves dysregulation of brain circuits that control the activities of certain hormones. Indeed, hormonal alterations in depressed patients have long been evident.

The hypothalamus of the brain lies at the top of the hierarchy regulating hormone secretion. It manufactures and releases peptides (small chains of amino acids) that act on the pituitary, at the base of the brain, stimulating or inhibiting the pituitary's release of various hormones into the blood. This hormones—among them the growth hormones, thyroid-stimulating hormone and adrenocorticotropic hormone (ACTH)—control the release of other hormones from target glands. In addition to functioning outside the nervous system, the hormones released in response to pituitary hormones feed back to the pituitary and hypothalamus. There they deliver inhibitory signals that keep hormone manufacture from becoming excessive.

Depressed patients have repeatedly been demonstrated to show a blunted response to a number of substances that normally stimulate the release of growth hormones. They also display aberrant responses to the hypothalamic substance that normally induces secretion from the thyroid-stimulating hormones derived from the pituitary. In addition, a common cause of nonresponse to antidepressants is the presence of previously undiagnosed thyroid insufficiency.

All these findings are intriguing, but so far the strongest case has been made for dysregulation of the hypothalamic-pituitary-adrenal (HPA) axis—the system that manages the body's response to stress. When a threat to physical or psychological well-being is detected, the hypothalamus amplifies production of corticotropin-releasing factors (CRF), which induces the pituitary to secrete ACTH. ACTH then instructs the adrenal gland atop each kidney to release cortisol. Together all the changes prepare the body to fight or flee and cause it to shut down activities that would distract from the self-protection. For instance, the cortisol enhances the delivery of fuel to muscles. At the same time, CRF depresses the appetite for food and sex and heightens alertness. Chronic activation of the HPA axis, however, may lay the ground for illness and, it appears, for depression.

As long ago as the late 1960s and early 1970s, several research groups reported increased activity in the HPA axis in unmedicated depressed patients, as evinced by raised levels of cortisol in urine, blood and cerebrospinal fluid, as well as by other measures. Hundreds, perhaps several thousands, of subsequent studies have agreeably confirmed, that substantial numbers of depressed patients—particularly most of the severely affected—display HPA-axis hyperactivity. Indeed, the finding is surely the most replicated one in all of biological psychiatry.

Deeper investigation of the phenomenon has now revealed alterations at each level of the HPA axis in depressed patients. For instance, both the adrenal gland and the pituitary are enlarged, and the adrenal gland hyper-secretes cortisol.

Notably, study after study has shown CRF concentrations in cerebrospinal fluid to be elevated in depressed patients, compared with control subjects or individuals with other psychiatric disorders. This magnification of CRF levels is reduced by treatment with antidepressants and by effective electroconvulsive therapy. Further, postmortem brain tissue studies have revealed a marked exaggeration both in the number of CRF-producing neurons in the hypothalamus and in the expression of the CRF gene (resulting in elevated CRF synthesis) in depressed patients as compared with controls. Moreover, delivery of CRF to the brains of laboratory animals produces behavioural effects that are cardinal features of depression in humans, namely, insomnia, decreased appetite, decreased libido and anxiety.

Neurobiologists do not yet know exactly how the genetic, monoamine and hormonal findings piece together, if indeed they always do. The discoveries nonetheless suggest a partial scenario for how people who endure traumatic childhoods become depressed later in life. I call this hypothesis the stress-diathesis model of mood disorders, in recognition of the interaction between experience (stress) and sensitive predisposition.

The observation that depression runs in families means that certain genetic traits in the affected families somehow lower the threshold for depression. Conceivably, the genetic features directly or indirectly diminish monoamine levels in synapses or increase reactivity of the HPA axis to stress. The genetically determined threshold is not necessarily low enough to induce depression in the absence of serious stress but may then be pushed still lower by early, adverse life experiences.

My colleagues and I propose that early abuse or neglect not only activates the stress response but induces persistently increased activity in CRF-containing neurons, which are known to be stress responsive and to be overactive in depressed people. If the hyperactivity in the neurons of children persisted through adulthood, these supersensitive cells would react vigorously even to mild stressors. This effect in people already innately predisposed to depression could then produce both the neuroendocrine and behavioural responses characteristic of the disorder.

To test the stress-diathesis hypothesis, we have conducted a series of experiments in which neonatal rats were neglected. We removed them from their mothers for brief periods on about 10 of their first 21 days of life, before allowing them to grow up (after weaning) in a standard rat colony. As adults, these maternally deprived rats showed clear signs of changes in CRF-containing neurons, all in the direction observed in depressed patients—such as rises in stress-induced ACTH secretion and elevations of CRF concentrations in several areas of the brain. Levels of corticosterone (the rat's cortisol) also rose. These findings suggested that a permanent increase in CRF gene expression and thus in CRF production occurred in the maternally deprived rats, an effect now confirmed by Paul M. Plotsky.

We have also found an increase in CRF-receptor density in certain brain regions of maternally deprived rats. Receptor amplification commonly reflects an attempt to compensate for a decrease in the substance that acts on the receptor. In this case, though, the rise in receptor density evidently occurs not as a balance to decreased CRF but in spite of an increase—the worst of all possibilities. Permanently elevated receptor concentrations would tend to magnify the action of CRF, thereby forever enhancing the depression-inducing effects of CRF and stress.

In an exciting preliminary finding, Plotsky has observed that treatment with one of the selective serotonin reuptake inhibitors (Paxil) returns CRF levels to normal, compensates for any gain in receptor sensitivity or number (as indicated by normal corticosterone production lower down in the axis) and normalizes behaviour (for instance, the rats become less fearful).

We do not know exactly how inhibition of serotonin reuptake would lead to normalization of the HPA axis. Even so, the finding implies that serotonin reuptake inhibitors might be particularly helpful in depressed patients with a history of childhood trauma. Plotsky further reports that all the HPA-axis and CRF abnormalities returned when treatment stopped, a hint that pharmaceutical therapy in analogous human patients might have to be continued indefinitely to block recurrences of depression.

Studies of Bonnet macaque monkeys, which as primates more closely resemble humans, yielded similar results. Newborns and their mothers encountered three foraging conditions for three months after the babies' birth: a plentiful, a scarce and a variable food supply. The variable situation (in which food was available unpredictably) evoked considerable anxiety in monkey mothers, who became so anxious and preoccupied that they basically ignored their offspring. As our model predicts, the neonates in the variable-foraging condition were less active, withdrew from interactions with other monkeys and froze in novel situations. In adulthood, they also exhibited marked elevations in CRF concentrations in spinal fluid.

The rat and monkey data raise profound clinical and public health questions. In the US alone in 1995, more than three million children were reportedly abused or neglected, and at least a million of those reports were verified. If the effects in human beings resemble those of the animals, the findings imply that abuse or neglect may produce permanent changes in the developing brain—changes that chronically boost the output of, and responsiveness to, CRF, and therefore increase the victims' lifelong vulnerability to depression.

If that conclusion is correct, investigators will be eager to determine whether noninvasive techniques able to assess the activity of CRF-producing neurons or the number of CRF receptors could identify abused individuals at risk for later depression. In addition, they will want to evaluate whether antidepressants or other interventions, such as psychotherapy, could help prevent depression in children who are shown to be especially susceptible. Researchers will also need to find out whether depressed adults with a history of abuse need to take antidepressants in perpetuity and whether existing drugs or psychotherapy can restore normal activity in CRF-producing neurons in humans.

The stress-diathesis model does not account for all cases of depression; not everyone who is depressed has been neglected or abused in childhood. But individuals who have both a family history of the condition and a traumatic childhood seem to be unusually prone to the condition. People who have no genetic predisposition to depression (as indicated by no family history of the disorder) could conceivably be relatively protected from serious depression even if they have a bad childhood or severe trauma later in life. Conversely, some people who are inherently vulnerability, will find them battling depression even when their childhoods and later life are free of trauma.

More work on the neurobiology of depression is clearly indicated, but the advances achieved so far are already being translated into ideas for new medications. Several pharmaceutical houses are developing blockers of CRF receptors to test the antidepressant value of such agents. Another promising class of drugs activates specific serotonin receptors; such agents can potentially exert powerful antidepressive effects without stimulating serotonin receptors on neurons that play no part in depression.

More therapies based on new understandings of the biology of mood disorders are sure to follow as well. As research into the neurobiological underpinnings progresses, treatment should become ever more effective and less likely to produce unwanted side effects.

Certain drugs work by interacting with receptors, special sites on the surface of body cells. Drugs may bind to a specific receptor, possibly preventing naturally occurring chemicals from binding to the receptor. In so doing, if a drug enhances cell activity, it is called an agonist; if it blocks cell activity, it is called an antagonist.

Drugs interact with cell receptors, small parts of proteins that control a multitude of chemical reactions and functions in the body. Receptors have a specific, chemical structure compatible only with certain drugs or endogenous compounds—substances that originate within the body such as hormones and neurotransmitters. This relationship can be compared to that of a lock and key: A drug molecule—the "key"—attaches briefly to its specific receptor—the "lock" that only this molecule can open. The lock-and-key combination of the drug and receptor results in a cascade of chemical events. The extent of the response is determined by the number of receptors activated. Stimulation of only a few receptors may not produce a response while stimulation of a certain number of receptors is needed to produce the desired effect.

Physician Vincent E. Friedewald, Jr., a specialist in cardiovascular medicine and the author of the "Ask the Doctor" series of medical books for laypersons, answers a wide variety of questions about illnesses and their treatments. Friedewald focuses in particular on hypertension, its causes, its symptoms, ways to prevent it, and the medications commonly used to combat it. He also discusses the new classes of drugs developed in recent years, explaining how ACE inhibitors, beta blockers, and calcium channel blockers work.

The same receptors can be found in different tissues and organs in the body, but receptors produce different responses depending on their location. As a result, a specific drug can affect the body in more than one way. Desirable effects are called therapeutic or beneficial responses. Undesirable or harmful effects are called adverse reactions. Some adverse reactions, or side effects, can be predicted. The most common side effects are drowsiness, headache, sleeplessness, nausea, and diarrhea. Other reactions, such as those that occur only in specific individuals for unexpected reasons, called idiosyncratic reactions, and those that occur with the triggering of the body's immune system, called allergic reactions, are less predictable.

Drug toxicity, or poisoning, can occur when drugs are given in too large a dose or when individuals take a particular drug over a long period of time, the drug may build up to dangerous levels in the kidneys and liver and damage these organs. For some drugs, such as those used to treat epilepsy, the difference between therapeutic and toxic concentrations is small. Physicians constantly monitor the precise levels of such drugs in an individual's bloodstream to prevent drug poisoning.

Other drugs, such as those used to treat cancer, are known to have toxic effects; However, the benefits outweigh the risks—that is, treatment without them may result in death.

When taken together, drugs can interact with one another and produce desirable or undesirable results. Some drugs have an additive effect—that is, they increase the effect of other drugs. For example, alcoholic beverages intensify the drowsiness-producing effect of some sedatives. Drugs that displace, or take the place of other drugs present in blood proteins, make the displaced drugs more active in the body, increasing their effect. Other drugs have a reducing effect—that is, they interfere with the action of drugs already present in the body. For example, antacids prevent antibiotics from being absorbed by the stomach. Some drugs combine with other drugs to create a substance that has no medical benefit. In some cases, however, drug interactions can produce desirable results. Doctors have found that using three drugs to fight AIDS is more effective than one drug used alone.

Drugs are most effective when properly prescribed by physicians and taken correctly by patients. Missing doses, taking drugs at the wrong time of the day or with instead of before meals, and stopping drug use too soon can markedly reduce the medical benefits of many drugs.

Drug abuse is characterized by taking more than the recommended dose of prescription drugs such as barbiturates without medical supervision, or using government-controlled substances such as marijuana, cocaine, heroin, or other illegal substances. Legal substances, such as alcohol and nicotine, are also abused by many people. Abuse of drugs and other substances can lead to physical and psychological dependence.

Drug abuse can cause a wide variety of adverse physical reactions. Long-term drug use may damage the heart, liver, and brain. Drug abusers may suffer from malnutrition if they habitually forget to eat, cannot afford to buy food, or eat foods lacking the proper vitamins and minerals. Individuals who abuse injectable drugs risk contracting infections such as hepatitis and HIV from dirty needles or needles shared with other infected abusers. One of the most dangerous effects of illegal drug use is the potential for overdosing—that is, taking too large or too strong a dose for the body's systems to handle. A drug overdose may cause an individual to lose consciousness and to breathe inadequately. Without treatment, an individual may die of a drug overdose.

Drug addiction is marked by a compulsive craving for a substance. Successful treatment methods vary and include psychological counselling, or psychotherapy, and detoxification programs—medically supervised programs that gradually wean an individual from a drug over a period of days or weeks. Detoxification and psychotherapy are often used together.

The illegal use of drugs was once considered a problem unique to residents of poor, urban neighbourhoods. Today, however, people from all economic levels, in both cities and suburbs, abuse drugs. Some people use drugs to relieve stress and to forget about their problems. Genetic factors may predispose other individuals to drug addiction. Environmental factors such as peer pressure, especially in young people, and the availability of drugs, also influence people to abuse drugs.

Humans have always experimented with substances derived from minerals, plants, and animal parts to treat pain, illness, and restore health. In ancient Egypt, physicians prescribed figs, dates, and castor oil as laxatives and used tannic acid to treat burns. The early Chinese and Greek pharmacies included opium, known for its pain-relieving qualities, while Hindus used the cannabis and henbane plants as anaesthetics and the root of the plant Rauwolfia serpentina, which contains reserpine, as a tranquillizer.

A school of pharmacy established in Arabia from 750 through until 1258 ad., discovering many substances effective against illness, such as burned sponge (which contains iodine) for the treatment of goiters—a noncancerous enlargement of the thyroid gland, visible as a swelling at the front of the neck. In Europe, the 15th century Swiss physician and chemist Philippus Aureolus Paracelsus identified the characteristics of numerous diseases such as syphilis, a chronic infectious disease usually transmitted in sexual intercourse, and used ingredients such as sulfur and mercury compounds to counter the diseases.

During the 17th and 18th centuries, physicians treated malaria, a disease transmitted by the bite of an infected mosquito, with the bark of the cinchona tree (which contains quinine). Heart failure was treated with the leaves of the foxglove plant (which contains digitalis); scurvy, a disease caused by vitamin C deficiency, was treated with citrus fruit (which contains vitamin C) and smallpox was prevented using inoculations of cells infected with a similar viral disease known as cowpox. The therapy developed for smallpox stimulated the body's immune system, which defends against disease-causing agents, to produce cowpox and smallpox-specific antibodies.

In the 19th century scientists continued to discover new drugs including ether, morphine, and a vaccine for rabies, an infectious, often fatal, viral disease of mammals that attacks the central nervous system and is transmitted by the bite of infected animals. These substances, however, were limited to those occurring naturally in plants, minerals, and animals. A growing understanding of chemistry soon changed, the way drugs were developed. Heroin and aspirin, two of the first synthetic drugs created from other elements or compounds using chemical reactions, were produced in the late 1800s. This development, combined with the establishment of a new discipline called pharmacology, the study of drugs and their actions on the body, signalled the birth of the modern drug industry.

Developing a new drug is a time-consuming, expensive process that often requires up to 10 years. The process begins with laboratory experiments resulting in the synthesis and purification of a possible new drug. The compound then goes through a series of tests in animal and human subjects to determine if it is safe and effective against disease. When those studies are completed, the Food and Drug Administration (FDA) decides whether to approve the drug for sale in the United States.

Today most drugs are synthesized by chemists in the laboratory. Synthetic drugs are better controlled than those occurring naturally, which ensures that each dose imparts the same effect. Some new synthetic drugs are developed by modifying the structure of existing substances. These new drugs are called analogues. For example, prednisone is an analogue of the hormone cortisone. Because scientists can selectively alter the drug's structure, analogues may be more effective and cause fewer side effects than the drugs from which they were derived.

One of the newer methods for developing drugs involves the use of gene splicing, or recombinant DNA. In drug research, this technique joins the DNA of a specific type of human cell to the DNA of a second organism, usually a harmless bacterium, to produce a recombinant (or "recombined") DNA. The altered organism then begins to produce the substance produced by the human cell. This substance is extracted from the bacteria and purified for use as a drug.

The first drug produced in this manner was the hormone insulin in 1982, which was created in large quantities by inserting the human insulin gene in The Escherichia coli (E coli) bacteria. Since 1982 other genetically engineered drugs for humans have been developed, including tissues plasminogen activators (tPA), an enzyme used to dissolve blood clots in people who have suffered heart attacks, and erythropoetin, a hormone used to stimulate the production of red blood cells in people with severe anaemia.

Because of the great expense and time involved, most new drugs are created by large, well-funded pharmaceutical companies. From idea to production, the development of a new drug can take up to ten years and cost about $200 million. The processing usually sparks aflame from the burning ambers of firing t o an idea that an existing chemical substance has therapeutic value or that the structure of an existing drug can be modified for new clinical uses. Out of 10,000 chemicals tested in a laboratory, only one may eventually become a drug.

Once drug researchers have determined that a new substance may have medical value, an elaborate testing program begins. The drug is tested first on small animals such as rats and mice, and then on larger animals such as monkeys and dogs. If these tests indicate that the new drug is effective against its intended target—such as a particular disease—and shows an acceptably low level of toxicity, the drug company requests permission from the Food and Drug Administration (FDA), an agency of the US Department of Health and Human Services, to test the drug in humans.

If the agency approves the request, clinical trials on humans can begin. These experiments are usually divided into three phases, each of which can last from several months to several years. In the first phase, the drug is tested on a small number of healthy individuals to determine its effect on the body. The second phase tests the drug on a small number of people who have the disease or disorder the drug manufacturer hopes the drug will treat. These individuals are divided into two groups. Those who receive the drug and those who receive a placebo, or inactive compound. Neither the investigating physicians nor the members of the test group know who is receiving the drug or who is receiving the placebo. This is privy to a double-blind study, ensures that no one consciously or unconsciously is due of the influence of the drug's effect. The third phase tests the drug on a much larger group of people and determines specific doses, possible interactions with other drugs, responses related to gender, and other information used for drug labelling. At the end of the third phase, a drug manufacturer compiles the results of the clinical trials and submits them to the FDA in a new product application. If the drug has been proven effective and safe, and its benefits outweigh any risks, the agency approves the drug for marketing. FDA approval of a new drug may take up to 18 months; however, the agency is working to reduce the time to 12 months for most drugs and 6 months for highly effective drugs that treat previously incurable conditions.

Because drugs can produce harmful effects when manufactured or taken improperly, most governments control drug development as well as availability. In the United States, the FDA determines how drugs are produced and how they are sold. Drugs that can be sold over the counter (OTC) that is, without a prescription from a physician are called proprietary drugs. They are considered safe for unsupervised use by the general population. Drugs that must be prescribed by physicians and dispensed by pharmacists are known as ethical drugs. Their use is monitored closely by medical personnel.

The FDA regulates the sale and manufacture of drugs in the United States as outlined in applicable laws enacted over the past century. Legal standards for composition and preparation of drugs in the United States are found in the publication known as the United States Pharmacopeia (USP). Drugs that can be abused, such as the powerful narcotic heroin, are regulated by the Drug Enforcement Administration (DEA) of the US Department of Justice to ensure that they are not prescribed or sold illegally.

Before 1900 any individual could sell a drug and claim it offered therapeutic benefits without medical proof. This changed after 1906 with the passage of the Pure Food and Drug Act, which required drug manufacturers to state the content, strength, and purity of each drug they produced. The Pure Food and Drug Act ended the practice of including morphine, cocaine, and heroin in drugs without the public's knowledge. In 1914 the US legislature began to strictly regulate the trade of narcotics with the enactment of the Harrison Narcotic Act; in 1937 the government added marijuana to this list of controlled substances (the Marijuana Tax Act).

The Federal Food, Drug, and Cosmetic Act was enacted in 1938 requiring that new drugs be safe for humans; however, it did not require that manufacturers prove their drugs' effectiveness. It would be 24 years before legislation was passed that would require proof of the efficacy of new drugs (the Kefaver-Harris Amendments, 1962). Enforcement of this law was entrusted to the FDA.

Two laws enacted in the 1960s strengthened the FDA's efforts to reduce drug abuse. The Drug Abuse Control Amendments of 1965 provided penalties for the illegal sale or possession of stimulants, sedatives, and hallucinogens, and the Narcotic Addict Rehabilitation Act of 1966 set up a federal program for addicts that provided them with the option of receiving treatment for their drug problems in place of a prison sentence.

In 1970 the Comprehensive Drug Abuse Prevention and Control Act established rules for manufacturing and prescribing habit-forming drugs. It stipulated that physicians can prescribe all drugs, but a special license is required to prescribe drugs with high abusive potential. This license is issued by the Drug Enforcement Administration.

The Anti-Drug Abuse Acts, signed into law in 1986 and 1988, set up funding for the treatment of drug abuse and for the creation of law-enforcement programs to fight the illegal sale of drugs. These acts also detailed severe punishments for individuals selling and possessing drugs illegally. Harsh penalties for using anabolic steroids (hormones that promote the storage of protein and the growth of tissue that are sometimes abused by competitive athletes) were included in the 1988 act, along with the requirement that all alcoholic beverages be labelled with warnings about alcohol's potentially dangerous effect on the body. The 1988 act also established the Office of National Drug Control Policy to develop an action plan that would involve the public, as well as private agencies, in eliminating the illegal sale of drugs, in helping individuals who use drugs to stop and preventing nonusers from ever starting to use drugs.

The US government and its regulatory agencies continually monitor the development and use of all drugs sold in the United States to ensure that the American public has access only to drugs that are safe and effective. Recently, the FDA introduced legislation requiring warning labels on all over-the-counter medication after research indicated that the nonaspirin pain reliever acetaminophen can cause liver damage when taken in high doses with large quantities of alcohol.

Some genes that cause genetic diseases interact in a dominant-recessive pattern. In these cases, two copies of the recessive gene are required for the disease to occur. A person who has just one copy of the recessive gene is termed a carrier, since he or she carries the gene but is not affected by it. In the illustration above, the dominant gene is represented in green, and the recessive in blue. For the couple on the left, the father has one copy of the dominant gene and one copy of the recessive gene. The mother has two copies of the dominant gene. Each parent can contribute just one gene to the child. The four children shown on the lower left represent the probabilities (not the actual children) for the combinations that can result from their parents. The children on the far left received the recessive gene from their father and the dominant gene from their mother, and are therefore carriers. For any child born to these parents, there is a 50 percent chance that the child will be a carrier. Since none of the children can inherit two copies of the recessive gene, none of the children will develop the disease. When both parents are carriers, however, as shown by the couple on the right, there is a 25 percent chance that any child born has the disease, a 50 percent chance that a child is a carrier, and a 25 percent chance that a child does not have the disease and is not a carrier.

A mutation in the gene responsible for producing oxygen-carrying haemoglobin in the blood causes a disease known as sickle-cell anaemia. In this disease the structure of haemoglobin in the human bloodstream is severely altered. The mutation changes the structure of red blood cells to a slender sickle shape.

Some genetic disorders have symptoms that are manifest at birth. These disorders may result from mutations in a single gene or from more general chromosomal abnormalities. Many diseases and conditions are inherited in a recessive manner: Neither parent may have the defect even though they both carry the causative gene. When both parents have a dominant gene A and a recessive gene a, their offspring may inherit one of four different combinations: AA, Aa, aA, or aa. If the recessive gene a is defective, the statistical probability is that one in four of the offspring will bear the defective trait. In other congenital disorders the presence of only one copy of the recessive gene is sufficient to cause the condition

Genetic disorders may result from defects in genes or from chromosomal abnormalities. Prenatal tests, performed early in a woman's pregnancy, can identify a fetus with a genetic abnormality. Prenatal diagnosis using amniocentesis or chorionic villus sampling pose a slight risk to the fetus, and health professionals generally recommend these tests only if the mother or father has a family history of a genetic disorder or an increased risk of having a child with a chromosomal abnormality.

Physical anthropologists studying human genetics use sophisticated laboratory techniques to analyze human chromosomes and DNA (deoxyribonucleic acid), the structures through which people inherit traits from their parents. With these techniques, researchers have identified human populations that have genetic predispositions to specific diseases, such as types of cancer. This knowledge has promoted increased focuses on the use of preventive measures among people with higher risk for disease.

Sometimes mutations are caused by transposition, in which long stretches of DNA (containing one or more genes) move from one chromosome to another. These jumping genes, called transposons, can disrupt transcription and change the type of amino acids inserted into a protein. Amino acid is an organic compound containing any amino group, carboxylic acid group and any of various groups, especially any of the 20 compounds that have the base formula that are linked together by peptide bonds in metabolisms. Transposons rearrange and interrupt genes in a way that generally improves the genetic variation of a species. While a segment of DNA that is capable of independently replicating itself and inserting the copy into a new position within the same or another chromosome or plasmid.

Mutations can occur spontaneously, some can be caused by exposure to physical or chemical agents in the environment called mutagens. Common environmental mutagens include ultraviolet rays from the sun and various chemicals, such as asbestos, cigarette smoke, and nitrous acid. High-energy radiation, such as medical X rays, can cause DNA strands to break, leading to the deletion of potentially important genetic information.

Lewis Edward devoted his entire academic career to the study of the fruit fly's genetic makeup. By studying mutations in the fruit fly and identifying which genes caused the mutations, he made two far-reaching discoveries about genes. The first was that a particular group of genes, called homeotic genes, controls the development of all the regions of the fly's body. These genes direct each cell to its proper location along the developing embryo's body. His second discovery was the principal of colinearity, or the linear sequence of the homeotic genes. He found that the homeotic genes are arranged on the chromosome in a linear order that exactly corresponds to the order of the body regions that each gene controls. This finding, which was subsequently found to hold true for other animals as well, won him the Nobel Prize.

Born in Lexington Kentucky, and educated at the State College of Kentucky, Morgan studied embryology at Johns Hopkins University, where he received his PhD in 1891. As professor of experimental zoology at Columbia University from 1904 to 1928, he was at first critical of Mendelian theory, which had not been physically demonstrated. Performing breeding experiments and cytological analyses on the vinegar fly, Drosophila melanogaster, Morgan and his graduate students Alfred Henry Sturtevant, Calvin Blackman Bridges, and Hermann Joseph Muller revealed that chromosomes behave very similarly to the ways in which Mendel believed genes segregate and become randomly assorted. Discovering also that genes for many character traits are arranged in a linear fashion on each chromosome, Morgan and his coworkers created linear chromosome maps in which each gene is assigned to a specific position. This work resulted in The Mechanism of Mendelian Heredity (1915), an influential book that was an important step in the development of modern genetics.

Morgan continued his experimental work, in the evincing presentation, to the 'Theory of the Gene' (1926) that genes are held together in different linkage groups, and that alleles (pairs of genes affecting the same trait) interchange, or cross over, in the same linkage group. In 1933 Morgan won the Nobel Prize for physiology or medicine.

Nettie Stevens (1861-1912), American biologist and geneticist whose research helped prove that chromosomes determine the sex of an organism. Researchers had previously believed that gender was influenced by food and temperature conditions during the early stages of an organism's development.

The Soviet government made development of science a national priority and showered top scientists with honours. Although day-to-day supervision was less oppressive than in the arts, there were countless episodes of arbitrary suppression of ideas. In the most notorious, the Ukrainian agronomist Trofim Lysenko rejected the chromosome theory of heredity generally accepted by modern genetics. Claiming his theories corresponded to Marxism, he convinced Stalin in 1948 to outlaw population genetics and several related fields of biological research; the decision was not reversed until the mid-1960s. Concern with freedom of inquiry and expression drew some scientists into the political realm. The best example is Andrey Sakharov, the nuclear physicist who became the most famous member of the hard-pressed liberal opposition in the 1970s. Sakharov was awarded the 1975 Nobel Peace Prize for his efforts, though the government would not allow him to go to Norway to accept the prize.

Kennedy's Telegram to Khrushchev After First Manned Space Mission. On April 12, 1961, the White House made public President John F. Kennedy's telegram to the Soviets, congratulating them on the first successful manned space mission. Cosmonaut Yuri Gagarin's orbit of the earth spurred American scientists and engineers to step up efforts to send United States astronauts into space.

The core of basic science was the Academy of Sciences, originally founded in 1725 and relocated from Leningrad to Moscow in 1934. It contained 250 research institutes and 60,500 full-time researchers in 1987, predominantly in the natural sciences. Several hundred scholars (330 in 1988) had the privileged status of "academician" and about twice as many had statuses of "corresponding members" of the academy. In addition, all of the union republics but the RSFSR had their own paradigm of science. About 90 percent of research was carried on outside the academy system. Most of this was of an applied character and much was related to weaponed systems and done in secret facilities in the defence-production ministries.

The launch of the artificial satellite Sputnik 1 by the Union of Soviet Socialist Republics (USSR) in 1957 marked the beginning of the space race. The satellite fell out of orbit three months after a launch, but it had an electrifying effect enhancing the international image of the USSR and creating the illusion of technological inferiority in the United States. In the aftermath, according to this 1978 National Aeronautics and Space Administration (NASA) report by historians Edward Clinton Ezell and Linda Neuman Ezell, tentative efforts to promote international cooperation in space gave way to competition.

Soviet scientists won lofty reputations in many fields. They were at the cutting edge of world science in mathematics and in several branches of physical science, notably theoretical and nuclear physics, chemistry, and astronomy. The physical chemist and physicist Nikolay Semenov was the first Soviet citizen to win a Nobel Prize, in 1956. Nobel Prizes were subsequently awarded in 1958 to the physicists Pavel Cherenkov, Ilya Frank, and Igor Tamm, for their discovery of the Cherenkov effect; in 1962 to the physicist Lev Landau, for his pioneer work in cryogenics, or low-temperature physics, as of 1964. Two physicists, Nikolay Basov and Aleksandr Prokhorov, for their development of the laser (light amplification) and the maser (microwave amplification) and in 1978 to the physicist Peter Kapitza, for his research in magnetism and low-temperature physics.

Soviet technology was most impressive in the areas of nuclear weaponry and space exploration, where the arms race with the West prodded policy makers to set aside the needed resources. By virtue of a crash program directed by Igor Kurchatov, the

Soviet Union was the second country to explode an atomic bomb, in 1949, four years after the United States. The Soviet Union detonated a hydrogen device in 1953, only ten months after the United States. In October 1957 it put the first artificial satellite, Sputnik 1, into an earth orbit, and in April 1961 a Russian cosmonaut, Yuri Gagarin, became the first man in space. Though disappointed that the United States beat them to the moon, the Soviets kept up a strong space program until economic problems led to cutbacks in the 1980s.

When new research is published, it often acts as a springboard for further work. Its impact can then be gauged by seeing how often the published research appears as a cited impaction, of which are, in time, major scientific breakthroughs that are cited through a times arrow, but at the other extreme, obscure pieces of research may be cited rarely or not at all. However, citation is not always a reliable guide to the value of scientific work. Sometimes a piece of research will go largely unnoticed, only to be rediscovered in subsequent years. Such was the case for the work on genes done by American geneticist Barbara McClintock during the 1940s. McClintock discovered a new phenomenon in corn cells known as transposable genes, sometimes referred to as jumping genes. McClintock observed that a gene could move from one chromosome to another, where it would break the second chromosome at a particular site, insert itself there, and influence the function of an adjacent gene. Her work was largely ignored until the 1960s when scientists found that transposable genes were of the essence for transferring genetic material in bacteria and more complex organisms. McClintock was awarded the 1983 Nobel Prize in physiology or medicine for her work in transposable genes, more than 35 years after performing the research.

After sperm are produced, they move out of the testes and into the epididymis, a long tube coiled against the testes, where the sperm are stored and mature. The vas deferens transports the sperm from the epididymis through the prostate, after which the vas deferens becomes the ejaculatory duct. Here, fluids from the prostate and seminal vesicles (small sacs that holds semen) combine with the sperm to form semen, a thick, yellowish-white fluid. The average discharged of semen, called ejaculate, contained approximately 300 million sperm.

There are two periods of marked sexual differentiation in human life. The first occurs prenatally and the second occurs at puberty. Although adult women and men may greatly differ in genital appearance and secondary sexual characteristics, they are almost identical during prenatal development. When an egg and a sperm unite during fertilization, they each bring to the new cell half the number of chromosomes (threadlike structures that contain genetic material) present in other cells. From fertilization through about the first six weeks of development, male and female embryos differ only in the pair of sex chromosomes they have in each cell—two X chromosome (XX) in females and one X and one Y chromosome (XY) in males. At this stage, both male and female embryos have undifferentiated gonads (ovaries or testes), two sets of ducts (one set capably of developing into male internal organs and the other into female organs), and undifferentiated external genital folds and swellings.

About six weeks after conception, if a Y chromosome is present in the embryo's cells (as it is in normal males), a gene on the chromosome directs the undifferentiated gonads to become testes. If the Y chromosome is not present (as in normal females), the undifferentiated gonads will become ovaries.

If the gonads become testes, they begin to produce androgens (male hormones, primarily testosterone) by about eight weeks after conception. These androgens stimulate development of the one set of the genital ducts into the epididymis, vas deferens, and ejaculatory duct. The presence of androgens also stimulates development of the penis and the scrotum. The testes later descend into the scrotum. Males also produce a substance that inhibits the development of the second set of ducts into female organs. In the absence of such hormonal stimulation, female structures develop.

Prenatal hormones also play a role in the sexual differentiation of the brain. For example, prenatal hormones direct the development of sex differences in some cells and the neural pathways in the hypothalamus (the part of the brain that controls the endocrine system). Beginning at puberty, based on prenatal sexual differentiation, the hypothalamus directs either the cyclic secretion of sex hormones that controls the female menstrual cycle or the relatively continuous production of male sex hormones. Other brain differences may be related to differences in sexual and aggressive behaviour or in cognitive and perceptual characteristics. Most of the research on sexual differentiation of the brain has been performed with animals or with biassed human samples, and there is much debate about the nature and behavioural relevance of these differences in humans.

In animals, the sex of an individual is generally determined at the time of fertilization by the sperm cell. If a sperm cell carrying an X chromosome fertilizes the egg, the offspring will be female (XX); if a sperm cell carrying a Y chromosome fertilizes the egg, the offspring will be male (XY). The term primary sexual characteristics denote the kind of gamete the gonad produces: The ovary produces egg cells in the female, and the testis produces sperm cells in the male. The term secondary sexual characteristics denote all other sexual distinctions that play indirect roles in uniting sperm and eggs. Secondary sexual characteristics include everything from the specialized male and female features of the genital tract, to the brilliant plumage of male birds or facial hair of humans, to behavioural features such as courtship.

Generally, the more highly evolved the species, the more elaborate are its secondary sexual characteristics. At the time the eggs of starfishes ripen, the male merely releases great quantities of sperm cells into the ocean water, and a tiny but sufficient number of them find and penetrate distant eggs. Frogs and toads are drawn to mates by calls, and they spawn in water; the male makes cloacal contact with the female and releases sperm externally, simultaneously with the eggs. Terrestrial animals, especially mammals, which do not have an environment of water through which sperm can propel itself, rely on herding and flocking, courtship, competition among males, and more specialized genitalia including an erectile penis, fallopian tubes, and a uterus in which eggs are fertilized and develop internally.

In mammals, the hormones that influence sexual differentiation and development are androgens (mainly testosterone), which stimulate later development of the ovary. In the sexually undifferentiated embryo, testosterone stimulates the development of the Wolffian duct system, the forerunner of the male genital tract. Later, testosterone, along with gonadotropins released by the pituitary gland, stimulates spermatogenesis. The Müllerian duct system, the forerunner of the female genital tract in the female embryo, probably differentiating spontaneously without hormonal stimuli, after which female sex is well defined, estradiol, produced in the ovaries and the placenta, plays a major role in the development and the functioning of the female reproductive tract.

Within the cytoplasm of all prokaryotes is deoxyribonucleic acid (DNA), a complex molecule in the form of a double helix, a shape similar to a spiral staircase. The DNA is about 1,000 times the length of the cell, and to fit inside, it repeatedly twists and folds to form a compact structure called a chromosome. The chromosome in prokaryotes is circular, and is located in a region of the cell called the nucleoid. Often, smaller chromosomes called Plasmids are located in the cytoplasm. The DNA is divided into units called genes, just like a long train is divided into separate cars. Depending on the species, the DNA contains several hundred or even thousands of genes. Typically, one gene contains coded instructions for building all or part of a single protein. Enzymes, which are specialized proteins, determine virtually all the biochemical reactions that support and sustain the cell.

The manufacture of ribosomes requires that the components of ribosomes—ribonucleic acid (RNA) and protein—be synthesized and brought together for assembly. The ribosomes of eukaryotic cells contain four strands of RNA and from 70 to 80 proteins. Using genes that reside on regions of chromosomes located in the nucleolus, three of the four ribosomal RNA strands are synthesized in the centre of the nucleolus. The fourth RNA strand is synthesized outside of the nucleolus, using genes at a different location. The fourth strand is then transported into the nucleolus to participate in ribosome assembly.

The genetic information for ribosomal proteins, found in the nucleus, is copied, or transcribed, into special chemical messengers called messenger RNA (mRNA), a different type of RNA than ribosomal RNA. The mRNA travels out of the nucleus into the cell's cytoplasm where its information is transferred, or translated, into the ribosomal proteins. The newly created proteins enter the nucleolus and bind with the four ribosomal RNA strands to create two ribosomal structures: the large and small subunits. These two subunits leave the nucleus and enter the cytoplasm. When protein synthesis is initiated, the two subunits merge to form the completed ribosome.

The nucleolus creates the two subunits for a single ribosome in about one hour. Thousands of subunits are manufactured by each nucleolus simultaneously, however, since several hundred to several thousand copies of the ribosomal RNA genes are present in the nucleolus. Before a cell divides, the nucleolus assembles about ten million ribosomal subunits, necessary for the large-scale protein production that occurs in cell division.

The nuclear envelope is attached to a network of membrane-enclosed tubules that extends throughout the cell called the endoplasmic reticulum. The nuclear envelope is perforated by many holes, called nuclear pores, that permit the movement of selected molecules between the nucleus and the rest of the cell, while blocking the passage of other molecules.

The nucleus contains the nucleolus, which manufactures protein-producing structures called ribosomes. Genetic information in the form of deoxyribonucleic acid (DNA) is stored in threadlike, tangled structures called chromatin within the nucleus. During the process of cell division known as mitosis, in which the nucleus divides, the chromatin condenses into several distinct structures called chromosomes. Each time the cell divides, the heredity information carried in the chromosomes is passed to the two newly formed cells.

The DNA in the nucleus also contains the instructions for regulating the amount and types of proteins made by the cell. These instructions are copied, or transcribed, into a type of ribonucleic acid (RNA) called messenger RNA (mRNA). The mRNA is transported from the nucleus to ribosomes, where proteins are assembled.

DNA Fingerprinting, method of identification that compares fragments of deoxyribonucleic acid (DNA) It is sometimes called DNA typing. DNA is the genetic material found within the cell nuclei of all living things. In mammals the strands of DNA are grouped into structures called chromosomes. With the exception of identical twins, the complete DNA of each individual is unique.

A DNA fingerprint is constructed by first extracting a DNA sample from body tissue or fluid such as hair, blood, or saliva. The sample distribution is then segmented using enzymes, and the segments are arranged by size using a process called electrophoresis. The segments are marked with probes and exposed on X-ray film, where they form a characteristic pattern of black bars—the DNA fingerprint. If the DNA fingerprints produced from two different samples match, the two samples probably came from the same person.

DNA fingerprinting was first developed as an identification technique in 1985. Originally used to detect the presence of genetic diseases, DNA fingerprinting soon came to be used in criminal investigations and forensic science. The first criminal conviction based on DNA evidence in the United States occurred in 1988. In criminal investigations, DNA fingerprints derived from evidence collected at the crime scene are compared to the DNA fingerprints of suspects. The DNA evidence can implicate or exonerate a suspect.

Generally, courts have accepted the reliability of DNA testing and admitted DNA test results into evidence. However, DNA fingerprinting is controversial in a number of areas: The accuracy of the results, the cost of testing, and the possible misuse of the technique.

The accuracy of DNA fingerprinting has been challenged for several reasons. First, because DNA segments rather than complete DNA strands are "fingerprinted," a DNA fingerprint may not be unique; large-scale research to confirm the uniqueness of DNA fingerprinting test results has not been conducted. In addition, DNA fingerprinting is often performed in private laboratories that may not follow uniform testing standards and quality controls. Also, since human beings must interpret the test, human error could lead to false results. DNA fingerprinting is expensive. Suspects who are unable to provide their own DNA experts may not be able to adequately defend themselves against charges based on DNA evidence.

In the United States, the Federal Bureau of Investigation (FBI) has created a national database of genetic information called the National DNA Index System. The database contains DNA obtained from convicted criminals and from evidence found at crime scenes. Some experts fear that this database might be used for unauthorized purposes, such as identifying individuals with stigmatizing illnesses such as acquired immunodeficiency syndrome (AIDS).

DNA Fingerprinting, method of identification that compares fragments of deoxyribonucleic acid (DNA) It is sometimes called DNA typing. DNA is the genetic material found within the cell nuclei of all living things. In mammals the strands of DNA are grouped into structures called chromosomes. With the exception of identical twins, the complete DNA of each individual is unique.

A DNA fingerprint is constructed by first extracting a DNA sample from body tissue or fluid such as hair, blood, or saliva. The sample is then segmented using enzymes, and the segments are arranged by size using a process called electrophoresis. The segments are marked with probes and exposed on X-ray film, where they form a characteristic pattern of black bars—the DNA fingerprint. If the DNA fingerprints produced from two different samples match, the two samples probably came from the same person.

DNA fingerprinting was first developed as an identification technique in 1985. Originally used to detect the presence of genetic diseases, DNA fingerprinting soon came to be used in criminal investigations and forensic science. The first criminal conviction based on DNA evidence in the United States occurred in 1988. In criminal investigations, DNA fingerprints derived from evidence collected at the crime scene are compared to the DNA fingerprints of suspects. The DNA evidence can implicate or exonerate a suspect.

Generally, courts have accepted the reliability of DNA testing and admitted DNA test results into evidence. However, DNA fingerprinting is controversial in a number of areas: The accuracy of the results, the cost of testing, and the possible misuse of the technique.

The accuracy of DNA fingerprinting has been challenged for several reasons. First, because DNA segments rather than complete DNA strands are "fingerprinted," a DNA fingerprint may not be unique; large-scale research to confirm the uniqueness of DNA fingerprinting test results has not been conducted. In addition, DNA fingerprinting is often performed in private laboratories that may not follow uniform testing standards and quality controls. Also, since human beings must interpret the test, human error could lead to false results. DNA fingerprinting is expensive. Suspects who are unable to provide their own DNA experts may not be able to adequately defend themselves against charges based on DNA evidence.

In the United States, the Federal Bureau of Investigation (FBI) has created a national database of genetic information called the National DNA Index System. The database contains DNA obtained from convicted criminals and from evidence found at crime scenes. Some experts fear that this database might be used for unauthorized purposes, such as identifying individuals with stigmatizing illnesses such as acquired immunodeficiency syndrome (AIDS).

Ribonucleic Acid (RNA), genetic material of certain viruses (RNA viruses) and, in cellular organisms, the molecule that directs the middle steps of protein production. In RNA viruses, the RNA directs two processes—protein synthesis (production of the virus's protein coat) and replication (the process by which RNA copies itself). In cellular organisms, another type of genetic material, called deoxyribonucleic acid (DNA), carries the information that determines protein structure. But DNA cannot act alone and rely upon RNA to transfer this crucial information during protein synthesis (production of the proteins needed by the cell for its activities and development).

Like DNA, RNA consists of a chain of chemical compounds called nucleotides. Each nucleotide is made up of a sugar molecule called ribose, as a phosphate group, and one of four different nitrogen-containing compounds called bases. The four bases are adenine, guanine, uracil, and cytosine. These components are joined together in the same manner as in a deoxyribonucleic acid

(DNA) molecule. RNA differs chemically from DNA in two ways: The RNA sugar molecule contains an oxygen atom not found in DNA, and RNA contains the base uracil in the place of the base thymine in DNA.

In cellular organisms, RNA is a single-stranded polynucleotide chain, a strand of many nucleotides linked together. There are three types of RNA. Ribosomal RNA (rRNA) is found in the cell's ribosomes, the specialized structures that are the sites of protein synthesis. Transfer RNA (tRNA) carries amino acids to the ribosomes for incorporation into a protein. Messenger RNA (mRNA) carries the genetic blueprint copied from the sequence of bases in a cell's DNA. This blueprint specifies the sequence of amino acids in a protein. All three types of RNA are formed as needed, using specific sections of the cell's DNA as templates.

Some RNA viruses have double-stranded RNA—that is, their RNA molecules consist of two parallel polynucleotide chains. The base of each RNA nucleotide in one chain pairs with a complementary base in the second chain—that is, adenine pairs with uracil, and guanine pairs with cytosine. For these viruses, the process of RNA replication in a host cell follows the same pattern as that of DNA replication, a method of replication called semi-conservative replication. In semi-conservative replication, each newly formed double-stranded RNA molecule contains one polynucleotide chain from the parent RNA molecule, and one complementary chain formed through the process of base pairing. The Colorado tick fever virus, which causes mild respiratory infections, is the double-stranded RNA virus.

There are two types of single-stranded RNA viruses. After entering a host cell, one type, a polio virus, becomes double-stranded by making an RNA strand complementary to its own. During replication, although the two strands separate, only the recently formed strand attracts nucleotides with complementary bases. Therefore, the polynucleotides chain that is produced as a result of replication is exactly the same as the original RNA chain. In that of a polymeric constituent of all living cells and many viruses, consisting of a long and usually single stranded chain of alternating phosphate and ribose units with the base adenine, guanine, cytosine and uracil bounded to the ribose. The structure and base sequence of RNA are determinants of protein synthesis and the transmission o f genetic information, nevertheless, then RNA-containing viruses is called the retrovirus.

The other types of single-stranded RNA viruses called retroviruses, including the human immunodeficiency virus (HIV), which causes AIDS, and other viruses that cause tumours. After entering a host cell, retroviruses make a DNA strand complementary to its own RNA strand using the host's DNA nucleotides. This new DNA strand then replicates and forms a double helix that becomes incorporated into the host cell's chromosomes, where it is replicated along with the host DNA. While in a host cell, the RNA-derived viral DNA produces single-stranded RNA viruses that then leave the host cell and enter other cells, where the replication process is repeated.

In 1981, American biochemist Thomas Cech discovered that certain RNA molecules appear to act as enzymes, molecules that speed up, or catalyze, some reactions inside cells. Until this discovery, biologists thought that all enzymes were proteins. Like other enzymes, these RNA catalysts, called ribosomes, show great specificity with respect to the reactions they speed up. The discovery of ribosomes added to the evidence that RNA, not DNA, was the earliest genetic material. Many scientists think that the earliest genetic molecule was simple in structure and capable of enzymatic activity. Furthermore, the molecule would necessarily exist in all organisms. The enzyme ribonuclease-P, which exists in all organisms, is made of protein and a form of RNA that has enzymatic activity. Based on this evidence, some scientists suspect that the RNA portion of ribonuclease-P may be the modern equivalent of the earliest genetic molecule, the molecule that first enabled replication to occur in primitive cells.

Nucleic acids are complex molecules produced by living cells and are essential to all living organisms. These acids govern the body's development and specific characteristics by providing hereditary information and triggering the production of proteins within the body. This computer-generated model shows two strands of deoxyribonucleic acid (DNA) and the double-helical structure typical of this class of nucleic acids.

Nucleic Acids, extremely complex molecules produced by living cells and viruses. Their name comes from their initial isolation from the nuclei of living cells. Certain nucleic acids, however, are found not in the cell nucleus but in cell cytoplasm. Nucleic acids have at least two functions: To pass on hereditary characteristics from one generation to the next, and to trigger the manufacture of specific proteins. How nucleic acids accomplish these functions is the object of some of the most intense and promising research currently under way. The nucleic acids are the fundamental substances of living things, believed by researchers to have first been formed about 3 billion years ago, when the most elementary forms of life began on earth. The origin of the so-called genetic code they carry has been accepted by researchers as being very close in time to the origin of life itself. Biochemists have succeeded in deciphering the code, that is, determining how the sequence of nucleic acids dictates the structure of proteins.

The two classes of nucleic acids are the deoxyribonucleic acids (DNA) and the ribonucleic acids (RNA). The backbones of both DNA and RNA molecules are shaped like helical strands. Their molecular weights are in the millions. To the backbones are connected a great number of smaller molecules (side groups) of four different types. The sequence of these molecules on the strand determines the code of the particular nucleic acid. This code, in turn, signals the cell how to reproduce either a duplicate of itself or the proteins it requires for survival.

All living cells contain the genetic material DNA. The cells of bacteria may have but one strand of DNA, but such a strand contains all the information needed by the cell in order to reproduce an identical offspring. The cells of mammals contain scores of DNA strands grouped together in chromosomes. In short, the structure of a DNA molecule or combination of DNA molecules determines the shape, form, and function of the offspring. Some viruses, called retroviruses, contain only RNA rather than DNA, but viruses in themselves are generally not considered true living organisms. The pioneering research that revealed the general structure of DNA was performed by the British biophysicists Francis Crick and Maurice Wilkins and by the American biochemist James Dewey Watson. Using an X-ray diffraction picture of the DNA molecule obtained by Wilkins in 1951, Crick and Watson were able to construct a model of the DNA molecule that was completed in 1953. For their work, the three scientists received the 1962 Nobel Prize in physiology or medicine. The American biochemist Arthur Kornberg synthesized DNA from "off-the-shelf" substances, for which he was awarded, with the American biochemist Severo Ochoa (for research on RNA), the 1959 Nobel Prize in physiology or medicine. The DNA that he synthesized, although structurally similar to natural DNA, was not biologically active. In 1967, however, Kornberg and a team of researchers at Stanford University succeeded in producing biologically active DNA from relatively simple chemicals.

Certain kinds of RNA have a slightly different function from that of DNA. They take part in the actual synthesis of the proteins a cell produces. This is of particular interest to virologists because many viruses reproduce by "forcing" the host cells to manufacture more viruses. The virus injects its own RNA into the host cell, and the host cell obeys the code of the invading RNA rather than that of its own. Thus the cell produces proteins that are, in fact, viruses instead of the proteins required for cell function. The host cell is destroyed, and the newly formed viruses are free to inject their RNA into other host cells.

The structure of two types of RNA and their function in protein production have been determined, one type by a team of Cornell University and US Department of Agriculture investigators led by Robert W. Holey of Cornell, and the other type by James T. Madison and George A. Everett of the Department of Agriculture. Important research into the interpretation of the genetic code and its role in protein synthesis was also performed by the Indian-born American chemist Har Gobind Khorana at the University of Wisconsin Enzyme Institute and the American biochemist Marshall W. Nirenberg of the National Heart Institute. In 1970 Khorana achieved the first complete synthesis of a gene and repeated his feat in 1973. Since then, one type of RNA has been synthesized. Also, in the early 1980s, American biochemists Thomas Robert Cech and Sidney Altman independently proved that certain types of RNA, called ribosomes, can function as true catalysts

Poliomyelitis, infectious viral disease that sometimes results in paralysis. The infection chiefly affects children and young adults and is caused by any one of three related viruses called polio viruses. In more than 95 percent of cases, the infection may pass without creating severe or even noticeable illness because the body's immune system neutralizes the invading virus and protects against future infection. In a small percentage of cases the virus penetrates to the central nervous system, infecting cells that control muscle function. Such infection can result in permanent paralysis of limbs. In its most perilous form, the infection attacks the brain, creating complications that sometimes result in death.

The term poliomyelitis derives from Greek words referring to inflammation (its) of the gray (polios) matter of the spinal cord (myelos). The shortened term polio is commonly used by the public and medical professionals, and the disease has also been referred to as infantile paralysis.

According to figures from the World Health Organization (WHO), approximately 7,100 cases of polio were reported throughout the world in 1999. Experts suspect that misdiagnosis and under reporting may make these numbers inaccurate. Thus, the actual number of polio cases may be roughly five times the reported figure—perhaps more than 20,000 cases, occurring primarily in Africa, the Middle East, and South Asia.

While still a health threat in many parts of the world, polio also represents one of the greatest medical success stories of the 20th century. The number of polio cases found worldwide today constitutes a 90 percent reduction from the number of cases reported in the late 1980s. Most health experts credit this achievement to a mass vaccination program called the Global Polio Eradication Initiative that WHO initiated in 1988 to eradicate polio worldwide by the year 2005.

In the United States and Canada, polio has been effectively eliminated, with fewer than ten cases reported in each country per year. This statistic contrasts strikingly with those from the first half of the 20th century, when epidemic polio was one of the most dreaded and feared diseases in North America. The first large-scale outbreak in the United States occurred in 1916, when over 37,000 cases were reported in 26 states, resulting in 6,000 deaths. Each year thereafter the number of polio cases in the United States averaged about 38,000 per year, including about 21,000 paralytic cases each year. In Canada the epidemic peaked in 1953, resulting in one of the highest national polio rates ever recorded in the world.

Fearing infection during epidemics in the first half of the 20th century, some people avoided beaches, public pools, theatres, fairs—any place of public gathering. Occasionally schools were closed until epidemics subsided. In response to the public's fear of this disease, in 1938 President Franklin Delano Roosevelt (who had himself lost the use of both legs to polio) founded the National Foundation for Infantile Paralysis. Now known as the March of Dimes Birth Defects Foundation, the organization raised millions of dollars for polio research and the support of victims.

The discovery in the 1950s of vaccines that protect against poliovirus infection eventually led to successful polio vaccination programs in North America, Latin America, and Europe. By the early 1990s, WHO declared the western hemisphere free of polio. But the struggle to eradicate polio continues in many developing nations. Furthermore, health officials stress that vaccination programs must be maintained in areas considered polio free. They warn that the virus could easily become dangerous again in populations of children who have not acquired immunity, the body's ability to resist infection from the polio virus. This danger was chillingly demonstrated in 1979 when an outbreak of paralytic polio erupted among unvaccinated members of an Amish sect in Pennsylvania and Maryland.

The three types of poliovirus belong to the virus family known as picornaviruses. This name derives from a combination of the words pico, meaning "small," and RNA, indicating that the viruses contain a core of the genetic material known as ribonucleic acid, or RNA. Three types of poliovirus have been identified: Type 1 (also known as Brunhilde), Type 2 (Lansing), and Type 3 (Leon). Type 1 is the most common form and the one most closely associated with polio's more severe, paralytic progression. A person who develops immunity from exposure of its single poliovirus type will not have immunity against the other polio viruses.

Poliovirus typically enter the body through the mouth and multiply in the tonsils and lymph nodes of the upper respiratory tract. Infection proceeds from the mouth into the gastrointestinal tract through the stomach to the intestines. The virus multiplies in the intestines and is shed from the body in faeces, often resulting in further infections. For example, a parent can become infected by an infant during diaper changes, or improper waste disposal can lead to contamination of a water supply. These infections, in turn, will spread the virus more widely.

Large quantities of poliovirus multiply in intestinal tissue known as Weyer's patches, where cells of the body's lymphatic system are concentrated. Passage of the virus into the body's lymphatic system stimulates the production of antibodies. These are themselves specialized immune-system defenders, in time, will destroy the viral intruder. From the lymphatic system, the virus typically invades the bloodstream.

Retrovirus, of any virus belonging to the family Retroviridae, whose members share a unique method of replicating (copying) themselves when they infect living cells. Retroviruses store their genetic information in molecules of ribonucleic acid (RNA). However, unlike other RNA viruses, retroviruses use RNA as a template (a master pattern) for forming deoxyribonucleic acid (DNA), the genetic material that puts viral replication instructions into effect. This process, called reverse transcription, is the exact opposite of the normal flow of genetic information in living things in which DNA serves as the template for RNA formation.

Retroviruses affect a wide range of animals, although the best-known types are those that target vertebrates. Some retroviruses are harmless, but many can cause malignant transformation—a genetic change that makes healthy cells cancerous. Disease-forming retroviruses can cause diseases such as leukemia (cancer of the blood) in mammals and malignant tumours and other disorders in birds. From a human perspective, by far the most significant retroviruses are a small group called lentiviruses, which include human immunodeficiency viruses (HIV), the virus that causes acquired immunodeficiency syndrome (AIDS).

Deoxyribonucleic Acid (DNA), genetic material of all cellular organisms and most viruses. DNA carries the information needed to direct protein synthesis and replication. Protein synthesis is the production of the proteins needed by the cell or virus for its activities and development. Replication is the process by which DNA copies itself for each descendant cell or virus, passing on the information needed for protein synthesis. In most cellular organisms, DNA is organized on chromosomes located in the nucleus of the cell.

The deoxyribonucleic acid (DNA) molecule is the genetic blueprint for each cell and ultimately the blueprint that determines every characteristic of a living organism. In 1953 American biochemist James Watson, left, and British biophysicist Francis Crick, right, described the structure of the DNA molecule as a double helix, somewhat like a spiral staircase with many individual steps. Their work was aided by X-ray diffraction pictures of the DNA molecule taken by British biophysicist Maurice Wilkins and British physical chemist Rosalind Franklin. In 1962 Crick, Watson, and Wilkins received the Nobel Prize for their pioneering work on the structure of the DNA molecule.

A molecule of DNA consists of two chains, strands composed of a large number of chemical compounds, called nucleotides, linked together to form a chain. These chains are arranged like a ladder showing of a twisted shape of a winding staircase, called a double helix. Each nucleotide consists of three units: a sugar molecule-called deoxyribose, a phosphate group, and one of four different nitrogen-containing compounds called bases. The four bases are adenine (A), guanine (G), thymine (T), and cytosine. The deoxyribose molecule occupies the centre position in the nucleotide, flanked by a phosphate group on one side and a base on the other. The phosphate group of each nucleotide is also linked to the deoxyribose of the adjacent nucleotide in the chain. These linked deoxyribose-phosphate subunits form the parallel side rails of the ladder. The bases face inward toward each other, forming the rungs of the ladder.

The nucleotides in one DNA strand have a specific association with the corresponding nucleotides in the other DNA strand. Because of the chemical affinity of the bases, nucleotides containing adenine are always paired with nucleotides containing thymine, and nucleotides containing cytosine are always paired with nucleotides containing guanine. The complementary bases are joined to each other by weak chemical bonds called hydrogen bonds.

In 1953 American biochemist James D. Watson and British biophysicist Francis Crick published the first description of the structure of DNA. Their model proved to be so important for the understanding of protein synthesis, DNA replication, and mutation that they were awarded the 1962 Nobel Prize for physiology or medicine for their work.

One of a cell's most important tasks is the synthesis of proteins, giant molecules that underlie most cellular functions. The hereditary material known as deoxyribonucleic acid (DNA), found within the nucleus of a cell, orchestrates a series of steps resulting in the manufacture of proteins tailored to meet the needs for a cell's development and growth.

DNA carries the instructions for the production of proteins. A protein is composed of smaller molecules called amino acids, and the structure and function of the protein is determined by the sequence of its amino acids. The sequence of amino acids, in turn, is determined by the sequence of nucleotide bases in the DNA. A sequence of three nucleotide bases, called a triplet, is the genetic code word, or codon, that specifies a particular amino acid. For instance, the triplet GAS (guanine, adenine, and cytosine) is the codon for the amino acid leucine, and the triplet CAG (cytosine, adenine, and guanine) is the codon for the amino acid valine. A protein consisting of 100 amino acids is thus encoded by a DNA segment consisting of 300 nucleotides. Of the two polynucleotide chains that form a DNA molecule, only one strand contains the information needed for the production of a given amino acid sequence. The other strand aids in replication.

Protein synthesis begins with the separation of a DNA molecule into two strands. In a process called transcription, a section of one strand acts as a template, or pattern, to produce a new strand called messenger RNA (mRNA). The mRNA leaves the cell nucleus and attaches to the ribosomes, specialized cellular structures that are the sites of protein synthesis. Amino acids are carried to the ribosomes by another type of RNA, called transfer RNA (tRNA). In a process called translation, the amino acids are linked together in a particular sequence, dictated by the mRNA, to form a protein.

A gene is a sequence of DNA nucleotides that specify the order of amino acids in a protein via an intermediary mRNA molecule. Substituting one DNA nucleotide with another containing of a different base causes all descendant cells or viruses to have the altered nucleotide base sequence. As a result of the substitution, the sequence of amino acids in the resulting protein may also be changed. Such a change in a DNA molecule is called a mutation. Most mutations are the result of errors in the replication process. Exposure of a cell or virus to radiation or to certain chemicals increases the likelihood of mutations.

In most cellular organisms, replication of a DNA molecule takes place in the cell nucleus and occurs just before the cell divides. Replication begins with the separation of the two polynucleotide chains, each of which then acts as a template for the assembly of a new complementary chain. As the old chains separate, each nucleotide in the two chains attracts a complementary nucleotide that has been formed earlier by the cell. The nucleotides are joined to one another by hydrogen bonds to form the rungs of a new DNA molecule. As the complementary nucleotides are fitted into place, an enzyme called DNA polymerase links them together by bonding the phosphate group of one nucleotide to the sugar molecule of the adjacent nucleotide, forming the side rail of the new DNA molecule. This process continues until a new polynucleotide chain has been formed alongside the old one, forming a new double-helix molecule.

Several tools and procedures facilitate are used by scientists for the study and manipulation of DNA. Specialized enzymes, called restriction enzymes, found in bacteria act like molecular scissors to cut the phosphate backbones of DNA molecules at specific base sequences. Strands of DNA that have been cut with restriction enzymes are left with single-stranded tails that are called sticky ends, because they can easily realign with tails from certain other DNA fragments. Scientists take advantage of restriction enzymes and the sticky ends generated by these enzymes to carry out recombinant DNA technology, or genetic engineering. This technology involves removing a specific gene from one organism and inserting the gene into another organism.

Another tool for working with DNA is a procedure called polymerase chain reaction (PCR). This procedure uses the enzyme DNA polymerase to make copies of DNA strands in a process that mimics the way in which DNA replicates naturally within cells. Scientists use PCR to obtain vast numbers of copies of a given segment of DNA.

DNA fingerprinting, also called DNA typing, makes it possible to compare samples of DNA from various sources in a manner that is analogous to the comparison of fingerprints. In this procedure, scientists use restriction enzymes to cleave a sample of DNA into an assortment of fragments. Solutions containing these fragments are placed at the surface of a gel to which an electric current is applied. The electric current causes the DNA fragments to move through the gel. Because smaller fragments move more quickly than larger ones, this process, called electrophoresis, separates the fragments according to their size. The fragments are then marked with probes and exposed on X-ray film, where they form the DNA fingerprint—a pattern of characteristic black bars that is unique for each type of DNA.

A procedure called DNA sequencing makes it possible to determine the precise order, or sequence, of nucleotide bases within a fragment of DNA. Most versions of DNA sequencing use a technique called primer extension, developed by British molecular biologist Frederick Sanger. In primer extension, specific pieces of DNA are replicated and modified, so that each DNA segment ends in a fluorescent form of one of the four nucleotide bases. Modern DNA sequencers, pioneered by American molecular biologist Leroy Hood, incorporate both lasers and computers. Scientists have completely sequenced the genetic material of several microorganisms, including the bacterium Escherichia coli. In 1998, scientists achieved the milestone of sequencing the complete genome of a multicellular organism—a roundworm identified as Caenorhabditis elegans. The Human Genome Project, is an accumulated representation of an international research correlation, having been established to determine the sequence of all of the three billion nucleotide base pairs that make up the human genetic material.

An instrument called an atomic force microscope enables scientists to manipulate the three-dimensional structure of DNA molecules. This microscope involves laser beams that act like tweezers—attaching to the ends of a DNA molecule and pulling on them. By manipulating these laser beams, scientists can stretch, or uncoil, fragments of DNA. This work is helping reveal how DNA changes its three-dimensional shape as it interacts with enzymes.

In the late 20th century scientists devised methods of altering the genetic makeup of food crops. Humans have modified crops for thousands of years to increase yield and resistance to pests, but changes on the molecular level have caused some people to wonder if science has gone too far. Recent studies suggest that some genetically altered crops may pose health risks and other dangers. Proponents of genetically modified food, however, point to increased yields and health benefits.

Research into DNA has had a significant impact on medicine. Through recombinant DNA technology, scientists can modify microorganisms so that they become so-called factories that produce large quantities of medically useful drugs. This technology is used to produce insulin, which is a drug used by diabetics, and interferon, in that which is used by some cancer patients. Studies of human DNA are revealing genes that are associated with specific diseases, such as cystic fibrosis and breast cancer. This information is helping physicians to diagnose various diseases, and it may lead to new treatments. For example, physicians are using a technology called chimeraplasty, which involves a synthetic molecule containing both DNA and RNA strands, in an effort to develop a treatment for a form of hemophilia.

Forensic science has been using techniques developed in DNA research to identify individuals who have committed crimes. DNA from semen, skin, or blood taken from the crime scene can be compared with the DNA of a suspect, and the results can be used in court as evidence.

In a landmark intersection of science and fiction, cloning leapt from the world's imagination to its front page in February 1997. It arrived in the innocent form of a sheep named Dolly: the first exact genetic duplicate of an adult mammal due to genetic engineering.

Scottish scientists had created Dolly from deoxyribonucleic acid (DNA)—the basic unit of heredity—taken from a single adult sheep cell. The accomplishment threw open the door to profound ethical as well as scientific controversy over the potential uses and abuses of cloning. "However the debate is resolved," wrote Los Angeles Times science reporter Thomas H. Maugh II, "the genie is irretrievably out of the bottle."

DNA has helped taxonomists determine evolutionary relationships among animals, plants, and other life forms. Closely related species have more similar DNA than do species that are distantly related. One surprising finding to emerge from DNA studies is that vultures of the Americas are more closely related to storks than to the vultures of Europe, Asia, or Africa.

Techniques of DNA manipulation are used in farming, in the form of genetic engineering and biotechnology. Strains of crop plants to which genes have been transferred may produce higher yields and may be more resistant to insects. Cattle have been similarly treated to increase milk and beef production, as have hogs, to yield more meat with less fat.

Despite the many benefits offered by DNA technology, some critics argue that its development should be monitored closely. One fear raised by such critics is that DNA fingerprinting could provide a means for employers to discriminate against members of various ethnic groups. Critics also fear that studies of people's DNA could permit insurance companies to deny health insurance to those people at risk for developing certain diseases. The potential use of DNA technology to alter the genes of embryos is a particularly controversial issue.

The use of DNA technology in agriculture has also sparked controversy. Some people question the safety, desirability, and ecological impact of genetically altered crop plants. In addition, animal rights groups have protested against the genetic engineering of farm animals.

Despite these and other areas of disagreement, many people agree that DNA technology offers a mixture of benefits and potential hazards. Many experts, also by agreeing, that information given directly to public scrutiny can help assure that DNA technology is used wisely.

Drugs in the class known as nitrosoureas interfere with DNA repair. They are primarily used in treating brain cancer. Another group of chemotherapy drugs, referred to as antimetabolites, interferes with cell replication by preventing the cell from assembling the building blocks of DNA and ribonucleic acid (RNA), the molecule that directs protein synthesis. Antimetabolites are used to treat breast cancer, ovarian cancer, and cancers of the gastrointestinal tract.

Mitotic inhibitors constitute another class of chemotherapeutic agents. As their name implies, these drugs interfere with mitosis, the part of the cell cycle when the cell actually divides. These agents are used to treat lung cancer, breast cancer, and testicular cancer. Another class of cancer drugs, known as antitumor antibiotics, of which treat a variety of cancers, including leukemias. These drugs work by inhibiting the synthesis of RNA.

In his early work beginning in the mid-1950s, Brenner Sydney studied how deoxyribonucleic acid (DNA), the genetic material of living things, instructs cells to make proteins. Working with French biologist and future Nobel laureate François Jacob and other scientists, in 1961 Brenner identified messenger ribonucleic acid (mRNA), a molecule that acts as an intermediary between

DNA and protein production. In that same year Brenner and British biophysicist Francis Crick, who won a Nobel Prize in 1962, identified codons, groups of three nucleotides (the building blocks of DNA and RNA). Brenner and Crick showed that codons provide instructions for the creation of all 20 amino acids that form the foundation of proteins.

The story of how cells evolved remains an open and actively investigated question in science. The combined expertise of physicists, geologists, chemists, and evolutionary biologists has been required to shed light on the evolution of cells from the nonliving matter of early Earth. The planet formed about 4.5 billion years ago, and for millions of years, violent volcanic eruptions blasted substances such as carbon dioxide, nitrogen, water, and other small molecules into the air. These small molecules, bombarded by ultraviolet radiation and lightning from intense storms, collided to form the stable chemical bonds of larger molecules, such as amino acids and nucleotides—the building blocks of proteins and nucleic acids. Experiments indicate that these larger molecules form spontaneously under laboratory conditions that simulate the probable early environment of Earth.

Scientists speculate that rain may have carried these molecules into lakes to create a primordial soup—a breeding ground for the assembly of proteins, the nucleic acid RNA, and lipids. Some scientists postulate that these more complex molecules formed in hydrothermal vents rather than in lakes. Other scientists propose that these key substances may have reached Earth on meteorites from outer space. Regardless of the origin or environment, however, scientists do agree that proteins, nucleic acids, and lipids provided the raw materials for the first cells. In the laboratory, scientists have observed lipid molecules joining to form spheres that resemble a cell's plasma membrane. As a result of these observations, scientists postulate that millions of years of molecular collisions resulted in lipid spheres enclosing RNA, the simplest molecule capable of self-replication. These primitive aggregations would have been the ancestors of the first prokaryotic cells.

Fossil studies indicate that cyanobacteria, bacteria capable of photosynthesis, were among the earliest bacteria to evolve, an estimated 3.4 billion to 3.5 billion years ago. In the environment of the early Earth, there was no oxygen, and cyanobacteria probably used fermentation to produce ATP. Over the eons, cyanobacteria performed photosynthesis, which produces oxygen as a byproduct; the result was the gradual accumulation of oxygen in the atmosphere. The presence of oxygen set the stage for the evolution of bacteria that used oxygen in aerobic respiration, a more efficient ATP-producing process than fermentation. Some molecular studies of the evolution of genes in archaebacteria suggest that these organisms may have evolved in the hot waters of hydrothermal vents or hot springs slightly earlier than cyanobacteria, around 3.5 billion years ago. Like cyanobacteria, archaebacteria probably relied on fermentation to synthesize ATP.

Eukaryotic cells may have evolved from primitive prokaryotes about 2 billion years ago. One hypothesis suggests that some prokaryotic cells lost their cell walls, permitting the cell's plasma membrane to expand and fold. These folds, ultimately, may have given rise to separate compartments within the cell—the forerunners of the nucleus and other organelles now found in eukaryotic cells. Another key hypothesis is known as endosymbiosis. Molecular studies of the bacteria-like DNA and ribosomes in mitochondria and chloroplasts indicate that mitochondrion and chloroplast ancestors were once free-living bacteria. Scientists propose that these free-living bacteria were engulfed and maintained by other prokaryotic cells for their ability to produce ATP efficiently and to provide a steady supply of glucose. Over generations, eukaryotic cells complete with mitochondria—the ancestors of animals—or with both mitochondria and chloroplasts—the ancestors of plants

Outside of a host cell, a virus is an inert particle. Once inside a cell, a virus can replicate many times, creating thousands of viruses that leave the cell to find host cells of their own. Viruses that cause disease do so by destroying or damaging cells as they leave them.

Like all viruses, human immunodeficiency viruses (HIV), is comprised of only genetic material, a few proteins, and a protective envelope. Its genetic material, carried by single-stranded RNA molecules, contains all the information, proven as necessary to make more viruses. HIV cannot reproduce itself outside of a cell, but when HIV invades a living cell, it turns the cell into a factory for making more HIV.HIV penetrates the cell membrane and releases its contents into the host cell.

Acquired Immunodeficiency Syndrome (AIDS), human viral disease that ravages the immune system, undermining the body's ability to defend itself from infection and disease. Caused by the human immunodeficiency virus (HIV), AIDS leaves an infected person vulnerable to opportunistic infections. Such infections are harmless in healthy people, but in those whose immune systems have been greatly weakened, they can prove fatal. Although there is no cure for AIDS, new drugs are available that can prolong the life spans and improve the quality of life of infected people.

The human immunodeficiency virus (HIV), which causes acquired immunodeficiency syndrome (AIDS), principally attacks CD4 T-cells, a vital part of the human immune system. As a result, the body's ability to resist opportunistic viral, bacterial, fungal, protozoal, and other infection is greatly weakened. Pneumocystis carinii pneumonia is the leading cause of death among people with HIV infection, but the incidence of certain types of cancers such as B-cell lymphomas and Kaposi's sarcoma is also increased. Neurological complications and dramatic weight loss, or "wasting," are characteristic of endstage HIV disease (AIDS). HIV can be transmitted sexually through contact with contaminated blood, tissue, or needles; and from mother to child during birth or breastfeeding. Full-blown symptoms of AIDS may not develop for more than 10 years after infection.

Infection with HIV does not necessarily mean that a person has AIDS. Some people who have HIV infection may not develop any of the clinical illnesses that define the full-blown disease of AIDS for ten years or more. Physicians prefer to use the term AIDS for cases where a person has reached the final, life-threatening stage of HIV infection.

More than 42 million people around the world are currently infected with human immunodeficiency viruses (HIV), the virus that causes acquired immunodeficiency syndrome (AIDS). New HIV infections have levelled off or even declined in most developed countries, but the virus is spreading rapidly through much of the developing world. In some areas of sub-Saharan Africa, one in four adults is carrying the virus.

AIDS was first identified in 1981 between homosexual men and intravenous drug users in New York and California. Shortly after its detection in the United States, evidence of AIDS epidemics grew among heterosexual men, women, and children in sub-Saharan Africa. AIDS quickly developed into a worldwide epidemic, affecting virtually every nation. By 2003 the United

Nations Program on HIV/AIDS (UNAIDS) and the World Health Organization (WHO) estimated that worldwide 40 million people, including 2.5 million children under the age of 15, were living with HIV infection or AIDS. The WHO, a specialized agency of the United Nations (UN), estimated that from 1981 to the end of 2002 about 20 million people died as a result of AIDS. About 4.5 million of those who died were children under the age of 15. UNAIDS and the WHO reported that 3 million people died in 2003 alone from AIDS, and 5 million more people became infected with HIV.

AIDS has struck sub-Saharan Africa particularly hard. In 2003 one in five adults in this region had AIDS or HIV infection, the highest rate of infection in the world since the epidemic began. Sub-Saharan Africa is the most severely affected region in the world with 26.6 million people living with HIV/AIDS as of 2003.

In the United States about 40,000 new HIV infections occur each year. More than 30 percent of these infections occur in women, and 60 percent occur in ethnic minorities. As of 2002 about 886,000 US residents were living with HIV/AIDS, and about 500,000 people had died of the disease since the epidemic began, according to the US Centres for Disease Control and Prevention. In Canada about 4,200 new HIV infections occur each year. Nearly 25 percent of these infections occur in women. In 2002 about 55,000 Canadians were living with HIV infection and about 18,000 people were living with full-blown AIDS.

The incidence of the new cases of HIV infections and AIDS deaths has significantly decreased in Canada and the United States since 1995. This decrease is attributed to the availability of new drug treatments and public health programs that target people most at risk for infection. But while the overall rate of

HIV infection seems to be on a downturn, certain populations appear to be at greater risk for the disease. In the United States in 1987, Caucasians accounted for 60 percent of AIDS cases and blacks and Hispanics presenting only 39 percent. But by 2000 the trend had reversed: 26 percent of new cases were diagnosed in Caucasians and 73 percent in blacks and Hispanics. Likewise the number of female AIDS patients in the United States has increased significantly in recent years, from 7 percent of all AIDS cases in 1985 to 30 percent in 2000. In the United States, African American and Hispanic women accounted for 82 percent of AIDS cases among women in 2000.

In western Europe the first cases of AIDS were detected in the early 1980s, and by the late 1990s, at least 30,000 new HIV infections occurred each year. In 2002 about 570,000 western Europeans were HIV positive, and 25 percent of these cases were women. Before the dissolution of the Union of Soviet Socialist Republics (USSR) in 1991, eastern Europe reported few HIV cases. But since 1995, HIV infection has spread rapidly in cities of several eastern European countries, including Ukraine, Belarus, and Moldova. The WHO estimates that the total number of HIV infections in this region may have risen from less than 30,000 in 1995 to about 1 million in 2002.

A road sign in Botswana about acquired immunodeficiency syndrome (AIDS) says "AIDS: Your Problem, Control With Condoms." Africa accounts for more than 70 percent of adults infected with human immunodeficiency virus (HIV), the cause of AIDS.

While cases of AIDS have been reported in every nation of the world, the disease affects some countries more than others. More than 95 percent of all HIV-infected people live in the developing world. In these areas, the disease has sapped the populations of young men and women who form the foundation of the labour force. Most die while in the peak of their reproductive years. Moreover, the epidemic has overwhelmed health-care systems, increased the number of orphans, and caused life expectancy rates to plummet. These problems have reached crisis proportions in some parts of the world already burdened by war, political upheaval, or unrelenting poverty.

In 1999 alone, 4 million people in sub-Saharan Africa became infected with the human immunodeficiency virus (HIV), the virus that causes acquired immunodeficiency syndrome (AIDS). In several African countries, at least half of males currently aged 15 will eventually die of AIDS. These and other shocking facts about the level of devastation that HIV/AIDS has inflicted and will inflict on the people and economies of Africa are documented in the Report on the Global HIV/AIDS Epidemic. The report, excerpted here, was published in June 2000 by the Joint United Nations Programme on HIV/AIDS, known as UNAIDS.

Nowhere is this better demonstrated than in sub-Saharan Africa, where the number of AIDS cases far exceeds that of all other geographic regions. Of the estimated 14,000 HIV infections that occur each day worldwide, about half of these infections occur in sub-Saharan Africa. About 70 percent of all people infected with HIV live in this region. In some countries in the southern part of the continent, including Botswana, Lesotho, Swaziland, and Zimbabwe, more than 30 percent of the population has HIV infection or AIDS.

In Asia and the Pacific Islands an estimated 7.2 million people were living with HIV infection by 2002. Health officials fear that as the virus spreads through China and India, the world's two most populous countries, cases of HIV infection in this region may surge up to 25 million cases by the year 2010, dwarfing the problems seen in sub-Saharan Africa.

Historical Essays reflect the knowledge and insight of leading historians. This collection of essays is assembled to support the National Standards for World History. In this essay, Oliver Osborne of the University of Washington argues that post-colonial rule and turmoil in Africa has not diminished the continent's diverse health care systems but rather demanded collaboration among them.

In 2002 the Chinese government reported that China had about 1 million HIV-positive people in a population of more than 1 billion. However, public health experts are concerned by the fast-rising number of new infections among intravenous drug users who share infected needles. In 2000 HIV prevalence among intravenous drug users ranged from 44 percent to 85 percent in selected communities of drug users in both Bunnan, in southern China, and Xinjiang, in northwestern China. The incidence of HIV infection will likely be exacerbated by the growing sex industry in China. Surveys indicate that as many as 4 million prostitutes work in China. Of these, four out of ten never use a condom to protect themselves or their clients from HIV infection or other sexually transmitted infections. In rural areas of China the incidence of HIV infection is rising because many poverty-stricken people regularly sell their blood. The people who buy the blood use unsterile methods to draw blood, including reusing contaminated needles, which can spread HIV infection.

In Latin America and the Caribbean region nearly 1.7 million people have been diagnosed with HIV infection or AIDS, twice the incidence in the United States and Canada. Brazil, Mexico,

Colombia, and Argentina are the Latin American countries with the highest number of cases of HIV infection or AIDS.

The human immunodeficiency virus (HIV), the cause of acquired immunodeficiency syndrome (AIDS), is genetically programmed to do one thing: highjack the reproductive machinery of a human cell, then trick it into churning out as many copies of the virus as it can before the cell dies. The current best hope for the treatment of AIDS requires that patients take a number of different drugs, each of which interferes with certain steps of the HIV infection process.

AIDS is the final stage of a chronic infection with the human immunodeficiency virus. There are two types of this virus: HIV-1, which is the primary cause of AIDS worldwide, and HIV-2, found mostly in West Africa. On its surface, HIV carries a protein structure that recognizes and binds only with a specific structure found on the outer surface of certain cells. HIV attacks any cell that has this binding structure. However, white blood cells of the immune system known as T cells, which orchestrate a wide variety of disease-fighting mechanisms, are especially vulnerable to HIV attack. Particularly vulnerable are certain T cells known as CD4 cells. When HIV infects a CD4 cell, it commandeers the genetic tools within the cell to manufacture new HIV virus. The newly formed HIV virus then leaves the cell, destroying the CD4 cell in the process. No existing medical treatment can completely eradicate HIV from the body once it has integrated into human cells.

The loss of CD4 cells endangers health because these immune cells help other types of immune cells respond to invading organisms. The average healthy person has over 1,000 CD4 cells per microliter of blood. In a person infected with HIV, the virus steadily destroys CD4 cells over a period of years, diminishing the cells' protective ability and weakening the immune system. When the density of CD4 cells drops to 200 cells per microliter of blood, the infected person becomes vulnerable to any of about 26 opportunistic infections and rare cancers, which take advantage of the weakened immune defences to cause disease.

Scientists have identified three ways that HIV infections spread: sexual intercourse with an infected person, contact with contaminated blood, and transmission from an infected mother to her child before or during birth or through breastfeeding.

HIV transmission occurs most commonly during intimate sexual contact with an infected person, including genital, anal, and oral sex. The virus is present in the infected person's semen or vaginal fluids. During sexual intercourse, the virus gains access to the bloodstream of the uninfected person by passing through openings in the mucous membrane—the protective tissue layer that lines the mouth, vagina, and rectum—and through breaks in the skin of the penis. In the United States and Canada, HIV is most commonly transmitted during sex between homosexual men, but the incidence of HIV transmission between heterosexual men and women has rapidly increased. In most other parts of the world, HIV is most commonly transmitted through heterosexual sex.

Direct contact with HIV-infected blood occurs when people who use heroin or other injected drugs share hypodermic needles or syringes contaminated with infected blood. Sharing of contaminated needles among intravenous drug users is the primary cause of HIV infection in eastern Europe, particularly in Ukraine, Russia, Belarus, and Moldova. Epidemics of HIV infection among drug users have also emerged in Georgia, Armenia, Azerbaijan, and Kazakhstan in Central Asia.

More or less, HIV infection results when health professionals accidentally stick themselves with needles containing HIV-infected blood or expose an open cut to contaminated blood. Some cases of HIV transmission from transfusions of infected blood, blood components, and organ donations were reported in the 1980s. Since 1985 government regulations in the United States and Canada have required that all donated blood and body tissues be screened for the presence of HIV before being used in medical procedures. As a result of these regulations, HIV transmission caused by contaminated blood transfusion or organ donations is rare in North America. However, the problem continues to concern health officials in sub-Saharan Africa. Less than half of the 46 nations in this region have blood-screening policies. By some estimates only 25 percent of blood transfusions are screened for the presence of HIV. WHO hopes to establish blood safety programs in more than 80 percent of sub-Saharan countries by 2003.

HIV can be transmitted from an infected mother to her baby while the baby is still in the woman's uterus or, more commonly, during childbirth. The virus can also be transmitted through the mother's breast milk during breastfeeding. Mother-to-child transmission accounts for 90 percent of all cases of AIDS in children. Mother-to-child transmission is particularly prevalent in Africa, where the number of women infected with HIV is ten times the rate found in other regions. Studies conducted in several cities in southern Africa in 1998 indicate that up to 45 percent of pregnant women in these cities carry HIV.

The routes of HIV transmission are well documented by scientists, but health officials continually grapple with the public's unfounded fears concerning the potential for HIV transmission by other means. HIV differs from other infectious viruses in that it dies quickly if exposed to the environment. No evidence has linked HIV transmission to casual contact with an infected person, such as a handshake, hugging, or kissing, or even sharing dishes or bathroom facilities. Studies have been unable to identify HIV transmission from modes common to other infectious diseases, such as an insect bite or inhaling virus-infected droplets from an infected person's sneeze or cough.

Without medical intervention, AIDS progresses along a typical course. Within one to three weeks after infection with HIV, most people experience flu-like symptoms, such as fever, sore throat, headache, skin rash, tender lymph nodes, and a vague feeling of discomfort. These symptoms last one to four weeks. During this phase, known as acute retroviral syndrome, HIV reproduces rapidly in the blood. The virus circulates in the blood throughout the body, particularly concentrating in organs of the lymphatic system.

The normal immune defences against viral infections eventually activate to battle HIV in the body, reducing but not eliminating HIV in the blood. Infected individuals typically enter a prolonged asymptomatic phase, a symptom-free period that can last ten years or more. While persons who have HIV may remain in good health during this period, HIV continues to replicate, progressively destroying the immune system. Often an infected person remains unaware that he or she carries HIV and unknowingly transmits the virus to others during this phase of the infection.

When HIV infection reduces the number of CD4 cells to around 200 per microliter of blood, the infected individual enters an early symptomatic phase that may last a few months to several years. HIV-infected persons in this stage may experience a variety of symptoms that are not life-threatening but may be debilitating. These symptoms include extensive weight loss and fatigue (wasting syndrome), periodic fever, recurring diarrhea, and thrush, a fungal mouth infection. An early symptom of HIV infection in women is a recurring vaginal yeast infection. Unlike earlier stages of the disease, in this early symptomatic phase the symptoms that develop are severe enough to cause people to seek medical treatment. Many at first may learn of their infection in this phase.

If CD4 cell levels drop below 200 cells per microliter of blood, the late symptomatic phase develops. This phase is characterized by the appearance of any of 26 opportunistic infections and rare cancers. The onset of these illnesses, sometimes referred to as AIDS-defining complications, is one sign that an HIV-infected person has developed full-blown AIDS. Without medical treatment, this stage may last from several months to years. The cumulative effects of these illnesses usually cause death.

Often the first opportunistic infection to develop is pneumocystis pneumonia, a lung infection caused by the fungus Pneumocystis carinii. This fungus infects most people in childhood, settling harmlessly in the lungs where it is prevented from causing disease by the immune system. But once the immune system becomes weakened, the fungus can block the lungs from delivering sufficient oxygen to the blood. The lack of oxygen leads to severe shortness of breath accompanied by fever and a dry cough.

In addition to pneumocystis pneumonia, people with AIDS often develop other fungal infections. Up to 23 percent of people with AIDS become infected with fungi from the genus Cryptococcus, which cause meningitis, inflammation of the membranes that surround the brain. Infection by the fungus Histoplasma capsulatum affects up to 10 percent of people with AIDS, causing general weight loss, fever, and respiratory complications.

Tuberculosis, a severe lung infection caused by the bacterium Mycobacterium tuberculosis, typically becomes more severe in AIDS patients than in those with a healthy immune system. Between the 1950s and the late 1980s, tuberculosis was practically eradicated in North America. In the early 1990s, doctors became alarmed when incidence of the disease dramatically escalated. This resurgence has been attributed to the increased susceptibility to tuberculosis of people infected with HIV. Infection by the bacterium Mycobacterium avium can cause fever, anaemia, and diarrhea. Other bacterial infections of the gastrointestinal tract contribute to wasting syndrome.

Opportunistic infections caused by viruses, especially members of the herpesvirus family, are common in people with AIDS. One of the herpesviruses, cytomegalovirus (CMV), infects the retina of the eye and can result in blindness. Another herpesvirus, Epstein-Barr viruses (EBV), may cause certain types of blood cancers. Infectious herpes of a simplex virus (HSV) types 1 or 2 may result in sores around the mouth, genital area, or anus.

Many people with AIDS develop cancers. The destruction of CD4 cells impairs the immune functions that halt the development of cancer. Kaposi's sarcoma is a cancer of blood vessels caused by a herpesvirus. This cancer produces purple lesions on the skin, which can spread to internal organs and cause death. B cell lymphoma affects certain cells of the lymphatic system that fight infection and perform other vital functions. Cervical cancer is more common in HIV-infected women than in women free from infection.

A variety of neurological disorders are common in the later stage of AIDS. Collectively called HIV-associated dementia, but they develop when HIV or another microbial organism infects the brain. The infection produces degeneration of intellectual processes such as memory and, sometimes, problems with movement and coordination.

HIV infection in children progresses more rapidly than in adults, most likely because the immune systems in children have not yet built up immunity to many infectious agents. The disease is particularly aggressive in infants—more than half of infants born with an HIV infection die before age two. Once a child is infected, the child's undeveloped immune system cannot prevent the virus from multiplying quickly in the blood. This extensive virus burden speeds the progression of the disease. In contrast, when adults become infected with HIV, their immune system generally fights the infection. Therefore, HIV levels in adults remain lower for an extended period, delaying the progression of the disease.

Children develop many of the opportunistic infections that befall adults but also exhibit symptoms not observed in older patients. Between infants and children, HIV infection produces wasting syndrome and slows growth (generally referred to as failure to thrive). HIV typically infects a child's brain early in the course of the disease, impairing intellectual development and coordination skills. While HIV can infect the brains of adults, it usually does so toward the later stages of the disease and produces different symptoms.

Children show a susceptibility to more bacterial and viral infections than adults. More than 20 percent of HIV-infected children develop serious, recurring bacterial infections, including meningitis and pneumonia. Some children suffer from repeated bouts of viral infections, such as chicken pox. Healthy children generally develop immunity to these viral illnesses after an initial infection.

Since HIV was first identified as the cause of AIDS in 1983, a variety of tests have been developed that help diagnose HIV infection as well as determine how far the infection has progressed. Other tests can be used to screen donated blood, blood products, and body organs for the presence of HIV.

Doctors determine if HIV is present in the body by identifying HIV antibodies, specialized proteins created by the immune system to destroy HIV. The presence of the antibodies indicates HIV infection because these antibodies form in the body only when HIV is present. HIV antibodies form anywhere from five weeks to three months after HIV infection occurs, depending upon the individual's immune system. The antibodies are produced continually throughout the course of the infection.

The standard test to detect HIV antibodies in the blood is the enzyme-linked immunosorbent assay (ELISA). In this test, a blood sample is mixed with proteins from HIV. If the blood contains HIV antibodies, they attach to the HIV proteins, producing a telltale colour change in the mixture. This test is highly reliable when performed two to three months after infection with HIV. The test is less reliable when used in the very early stage of HIV infection, before detectable levels of antibodies have had a chance to form. Doctors routinely confirm a positive result from an ELISA test by using the Western Blot test, which can detect lower levels of HIV antibodies. In this test a blood sample is applied to a paper strip containing HIV proteins. If HIV antibodies are present in the blood, they bind to the HIV proteins, producing a colour change on the paper. The combination of the ELISA and the Western Blot test is more than 99.9 percent accurate in detecting HIV infection within 12 weeks following exposure.

Once tests confirm an HIV infection, doctors monitor the health of the infected person's immune system by periodically measuring CD4 cell counts in the blood. The progressive loss of CD4 cells corresponds to a worsening of the disease as the immune system becomes increasingly impaired. Doctors also measure the viral load—the amounting of the virus in the blood—using polymerase chain reaction (PCR) technology. PCR tests measure the level of viral ribonucleic acid (RNA), a type of nucleic acid, in blood to determine the rate of HIV growth in an infected person. Knowing the viral load helps doctors estimate an infected person's survival time. For example, studies show that without treatment, the average survival time for people with an HIV viral load greater than 30,000 per microliter of blood is 4.4 years, while those with a viral load below 10,000 per microliter of blood live for an average of ten years.

A modified ELISA test that detects p24 antigen, a protein produced by HIV, can determine if specific drug treatments are having a positive effect on a patient. Blood banks, plasma Centres, clinical laboratories, private clinics, and public health departments also use this p24 antigen test to screen for the presence of HIV in blood, blood components, and organs before they are used in medical procedures.

Physicians prefer to differentiate between people who have HIV infection and those who have AIDS. The Centres for Disease Control and Prevention (CDC), based in Atlanta, Georgia, recommends that physicians reserve the diagnosis of AIDS for HIV-infected individuals whose CD4 count falls below 200 cells per microliter of blood. A diagnosis of AIDS can also be made without confirmation of CD4 levels if someone who has no other reason for immune system damage develops an opportunistic disease.

Research into the human immunodeficiency virus (HIV), the virus that causes acquired immunodeficiency syndrome (AIDS), has made remarkable progress since it began in the early 1980s. Preventive efforts have reduced the number of new cases of the disease, and for people already living with HIV/AIDS, the survival rate is increasing because of advances in drug therapy. But the majority of those affected by the disease live in developing nations, which, like many minority communities of the United States, are unable to afford the latest drug therapies and are still seriously threatened by the disease.

While no medical treatment cures AIDS, in the relatively short time since the disease was first recognized, new methods to treat the disease have developed rapidly. Health-care professionals focus on three areas of therapy for people living with HIV infection or AIDS: antiretroviral therapy using drugs that suppress HIV replication medication and other treatments that fight the opportunistic infections and cancers that commonly accompany HIV infection; and support mechanisms that help people deal with the emotional repercussions as well as the practical considerations of living with a disabling, potentially fatal disease.

A National Geographic article discusses ways the human body's immune system fights diseases, as well as attempts by scientists to develop vaccines for many virulent viruses including AIDS. Since this account was published early in the AIDS epidemic, it contains some information that has subsequently been revised or updated.

Understanding the specific steps in the HIV replication cycle is critical in order for scientists to develop drugs that attack vulnerable stages within the cycle. HIV belonged to a unique group of viruses known as retroviruses, so named because these viruses reverse the usual flow of genetic information within an infected cell. Most viruses store their genetic material in deoxyribonucleic acid (DNA), the double-helix structure that makes up genes. When a virus infects a cell, the viral DNA forms the template for the creation of messenger RNA, a type of ribonucleic acid. This messenger RNA directs the formation of specific proteins, and these proteins, in turn, builds new virus particles. In HIV, however, genetic material is stored in two single-stranded RNA molecules. When HIV infects a cell, an enzyme called reverse transcriptase copies the genetic instructions in the virus's RNA and moved it into the DNA. This movement of genetic information from RNA to DNA is the opposite of that which occurs in most cells during protein synthesis.

Another HIV enzyme, called integrase, helps the newly formed viral DNA to become part of the structure of the infected cell's DNA. The viral DNA then forces the infected cell to manufacture HIV particles. A third HIV enzyme, called protease, packages these HIV particles into a complete and functional HIV virus. Over the last decade researchers have created a variety of drugs that block the action of some of the enzymes used in HIV replication. The main classes of drugs used against HIV are nucleoside analogues, non-nucleoside reverse transcriptase inhibitors, protease inhibitors, and fusion inhibitors.

Nucleoside analogues impede the action of reverse transcriptase, the HIV enzyme that converts the virus's genetic material into DNA. During this conversion process, these drugs incorporate themselves into the structure of the viral DNA, rendering the

DNA useless and preventing it from instructing the infected cell to make additional HIV. The nucleoside analogue known as azidothymidine (AZT), which became available in 1987, was the first drug approved by the United States Food and Drug Administration (FDA) to treat AIDS. AZT slows HIV growth in the body, permitting an increase in the number of CD4 cells, which boosts the immune system. AZT also prevents transmission of HIV from an infected mother to her newborn. Since the introduction of AZT, additional nucleoside analogues have been developed, including didanosine (sold under the trade name Videx), zalcitabine (HIVID), stavudine (Zerit), lamivudine (Epivir), and abacavir (Ziagen). These drugs are not particularly powerful when used alone, and often their benefits last for only 6 to 12 months. But when nucleoside analogues are used in combination with each other, they provide longer-lasting and more effective results.

Non-nucleoside reverse transcriptase inhibitors (NNRTIs), introduced in 1996, use a different mechanism to block reverse transcriptase. These drugs bind directly to reverse transcriptase, preventing the enzyme from converting RNA to DNA. Three NNRTIs are available: nevirapine (Viramune), delavirdine (Rescriptor), and efavirenz (Sustiva). NNRTIs work best when used in combination with nucleoside analogues.

The third group of antiviral drugs, called protease inhibitors, cripples protease, the enzyme vital to the formation of new HIV. When these drugs block protease, defective HIV forms that is unable to infect new cells. Protease inhibitors are more powerful than nucleosides and NNRTIs, producing dramatic decreases in HIV levels in the blood. This reduced a viral load, in turn, enabled CD4 cell levels to skyrocket. The first protease inhibitor, saquinavir (Invirase), was approved in 1995. Since then other protease inhibitors have been approved, including ritonavir (Norvir), indinavir (Crixivan), nelfinavir (Viracept), and amprenavir (Agenerase).

A new class of drugs, known as fusion inhibitors, became available in 2003 when the FDA approved the use of enfuvirtide, sold under the brand name Fuzeon. Fusion inhibitors prevent the binding or fusion of HIV to CD4 cells. When used with other antiretroviral medicines, fusion inhibitors can reduce the amount of HIV in the blood and increase the number of CD4 cells.

Clinical studies of treatment with antiretroviral drugs immediately showed that their benefits are short-lived when a single drug is used alone. This short-term effectiveness results when HIV mutates, or changes its genetic structure, becoming resistant to the drug. The genetic material in HIV provides instructions for the manufacture of critical enzymes needed to replicate the virus. Scientists design current antiretroviral drugs to impede the activity of these enzymes. If the virus mutates, the structure of the virus's enzymes changes. Drugs no longer work against the enzymes, making the drugs ineffective against viral infection.

Genes mutate during the course of viral replication, so the best way to prevent mutation is to halt replication. Studies have shown that the most effective treatment to halt HIV replication employs a combination of three drugs taken together—for instances, a combination of two nucleoside analogues with a protease inhibitor. This regimen, called triple therapy, maximizes drug potency while reducing the chance for drug resistance. The combination of three drugs is often referred to as an AIDS cocktail. In HIV-infected patients who have undergone triple therapy, the viral loads reduced significantly, sometimes to undetectable levels. Their CD4 cell counts gradually increased, and they sustained good health with

586

no complications. With this treatment, some patients who were near death were able to return to normal physical activity. Triple therapy was introduced in the United States in 1996. That year AIDS deaths in the United States decreased 26 percent, the first decrease since the beginning of the epidemic. In 1997 US AIDS deaths decreased by 56 percent from the year before.

Despite phenomenal success, triple therapy has some drawbacks. This multidrug therapy is quite complicated, requiring patients to take anywhere from 5 to 20 pills a day on a specific schedule. Some drugs must be taken with food, while others cannot be taken at the same time as certain other pills. Even the most organized of people find it difficult to take pills correctly. Yet, just one or two lapses in treatment may cause the virus to develop resistance to the drug regimen.

Many people also find it difficult to deal with the unpleasant side effects produced by antiretroviral drugs. Common side effects include nausea, diarrhea, headache, fatigue, abdominal pain, kidney stones, anaemia, and tingling or numbness in the hands and feet. Some patients may develop diabetes mellitus, while other patients develop collections of fat deposits in the abdomen or back, causing a noticeable change in body configurations. Some antiretroviral drugs produce an increase in blood fat levels, placing a patient at risk for heart attack or stroke. Some patients suffer more misery from the drug treatment than they do from the illnesses produced by HIV infection.

Perhaps the greatest drawback to triple therapy is its cost, which ranges from $10,000 to $12,000 a year. This high cost is well beyond the means of people with low incomes or those with limited health-care insurance. As a result, the most effective therapies currently available remain beyond the reach of the majority of HIV-infected people worldwide.

To decrease the toxic effects of drugs and to defer costly therapy, in 2001 United States federal health officials recommended delaying drug treatment for HIV infection in people showing no symptoms and who have been infected with HIV for more than six months. The new guidelines call for delaying treatment until an infected person's CD4 cells fall below 350 cells per microliter of blood or the HIV viral load exceeds 30,000 per microliter of blood. Evidence suggests, that delaying treatment poses no harm to infected people and, in fact, benefits them by deferring the toxic side effects of the drugs.

Studies show that under certain circumstances, administering antiretroviral drugs within 24 hours (preferably within one to two hours) after exposure to HIV can protect a person from becoming infected with the virus. Although the effectiveness of postexposure antiretroviral therapy following sexual exposure to HIV remains uncertain, the CDC recommends that health-care personnel exposed to HIV infection from a needle stick or other accident take antiretroviral drugs.

Scientists continue to develop more powerful HIV treatments that have fewer side effects and fewer resistance problems. Some drugs under investigation block the HIV enzyme integrase from inserting viral DNA into the infected cell. Other drugs prevent HIV from binding with a CD4 cell in the first place, thereby barring HIV entry into cells.

Some scientists focus on ways to fortify the immune system. A biological molecule called interleukin-2 shows promise in boosting the immune system's arsenal of infection-fighting cells.

Interleukin-2 stimulates the production of CD4 cells. If enough CD4 cells can be created, they may trigger other immune cell responses that can overpower HIV infection.

In other research, doctors hope to bolster the immune system with a vaccine. Most vachines available today, including those that prevent measles or poliomyelitis, work by helping the body to create antibodies. Such vaccines mark specific infectious agents, such as the measles and polio viruses, for destruction. But many experts believe that an effective HIV vaccine will need to do more than just stimulate anti-HIV antibodies. Studies are underway to develop vaccines that also elevate the production of T cells in the immune system. Scientists hope that this dual approach will prime the immune system to attack HIV as soon as it appears in the body, perhaps containing the virus before it spreads through the body in a way that natural immune defence cannot. The genetic variability of HIV frustrates efforts to develop a vaccine: A vaccine effective against one type of HIV may not work on a virus that has undergone genetic mutation.

In addition to antiretroviral therapy to combat HIV infection, effective drug treatments are available to fight many of the medical complications that result from HIV infection. Doctors try to prevent infections before they begin to avoid taxing a patient's weakened immune system unnecessarily. A doctor instructs an HIV-infected person on ways to avoid exposure to infectious agents that produce opportunistic infections common in people with a weakened immune system. Doctors usually prescribe more than one drug to forestall infections. For example, for those who have a history of pneumocystic pneumonia and a CD4 cell count of less than 200 cells per microliter, doctors may prescribe the antibiotic sulfamethoxazole and trimethoprim to prevent further bouts of pneumonia. Patients suffering from recurring thrush may be given the antifungal drug fluconazole for prolonged periods. For people with CD4 cell counts of less than 100 cells per microliter, doctors may prescribe clarithromycin or azithromycin to prevent Mycobacterium avium infections.

The AIDS quilt travels on display to promote public awareness of acquired immunodeficiency syndrome (AIDS). The quilt project, initiated in 1986 by the NAMES Project organization, consists of thousands of panels. Each panel is individually designed and is dedicated to the memory of someone who has died of AIDS.

A person diagnosed with HIV infection, he faces many challenges, including choosing the best course of treatment, paying for health care, and providing for the needs of children in the family while ill. In addition to these practical considerations, people with HIV infection must cope with the emotional toll associated with the diagnosis of a potentially fatal illness. The social stigma that continues to surround a diagnosis of AIDS because of the disease's prevalence among gay men or drug users causes many people to avoid telling family or friends about their illness. People with AIDS often feel incredibly lonely as they try to cope with a devastating illness on their own. Loneliness, anxiety, fear, anger, and other emotions often require as much attention as the medical illnesses common to HIV infection.

Since the AIDS epidemic began in the United States in 1981, grassroots organizations have been created to meet the medical and emotional needs of people who have AIDS and also to protect their civil rights. The Gay Men's Health Crisis, founded in 1982, was the first nonprofit organization to provide medical, education, and advocacy services for people with AIDS. The Los Angeles Shanti Group was established in 1983 to provide emotional support and medical guidance to people with AIDS and other life-threatening illnesses. Activist organizations such as the AIDS Coalition to Unleash Power (ACT UP), founded in 1986, have been created to initiate faster change in public policies and to speed up the course of AIDS clinical research. American Foundation for AIDS Research (AMFAR), created in 1985, is the nation's leading nonprofit organization dedicated to the support of AIDS research and the advocacy of fair and compassionate AIDS-related public policies. In Canada, the AIDS Committee of Toronto (ACT) was established in 1983 by community activists intent on fighting for the civil rights of people infected with HIV. As the AIDS epidemic grew, ACT expanded its mission to help people disabled by the disease and to spread health information to halt the spread of the disease. AIDS Vancouver (AV), also established in 1983, became the principal education, prevention, and support service organization for that city.

Counselling Centres and churches provide individual or group counselling to help people with HIV infection or AIDS are shared by feelings, problems, and coping mechanisms with others. Family counselling can address the emotions of other family members who are disturbed by the diagnosis of HIV infection in another family member. Grief counselling also helps people who have lost friends or family members to AIDS.

In the United States and Canadian government-funded and privately funded organizations help people cope with disease. For instance, local, city-funded clinics provide AIDS testing as well as counselling to prepare people for a test result that indicates HIV infection. Health experts at clinics explain the medical progression of the illness, arrange medical appointments with health-care specialists, and help people choose appropriate treatment options. State-appointed social workers and community nonprofit organizations help people find federally funded programs that offset the high cost of medical care and child care.

The United States Congress has passed legislation to help HIV-infected individuals. In 1990 the Americans with Disabilities Act (ADA), was enacted, protecting people with disabling diseases, including AIDS, from discrimination in activities such as applying for jobs or buying a house. The Ryan White Comprehensive AIDS Resources Emergency Act was established in 1990 and reauthorized in 1996. This program provides medical and dental care, counselling, transportation, and home and hospice care for low-income or uninsured people living with AIDS. The AIDS Drug Assistance Program (ADAP) is funded in large part by this act and administered by all 50 states. It pays for costly AIDS medications for people who do not have private insurance and who are not poor enough to be eligible for Medicaid.

A landmark United Nations (UN) report, issued in June 2000, documents the terrible effect that acquired immunodeficiency syndrome (AIDS) has had on millions of people around the world. Some of the successes to those individual nations have achieved in stabilizing or halting the spread of the disease and what other countries can learn from those successes.

With a vaccine for AIDS years away and no cure on the horizon, experts believe that the most effective treatment for AIDS is to prevent the occurrence of HIV infection. Health officials focus public education programs on altering risky behaviours linked to HIV transmission, particularly unsafe sexual practices and needle-sharing by intravenous drug users. Safe-sex campaigns sponsored by health clinics, social Centres, schools, and churches encourage sexual abstinence or monogamy (sexual relations with only one partner). Education programs instruct about the proper way to use condoms to provide a protective barrier against transmission of HIV during sexual intercourse. Needle-exchange programs, which provide clean needles to drug users, enable intravenous drug abusers to avoid sharing HIV-contaminated needles. Needle-exchange programs have been widely criticized because they seem to condone illicit drug use. However, numerous US government-funded studies have indicated that such programs reduce HIV transmission without promoting greater drug use. To reduce the accidental transmission of HIV during medical procedures, both the United States and Canada have established strict guidelines for health-care settings, including the use of protective clothing and proper instrument disposal.

In the United States, the effectiveness of public education programs that target people at risk for HIV infection was well demonstrated in the gay community of San Francisco, California, in the 1980s. In 1982 and 1983, 6,000 to 8,000 people in San Francisco became infected with HIV. The gay community rallied to promote condom use and advocate monogamy through extensive education programs and public health advertisements geared for gay men. These public education programs were credited with reducing the number of gay men in San Francisco who became HIV infected. By 1993 the number of new infections declined to 1,000, and by 1999, fewer than 500 people were infected each year.

Public education about AIDS has also proven effective in other countries. Uganda was one of the first African countries to report cases of HIV infection. The first cases of AIDS were reported there in 1982, and by the late 1980s Uganda had one of the highest rates of HIV infection in the world. The Ugandan government was one of the first countries to set up a partnership with WHO to create a national AIDS control program called the AIDS Information Centre (AIC). The AIC has established extensive education programs promoting condom use and other methods to prevent HIV from spreading further. The program has also worked with community organizations to change social behaviours that increase the risk of HIV infection. The AIC promotes its message using innovative drama, song, and dance programs, a particularly effective communication method for African communities. AIC established confidential HIV testing services that provide same-day results and community counselling programs. As a result of Uganda's quick response to the AIDS epidemic, the totals of HIV infected people in that country has declined significantly since 1993, during a time when most other African nations faced a frightening increase in the incidence of HIV infection.

Public health officials have learned that education programs that teach and reinforce safe behaviours through a series of meetings are more effective than one-time exposure to public-health information provided in a class lecture, magazine article, advertisement, or pamphlet. Education programs tailored to reflect specific ethnic and cultural preferences prove even more effective. For example, the Canadian Aboriginal AIDS Network creates HIV education programs that fight the common misperception among the indigenous peoples of Canada that AIDS is primarily a disease of white, affluent people. Among indigenous communities, the network promotes programs that use colloquial language to increase awareness about safe sex practices and needle use.

In the short time since the first cases of the AIDS epidemic were reported in 1981, scientists have identified the viral cause of the illness, the basic modes of transmission, accurate tests for the presence of infection, and effective drugs that slow or halt the progression of the disease. During that same period, governments and grassroots organizations around the world were spurred into action to meet the growing need for AIDS education, counselling, patients' rights, and clinical research. Despite these advances, critics observe that many governments were slow to respond to the crisis. For example, United States president Ronald Reagan did not discuss AIDS in public until 1987, more than six years after the start of the AIDS epidemic. By that time, 41,000 Americans had already died of the disease. AIDS advocates believe that the lack of federal support for AIDS research in these early years delayed the development of an effective vaccine or a cure for the disease.

Using computer technology to study the structure of HIV, scientists have determined that HIV originated around 1930 in rural areas of Central Africa, where the virus may have been present for many years in isolated communities. The virus probably did not spread because members of these rural communities had limited contact with people from other areas. But in the 1960s and 1970s, political upheaval, wars, drought, and famine forced many people from these rural areas to migrate to cities to find jobs. During this time, the incidence of sexually transmitted infections, including HIV infection, accelerated and quickly spread throughout Africa. As world travel became more prevalent, HIV infection developed into a worldwide epidemic. Studies of stored blood from the United States suggest that HIV infection was well established there by 1978.

In 1970, at about the same time that the HIV epidemic was taking hold in Africa, American molecular biologist David Baltimore and American virologist Howard Temin independently discovered the enzyme reverse transcriptase, which could be used to identify retroviruses. Over the next ten years, many retroviruses were identified in animals. But not until 1980, shortly before the first AIDS cases were recognized in the United States, did American virologist Robert Gallo identify the first human retroviruses, HTLV-I and HTLV-II (HTLV stands for human T cell lymphotropic viruses).

Other studies demonstrated that these human retroviruses were more closely related to a retrovirus found in African chimpanzees than to each other. This discovery suggests that the human retroviruses may have evolved from retroviruses that originally infected chimpanzees. The chimpanzee retrovirus likely infected people and underwent mutations to form the human retrovirus. In 1999 scientists confirmed that HIV had been spread from chimpanzees to humans on at least three separate occasions in Central Africa, probably beginning in the 1940s or 1950s.

In 1983 the French biologist and cancer specialist Luc Montagnier and his research team isolated the human immunodeficiency virus (HIV), the virus that causes AIDS. Montagnier has since become a champion of AIDS prevention education and has devoted his career to developing an AIDS vaccine.

Beginning in June 1981 the CDC published reports on clusters of gay men in New York and California who had been diagnosed with pneumocystic pneumonia or Kaposi's sarcoma. These two rare illnesses had previously been observed only in people whose immune systems had been damaged by drugs or disease. These reports triggered concern that a disease of the immune system was spreading quickly in the homosexual community. Initially called gay-related immunodeficiency disease (GRID). The new illness to be identified in population groups outside the gay community, including users of intravenous drugs, recipients of blood transfusions, and heterosexual partners of infected people. In 1982 the name for the new illness was changed to acquired immunodeficiency syndrome, or AIDS.

While the disease was making headlines for the speed with which it was spreading around the world, the cause of AIDS remained unidentified. Fear of AIDS and ignorance of its causes resulted in some outlandish theories. Some thought the disease was God's punishment for behaviours that they considered immoral. These early theories created a social stigma surrounding the disease that still lingers.

Scientists quickly identified the primary modes of transmission—sexual contact with an infected person, contact with infected blood products, and mother-to-child transmission. From these modes of transmission it was clear that the new illness was spread in a specific manner that matched the profile of a viral infection. In 1983 French cancer specialist Luc Montagnier and his colleagues isolated what appeared to be a new human retrovirus from AIDS patients. They named it lymphadenopathy virus (LAV). Eight months later Gallo and his colleagues isolated the same virus in AIDS patients, naming the virus HTLV-III. Eventually, scientists agreed to call the infectious agent human immunodeficiency virus (HIV). In 1985 a new AIDS-causing virus was discovered in West Africa. Named HIV-2, the new virus is closely related to the first HIV, but it appears to be less harmful to cells of the immune system and reproduces more slowly than HIV-1.

Research leading to the development of the ELISA test was conducted simultaneously by teams led by Gallo in the United States and Montagnier in France. In 1985 the ELISA test to identify HIV in blood became available, followed by the development of the Western Blot test. These tests were first employed to screen blood for the presence of HIV before the blood was used in medical procedures. The tests were later used to identify HIV-infected people, many of whom did not know they were infected. These diagnostic tests also helped scientists study the course of HIV infection in populations.

The CDC presented its first definition of AIDS in 1982. The CDC recommended that physicians diagnose AIDS if a person has an illness known to be caused by immune deficiency, as long as there is no known cause for this immune deficiency (people who undergo radiation therapy or who take certain drugs may impair their immune systems). As more information became known about the course of HIV infection and the nature of the virus itself, this definition of AIDS was revised repeatedly to expand the list of illnesses considered diagnostic indicators of the disease. Early definitions were based on the opportunistic infections commonly found in HIV-infected men. As a result, many women who did not have symptoms covered in the official AIDS definition were denied disability benefits and AIDS-related drug therapies.

The current definition of AIDS was created in 1993 and includes 26 opportunistic infections and cancers, known as diagnostic indicators, that affect both men and women. The definition also emphasizes the importance of the level of CD4 cells in the blood. Today doctors make the diagnosis of AIDS in anyone with a CD4 count below 200 cells per microliter of blood, regardless of the associated illnesses they may have.

Although new and effective AIDS drugs have brought hope to many HIV-infected persons, a number of social and ethical dilemmas still confront researchers and public-health officials. The latest combination drug therapies are far too expensive for infected persons in the developing world—particularly in sub-Saharan Africa, where the majority of AIDS deaths have occurred. In these regions, where the incidence of HIV infection continues to soar, the lack of access to drugs can be catastrophic. In 1998, responding to an international outcry, several pharmaceutical firms announced that they would slash the price of AIDS drugs in developing nations by as much as 75 percent. However, some countries argued that drug firms had failed to deliver on their promises, more or less of the expensive drugs. In South Africa government officials developed legislation that would enable the country to override the patent rights of drug firms by importing cheaper generic medicines made in India and Thailand to treat HIV infection. In 1998, 39 pharmaceutical companies sued the South African government on the grounds that the legislation violated international trade agreements. Pharmaceutical companies eventually dropped their legal efforts in April 2001, conceding that South Africa's legislation did comply with international trading laws. The end of the legal battle was expected to pave the way for other developing countries to gain access to more affordable AIDS drugs.

AIDS research in the developing world has raised ethical questions pertaining to the clinical testing of new therapies and potential vaccines. For example, controversy erupted over 1997 clinical trials that tested a shorter course of AZT therapy in HIV-infected pregnant women in developing countries. Earlier studies had shown that administering AZT to pregnant women for up to six months prior to birth could cut mother-to-child transmission of HIV by up to two-thirds. The treatment's $800 cost, however, made it too expensive for patients in developing nations.

The controversial 1997 clinical trials, which were conducted in Thailand and other regions in Asia and Africa, tested a shorter course of AZT treatment, costing only $50. Some pregnant women received AZT, while others received a placebo—a medically inactive substance often used in drug trials to help scientists determine the effectiveness of the drug under study. Ultimately the shorter course of AZT treatment proved to be successful and is now standard practice in a growing number of developing nations. However, at the time of the trials, critics charged that using a placebo on HIV-infected pregnant women—when AZT had already been shown to prevent mother-to-child transmission—was unethical and needlessly placed babies at fatal risk. Defenders of the studies countered that a placebo was necessary to accurately gauge the effectiveness of the AZT short-course treatment. Some critics speculated whether such a trial, while apparently acceptable in the developing nations of Asia and Africa, would ever have been viewed as ethical, or even permissible, in a developed nation like the United States.

Similar ethical questions surround the testing of AIDS vaccines in developing nations. Vaccines typically use weakened or killed HIV to spark antibody production. In some vaccines, these weakened or killed viruses have the potential to cause infection and disease. Critics questioned whether it is ethical to place all the risk on test subjects in developing regions such as sub-Saharan Africa, where a person infected by a vaccine would have little or no access to medical care. At the same time, with AIDS causing up to 5,500 deaths a day in Africa, others feel that developing nations must pursue any medical avenue for stemming the epidemic and protecting people from the virus.

For the struggling economies of some developing nations, AIDS has brought yet another burden: AIDS tends to kill young adults in the prime of their lives—the primary breadwinners and caregivers in families. According to figures released by the United Nations in 1999, AIDS has shortened the life expectancy in some African nations by an average of seven years. In Zimbabwe, life expectancy for adults declined from 61 years in 1993 to 38 in

2003, according to the World Health Organization (WHO). The next few decades may see average life expectance fall even lower in sub-Saharan Africa. As of 2003, 14 million children around the world had been orphaned by the AIDS epidemic. Those children who survive face a lack of income, a higher risk of malnutrition and disease, and the breakdown of family structure.

In Africa, the disease has had a heavy impact on urban professionals—educated, skilled workers who play a critical role in the labour force of industries such as agriculture, education, transportation, and government. The decline in the skilled workforce has already damaged economic growth in Africa, and economists warn of disastrous consequences in the future.

The grassroots AIDS organization AIDS Coalition to Unleash Power, commonly known as ACT UP, uses nonviolent civil disobedience to protest against government and societal indifference to the AIDS epidemic.

From the early days of the identification of AIDS, the disease has been powerfully linked to behaviours that are illegal (such as illicit drug use) or are considered immoral by many people (such as promiscuity and homosexuality). Consequently, a diagnosis of AIDS was a mark of disgrace, although medical research revealed that the disease follows well-defined modes of transmission that can affect any person. As the extent of the epidemic unfolded, giving the misinformation about AIDS and how it is transmitted triggered widespread fear of contracting the disease. Some communities responded with hysteria that resulted in violence. In the United States, in 1987, a Florida family was contained of three HIV-positive sons who had been infected from blood transfusions, they were driven from their home when it was torched by an arsonist. In other communities, parents protested when HIV-infected children attended school. In many areas of the world, women in particular may face consequences if their HIV status is discovered. Reports indicate that many HIV-infected women are subject to domestic violence at the hands of their husbands—even if the husbands themselves are the source of infection. As a result, some women in developing nations fear being tested for HIV infection and cut themselves off from medical care and counselling.

In addition to social stigmas, HIV-infected persons must grapple with more immediate concerns—daily struggles for basic medical care and other basic rights in the face of discrimination and fear because of their HIV status. In China, for example, the number of HIV-positive individuals is a comparatively small problem so far. Yet nurses and other medical personnel who fear infection commonly refuse to perform procedures on HIV-infected people. This sort of discrimination against HIV-infected individuals has long been a problem in the United States. In 1998 the United States Supreme Court heard the case of Sidney Abbott, a young woman in Maine who sued dentist Randon Bragdon after he refused to treat her when he learned of her HIV-positive status. Basing its ruling on the Americans with Disabilities Act, the Supreme Court ruled in Bragdon v. Abbott that the woman's HIV infection constituted a disability, even though she suffered from no disease symptoms. AIDS advocates expect this decision to protect the rights of many people with AIDS in the United States.

Some developing nations, such as Uganda, have met the AIDS crisis head-on, attempting to educate citizens and change high-risk behaviours in the population. However, other nations have been slow to even acknowledge the disease. In India, for example, the nation's prime minister did not speak publicly about the dangers posed by the epidemic until 1999.

In developed nations, some of the stigmas attached to a diagnosis of AIDS has lessened in recent years, in part due to the admissions by public figures and celebrities, especially in the United States, that they were HIV infected. The deaths from AIDS of actor Rock Hudson and tennis players Arthur Ashe, and the AIDS advocacy roles of basketball player Magic Johnson and Olympic diver Greg Louganis have personalized the disease and helped society come to terms with the enormity of the epidemic.

To some scientists, the AIDS epidemic signals a troubling trend in humanity's future. Along with other deadly microbial threats of recent years—most notably Ebola virus, which has caused sporadic epidemics in Africa, and hantavirus, which broke out in the American Southwest in the early 1990s—AIDS is viewed by some as yet another in a series of emerging diseases that demonstrate how vulnerable humans are to newly encountered microbes. With population and land development increasing, humans have encroached farther into rain forests and other formerly wild areas, unleashing previously unknown disease agents. Meanwhile, global travel has become faster, more convenient, and more accessible to many people. Some scientists are worried by these trends, fearing the potential for an as-yet-unknown pathogen to arise and spread quickly and lethally around the globe.

The social, ethical, and economic effects of the AIDS epidemic are still being played out, and no one is entirely certain what the consequences will be. Despite the many grim facts of the AIDS epidemic, however, humanity is armed with proven, effective weapons against the disease: Knowledge, education, prevention, and the ever-growing store of information about the virus's actions.

Human Immunodeficiency Virus, infectious agent that causes acquired immunodeficiency syndrome (AIDS), a disease that leaves a person vulnerable to life-threatening infections. Scientists have identified two types of this virus. HIV-1 is the primary cause of AIDS worldwide. HIV-2 is found mostly in West Africa.

The human immunodeficiency virus (HIV), the cause of acquired immunodeficiency syndrome (AIDS), is genetically programmed to do one thing: highjack the reproductive machinery of a human cell, then trick it into churning out as many copies of the virus as it can before the cell dies. The current best hope for the treatment of AIDS requires that patients take a number of different drugs, each of which interferes with certain steps of the HIV infection process.

The human immunodeficiency virus (HIV) consists of a nucleoid core and the surrounding protein matrix, both enclosed in a lipid envelope. The nucleoid core contains the viral genetic material and the reverse transcriptase enzyme, which are used in viral replication. The transmembrane glycoprotein gp41 and the envelope glycoprotein gp120 are attached to the envelope; these proteins enable HIV to bind and fuse with a target host cell.

Human immunodeficiency viruses (HIV), is the causing of acquired immunodeficiency syndrome (AIDS). By infecting CD4 T-lymphocytes, a type of white blood cell, HIV weakens the immune system and leaves the infected individual open to deadly infections. The viruses gain access to a T-lymphocyte by attaching to CD4 proteins on the outer surface of the cell membrane.

In 1999 alone, 4 million people in sub-Saharan Africa became infected with the human immunodeficiency virus (HIV), the virus that causes acquired immunodeficiency syndrome (AIDS).

In several African countries, at least half of males currently aged 15 will eventually die of AIDS. These and other shocking facts about the level of devastation that HIV/AIDS has inflicted and will inflict on the people and economies of Africa are documented in the Report on the Global HIV/AIDS Epidemic. The report, excerpted here, was published in June 2000 by the Joint United Nations Programme on HIV/AIDS, known as UNAIDS.

A landmark United Nations (UN) report, issued in June 2000, documents the terrible effects that acquired immunodeficiency syndromes having had millions of people around the world. Of which focuses on some of the successes of individual nations have achieved in stabilizing or halting the spread of the disease and what other countries can learn from those successes.

HIV is the retrovirus and associated wi th members that share a unique method of replicating themselves when they infect living cells. Retroviruses store their genetic information in molecules of ribonucleic acid (RNA). However, unlike other RNA viruses, retroviruses use RNA as a template (a master pattern) for forming deoxyribonucleic acid (DNA), the genetic material that puts viral replication instructions into effect. This process, called reverse transcription, is the exact opposite of the normal flow of genetic information in living things, in which DNA serves as the template for RNA formation.

HIV consisted of a flexible outer membrane, called the envelope, that surrounds a protein case known as the capsid. The envelope is studded with glycoproteins, chemical receptors that enable the virus to lock onto target cells. Inside the capsid has for residing of two identical strands of RNA. These RNA strands make up the virus's genetic program and store all the instructions needed to replicate HIV once it has infected a host cell. HIV also contains molecules of an enzyme called reverse transcriptase. When HIV infects a cell, reverse transcriptase copies the genetic instructions in the virus's RNA and uses the instructions to build complementary strands of DNA.

HIV transmission occurs when a person is exposed to body fluids infected with the virus, such as blood, semen, vaginal secretions, and breast milk. The primary modes of HIV transmission are (1) sexual relations with an infected person. (2) Sharing hypodermic needles or accidental pricking by a needle contaminated with infected blood; (3) transfer of the virus from an infected mother to her baby during pregnancy, childbirth, or through breast-feeding.

When HIV takes into the body it infects lymphocytes, in that which are a type of white blood cell in the immune system. HIV uses its glycoproteins to attach itself to receptors on the surface of a lymphocyte. The outer envelope of HIV then fuses with the lymphocyte, enabling the HIV capsid to enter the lymphocyte itself. HIV commandeers the genetic material of the lymphocyte, instructing the cell to replicate more viruses. The newly formed viruses break free from the host, destroying the cell in the process. The new viruses go on to infect and destroy other lymphocytes.

Over a period that may last from a few months to up to 15 years, HIV may destroy enough lymphocytes that the immune system becomes unable to function properly. An infected person develops multiple life-threatening illnesses from infections that normally do not cause illnesses in people with a healthy immune system. Some people who have HIV infection may not develop any of the clinical illnesses that define the full-blown disease of AIDS for ten years or more. Doctors prefer to use the term AIDS for cases where a person has reached the final, life-threatening stages of HIV infection.

No treatment is available that cures AIDS, but a number of drugs have been developed that suppress HIV replication, thereby preventing the destruction of the immune system. Known as antiretroviral therapy, these drugs target different stages in the life cycle of HIV. There are four main classes of drugs used against HIV: Nucleoside analogues, non-nucleoside reverses transcriptase inhibitors, protease inhibitors, and fusion inhibitors. Nucleoside analogues and non-nucleoside reverse transcriptase inhibitors use different mechanisms to block the action of the enzyme reverse transcriptase. Protease inhibitors interfere with protease, an enzyme vital to the formation of new HIV. When these drugs block protease, defective HIV forms that is unable to infect new cells. In 2003 the US Food and Drug Administration approved the use of enfuvirtide, sold under the brand name Fuzeon. This drug belongs to a new class of drugs called fusion inhibitors, which prevent the binding or fusion of HIV to lymphocytes.

Ribonucleic Acid (RNA), genetic material of certain viruses (RNA viruses) and, in cellular organisms, the molecule that directs the middle steps of protein production. In RNA viruses, the RNA directs two processes—protein syntheses (production of the virus's protein coat) and replication (the process by which RNA copies itself). In cellular organisms, another type of genetic material, called deoxyribonucleic acid (DNA), carries the information that determines protein structure. But DNA cannot act alone and rely upon RNA to transfer this crucial information during protein synthesis (production of the proteins needed by the cell for its activities and development).

Like DNA, RNA consists of a chain of chemical compounds called nucleotides. Each nucleotide is made up of a sugar molecule called ribose, from which of a group and placed in one of four different nitrogen-containing compounds called bases. The four bases are adenine, guanine, uracil, and cytosine. These constituents are components that are joined together in the same manner as the deoxyribonucleic acid (DNA) molecule. Simply, a nucleic acid t hat carries genetic information in the cell is capable of self-replication and synthesis of RNA. DNA consists of two long chains of nucleotides twisted into a double helix and joined by hydrogen bonds between the complementary bases adenine and thymine or cytosine and guanine. The sequence of nucleotides determines individual hereditary characteristics.

RNA differs chemically from DNA in two ways: The RNA sugar molecule contains an oxygen atom not found in DNA, and RNA contains the base uracil in the place of the base thymine in DNA. As a polymeric constituent of all living cells and many viruses, consisting of a long, usually a single -stranded chain of alternating phosphate and ribose units with the bases adenine, guanine, cytosine and uracil bonded to the ribose. The structure and base sequence of RNA are determinants of protein synthesis and the transmission of genetic information.

In cellular organisms, RNA is a single-stranded polynucleotide chain, a strand of many nucleotides linked together. There are three types of RNA. Ribosomal RNA (rRNA) is found in the cell's ribosomes, the specialized structures that are the sites of protein synthesis. Transfer RNA (tRNA) carries amino acids to the ribosomes for incorporation into a protein. Messenger RNA (mRNA) carries the genetic blueprint copied from the sequence of bases in a cell's DNA. This blueprint specifies the sequence of amino acids in a protein. All three types of RNA are formed as needed, using specific sections of the cell's DNA as templates.

Some RNA viruses have double-stranded RNA—that is, their RNA molecules consist of two parallel polynucleotide chains.

The base of each RNA nucleotide in one chain pairs with a complementary base in the second chain—that is, adenine pairs with uracil, and guanine pairs with cytosine. For these viruses, the process of RNA replication in a host cell follows the same pattern as that of DNA replication, a method of replication called semi-conservative replication. In semi-conservative replication, each newly formed double-stranded RNA molecule contains one polynucleotide chain from the parent RNA molecule, and one complementary chain formed through the process of base pairing. The Colorado tick fever virus, which causes mild respiratory infections, the double-stranded helix virus.

There are two types of single-stranded RNA viruses. After entering a host cell, one type, a polio virus, becomes double-stranded by making an RNA strand complementary to its own. During replication, although the two strands separate, only the recently formed strand attracts nucleotides with complementary bases. Therefore, the polynucleotide chain that is produced as a result of replication is exactly the same as the original RNA chain.

The other type of single-stranded RNA viruses, called retroviruses, include the human immunodeficiency virus (HIV), which causes AIDS, and other viruses that cause tumours. After entering a host cell, a retrovirus makes a DNA strand complementary to its own RNA strand using the host's DNA nucleotides. This new DNA strand then replicates and forms a double helix that becomes incorporated into the host cell's chromosomes, where it is replicated along with the host DNA. While in a host cell, the RNA-derived viral DNA produces single-stranded RNA viruses that then leave the host cell and enter other cells, where the replication process is repeated.

In 1981, American biochemist Thomas Cech discovered that certain RNA molecules appear to act as enzymes, molecules that speed up, or catalyze, some reactions inside cells. Until its discovery biologists thought that all enzymes were proteins. Like other enzymes, these RNA catalysts, called ribozymes, show great specificity with respect to the reactions they speed up. The discovery of ribozymes added to the evidence that RNA, not DNA, was the earliest genetic material. Many scientists think that the earliest genetic molecule was simple in structure and capable of enzymatic activity. Furthermore, the molecule would necessarily exist in all organisms. The enzyme ribonuclease-P, which exists in all organisms, is made of protein and a form of RNA that has enzymatic activity. Based on this evidence, some scientists suspect that the RNA portion of ribonuclease-P may be the modern equivalent of the earliest genetic molecule, the molecule that first enabled replication to occur in primitive cells.

Deoxyribonucleic acid (DNA), one of the nucleic acids, stores genetic information within cells, while enzymes are protein molecules that cause cellular reactions. RNA is the go-between, translating genetic information to protein by means of small molecules called transfer RNA (tRNA). While studying the formation of tRNA in 1978, Altman discovered an enzyme called ribonuclease P (RNase P), composed of both RNA and a protein. He noted that RNase P caused the splicing of tRNA molecules and assumed that the protein portion of the enzyme had caused this reaction. He then noted that the protein component acting alone did not splice the transfer RNA molecule. After isolating the RNA component (called M1 RNA) and repeating the experiment, Altman demonstrated that the M1 RNA had acted alone to cause the reaction. Because this process violated an absolute of molecular biology (that only proteins function as catalysts),

Altman's findings were initially greeted with skepticism and indifference. But Thomas Robert Cech, working independently of Altman, documented a cellular reaction in which RNA acted as a self-catalyst. Cech called this self-acting RNA a ribozyme.

These discoveries astounded the scientific community. It was now possible to suggest that RNA, not proteins, may have served as the regulator in primitive cells when life was first formed. Since DNA cannot form without a catalyst, and proteins cannot act as a catalyst without DNA, it now appears that RNA serves both functions. Altman and Cech had basically provided a new theory as to how life develops.

Individual viruses, or virus particles, also called virions, contain genetic material, or genomes, in one of several forms. Unlike cellular organisms, in which the genes always are made up of DNA, viral genes may consist of either DNA or RNA. Like cell DNA, almost all viral DNA is double-stranded, and it can have either a circular or a linear arrangement. Almost all viral RNA is single-stranded; it is usually linear, and it may be either segmented (with different genes on different RNA molecules) or nonsegmented (with all genes on a single piece of RNA).

Nucleic acids are complex molecules produced by living cells and are essential to all living organisms. These acids govern the body's development and specific characteristics by providing hereditary information and triggering the production of proteins within the body. This computer-generated model shows two strands of deoxyribonucleic acid (DNA) and the double-helical structure typical of this class of nucleic acids.

One of a cell's most important tasks is the synthesis of proteins, giant molecules that underlie most cellular functions. The hereditary material known as deoxyribonucleic acid (DNA), found within the nucleus of a cell, orchestrates a series of steps resulting in the manufacture of proteins tailored to meet the needs for a cell's development and growth.

A Gene, is the basic unit of heredity found in the cells of all living organisms, from bacteria to humans. Genes determine the physical characteristics that an organism inherits, such as the shape of a tree's leaf, the markings on a cat's fur, and the colour of a human hair.

Genes are composed of segments of deoxyribonucleic acid (DNA), a molecule that forms the long, threadlike structures called chromosomes. The information encoded within the DNA structure of a gene directs the manufacture of proteins, molecular workhorses that carry out all life-supporting activities within a cell.

Chromosomes within a cell occur in matched pairs. Each chromosome contains many genes, and each gene is located at a particular site on the chromosome, known as the locus. Like chromosomes, genes typically occur in pairs. A gene found on one chromosome in a pair usually has the same locus as another gene in the other chromosome of the pair, and these two genes are called alleles. Alleles are alternate forms of the same gene. For example, a pea plant has one gene that determines height, but that gene appears in more than one form—the gene that produces a short plant is an allele of the gene that produces a tall plant. The behaviour of alleles and how they influence inherited traits that follow a predictable pattern. Austrian monk Gregor Mendel first identified these patterns in the 1860.

In organisms that use sexual reproduction, offspring inherit one-half of their genes from each parent and then mix the two sets of genes together. This produces new combinations of genes, so that each individual is unique but still possesses the same genes as its parents. As a result, sexual reproduction ensures that the basic characteristics of a particular species remain largely the same for generations. However, mutations, or alterations in DNA, occur constantly. They create variations in the genes that are inherited. Some mutations may be neutral, or silent, and do not affect the function of a protein. Occasionally a mutation may benefit or harm an organism and over the course of evolutionary time, these mutations serve the crucial role of providing organisms with previously nonexistent proteins. In this way, mutations are a driving force behind genetic diversity and the rise of new or more competitive species that are better able to adapt to changes, such as climate variations, depletion of food sources, or the emergence of new types of disease.

Geneticists are scientists who study the function and behaviour of genes. Since the 1970s geneticists have devised techniques, cumulatively known as genetic engineering, to alter or manipulate the DNA structure within genes. These techniques enable scientists to introduce one or more genes from one organism into a second organism. The second organism incorporates the new DNA into its own genetic material, thereby altering its own genetic characteristics by changing the types of proteins it can produce. In humans these techniques form the basis of gene therapy, a group of experimental procedures in which scientists try to substitute one or more healthy genes for defective ones in order to eliminate symptoms of disease.

Genetic engineering techniques have also enabled scientists to determine the chromosomal location and DNA structure of all the genes found within a variety of organisms. In April 2003 the Human Genome Project, a publicly funded consortium of academic scientists from around the world, identified the chromosomal locations and structure of the estimated 20,000 to 25,000 genes found within human cells. The genetic makeup of other organisms has also been identified, including that of the bacterium stem from Escherichia coli, the yeast Saccharomyces cerevisiae, the roundworm Caenorhabditis elegans, and the fruit fly Drosophila melanogaster. Scientists hope to use this genetic information to develop life-saving drugs for a variety of diseases, to improve agricultural crop yields, and to learn more about plant and animal physiology and evolutionary history.

American neurologist Stanley B. Prusiner was awarded the 1997 Nobel Prize in physiology or medicine for his discovery of a class of infectious proteins called prions. Prions are implicated in several degenerative brain diseases of mammals, including bovine spongiform encephalopathy, commonly known as mad cow disease.

Prion, shortened term for proteinaceous, as a infectious particle, a small protein linked to certain rare, fatal brain diseases in cows, sheep, humans, and other mammals. If the prion is an infectious agent, it is the first infectious agent identified that does not contain the nucleic acids deoxyribonucleic acid (DNA) or ribonucleic acid (RNA). While the prion's role in causing disease is still controversial, its discovery has opened the door to alternative ideas about how infectious diseases may be transmitted.

American neurologist Stanley B. Prusiner was awarded the 1997 Nobel Prize in physiology or medicine for his discovery of a class of infectious proteins called prions. Prions are implicated in several degenerative brain diseases of mammals, including bovine spongiform encephalopathy, commonly known as mad cow disease.

Discovered by American neurologist Stanley B. Prusiner, prions are proteins with an abnormal shape, believed to be caused by a mutation to the gene that encodes for the protein. Normal proteins are found on the surfaces of nerve cells in the brain, white blood cells, muscle cells, and cells of many other tissues. The role of the normal protein is not yet understood, but the mystery of its structure has been solved. A hundred times smaller than the smallest virus, the normal protein is composed of 208 amino acids twisted into three long, and telephone cordlike coils known as helices. A floppy tail of 97 amino acids extends from the end of one of the helices. The abnormal protein is built of the same amino acids. However, instead of the coil shape, the abnormal protein is folded like the flat pleats of a partly opened accordion.

In the mid-1980s American neurologist Stanley Prusiner first proposed the existence of infectious agents that contain no genetic material and are made entirely of protein. Prusiner suggested that these particles—which he called prions—were responsible for neurodegenerative diseases, such as bovine spongiform encephalopathy (BSE), or "mad cow disease," in cows and Creutzfeldt-Jakob disease (CJD) in humans. He described his research on prions in a 1995 Scientific American article. In 1997 Prusiner was the sole recipient of the Nobel Prize in physiology or medicine "for his discovery of Prions—a new biological principle of infection." The award was unusual because it went to a single recipient and because Prusiner's findings still lack a scientific consensus. Some scientists believe a slow-acting virus may cause the spongiform encephalopathy diseases.

Some scientists think that the abnormal protein causes disease when it contacts the normal protein and triggers part of it to switch from the coiled to the pleated form. A chain reaction follows, resulting in a cluster of tangled, nonfunctional proteins called plaques. These plaques are found in the brains of animals that die of prion-related diseases. The plaques destroy the brain cells, resulting in one of the diseases collectively known as transmissible spongiform encephalopathies (TSEs).

TSEs cause inflammation and characteristic spongelike holes in the delicate membranes surrounding brain cells. This physical damage results in loss of coordination, dementia, and, eventually, death. Perhaps the best-known TSE is bovine spongiform encephalopathy (BSE), more popularly known as mad cow disease. BSE made headlines in 1996 when about a million cattle in the United Kingdom became infected with the disease. Most scientists believe the infection originally spread when cows contracted BSE after eating animal feed containing sheep's brains and other sheep byproducts infected with scrapie, a fatal spongiform disease affecting sheep and goats. Later, the epidemic spread when brains and other tissues from infected cattle were used in protein supplements distributed to cattle throughout Britain. By 2003 ingestion of the infected cow meat had caused about 150 people in Britain and Europe to develop an unusual form of Creutzfeldt-Jakob disease known as variant Creutzfeldt-Jakob disease (vCJD). Other TSEs include kuru, a rare disease contracted by natives of New Guinea who ate the infected brains of their dead relatives during ritual cannibalism.

The province of psychiatry is unusually broad for a medical specialty. Mental disorders may affect most aspects of a patient's life, including physical functioning, behaviour, emotions, thought, perception, interpersonal relationships, sexuality, work, and play. These disorders are caused by a poorly understood combination of biological, psychological, and social determinants. Psychiatry's task is to account for the diverse sources and manifestations of mental illness.

Physicians in the 18th and 19th centuries had of using crude devices to treat mental illness, none of which offered any real relief. The circulating swing, top left, was used to spin depressed patients at high speed. American physician Benjamin Rush devised the tranquillizing chair, top right, to calm people with mania. The crib, bottom, was widely used to restrain violent patients.

Physicians in the Western world began specializing in the treatment of the mentally ill in the 19th century. Known as alienists, psychiatrists of that era worked in large asylums, practising what was then called moral treatment, a humane approach aimed at quieting mental turmoil and restoring reason. During the second half of the century, psychiatrists abandoned this mode of treatment and, with it, the tacit recognition that mental illness is caused by both psychological and social influences. For a while, their attention focussed almost exclusively on biological factors. Drugs and other forms of somatic (physical) treatments were common. The German psychiatrist Emil Kraepelin identified and classified mental disorders into a system that is the foundation for modern diagnostic practices. Another important figure was the Swiss psychiatrist Eugen Bleuler, who coined the word schizophrenia and described its characteristics.

The discovery of unconscious sources of behaviour—an insight dominated by the psychoanalytic writings of Sigmund Freud in the early 20th century—enriched psychiatric thought and changed the direction of its practice. Attention shifted to processes within the individual psyche, and psychoanalysis came to be regarded as the preferred mode of treatment for most mental disorders. In the 1940s and 1950s emphasis shifted again: this time to the social and physical environment. Many psychiatrists had all but ignored biological influences, but others were studying those involved in mental illness and were using somatic forms of treatment such as electroconvulsive therapy (electric shock) and psychosurgery.

Dramatic changes in the treatment of the mentally ill in the United States began in the mid-1950s with the introduction of the first effective drugs for treating psychotic symptoms. Along with drug treatment, new, more liberal and humane policies and treatment strategies were introduced into mental hospitals. More and more patients were treated in community settings in the 1960s and 1970s. Support for mental health research led to significant new discoveries, especially in the understanding of genetic and biochemical determinants in mental illness and the functioning of the brain. Thus, by the 1980s, psychiatry had once again shifted in emphasis to the biological, to the relative neglect of psychosocial influences in mental health and illness.

Psychiatrists use a variety of methods to detect specific disorders in their patients. The most fundamental is the psychiatric interview, during which the patient's psychiatric history is taken and mental status is evaluated. The psychiatric history is a picture of the patient's personality characteristics, relationships with others, and past and present experience with psychiatric problems—all told in the patient's words (sometimes supplemented by comments from other family members). Psychiatrists use mental-status examinations much as internists use physical examinations. They elicit and classify aspects of the patient's mental functioning.

Some diagnostic methods rely on testing by other specialists. Psychologists administer intelligence and personality tests, as well as tests designed to detect damage to the brain or other parts of the central nervous system. Neurologists also test psychiatric patients for evidence of impairment of the nervous system. Other physicians sometimes examine patients who complain of physical symptoms. Psychiatric social workers explore family and community problems. The psychiatrist integrates all this information in making a diagnosis according to criteria established by the psychiatric profession.

Psychiatric treatments fall into two classes, as the organic and nonorganic categories or formed in the organic treatments, such as drugs, are those that affect the body directly. Nonorganic types of treatment improve the patient's functioning by psychological means, such as psychotherapy, or by altering the social environment.

Besides psychotherapy, the other major form of nonorganic treatment used in psychiatry is milieu therapy. Usually carried out in psychiatric wards, milieu therapy directs social relations between patients and staff toward therapeutic ends. Ward activities, too, are planned to serve specific therapeutic goals.

In general, psychotherapy is relied on more heavily for the treatment of neuroses and other nonpsychotic conditions than it is for psychoses. In psychotic patients, who usually receive psychoactive drugs, psychotherapy is used to improve social and vocational functioning. Milieu therapy is limited to hospitalized patients. Increasingly, psychiatrists use a combination of organic and nonorganic techniques for all patients, depending on their diagnosis and response to treatment.

William James (1842-1910), American philosopher and psychologist, who developed the philosophy of pragmatism. American psychologist and philosopher William James helped to popularize the philosophy of pragmatism with his book

Pragmatism: A New Name for Old Ways of Thinking (1907). Influenced by a theory of meaning and verification developed for scientific hypotheses by American philosopher C. S. Peirce, James held that truth is whatever work or has good experimental results. In a related theory, James argued the existence of God is partly verifiable because many people derive benefits from believing.

James was born in New York City. His father, Henry James, Sr., was a Swedenborgian theologian; one of his brothers was the writer Henry James. William James attended private schools in the United States and Europe, the Lawrence Scientific School at Harvard University, and the Harvard Medical School, from which he received a degree in 1869. Before finishing his medical studies, he went on an exploring expedition in Brazil with Swiss American naturalist Louis Agassiz and also studied physiology in Germany. After three years of retirement due to illness, James became an instructor in physiology at Harvard in 1872. He taught psychology and philosophy at Harvard after 1880; he left Harvard in 1907 and gave highly successful lectures at Columbia University and the University of Oxford. James died in Chocorua, New Hampshire.

Scientists have long considered the nature of consciousness without producing a fully satisfactory definition. In the early 20th century American philosopher and psychologist William James suggested that consciousness is a mental process involving both attention to external stimuli and short-term memory. Later scientific explorations of consciousness mostly expanded upon James's work. In this article from a 1997 special issue of Scientific American, Nobel laureate Francis Crick, who helped determine the structure of a DNA, and fellow biophysicist Christof Koch explain how experiments on vision might deepen our understanding of consciousness.

The Association for International Conciliation first published William James's pacifist statement, "The Moral Equivalent of War," in 1910. James, a highly respected philosopher and psychologist, was one of the founders of pragmatism—a philosophical movement holding that ideas and theories must be tested in practice to assess their worth. James hoped to find a way to convince men with a long-standing history of pride and glory in war to evolve beyond the need for bloodshed and to develop other avenues for conflict resolution. Spelling and grammar represent standards of the time.

At the turn of the century, American psychologist and philosopher William James gave a series of lectures on religion at Scotland's University of Edinburgh. In the 20 lectures he delivered between 1901 and 1902, published together as The Varieties of Religious Experience (1902), James discussed such topics as the existence of God, religious conversions, and immortality. In his lectures on mysticism, excerpted here, James defined the characteristics of a mystical experience—a state of consciousness in which God is directly experienced. He also quoted accounts of mystical experiences as given by important religious figures from many different religious traditions.

James's first book, the monumental Principles of Psychology (1890), established him as one of the most influential thinkers of his time. The work advanced the principle of functionalism in psychology, thus removing psychology from its traditional place as a branch of philosophy and establishing it among the laboratory sciences based on experimental method.

In the next decade James applied his empirical methods of investigation to philosophical and religious issues. He explored the questions of the existence of God, the immortality of the soul, free will, and ethical values by referring to human religious and moral experience as a direct source. His views on these subjects were presented in the lectures and essays published in such books as The Will to Believe and Other Essays in Popular Philosophy (1897), Human Immortality (1898), and The Varieties of Religious Experience (1902). The last-named work is a sympathetic psychological account of religious and mystical experiences.

Later lectures published as Pragmatism: A New Name for Old Ways of Thinking (1907) summed up James's original contributions to the theory called pragmatism, a term first used by the American logician C. S. Peirce. James generalized the pragmatic method, developing it from a critique of the logical basis of the sciences into a basis for the evaluation of all experience. He maintained that the meaning of ideas is found only in terms of their possible consequences. If consequences are lacking, ideas are meaningless. James contended that this is the method used by scientists to define their terms and to test their hypotheses, which, if meaningful, entail predictions. The hypotheses can be considered true if the predicted events take place. On the other hand, most metaphysical theories are meaningless, because they entail no testable predictions. Meaningful theories, James argued, are instruments for dealing with problems that arise in experience.

According to James's pragmatism, then, truth is that which works. One determines what works by testing propositions in experience. In so doing, one finds that certain propositions become true. As James put it, "Truth is something that happens to an idea" in the process of its verification; it is not a static property. This does not mean, however, that anything can be true. "The true is only the expedient in the way of our thinking, just as 'the right' is only the expedient in the way of our behaving," James maintained.

One cannot believe whatever one wants to believe, because such self-centred beliefs would not work out.

James was opposed to absolute metaphysical systems and argued against doctrines that describe reality as a unified, monolithic whole. In Essays in Radical Empiricism (1912), he argued for a pluralistic universe, denying that the world can be explained in terms of an absolute force or scheme that determines the interrelations of things and events. He held that the interrelations, whether they serve to hold things together or apart, are just as real as the things themselves.

By the end of his life, James had become world-famous as a philosopher and psychologist. In both fields, he functioned more as an originator of new thought than as a founder of dogmatic schools. His pragmatic philosophy was further developed by American philosopher John Dewey and others; later studies in physics by Albert Einstein made the theories of interrelations advanced by James appear prophetic.

Of Associationism, in psychology, is the theory that the mind learns by combining simple, irreducible elements through association. Aristotle recognized four methods by which the mind associates one idea with another: similarity (for example, an orange and a lemon), difference (hot and cold), contiguity in time (sunrise and a rooster's crow), and contiguity in space (cup and saucer). The British empiricist philosophers John Locke and David Hume stressed the importance of sensory perceptions in the associationism. Other philosophers, such as David Hartley, John Stuart Mill, and Alexander Bain, continued formulating theories of associationism during the 19th century and were responsible for an associationist school of psychology. In addition to Aristotle's original four methods of association, the school included such laws as intensity, inseparability, and repetition. The appearance of James Mill's Analysis of the Phenomena of the Human Mind (1829) probably marked the moment of associationism's greatest influence.

The birth of modern experimental psychology in the late 19th century gave rise to a new adaptation of a conceptual associationism. Now the "irreducible elements" associated were called stimuli and responses. A stimulus could be associated with a response; a stimulus could be associated with another stimulus; a response could be associated with a response; or one stimulus-response combination could be associated with another stimulus-response combination.

Every major behavioural psychologist has utilized the mechanism of an associationism. Although behaviorists believe all thought processes can be accounted for through associations of stimuli and responses, other psychologists strongly reject such an approach as inadequate to explain creative thought and verbal behaviour.

The association of ideas, images, and objects has practical uses beyond its disputed role in formulating psychological theories. Free association, in which a person voices thoughts as they occur without considering their effect and with no regard to logic, is a basic, proven tool of psychotherapy. Free association is also used in the business world, in "brainstorming" sessions in which staff members are encouraged to express their views freely and thereby develop new concepts or solutions for problems.

Deliberate associative devices are employed in all modern teaching, but especially in the language arts and in the teaching of foreign languages. Music, movement, and colour aid students with the recall of vocabulary and the sounds of most words.

Attention-Deficit Hyperactivity Disorder or Hyperactivity (ADHD), is a disorder beginning in childhood, characterized by a persistent inability to sit still, focus attention on specific tasks, and control impulses. Children with ADHD show these behaviours more frequently and severely than other children of the same age. A person with ADHD may have difficulty with school, work, friendships, or family life. ADHD has also been referred to as attention-deficit disorder, hyperkinesias, minimal brain dysfunction, and minimal brain damage.

A child with attention-deficit hyperactivity disorder (ADHD) may be described by parents or teachers as lacking self-control. As Russell Barkly, a professor of psychiatry and neurology, explains in a 1998 Scientific American article, recent research has indicated that ADHD is indeed caused by impaired functioning of the brain pathways governing inhibition and self-control. Contrary to earlier theories that implicated dietary sugar or parenting techniques, ADHD appears most often to be genetically based and inheritable.

Attention-deficit hyperactivity disorder is one of the most common mental disorders of childhood, affecting 3 to 5 percent of school-age children. The disorder, occurring at least four times more often in boys than in girls. Although the symptoms sometimes disappear with age, ADHD can persist into adolescence and adulthood. Some estimates show that up to 2 percent of adults have ADHD.

Diagnosing ADHD is difficult because most children are inattentive, hyperactive, and impulsive at least some of the time. In diagnosing ADHD, experts use guidelines listed in the Diagnostic and Statistical Manual of Mental Disorders. These guidelines require that a child show behaviours typical of ADHD before the age of seven. The behaviours must last for at least six months, and must occur more frequently than in other children of the same age. The behaviours also must occur, in at least, two settings, such as classroom and home, rather than just at a single setting.

Controversy exists over the diagnosis of ADHD. Physicians in the United States diagnose the disorder more often than doctors elsewhere in the world. Critics regard this discrepancy as evidence that physicians and psychologists too often apply psychiatric labels to children who are naturally more active or simply nuisances to teachers and parents.

Children and adults with ADHD consistently show various degrees of inattention, hyperactivity, and impulsiveness. Inattention means that people with ADHD have difficulty keeping their minds on one thing. They may get bored with homework or other tasks after a few minutes, make careless mistakes, have trouble listening, and seem to daydream. However, children with ADHD sometimes can concentrate on and complete new or unusually interesting tasks. Hyperactivity involves almost constant motion, as if driven by a motor. Children may squirm and fidget at their desks in school, get up often to roam around the room, constantly touch things, disturb other people, tap pencils, and talk constantly. ADHD also makes children unusually impulsive, so that they act before thinking. They may run into the street without looking, blurt out inappropriate comments in class, interrupt conversations, and be unusually clumsy or accident-prone.

Children with ADHD often have severe learning problems because of their difficulties in paying attention, following instructions, and completing tasks. In addition, their disruptive, demanding behaviour makes them unpopular with peers. Children with ADHD often receive constant criticism and correction from teachers and parents, who believe the behaviour is intentional. The combination of negative feedback, poor academic achievement, and social problems may contribute to low self-esteem and other emotional problems.

Scientists do not know what causes ADHD. However, they have discredited many theories that once were widely accepted. One theory contended that ADHD resulted from minor head injuries or undetectable brain damage due to infections or complications during birth. Experts called ADHD as the "minimal brain damage" and "minimal brain dysfunction" when this theory was popular in the early 1970s. Another theory linked ADHD with consumption of refined sugar and food additives. Scientists questioned this theory when studies showed that few children with ADHD benefited from diets restricting sugar and food colourings. Most experts also reject the idea that poor parenting or a dysfunctional home environment causes ADHD.

Most scientists regard ADHD as a biological disorder caused by abnormalities in the brain. Studies have shown that areas or regions of the brain can control attention span and limit impulsive and behaviours are less active in people with ADHD. In addition, ADHD seems to run in families, suggesting that genetic factors may play an important role. One study showed that more or less of one-third of the fathers who had ADHD in childhood have children with ADHD.

Although there is no cure for ADHD, a variety of treatments may help children with this disorder. These include medication, counselling, social skills training, and other methods.

Drugs are the most common treatment for ADHD and can help reduce symptoms of the disorder. Physicians usually prescribe one of three drugs: methylphenidate (Ritalin), dextroamphetamine (Dexedrine or DextroStat), and pemoline (Cylert). These drugs are normally stimulants, yet they ease hyperactivity and other symptoms in 90 percent of children with ADHD. The drugs work by altering levels of neurotransmitters, brain chemicals that transmit nerve signals. A newer stimulant used to treat ADHD, Adderall, combined dextroamphetamine and amphetamine.

Medical experts regard stimulants as safe. The most common side effects include stomachaches, loss of appetite, nervousness, and insomnia. Drug therapy may slow a child's rate of growth temporarily, but growth usually returns to normal during adolescence. Low doses of stimulants do not cause a "high" sensation, sedate the child, or cause addiction. Experts often recommend that children take medication only during school, with medication breaks on weekends and holidays to reduce unwanted side effects. Doctors may prescribe other types of drugs if stimulants do not prove effective.

Critics argue that physicians medicate too many children who do not have ADHD. They point out that allergies, depression, anxiety, conflicts with teachers or parents, and other problems can make normal children seem hyperactive, impulsive, and distracted.

Most children with ADHD need more than medication. Drugs only relieve symptoms of ADHD, which usually return when medication is discontinued. Although drugs help a child to concentrate and complete schoolwork, they cannot increase a child's knowledge, teach academic skills, or directly alter underlying learning disorders or other problems. Experts cite the need for more information on whether medication improves a child's chances for a successful career.

Children may benefit from several different kinds of therapy. Psychological counselling, for instance, can help them recognize and deal with negative feelings that result from their symptoms. Social skills training can help them recognize how their behaviour affects other people and help them develop more appropriate behaviour. Children with ADHD also may benefit from special academic tutors who show them how to break school assignments down into small parts that can be completed one at a time.

Because children with ADHD often cause family turmoil, parents and other family members may benefit from therapy or support groups in which other parents share their experiences. Parental skills training can teach parents to manage a child's behaviour with praise and other rewards, and with penalties such as "time-outs" in which a child must sit alone to calm down.

Many children with ADHD continue to have problems as adolescents and adults. Adults with ADHD may be unusually impatient and restless and may become bored before finishing a task. They may constantly arrive late for appointments, lose things, change jobs often, fail to organize their time or set priorities, and have difficulty maintaining friendships and other relationships. Studies suggest they are more likely than others to develop other mental illnesses such as anxiety and depression, as well as substance-abuse problems such as alcoholism and drug dependence.

Biopsychology, the scientific study of the biology of behaviour and mental processes. People also refer to this field as biological psychology, psychobiology, behavioural biology, or behavioural neuroscience.

Weighing about of 1.3 kg (3 lb) and containing 100 billion neurons, the human brain is a marvel of evolution. Complex interactions between neurons produce psychological processes, including learning, memory, emotion, thinking, and perception.

The term biopsychology refer to a biological approach to psychology, rather than a psychological approach to biology. Most biopsychologists are trained experimental psychologists who have brought their knowledge of biology to the study of psychological phenomena. These phenomena include behaviour and underlying psychological processes, such as learning, memory, perception, attention, motivation, emotion, and cognition.

Biopsychologists work in a variety of overlapping fields of study. Scientists in cognitive neuroscience primarily study the brain to understand the neural mechanisms of mental processes. Researchers in the field of psychopharmacology examine how drugs affect the psychological functions of the brain. Scientists in the field of neuropsychology study the psychological effects of brain damage in humans. Researchers in behavioural genetics study how genes influence behaviour and psychological traits. Evolutionary psychologists investigate how evolution shapes psychological processes. Comparative psychologists study animal behaviour by comparing findings among different species. Comparative psychology often entails ethology, in the scientific studies of the way animals behave in their natural habitat.

Because biopsychology combines biological and psychological approaches, it can be viewed either as a specialized field of psychology or as a specialized field of biology. However, most biopsychologists receive the majority of their training from university psychology departments.

Unlike other branches of psychology, Biopsychology is characterized by its approach rather than its subject matter. Most other branches of psychology focus on particular psychological phenomena. For example, clinical psychology is dedicated to the study of mental illness, and social psychology studies human behaviour in social situations. In contrast, biopsychologists study the entire range of psychological phenomena but always from a biological perspective. Consequently, biopsychological research has made important contributions to many fields of psychology—particularly developmental psychology, learning and memory, perception, motivation, cognition, and emotion.

Although scholars and philosophers have long speculated about the involvement of biological factors in psychological phenomena, biopsychology did not coalesce as a field of scientific research until the 20th century. The publication of The Organization of Behaviour in 1949 by Canadian psychologist Donald O. Hebb played a key role in the emergence of the field. In his book, Hebb developed the first comprehensive theory of how brain activity might produce various complex psychological phenomena. Hebb's book stimulated the emergence of biopsychology by discrediting the widely held view that psychological functioning was too complex to have its roots in the chemistry and physiology of the brain. Hebb based his theories on experiments involving humans and animals, on clinical case studies, and on logical arguments developed from his own observations of daily life. This eclectic approach became a hallmark of biopsychological analysis.

In 1949, the year that The Organization of Behaviour was published, few scientists studied the biology of psychological processes, and scholars seldom used the term biopsychology. Moreover, few universities offered courses that expressly focussed on the biology of psychological processes, and only two or three journals specialized in publishing biopsychological research. Today, however, biopsychology is among the most active fields of psychology. Most universities offer several courses in the various fields of biopsychology and employ biopsychologists to teach students and to conduct research. Dozens of academic journals now specialize in the publication of biopsychological research.

To investigate the biological bases of behaviour and mental processes, biopsychologists must find ways to observe and record the internal activities of the brain and body. The research methods of biopsychology fall into two general categorical methods of manipulating and measuring behaviour, and methods of manipulating and measuring biological factors, most often brain activity. The first group of methods originated in other fields of psychology, whereas the second group of methods has come from relevant biological fields, primarily neuroscience (the scientific study of the brain and nervous system). This article discusses the biological methods, including lesion methods, stimulation methods, recording methods, imaging methods, and genetic engineering techniques.

A lesion is a wound or area of damage. Researchers using lesion methods damage, destroy, or remove a particular part of a laboratory animal's brain. After this is done, the researcher carefully assesses the psychological consequences in an effort to determine the function of the damaged part. For example, biopsychologists interested in memory may surgically remove a small part of a rat's brain and then devise an experiment to compare the rat's memory to that of normal rats. A similar technique, called cryogenic blockade, temporarily deactivates an area of brain tissue by cooling it with a probe to near-freezing temperatures. Ethical considerations prohibit experimental brain lesions in human subjects. However, researchers can conduct tests on patients with existing brain damage to try to learn about the brain mechanisms involved in psychological processes.

One problem with lesion methods is that neural circuits (brain circuits) that control particular psychological processes are often intermeshed with neural circuits that perform other functions. So when using this method, researchers may find it difficult to determine exactly which neural circuits are involved in a given psychological process, accountably, a surgical lesion destroys all the neurons in the target area. Today, researchers can largely circumvent this problem by using selective neurotoxins, chemicals that destroy only particular kinds of neurons (brain cells) in a given area of the brain. For example, there are selective neurotoxins that destroy only those neurons that release the neurotransmitters of norepinephrine or dopamine.

Stimulation methods activate the neurons in a specific part of the brain. The researcher then assesses the effects of the activation on behaviour. Researchers usually do this by implanting an electrode into a particular area of a laboratory animal's brain and passing a weak electrical current across the tip. One weakness of this method is that electrical stimulation indiscriminately activates all neurons at the electrode tip. However, a variety of neurochemical techniques now exist that selectively activate neurons that release a particular neurotransmitter or that containing a particular receptor. Although scientists rarely conduct stimulation studies on humans, surgeons occasionally use stimulation techniques on conscious patients just before brain surgery. By assessing the reactions of the patient, the surgeon can determine which brain tissue to remove and which tissue to leave intact.

The electroencephalograph (EEG) pattern of a normal individual, left, shows low amplitude tracings from each of the electrodes that have been placed on the head. In an EEG pattern from an individual suffering from a grand mal seizure, right, these tracings exhibit both a high amplitude and an erratic pattern lasting for several minutes.

EEG studies of laboratory animals, experimenters may implant the electrodes directly in an animal's brain. Experimenters can record the electrical activity of an individual neuron by inserting a tiny electrode, call a microelectrode, either inside it or adjacent to it.

Other useful recording methods include electromyography, a procedure for measuring muscle tension, and electrooculography, a procedure for recording eye movements. Psychologists sometimes measure how the skin's ability to conduct electricity, known as skin conductance, changes in different situations. Psychologists studying the relationship between emotion and cardiovascular activity may measure blood pressure, blood volume in various parts of the body, or electrocardiographic activity (the electrical activity of the heart).

Beginning in the early 1970s, advances in technology enabled scientists to see inside the human brain without cutting into it. Today psychologists use a number of brain imaging methods to study brain activity during various cognitive processes, h as perceiving, reading, and imagining, and to investigate the biological bases of mental illnesses, such as schizophrenia. These methods include computed tomography (CT), magnetic resonance imaging (MRI), functional magnetic resonance imaging (functional MRI), and positron emission tomography. Some methods, such as functional MRI, produce three-dimensional images of the human brain with different colours indicating the different levels of activity in each part.

Brain imaging research has spawned an important new field of biopsychology, cognitive neuroscience. One particularly important line of cognitive neuroscience experiments assessed patterns of people's brain activity as they perceived various types of visual stimuli. The experimenters found that different areas of the cerebral cortex specialize in analyzing different aspects of a visual image, for example, position, speed, angle of motion, shape, and colour. These findings confirmed earlier studies on monkeys that had used recording rather than imaging methods.

Advances in genetics have taken biopsychology to the threshold of a new era in research on behavioural genetics. Historically, research into the role of genes in the developing of normal and abnormal psychological traits was largely restricted to two kinds of studies: Of those that trace the flow of particular traits from generation to generation, and those that compared the similarity of identical twins with the similarity of fraternal twins. The creation of genetic engineering techniques to insert or "knock out" specific genes in organisms has allowed psychologists to experimentally assess how genes affect the development of psychological traits.

Behavioural geneticists most often use genetic engineering techniques on invertebrate animals, such as snails and slugs. Recently, experimenters have used these techniques on mice, creating so-called transgenic mice by transferring genes from another species into the mice. Although research of this kind is in its infancy, many biopsychologists believe that it will lead to important discoveries about behaviour and to treatments for some psychological disorders.

Delusion, is the false belief firmly held by a person even though other people recognize the belief as obviously untrue. For example, a person who truly believes he is Napoleon Bonaparte is delusional. Religious beliefs or popular conceptions, as in that the belief that people have been abducted by aliens, are not delusions because they are widely held beliefs. Delusions are a type of psychotic symptom that indicate a person has lost contact with reality.

There are many different types of delusions. A person with a paranoid delusion believes that others—as the FBI, CIA, or the Mafia—are trying to harm or plot against him or her. A person with a delusion of reference believes that events or people refer specifically to him or her when they do not. For example, a woman with schizophrenia may believe that a television news broadcaster is talking personally to her rather than to the entire viewing audience. A grandiose delusion is a belief that one is extremely famous or that one has special powers, such as the ability to magically heal people.

A delusion of control is a belief that others are able to control one's thoughts, feelings, or actions. For example, a man with this type of delusion may believe that someone has implanted a microchip in his brain that enables other people to control his thoughts. A somatic delusion is a belief that something is wrong with one's body—for example, that one's brain is rotting away—even though no medical evidence supports this belief. A person with an erotic delusion believes that someone is in love with him or her despite a lack of evidence for this belief. In a delusion of jealousy, a person believes that his or her spouse or lover is unfaithful despite evidence to the contrary.

Delusions commonly occur in certain severe mental illnesses, such as schizophrenia, bipolar disorder (also called manic-depressive illness), some cases of major depression, dissociative disorders, post-traumatic stress disorder, and paranoid personality disorder. In addition, delusions may result from abuse of certain drugs, including alcohol, cocaine, amphetamines, and hallucinogens such as lysergic acid diethylamide (LSD), phencyclidine (PCP), and mescaline. Medical conditions affecting the brain, such as syphilis and brain tumours, may also cause delusions.

Delusional disorder is a relatively uncommon mental illness characterized by delusions. People with this disorder have one or more delusions that persist for at least one month. In addition, they do not suffer from other symptoms of schizophrenia, such as disorganized speech and bizarre behaviour. Usually their delusions are less bizarre than those that occur in schizophrenia and seem merely odd or unsupported by facts. Examples of nonbizarre delusions include beliefs that one is being followed, loved by someone famous, or deceived by one's spouse. Because delusional disorder is relatively rare, little research has systematically examined its peculiarity. However, doctors most often use antipsychotic drugs (also called neuroleptics) to treat this disorder. These drugs help reduce or eliminate delusions, hallucinations, and other psychotic symptoms.

As Emotion, is a term frequently and familiarly used as synonymous with feeling. In psychology it signified a reaction involving certain physiological changes, such as an accelerated or retarded pulse rate, the diminished or increased activities of certain glands, or a change in body temperature, which stimulate the individual, or some component part of his or her body, to further activity. The three primary reactions of this type are anger, love, and fear, which either occur as an immediate response to external stimuli or are the result of an indirect subjective process, such as memory, association, or introspection. The American psychologist John Watson proved in a series of experiments that infants are capable of these three emotions; he also demonstrated that emotional reactions may be conditioned.

The external stimuli diminish in importance, as a direct cause of the individual's emotional reaction, in proportion to the individual's maturity, and the stimuli that elicit these emotions develop more plexuities. Thus, the same environmental condition that inspires anger in a child may cause fear in an adult. As the emotional degree of the reaction rises, however, the resemblance between the various kinds of reaction increases as well; thus, extreme anger, fear, or resentment has to a greater extent than in common than the same reactions in fewer exaggerated phases. Momentary physiological change or distortion accompanies all emotional reactions, as in the instance of the accelerated heart action during a fit of anger. Fear, for example, may result in a violent physical manifestation such as the quaking of the limbs or a momentary loss of voice. It may also, by way of contrast, result in an attempt to disguise itself through means as something assumed coolness or even boasting features.

Most of our knowledge about how the brain links memory and emotion has been gleaned through the study of so-called classical fear conditioning. In this process the subject, usually a rat, hears a noise or sees a flashing light that is paired with a brief, mild electric shock to its feet. After a few such experiences, the rat responds automatically to the sound or light, even in the absence of the shock. Its reactions are typical to any threatening situation: the animal freezes, its blood pressure and heart rate increase, and it startles easily. In the language of such experiments, the noise or flash is a conditioned stimulus, the foot shock is an unconditioned stimulus, and the rat's reaction is a conditioned response, which consists of readily measured behavioural and physiological changes.

Conditioning of this kind happens quickly in rats—indeed, it takes place as rapidly as it does in humans. A single pairing of the shock to the sound or sight can bring on the conditioned effect. Once established, the fearful reaction is relatively permanent. If the noise or light is administered many times without an accompanying electric shock, the rat's response diminishes. This change is called extinction. But considerable evidence suggests that this behavioural alteration is the result of the brain's controlling the fear response rather than the elimination of the emotional memory. For example, an apparently extinguished fear response can recover spontaneously or can be reinstated by an irrelevant stressful experience. Similarly, stress can cause the reappearance of phobias in people who have been successfully treated. This resurrection demonstrates that the emotional memory underlying the phobia was rendered dormant rather than erased by treatment.

Fear conditioning has proved an ideal starting point for studies of emotional memory for several reasons. First, it occurs in nearly every animal group in which it has been examined: fruit flies, snails, birds, lizards, fish, rabbits, rats, monkeys and people. Although no one claims that the mechanisms are precisely the same in all these creatures, it seems clear from studies to date that the pathways are very similar in mammals and possibly in all vertebrates. We therefore are confident in believing that many of the findings in animals apply to humans. In addition, the kinds of stimuli most commonly used in this type of conditioning are not signals that rats—or humans, for that matter—encounter in their daily lives. The novelty and irrelevance of these lights and sounds help to ensure that the animals have not already developed strong emotional reactions to them. So researchers are clearly observing learning and memory at work. At the same time, such cues do not require complicated cognitive processing from the brain. Consequently, the stimuli permit us to study emotional mechanisms relatively directly. Finally, our extensive knowledge of the neural pathways involved in processing acoustic and visual information serves as an excellent starting point for examining the neurological foundations of fear elicited by such stimuli.

Memory is generally thought to be the process by which we bring back to mind some earlier conscious experience. The original learning and the remembering, in this case, are both conscious events. Workers have determined that declarative memory is mediated by the Hippocampus and the cortex. But removal of the Hippocampus has little effect on fear conditioning—except conditioning to context.

In contrast, emotional learning that comes about through fear conditioning is not declarative learning. Rather it is mediated by a different system, which in all likelihood operates independently of our conscious awareness. Emotional information may be stored within declarative memory, but it is kept there as a cold declarative fact. For example, if a person is injured in an automobile accident in which the horn gets stuck in the on position, he or she may later have a reaction when hearing the blare of car horns. The person may remember the details of the accident, such as where and when it occurred, who else was involved and how awful it was. These are declarative memories that are dependent on the Hippocampus. The individual may also become tense, anxious and depressed, as the emotional memory is reactivated through the amygdalic system. The declarative system has stored the emotional content of the experience, but it has done so as a fact.

Emotional and declarative memories are stored and retrieved in parallel, and their activities are joined seamlessly in our conscious experience. That does not mean that we have direct conscious access to our emotional memory; it means instead that we have access to the consequences—such as the way we behave, the way our bodies feel. These consequences combine with current declarative memory to form a new declarative memory. Emotion is not just unconscious memory: it exerts a powerful influence on declarative memory and other thought processes. As James L. McGaugh and his colleagues at the University of California at Irvine have convincingly shown, the amygdala plays an essential part in modulating the storage and strength of memories.

The distinction between declarative memory and emotional memory is an important one. W. J. Jacobs of the University of British Columbia and Lynn Nadel of the University of Arizona have argued that we are unable to remember traumatic events that take place early in life because the Hippocampus has not yet matured to the point of forming consciously accessible memories. The emotional memory system, which may develop earlier, clearly forms and stores its unconscious memories of these events. And for this reason, the trauma may affect mental and behavioural functions in later life, albeit through processes that remain inaccessible to consciousness.

Because pairing a tone and a shock can bring about conditioned responses in animals throughout the phyla, it is clear that fear conditioning cannot be dependent on consciousness. Fruit-flies and snails, for example, are not creatures known for their conscious mental processes. My way of interpreting this phenomenon is to consider fear a subjective state of awareness brought about when brain systems react to danger. Only if the organism possesses a sufficiently advanced neural mechanism does conscious fear accompany bodily response. This is not to say that only humans experience fear but, rather, that consciousness is a prerequisite to subjective emotional states.

Thus, emotions or feelings are conscious products of unconscious processes. It is crucial to remember that the subjective experiences we call feelings are not the primary business of the system that generates them. Emotional experiences are the result of triggering systems of behavioural adaptation that have been preserved by evolution. Subjective experience of any variety is challenging turf for scientists. We have, however, gone a long way toward understanding the neural system that underlies fear responses, and this same system may in fact give rise to subjective feelings of fear. If so, studies of the neural control of emotional responses may hold the key to understanding subjective emotion as well.

Behaviour Modification, psychological methods for treating maladjustment and for changing observable Behaviour patterns. In the Behaviour modification process, the procedures used are monitored so that changes can be made when necessary. Physical and mental coercion, brain surgery, brainwashing, drug use, and psychotherapy are often considered methods of Behaviour modification because they try to, and frequently do, change Behaviour. None of them, however, is Behaviour modification as the term is used in present-day psychology.

Russian physiologist Ivan Pavlov won the 1904 Nobel Prize in physiology or medicine. Pavlov is best known for his work on reflex Behaviour.

The foundation for Behaviour modification was laid at the beginning of the 20th century in the experimental laboratory of the Russian physiologist Ivan P. Pavlov. A dog was being trained to salivate when a circle was projected on a screen and not to salivate when an ellipse was shown. The shape of the ellipse was gradually modified to resemble the circle. When only a slight difference between the circle and the ellipse could be perceived, the dog became agitated and no longer displayed the conditioned response it had acquired. This type of disturbance was called an "experimentally induced neurosis."

A second landmark event for Behaviour modification took place when Pavlov's conditioning principles were extended to humans. In 1920 the American psychologists John B. Watson and Rosalie Rayner reported an experimental study in which an 11-month-old baby who had previously played with a white laboratory rat was conditioned to be fearful of the rat by associating a loud noise with the animal, a process known as pairing. The psychologist Mary Cover Jones later performed experiments designed to reduce already established fears in children. She found two methods particularly effective: (1) Associating a feared object with a different stimulus capable of arousing a positive reaction, and (2) placing the child, who feared a certain object with other children who did not.

Behaviour modification techniques were used in the 1940s and '50s by psychologists in South Africa, England, and the United States. Joseph P. Wolpe, a South African physician, questioned the effectiveness of psychotherapy for treating disturbed young adults, especially those with disabling fear reactions. To deal with anxiety disturbances, Wolpe devised treatment procedures based on Pavlov's classical-conditioning model. At about the same time, a group of psychologists in London, headed by Hans J. Eysenck and M. B. Shapiro, launched a new program of research on the development of treatment techniques, basing their investigations on the learning theory of the American psychologist's Clark L. Hull and Kenneth W. Spence.

In the US two kinds of investigations helped to establish the field of Behaviour modification. One was a further extension of the classical-conditioning principles to clinical problems such as bed-wetting and alcoholism. The other was the application of the operant-conditioning principles developed by B. F. Skinner to the education and training of handicapped children in schools and institutions and to the treatment of adults in psychiatric hospitals.

By the early 1960s, Behaviour modification had become a clearly identifiable applied psychology movement with two components: Behaviour therapy and applied Behaviour analysis.

Some of the treatment techniques used in Behaviour therapy became prominent enough to acquire specific names. Among them are systematic desensitization, aversion therapy, and biofeedback.

Systematic desensitization, the most widely used technique, attempts to treat disturbances having identifiable sources, such as a paralyzing fear of closed spaces. This method usually involves training the individual to relax in the presence of fear-producing stimuli. The therapist assumes that the anxiety reaction will be replaced gradually with the new relaxation response; this is called reciprocal inhibition.

Aversion therapy is used to break disabling bad habits. An aversive stimulus, such as an electric shock, is given together with the "bad habit," such as an alcoholic drink. Repeated pairings result in changing the values of such stimuli from positive attraction to repulsion.

Biofeedback is most often used in treating disturbed Behaviour that has a physical basis. It provides an individual with information about an ongoing physiological process such as blood pressure or heartbeat rates. By the use of a mechanical device, indications of moment-to-moment variations in bodily functioning can be observed and monitored by the individual. The therapist may provide some reward for desirable changes, such as a decrease in blood pressure.

Applied Behaviour analysis is used to develop educational and treatment techniques that can be tailored to each individual's requirements while still following a constant format, whether the patients are retarded or disturbed children in a school or residential setting, or adults in a psychiatric hospital or rehabilitation centre. Five essential steps characterize this approach: (1) Deciding what the individual can do to ameliorate the problem; (2) Devising a program to weaken undesirable Behaviour and strengthen desirable substitute Behaviour; (3) The enacting or carrying of duties, are the behavioural principles as accorded by the treatment programs. (4) Keeping careful and objective records, and (5) altering the program if progress can thereby be improved.

Is consciousness determinative, or is it determined? English philosophers such as John Locke equated consciousness with physical sensations and the information they provide, whereas European philosophers such as Gottfried Wilhelm Leibniz and Immanuel Kant gave a more central and active role to consciousness.

The philosopher who most directly influenced subsequent exploration of the subject of consciousness was the 19th-century German educator Johann Friedrich Herbert, who wrote that ideas had quality and intensity and that they may inhibit or facilitate one another. Thus, ideas may pass from "states of reality" (consciousness) to "states of tendency" (unconsciousness), with the dividing line between the two states being described as the threshold of consciousness. This formulation of Herbert clearly presages the development, by the German psychologist and physiologist Gustav Theodor Fechner, of the psychophysical measurement of sensation thresholds, and the later development by Sigmund Freud of the concept of the unconscious.

The experimental analysis of consciousness dates from 1879, when the German psychologist Wilhelm Max Wundt started his research laboratory. For Wundt, the task of psychology was the study of the structure of consciousness, which extended well beyond sensations and included feelings, images, memory, attention, duration, and movement. Because early interest focussed on the content and dynamics of consciousness, it is not surprising that the central methodology of such studies was introspection; that is, subjects reported on the mental contents of their own consciousness. This introspective approach was developed most fully by the American psychologist Edward Bradford Titchener at Cornell University. Setting his task as that of describing the structure of the mind, Titchener attempted to detail, from introspective self-reports, the dimensions of the elements of consciousness. For example, taste was "dimensionalized" into four basic categories: sweet, sour, salt, and bitter. This approach was known as structuralism.

By the 1920s, however, a remarkable revolution had occurred in psychology that was to essentially remove considerations of consciousness from psychological research for some 50 years: Behaviourism captured the field of psychology. The main initiator of this movement was the American psychologist John Broadus Watson. In a 1913 article, Watson stated, "I believe that we can write a psychology and never use the terms consciousness, mental states, mind . . . imagery and the like." Psychologists then turned almost exclusively to Behaviour, as described in terms of stimulus and response, and consciousness was totally bypassed as a subject. A survey of eight leading introductory psychology texts published between 1930 and the 1950s found no mention of the topic of consciousness in five texts, and in two it was treated as a historical curiosity.

Set about in or around the later part of the 1950s, however, interest in the subject of consciousness returned, specifically in those subjects and techniques relating to altered states of consciousness: In that of an internalized sleep and dreams, meditation, biofeedback, hypnosis, and drug-induced states. The surge in sleep and dream research was directly fuelled by a discovery relevant to the nature of consciousness. A physiological indicator of the dream state was found: At roughly 90-minute intervals, the eyes of sleepers were observed to move rapidly, and at the same time the sleepers' brain waves would show a pattern resembling the waking state. When people were awakened during these periods of rapid eye movement, they almost always reported dreams, whereas if awakened at other times they did not. This and other research clearly indicated that sleep, once considered a passive state, was instead an active state of consciousness.

During the 1960s, an increased search for "higher levels" of consciousness through meditation resulted in a growing interest in the practices of Zen Buddhism and Yoga from Eastern cultures. A full flowering of this movement in the United States was seen in the development of training programs, such as Transcendental Meditation, that were self-directed procedures of physical relaxation and focussed attention. Biofeedback techniques also were developed to bring body systems involving factors such as blood pressure or temperature under voluntary control by providing feedback from the body, so that subjects could learn to control their responses. For example, researchers found that persons could control their brain-wave patterns to some extent, particularly the so-called alpha rhythms generally associated with a relaxed, meditative state. This finding was especially relevant to those interested in consciousness and meditation, and a number of "alpha training" programs emerged.

Another subject that led to increased interest in altered states of consciousness was hypnosis, which involves a transfer of conscious control from the subject to another person. Hypnotism has had a long and intricate history in medicine and folklore and has been intensively studied by psychologists. Much has become known about the hypnotic state, relative to individual suggestibility and personality traits; the subject has now largely been demythologized, and the limitations of the hypnotic state are fairly well known. Despite the increasing use of hypnosis, however, much remains to be learned about this unusual state of focussed attention.

Finally, many people in the 1960s experimented with the psychoactive drugs known as hallucinogens, which produce a disordering of consciousness. The most prominent of these drugs are lysergic acid diethylamide or LSD. Mescaline and psilocybin have long been associated with religious ceremonies in various cultures. LSD, because of its radical thought-modifying properties, was initially explored for its so-called mind-expanding potential and for its psychotomimetic effects (imitating psychoses). Little positive use, however, has been found for these drugs, and their use is highly restricted.

Scientists have long considered the nature of consciousness without producing a fully satisfactory definition. In the early 20th century American philosopher and psychologist William James suggested that consciousness is a mental process involving both attention to external stimuli and short-term memory. Later scientific explorations of consciousness mostly expanded upon James's work. In this article from a 1997 special issue of

Scientific American, Nobel laureate Francis Crick, who helped determine the structure of the DNA, and fellow biophysicist Christof Koch explain how experiments on vision might deepen our understanding of consciousness.

As the concept of a direct, simple linkage between environment and Behaviour became unsatisfactory in recent decades, the interest in altered states of consciousness may be taken as a visible sign of renewed interest in the topic of consciousness. That persons are active and intervening participants in their Behaviour has become increasingly clear. Environments, rewards, and punishments are not simply defined by their physical character. Memories are organized, not simply stored. An entirely new area called cognitive psychology has emerged that centres on these concerns. In the study of children, increased attention is being paid to how they understand, or perceive, the world at different ages. In the field of animal Behaviour, researchers increasingly emphasize the inherent characteristics resulting from the way a species has been shaped to respond adaptively to the environment. Humanistic psychologists, with a concern for self-actualization and growth, have emerged after a long period of silence. Throughout the development of clinical and industrial psychology, the conscious states of persons in terms of their current feelings and thoughts were of obvious importance. The role of consciousness, however, was often de-emphasised in favour of unconscious needs and motivations. Trends can be seen, however, toward a new emphasis on the nature of states of consciousness.

As accorded to states of consciousness, is that, no simple, agreed-upon definition of consciousness exists. Attempted definitions tend to be tautological (for example, consciousness defined as awareness) or merely descriptive (for example, consciousness described as sensations, thoughts, or feelings).

Despite this problem of definition, the subject of consciousness has had a remarkable history. At one time the primary subject matter of psychology, consciousness as an area of study suffered an almost total demise, later reemerging to become a topic of current interest.

French thinker René Descartes applied rigorous scientific methods of deduction to his exploration of philosophical questions. Descartes is probably best known for his pioneering work in philosophical skepticism. Author Tom Sorell examines the concepts behind Descartes's work Meditationes de Prima Philosophia (1641, Meditations on First Philosophy) focussing on its unconventional use of logic and the reactions it aroused.

Most of the philosophical discussions of consciousness arose from the mind-body issues posed by the French philosopher and mathematician René Descartes in the 17th century. Descartes asked: Is the mind, or consciousness, independent of matter? Is consciousness extended (physical) or unextended (nonphysical)? Is consciousness determinative, or is it determined? English philosophers such as John Locke equated consciousness with physical sensations and the information they provide, whereas European philosophers such as Gottfried Wilhelm Leibniz and Immanuel Kant gave a more central and active role to consciousness.

The philosopher who most directly influenced subsequent exploration of the subject of consciousness was the 19th-century German educator Johann Friedrich Herbert, who wrote that ideas had quality and intensity and that they may inhibit or facilitate each another. Thus, ideas may pass from "states of reality" (consciousness) to "states of a tendency" (unconsciousness), with the dividing line between the two states being described as the threshold of consciousness. This formulation of Herbert clearly presages the development, by the German psychologist and physiologist Gustav Theodor Fechner, of the psychophysical measurement of sensation thresholds, and the later development by Sigmund Freud of the concept of the unconscious.

The experimental analysis of consciousness dates from 1879, when the German psychologist Wilhelm Max Wundt started his research laboratory. For Wundt, the task of psychology was the study of the structure of consciousness, which extended well beyond sensations and included feelings, images, memory, attention, duration, and movement. Because early interest focussed on the content and dynamics of consciousness, it is not surprising that the central methodology of such studies was introspection; that is, subjects reported on the mental contents of their own consciousness. This introspective approach was developed most fully by the American psychologist Edward Bradford Titchener at Cornell University. Setting his task as that of describing the structure of the mind, Titchener attempted to detail, from introspective self-reports, the dimensions of the elements of consciousness. For example, taste was "dimensionalized" into four basic categories: sweet, sour, salt, and bitter. This approach was known as structuralism.

By the 1920s, however, a remarkable revolution had occurred in psychology that was to essentially remove considerations of consciousness from psychological research for some 50 years: Behaviourism captured the field of psychology. The main initiator of this movement was the American psychologist John Broadus Watson. In a 1913 article, Watson stated, "I believe that we can write a psychology and never use the terms consciousness, mental states, mind . . . imagery and the like." Psychologists then turned almost exclusively to Behaviour, as described in terms of stimulus and response, and consciousness was totally bypassed as a subject.

A survey of eight leading introductory psychology texts published between 1930 and the 1950s found no mention of the topic of consciousness in five texts, and in two it was treated as a historical curiosity.

Set about in the later parts of the 1950s, the subject of consciousness returned, specifically in those subjects and techniques relating to altered states of consciousness: sleep and dreams, meditation, biofeedback, hypnosis, and drug-induced states. Much of the surge in sleep and dream research was directly fuelled by a discovery relevant to the nature of consciousness. A physiological indicator of the dream state was found: At roughly 90-minute intervals, the eyes of sleepers were observed to move rapidly, and at the same time the sleepers' brain waves would show a pattern resembling the waking state. When people were awakened during these periods of rapid eye movement, they almost always reported dreams, whereas if awakened at other times they did not. This and other research clearly indicated that sleep, once considered a passive state, was instead an active state of consciousness.

During the 1960s, an increased search for "higher levels" of consciousness through meditation resulted in a growing interest in the practices of Zen Buddhism and Yoga from Eastern cultures. A full flowering of this movement in the United States was seen in the development of training programs, such as Transcendental Meditation, that were self-directed procedures of physical relaxation and focussed attention. Biofeedback techniques also were developed to bring body systems involving factors such as blood pressure or temperature under voluntary control by providing feedback from the body, so that subjects could learn to control their responses. For example, researchers found that persons could control their brain-wave patterns to some extent, particularly the so-called alpha rhythms generally associated with a relaxed, meditative state. This finding was especially relevant to those interested in consciousness and meditation, and a number of "alpha training" programs emerged.

Another subject that led to increased interest in altered states of consciousness was hypnosis, which involves a transfer of conscious control from the subject to another person. Hypnotism has had a long and intricate history in medicine and folklore and has been intensively studied by psychologists. Much has become known about the hypnotic state, relative to individual suggestibility and personality traits; the subject has now largely been demythologized, and the limitations of the hypnotic state are fairly well known. Despite the increasing use of hypnosis, however, much remains to be learned about this unusual state of focussed attention.

Finally, many people in the 1960s experimented with the psychoactive drugs known as hallucinogens, which produce some disorders of consciousness. The most prominent of these drugs are lysergic acid diethylamide, or LSD. Mescaline and psilocybin have long been associated with religious ceremonies in various cultures. LSD, because of its radical thought-modifying properties, was initially explored for its so-called mind-expanding potential and for its psychotomimetic effects (imitating psychoses). Little positive use, however, has been found for these drugs, and their use is highly restricted.

Scientists have long considered the nature of consciousness without producing a fully satisfactory definition. In the early 20th century American philosopher and psychologist William James suggested that consciousness is a mental process involving both attention to external stimuli and short-term memory. Later scientific explorations of consciousness mostly expanded upon

James's work. In this article from a 1997 special issue of Scientific American, Nobel laureate Francis Crick, who helped determine the structure of DNA, and fellow biophysicist Christof Koch explain how experiments on vision might deepen our understanding of consciousness.

As the concept of a direct, simple linkage between environment and Behaviour became unsatisfactory in recent decades, the interest in altered states of consciousness may be taken as a visible sign of renewed interest in the topic of consciousness. That persons are active and intervening participants in their Behaviour has become increasingly clear. Environments, rewards, and punishments are not simply defined by their physical character. Memories are organized, not simply stored. An entirely new area called cognitive psychology has emerged that centres on these concerns. In the study of children, increased attention is being paid to how they understand, or perceive, the world at different ages. In the field of animal Behaviour, researchers increasingly emphasize the inherent characteristics resulting from the way a species has been shaped to respond adaptively to the environment. Humanistic psychologists, with a concern for self-actualization and growth, have emerged after a long period of silence. Throughout the development of clinical and industrial psychology, the conscious states of persons in terms of their current feelings and thoughts were of obvious importance. The role of consciousness, however, was often de-emphasised in favour of unconscious needs and motivations. Trends can be seen, however, toward a new emphasis on the nature of states of consciousness

Psychoactive Drugs, chemical substances that alter mood, Behaviour, perception, or mental functioning. Throughout history, many cultures have found ways to alter consciousness through the ingestion of substances. In current professional practice, psychoactive substances known as psychotropic drugs have been developed to treat patients with severe mental illness. That of having an altering effect on perception, emotion, or behaviour and used of a Psychotropic drug or other agent.

Psychoactive substances exert their effects by modifying biochemical or physiological processes in the brain. The message system of nerve cells, or neurons, relies on both electrical and chemical transmission. Neurons rarely touch each other; the microscopic gap between one neuron and the next, called the synapse, is bridged by chemicals called neuroregulators, or neurotransmitters. Psychoactive drugs act by altering neurotransmitter function. The drugs can be divided into six major pharmacological classes based on their desired behavioural or psychological effect: Alcohol, sedative-hypnotics, narcotic analgesics, stimulant-euphoriants, hallucinogens, and psychotropic agents.

Psychotropic drugs have been in use since the early 1950s. Antipsychotic drugs decrease the symptoms of schizophrenia, allowing many schizophrenic patients to leave the hospital and rejoin community life. Antidepressant drugs help the majority of patients with severe depression recover from their disorder. Lithium salts eliminate or diminish the episodes of mania and depression experienced by manic-depressive patients.

Alfred Adler (1870-1937), Austrian psychologist and psychiatrist, born in Vienna, and educated at Vienna University. After leaving the university he studied and was associated with Sigmund Freud, the founder of psychoanalysis. In 1911 Adler left the orthodox psychoanalytic school to found a neo-Freudian school of psychoanalysis. After 1926 he was a visiting professor at Columbia University, and in 1935 he and his family moved to the United States.

In his analysis of individual development, Adler stressed the sense of inferiority, rather than sexual drives, as the motivating force in human life. According to Adler, conscious or subconscious feelings of inferiority (to which he gave the name inferiority complex), combined with compensatory defence mechanisms, are the basic causes of psychopathological Behaviour. The function of the psychoanalyst, furthermore, is to discover and rationalize such feelings and break down the compensatory, neurotic will for power that they engender in the patient. Adler's works include The Theory and Practice of Individual Psychology (1918) and The Pattern of Life (1930).

Johann Friedrich Herbert (1776-1841) saying that, inferiority from which the philosophy stems from the analysis of experience. The system includes logic, metaphysics, and aesthetics as coordinate elements. He rejected all concepts of separate mental faculties, postulating instead that all mental phenomena result from interaction of elementary ideas. Herbert believed that educational methods and systems should be based on psychology and ethics: psychology to furnish necessary knowledge of the mind and ethics to be used as a basis for determining the social ends of education. Among his major works is A Textbook in Psychology (1816; trs., 1894).

In the philosophy expounded by Leibniz, the universe is composed of countless conscious centres of spiritual force or energy, known as monads. Each monad represents an individual microcosm, mirroring the universe in varying degrees of perfection and developing independently of all other monads. The universe that these monads constitute is the harmonious result of a divine plan. Humans, however, with their limited vision, cannot accept such evils as disease and death as part of a universal harmony. This Leibnizian universe, "the best of all possible worlds," is satirized as a utopia by the French author Voltaire in his novel Candide (1759).

Behaviourism was first developed in the early 20th century by the American psychologist John B. Watson. The dominant view of that time was that psychology is the study of inner experiences or feelings by subjective, introspective methods. Watson did not deny the existence of inner experiences, but he insisted that these experiences could not be studied because they were not observable. He was greatly influenced by the pioneering investigations of the Russian physiologists Ivan P. Pavlov and Vladimir M. Bekhterev on conditioning of animals (classical conditioning). Watson proposed to make the study of psychology scientific by using only objective procedures such as laboratory experiments designed to establish statistically significant results. The behaviouristic view led him to formulate a stimulus-response theory of psychology. In this theory all complex forms of Behaviour—emotions, habits, and such—are seen as composed of simple muscular and glandular elements that can be observed and measured. He claimed that emotional reactions are learned in much the same way as other skills.

Watson's stimulus-response theory resulted in a tremendous increase in research activity on learning in animals and in humans, from infancy to early adulthood. Between 1920 and midcentury, Behaviourism dominated psychology in the United States and also had wide international influence. By the 1950s, the new behavioural movement had produced a mass of data on learning that led such American experimental psychologists as Edward C. Tolman, Clark L. Hull, and B. F. Skinner to formulate their own theories of learning and Behaviour based on laboratory experiments instead of introspective observations.

American psychologist B. F. Skinner became famous for his pioneering research on learning and Behaviour. During his 60-year career, Skinner discovered important principles of operant conditioning, a type of learning that involves reinforcement and punishment. A strict behaviorist, Skinner believed that operant conditioning could explain even the most complex of human behaviours.

Skinners' position, known as radical (or basic) Behaviourism, is similar to Watson's view that psychology is the study of the observable Behaviour of individuals interacting with their environment. Skinner, however, disagrees with Watson's position that inner processes, such as feelings, should be excluded from study. He maintains that these inner processes should be studied by the usual scientific methods, with particular emphasis on controlled experiments using individual animals and humans. His research with animals, focussing on the kind of learning—known as operant conditioning—that occurs as a consequence of stimuli, demonstrates that complex Behaviour such as language and problem solving can be studied scientifically. He postulated a type of psychological conditioning known as reinforcement.

Since 1950, behavioural psychologists have produced an impressive amount of basic research directed at understanding how various forms of Behaviour are developed and maintained. These studies have included the role of (1) the interactions preceding Behaviour, such as the attention span and perceptual processes; (2) changes in Behaviour itself, such as the formation of skills; (3) interactions following Behaviour, such as the effects of incentives or rewards and punishments; and (4) conditions prevailing over all the events, such as prolonged emotional stress and deprivations of the essentials of life.

Some of these studies were conducted with humans in rooms especially equipped with observational devices and also in natural settings, as in school or at home. Other studies used animals, particularly rats and pigeons, as subjects, in standard laboratory settings. Most studies with animals required simple responses. For example, the animal was trained to press a lever or peck a disk in order to receive something of value, such as food, or to avoid painful stimulation, such as a slight electric shock.

At the same time, psychologists have undertaken studies using behavioural principles on practical problems. This work has yielded a body of knowledge known as Behaviour modification, or applied Behaviour analysis. Applied behavioural research has been carried out in three main areas. The first focuses on the techniques of psychological treatment for troubled adults and children with Behaviour disorders. This area is known as Behaviour therapy. The second centres on improving teaching and training methods. Some studies have explored the teaching processes used in the educational system from preschool to college; others have focussed on training in business and industry and in the armed forces. Methods of programmed instruction have been developed. Many studies have dealt with the problems of improving teaching and training methods for handicapped children at home, in school, or in institutions. The third area of applied research is concerned with the long and short-term effects of drugs on Behaviour. In these studies, drugs usually are administered to animals in various dosages and combinations. Changes are then observed in the way in which these animals perform repetitious tasks, such as pressing a lever.

The initial influence of Behaviourism on psychology was to minimize the introspective study of the mental processes, emotions, and feelings and to substitute the study of the objective

Behaviour of individuals in relation to their environment by means of experimental methods. This orientation suggested a way to relate human and animal research and to bring psychology into line with the natural sciences, such as physics, chemistry, and biology.

Present-day Behaviourism has extended its influence on psychology in three ways functional concept that emphasizes the meaningfulness of stimulating conditions to the individual. It has introduced a research method for the experimental study of a single individual. Finally, it has demonstrated that behavioural concepts and principles can be applied to many practical problems.

The term psychology comes from two Greek words 'psyche' which means "soul," and logos, "the study of." These root words were first combined in the 16th century, at a time when the human soul, spirit, or mind was seen as distinct from the body.

Psychology overlaps with other sciences that investigate Behaviour and mental processes. Certain parts of the field share much with the biological sciences, especially physiology, the biological study of the functions of living organisms and their parts. Like physiologists, many psychologists study the inner workings of the body from a biological perspective. However, psychologists usually focus on the activity of the brain and nervous system.

The social sciences of sociology and anthropology, which study human societies and cultures, also intersect with psychology. For example, both psychology and sociology explore how people behave when they are in groups. However, psychologists try to understand Behaviour from the vantage point of the individual, whereas sociologists focus on how Behaviour is shaped by social forces and social institutions. Anthropologists investigate

Behaviour as well, paying particular attention to the similarities and differences between human cultures around the world.

Psychology is closely connected with psychiatry, which is the branch of medicine specializing in mental illnesses. The study of mental illness is one of the largest areas of research in psychology. Psychiatrists and psychologists differ in their training. A person seeking to become a psychiatrist first obtains a medical degree and then engages in further formal medical education in psychiatry. Most psychologists have a doctoral graduate degree in psychology.

The study of psychology draws on two kinds of research: Basic and applied. Basic researchers seek to test general theories and build a foundation of knowledge, while applied psychologists study people in real-world settings and use the results to solve practical human problems. There are five major areas of research: biopsychology, clinical psychology, cognitive psychology, developmental psychology, and social psychology. Both basic and applied research is conducted in each of these fields of psychology.

In 1860 German physicist Gustav Fechner theorized that if the human brain were divided into right and left halves, each side would have its own stream of consciousness. Modern medicine has actually allowed scientists to investigate this hypothesis. People who suffer from life-threatening epileptic seizures sometimes undergo a radical surgery that severs the corpus callosum, a bridge of nerve tissue that connects the right and left hemispheres of the brain. After the surgery, the two hemispheres can no longer communicate with each other.

Wilhelm Wundt (1832-1920), German psychologist, generally recognized as the founder of scientific psychology as an independent discipline. He was born in Neckarau (now part of Mannheim), and educated at the universities of Tübingen and Heidelberg and the Institute of Physiology in Berlin. After teaching physiology at the University of Heidelberg (1858-74), he taught inductive philosophy at the University of Zürich (1874-75). He was professor of philosophy at the University of Leipzig from 1875 to 1917. Wundt offered in 1862 the first academic course in psychology and established the first laboratory for experimental psychology in 1879. He founded the first psychological journal, Philosophische Studien (Studies in Philosophy), in 1881.

Wundt promoted what is known as structuralist or content psychology, emphasizing observations of the conscious mind rather than inference. Wundt also carried out extensive experimental research on perception, feeling, and apperception. His more than 500 published works include Principles of Physiological Psychology (2 volumes, 1873-74; trans. 1904) and the monumental work Elements of Folk Psychology (containing 10 volumes, 1900-20; trs., 1916). He also wrote Logik (1880), Ethik (1886), and System der Philosophie (1889).

The human brain is the most highly organized form of matter known, and in complexity the brains of the other higher animals are not greatly inferior. For certain purposes it is expedient to regard the brain as being analogous to a machine. Even if it is so regarded, however, it is a machine of a totally different kind from those made by man. In trying to understand the workings of his own brain man meets his highest challenge. Nothing is given; there are no operating diagrams, no maker's instructions.

The first step in trying to understand the brain is to examine its structure in order to discover the components from which it is built and how they are related to one another. After that one can attempt to understand the mode of operation of the simplest components.

These two modes of investigation—the morphological and the physiological—have now becomes complementary. In studying the nervous system with today's sensitive electrical device, however, it is all too easy to find physiological events that cannot be correlated with any known anatomical structure. Conversely, the electron microscope reveals many structural details whose physiological significance is obscure or unknown.

At the close of the past century the Spanish anatomist Santiago Ramón y Cajal showed how all parts of the nervous system are built up of individual nerve cells of many different shapes and sizes. Like other cells, each nerve cell has a nucleus and the surrounding cytoplasm. Its outer surface consists of many fine branches—the Dendrites-that receive nerve impulses from other nerve cells, and one relatively long branch—the axon—that transmits nerve impulses. Near its end the axon divides into branches that terminate at the dendrites or bodies of other nerve cells. The axon can be as short as a fraction of a millimetre or as long as a metre, depending on its place and function. It has many of the properties of an electric cable and is uniquely specialized to conduct the brief electrical waves called nerve impulses. In very thin axons these impulses travel at less than one metre per second; in others, for example in the large axons of the nerve cells that activate muscles, they travel as fast as 100 metres per second.

The electrical impulse that travels along the axon ceases abruptly when it comes to the point where the axon's terminal fibres make contact with another nerve cell. These junction points were given the name "synapses" by Sir Charles Sherrington, who laid the foundations of what is sometimes called synaptology. If the nerve impulse is to continue beyond the synapse, it must be regenerated afresh on the other side. As recently as 15 years ago some physiologists held that transmission at the synapse was predominantly, if not exclusively, an electrical phenomenon. Now, however, there is abundant evidence that transmission is effectuated by the release of specific chemical substances that trigger a regeneration of the impulse. In fact, the first strong evidence showing that transmitter substances act across the synapse was provided over 40 years ago by Sir Henry Dale and Otto Loewi.

It has been estimated that the human central nervous system, which of course includes the spinal cord as well as the brain itself, consists of about 10 billion (1010) nerve cells. With rare exceptions each nerve cell receives information directly in the form of impulses from many other nerve cells—often hundreds—and transmits information to a like number. Depending on its threshold of response, a given nerve cell may fire an impulse when stimulated by only a few incoming fibres or it may not fire until stimulated by many incoming fibres. It has long been known that this threshold can be raised or lowered by various factors. Moreover, it was conjectured some 60 years ago that some of the incoming fibres must inhibit the firing of the receiving cell rather than excite it. The conjecture was subsequently confirmed, and the mechanism of the inhibitory effect has now been clarified. This mechanism and its equally fundamental counterpart—nerve-cell excitation

The electron microscope has revealed structural details of synapses that fit in nicely with the view that a chemical transmitter is involved in nerve transmission. Enclosed in the synaptic knob are many vesicles, or tiny sacs, which appear to contain the transmitter substances that induce synaptic transmission. Between the synaptic knob and the synaptic membrane of the adjoining nerve cell is a remarkably uniform space of about 20 millimicrons that is termed the synaptic cleft. Many of the synaptic vesicles are concentrated adjacent to this cleft; it seems plausible that the transmitter substance is discharged from the nearest vesicles into the cleft, where it can act on the adjacent cell membrane. This hypothesis is supported by the discovery that the transmitter is released in packets of a few thousand molecules.

The study of synaptic transmission was revolutionized in 1951 by the introduction of delicate techniques for recording electrically from the interior of single nerve cells. This is done by inserting into the nerve cell an extremely fine glass pipette with a diameter of .5 microns, about a fifty-thousandth of an inch. The pipette is filled with an electrically conducting salt solution such as concentrated potassium chloride. If the pipette is carefully inserted and held rigidly in place, the cell membrane appears to seal quickly around the glass, thus preventing the flow of a short-circuiting current through the puncture in the cell membrane. Impaled in this fashion, nerve cells can function normally for hours. Although there is no way of observing the cells during the insertion of the pipette, the insertion can be guided by using as clues the electric signals that the pipette picks up when close to active nerve cells.

To study the large nerve cells called motoneurons, which lie in the spinal cord and whose function is to activate muscles. This was a fortunate choice: intracellular investigations with motoneurons have proved to be easier and more rewarding than those with any other kind of mammalian nerve cell.

Finding that when the nerve cell responds to the chemical synaptic transmitter, the response depends in part on characteristic features of ionic composition that are also concerned with the transmission of impulses in the cell and along its axon. When the nerve cell is at rest, its physiological makeup resembles that of most other cells in that the water solution inside the cell is quite different in composition from the solution in which the cell is bathed. The nerve cell is able to exploit this difference between external and internal composition and use it in quite different ways for generating an electrical impulse and for synaptic transmission.

The composition of the external solution is well established because the solution is essentially the same as blood from which cells and proteins have been removed. The composition of the internal solution is known only approximately. Indirect evidence indicates that the concentrations of sodium and chloride ions outside the cell are respectively some 10 and 14 times higher than the concentrations inside the cell. In contrast, the concentration of potassium ions inside the cell is about 30 times higher than the concentration outside.

How can one account for this remarkable state of affairs? Part of the explanation is that the interior of the cell is negatively charged with respect to the outside of the cell by about 70 millivolts. Since like charges repel each other, this internal negative charge tends to drive chloride ions (Cl-) outward through the cell membrane and, at the same time, to impede their inward movement. In fact, a potential difference of 70 millivolts is just sufficient to maintain the observed disparity in the concentration of chloride ions inside the cell and outside it; chloride ions diffuse inward and outward at equal rates. A drop of 70 millivolts across the membrane therefore defines the "equilibrium potential" for chloride ions.

To obtain a concentration of potassium ions (K+) that is 30 times higher inside the cell than outside would require that the interior of the cell membrane be about 90 millivolts negative with respect to the exterior. Since the actual interior is only 70 millivolts negative, it falls short of the equilibrium potential for potassium ions by 20 millivolts. Evidently the thirty-fold concentration can be achieved and maintained only if there is some auxiliary mechanism for "pumping" potassium ions into the cell at a rate equal to their spontaneous net outward diffusion.

The pumping mechanisms have more of a difficult form to which is to carry out a specific task, of pumping sodium ions (Na+) out of the cell against a potential gradient of 130 millivolts. This figure is obtained by adding the 70 millivolts of internal negative charge to the equilibrium potential for sodium ions, which is 60 millivolts of internal positive charge. If it were not for this postulated pump, the concentration of sodium ions inside and outside the cell would be almost the reverse of what is observed.

In their classic studies of nerve-impulse transmission in the giant axon of the squid, A. L. Hodgkin, A. F. Huxley and Bernhard Katz of Britain demonstrated that the propagation of the impulse coincides with abrupt changes in the permeability of the axon membrane. When a nerve impulse has been triggered in some way, what can be described as a gate opens and lets sodium ions pour into the axon during the advance of the impulse, making the interior of the axon locally positive. The process is self-reinforcing in that the flow of some sodium ions through the membrane opens the gate further and makes it easier for others to follow. The sharp reversal of the internal polarity of the membrane constitutes the nerve impulse, which moves like a wave, until it has travelled the length of the axon. In the wake of the impulse the sodium gate closes and a potassium gate opens, thereby restoring the normal polarity of the membrane within a millisecond or less.

With this understanding of the nerve impulse in hand, one is ready to follow the electrical events at the excitatory synapse. One might guess that if the nerve impulse results from an abrupt inflow of sodium ions and a rapid change in the electrical polarity of the axon's interior, something similar must happen at the body and dendrites of the nerve cell in order to generate the impulse in the first place. Indeed, the function of the excitatory synaptic terminals on the cell body and its dendrites is to depolarize the interior of the cell membrane essentially by permitting an inflow of sodium ions. When the depolarization reaches a threshold value, a nerve impulse is triggered.

As a simple instance of this phenomenon we have recorded the depolarization that occurs in a single motoneurons activated directly by the large nerve fibres that enter the spinal cord from special stretch-receptors known as annulospiral endings. These receptors in turn are located in the same muscle that is activated the motoneurons under study. Thus the whole system forms a typical reflex arc, such as the arc responsible for the patellar reflex, or "knee jerk."

To conduct the experiment we anaesthetize an animal (most often a cat) and free by dissection muscle nerves, which contains these large nerve fibres. By applying a mild electric shock to the exposed nerve one can produce a single impulse in each of the fibres; since the impulses travel to the spinal cord almost synchronously they are referred to collectively as a volley. The number of impulses contained in the volley can be reduced by reducing the stimulation applied to the nerve. The volley strength is measured at a point just outside the spinal cord and is displayed on an oscilloscope. About half a millisecond after detection of a volley there is a wavelike change in the voltage inside the motoneurons that has received the volley. The change is detected by a microelectrode inserted in the motoneurons and is displayed on another oscilloscope.

What we find is that the negative voltage inside the cell becomes progressively fewer negative and for more of the fibres impinging on the cell are stimulated to fire. This observed depolarization is in fact a simple summation of the depolarisation produced by each individual synapse. When the depolarization of the interior of the motoneurons reaches a critical point, a "spike" suddenly appears on the second oscilloscope, showing that a nerve impulse has been generated. During the spike the voltage inside the cell changes from about 70 negative millivolts, as much as 30 millivolts positive. The spike regularly appears when the depolarization, or reduction of membrane potential, reaches a critical level, which is usually between 10 and 18 millivolts. The only effect of a further strengthening of the synaptic stimulus is to shorten the time needed for the motoneurons to reach the firing threshold. The depolarizing potentials produced in the cell membrane by excitatory synapses are called excitatory postsynaptic potentials, or EPSP's.

Through one barrel of a double-barrelled microelectrode one can apply a background current to change the resting potential of the interior of the cell membrane, either increasing it or decreasing it. When the potential is made more negative, the EPSP rises more steeply to an earlier peak. When the potential is made less negative, the EPSP rises more slowly to a lower peak. Finally, when the charge inside the cell is reversed so as to be positive with respect to the exterior, the excitatory synapses give rise to an EPSP that is actually the reverse of the normal one.

These observations support the hypothesis that excitatory synapses produce what amounts virtually to a short circuit in the synaptic membrane potential. When this occurs, the membrane no longer acts as a barrier to the passage of ions but lets them flow through in response to the differing electric potential on the two sides of the membrane. In other words, the ions are momentarily allowed to travel freely down their electrochemical gradients, which means that sodium ions would flow into the cell and, to a lesser degree, potassium ions flow out. It is this net flow of positive ions that creates the excitatory postsynaptic potential. The flow of negative ions, such as the chloride ion, is apparently not involved. By artificially altering the potential inside the cell one can establish that there is no flow of ions, and therefore no EPSP, when the voltage drop across the membrane is zero.

How is the synaptic membrane converted from a strong ionic barrier into an ion-permeable state? It is currently accepted that the agency of conversion is the chemical transmitter substance contained in the vesicles inside the synaptic knob. When a nerve impulse reaches the synaptic knob, some of the vesicles are caused to eject the transmitter substance into the synaptic cleft. The molecules of the substance would take only a few microseconds to diffuse across the cleft and become attached to specific receptor sites on the surface membrane of the adjacent nerve cell.

Presumably the receptor sites are associated with fine channels in the membrane that are opened in some way by the attachment of the transmitter-substance molecules to the receptor sites. With the channels thus opened, sodium and potassium ions flow through the membrane thousands of times more readily than they normally do, thereby producing the intense ionic flux that depolarizes the cell membrane and produces the EPSP. In many synapses the current flows strongly for only about a millisecond before the transmitter substance is eliminated from the synaptic cleft, either by diffusion into the surrounding regions or as a result of being destroyed by enzymes. The latter process is known to occur when the transmitter substance is acetylcholine, which is destroyed by the enzyme acetylcholinesterase.

The substantiation of this general picture of synaptic transmission requires the solution of many fundamental problems. Since we do not know the specific transmitter substance for the vast majority of synapses in the nervous system we do not know if there are many different substances or only a few. The only one identified with reasonable certainty in the mammalian central nervous system is acetylcholine. We know practically nothing about the mechanism by which a presynaptic nerve impulse causes the transmitter substance to be injected into the synaptic cleft. Nor do we know how the synaptic vesicles not immediately adjacent to the synaptic cleft are moved up to the firing line to replace the emptied vesicles. It is conjectured that the vesicles contain the enzyme systems needed to recharge themselves. The entire process must be swift and efficient: The total amount of transmitter substance in synaptic terminals is enough for only a few minutes of synaptic activity at normal operating rates. There are also knotty problems to be solved on the other side of the synaptic cleft. What, for example, is the nature of the receptor sites? How are the ionic channels in the membrane opened up?

Let us turn now to the second type of synapse that has been identified in the nervous system. These are the synapses that can inhibit the firing of a nerve cell even though it may be receiving a volley of excitatory impulses. When inhibitory synapses are examined in the electron microscope, they look very much like excitatory synapses. Microelectrode activity was recorded by a single motoneurons and other nerve cells have now shown that the inhibitory postsynaptic potential (IPSP) is virtually a mirror image of the EPSP. Moreover, individual inhibitory synapses, like excitatory synapses, have a cumulative effect. The chief difference is simply that the IPSP makes the cell's internal voltage more negative than it is normally, which is in a direction opposite to that needed for generating a spike discharge.

By driving the internal voltage of a nerve cell in the negative direction inhibitory synapses oppose the action of excitatory synapses, which of course drive it in the positive direction. Hence if the potential inside a resting cell is 70 millivolts negative, a strong volley of inhibitory impulses can drive the potential to 75 or 80 negative millivolts. One can easily see that if the potential is made more negative in this way the excitatory synapses find it more difficult to raise the internal voltage to the threshold point for the generation of a spike. Thus the nerve cell responds to the algebraic sum of the internal voltage changes produced by excitatory and inhibitory synapses.

If, as in the experiment described earlier, the internal membrane potential is altered by the flow of an electric current through one barrel of a double-barrelled microelectrode, one can observe the effect of such changes on the inhibitory postsynaptic potential. When the internal potential is made less negative, the inhibitory postsynaptic potential is deepened. Conversely, when the potential is made more negative, the IPSP diminishes; it finally reverses when the internal potential is driven below minus 80 millivolts.

We can easily conclude, that inhibitory synapses' share with excitatory synapses', the ability to change the ionic permeability of the synaptic membrane. The difference is that inhibitory synapses enable ions to flow freely down an electrochemical gradient that has an equilibrium point at minus 80 millivolts rather than at zero, as is the case for excitatory synapses. This effect could be achieved by the outward flow of positively charged ions such as potassium or the inward flow of negatively charged ions such as chloride, or by a combination of negative and positive ionic flows such that the interior reaches equilibrium at minus 80 millivolts.

In an effort to discover the permeability changes associated with the inhibitory potential my colleagues and I have altered the concentration of ions normally found in motoneurons and have introduced a variety of other ions that are not normally present. This can be done by impaling nerve cells with micropipettes that are filled with a salt solution containing the ion to be injected. The actual injection is achieved by passing a brief current through the micropipette.

If the concentration of chloride ions within the cell is in this way increased as much as three times, the inhibitory postsynaptic potential reverses and acts as a depolarizing current; that is, it resembles that of excitatory potential. On the other hand, if the cell is heavily injected with sulfate ions, which are also negatively charged, there is no such reversal. This simple test shows that under the influence of the inhibitory transmitter substance, which is still unidentified, the subsynaptic membrane becomes permeable momentarily to chloride ions but not to sulfate ions. During the generation of the IPSP the outflow of chloride ions is so rapid that it more than outweighs the flow of other ions that generate the normal inhibitory potential.

The effect of injecting motoneurons with more than 30 kinds of negatively charged ions. With one exception the hydrated ions (ions bound to water) to which the cell membrane is permeable under the influence of the inhibitory transmitter substance are smaller than the hydrated ions to which the membrane is impermeable. The exception is the formate ion (HCO_2-), which may have an ellipsoidal shape and so be able to pass through membrane pores that block smaller spherical ions.

Apart from the formate ion all the ions to which the membrane is permeable have a diameter not greater than 1.14 times the diameter of the potassium ion; that is, they are less than 2.9 angstrom units in diameter. Comparable investigations in other laboratories have found the same permeability effects, including the exceptional behaviour of the formate ion, in fishes, toads and snails. It may well be that the ionic mechanism responsible for synaptic inhibition is the same throughout the animal kingdom.

The significance of these and other studies is that they strongly indicate that the inhibitory transmitter substance opens the membrane to the flow of potassium ions but not to sodium ions. It is known that the sodium ion is somewhat larger than any of the negatively charged ions, including the formate ion, that are able to pass through the membrane during synaptic inhibition. It is not possible, however, to test the effectiveness of potassium ions by injecting excess amounts into the cell because the excess is immediately diluted by an osmotic flow of water into the cell.

The concentration of potassium ions inside the nerve cell is about 30 times greater than the concentration outside, and to maintain this large difference in concentration without the help of a metabolic pump, the interior of the membrane would have to be charged 90 negative millivolts with respect to the exterior. This implies that if the membrane were suddenly made porous to potassium ions, the resulting outflow of ions would make the inside potential of the membrane even more negative than it is in the resting state, and that is just what happens during synaptic inhibition. The membrane must not simultaneously become porous to sodium ions, because they exist in much higher concentration outside the cell than inside and their rapid inflow would more than compensate for the potassium outflow. In fact, the fundamental difference between synaptic excitation and synaptic inhibition is that the membrane freely passes sodium ions in response to the former and largely excludes the passage of sodium ions in response to the latter.

This fine discrimination between ions that are not very different in size must be explained by any hypothesis of synaptic action. It is most unlikely that the channels through the membrane are created afresh and accurately maintained for a thousandth of a second every time a burst of transmitter substance is released into the synaptic cleft. It is more likely that channels of at least two different sizes are built directly into the membrane structure. In some way the excitatory transmitter substance would selectively unplug the larger channels and permit the free inflow of sodium ions. Potassium ions would simultaneously flow out and thus would tend to counteract the large potential change that would be produced by the massive sodium inflow. The inhibitory transmitter substance would selectively unplug the smaller channels that are large enough to pass potassium and chloride ions but not sodium ions.

To explain certain types of inhibition other features must be added to this hypothesis of synaptic transmission. In the simple hypothesis chloride and potassium ions can flow freely through pores of all inhibitory synapses. It has been shown, however, that the inhibition of the contraction of heart muscle by the vagus nerve is due almost exclusively to potassium-ion flow. On the other hand, in the muscles of crustaceans and in nerve cells in the snail's brain synaptic inhibition is due largely to the flow of chloride ions. This selective permeability could be explained if there were fixed charges along the walls of the channels. If such charges were negative, they would repel negatively charged ions and prevent their passage; if they were positive, they would similarly prevent the passage of positively charged ions. One can now suggest that the channels opened by the excitatory transmitter are negatively charged and so do not permit the passage of the negatively charged chloride ion, even though it is small enough to move through the channel freely.

One might wonder if a given nerve cell can have excitatory synaptic action at some of its axon terminals and inhibitory action at others. The answer is no. Two different kinds of nerve cell are needed, one for each type of transmission and synaptic transmitter substance. This can readily be demonstrated by the effect of strychnine and tetanus toxin in the spinal cord; they specifically prevent inhibitory synaptic action and leave excitatory action unaltered. As a result the synaptic excitation of nerve cells is uncontrolled and convulsions result. The special types of cell responsible for inhibitory synaptic action are now being recognized in many parts of the central nervous system.

This account of communication between nerve cells is necessarily oversimplified, yet it shows that some significant advances are being made at the level of individual components of the nervous system. By selecting the most favourable situations we have been able to throw light on some details of nerve-cell behaviour. We can be encouraged by these limited successes. But the task of understanding in a comprehensive way how the human brain operates staggers its own imagination

In general, each neuron uses only a single compound as its neurotransmitter. However, some neurons outside the central nervous system are able to release both an amine and a peptide neurotransmitter.

Neurotransmitters are manufactured from precursor compounds like amino acids, glucose, and the dietary amine-called choline.

Neurons modify the structure of these precursor compounds in a series of reactions with enzymes. Neurotransmitters that come from amino acids include serotonin, which is derived from tryptophan, dopamine and norepinephrine, which are formed from tyrosine and glycine, which is derived from threonine. Among the neurotransmitters made from glucose are glutamate, aspartate, and GABA. Choline serves as the precursor for acetylcholine.

In the nervous system, a message-carrying impulse travels from one end of a nerve cell to the other by means of an electrical impulse. When it reached the terminal end of a nerve cell, the impulse trigger tiny sacs called presynaptic vessicles to release their contents, chemical messengers called neurotransmitters. The neurotransmitters float across the synapse, or gap between adjacent nerve cells. When they reach the neighbouring nerve cell, the neurotransmitters fit into specialized receptor sites much as a key fits into a lock, causing that nerve cell to "fire," or generate an electric message-carrying impulse. As the message continues through the nervous system, the presynaptic cell absorbs the excess neurotransmitters, and repackages them in presynaptic vessicles in a process called neurotransmitter.

Neurotransmitters are released into a microscopic gap, called a synapse, that separates the transmitting neuron from the cell receiving the chemical signal. The cell that generates the signal is called the presynaptic cell, while the receiving cell is termed the postsynaptic cell.

After their release into the synapse, neurotransmitters combine chemically with highly specific protein molecules, termed receptors, that are embedded in the surface membranes of the postsynaptic cell. When this combination occurs, the voltage, or electrical force, of the postsynaptic cell is either increased (excited) or decreased (inhibited).

When a neuron is in its resting state, its voltage is about -70 millivolts. An excitatory neurotransmitter alters the membrane of the postsynaptic neuron, making it possible for ions (electrically charged molecules) to move back and forth across the neuron's membranes. This flow of ions makes the neuron's voltage rise toward zero. If enough excitatory receptors have been activated, the postsynaptic neuron responds by firing, generating a nerve impulse that causes its own neurotransmitter to be released into the next synapse. An inhibitory neurotransmitter causes different ions to pass back and forth across the postsynaptic neuron's membrane, lowering the nerve cell's voltage to -80 or -90 millivolts. The drop in voltage makes it less likely that the postsynaptic cell will fire.

If the postsynaptic cell is a muscle cell rather than a neuron, an excitatory neurotransmitter will cause the muscle to contract. If the postsynaptic cell is a gland cell, an excitatory neurotransmitter will cause the cell to secrete its contents.

While most neurotransmitters interact with their receptors to create new electrical nerve impulses that energize or inhibit the adjoining cell, some neurotransmitter interactions do not generate or suppress nerve impulses. Instead, they interact with a second type of receptor that changes the internal chemistry of the postsynaptic cell by either causing or blocking the formation of chemicals called second messenger molecules. These second messengers regulate the postsynaptic cell's biochemical processes and enable it to conduct the maintenance necessary to continue synthesizing neurotransmitters and conducting nerve impulses. Examples of second messengers, which are formed and entirely contained within the postsynaptic cell, include cyclic adenosine monophosphate, diacylglycerol, and inositol phosphates.

Once neurotransmitters have been secreted into synapses and have passed on their chemical signals, the presynaptic neuron clears the synapse of neurotransmitter molecules. For example, acetylcholine is broken down by the enzyme acetylcholinesterase into choline and acetate. Neurotransmitters like dopamine, serotonin, and GABA are removed by a physical process called reuptake. In reuptake, a protein in the presynaptic membrane acts as a sort of sponge, causing the neurotransmitters to reenter the presynaptic neuron, where they can be broken down by enzymes or repackaged for reuse.

Neurotransmitters are known to be involved in a number of disorders, including Alzheimer's disease. Victims of Alzheimer's disease suffer from loss of intellectual capacity, disintegration of personality, mental confusion, hallucinations, and aggressive— even violent—behaviour. These symptoms are the result of progressive degeneration in many types of neurons in the brain. Forgetfulness, one of the earliest symptoms of Alzheimer's disease, is partly caused by the destruction of neurons that normally release the neurotransmitter acetylcholine. Medications that increase brain levels of acetylcholine have helped restore short-term memory and reduce mood swings in some Alzheimer's patients.

Neurotransmitters also play a role in Parkinson disease, which slowly attacks the nervous system, causing symptoms that worsen over time. Fatigue, mental confusion, a masklike facial expression, stooping posture, shuffling gait, and problems with eating and speaking are among the difficulties suffered by Parkinson victims. These symptoms have been partly linked to the deterioration and eventual death of neurons that run from the base of the brain to the basal ganglia, a collection of nerve cells that manufacture the neurotransmitter dopamine. The reasons why such neurons die are yet to be understood, but the related symptoms can be alleviated. L-dopa, or levodopa, widely used to treat Parkinson disease, acts as a supplementary precursor for dopamine. It causes the surviving neurons in the basal ganglia to increase their production of dopamine, thereby compensating to some extent for the disabled neurons.

Many other effective drugs have been shown to act by influencing neurotransmitter behaviour. Some drugs work by interfering with the interactions between neurotransmitters and intestinal receptors. For example, belladonna decreases intestinal cramps in such disorders as irritable bowel syndrome by blocking acetylcholine from combining with receptors. This process reduces nerve signals to the bowel wall, which prevents painful spasms.

Other drugs block the reuptake process. One well-known example is the drug fluoxetine (Prozac), which blocks the reuptake of serotonin. Serotonin then remains in the synapse for a longer time, and its ability to act as a signal is prolonged, which contributes to the relief of depression and the control of obsessive-compulsive behaviour.

In general, each neuron uses only a single compound as its neurotransmitter. However, some neurons outside the central nervous system are able to release both an amine and a peptide neurotransmitter.

After their release into the synapse, neurotransmitters combine chemically with highly specific protein molecules, termed receptors, that are embedded in the surface membranes of the postsynaptic cell. When this combination occurs, the voltage, or electrical force, of the postsynaptic cell is either increased (excited) or decreased (inhibited).

When a neuron is in its resting state, its voltage is about -70 millivolts. An excitatory neurotransmitter alters the membrane of the postsynaptic neuron, making it possible for ions (electrically charged molecules) to move back and forth across the neuron's membranes. This flow of ions makes the neuron's voltage rise toward zero. If enough excitatory receptors have been activated, the postsynaptic neuron responds by firing, generating a nerve impulse that causes its own neurotransmitter to be released into the next synapse. An inhibitory neurotransmitter causes different ions to pass back and forth across the postsynaptic neuron's membrane, lowering the nerve cell's voltage to -80 or -90 millivolts. The drop in voltage makes it less likely that the postsynaptic cell will fire.

If the postsynaptic cell is a muscle cell rather than a neuron, an excitatory neurotransmitter will cause the muscle to contract. If the postsynaptic cell is a gland cell, an excitatory neurotransmitter will cause the cell to secrete its contents.

While most neurotransmitters interact with their receptors to create new electrical nerve impulses that energize or inhibit the adjoining cell, some neurotransmitter interactions do not generate or suppress nerve impulses. Instead, they interact with a second type of receptor that changes the internal chemistry of the postsynaptic cell by either causing or blocking the formation of chemicals called second messenger molecules. These second messengers regulate the postsynaptic cell's biochemical processes and enable it to conduct the maintenance necessary to continue synthesizing neurotransmitters and conducting nerve impulses. Examples of second messengers, which are formed and entirely contained within the postsynaptic cell, include cyclic adenosine monophosphate, diacylglycerol, and inositol phosphates.

Once neurotransmitters have been secreted into synapses and have passed on their chemical signals, the presynaptic neuron clears the synapse of neurotransmitter molecules. For example, acetylcholine is broken down by the enzyme acetylcholinesterase into choline and acetate. Neurotransmitters like dopamine, serotonin, and GABA is removed by a physical process called reuptake. In reuptake, a protein in the presynaptic membrane acts as a sort of sponge, causing the neurotransmitters to reenter the presynaptic neuron, where they can be broken down by enzymes or repackaged for reuse.

Neurotransmitters are known to be involved in a number of disorders, including Alzheimer's disease. Victims of Alzheimer's disease suffer from loss of intellectual capacity, disintegration of personality, mental confusion, hallucinations, and aggressive— even violent—behaviour. These symptoms are the result of progressive degeneration in many types of neurons in the brain. Forgetfulness, one of the earliest symptoms of Alzheimer's disease, is partly caused by the destruction of neurons that normally release the neurotransmitter acetylcholine. Medications that increase brain levels of acetylcholine have helped restore short-term memory and reduce mood swings in some Alzheimer's patients.

Neurotransmitters also play a role in Parkinson disease, which slowly attacks the nervous system, causing symptoms that worsen over time. Fatigue, mental confusion, a masklike facial expression, stooping posture, shuffling gait, and problems with eating and speaking are among the difficulties suffered by Parkinson victims. These symptoms have been partly linked to the deterioration and eventual death of neurons that run from the base of the brain to the basal ganglia, a collection of nerve cells that manufacture the neurotransmitter dopamine. The reasons why such neurons die are yet to be understood, but the related symptoms can be alleviated. L-dopa, or levodopa, widely used to treat Parkinson disease, acts as a supplementary precursor for dopamine. It causes the surviving neurons in the basal ganglia to increase their production of dopamine, thereby compensating to some extent for the disabled neurons.

Many other effective drugs have been shown to act by influencing neurotransmitter behaviour. Some drugs work by interfering with the interactions between neurotransmitters and intestinal receptors. For example, belladonna decreases intestinal cramps in such disorders as irritable bowel syndrome by blocking acetylcholine from combining with receptors. This process reduces nerve signals to the bowel wall, which prevents painful spasms.

Other drugs block the reuptake process. One well-known example is the drug fluoxetine (Prozac), which blocks the reuptake of serotonin. Serotonin then remains in the synapse for a longer time, and its ability to act as a signal is prolonged, which contributes to the relief of depression and the control of obsessive-compulsive behaviour.

Some evidence suggests that schizophrenia may result from an imbalance of chemicals in the brain called neurotransmitters. These chemicals enable neurons (brain cells) to communicate with each other. Some scientists suggest that schizophrenia result from excess activity of the neurotransmitter dopamine in certain parts of the brain or from an abnormal sensitivity to dopamine. Support for this hypothesis comes from antipsychotic drugs, which reduce psychotic symptoms in schizophrenia by blocking brain receptors for dopamine. In addition, amphetamines, which increase dopamine activity, intensify psychotic symptoms in people with schizophrenia. Despite these findings, many experts believe that excess dopamine activity alone cannot account for schizophrenia. Other neurotransmitters, such as serotonin and norepinephrine, may play important roles as well.

Other mechanisms reduce pain sensation by blocking, or inhibiting, the transmission of the pain message to the brain. To alter the pain sensation, the brain and spinal cord release specialized neurotransmitters called endorphins and enkephalins. These chemicals interfere with pain impulse transmission by occupying the nerve cell receptors required to send the impulse across the synapse. By making the pain impulse travel less efficiently, endorphins and enkephalins can significantly lessen the perception of pain. In extreme circumstances, they can even make severe injuries nearly painless. If an athlete is injured during the height of competition, or a soldier injured during combat, they may not realize they have been injured until after the stressful situation has ended. This happens because the brain produces abnormally high levels of endorphins or enkephalins in periods of intense stress or excitement.

Concentrated chemical substances, or hormones, which control 10 to 12 functions in the body, have been obtained as extracts from the anterior pituitary glands of cattle, sheep, and swine. Eight hormones have been isolated, purified, and identified; all of them are peptides, that is, they are composed of amino acids. Developmental hormones (GH) or the somatotropic hormones (STH) are essential for normal skeletal growth and is neutralized during adolescence by the gonadal sex hormones. A thyroid-stimulating hormone (TSH) controls the normal functioning of the thyroid gland; and the adrenocorticotropic hormone (ACTH) controls the activity of the cortex of the adrenal glands and takes part in the stress reaction. Prolactin, also called lactogenic, luteotropic, or mammotropic hormone, initiates milk secretion in the mammary gland after the mammary tissues have been prepared during pregnancy by the secretion of other pituitary and sex hormones. The two gonadotropic hormones are follicle-stimulating hormones (FSH) and Luteinizing hormones (LH). Follicle-stimulating hormones stimulate the formation of the Graafian follicle in the female ovary and the development of spermatozoa in the male. The luteinizing hormone stimulates the formation of ovarian hormones after ovulation and initiates lactation in the female; in the male, it stimulates the tissues of the testes to elaborate testosterone. In 1975 scientists identified the pituitary peptide endorphin, which acts in experimental animals as a natural pain reliever in times of stress. Endorphin and ACTH is made as parts of a single large protein, which subsequently splits. This may be the body's mechanism for coordinating the physiological activities of two stress-induced hormones. The same large prohormone that contains ACTH and endorphin also contains short peptides called melanocyte-stimulating hormones. These substances are analogous to the hormone that regulates pigmentation in fish and amphibians, but in humans they have no known function.

Many people learn to control their pain with strategies that do not rely on drugs or surgery. Some people control the normally involuntary components of pain message transmission using a behaviour modification technique-called biofeedback. Acupuncture is widely used for pain relief. Many scientists now believe that this ancient medical procedure may trigger the release of endorphins and enkephalins, the body's own pain-inhibiting neurotransmitters. Others suspect that the pain-relieving attributes of acupuncture are due, in part, to a patient's expectation of relief. Although it is not completely understood, physicians and pain specialists have found that when a person suffering from pain expects that a particular procedure—in this case acupuncture—will make their pain subside, it actually does.

In cases where no treatment effectively relieves pain, doctors may recommend a surgical procedure in which pain-transmitting nerves in the brain or spinal cord are severed. Only small fractions of pain sufferers need not receive the surgical treatment. Another pain-relieving procedure involves placing electrical stimulators on the skin, nerves, spinal cord, or brain to reduce pain sensation.

Some injuries take a long time to heal, and even then, pain does not always completely subside. People suffering from this condition, known as chronic pain, may continue to experience debilitating pain for years, without having any apparent tissue damage. This may be the result of permanent damage to the nervous system. There is new evidence that the nerves in the spinal cord and brain can alter their connections after severe pain—that is, even after healing, the nervous system never returns to normal. Pain that subsides and then returns periodically, such as headaches or low back pain, also falls under the category of chronic pain. In their search for pain relief, many chronic pain sufferers become dependent on strong painkilling medicines, and they often fall into an endless cycle of pain, depression, and inactivity.

The complexity of human pain often requires a combination of pain therapies to achieve relief. Pain management specialists are usually medical doctors with specialized training in neurology, psychiatry, or surgery who have restricted their practice to the analysis and treatment of pain. Psychologists are usually important members of a pain management team. Many people are turning to alternative healthcare practitioners, such as those that specialize in acupuncture or chiropractic, for pain relief. Often, pain management specialists and practitioners of alternative pain therapies join forces in multidisciplinary pain clinics.

The complexity of human pain often requires a combination of pain therapies to achieve relief. Pain management specialists are usually medical doctors with specialized training in neurology, psychiatry, or surgery who have restricted their practice to the analysis and treatment of pain. Psychologists are usually important members of a pain management team. Many people are turning to alternative healthcare practitioners, such as those that specialize in acupuncture or chiropractic, for pain relief. Often, pain management specialists and practitioners of alternative pain therapies join forces in multidisciplinary pain clinics.

Acetaminophen, a nonprescription drug used for the relief of minor pain, such as headaches and structural muscle aches, and for the reduction of fever. Like the other common analgesic drugs aspirin and ibuprofen, acetaminophen relieves pain by inhibiting the synthesis of prostaglandins in the body. It does not reduce inflammation as do those other two analgesics, but it also does not irritate the stomach lining, as aspirin tends to do for some users. A large overdose of acetaminophen may cause severe liver damage.

Aspirin, synthetic chemical compound, acetylsalicylic acid. It is made from salicylic acid, found in the bark of the willow tree, which was used by the ancient Greeks and Native Americans, among others, to counter fever and pain. Salicylic acid is bitter, however, and irritates the stomach. The German chemist Felix

Hoffman synthesized the acetyl derivative of salicylic acid in 1893 in response to the urging of his father, who took salicylic acid for rheumatism. Aspirin is currently the first-choice drug for fever, mild to moderate pain, and inflammation due to arthritis or injury. It is a more effective analgesic than codeine. Aspirin causes insignificant gastrointestinal bleeding that can over time, however, cause iron deficiency; gastric ulcers may also occur with long-term use. Complications can be avoided by using enteric-coated aspirin, which does not dissolve until reaching the intestine. Aspirin should not be given to children who have chicken pox or influenza, because it increases the risk of contracting the rare and frequently fatal Reye's syndrome, a disease of the brain and some abdominal organs.

Aspirin is thought to act by interfering with synthesis of prostaglandins, which are implicated in inflammation and fever. Studies of aspirin's anticlotting activities suggest that half an aspirin tablet per day may reduce the risk of heart attack and stroke in some persons.

Ibuprofen, drug used to reduce inflammation, fever, and the sensation of pain. In prescription form, ibuprofen is usually taken to relieve the more severe symptoms associated with arthritis. The nonprescription form available over the counter is taken for low-intensity pain, inflammation, or fever.

Ibuprofen works by inhibiting the action of prostaglandins (chemicals that cause inflammation and contribute to the brain's perception of pain). Ibuprofen reduces fever by blocking prostaglandin synthesis in the hypothalamus, a structure in the brain that regulates body temperature. Ibuprofen also acts as an anticoagulant, suppressing the formation of blood clots.

In adults, the dosage of ibuprofen commonly prescribed for arthritis is 1200 to 3200mg per day, usually divided into 3 or 4 doses. For mild to moderate pain in nonprescription uses, the dosage is generally 400mg taken every 4 to 6 hours as necessary. Because ibuprofen can cause stomach upset, pills should be swallowed with a full glass of water, and may be taken with food. Ibuprofen is not recommended for use by pregnant women.

Prolonged use of ibuprofen can result in ulcers and internal bleeding because it blocks the production of the stomach lining's protective mucous barrier.

Ibuprofen prevents the body from excreting salt and water properly, and it should be used with caution by people who suffer from kidney disease, liver disease, or high blood pressure. The anticoagulant effect of ibuprofen can also result in excessive bleeding when taken prior to tooth extraction or minor surgery. When taken in excessive amounts, ibuprofen can produce a potentially fatal overdose syndrome, which usually involves vomiting, diarrhea, rapid breathing, or rapid heartbeat. Alcoholic beverages should be avoided while taking this medication.

The opium poppy's green, unripe seed capsule, revealed when the flower petals drop, contains a milky sap that is the source of opium. To collect the sap, slits are made along the circumference of the seed capsules, enabling the milky sap to ooze out and dry. It is then scraped from the capsules, pressed into cakes, and dried to form the rubbery, yellow-brown opium. Natural derivatives of opium include morphine and codeine, used extensively in medicine as sedatives and pain killers. Heroin is a synthetic derivative of morphine. Morphine and codeine are habit forming. Heroin, which is especially addictive, is illegal in the United States.

Opium is the narcotic drug that produces, from the drying resin of unripe capsules of the opium poppy, the Papaver somniferum. Opium is grown mainly in Myanmar (formerly Burma) and Afghanistan. The legitimate world demand for opium amounts to about 680 metric tons a year, but many times that amount is distributed illegally.

In its commercial form, opium is a chestnut-coloured globular mass, sticky and rather soft, but hardening from within as it ages. It is processed into the alkaloid morphine which has long served as the chief painkiller in medical practice, although synthetic substitutes such as meperidine (trade name Demerol) are now available. Heroin, a derivative of morphine, is about three times more potent. Codeine is another important opium alkaloid.

The molecules of opiates have painkilling properties similar to those of compounds called endorphins or enkephalins produced in the body. Being of similar structure, the opiate molecules occupy many of the same nerve-receptor sites and bring on the same analgesic effect as the body's natural painkillers. Opiates first produce a feeling of pleasure and euphoria, but with their continued use the body demands larger amounts to reach the same sense of well-being. Withdrawal is extremely uncomfortable, and addicts typically continue taking the drug to avoid pain rather than to attain the initial state of euphoria. Malnutrition, respiratory complications, and low blood pressure are some of the illnesses associated with addiction.

As long ago as 100 Ad, opium had been used as a folk medicine, taken with a beverage or swallowed as a solid. Only toward the middle of the 17th century, when opium smoking was introduced into China, did any serious addiction problems arise. In the 18th century opium addiction was so serious there that the Chinese made many attempts to prohibit opium cultivation and opium trade with Western countries. At the same time opium made its way to Europe and North America, where addiction grew out of its prevalent use as a painkiller.

With the invention of the hypodermic syringe during the American Civil War, the injection of morphine became indispensable in treating patients who had to undergo some of the newly developed surgical operations. Physicians of that time hoped that injecting morphine directly into the blood stream would avoid the addictive effects of smoking or eating opium, but instead it proved more addictive. With the discovery of heroin in 1898, there came a similar hope, but this more potent drug created a much stronger dependency than opium or morphine.

Today opium is sold on the street as a powder or dark brown solid and is smoked, eaten, or injected. Heroin addicts residing in the United States number around 2 million people. Although the synthetic narcotic methadone has been used to offer addicts some relief from opiates, it is itself addictive. Complete recovery from opiate addiction requires years of social and psychological rehabilitation

Narcotics, term originally applied to all compounds that produce insensibility to external stimuli through depression of the central nervous system, but now applied primarily to the drugs known as opiates—compounds extracted from the opium poppy and their chemical derivatives. Also classed as narcotics are the opioids, chemical compounds that are wholly synthesized, but which resemble the opiates in their actions.

The most important attribute of narcotics is their capacity to decrease pain, not only by decreasing the perception of pain, but also by altering the reaction to it. Although they do have sedative properties when used in large doses, they are not used primarily for sedation.

The major constituent of opium and the prototype of all narcotic analgesics is morphine, which was isolated and chemically analyzed by the German apothecary F. W. A. Setürner between 1805 and 1817. Other narcotics used in the US are meperidine (as the trade name Demerol), codeine, and propoxyphene (trade name Darvon). Heroin, synthesized from morphine, is a potent analgesic, but its use is forbidden in the US Some of the newer synthetic compounds are 1000 to 10,000 times more potent than morphine.

In addition to their painkilling properties, the narcotic analgesics cause a profound feeling of well-being (euphoria). It is this feeling that is in part responsible for the psychological drive of certain persons to obtain and self-administer these drugs. When taken chronically in large doses, the narcotics have the capacity to induce tolerance (whereby a larger and larger dose is required by the body to achieve the same effect), and ultimately psychological and physical dependence, or addiction. In this respect they are similar to the barbiturates and to alcohol. These properties make the medical use in narcotics extremely difficult and have led to strict regulation of the prescription and dispensing of this class of drugs. Even so, they are widely abused.

The mode of action of the narcotic analgesics is still not fully understood. Recent research has determined that specific regions of the brain and spinal cord have an affinity for binding opiates, and the binding sites in the brain are in the same general areas where pain centres are believed to be. This research has also succeeded in isolating compounds, called enkephalins, that are produced in the body to reduce pain; the compounds consist of five amino acids. Apparently they can depress neurons throughout the central nervous system. They belong to a group of larger compounds called endorphins, consisting of many amino acids, that have also been isolated in the body and that are produced by the pituitary gland. Administration of endorphins, including the enkephalins, results in effects similar to those produced by opiates.

The discovery of a class of compounds that are specific antagonists to the action of the opiates has made it possible to treat opiate over dosage quickly and efficiently. The standard drug for this use is naloxone. Some of the antagonists also have opiate like properties, and this has led to the introduction of a new class of analgesics, the mixed agonists-antagonists. It is hoped that these drugs will produce analgesia without euphoria, reducing their potential for abuse. The three drugs of this class approved so far in the US—pentazocine, butorphanol, and nalbuphine—are as analgesic as morphine for many uses that induce little or no euphoria. All appear to have a lower abuse potential than morphine or propoxyphene.

Chromosome, are the microscopic structure within cells that carries the molecule deoxyribonucleic acid (DNA)—the hereditary material that influences the development and characteristics of each organism. In bacteria and bacteria-like organisms called archaebacteria, chromosomes consist of simple circles of DNA floating freely in the organism. In all other life forms, collectively called eukaryotes, chromosomes reside within a well-defined nucleus. In eukaryotes, chromosomes are highly complex structures in which the shape of the DNA molecules is linear, rather than circular.

Chromosomes consist chiefly of proteins and DNA. Tiny chemical subunits called nucleotide bases its form in the structure of DNA. A sequence of bases along a DNA strand that codes for the production of a protein is known as a gene, Genes occupy precise locations on the chromosome.

Each cell contains enough DNA to form a thread extending about 2 m (about 7 ft). Proteins called histones play a key role in packaging DNA within chromosomes. Sections of the DNA molecule wind around clusters of histones to form units called nucleosomes, which resemble spools encircled with thread. Another type of protein, called nonhistone chromosomal protein, further compresses nucleosomes into a compact, narrow coil. Chromosomes become most condensed when a cell is preparing to divide.

The chromosome structure ensures that even when the DNA is highly confined, it is free to carry out transcription, or the production of messenger ribonucleic acid (mRNA). The messenger ribonucleic acid is the molecule that carries the DNA instructions that determine the types of proteins a cell will reproduce to the sites where proteins are constructed. In addition, chromosomes permit DNA to replicate, or reproduce itself, so that as a cell divides to produce two cells, each of these new cells will contain all of the necessary genetic information.

Scientists are learning how DNA loosens its connection with histones in order to replicate itself and participate in the synthesis of mRNA. Evidence suggests that enzymes interact with the tails of histones, which protrude from the nucleosomes. These interactions may temporarily disrupt the nucleosome structure so that the DNA is free to interact with the enzymes that help to generate either mRNA or new copies of DNA.

The chromosomes of nearly all eukaryotic life forms contain two important structures: Centromeres and telomeres. During cell division, the centromere—visible through a microscope as a knotlike structure—connects to an apparatus called the spindle. The spindle contains fibres that move the centromeres around, causing the rest of each chromosome to follow. This process ensures that each chromosome moves to its proper place during mitosis, when a cell divides to give rise to two cells, and during meiosis, the process of cell division that gives rise to eggs or sperm.

Telomeres occur at the ends of a chromosome, as a specialized sequence of DNA that are found at the tips of chromosomes. Telomeres serve as a kind of cap that prevents the ends of chromosomes from attaching to the ends of other chromosomes. Scientists suspect that telomeres may influence the activity of nearby genes and may play a role in determining the life span of a cell.

In the cells of most organisms that reproduce sexually, chromosomes occur in pairs: One chromosome is inherited from the female parent, and one is inherited from the male parent. The two chromosomes of each pair contain genes that correspond to the same inherited characteristics. Each pair of chromosomes is different from every other pair of chromosomes in the same cell.

The number of chromosome pairs in an organism varies depending on the species. The number of chromosomes characteristic of a particular organism is known as the diploid number. Dogs, for example, have 38 pairs of chromosomes and a diploid number of 76, while tomato plants have 12 pairs of chromosomes and a diploid number of 24.

Sex cells (eggs or sperm) contain only half the number of chromosomes found in the other cells of an organism. This reduced number of chromosomes in the sex cells is known as the haploid number. During fertilization, an egg and sperm unite to form a cell known as a zygote, the first cell of the offspring. The zygote contains the diploid number of chromosomes characteristic of the species.

Most organisms have complete sets of matching chromosomal pairs, known as autosomes. In mammals, birds, and some other organisms, one pair of chromosomes is not identical. Known as the sex chromosomes, this pair plays a dominant role in determining the sex of an organism. Females have two copies of the X chromosome, while males have one Y chromosome and one X chromosome. Both males and females inherit one sex chromosome from the mother (always an X chromosome) and one sex chromosome from the father (an X in female offspring and a Y in male offspring). The presence of the Y chromosome determines that a zygote will develop into a male.

The Y chromosome is about one-third the size of the X chromosome and contains only a fraction of the number of genes. At one point in evolutionary history, the X and Y chromosomes were equal in size and gene number, but the two chromosomes gradually diverged over the course of 300 million years. These unmatched sex chromosomes produce a pattern of gene inheritance known as sex-linked inheritance, which differs from genes found on autosomes. In males, which carry an X and a Y chromosome, some genes found on the X chromosome may be missing on the Y chromosome. As a result, the organism will usually develop the trait associated with the gene on the X chromosome. In fruit flies, for instance, the gene for eye colour is located on the X chromosome. A male fruit fly will inherit the eye colour found on the X chromosome, since no gene for eye colour is found on the Y chromosome.

A karyotype, like the ones shown here, is a photographic image that depicts all of the chromosomes in an individual cell. Laboratory workers use computers to rearrange the images so that the chromosomes are lined up in pairs, typically beginning with the autosomes—chromosomes 1 through 22—and ending with the sex chromosomes—normally XX or XY. A complete karyotype helps doctors determine if a person has extra chromosomes, missing chromosomes, or chromosomes that have attached to one another in unusual ways.

Humans have 23 pairs of chromosomes, with a diploid number of 46. Scientists number these chromosome pairs according to their size—the largest is chromosome 1 and the smallest is chromosome 23. In human chromosomes, errors may occur that give rise to embryos with more or less genetic material, sometimes resulting in developmental disabilities or health problems. In a process called nondisjunction, paired members of chromosomes fail to separate from one another during meiosis. Nondisjunction can lead to a condition known as Down syndrome, in which a person inherits three copies of chromosome 21. Another condition that may result from nondisjunction is Turner syndrome, a disorder in which a female inherits only a single X chromosome.

Genetic errors occur if part of a chromosome is either missing or duplicated. Chromosomes sometimes undergo changes called translocation, in which part of one chromosome breaks off and attaches to another chromosome. A translocation involving chromosomes 9 and 22 is linked to a type of leukemia called chronic myelogenic leukemia. On the sex chromosomes, problems arise in men when an abnormal gene is present on the X chromosome.

With no healthy gene found on the Y chromosome to override the abnormal gene, disease may result. For example, men who inherit a mutated gene that causes hemophilia from their mother on the X chromosome will develop this bleeding disorder since they are missing a normal version of the gene on their Y chromosome.

Scientists called cytogeneticists for look at a person's chromosomes in the laboratory to determine whether the individual has the usual number of chromosomes and whether these chromosomes have missing or extra segments. To examine chromosomes, cytogeneticists grow samples of a person's blood cells in the laboratory and expose the cells to a chemical called colchicine, which disrupts the spindle apparatus that is normally present in dividing cells. This disruption immobilizes the chromosomes during cell division, when they are most condensed and visible. Chromosomes are then stained with various dyes, which produce a pattern of vertical bands. Cytogeneticists take photographs of the banded chromosomes through a microscope to create images called karyotypes, in which the members of each chromosome pair are arranged next to each other for easy comparison. The analysis of karyotypes reveals whether a person has extra or missing chromosomes, as well as whether large segments of chromosome are absent, rearranged, or duplicated. The Karyotype are the characterization of the chromosomal complement of an individual of a species, including number, form, and size of the chromosomes, in that which the chromosomes are arranged according to a standard classification. To which of a class complement that any standardized complement measures of number, form, shape and other characteristics of the chromosomes.

Experiments involving artificial chromosomes—chromosomes are synthesized in the laboratory—are providing new insights into the structure and function of chromosomes. The first artificial chromosomes, produced in the 1980s, were chromosomes of yeast cells. The first artificial human chromosomes were created in 1997.

Researchers have successfully identified all the genes located on chromosomes 5, 16, 19, 21, and 22. This research has revealed a number of disease-causing genes associated with these chromosomes. For instance, genes found on chromosome 5 having been linked to colorectal cancer, basal cell carcinomas (a form of skin cancer), and a type of dwarfism. Chromosome 16 contains genes implicated in adult polycystic renal disease, which affects 5 million people worldwide. Identifying disease-causing genes and their chromosome locations will help researchers devise new diagnostic tools to determine a person's risk for disease as well as new therapies to replace or repair faulty genes.

Heredity, process of transmitting biological traits from parent to offspring through genes, the basic units of heredity. Heredity also refers to the inherited characteristics of an individual, including traits such as height, eye colour, and blood type.

This karyotype of a human male shows the 23 pairs of chromosomes that are typically present in human cells. The chromosome pairs labelled 1 through 22 are called autosomes, and have a similar appearance in males and females. The 23rd pair, shown on the bottom right, represents the sex chromosomes. Females have two identical-looking sex chromosomes that are both labelled X, whereas males have a single X chromosome and a smaller chromosome labelled Y.

Heredity accounts for why offspring look like their parents: when two dogs mate, for example, they have puppies, not kittens. If the parents are both Chihuahuas, the puppies will also be Chihuahuas, not great Danes or Labrador retrievers. The puppies may be a little taller or shorter, a little lighter or a lot heavier than their parents are. Their faces may look a little different, or they may have different talents and temperaments. In all the important characteristics, however—the number of limbs, arrangement of organs, general size, fur type—they will share the traits of their parents. The principles of heredity hold true not only for a puppy but also for a virus, a roundworm, a pansy, or a human.

Genetics is the study of how heredity works and, in particular, of genes. A gene is a section of a long deoxyribonucleic acid (DNA) molecule, and it carries information for the construction of a protein or part of a protein. Through the diversity of proteins they code for, genes influence or determine such traits as eye colour, the ability of a bacterium to eat a certain sugar, or the number of peas in a pod. A virus has as few as a dozen genes. A simple roundworm has 5000 to 8000 genes, while a corn plant has 60,000. The construction of a human requires an estimated 50,000 genes.

If the DNA in a single human cell could be unravelled, it would form a single thread about five feet long and about 50 trillionths of an inch thick. To prevent this fine string of DNA from becoming knotted like a big tangle of yarn, parts of the strand are wrapped around proteins like a thread is wound around spools. These units of wrapped DNA are called nucleosomes, and they coil and fold into structures called chromosomes. Humans have 23 pairs of chromosomes. In each pair, one chromosome comes from the mother and the other from the father. Twenty-two of the pairs are the same in both men and women, and these are called autosomes. The twenty-third pair consisted of the sex chromosomes, so called because they are the primary factor in determining the gender of a child. The sex chromosomes are known as the X and Y chromosomes.

Females have two X chromosomes, and males have one X and one Y chromosomes. The Y chromosome is about one-third the size of the X chromosome. A sperm, the reproductive cell produced by the male, can carry either one X or one Y chromosome. An egg, the reproductive cell produced by the female, can carry only the X chromosome. When a sperm with an X chromosome unites with an egg, the result is a child with two x-chromosomes-a females. When a sperm with a Y chromosome unites with an egg, however, the result is a child with one X and one Y chromosome—a male. Thus, the father determines the gender of the child.

The single-celled amoeba demonstrates a simple method of asexual reproduction; it divides in half by a process called fission, producing two smaller daughter cells. After a period of feeding and growth, these two daughter cells will themselves divide in half.

Throughout the entire world of life, evolution has brought about only two types of reproduction—asexual and sexual. Asexual reproduction does not require a mate and is less complicated than sexual reproduction. It is used by simple life forms, such as bacteria as complex one-celled organisms, such as amoebas and diatoms, with certain worms, such as flatworms: Fungi and several plants.

In asexual reproduction, one parent transmits all of its genetic information to the offspring, and the offspring is therefore identical to the parent. Asexual reproduction typically is a rapid and reliable method of reproduction. It is limited, however, because the genetic uniformity in the offspring makes them all equally susceptible to a change in the environment. If a new disease, a new predator, or a climate change is lethal to one individual, it is lethal to all genetically identical organisms. Such changes can effectively wipe out entire populations of genetically identical organisms. Sexual reproduction results in offspring with diverse traits, and is the predominant form of reproduction among plants, animals, and most other organisms.

In contrast to asexual reproduction, sexual reproduction requires two parents. Each parent creates sex cells, or gametes that contain half the parent's genetic information. Human sex cells—sperm and eggs—contain 23 single, unpaired chromosomes rather than the 23 paired chromosomes found in all other body cells, or somatic cells. When egg and sperm unite in the process called fertilization, they form one cell that contains 23 pairs of chromosomes, the normal number for human body cells? The cell develops into a child that has a mixture of genetic information from both parents. As a result, the child is similar to each of the parents but not identical to either of them.

If these same parents have a second child, it is the product of fertilization of a different sperm and a different egg. Therefore the second child is unique, because each sperm and egg contains a unique set of chromosomes. Scientists estimate that each person is capable of producing 223 or 8,388,608 unique sex cells. The total number of unique children possible from one couple is a phenomenal 223 ´ 223 or 246. This genetic diversity that results from sexual reproduction enables populations to withstand changing environments through evolution.

With the exception of the X and Y chromosomes, genes come in twos on the paired chromosomes, but the genes are not necessarily identical. The hair colour gene from the father may carry information for black hair, but its partner on the chromosome from the mother may specify red hair. These different forms of genes that carry information for specific traits are called alleles. A person's hair colour depends on several alleles interacting in complex ways to determine the actual trait of the offspring.

The pattern of inheritance describes how alleles work together to produce traits. Understanding inheritance patterns enables geneticists to predict the probability that a child will inherit a certain trait. A variety of inheritance patterns influence the diverse traits found not only in humans, but in other animals, plants, fungi, and bacteria.

Some genes that cause genetic diseases interact in a dominant-recessive pattern. In these cases, two copies of the recessive gene are required for the disease to occur. A person who has just one copy of the recessive gene is termed a carrier, since he or she carries the gene but is not affected by it. In the illustration above, the dominant gene is represented in green, and the recessive in blue. For the couple on the left, the father has one copy of the dominant gene and one copy of the recessive gene. The mother has two copies of the dominant gene. Each parent can contribute just one gene to the child. The four children shown on the lower left represent the probabilities (not the actual children) for the combinations that can result from their parents. The children on the far left received the recessive gene from their father and the dominant gene from their mother, and are therefore carriers. For any child born to these parents, there is a 50 percent chance that the child will be a carrier. Since none of the children can inherit two copies of the recessive gene, none of the children will develop the disease. When both parents are carriers, however, as shown by the couple on the right, there is a 25 percent chance that any child born has the disease, a 50 percent chance that a child is a carrier, and a 25 percent chance that a child does not have the disease and is not a carrier.

The dominant-recessive pattern of inheritance, a relatively simple pattern, involves paired alleles that influence one trait. In this pattern, one of the two alleles contains information for a certain characteristic—the lavender colour of sweet pea flowers, for example—while the second allele directs the production of an alternate characteristic—the white flower colour. In sweet peas, if these two alleles occur together, the allele for lavender flowers is expressed, and the flowers are lavender. The allele for lavender is therefore called the dominant allele. The allele for white is known as the recessive allele. Lavender flowers also occur when two alleles for lavender colour are paired. Only when two alleles for the recessive characteristic are paired do white flowers appear. This genetic rule applies regardless of the organism or the trait. In the dominant recessive pattern, the recessive trait shows up only when two recessive alleles are paired.

In humans, several hundred genetic diseases and disorders follow the dominant-recessive pattern. These conditions result when a mutation, or a change in a normal allele, is found in a sperm or egg, and the mutation causes disease when the child inherits a pair of mutated alleles. If a child inherits one dominant allele and one recessive allele, he or she typically does not have the disease. Such individuals are termed carriers, since although healthy, they carry the recessive allele. A carrier can pass either the dominant or recessive allele to their child. If both parents are carriers, these alleles can be passed along in four ways. The child can receive a normal allele from each parent, in which case it does not develop the disease. It can receive a mutated allele from the mother and a normal allele from the father, or a normal allele from the mother and a mutated allele from the father. In both of these cases, the child will be a carrier. The child develops the disease only if he or she receives a mutated allele from each parent. When both parents are carriers, there is a 25 percent chance that a child will be disease-free, a 25 percent chance that it will have the disease, and a 50 percent chance that it will be a carrier. Examples of genetic diseases that follow the dominant-recessive pattern include sickle-cell anaemia, beta-thalassemia, cystic fibrosis, and severe combined immunodeficiency disease.

A significant number of human traits, such as eye colour, skin colour, height, weight, and muscle strength are typically regulated by more than one allele in a pattern known as polygenic inheritance. Several thousand alleles, for example, may combine to determine a person's potential for pole-vaulting, and several hundred may play a role in establishing a person's normal weight. Certain diseases may result from mutations in one or more alleles involved in polygenic inheritance. Researchers have identified nearly a dozen mutated alleles that are associated with diabetes mellitus, and a similar number are linked to asthma. Heart disease may be linked to two or three times that number. Some types of cancer may be correlated with more than 100 different genes. Polygenic inheritance is quite complex, and the ways in which multiple genes interact to produce traits are not fully understood.

X-Y linked, or sex-linked, inheritance results from the size differences between the X and Y chromosomes. The longer X chromosome carries an estimated 250 genes, which are responsible for critical biochemical functions such as normal blood clotting. The shorter Y chromosome carries 6 genes, which are responsible for other traits, such as producing significant amounts of testosterone, the male sex hormone.

X-Y linked conditions typically occur in a male when the single X chromosome carries a mutated allele, one that prevents normal blood clotting, for example. A male does not have a second X chromosome with a normal allele to override the mutation. As a result, the male in this case will have hemophilia, a disease in which blood does not clot normally. If one of the female's X chromosomes carries the mutated allele, however, her second X chromosome is usually normal. The normal allele is the dominant allele, so the female does not have hemophilia. Thus, females are typically carriers of X-Y linked diseases but do not develop them unless they receive a mutated allele from each parent, an unusual event. Among the genetic disorders typically carried by females but inherited by males are hemophilia, colour blindness, and Duchenne's muscular dystrophy.

In most organisms, the chromosomes located in the cell nucleus contain the vast majority of the DNA. But another structure in the cell, called a mitochondrion, also holds a chromosome. The DNA on this chromosome is referred to as mitochondrial DNA. While both sperm and egg contain mitochondria, only the egg's mitochondria are transmitted to the offspring. The sperm's mitochondria are contained in the sperm's tail, which never penetrates the egg.

Mutations in mitochondrial DNA have been implicated in a number of genetic diseases. These diseases include diabetes mellitus, deafness, heart disease, Alzheimer's disease, Parkinson disease, and Leber's hereditary optic neuropathy, a condition of complete or partial blindness resulting from degeneration of the optic nerve. Mitochondrial medicine is a relatively new specialty that seeks to explain the disorders and the patterns of inheritance associated with mitochondrial DNA.

Since mitochondrial DNA is inherited only from the mother—a type of inheritance known as maternal inheritance—scientists can trace these genes from one generation to the next, a simpler task than tracing genes that might come from either the mother or the father. The study of mitochondrial DNA has been employed to study human evolution. Recently scientists extracted mitochondrial DNA from Neanderthal bones believed to be between 30,000 and 100,000 years old. They compared these ancient genes with those of hundreds of people around the world. As a result, they determined that Neanderthal is a different species than humans and not their ancestors, as was formerly believed.

Alleles differ in the degree to which they determine traits. If a person inherits the alleles for Type A blood, for example, they have Type A blood from birth to death. Traits associated with some alleles, however, show up only under certain circumstances. For example, a specific allele might place a person at risk for developing diabetes mellitus, but only if they suffer a particular viral infection. Alleles that influence depression may make an individual more likely to become depressed, but only if they encounter life experiences that enhance the allele's effects. Researchers increasingly find evidence that many alleles are associated only with a tendency toward particular traits. The expression of these alleles can vary during a person's lifetime. Some alleles appear to be involved in an interplay with the environment: triggers such as toxins, light, certain nutrients, or stress may "turn on" an allele, resulting in expression of the trait.

Psychologists and biologists have long debated whether interaction with the environment—a person's family and culture, for instance—is more important than genes in shaping disease, character, and behaviour. It is becoming more obvious that environment and genes have different degrees of influence, depending on the trait. Some traits such as eye colour appear to depend on only a genetic component with little or no environmental input. However, others such as muscle strength or musical achievement seem to require contributions from both genes and the environment. If a person is born with the alleles for great athletic or musical potential, for example, those talents will not develop without practice. A child may be born with the alleles for potentially high academic intelligence, but lack of stimulation and limited exposure to new experiences in early childhood may keep the child from realizing that potential. Lack of nutrition during childhood can turn a person with the potential to be six feet tall into someone who barely clears five feet. Current research indicates that expression of alleles in certain individuals may also depend on their unique internal environment—their nervous system, hormone balance, or other aspects of their biochemistry.

Gregor Mendel developed the principles of heredity by studying the variation and heredity of seven pairs of inherited characteristics in pea plants. Although the significance of his work was not recognized during his lifetime, it became the basis for the present day field of genetics.

Current knowledge of heredity is the result of more than 2000 years of contemplation of how inheritance works. The ancient Babylonians knew that pollen from a male date palm tree must be applied to the carpels of a female flower to obtain fruit, but they did not know about the reproductive cells in humans. The Greek scientist and philosopher Aristotle believed that inheritance was passed through the blood. This concept was embraced for centuries and persists today in such terminology as bloodlines, half bloods, and blue bloods.

The past few centuries have witnessed tremendous advances in understanding the role of reproductive cells in heredity. In 1651 the British scientist William Harvey proposed the idea, based on his experiments with embryos of different organisms, that all animals develop from eggs. In 1677 a different view was advocated by the Dutch naturalist Anton van Leeuwenhoek, who was the first to observe human sperm under the microscope. Leeuwenhoek believed that sperm contained a child in miniature, which grew larger inside the female's body. Two centuries of experiment and debate followed. Then in 1879, with the use of improved microscopes, German zoologists Herman Fol and Oscar Hertwig observed the union of egg and sperm in animals. This observation crystallized our understanding of the roles of male and female sex cells in reproduction.

Exactly how traits are transmitted to offspring from the sperm and egg was a topic of vigorous discussion in the 19th century. In 1866, the Austrian monk Gregor Mendel published his groundbreaking studies on inheritance in peas. At the time of his work, chromosomes, genes, and DNA were unknown. Even so, Mendel discovered a variety of genetic rules, including the concept of dominant and recessive genes. Mendel hypothesized that plants contain two factors for each plant trait, such as height, seed shape, and flower colour, and that each plant received one factor from each parent. His work anticipated the discoveries that chromosomes are the factors that transmit heredity and that parents contribute one of each member of a pair of chromosomes to their offspring.

Known as the father of modern genetics, Gregor Mendel developed the principles of heredity by studying the variation and heredity of seven pairs of inherited characteristics in pea plants. Although the significance of his work was not recognized during his lifetime, it became the basis for the present day field of genetics.

Gregor Mendel (1822-1884), an Austrian monk, whose experimental work became the basis of modern hereditary theory.

Mendel was born on July 22, 1822, to a peasant family in Heinzendorf (now Hyn_ice, Czech Republic). He entered the Augustinian monastery at Brünn (now Brno, Czech Republic), which was known as a centre of learning and scientific endeavour. He later became a substitute teacher at the technical school in Brünn. There Mendel became actively engaged in investigating variation, heredity, and evolution in plants at the monastery's experimental garden. Between 1856 and 1863 he cultivated and tested at least 28,000 pea plants, carefully analyzing seven pairs of seed and plant characteristics. His tedious experiments resulted in the enunciation of two generalizations that later became known as the laws of heredity. His observations also led him to coin two terms still used in present-day genetics: dominance, for a trait that shows up in an offspring, and recessiveness, for a trait masked by a dominant gene.

Mendel's Laws, principles of hereditary transmission of physical characteristics. They were formulated in 1865 by the Augustinian monk Gregor Johann Mendel. Experimenting with seven contrasting characteristics of pure-breeding garden peas, Mendel discovered that by crossing tall and dwarf parents, for example, he got hybrid offspring that resembled the tall parent rather than being a medium-height blend. To explain this he conceived of hereditary units, now called genes, which often expressed dominant or recessive characteristics. Formulating his first principle (the law of segregation), Mendel stated that genes normally occur in pairs in the ordinary body cells, but segregate in the formation of sex cells (eggs or sperm), each member of the pair becoming part of the separate sex cell. When egg and sperm unite, forming a gene pair, the dominant gene (tallness) masks the recessive gene (shortness?).

To corroborate the existence of such hereditary units, Mendel went on to interbreed the first generation of hybrid tall peas and found that the second generation turned out in a ratio of three tall to each short offspring. He then correctly conceived that the genes paired into AA, Aa, and aa ("A" representing dominant and "a" representing recessive). Continuing the breeding experiments, he found that the self-pollinated AA bred true to produce pure tall plants, that the aa plant produced pure dwarf plants, and that the Aa, or hybrid, tall plants produced the same three-to-one ratio of offspring. From this Mendel could see that hereditary units did not blend, as his predecessors believed, but remained unchanged from one generation to another. He thus formulated his second principle (the law of an independent assortment), in which the expression of a gene for any single characteristic is usually not influenced by the expression of another characteristic. Mendel's laws became the theoretical basis for modern genetics and heredity.

Mendel published his important work on heredity in 1866. Despite, or perhaps because of, its descriptions of large numbers of experimental plants, which allowed him to express his results numerically and subject them to statistical analysis, this work made virtually no impression for the next 34 years. Only in 1900 was his work recognized more or less independently by three investigators, one of whom was the Dutch botanist Hugo Marie de Vries, and not until the late 1920s and the early '30s was its full significance realized, particularly in relation to evolutionary theory. As a result of years of research in population genetics, investigators were able to demonstrate that Darwinian evolution can be described in terms of the change in gene frequency of Mendelian pairs of characteristics in a population over successive generations.

Mendel's later experiments with the hawkweed Hieracium proved inconclusive, and because of the pressure of other duties he ceased his experiments on heredity by the 1870s. He died in Brünn on January 6, 1884.

Mendel's work was initially ignored, however, while other theories of heredity were advanced. French naturalist Jean-Baptiste Lamarck proposed that characteristics acquired during an individual's lifetime are passed to offspring. This idea was embraced by many 19th-century scientists, including the British naturalist Charles Darwin. Darwin and others believed that particles in the body, called gemmules, reside in the limbs and organs. The gemmules become imprinted with any changes acquired by the body, such as development of a strong heart through exercise. The gemmules then move to the reproductive cells and transfer information about the body's alterations to these cells. The reproductive cells transmit the acquired traits to the offspring through particles called pangenes. Darwin's theory of heredity, known as pangenesis, attempted to account for both the process of heredity and the variety of traits seen among offspring.

The deoxyribonucleic acid (DNA) molecule is the genetic blueprint for each cell and ultimately the blueprint that determines every characteristic of a living organism. In 1953 American biochemist James Watson, left, and British biophysicist Francis Crick, right, described the structure of the DNA molecule as a double helix, somewhat like a spiral staircase with many individual steps. Their work was aided by X-ray diffraction pictures of the DNA molecule taken by British biophysicist Maurice Wilkins and British physical chemist Rosalind Franklin. In 1962 Crick, Watson, and Wilkins received the Nobel Prize for their pioneering work on the structure of the DNA molecule.

In 1889 the German biologist August Weismann published his opposition to this view. His experiments with reproduction in jellyfish and similar animals led him to believe that variations in offspring results from the union of a substance from the parents. He referred to this substance as germ plasm. Other scientists observed the movement of chromosomes in cell division and suggested that chromosomes transmit the hereditary information from parent to offspring. About the same time, Aristotle's belief that blood transmitted inheritance was disproved by the British scientist Francis Galton. To do this, Galton transfused blood from black rabbits into white rabbits. If traits were indeed transmitted through blood, those white rabbits should have produced black offspring, but their offspring were, in fact, white.

In 1900 several biologists independently theorized that the union of sperm and egg, which resulted in a combination of the male and female chromosomes, corresponds to Mendel's description of inheritance through factors. With the rediscovery of Mendel's principles, genetics studies accelerated. In the early decades of the 19th century, the work of the American geneticist Thomas Hunt Morgan spearheaded these investigations. Working with fruit flies, Morgan's proof that Mendel's factors or genes (shortened from the word pangenes), are transmitted from parent to offspring through the action of chromosomes. Morgan also found that genes for many traits are arranged in a linear fashion on each chromosome. He created the first chromosome maps, which laid the groundwork for modern genetics.

During the first few decades of the 20th century, researchers established that chromosomes are composed of DNA and protein. At that time, it was widely held that proteins contained the genetic information. In 1928, however, the British scientist Frederick Griffith carried out experiments that ruled out proteins as the genetic material. In 1944, the American geneticist Oswald T. Avery and his colleagues clearly demonstrated that DNA carried the genetic information in bacteria. Avery's work was not generally accepted until 1952, when American scientists Alfred Hershey and Martha Chase showed that the hereditary material of the T2 virus, a virus that infects bacteria, is also DNA. The work of Avery, Hershey, and Chase led scientists to the understanding that DNA is the heredity molecule for all organisms. Related experiments were carried out in the early 1940s by the American biologist George Beadle and the American geneticist Edward Tatum. Their investigations with the fungus Neurospora demonstrated that mutations in genes result in defective enzymes, the specialized proteins that speed up biochemical reactions. Thus, the link between genes and proteins was established.

United States biochemist Marshall Nirenberg won the 1968 Nobel Prize in physiology or medicine. His independent investigation into the genetic code revealed how different combinations of bases within amino acids instruct cells to build protein.

While many researchers accepted the role of DNA in inheritance, they did not understand how it could transmit genetic information from one generation to the next. In 1953, American biochemist James Watson and British biophysicist Francis Crick proposed the now-famous double-helix model of DNA. They offered compelling evidence that DNA consists of two parallel strands twisted like a spiral staircase. The "banisters" of this staircase are formed from sugar and phosphate molecules. Other molecules, called bases, form the "stairs." Watson and Crick demonstrated that one "stair" consists of a base pair, which is either an adenine bonded to thymine or cytosine bonded to guanine. Hundreds of thousands of these paired bases run the length of a DNA molecule. The Watson-Crick model suggested that during cell division, the bond between the base pairs is broken, causing the strands of the double helix to separate. Each of the two strands serves as a template to construct a second strand of DNA, and two new DNA molecules are formed. The two DNA molecules are exactly the same and one goes to each new cell, resulting in cells with the same hereditary information. The dramatic discovery of DNA architecture stimulated a quest to uncover its precise role in determining heredity.

Drawing on the work of Beadle and Tatum, and using the Watson-Crick model of DNA, scientists determined that DNA must be a code that directs the construction of proteins. Proteins are built of small molecules called amino acids, which link together to form the protein. The amino acids must be lined up in a particular order, like letters in a correctly spelled word, for the protein to form correctly. Scientists inferred that DNA instructs the cell to link amino acids in the proper order. They further determined that a unique sequence of three bases on DNA, a triplet, is a code for one amino acid, and that unique triplets code for each of the twenty amino acids. In 1961 American biochemist Marshall W. Nirenberg and his colleagues began to unravel the code. Using an artificial mixture of amino acids and ribonucleic acid (RNA), a molecule similar to DNA, they showed that the base adenine repeated three times in a row is the code for the amino acid phenylalanine.

By 1967 scientists had translated the genetic code for all twenty amino acids. They had also confirmed that one gene, a section of DNA, is a code for one protein or part of a protein. Within 15 years, researchers had developed the capability of inserting genes from one organism into another, a breakthrough that ushered in the field of biotechnology. In the not-too-distant future, scientists may perfect the technology for inserting or removing genes from an egg, sperm, or embryo. This development may drastically alter the traditional principles of heredity, opening the door to a new array of rules governing the transmission of traits from parent to offspring.

Gene, representing the basic unit of heredity found in the cells of all living organisms, from bacteria to humans. Genes determine the physical characteristics that an organism inherits, such as the shape of a tree's leaf, the markings on a cat's fur, and the colour of a human hair.

Genes are composed of segments of deoxyribonucleic acid (DNA), a molecule that forms the long, threadlike structures called chromosomes. The information encoded within the DNA structure of a gene directs the manufacture of proteins, molecular workhorses that carry out all life-supporting activities within a cell.

Chromosomes within a cell occur in matched pairs. Each chromosome contains many genes, and each gene is located at a particular site on the chromosome, known as the locus. Like chromosomes, genes typically occur in pairs. A gene found on one chromosome in a pair usually has the same locus as another gene in the other chromosome of the pair, and these two genes are called alleles. Alleles are alternate forms of the same gene. For example, a pea plant has one gene that determines height, but that gene appears in more than one form—the gene that produces a short plant is an allele of the gene that produces a tall plant.

The behaviour of alleles and how they influence inherited traits follow predictable patterns. Austrian monk Gregor Mendel first identified these patterns in the 1860s

In organisms that use sexual reproduction, offspring inherit one-half of their genes from each parent and then mix the two sets of genes together. This produces new combinations of genes, so that each individual is unique but still possesses the same genes as its parents. As a result, sexual reproduction ensures that the basic characteristics of a particular species remain largely the same for generations. However, mutations, or alterations in DNA, occur constantly. They create variations in the genes that are inherited. Some mutations may be neutral, or silent, and do not affect the function of a protein. Occasionally a mutation may benefit or harm an organism and over the course of evolutionary time, these mutations serve the crucial role of providing organisms with previously nonexistent proteins. In this way, mutations are a driving force behind genetic diversity and the rise of new or more competitive species that are better able to adapt to changes, such as climate variations, depletion of food sources, or the emergence of new types of disease.

Geneticists are scientists who study the function and behaviour of genes. Since the 1970s geneticists have devised techniques, cumulatively known as genetic engineering, to alter or manipulate the DNA structure within genes. These techniques enable scientists to introduce one or more genes from one organism into a second organism. The second organism incorporates the new DNA into its own genetic material, thereby altering its own genetic characteristics by changing the types of proteins it can produce. In humans these techniques form the basis of gene therapy, a group of experimental procedures in which scientists try to substitute one or more healthy genes for defective ones in order to eliminate symptoms of disease.

Genetic engineering techniques have also enabled scientists to determine the chromosomal location and DNA structure of all the genes found within a variety of organisms. In April 2003 the Human Genome Project, a publicly funded consortium of academic scientists from around the world, identified the chromosomal locations and structure of the estimated 20,000 to 25,000 genes found within human cells. The genetic makeup of other organisms has also been identified, including that of the bacterium Escherichia coli, the yeast Saccharomyces cerevisiae, the roundworm Caenorhabditis elegans, and the fruit fly Drosophila melanogaster. Scientists hope to use this genetic information to develop lifesaving drugs for a variety of diseases, to improve agricultural crop yields, and to learn more about plant and animal physiology and evolutionary history.

Plasmid, small, usually ring-shaped molecule of deoxyribonucleic acid (DNA), which is the hereditary material in all living cells. Plasmids are present in almost all bacteria and may also be found in some yeasts and other fungi, protozoa, and even some plants and animals. They are separate from chromosomes, the primary structures that contain DNA in cells. Plasmids are important tools used in genetic engineering—the deliberate manipulation of an organism's genetic material—and they are also key to scientists' understanding of how bacteria cause human disease.

Plasmids carry hereditary information in the form of genes, the basic units of inheritance. Plasmids generally carry fewer genes than do chromosomes, and the genes that they carry are useful, but not essential, to the survival of the cell. For example, some Plasmids help bacteria make use of unusual food sources, such as camphor or petroleum. Fertility Plasmids carry genes that a bacterial cell must have in order to transfer DNA to another bacterium. Resistance Plasmids enable bacteria to degrade or inactivate antibiotics used to halt bacterial growth, or to survive in the presence of heavy metals by converting the metals into less toxic forms. Other Plasmids enable bacteria to produce chemicals that are toxic to other organisms, including insects, humans, and other bacteria.

Bacterium cells typically are surrounded by a rigid, protective cell wall. The cell membrane, also called the plasma membrane, regulates passage of materials into and out of the cytoplasm, the semifluids that fill the cell. The DNA, located in the nucleoid region, contains the genetic information for the cell. Ribosomes carry out protein synthesis. Many bacteria contain a pilus (plural pili), a structure that extends out of the cell to transfer DNA to another bacterium. The flagellum, found in numerous species, is used for the locomotion. Some bacteria contain a plasmid, a small loop of DNA with extra genes. Others have a capsule, a sticky substance external to the cell wall that protects bacteria from attack by white blood cells. Mesosomes were formerly thought to structures with unknown functions, but now are known to be artifacts created when cells are prepared for viewing with electron microscopes.

Most bacteria have only one chromosome under normal circumstances, but may contain 1 to 100 or more copies of a given plasmid. Plasmids replicate independently of cell division, and when a cell containing Plasmids divides, the Plasmids distribute randomly among the two resulting daughters' cells. In this way, each daughter cell receives approximately—but not always exactly—the same number of Plasmids.

Genetic engineering enables scientists to produce clones of cells or organisms that contain the same genes. (1) Scientists use restriction enzymes to isolate a segment of deoxyribonucleic acid (DNA) that contains a gene of interest—for example, the gene regulating insulin production. (2) A plasmid removed from a bacterium and treated with the same restriction enzyme binds with the DNA fragment to form hybrid plasma. (3) The hybrid Plasmid is reinserted back into the bacterium, in which it replicates as part of the cell's DNA. (4) A large number of identical daughter cells (clones) can be cultured and their gene products extracted for human use.

Plasmids are important tools that are used in genetic engineering. The structure of DNA is the same in all living cells, so DNA from almost any organism can be combined with plasmid DNA. Plasmids thus serve as convenient vehicles for transferring genes from one organism to another.

In 1977 scientists successfully manipulated bacteria to produce a human protein. That same year American molecular biologist Walter Gilbert found a way to accelerate dramatically the labourious task of sequencing the chemicals that make up a strand of genetic material. He shared the 1980 Nobel Prize in chemistry for this achievement. In a 1980 Scientific American article, Gilbert and American molecular biologist Lydia Villa-Komaroff describe basic biotechnology techniques and their laboratory's success in producing rat insulin with genetically engineered bacteria. Human insulin was first produced in the lab using recombinant (genetically engineered) bacteria in 1978, and five years later recombinant human insulin, used to treat diabetes mellitus, became the first biopharmaceutical on the market.

Using enzymes known as restriction endonucleases and DNA ligase, which act, respectively, like molecular scissors and glue, scientists cut and paste pieces of DNA from different sources together to create molecules known as recombinant DNA. A recombinant plasmid made by such techniques can then be introduced into a bacterial cell to produce bacteria with useful characteristics.

The ability to combine human and bacterial DNA has given rise to a number of medical advances. The first commercial use of a recombinant plasmid came in 1982, when scientists created a genetically engineered bacterium able to produce human insulin. Insulin is a hormone that helps regulate blood sugar and is needed by many people with diabetes. To create the insulin-producing bacterium, scientists inserted the gene that directs the production of human insulin into a plasmid, and then introduced the plasmid into bacterial cells. As the bacteria grew and multiplied in the laboratory, they produced large quantities of human insulin that could be collected and packaged for use by diabetics. Previously, insulin for diabetics had been harvested from slaughtered cattle. Insulin produced by recombinant bacteria is cheaper and of better quality than insulin from cattle. In addition, it is virtually identical to the hormone produced in the human body and does not cause allergic reactions.

Other useful medical substances now manufactured with the aid of recombinant Plasmids include a human grown hormone, an immune system protein known as interferon, blood-clotting proteins, and proteins that are used in making vaccines. Not all applications of recombinant Plasmids are medical. Scientists have produced bacteria that can remove mercury and other harmful chemicals from the soil or water in a process known as bioremediation. Other bacteria that contain recombinant Plasmids make insecticides that may be safer than traditional synthetic insecticides.

Bacterial Plasmids are also used to transfer foreign genes to plants. Genetic engineering of plants often involves a plasmid known as a tumour inducing, or Ti, plasmid found in Agrobacterium tumefaciens, the bacterium that causes crown gall disease in plants. Typically, when Agrobacterium tumefaciens bacteria enter a plant through a wound, they transfer the Ti plasmid into nearby plant cells. The presence of this plasmid drastically changes the growth of the plant cells, resulting in the formation of a large tumour on the plant. Scientists manipulate this natural process by removing the Ti Plasmids from Agrobacterium tumefaciens cells to replace the plasmids' tumour-causing genes with genes that code for desirable characteristics. These recombinant Plasmids are then introduced into plant cells to produce, for example, crop plants that are resistant to certain diseases, insect pests, or herbicides. These techniques may someday be used to improve the nutritional value of food plants.

Overuse of antibiotics in recent years has enabled the development of strains of bacteria that are resistant to antibiotics. Resistance Plasmids, which may be transferred from bacterium to bacterium, are responsible for antibiotic resistance. This scanning electron micrograph shows disease-causing Streptococcus bacteria, commonly found in the human mouth, throat, respiratory tract, bloodstream, and wounds.

Plasmids also help scientists understand how bacteria cause human disease. Some bacteria carry Plasmids known as virulence Plasmids that make them harmful to humans. Without a virulence plasmid, these bacteria are harmless, but when they carry such a plasmid they can cause disease. For example, the bacterium Clostridium tetani causes tetanus only if it carries a virulence plasmid containing the gene for the tetanus toxin. Certain strains of Staphylococcus aureus cause food poisoning and certain strains of Escherichia coli cause diarrhea only because they contain virulence Plasmids.

Resistance Plasmids are currently a topic of intense research because of the growing problem with disease-causing bacteria that are resistant to penicillin and other commonly used antibiotics. Scientists have learned that bacteria can readily transfer resistance Plasmids to other bacteria. When a bacterial cell acquires two different antibiotic resistance Plasmids, the antibiotic resistance genes carried on the two Plasmids are sometimes assembled onto a single plasmid. This new plasmid may then be transferred to other bacteria, where it may acquire additional antibiotic resistance genes. This process may be repeated several times, giving rise to a plasmid that will make bacteria resistant to a number of different antibiotics. Infections caused by such bacteria are extremely difficult to treat.

Inappropriate use of antibiotics contributes to the spread of antibiotic resistant bacteria. When physicians prescribe drugs unnecessarily or when patients fail to take the full course of antibiotics prescribed because they are feeling better, resistant bacterial strains are more likely to survive. Scientists are studying how resistance Plasmids are maintained and transferred in populations of bacteria in hope of learning how to stop the spread of antibiotic resistance.

Chromosomal disorders are caused by the presence of an extra or missing whole or partial chromosome. In some cases, whole chromosomes or pieces of chromosomes are attached to one another in abnormal ways, which cause a person or their offspring to have an incorrect amount of chromosomal material. Chromosomal disorders are sometimes caused by an error in a type of cell division called meiosis, which occurs during the formation of eggs and sperm. Chromosomal disorders disrupt the biological functions of many genes. They produce multiple problems in the affected individual, often including mild or severe mental retardation. More than 600 chromosomal syndromes have been identified.

Down syndrome is the most common chromosomal disorder, affecting about 1 in 800 newborns. People with Down syndrome characteristically have three copies of the autosomal chromosome known as number 21 instead of the normal pair of number 21 chromosomes. For this reason, Down syndrome is commonly called trisomy 21. People with Down syndrome usually have mild to severe learning disabilities and physical symptoms that include a small skull, an extra folds of skin at the inner corner of each eye, and a flattened bridge of the nose. They also may have heart defects and other serious health problems.

Some chromosomal disorders involve the sex chromosomes. In many instances, an extra or missing sex chromosome is less life threatening than an extra or missing autosome. A person with Klinefelter syndrome, which affects about 1 in 500 males, has two X chromosomes and one Y chromosome. Males with Klinefelter syndrome are typically tall, and they may have small testes and slight breast development. They also may have minor problems with learning and are usually infertile.

Another chromosomal disorder that affects the sex chromosomes is Turner syndrome, which affects 1 in 2,500 females. In this disorder, a female has one functioning X chromosome instead of two. Females with this condition are typically short, with a thick, webbed neck. They may have mild problems with learning, and they usually are infertile because they lack normal ovaries.

Multifactorial disorders are caused by several genes as well as the influence of a person's environment, such as diet or lifestyle. An example of a multifactorial disorder is a category of birth defects called neural tube defects. In a neural tube defect, a fetus's neural tube—the structure that develops into the spinal cord and brain—is damaged. The two most common types of neural tube defects are anencephaly and spina bifida. Anencephaly is a fatal condition in which a baby is born with only a partial brain or no brain at all. About 1,000 to 2,000 babies with anencephaly are born each year in the United States. Spina bifida results when a neural tube defect causes an opening in the spine. In the United States, about one infant in every 2,000 live births is born with spina bifida. These infants need surgery to close the opening in the spine, and they may develop problems with walking or with bowel or bladder control. Geneticists believe that certain genes may play a role in damage to the neural tube, but the mother's diet during pregnancy also plays a role. A woman's risk of giving birth to an infant with a neural tube defect significantly decreases if she consumes adequate amounts of folic acid, a vitamin in the B complex, during the first three months of pregnancy and one month before conception.

Some common diseases that run in families but do not display an obvious pattern of inheritance are also thought to be multifactorial. Two examples are coronary heart disease and diabetes mellitus. In both cases, genes may cause a person to be predisposed to develop the disease, but lifestyle choices can help to prevent the disease from developing or from worsening after it occurs.

Thousands of inherited diseases caused by altered genes and chromosomal abnormalities effect humans. These disorders cause problems such as physical deformities, metabolic dysfunction, and developmental problems. Medical surveys indicate that roughly

1 percent of newborns in the United States have a single-gene defect. As many as 1 baby in 200 is born with a chromosomal abnormality serious enough to produce physical defects or mental retardation.

Genetic causes include single-gene defects such as Fragile X syndrome and chromosomal disorders such as Down syndrome. Scientists in 1992 identified Fragile X syndrome as the most common inherited cause of mental retardation, responsible for up to 10 percent of cases. People with this condition inherit a defective gene that results in a weak spot on the X chromosome, a sex chromosome. The weak part of the chromosome is susceptible to breaking. Fragile X syndrome is more likely to cause retardation in males then females.

Chromosomal disorders, which occur in about 7 out of every 1000 infants, involve an abnormal number of chromosomes or changes in the structure of a chromosome. Down syndrome occurs when people inherit all or part of an extra copy of a pair of chromosomes known together as chromosome 21. Although regarded as genetic disorders, chromosomal disorders are not necessarily inherited. Both parents may have normal genes, with the defect resulting from a random error when chromosomes reproduce.

Other genetic causes of mental retardation are inborn errors of a metabolism. They involve inheritance of a defective gene unable to produce enzymes or proteins needed for critical cell functions. Scientists have identified more than 300 gene disorders involving inborn errors of a metabolism. Many can result in mental retardation, including phenylketonuria (PKU), Tay-Sachs disease, galactosemia, homocystinuria, maple syrup urine disease, and biotinidase deficiency.

Another common cause of mental retardation, congenital hypothyroidism, occurs in about 1 in every 4000 births. Infants with this disorder are unable to produce enough thyroxine, a hormone secreted by the thyroid gland. Mental retardation and stunted growth results unless they receive thyroid replacement therapy.

A number of other disorders may include characteristics of autism. In fragile X syndrome, which results from a defective X chromosome, people may show poor eye contact, limited speech, hand flapping, and hyperactivity. People with Asperger's disorder may show some symptoms of autism such as difficulties in social interactions, poor eye contact, repetitive body movements, and an insistence on routines and rituals. However, they have normal language development and do not have mental retardation. Rett's disorder involves repetitive hand movements, social withdrawal, and impaired language development. The disorder appears before the age of four and affects only girls. Some experts regard these disorders as mild forms of autism rather than as separate disorders.

One of the most common fatal genetic disorders in the United States, cystic fibrosis occurs in about one in every 3,900 babies. About 1,000 new cases are diagnosed each year, usually before a child reaches three years of age. Approximately 30,000 American children and young adults have cystic fibrosis. The disease affects white people more often than black people: One in every 3,300 white babies is born with cystic fibrosis, but only one in every 15,300 black babies is born with the disease.

Cystic fibrosis is caused by a defect in the gene responsible for manufacturing cystic fibrosis transmembrane conductance regulators (CFTR), a protein that controls the flow of chloride ions into and out of certain cells. In healthy people, CFTR forms a channel in the plasma membrane through which chloride ions enter and leave the cells lining the lungs, pancreas, sweat glands and the small intestine. In people with cystic fibrosis, malfunctioning (or absent) CFTR prevents chloride from entering or leaving cells, resulting in production of a thick, sticky mucus that clogs ducts or tubes in these organs. In the lungs, this mucus blocks airways and impedes natural infection-fighting mechanisms, eventually turning the body's immune system against its own lung tissue. A similar blockage prevents crucial digestive enzymes produced in the pancreas from reaching the intestines, impairing the ability to break down certain foods. In healthy people most of the chloride in sweat is reabsorbed, but in people with cystic fibrosis, sweat glands cannot take up chloride ions, enabling excessive amounts of salt to escape in the sweat.

Cystic fibrosis is an autosomal recessive genetic disorder. This means that to have the disease, a child must inherit two copies of the defective gene, one from each parent. Many people carry a single cystic fibrosis gene, although they do not experience any significant health problems as a result; in the general population, approximately 1 in 31 Americans carries the gene. The disease can only occur in babies with two carrier parents. When both parents are carriers, they have a 25 percent chance with every pregnancy of passing two copies of the defective gene to their child. Prospective parents may elect to undergo genetic testing to determine if one or both of them carry the defective gene.

Researchers identified the gene responsible for cystic fibrosis in 1989. Since that time more than 200 different defects in the cystic fibrosis gene have been described, many of which produce cystic fibrosis in varying degrees of severity. Researchers have also learned of two different gene defects. One from each parent can combine to produce varying effects.

Depending on the disease's severity, symptoms may be apparent soon after birth, or they may intestinal blockages detection for months or years. In nearly 20 percent of all cases, the first symptom is meconium ileus, intestinal blockages in newborns. In other babies, the first evidence of cystic fibrosis is bulky stool, poor weight gain, flabby muscle tone, or slow growth, all products of low levels of digestive enzymes in the intestines. About half of all children with cystic fibrosis first see the doctor for coughing, wheezing, or respiratory tract infections. Teenagers with cystic fibrosis may grow and mature slowly and enter puberty later than their peers. Cystic fibrosis often causes impaired reproductive function. About 98 percent of adult men who have cystic fibrosis produce little or no sperm, and females have decreased fertility and are more likely to experience complications during pregnancy and childbirth. Cystic fibrosis patients of all ages are prone to dehydration because they lose so much salt in their sweat. Infections, particularly in the lungs, plague people with cystic fibrosis throughout their lives. These chronic infections destroy lung tissue, a complication that ultimately takes the lives of most people with cystic fibrosis.

The earlier a diagnosis is made the better so that early treatment can slow the progression of lung damage caused by infection. Prenatal tests are available to determine if a baby will be born with cystic fibrosis. In newborns, blood tests indicating high levels of digestive enzymes suggest cystic fibrosis, but a certain diagnosis requires a sweat test to determine the amount of salt in the sweat. Sweat tests provide a valid diagnosis in babies over 24 hours old, and this test is also used to confirm diagnosis in older children and adults.

Cystic fibrosis remains incurable; existing treatments aim to relieve discomfort and delay the devastating and inevitable effects of the disease. Meconium ileus, the intestinal obstruction occurring in newborns, may require surgery. Patients with pancreatic blockages must take pancreatic enzymes with meals. Even with such enzymes, people with cystic fibrosis must consume adequate amounts of protein, vitamins, and higher-than-normal amounts of fat to ensure growth. Those with respiratory infections are treated with antibiotics, often in aerosol form. When inhaled, these medicated vapours fight infection and relieve constriction of the airways. Using a procedure called chest physical therapy or postural drainage, caregivers of people with cystic fibrosis repeatedly and vigorously pound on the patient's back and chest to dislodge mucus obstructing the airways. Increasingly, cystic fibrosis patients with severe irreparable lung damage turn to lung transplantation surgery. Although complications with transplantation surgery may pose problems for some patients, lung or combination heart and lung transplants provide nearly 80 percent of cystic fibrosis patients with severe lung damage an entirely new lease on life.

Although no cure has yet been found, cystic fibrosis presents one of the most promising areas of research in modern medicine. Scientists are investigating the use of gene therapy to introduce healthy copies of the CFTR gene into the cells of patients with cystic fibrosis. Scientists hope that once inside the cells, healthy copies of the gene will manufacture functional CFTR protein, permitting the flow of chloride into and out of cells in affected organs and restoring healthy function. Just one of many new treatment strategies under investigation, such research provides the cystic fibrosis community—scientists, patients, and families—with hope that more-effective treatments and possibly a cure may soon be discovered.

Down syndrome occurs in about 1 out of every 800 births worldwide. In the United States each year, about 1,600 babies are born with this condition. Down syndrome results when a person inherits all or part of an extra copy of chromosome 21. This can occur in a variety of ways, the causes of which are unknown. The most common chromosomal abnormality that produces Down syndrome (accounting for about 95 percent of all cases) is Trisomy 21, a defect in which an extra, third copy of chromosome 21 is present in every cell in the body. The risk of Trisomy 21 is directly related to the age of the mother. The number of Down syndrome births is relatively low for 18-year-old mothers—about 1 in 2,100 births. In the later childbearing years the risk increases significantly—from 1 in 1,000 births for 30-year-old women to 1 in 100 births for 40-year-old women.

Two other chromosomal abnormalities cause Down syndrome and occur in about 2 to 3 percent of all cases. The first, translocation, takes place when a child inherits a small, extra pieces of the 21st chromosome that is attached to another chromosome. If, in addition to the translocation, two normal 21st chromosomes are also present, the person will have some of the features of Down syndrome. If there is only one normal 21st chromosome, the person will not display symptoms but the children may inherit Down syndrome. Mosaic Down syndrome results from a second type of chromosomal abnormality in which only some cells in the body have an extra chromosome.

There is no cure for Down syndrome. However, prenatal tests are available to identify fetuses with the disorder. The American College of Obstetricians and Gynecologists recommends that the so-called triple-screen blood test be offered to all pregnant women. This test measures the levels of three chemicals in the blood of the pregnant woman to indicate the baby's risk of Down syndrome. If the risk is high, amniocentesis, a procedure for removing a sample of the amniotic fluid surrounding the fetus, is administered to confirm the findings from the blood tests. Fetal cells are present in the amniotic fluid and can be checked for the presence of the chromosomal disorder.

People with Down syndrome are subject to a variety of medical conditions. Heart abnormalities that may require surgery are present in about half of all Down syndrome cases. Thyroid problems (underproduction or overproduction of thyroid hormones) affect 10 to 20 percent of people with Down syndrome, but these problems respond well to treatment. The risk of acute leukemia is somewhat increased, although treatment is successful in the majority of cases.

There have been dramatic increases in the survival rates of people with Down syndrome since the 1970s. As the risks of medical problems specific to Down syndrome have become known, doctors are now able to recognize those problems earlier, and develop more effective treatments. Today, 44 percent of people with Down syndrome survive to age 60, and this life expectancy is slowly approaching that of people without Down syndrome.

Although people with Down syndrome have a range of learning disabilities, physicians, educators, and parents now recognize that these people's achievements may be most influenced by what is expected of them. This so-called environmental expectation is perhaps the most important factor in determining the educational and vocational potential of people with Down syndrome. On the other hand, intelligence-quotient test scores, once considered an authoritative indicator of educational potential, are now seen to be of questionable value.

Educational and vocational opportunities have also advanced. In the recent past, children with Down syndrome were relegated to institutions, receiving minimal social interaction or educational opportunities. Today, children with Down syndrome usually remain with their families and are enrolled in public schools. Often they attend regular classes and learn skills such as reading and writing alongside children without Down syndrome. Adults with Down syndrome are employed in a range of fields. Some may live in supervised group homes, while others live independently.

Primary immune deficiencies caused by genetic factors have been studied extensively, and a number of genes responsible for these defects have been identified. Some genes have been found on the X chromosome, the sex chromosome inherited from the mother. These X-linked diseases include x-linked agammaglobulinemia, Wiskott-Aldrich Syndrome, and some forms of SCID.

Klinefelter's Syndrome, genetic disease affecting 1 in 850 males. It occurs when a male inherits an extra X, or female, sex chromosome that interferes with the development of male characteristics. Klinefelter's syndrome is characterized by enlarged breasts (gynecomastia), little or no facial and body hair, a small penis and testes, reduced sex drive, and the inability to produce sperm. Although a child with the condition is not developmentally disabled, he may learn to speak later than other children and have difficulty learning to read and write. The disorder was first described by American endocrinologist Harry F. Klinefelter in 1942.

Both men and women normally have 23 pairs of chromosomes. One of these pairs is the sex chromosome. A female normally inherits an X chromosome from each parent so that her chromosomal complement is XX. A male inherits an X chromosome from his mother and a Y chromosome from his father so that his chromosomal complement is XY. It is the presence of the Y chromosome that determines maleness. A male with Klinefelter's syndrome inherits an extra X chromosome, giving him an abnormal chromosomal complement of XXY. In some cases, more than one extra X chromosome is inherited. The cause of Klinefelter's syndrome is unknown, although has of occurring to a slightly more in boys born to older mothers.

In most cases, a boy with Klinefelter's syndrome has a normal physical appearance until he reaches puberty. Diagnosis of the disorder may be delayed until physical symptoms develop, or until the adult male is tested for infertility. Diagnosis of the disorder is made by performing a chromosomal analysis in which body cells are studied in the laboratory to identify any chromosomal irregularities.

There is no treatment for Klinefelter's syndrome, although regular injections of the male sex hormone testosterone may increase muscle size and strength, stimulate the growth of facial and body hair, and produce a normal sex drive in some cases. Enlarged breasts may be reduced surgically. Reversing infertility associated with Klinefelter's syndrome may not be possible. Some men with the disorder may produce a small number of sperm, and they may benefit from modern fertility techniques in which a single sperm is injected into an egg to achieve fertilization

Turner syndrome is caused, partially or completely missing sex chromosomes, chromosomes are gene-carrying structures found within the nuclei of cells. In the human body, all cells except for sperm and egg cells contain 46 chromosomes arranged in 23 pairs. Of these, 22 of the pairs each consist of chromosomes that are almost identical, while the 23rd pair contains special chromosomes that determine the sex of the individual. The sex chromosome pair in healthy males contains an X and a Y chromosome, while the sex chromosome pair in females contains two X chromosomes. In a female born with Turner syndrome, part or all of one X chromosome in her sex chromosome pair is absent. Scientists do not know what causes this chromosomal abnormality. But—it apparently occurs randomly and is not linked to factors known to increase the risk of a birth defect, such as a pregnant woman's exposure to drugs, radiation, or disease-causing viruses or bacteria.

Chromosomal disorders are caused by the presence of an extra or missing whole or partial chromosome. In some cases, whole chromosomes or pieces of chromosomes are attached to each another in abnormal ways, which cause a person or their offspring to have an incorrect amount of chromosomal material. Chromosomal disorders are sometimes caused by an error in a type of cell division called meiosis, which occurs during the formation of eggs and sperm. Chromosomal disorders disrupt the biological functions of many genes. They produce multiple problems in the affected individual, often including mild or severe mental retardation. More than 600 chromosomal syndromes have been identified.

Twenty percent, more or less, of malformed fetuses are spontaneously aborted; The rest result in a newborn with a birth defect. Although each single type of birth defect is rare, taken together they make up almost 5 percent of all live births and cause about 20 percent of infant deaths in the period immediately after birth. About one in ten developmental disorders is hereditary and arises from an abnormality in a single gene. Another 5 percent of birth defects arise from physical abnormalities in the chromosome.

Some genes that cause genetic diseases interact in a dominant-recessive pattern. In these cases, two copies of the recessive gene are required for the disease to occur. A person who has just one copy of the recessive gene is termed a carrier, since he or she carries the gene but is not affected by it. In the illustration above, the dominant gene is represented in green, and the recessive in blue. For the couple on the left, the father has one copy of the dominant gene and one copy of the recessive gene. The mother has two copies of the dominant gene. Each parent can contribute just one gene to the child. The four children shown on the lower left represent the probabilities (not the actual children) for the combinations that can result from their parents. The children on the far left received the recessive gene from their father and the dominant gene from their mother, and are therefore carriers. For any child born to these parents, there is a 50 percent chance that the child will be a carrier. Since none of the children can inherit two copies of the recessive gene, none of the children will develop the disease. When both parents are carriers, however, as shown by the couple on the right, there is a 25 percent chance that any child born has the disease, a 50 percent chance that a child is a carrier, and a 25 percent chance that a child does not have the disease and is not a carrier.

A mutation in the gene responsible for producing oxygen-carrying haemoglobin in the blood causes a disease known as sickle-cell anaemia. In this disease the structure of haemoglobin in the human bloodstream is severely altered. The mutation changes the structure of red blood cells to a slender sickle shape.

Some genetic disorders have symptoms that are manifest at birth. These disorders may result from mutations in a single gene or from more general chromosomal abnormalities. Many diseases and conditions are inherited in a recessive manner: Neither parent may have the defect even though they both carry the causative gene. When both parents have a dominant gene A and a recessive gene a, their offspring may inherit one of four different combinations: AA, Aa, aA, or aa. If the recessive gene a is defective, the statistical probability is that one in four of the offspring will bear the defective trait. In other congenital disorders the presence of only one copy of the recessive gene is sufficient to cause the condition

Genetic disorders may result from defects in genes or from chromosomal abnormalities. Prenatal tests, performed early in a woman's pregnancy, can identify a fetus with a genetic abnormality. Prenatal diagnosis using amniocentesis or chorionic villus sampling pose a slight risk to the fetus, and health professionals generally recommend these tests only if the mother or father has a family history of a genetic disorder or an increased risk of having a child with a chromosomal abnormality.

Physical anthropologists studying human genetics use sophisticated laboratory techniques to analyze human chromosomes and DNA (deoxyribonucleic acid), the structures through which people inherit traits from their parents. With these techniques, researchers have identified human populations that have genetic predispositions to specific diseases, such as types of cancer. This knowledge has promoted an increased focus on the use of preventive measures among people with higher risk for disease.

Sometimes mutations are caused by transposition, in which long stretches of DNA (containing one or more genes) move from one chromosome to another. These jumping genes, called transposons, can disrupt transcription and change the type of amino acids inserted into a protein. Transposons rearrange and interrupt genes in a way that generally improves the genetic variation of a species.

While mutations can occur spontaneously, some can be caused by exposure to physical or chemical agents in the environment called mutagens. Common environmental mutagens include ultraviolet rays from the sun and various chemicals, such as asbestos, cigarette smoke, and nitrous acid. High-energy radiation, such as medical X rays, can cause DNA strands to break, leading to the deletion of potentially important genetic information.

Lewis Edward devoted his entire academic career to the study of the fruit fly's genetic makeup. By studying mutations in the fruit fly and identifying which genes caused the mutations, he made two far-reaching discoveries about genes. The first was that a particular group of genes, called homeotic genes, controls the development of all the regions of the fly's body. These genes direct each cell to its proper location along the developing embryo's body. His second discovery was the principal of colinearity, or the linear sequence of the homeotic genes. He found that the homeotic genes are arranged on the chromosome in a linear order that exactly corresponds to the order of the body regions that each gene controls. This finding, which was subsequently found to hold true for other animals as well, won him the Nobel Prize.

Born in Lexington, Kentucky, and educated at the State College of Kentucky, Morgan studied embryology at Johns Hopkins University, where he received his PhD in 1891. As professor of experimental zoology at Columbia University from 1904 to 1928, he was at first critical of Mendelian theory, which had not been physically demonstrated. Performing breeding experiments and cytological analyses on the vinegar fly, Drosophila melanogaster, Morgan and his graduate students Alfred Henry Sturtevant, Calvin Blackman Bridges, and Hermann Joseph Muller revealed that chromosomes behave very similarly to the ways in which Mendel believed genes segregate and become randomly assorted.

Discovering also that genes for many character traits are arranged in a linear fashion on each chromosome, Morgan and his coworkers created linear chromosome maps in which each gene is assigned to a specific position. This work resulted in The Mechanism of Mendelian Heredity (1915), an influential book that was an important step in the development of modern genetics.

Morgan continued his experimental work, demonstrating in Theory of the Gene (1926) that genes are held together in different linkage groups, and that alleles (pairs of genes affecting the same trait) interchange, or cross over, in the same linkage group. In 1933 Morgan won the Nobel Prize for physiology or medicine.

Nettie Stevens (1861-1912), American biologist and geneticist whose research helped prove that chromosomes determine the sex of an organism. Researchers had previously believed that gender was influenced by food and temperature conditions during the early stages of an organism's development.

The Soviet government made development of science a national priority and showered top scientists with honours. Although day-to-day supervision was less oppressive than in the arts, there were countless episodes of arbitrary suppression of ideas. In the most notorious, the Ukrainian agronomist Trofim Lysenko rejected the chromosome theory of heredity generally accepted by modern genetics. Claiming his theories corresponded to Marxism, he convinced Stalin in 1948 to outlaw population genetics and several related fields of biological research; the decision was not reversed until the mid-1960s. Concern with freedom of inquiry and expression drew some scientists into the political realm. The best example is Andrey Sakharov, the nuclear physicist who became the most famous member of the hard-pressed liberal opposition in the 1970s. Sakharov was awarded the 1975 Nobel

Peace Prize for his efforts, though the government would not allow him to go to Norway to accept the prize.

Kennedy's Telegram to Khrushchev After First Manned Space Mission On April 12, 1961, the White House made public President John F. Kennedy's telegram to the Soviets, congratulating them on the first successful manned space mission. Cosmonaut Yuri Gagarin's orbit of the earth spurred American scientists and engineers to step up efforts to send United States astronauts into space.

The core of basic science was the Academy of Sciences, originally founded in 1725 and relocated from Leningrad to Moscow in 1934. It contained 250 research institutes and 60,500 full-time researchers in 1987, predominantly in the natural sciences. Several hundred scholars (330 in 1988) had the privileged status of "academician" and about twice as many had the status of "corresponding members" of the academy. In addition, all of the union republics but the RSFSR had their own paradigms of science. About 90 percent of research was carried on outside the academy system. Most of this was of an applied character and much of it was related to weapons systems and done in secret facilities in the defence-production ministries.

The launch of the artificial satellite Sputnik 1 by the Union of Soviet Socialist Republics (USSR) in 1957 marked the beginning of the space race. The satellite fell out of orbit three months after launch, but it had an electrifying effect—enhancing the international image of the USSR and creating the illusion of technological inferiority in the United States. In the aftermath, according to this 1978 National Aeronautics and Space Administration (NASA) report by historians Edward Clinton Ezell and Linda Neuman Ezell, tentative efforts to promote international cooperation in space gave way to competition.

Soviet scientists won lofty reputations in many fields. They were at the cutting edge of world science in mathematics and in several branches of physical science, notably theoretical and nuclear physics, chemistry, and astronomy. The physical chemist and physicist Nikolay Semenov was the first Soviet citizen to win a Nobel Prize, in 1956. Nobel Prizes were subsequently awarded in 1958 to the physicists Pavel Cherenkov, Ilya Frank, and Igor Tamm, for their discovery of the Cherenkov effect; in 1962 to the physicist Lev Landau, for his pioneer work in cryogenics, or low-temperature physics in 1964. Two physicists, Nikolay Basov and Aleksandr Prokhorov, worked to development of the laser (light amplification) and the maser (microwave amplification); and in 1978 to the physicist Peter Kapitza, for his research in magnetism and low-temperature physics.

Soviet technology was most impressive in the areas of nuclear weaponry and space exploration, where the arms race with the West prodded policy makers to set aside the needed resources. By virtue of a crash program directed by Igor Kurchatov, the Soviet Union was the second country to explode an atomic bomb, in 1949, four years after the United States. The Soviet Union detonated a hydrogen device in 1953, only ten months after the United States. In October 1957 it put the first artificial satellite, Sputnik 1, into an earth orbit, and in April 1961 a Russian cosmonaut, Yuri Gagarin, became the first man in space. Though disappointed that the United States beat them to the moon, the Soviets kept up a strong space program until economic problems led to cutbacks in the 1980s.

When new research is published, it often acts as a springboard for further work. Its impact can then be gauged by seeing how often the published research appears as a major scientific breakthroughs of which arrived thousands of times a year, but at the other extreme, obscure pieces of research may be cited rarely or not at all. However, citation is not always a reliable guide to the value of scientific work. Sometimes a piece of research will go largely unnoticed, only to be rediscovered in subsequent years. Such was the case for the work on genes done by American geneticist Barbara McClintock during the 1940s. McClintock discovered a new phenomenon in corn cells known as transposable genes, sometimes referred to as jumping genes. McClintock observed that a gene could move from one chromosome to another, where it would break the second chromosome at a particular site, insert itself there, and influence the function of an adjacent gene. Her work was largely ignored until the 1960s when scientists found that transposable gene is a primary means for transferring genetic material in bacteria and more complex organisms. McClintock was awarded the 1983 Nobel Prize in physiology or medicine for her work in transposable genes, more than 35 years after performing the research.

After sperm are produced, they move out of the testes and into the epididymis, a long tube coiled against the testes, where the sperm are stored and mature. The vas deferens transports the sperm from the epididymis through the prostate, after which the vas deferens becomes the ejaculatory duct. Here, fluids from the prostate and seminal vesicles (small sacs that hold semen) combine with the sperm to form semen, a thick, yellowish-white fluid. The average discharges of semen, called ejaculate, contains approximately 300 million sperm.

There are two periods of marked sexual differentiation in human life. The first occurs prenatally and the second occurs at puberty. Although adult women and men may differ to a greater degree, in genital appearance and secondary sexual characteristics, they are almost identical during prenatal development. When an egg and a sperm unite during fertilization, they each bring to the new cell half the number of chromosomes (threadlike structures that contain genetic material) present in other cells. From fertilization through about the first six weeks of development, male and female embryos differ only in the pair of sex chromosomes they have in each cell—two X chromosome (XX) in females and one X and one Y chromosome (XY) in males. At this stage, both male and female embryos have undifferentiated gonads (ovaries or testes), two sets of ducts (one set capable of developing into male internal organs and the other into female organs), and undifferentiated external genital folds and swellings.

About six weeks after conception, if a Y chromosome is present in the embryo's cells (as it is in normal males), a gene on the chromosome directs the undifferentiated gonads to become testes. If the Y chromosome is not present (as in normal females), the undifferentiated gonads will become ovaries.

If the gonads become testes, they begin to produce androgens (male hormones, primarily testosterone) by about eight weeks after conception. These androgens stimulate development of the one set of the genital ducts into the epididymis, vas deferens, and ejaculatory duct. The presence of androgens also stimulates development of the penis and the scrotum. The testes later descend into the scrotum. Males also produce a substance that inhibits the development of the second set of ducts into female organs. In the absence of such hormonal stimulation, female structures develop.

Prenatal hormones also play a role in the sexual differentiation of the brain. For example, prenatal hormones direct the development of sex differences in some cells and the neural pathways in the hypothalamus (the part of the brain that controls the endocrine system). Beginning at puberty, based on prenatal sexual differentiation, the hypothalamus directs either the cyclic secretion of sex hormones that controls the female menstrual cycle or the relatively continuous production of male sex hormones. Other brain differences may be related to differences in sexual and aggressive behaviour or in cognitive and perceptual characteristics. Most of the research on sexual differentiation of the brain has been performed with animals or with biassed human samples, and there is much debate about the nature and behavioural relevance of these differences in humans.

In animals, the sex of an individual is generally determined at the time of fertilization by the sperm cell. If a sperm cell carrying an X chromosome fertilizes the egg, the offspring will be female (XX); if a sperm cell carrying a Y chromosome fertilizes the egg, the offspring will be male (XY). The term primary sexual characteristics denote the kind of gamete the gonad produces: The ovary produces egg cells in the female, and the testis produces sperm cells in the male. The term secondary sexual characteristics denote all other sexual distinctions that play indirect roles in uniting sperm and eggs. Secondary sexual characteristics include everything from the specialized male and female features of the genital tract, to the brilliant plumage of male birds or facial hair of humans, to behavioural features such as courtship.

Generally, the more highly evolved the species, the more elaborate are its secondary sexual characteristics. At the time the eggs of starfish ripen, the male merely releases great quantities of sperm cells into the ocean water, and a tiny but sufficient number of them find and penetrate distant eggs. Frogs and toads are drawn to mates by calls, and they spawn in water; the male makes cloacal contact with the female and releases sperm externally, simultaneously with the eggs. Terrestrial animals, especially mammals, which do not have an environment of water through which sperm can propel itself, rely on herding and flocking, courtship, competition among males, and more specialized genitalia including an erectile penis, fallopian tubes, and a uterus in which eggs are fertilized and develop internally.

In mammals, the hormones that influence sexual differentiation and development are androgens (mainly testosterone), which stimulate later development of the ovary. In the sexually undifferentiated embryo, testosterone stimulates the development of the Wolffian duct system, the forerunner of the male genital tract. Later, testosterone, along with gonadotropins released by the pituitary gland, stimulates spermatogenesis. The Müllerian duct system, the forerunner of the female genital tract in the female embryo, probably differentiates spontaneously without hormonal stimuli. After female sex is well defined, estradiol, produced in the ovaries and the placenta, plays a major role in the development and the functioning of the female reproductive tract.

Within the cytoplasm of all prokaryotes is deoxyribonucleic acid (DNA), a complex molecule in the form of a double helix, a shape similar to a spiral staircase. The DNA is about 1,000 times the length of the cell, and to fit inside, it repeatedly twists and folds to form a compact structure called a chromosome. The chromosome in prokaryotes is circular, and is located in a region of the cell called the nucleoid. Often, smaller chromosomes called Plasmids are located in the cytoplasm. The DNA is divided into units called genes, just like a long train is divided into separate cars. Depending on the species, the DNA contains several hundred or even thousands of genes. Typically, one gene contains coded instructions for building all or part of a single protein. Enzymes, which are specialized proteins, determine virtually all the biochemical reactions that support and sustain the cell.

The manufacture of ribosomes requires that the components of ribosomes—ribonucleic acid (RNA) and protein—be synthesized and brought together for assembly. The ribosomes of eukaryotic cells contain four strands of RNA and from 70 to 80 proteins. Using genes that reside on regions of chromosomes located in the nucleolus, three of the four ribosomal RNA strands are synthesized in the centre of the nucleolus. The fourth RNA strand is synthesized outside of the nucleolus, using genes at a different location. The fourth strand is then transported into the nucleolus to participate in ribosome assembly.

The genetic information for ribosomal proteins, found in the nucleus, is copied, or transcribed, into special chemical messengers called messenger RNA (mRNA), a different type of RNA than ribosomal RNA. The mRNA travels out of the nucleus into the cell's cytoplasm where its information is transferred, or translated, into the ribosomal proteins. The newly created proteins enter the nucleolus and bind with the four ribosomal RNA strands to create two ribosomal structures: the large and small subunits. These two subunits leave the nucleus and enter the cytoplasm. When protein synthesis is initiated, the two subunits merge to form the completed ribosome.

The nucleolus creates the two subunits for a single ribosome in about one hour. Thousands of subunits are manufactured by each nucleolus simultaneously, however, since several hundred to several thousand copies of the ribosomal RNA genes are present in the nucleolus. Before a cell divides, the nucleolus assembles about ten million ribosomal subunits, necessary for the large-scale protein production that occurs in cell division.

The nuclear envelope is attached to a network of membrane-enclosed tubules that extends throughout the cell called the endoplasmic reticulum. The nuclear envelope is perforated by many holes, called nuclear pores, that permit the movement of selected molecules between the nucleus and the rest of the cell, while blocking the passage of other molecules.

The nucleus contains the nucleolus, which manufactures protein-producing structures called ribosomes. Genetic information in the form of deoxyribonucleic acid (DNA) is stored in threadlike, tangled structures called the chromatin within the nucleus. During the process of cell division known as mitosis, in which the nucleus divides, the chromatin shrinks into several distinct structures called chromosomes. Each time the cell divides, the heredity information carried in the chromosomes is passed to the two newly formed cells.

The DNA in the nucleus also contains the instructions for regulating the amount and types of proteins made by the cell. These instructions are copied, or transcribed, into a type of ribonucleic acid (RNA) called messenger RNA (mRNA). The mRNA is transported from the nucleus to ribosomes, where proteins are assembled.

DNA Fingerprinting, method of identification that compares fragments of deoxyribonucleic acid (DNA) It is sometimes called DNA typing. DNA is the genetic material found within the cell nuclei of all living things. In mammals the strands of DNA are grouped into structures called chromosomes. With the exception of identical twins, the complete DNA of each individual is unique.

A DNA fingerprint is constructed by first extracting a DNA sample from body tissue or fluid such as hair, blood, or saliva. The samples are then segmented using enzymes, and the segments are arranged by size using a process called electrophoresis. The segments are marked with probes and exposed on X-ray film, where they form a characteristic pattern of black bars—the DNA fingerprint. If the DNA fingerprints produced from two different samples match, the two samples probably came from the same person.

DNA fingerprinting was first developed as an identification technique in 1985. Originally used to detect the presence of genetic diseases, DNA fingerprinting soon came to be used in criminal investigations and forensic science. The first criminal conviction based on DNA evidence in the United States occurred in 1988. In criminal investigations, DNA fingerprints derived from evidence collected at the crime scene are compared to the DNA fingerprints of suspects. The DNA evidence can implicate or exonerate a suspect.

Generally, courts have accepted the reliability of DNA testing and admitted DNA test results into evidence. However, DNA fingerprinting is controversial in a number of areas: the accuracy of the results, the cost of testing, and the possible misuse of the technique.

The accuracy of DNA fingerprinting has been challenged for several reasons. First, because DNA segments rather than complete DNA strands are "fingerprinted," a DNA fingerprint may not be unique; large-scale research to confirm the uniqueness of DNA fingerprinting test results has not been conducted. In addition, DNA fingerprinting is often performed in private laboratories that may not follow uniform testing standards and quality controls. Also, since human beings must interpret the test, human error could lead to false results. DNA fingerprinting is expensive. Suspects who are unable to provide their own DNA experts may not be able to adequately defend themselves against charges based on DNA evidence.

In the United States, the Federal Bureau of Investigation (FBI) has created a national database of genetic information called the National DNA Index System. The database contains DNA obtained from convicted criminals and from evidence found at crime scenes. Some experts fear that this database might be used for unauthorized purposes, such as identifying individuals with stigmatizing illnesses such as acquired immunodeficiency syndrome (AIDS).

DNA Fingerprinting, method of identification that compares fragments of deoxyribonucleic acid (DNA) It is sometimes called DNA typing. DNA is the genetic material found within the cell nuclei of all living things. In mammals the strands of DNA are grouped into structures called chromosomes. With the exception of identical twins, the complete DNA of each individual is unique.

DNA fingerprinting was first developed as an identification technique in 1985. Originally used to detect the presence of genetic diseases, DNA fingerprinting soon came to be used in criminal investigations and forensic science. The first criminal conviction based on DNA evidence in the United States occurred in 1988. In criminal investigations, DNA fingerprints derived from evidence collected at the crime scene are compared to the DNA fingerprints of suspects. The DNA evidence can implicate or exonerate a suspect.

Generally, courts have accepted the reliability of DNA testing and admitted DNA test results into evidence. However, DNA fingerprinting is controversial in a number of areas: the accuracy of the results, the cost of testing, and the possible misuse of the technique.

The accuracy of DNA fingerprinting has been challenged for several reasons. First, because DNA segments rather than complete DNA strands are "fingerprinted," a DNA fingerprint may not be unique; large-scale research to confirm the uniqueness of DNA fingerprinting test results has not been conducted. In addition, DNA fingerprinting is often performed in private laboratories that may not follow uniform testing standards and quality controls. Also, since human beings must interpret the test, human error could lead to false results. DNA fingerprinting is expensive. Suspects who are unable to provide their own DNA experts may not be able to adequately defend themselves against charges based on DNA evidence.

In the United States, the Federal Bureau of Investigation (FBI) has created a national database of genetic information called the National DNA Index System. The database contains DNA obtained from convicted criminals and from evidence found at crime scenes. Some experts fear that this database might be used for unauthorized purposes, such as identifying individuals with stigmatizing illnesses such as acquired immunodeficiency syndrome (AIDS).

Ribonucleic Acid (RNA), genetic material of certain viruses (RNA viruses) and, in cellular organisms, the molecule that directs the middle steps of protein production. In RNA viruses, the RNA directs two processes—protein synthesis (production of the virus's protein coat) and replication (the process by which RNA copies itself). In cellular organisms, another type of genetic material, called deoxyribonucleic acid (DNA), carries the information that determines protein structure. But DNA cannot act alone but relies upon RNA to transfer this crucial information during protein synthesis (production of the proteins needed by the cell for its activities and development).

Like DNA, RNA consists of a chain of chemical compounds called nucleotides. Each nucleotide is made up of a sugar molecule called ribose, a phosphate group, and one of four different nitrogen-containing compounds called bases. The four bases are adenine, guanine, uracil, and cytosine. These components are joined together in the same manner as in a deoxyribonucleic acid (DNA) molecule. RNA differs chemically from DNA in two ways: The RNA sugar molecule contains an oxygen atom not found in DNA, and RNA contains the base uracil in the place of the base thymine in DNA.

In cellular organisms, RNA is a single-stranded polynucleotide chain, a strand of many nucleotides linked together. There are three types of RNA. Ribosomal RNA (rRNA) is found in the cell's ribosomes, the specialized structures that are the sites of protein synthesis. Transfer RNA (tRNA) carries amino acids to the ribosomes for incorporation into a protein. Messenger RNA (mRNA) carries the genetic blueprint copied from the sequence of bases in a cell's DNA. This blueprint specifies the sequence of amino acids in a protein. All three types of RNA are formed as needed, using specific sections of the cell's DNA as templates.

Some RNA viruses have double-stranded RNA—that is, their RNA molecules consist of two parallel polynucleotide chains. The base of each RNA nucleotide in one chain pair with a complementary base in the second chain—that is, adenine pairs with uracil, and guanine pairs with cytosine. For these viruses, the process of RNA replication in a host cell follows the same pattern as that of DNA replication, a method of replication called semi-conservative replication. In semi-conservative replication, each newly formed double-stranded RNA molecule contains one polynucleotide chain from the parent RNA molecule, and one complementary chain formed through the process of base pairing. The Colorado tick fever virus, which causes mild respiratory infections, is a double stranded RNA virus.

There are two types of single-stranded RNA viruses. After entering a host cell, one type, polio viruses have become double-stranded by making an RNA strand complementary to its own. During replication, although the two strands separate, only the recently formed strand attracts nucleotides with complementary bases. Therefore, the polynucleotide chain that is produced as a result of replication is exactly the same as the original RNA chain.

The other types of single-stranded RNA virus, called retro viruses, include the human immunodeficiency virus (HIV), which causes AIDS, and other viruses that cause tumours. After entering a host cell, a retrovirus makes a DNA strand complementary to its own RNA strand using the host's DNA nucleotides. This new DNA strand then replicates and forms a double helix that becomes incorporated into the host cell's chromosomes, where it is replicated along with the host DNA. While in a host cell, the RNA-derived viral DNA produces single-stranded RNA viruses that then leave the host cell and enter other cells, where the replication process is repeated.

In 1981, American biochemist Thomas Cech discovered that certain RNA molecules appear to act as enzymes, molecules that speed up, or catalyze, some reactions inside cells. Until this discovery biologist thought that all enzymes were proteins. Like other enzymes, these RNA catalysts, called ribozymes, show great specificity with respect to the reactions they speed up. The discovery of ribozymes added to the evidence that RNA, not DNA, was the earliest genetic material. Many scientists think that the earliest genetic molecule was simple in structure and capable of enzymatic activity. Furthermore, the molecule would necessarily exist in all organisms. The enzyme ribonuclease-P, which exists in all organisms, is made of protein and a form of RNA that has enzymatic activity. Based on this evidence, some scientists suspect that the RNA portion of ribonuclease-P may be the modern equivalent of the earliest genetic molecule, the molecule that first enabled replication to occur in primitive cells.

Nucleic acids are complex molecules produced by living cells and are essential to all living organisms. These acids govern the body's development and specific characteristics by providing hereditary information and triggering the production of proteins within the body. This computer-generated model shows two strands of deoxyribonucleic acid (DNA) and the double-helical structure typical of this class of nucleic acids.

Nucleic Acids, extremely complex molecules produced by living cells and viruses. Their name comes from their initial isolation from the nuclei of living cells. Certain nucleic acids, however, are found not in the cell nucleus but in cell cytoplasm. Nucleic acids have at least two functions: to pass on hereditary characteristics from one generation to the next, and to trigger the manufacture of specific proteins. How nucleic acids accomplish these functions is the object of some of the most intense and promising research currently under way. The nucleic acids are the fundamental substances of living things, believed by researchers to have first been formed about 3 billion years ago, when the most elementary forms of life began on earth. The origin of the so-called genetic code they carry has been accepted by researchers as being very close in time to the origin of life itself. Biochemists have succeeded in deciphering the code, that is, determining how the sequence of nucleic acids dictates the structure of proteins.

The two classes of nucleic acids are the deoxyribonucleic acids (DNA) and the ribonucleic acids (RNA). The backbones of both DNA and RNA molecules are shaped like helical strands. Their molecular weights are in the millions. To the backbones are connected a great number of smaller molecules (side groups) of four different types. The sequence of these molecules on the strand determines the code of the particular nucleic acid. This code, in turn, signals the cell how to reproduce either a duplicate of itself or the proteins it requires for survival.

All living cells contain the genetic material DNA. The cells of bacteria may have but one strand of DNA, but such a strand contains all the information needed by the cell in order to reproduce an identical offspring. The cells of mammals contain scores of DNA strands grouped together in chromosomes. In short, the structure of a DNA molecule or combination of DNA molecules determines the shape, form, and function of the offspring. Some viruses, called retroviruses, contain only RNA rather than DNA, but viruses in themselves are generally not considered true living organisms.

The pioneering research that revealed the general structure of DNA was performed by the British biophysicists Francis Crick and Maurice Wilkins and by the American biochemist James Dewey Watson. Using an X-ray diffraction picture of the DNA molecule obtained by Wilkins in 1951, Crick and Watson were able to construct a model of the DNA molecule that was completed in 1953. For their work, the three scientists received the 1962 Nobel Prize in physiology or medicine. The American biochemist Arthur Kornberg synthesized DNA from "off-the-shelf" substances, for which he was awarded, with the American biochemist Severo Ochoa (for research on RNA), the 1959 Nobel Prize in physiology or medicine. The DNA that he synthesized, although structurally similar to natural DNA, was not biologically active. In 1967, however, Kornberg and a team of researchers at Stanford University succeeded in producing biologically active DNA from relatively simple chemicals.

Certain kinds of RNA have a slightly different function from that of DNA. They take part in the actual synthesis of the proteins a cell produces. This is of particular interest to virologists because many viruses reproduce by "forcing" the host cells to manufacture more viruses. The virus injects its own RNA into the host cell, and the host cell obeys the code of the invading RNA rather than that of its own. Thus the cell produces proteins that are, in fact, viruses instead of the proteins required for cell function. The host cell is destroyed, and the newly formed viruses are free to inject their RNA into other host cells.

The structure of two types of RNA and their function in protein production have been determined, one type by a team of Cornell University and US Department of Agriculture investigators led by Robert W. Holey of Cornell, and the other type by James T. Madison and George A. Everett of the Department of Agriculture. Important research into the interpretation of the genetic code and its role in protein synthesis was also performed by the Indian-born American chemist Har Gobind Khorana at the University of Wisconsin Enzyme Institute and the American biochemist Marshall W. Nirenberg of the National Heart Institute. In 1970 Khorana achieved the first complete synthesis of a gene and repeated his feat in 1973, since one type of RNA has been synthesized. Also, in the early 1980s, American biochemists Thomas Robert Cech and Sidney Altman independently proved that certain types of RNA, called ribozymes, can function as true catalysts

Poliomyelitis, infectious viral disease that sometimes results in paralysis. The infection chiefly affects children and young adults and is caused by any one of three related viruses called polio viruses. In more than 95 percent of cases, the infection may pass without creating severe or even noticeable illness because the body's immune system neutralizes the invading virus and protects against future infection. In a small percentage of cases the virus penetrates to the central nervous system, infecting cells that control muscle function. Such infection can result in permanent paralysis of limbs. In its most perilous form, the infection attacks the brain, creating complications that sometimes result in death.

The term poliomyelitis derives from Greek words referring to inflammation (its) of the gray (polios) matter of the spinal cord (myelos). The shortened term polio is commonly used by the public and medical professionals, and the disease has also been referred to as infantile paralysis.

According to figures from the World Health Organization (WHO), approximately 7,100 cases of polio were reported throughout the world in 1999. Experts suspect that misdiagnosis and under-reporting may make these numbers inaccurate. Thus, the actual number of polio cases may be roughly five times the reported figure—perhaps more than 20,000 cases, occurring primarily in Africa, the Middle East, and South Asia.

While still a health threat in many parts of the world, polio also represents one of the greatest medical success stories of the 20th century. The number of polio cases found worldwide today constitutes a 90 percent reduction from the number of cases reported in the late 1980s. Most health experts credit this achievement to a mass vaccination program called the Global Polio Eradication Initiative that WHO initiated in 1988 to eradicate polio worldwide by the year 2005.

In the United States and Canada, polio has been effectively eliminated, with fewer than ten cases reported in each country per year. This statistic contrasts strikingly with those from the first half of the 20th century, when epidemic polio was one of the most dreaded and feared diseases in North America. The first large-scale outbreak in the United States occurred in 1916, when over 37,000 cases were reported in 26 states, resulting in 6,000 deaths. Each year thereafter the number of polio cases in the United States averaged about 38,000 per year, including about 21,000 paralytic cases each year. In Canada the epidemic peaked in 1953, resulting in one of the highest national polio rates ever recorded in the world.

Fearing infection during epidemics in the first half of the 20th century, some people avoided beaches, public pools, theatres, fairs—any place of public gathering. Occasionally schools were closed until epidemics subsided. In response to the public's fear of this disease, in 1938 President Franklin Delano Roosevelt (who had himself lost the use of both legs to polio) founded the National Foundation for Infantile Paralysis. Now known as the March of Dimes Birth Defects Foundation, the organization raised millions of dollars for polio research and the support of victims.

The discovery in the 1950s of vaccines that protect against poliovirus infection eventually led to successful polio vaccination programs in North America, Latin America, and Europe. By the early 1990s, WHO declared the western hemisphere free of polio.

But the struggle to eradicate polio continues in many developing nations. Furthermore, health officials stress that vaccination programs must be maintained in areas considered polio free. They warn that the virus could easily become dangerous again in populations of children who have not acquired immunity, the body's ability to resist infection from the polio virus. This danger was chillingly demonstrated in 1979 when an outbreak of paralytic polio erupted among unvaccinated members of an Amish sect in Pennsylvania and Maryland.

The three types of poliovirus belong to the virus family known as picornaviruses. This name derives from a combination of the words pico, meaning "small," and RNA, indicating that the viruses contain a core of the genetic material known as ribonucleic acid, or RNA. Three types of poliovirus have been identified: Type 1 (also known as Brunhilde), Type 2 (Lansing), and Type 3 (Leon). Type 1 is the most common form and the one most closely associated with polio's more severe, paralytic progression. A person who develops immunity from exposure to one poliovirus type will not have immunity against the other polio viruses.

Poliovirus typically enters the body through the mouth and multiplies in the tonsils and lymph nodes of the upper respiratory tract. Infection proceeds from the mouth into the gastrointestinal tract through the stomach to the intestines. The virus multiplies in the intestines and is shed from the body in faeces, often resulting in further infections. For example, a parent can become infected by an infant during diaper changes, or improper waste disposal can lead to contamination of a water supply. These infections, in turn, will spread the virus more widely.

Large quantities of poliovirus multiply in intestinal tissue known as Weyer's patches, where cells of the body's lymphatic system are concentrated. Passage of the virus into the body's lymphatic system stimulates the production of antibodies. These specializing immune-system defenders, in time, will destroy the viral intruder. From the lymphatic system, the virus typically invades the bloodstream.

Retrovirus, of any virus belonging to the family Retroviridae, whose members share a unique method of replicating (copying) themselves when they infect living cells. Retroviruses store their genetic information in molecules of ribonucleic acid (RNA). However, unlike other RNA viruses, retroviruses use RNA as a template (a master pattern) for forming deoxyribonucleic acid (DNA), the genetic material that puts viral replication instructions into effect. This process, called reverse transcription, is the exact opposite of the normal flow of genetic information in living things in which DNA serves as the template for RNA formation.

Retroviruses affect a wide range of animals, although the best-known types are those that target vertebrates. Some retroviruses are harmless, but many can cause malignant transformation—a genetic change that makes healthy cells cancerous. Disease-forming retroviruses can cause diseases such as leukemia (cancer of the blood) in mammals and malignant tumours and other disorders in birds. From a human perspective, by far the most significant retroviruses are a small group called lentiviruses, which include a human immunodeficiency virus (HIV), the virus that causes acquired immunodeficiency syndrome (AIDS).

Deoxyribonucleic Acid (DNA), genetic material of all cellular organisms and most viruses. DNA carries the information needed to direct protein synthesis and replication. Protein synthesis is the production of the proteins needed by the cell or virus for its activities and development. Replication is the process by which DNA copies itself for each descendant cell or virus, passing on the information needed for protein synthesis. In most cellular organisms, DNA is organized on chromosomes located in the nucleus of the cell.

The deoxyribonucleic acid (DNA) molecule is the genetic blueprint for each cell and ultimately the blueprint that determines every characteristic of a living organism. In 1953 American biochemist James Watson, left, and British biophysicist Francis Crick, right, described the structure of the DNA molecule as a double helix, somewhat like a spiral staircase with many individual steps. Their work was aided by X-ray diffraction pictures of the DNA molecule taken by British biophysicist Maurice Wilkins and British physical chemist Rosalind Franklin. In 1962 Crick, Watson, and Wilkins received the Nobel Prize for their pioneering work on the structure of the DNA molecule.

A molecule of DNA consists of two chains, strands composed of a large number of chemical compounds, called nucleotides, linked together to form a chain. These chains are arranged like a ladder that has been twisted into the shape of a winding staircase, called a double helix. Each nucleotide consists of three units: a sugar molecule-called deoxyribose, a phosphate group, and one of four different nitrogen-containing compounds called bases. The four bases are adenine (A), guanine (G), thymine (T), and cytosine. The deoxyribose molecule occupies the centre position in the nucleotide, flanked by a phosphate group on one side and a base on the other. The phosphate group of each nucleotide is also linked to the deoxyribose of the adjacent nucleotide in the chain. These linked deoxyribose-phosphate subunits form the parallel side rails of the ladder. The bases face inward toward each other, forming the rungs of the ladder.

The nucleotides in one DNA strand have a specific association with the corresponding nucleotides in the other DNA strand. Because of the chemical affinity of the bases, nucleotides containing adenine are always paired with nucleotides containing thymine, and nucleotides containing cytosine are always paired with nucleotides containing guanine. The complementary bases are joined to each other by weak chemical bonds called hydrogen bonds.

In 1953 American biochemist James D. Watson and British biophysicist Francis Crick published the first description of the structure of DNA. Their model proved to be so important for the understanding of protein synthesis, DNA replication, and mutation that they were awarded the 1962 Nobel Prize for physiology or medicine for their work.

One of a cell's most important tasks is the synthesis of proteins, giant molecules that underlie most cellular functions. The hereditary material known as deoxyribonucleic acid (DNA), found within the nucleus of a cell, orchestrates a series of steps resulting in the manufacture of proteins tailored to meet the needs for a cell's development and growth.

DNA carries the instructions for the production of proteins. A protein is composed of smaller molecules called amino acids, and the structure and function of the protein is determined by the sequence of its amino acids. The sequence of amino acids, in turn, is determined by the sequence of nucleotide bases in the DNA. A sequence of three nucleotide bases, called a triplet, is the genetic code word, or codon, that specifies a particular amino acid. For instance, the triplet GAS (guanine, adenine, and cytosine) is the codon for the amino acid leucine, and the triplet CAG (cytosine, adenine, and guanine) is the codon for the amino acid valine. A protein consisting of 100 amino acids is thus encoded by a DNA segment consisting of 300 nucleotides. Of the two polynucleotide chains that form a DNA molecule, only one strand contains the information needed for the production of a given amino acid sequence. The other strand aids in replication.

Protein synthesis begins with the separation of a DNA molecule into two strands. In a process called transcription, a section of one strand acts as a template, or pattern, to produce a new strand called messenger RNA (mRNA). The mRNA leaves the cell nucleus and attaches to the ribosomes, specialized cellular structures that are the sites of protein synthesis. Amino acids are carried to the ribosomes by another type of RNA, called transfer RNA (tRNA). In a process called translation, the amino acids are linked together in a particular sequence, dictated by the mRNA, to form a protein.

A gene is a sequence of DNA nucleotides that specify the order of amino acids in a protein via an intermediary mRNA molecule. Substituting one DNA nucleotide with another containing a different base causes all descendant cells or viruses to have the altered nucleotide base sequence. As a result of the substitution, the sequence of amino acids in the resulting protein may also be changed. Such a change in a DNA molecule is called a mutation. Most mutations are the result of errors in the replication process. Exposure of a cell or virus to radiation or to certain chemicals increases the likelihood of mutations.

In most cellular organisms, replication of a DNA molecule takes place in the cell nucleus and occurs just before the cell divides. Replication begins with the separation of the two polynucleotide chains, each of which then acts as a template for the assembly of a new complementary chain. As the old chains separate, each nucleotide in the two chains attracts a complementary nucleotide that has been formed earlier by the cell. The nucleotides are joined to one another by hydrogen bonds to form the rungs of a new DNA molecule. As the complementary nucleotides are fitted into place, an enzyme called DNA polymerase links them together by bonding the phosphate group of one nucleotide to the sugar molecule of the adjacent nucleotide, forming the side rail of the new DNA molecule. This process continues until a new polynucleotide chain has been formed alongside the old one, forming a new double-helix molecule.

Several tools and procedures are used by scientists for the study and manipulation of DNA. Specialized enzymes, called restriction enzymes, found in bacterium' act like molecular scissors to cut the phosphate backbones of DNA molecules at specific base sequences. Strands of DNA that have been cut with restriction enzymes are left with single-stranded tails that are called sticky ends, because they can easily realign with tails from certain other DNA fragments. Scientists take advantage of restriction enzymes and the sticky ends generated by these enzymes to carry out recombinant DNA technology, or genetic engineering. This technology involves removing a specific gene from one organism and inserting the gene into another organism.

Another tool for working with DNA is a procedure called polymerase chain reaction (PCR). This procedure uses the enzyme DNA polymerase to make copies of DNA strands in a process that mimics the way in which DNA replicates naturally within cells. Scientists use PCR to obtain vast numbers of copies of a given segment of DNA.

DNA fingerprinting, also called DNA typing, makes it possible to compare samples of DNA from various sources in a manner that is analogous to the comparison of fingerprints. In this procedure, scientists use restriction enzymes to cleave a sample of DNA into an assortment of fragments. Solutions containing these fragments are placed at the surface of a gel to which an electric current is applied. The electric current causes the DNA fragments to move through the gel. Because smaller fragments move more quickly than larger ones, this process, called electrophoresis, separates the fragments according to their size. The fragments are then marked with probes and exposed on X-ray film, where they form the DNA fingerprint—a pattern of characteristic black bars that is unique for each type of DNA.

A procedure called DNA sequencing makes it possible to determine the precise order, or sequence, of nucleotide bases within a fragment of DNA. Most versions of DNA sequencing use a technique called primer extension, developed by British molecular biologist Frederick Sanger. In primer extension, specific pieces of DNA are replicated and modified, so that each DNA segment ends in a fluorescent form of one of the four nucleotide bases. Modern DNA sequencers, pioneered by American molecular biologist Leroy Hood, incorporate both lasers and computers. Scientists have completely sequenced the genetic material of several microorganisms, including the bacterium Escherichia coli. In 1998, scientists achieved the milestone of sequencing the complete genome of a multicellular organism—a roundworm identified as Caenorhabditis elegans. The Human Genome Project, an international research collaboration, has been established to determine the sequence of all of the three billion nucleotide base pairs that make up the human genetic material.

An instrument called an atomic force microscope enables scientists to manipulate the three-dimensional structure of DNA molecules. This microscope involves laser beams that act like tweezers—attaching to the ends of a DNA molecule and pulling on them. By manipulating these laser beams, scientists can stretch, or uncoil, fragments of DNA. This work is helping reveal how DNA changes its three-dimensional shape as it interacts with enzymes.

In the late 20th century scientists devised methods of altering the genetic makeup of food crops. Humans have modified crops for thousands of years to increase yield and resistance to pests, but changes on the molecular level have caused some people to wonder if science has gone too far. Recent studies suggest that some genetically altered crops may pose health risks and other dangers. Proponents of genetically modified food, however, point to increased yields and health benefits.

Research into DNA has had a significant impact on medicine. Through recombinant DNA technology, scientists can modify microorganisms so that they become so-called factories that produce large quantities of medically useful drugs. This technology is used to produce insulin, which is a drug used by diabetics, and interferon, which is used by some cancer patients. Studies of human DNA are revealing genes that are associated with specific diseases, such as cystic fibrosis and breast cancer. This information is helping physicians to diagnose various diseases, and it may lead to new treatments. For example, physicians are using a technology called chimeraplasty, which involves a synthetic molecule containing both DNA and RNA strands, in an effort to develop a treatment for a form of hemophilia.

Forensic science uses techniques developed in DNA research to identify individuals who have committed crimes. DNA from semen, skin, or blood taken from the crime scene can be compared with the DNA of a suspect, and the results can be used in court as evidence.

In a landmark intersection of science and fiction, cloning leapt from the world's imagination to its front page in February 1997. It arrived in the innocent form of a sheep named Dolly: the first exact genetic duplicate of an adult mammal due to genetic engineering. Scottish scientists had created Dolly from deoxyribonucleic acid (DNA)—the basic unit of heredity—taken from a single adult sheep cell. The accomplishment threw open the door to profound ethical as well as scientific controversy over the potential uses and abuses of cloning. "However the debate is resolved," wrote Los Angeles Times science reporter Thomas H. Maugh II, "the genie is irretrievably out of the bottle."

DNA has helped taxonomists determine evolutionary relationships among animals, plants, and other life forms. Closely related species have more similar DNA than do species that are distantly related. One surprising finding to emerge from DNA studies is that vultures of the Americas are more closely related to storks than to the vultures of Europe, Asia, or Africa.

Techniques of DNA manipulation are used in farming, in the form of genetic engineering and biotechnology. Strains of crop plants to which genes have been transferred may produce higher yields and may be more resistant to insects. Cattle have been similarly treated to increase milk and beef production, as have hogs, to yield more meat with less fat.

Despite the many benefits offered by DNA technology, some critics argue that its development should be monitored closely. One fear raised by such critics is that DNA fingerprinting could provide a means for employers to discriminate against members of various ethnic groups. Critics also fear that studies of people's DNA could permit insurance companies to deny health insurance to those people at risk for developing certain diseases. The potential use of DNA technology to alter the genes of embryos is a particularly controversial issue.

The use of DNA technology in agriculture has also sparked controversy. Some people question the safety, desirability, and ecological impact of genetically altered crop plants. In addition, animal rights groups have protested against the genetic engineering of farm animals.

Despite these and other areas of disagreement, many people agree that DNA technology offers a mixture of benefits and potential hazards. Many experts also agree that an informed public can help assure that DNA technology is used wisely.

Drugs in the class known as nitrosoureas interfere with DNA repair. They are primarily used in treating brain cancer. Another group of chemotherapy drugs, as referred to as antimetabolites, that interfere with cell replication by preventing the cell from assembling the building blocks of DNA and ribonucleic acid (RNA), the molecule that directs protein synthesis. Antimetabolites are used to treat breast cancer, ovarian cancer, and cancers of the gastrointestinal tract.

Mitotic inhibitors constitute another class of chemotherapeutic agents. As their name implies, these drugs interfere with mitosis, the part of the cell cycle when the cell actually divides. These agents are used to treat lung cancer, breast cancer, and testicular cancer. Another class of cancer drugs, known as antitumor antibiotics, treat a variety of cancers, including leukemias. These drugs work by inhibiting the synthesis of RNA.

In his early work beginning in the mid-1950s, Brenner Sydney studied how deoxyribonucleic acid (DNA), the genetic material of living things, instructs cells to make proteins. Working with French biologist and future Nobel laureate François Jacob and other scientists, in 1961 Brenner identified messenger ribonucleic acid (mRNA), a molecule that acts as an intermediary between DNA and protein production. In that same year Brenner and British biophysicist Francis Crick, who won a Nobel Prize in 1962, identified codons, groups of three nucleotides (the building blocks of DNA and RNA). Brenner and Crick showed that codons provide instructions for the creation of all 20 amino acids that form the foundation of proteins.

The story of how cells evolved remains an open and actively investigated question in science. The combined expertise of physicists, geologists, chemists, and evolutionary biologists has been required to shed light on the evolution of cells from the nonliving matter of early Earth. The planet formed about 4.5 billion years ago, and for millions of years, violent volcanic eruptions blasted substances such as carbon dioxide, nitrogen, water, and other small molecules into the air. These small molecules, bombarded by ultraviolet radiation and lightning from intense storms, collided to form the stable chemical bonds of larger molecules, such as amino acids and nucleotides—the building blocks of proteins and nucleic acids. Experiments indicate that these larger molecules form spontaneously under laboratory conditions that simulate the probable early environment of Earth.

Scientists speculate that rain may have carried these molecules into lakes to create a primordial soup—a breeding ground for the assembly of proteins, the nucleic acid RNA, and lipids. Some scientists postulate that these more complex molecules formed in hydrothermal vents rather than in lakes. Other scientists propose that these key substances may have reached Earth on meteorites from outer space. Regardless of the origin or environment, however, scientists do agree that proteins, nucleic acids, and lipids provided the raw materials for the first cells. In the laboratory, scientists have observed lipid molecules joining to form spheres that resemble a cell's plasma membrane. As a result of these observations, scientists postulate that millions of years of molecular collisions resulted in lipid spheres enclosing RNA, the simplest molecule capable of self-replication. These primitive aggregations would have been the ancestors of the first prokaryotic cells.

Fossil studies indicate that cyanobacteria, bacteria capable of photosynthesis, were among the earliest bacteria to evolve, an estimated 3.4 billion to 3.5 billion years ago. In the environment of the early Earth, there was no oxygen, and cyanobacteria probably used fermentation to produce ATP. Over the eons, cyanobacteria performed photosynthesis, which produces oxygen as a byproduct; the result was the gradual accumulation of oxygen in the atmosphere. The presence of oxygen set the stage for the evolution of bacteria that used oxygen in aerobic respiration, a more efficient ATP-producing process than fermentation. Some molecular studies of the evolution of genes in archaebacteria suggest that these organisms may have evolved in the hot waters of hydrothermal vents or hot springs slightly earlier than cyanobacteria, around 3.5 billion years ago. Like cyanobacteria, archaebacteria probably relied on fermentation to synthesize ATP.

Eukaryotic cells may have evolved from primitive prokaryotes about 2 billion years ago. One hypothesis suggests that some prokaryotic cells lost their cell walls, permitting the cell's plasma membrane to expand and fold. These folds, ultimately, may have given rise to separate compartments within the cell—the forerunners of the nucleus and other organelles now found in eukaryotic cells. Another key hypothesis is known as endosymbiosis. Molecular studies of the bacteria-like DNA and ribosomes in mitochondria and chloroplasts indicate that mitochondrion and chloroplast ancestors were once free-living bacteria. Scientists propose that these free-living bacteria were engulfed and maintained by other prokaryotic cells for their ability to produce ATP efficiently and to provide a steady supply of glucose. Over generations, eukaryotic cells complete with mitochondria—the ancestors of animals—or with both mitochondria and chloroplasts—the ancestors of plants

Outside of a host cell, a virus is an inert particle. Once inside a cell, a virus can replicate many times, creating thousands of viruses that leave the cell to find host cells of their own. Viruses that cause disease do so by destroying or damaging cells as they leave them.

Like all viruses, human immunodeficiency viruses (HIV) are comprised of only genetic material, a few proteins, and a protective envelope. Its genetic material, carried by single-stranded RNA molecules, contains all of the information to make more viruses. HIV cannot reproduce itself outside of a cell, but when HIV invades a living cell, it turns the cell into a factory for making more HIV.HIV penetrates the cell membrane and releases its contents into the host cell.

Acquired Immunodeficiency Syndrome (AIDS), human viral disease that ravages the immune system, undermining the body's ability to defend itself from infection and disease. Caused by the human immunodeficiency virus (HIV), AIDS leaves an infected person vulnerable to opportunistic infections. Such infections are harmless in healthy people, but in those whose immune systems have been greatly weakened, they can prove fatal. Although there is no cure for AIDS, new drugs are available that can prolong the life spans and improve the quality of life of infected people.

The human immunodeficiency virus (HIV), which causes acquired immunodeficiency syndrome (AIDS), principally attacks CD4 T-cells, a vital part of the human immune system. As a result, the body's ability to resist opportunistic viral, bacterial, fungal, protozoal, and other infection is greatly weakened. Pneumocystis carinii pneumonia is the leading cause of death among people with HIV infection, but the incidence of certain types of cancers such as B-cell lymphomas and Kaposi's sarcoma is also increased. Neurological complications and dramatic weight loss, or "wasting," are characteristic of endstage HIV disease (AIDS). HIV can be transmitted sexually, through contact with contaminated blood, tissue, or needles, and from mother to child during birth or breastfeeding. Full-blown symptoms of AIDS may not develop for more than 10 years after infection.

Infection with HIV does not necessarily mean that a person has AIDS. Some people who have HIV infection may not develop any of the clinical illnesses that define the full-blown disease of AIDS for ten years or more. Physicians prefer to use the term AIDS for cases where a person has reached the final, life-threatening stage of HIV infection.

More than 42 million people around the world are currently infected with human immunodeficiency viruses (HIV), the virus that causes immunodeficiency syndrome (AIDS). New HIV infections have levelled off or even declined in most developed countries, but the virus is spreading rapidly through much of the developing world. In some areas of sub-Saharan Africa, one in four adults is carrying the virus.

AIDS was first identified in 1981 among homosexual men and intravenous drug users in New York and California. Shortly after its detection in the United States, evidence of AIDS epidemics grew among heterosexual men, women, and children in sub-Saharan Africa. AIDS quickly developed into a worldwide epidemic, affecting virtually every nation. By 2003 the United Nations Program on HIV/AIDS (UNAIDS) and the World Health Organization (WHO) estimated that worldwide 40 million people, including 2.5 million children under the age of 15, were living with HIV infection or AIDS. The WHO, a specialized agency of the United Nations (UN), estimated that from 1981 to the end of 2002 about 20 million people died as a result of AIDS. About 4.5 million of those who died were children under the age of 15. UNAIDS and the WHO reported that 3 million people died in 2003 alone from AIDS, and 5 million more people became infected with HIV.

AIDS has struck sub-Saharan Africa particularly hard. In the year 2003 one in five adults in this region had AIDS or HIV infection, the highest rate of infection in the world since the epidemic began. Sub-Saharan Africa is the most severely affected region in the world with 26.6 million people living with HIV/AIDS as of 2003.

In the United States about 40,000 new HIV infections occur each year. More than 30 percent of these infections occur in women, and 60 percent occur in ethnic minorities. As of 2002 about 886,000 US residents were living with HIV/AIDS, and about 500,000 people had died of the disease since the epidemic began, according to the US Centres for Disease Control and Prevention. In Canada about 4,200 new HIV infections occur each year. Nearly 25 percent of these infections occur in women. In 2002 about 55,000 Canadians were living with HIV infection and about 18,000 people were living with full-blown AIDS.

The incidence of the new cases of HIV infections and AIDS deaths has significantly decreased in Canada and the United States since 1995. This decrease is attributed to the availability of new drug treatments and public health programs that target people most at risk for infection. But while the overall rate of HIV infection seems to be on a downturn, certain populations appear to be at greater risk for the disease. In the United States in 1987, Caucasians accounted for 60 percent of AIDS cases and blacks and Hispanics only 39 percent. But by 2000 the trend had reversed: 26 percent of new cases were diagnosed in Caucasians and 73 percent in blacks and Hispanics. Likewise the number of female AIDS patients in the United States has increased significantly in recent years, from 7 percent of all AIDS cases in 1985 to 30 percent in 2000. In the United States, African American and Hispanic women accounted for 82 percent of AIDS cases among women in 2000.

In western Europe the first cases of AIDS were detected in the early 1980s, and by the late 1990s, at least 30,000 new HIV infections occurred each year. In 2002 about 570,000 western Europeans were HIV positive, and 25 percent of these cases were women. Before the dissolution of the Union of Soviet Socialist Republics (USSR) in 1991, eastern Europe reported few HIV cases. But since 1995, HIV infection has spread rapidly in cities of several eastern European countries, including Ukraine, Belarus, and Moldova. The WHO estimates that the total number of HIV infections in this region may have risen from less than 30,000 in 1995 to about 1 million in 2002.

A road sign in Botswana about acquired immunodeficiency syndrome (AIDS) says "AIDS: Your Problem, Control With Condoms." Africa accounts for more than 70 percent of adults infected with human immunodeficiency viruses (HIV), the cause of AIDS.

While cases of AIDS have been reported in every nation of the world, the disease affects some countries more than others. More than 95 percent of all HIV-infected people live in the developing world. In these areas, the disease has sapped the populations of young men and women who form the foundation of the labour force. Most die while in the peak of their reproductive years. Moreover, the epidemic has overwhelmed health care systems, increased the number of orphans, and caused life expectancy rates to plummet. These problems have reached crisis proportions in some parts of the world already burdened by war, political upheaval, or unrelenting poverty.

In 1999 alone, 4 million people in sub-Saharan Africa became infected with the human immunodeficiency virus (HIV), the virus that causes acquired immunodeficiency syndrome (AIDS). In several African countries, at least half of the males currently aged 15 will eventually die of AIDS. These and other shocking facts about the level of devastation that HIV/AIDS has inflicted and will inflict on the people and economies of Africa are documented in the Report on the Global HIV/AIDS Epidemic. The report, excerpted here, was published in June 2000 by the Joint United Nations Programme on HIV/AIDS, known as UNAIDS.

Nowhere is this better demonstrated than in sub-Saharan Africa, where the number of AIDS cases far exceeds that of all other geographic regions. Of the estimated 14,000 HIV infections that occur each day worldwide, about half of these infections occur in sub-Saharan Africa. About 70 percent of all people infected with HIV live in this region. In some countries in the southern part of the continent, including Botswana, Lesotho, Swaziland, and Zimbabwe, more than 30 percent of the population has HIV infection or AIDS.

In Asia and the Pacific Islands an estimated 7.2 million people were living with HIV infection by 2002. Health officials fear that as the virus spreads through China and India, the world's two most populous countries, cases of HIV infection in this region may surge up to 25 million cases by the year 2010, dwarfing the problems seen in sub-Saharan Africa.

Historical Essays reflect the knowledge and insight of leading historians. This collection of essays is assembled to support the National Standards for World History. In this essay, Oliver Osborne of the University of Washington argues that post-colonial rule and turmoil in Africa has not diminished the continent's diverse health care systems but rather demanded collaboration among them.

In 2002 the Chinese government reported that China had about 1 million HIV-positive people in a population of more than 1 billion. However, public health experts are concerned by the fast-rising number of new infections among intravenous drug users who share infected needles. In 2000 HIV prevalence among intravenous drug users ranged from 44 percent to 85 percent in selected communities of drug users in both Bunnan, in southern China, and Xinjiang, in northwestern China. The incidence of HIV infection will likely be exacerbated by the growing sex industry in China. Surveys indicate that as many as 4 million prostitutes work in China. Of these, four out of ten never use a condom to protect themselves or their clients from HIV infection or other sexually transmitted infections. In rural areas of China the incidence of HIV infection is rising because many poverty-stricken people regularly sell their blood. The people who buy the blood use unsterile methods to draw blood, including reusing contaminated needles, which can spread HIV infection.

In Latin America and the Caribbean region nearly 1.7 million people have been diagnosed with HIV infection or AIDS, twice the incidence in the United States and Canada. Brazil, Mexico, Colombia, and Argentina are the Latin American countries with the highest number of cases of HIV infection or AIDS.

The human immunodeficiency virus (HIV), the cause of acquired immunodeficiency syndrome (AIDS), is genetically programmed to do one thing: highjack the reproductive machinery of a human cell, then trick it into churning out as many copies of the virus as it can before the cell dies. The current best hope for the treatment of AIDS requires that patients take a number of different drugs, each of which interferes with certain steps of the HIV infection process.

AIDS is the final stage of a chronic infection with the human immunodeficiency virus. There are two types of this virus: HIV-1, which is the primary cause of AIDS worldwide, and HIV-2, found mostly in West Africa. On its surface, HIV carries a protein structure that recognizes and binds only with a specific structure found on the outer surface of certain cells. HIV attacks any cell that has this binding structure.

However, white blood cells of the immune system known as T cells, which orchestrate a wide variety of disease-fighting mechanisms, are especially vulnerable to HIV attack. Particularly vulnerable are certain T cells known as CD4 cells. When HIV infects a CD4 cell, it commandeers the genetic tools within the cell to manufacture new HIV virus. The newly formed HIV virus then leaves the cell, destroying the CD4 cell in the process. No existing medical treatment can completely eradicate HIV from the body once it has integrated into human cells.

The loss of CD4 cells endangers health because these immune cells help other types of immune cells respond to invading organisms. The average healthy person has over 1,000 CD4 cells per microliter of blood. In a person infected with HIV, the virus steadily destroys CD4 cells over a period of years, diminishing the cells' protective ability and weakening the immune system. When the density of CD4 cells drops to 200 cells per microliter of blood, the infected person becomes vulnerable to any of about 26 opportunistic infections and rare cancers, which take advantage of the weakened immune defences to cause disease.

Scientists have identified three ways that HIV infections spread: sexual intercourse with an infected person, contact with contaminated blood, and transmission from an infected mother to her child before or during birth or through breastfeeding.

HIV transmission occurs most commonly during intimate sexual contact with an infected person, including genital, anal, and oral sex. The virus is present in the infected person's semen or vaginal fluids. During sexual intercourse, the virus gains access to the bloodstream of the uninfected person by passing through openings in the mucous membrane—the protective tissue layer that lines the mouth, vagina, and rectum—and through breaks in the skin of the penis. In the United States and Canada, HIV is most commonly transmitted during sex between homosexual men, but the incidence of HIV transmission between heterosexual men and women has rapidly increased. In most other parts of the world, HIV is most commonly transmitted through heterosexual sex.

Direct contact with HIV-infected blood occurs when people who use heroin or other injected drugs share hypodermic needles or syringes contaminated with infected blood. Sharing of contaminated needles among intravenous drug users is the primary cause of HIV infection in eastern Europe, particularly in Ukraine, Russia, Belarus, and Moldova. Epidemics of HIV infection among drug users have also emerged in Georgia, Armenia, Azerbaijan, and Kazakhstan in Central Asia.

Less frequently, it is, that HIV infection results when health professionals accidentally stick themselves with needles containing HIV-infected blood or expose an open cut to contaminated blood. Some cases of HIV transmission from transfusions of infected blood, blood components, and organ donations were reported in the 1980s. Since 1985 government regulations in the United States and Canada have required that all donated blood and body tissues be screened for the presence of HIV before being used in medical procedures. As a result of these regulations, HIV transmission caused by contaminated blood transfusion or organ donations is rare in North America. However, the problem continues to concern health officials in sub-Saharan Africa. Less than half of the 46 nations in this region have blood-screening policies. By some estimates only 25 percent of blood transfusions are screened for the presence of HIV. WHO hopes to establish blood safety programs in more than 80 percent of sub-Saharan countries by 2003.

HIV can be transmitted from an infected mother to her baby while the baby is still in the woman's uterus or, more commonly, during childbirth. The virus can also be transmitted through the mother's breast milk during breastfeeding. Mother-to-child transmission accounts for 90 percent of all cases of AIDS in children. Mother-to-child transmission is particularly prevalent in Africa, where the number of women infected with HIV is ten times the rate found in other regions. Studies conducted in several cities in southern Africa in 1998 indicate that up to 45 percent of pregnant women in these cities carry HIV.

The routes of HIV transmission are well documented by scientists, but health officials continually grapple with the public's unfounded fears concerning the potential for HIV transmission by other means. HIV differs from other infectious viruses in that it dies quickly if exposed to the environment. No evidence has linked HIV transmission to casual contact with an infected person, such as a handshake, hugging, or kissing, or even sharing dishes or bathroom facilities. Studies have been unable to identify HIV transmission from modes common to other infectious diseases, such as an insect bite or inhaling virus-infected droplets from an infected person's sneeze or cough.

Without medical intervention, AIDS progresses along a typical course. Within one to three weeks after infection with HIV, most people experience flu-like symptoms, such as fever, sore throat, headache, skin rash, tender lymph nodes, and a vague feeling of discomfort. These symptoms last one to four weeks. During this phase, known as acute retroviral syndrome, HIV reproduces rapidly in the blood. The virus circulates in the blood throughout the body, particularly concentrating in organs of the lymphatic system.

The normal immune defences against viral infections eventually activate to battle HIV in the body, reducing but not eliminating HIV in the blood. Infected individuals typically enter a prolonged asymptomatic phase, a symptom-free period that can last ten years or more. While persons who have HIV may remain in good health during this period, HIV continues to replicate, progressively destroying the immune system. Often an infected person remains unaware that he or she carries HIV and unknowingly transmits the virus to others during this phase of the infection.

When HIV infection reduces the number of CD4 cells to around 200 per microliter of blood, the infected individual enters an early symptomatic phase that may last a few months to several years. HIV-infected persons in this stage may experience a variety of symptoms that are not life-threatening but may be debilitating. These symptoms include extensive weight loss and fatigue (wasting syndrome), periodic fever, recurring diarrhea, and thrush, a fungal mouth infection. An early symptom of HIV infection in women is a recurring vaginal yeast infection. Unlike earlier stages of the disease, in this early symptomatic phase the symptoms that develop are severe enough to cause people to seek medical treatment. Many may first learn of their infection in this phase.

If CD4 cell levels drop below 200 cells per microliter of blood, the late symptomatic phase develops. This phase is characterized by the appearance of any of 26 opportunistic infections and rare cancers. The onset of these illnesses, sometimes referred to as AIDS-defining complications, is one sign that an HIV-infected person has developed full-blown AIDS. Without medical treatment, this stage may last from several months to years. The cumulative effects of these illnesses usually cause death.

Often the first opportunistic infection to develop is pneumocystis pneumonia, a lung infection caused by the fungus Pneumocystis carinii. This fungus infects most people in childhood, settling harmlessly in the lungs where it is prevented from causing disease by the immune system. But once the immune system becomes weakened, the fungus can block the lungs from delivering sufficient oxygen to the blood. The lack of oxygen leads to severe shortness of breath accompanied by fever and a dry cough.

In addition to pneumocystis pneumonia, people with AIDS often develop other fungal infections. Up to 23 percent of people with AIDS become infected with fungi from the genus Cryptococcus, which cause meningitis, inflammation of the membranes that surround the brain. Infection by the fungus Histoplasma capsulatum affects up to 10 percent of people with AIDS, causing general weight loss, fever, and respiratory complications.

Tuberculosis, a severe lung infection caused by the bacterium Mycobacterium tuberculosis, typically becomes more severe in AIDS patients than in those with a healthy immune system. Between the 1950s and the late 1980s, tuberculosis was practically eradicated in North America. In the early 1990s, doctors became alarmed when incidence of the disease dramatically escalated. This resurgence has been attributed to the increased susceptibility to tuberculosis of people infected with HIV. Infection by the bacterium Mycobacterium avium can cause fever, anaemia, and diarrhea. Other bacterial infections of the gastrointestinal tract contribute to wasting syndrome.

Opportunistic infections caused by viruses, especially members of the herpesvirus family, are common in people with AIDS. One of the herpesviruses, cytomegalovirus (CMV), infects the retina of the eye and can result in blindness. Another herpesvirus, Epstein-Barr virus (EBV), may cause certain types of blood cancers. Infections with herpes simplex virus (HSV) types 1 or 2 may result in sores around the mouth, genital area, or anus.

Many people with AIDS develop cancers. The destruction of CD4 cells impairs the immune functions that halt the development of cancer. Kaposi's sarcoma is a cancer of blood vessels caused by a herpesvirus. This cancer produces purple lesions on the skin, which can spread to internal organs and cause death. B cell lymphoma affects certain cells of the lymphatic system that fight infection and perform other vital functions. Cervical cancer is more common in HIV-infected women than in women free from infection.

A variety of neurological disorders are common in the later stage of AIDS. Collectively called HIV-associated dementia, they develop when HIV or another microbial organism infects the brain. The infection produces degeneration of intellectual processes such as memory and, sometimes, problems with movement and coordination.

HIV infection in children progresses more rapidly than in adults, most likely because the immune systems in children have not yet built up immunity to many infectious agents. The disease is particularly aggressive in infants—more than half of infants born with an HIV infection die before age two. Once a child is infected, the child's undeveloped immune system cannot prevent the virus from multiplying quickly in the blood. This extensive virus burden speeds the progression of the disease. In contrast, when adults become infected with HIV, their immune system generally fights the infection. Therefore, HIV levels in adults remain lower for an extended period, delaying the progression of the disease.

Children develop many of the opportunistic infections that befall adults but also exhibit symptoms not observed in older patients. Among infants and children, HIV infection produces wasting syndrome and slows growth (generally referred to as failure to thrive). HIV typically infects a child's brain early in the course of the disease, impairing intellectual development and coordination skills. While HIV can infect the brains of adults, it usually does so toward the later stages of the disease and produces different symptoms.

Children show a susceptibility to more bacterial and viral infections than adults. More than 20 percent of HIV-infected children develop serious, recurring bacterial infections, including meningitis and pneumonia. Some children suffer from repeated bouts of viral infections, such as chicken pox. Healthy children generally develop immunity to these viral illnesses after an initial infection.

Since HIV was first identified as the cause of AIDS in 1983, a variety of tests have been developed that help in the diagnoses. That HIV infection, as well as to ascertain how far the infection has progressed. Other tests can be used to screen donated blood, blood products, and body organs for the presence of HIV.

Doctors determine if HIV is present in the body by identifying HIV antibodies, specialized proteins created by the immune system to destroy HIV. The presence of the antibodies indicates HIV infection because these antibodies form in the body only when HIV is present. HIV antibodies form anywhere from five weeks to three months after HIV infection occurs, depending upon the individual's immune system. The antibodies are produced continually throughout the course of the infection.

The standard test to detect HIV antibodies in the blood is the enzyme-linked immunosorbent assay (ELISA). In this test, a blood sample is mixed with proteins from HIV. If the blood contains

HIV antibodies, they attach to the HIV proteins, producing a telltale colour change in the mixture. This test is highly reliable when performed two to three months after infection with HIV. The test is less reliable when used in the very early stage of HIV infection, before detectable levels of antibodies have had a chance to form. Doctors routinely confirm a positive result from an ELISA test by using the Western Blot test, which can detect lower levels of HIV antibodies. In this test a blood sample is applied to a paper strip containing HIV proteins. If HIV antibodies are present in the blood, they bind to the HIV proteins, producing a colour change on the paper. The combination of the ELISA and the Western Blot test is more than 99.9 percent accurate in detecting HIV infection within 12 weeks following exposure.

Once tests confirm an HIV infection, doctors monitor the health of the infected person's immune system by periodically measuring CD4 cell counts in the blood. The progressive loss of CD4 cells corresponds to a worsening of the disease as the immune system becomes increasingly impaired. Doctors also measure the viral load—the amounting of the virus in the blood—using polymerase chain reaction (PCR) technology. PCR tests measure the level of viral ribonucleic acid (RNA), a type of nucleic acid, in blood to determine the rate of HIV growth in an infected person. Knowing the viral load helps doctors estimate an infected person's survival time. For example, studies show that without treatment, the average survival time for people with an HIV viral load greater than 30,000 per microliter of blood is 4.4 years, while those with a viral load below 10,000 per microliter of blood live for an average of ten years.

A modified ELISA test that detects p24 antigen, a protein produced by HIV, can determine if specific drug treatments are having a positive effect on a patient. Blood banks, plasma Centres, clinical laboratories, private clinics, and public health departments also use this p24 antigen test to screen for the presence of HIV in blood, blood components, and organs before they are used in medical procedures.

Physicians prefer to differentiate between people who have HIV infection and those who have AIDS. The Centres for Disease Control and Prevention (CDC), based in Atlanta, Georgia, recommends that physicians reserve the diagnosis of AIDS for HIV-infected individuals whose CD4 count falls below 200 cells per microliter of blood. A diagnosis of AIDS can also be made without confirmation of CD4 levels if someone who has no other reason for immune system damage develops an opportunistic disease.

Research into the human immunodeficiency virus (HIV), the virus that causes acquired immunodeficiency syndrome (AIDS), has made remarkable progress since it began in the early 1980s. Preventive efforts have reduced the number of new cases of the disease, and for people already living with HIV/AIDS, the survival rate is increasing because of advances in drug therapy. But the majority of those affected by the disease live in developing nations, which, like many minority communities of the United States, are unable to afford the latest drug therapies and are still seriously threatened by the disease.

While no medical treatment cures AIDS, in the relatively short time since the disease was first recognized, new methods to treat the disease have developed rapidly. Health care professionals focus on three areas of therapy for people living with HIV infection or AIDS: antiretroviral therapy using drugs that suppress HIV replication medication and other treatments that fight the opportunistic infections and cancers that commonly accompany

HIV infection; and support mechanisms that help people deal with the emotional repercussions as well as the practical considerations of living with a disabling, potentially fatal disease.

This National Geographic article discusses ways the human body's immune system fights diseases, as well as attempts by scientists to develop vaccines for many virulent viruses including AIDS. Since this account was published early in the AIDS epidemic, it contains some information that has subsequently been revised or updated.

Understanding the specific steps in the HIV replication cycle is critical in order for scientists to develop drugs that attack vulnerable stages within the cycle. HIV belonged to a unique group of viruses known as retroviruses, so named because these viruses reverse the usual flow of genetic information within an infected cell. Most viruses store their genetic material in deoxyribonucleic acid (DNA), the double-helix structure that makes up genes. When a virus infects a cell, the viral DNA forms the template for the creation of messenger RNA, a type of ribonucleic acid. This messenger RNA directs the formation of specific proteins, and these proteins, in turn, builds new virus particles. In HIV, however, genetic material is stored in two single-stranded RNA molecules. When HIV infects a cell, an enzyme called reverse transcriptase copies the genetic instructions in the virus's RNA and moves it into the DNA. This movement of genetic information from RNA to DNA is the opposite of that which occurs in most cells during protein synthesis.

Another HIV enzyme, called integrase, helps the newly formed viral DNA to become part of the structure of the infected cell's DNA. The viral DNA then forces the infected cell to manufacture HIV particles. A third HIV enzyme, called protease, packages these HIV particles into a complete and functional HIV virus. Over the last decade researchers have created a variety of drugs that block the action of some of the enzymes used in HIV replication. The main classes of drugs used against HIV are nucleoside analogues, non-nucleoside reverse transcriptase inhibitors, protease inhibitors, and fusion inhibitors.

Nucleoside analogues impede the action of reverse transcriptase, the HIV enzyme that converts the virus's genetic material into DNA. During this conversion process, these drugs incorporate themselves into the structure of the viral DNA, rendering the DNA useless and preventing it from instructing the infected cell to make additional HIV. The nucleoside analogue known as azidothymidine (AZT), which became available in 1987, was the first drug approved by the United States Food and Drug Administration (FDA) to treat AIDS. AZT slows HIV growth in the body, permitting an increase in the number of CD4 cells, which boosts the immune system. AZT also prevents transmission of HIV from an infected mother to her newborn. Since the introduction of AZT, additional nucleoside analogues have been developed, including didanosine (sold under the trade name Videx), zalcitabine (HIVID), stavudine (Zerit), lamivudine (Epivir), and abacavir (Ziagen). These drugs are not particularly powerful when used alone, and often their benefits last for only 6 to 12 months. But when nucleoside analogues are used in combination with each other, they provide longer-lasting and more effective results.

Non-nucleoside reverse transcriptase inhibitors (NNRTIs), introduced in 1996, use a different mechanism to block reverse transcriptase. These drugs bind directly to reverse transcriptase, preventing the enzyme from converting RNA to DNA. Three NNRTIs are available: nevirapine (Viramune), delavirdine

(Rescriptor), and efavirenz (Sustiva). NNRTIs work best when used in combination with nucleoside analogues.

The third group of antiviral drugs, called protease inhibitors, cripples protease, the enzyme vital to the formation of new HIV. When these drugs block protease, defective HIV forms that is unable to infect new cells. Protease inhibitors are more powerful than nucleosides and NNRTIs, producing dramatic decreases in HIV levels in the blood. This reduced a viral load, in turn, enables CD4 cell levels to skyrocket. The first protease inhibitor, saquinavir (Invirase), was approved in 1995. Since then other protease inhibitors have been approved, including ritonavir (Norvir), indinavir (Crixivan), nelfinavir (Viracept), and amprenavir (Agenerase).

A new class of drugs, known as fusion inhibitors, became available in 2003 when the FDA approved the use of enfuvirtide, sold under the brand name Fuzeon. Fusion inhibitors prevent the binding or fusion of HIV to CD4 cells. When used with other antiretroviral medicines, fusion inhibitors can reduce the amount of HIV in the blood and increase the number of CD4 cells.

Clinical studies of treatment with antiretroviral drugs immediately showed that their benefits are short-lived when a single drug is used alone. This short-term effectiveness results when HIV mutates, or changes its genetic structure, becoming resistant to the drug. The genetic material in HIV provides instructions for the manufacture of critical enzymes needed to replicate the virus. Scientists design current antiretroviral drugs to impede the activity of these enzymes. If the virus mutates, the structure of the virus's enzymes changes. Drugs no longer work against the enzymes, making the drugs ineffective against viral infection.

Genes mutate during the course of viral replication, so the best way to prevent mutation is to halt replication. Studies have shown that the most effective treatment to halt HIV replication employs a combination of three drugs taken together—for instances, a combination of two nucleoside analogues with a protease inhibitor. This regimen, called triple therapy, maximizes drug potency while reducing the chance for drug resistance. The combination of three drugs is often referred to as an AIDS cocktail. In HIV-infected patients who have undergone triple therapy, the viral loads reduced significantly, sometimes to undetectable levels. Their CD4 cell counts gradually increased, and they sustained good health with no complications. With this treatment, some patients who were near death were able to return to work and normal physical activity. Triple therapy was introduced in the United States in 1996. That year AIDS deaths in the United States decreased 26 percent, the first decrease since the beginning of the epidemic. In 1997 US AIDS deaths decreased by 56 percent from the year before.

Despite phenomenal success, triple therapy has some drawbacks. This multidrug therapy is quite complicated, requiring patients to take anywhere from 5 to 20 pills a day on a specific schedule. Some drugs must be taken with food, while others cannot be taken at the same time as certain other pills. Even the most organized of people find it difficult to take pills correctly. Yet, just one or two lapses in treatment may cause the virus to develop resistance to the drug regimen.

Many people also find it difficult to deal with the unpleasant side effects produced by antiretroviral drugs. Common side effects include nausea, diarrhea, headache, fatigue, abdominal pain, kidney stones, anaemia, and tingling or numbness in the hands and feet. Some patients may develop diabetes mellitus, while other patients develop collections of fat deposits in the abdomen or back, causing a noticeable change in body configurations. Some antiretroviral drugs produce an increase in blood fat levels, placing a patient at risk for heart attack or stroke. Some patients suffer more misery from the drug treatment than they do from the illnesses produced by HIV infection.

Perhaps the greatest drawback to triple therapy is its cost, which ranges from $10,000 to $12,000 a year. This high cost is well beyond the means of people with low incomes or those with limited health care insurance. As a result, the most effective therapies currently available remain beyond the reach of the majority of HIV-infected people worldwide.

To decrease the toxic effects of drugs and to defer costly therapy, in 2001 United States federal health officials recommended delaying drug treatment for HIV infection in people showing no symptoms and who have been infected with HIV for more than six months. The new guidelines call for delaying treatment until an infected person's CD4 cells fall below 350 cells per microliter of blood or the HIV viral load exceeds 30,000 per microliter of blood. Evidence suggests, that delaying treatment poses no harm to infected people and, in fact, benefits them by deferring the toxic side effects of the drugs.

Studies show that under certain circumstances, administering antiretroviral drugs within 24 hours (preferably within one to two hours) after exposure to HIV can protect a person from becoming infected with the virus. Although the effectiveness of postexposure antiretroviral therapy following sexual exposure to HIV remains uncertain, the CDC recommends that health care personnel exposed to HIV infection from a needle stick or other accident take antiretroviral drugs.

Scientists continue to develop more powerful HIV treatments that have fewer side effects and fewer resistance problems. Some drugs under investigation block the HIV enzyme integrase from inserting viral DNA into the infected cell. Other drugs prevent HIV from binding with a CD4 cell in the first place, thereby barring HIV entry into cells.

Some scientists focus on ways to fortify the immune system. A biological molecule called interleukin-2 shows promise in boosting the immune system's arsenal of infection-fighting cells. Interleukin-2 stimulates the production of CD4 cells. If enough CD4 cells can be created, they may trigger other immune cell responses that can overpower HIV infection.

In other research, doctors hope to bolster the immune system with a vaccine. Most vaccines available today, including those that prevent measles or poliomyelitis, work by helping the body to create antibodies. Such vaccines mark specific infectious agents, such as the measles and polio viruses, for destruction. But many experts believe that an effective HIV vaccine will need to do more than just stimulate anti-HIV antibodies. Studies are underway to develop vaccines that also elevate the production of T cells in the immune system. Scientists hope that this dual approach will prime the immune system to attack HIV as soon as it appears in the body, perhaps containing the virus before it spreads through the body in a way that natural immune defence cannot. The genetic variability of HIV frustrates efforts to develop a vaccine: A vaccine effective against one type of HIV may not work on a virus that has undergone genetic mutation.

In addition to antiretroviral therapy to combat HIV infection, effective drug treatments are available to fight many of the medical complications that result from HIV infection. Doctors try to prevent infections before they begin to avoid taxing a patient's weakened immune system unnecessarily. A doctor instructs an HIV-infected person on ways to avoid exposure to infectious agents that produce opportunistic infections common in people with a weakened immune system. Doctors usually prescribe more than one drug to forestall infections. For example, for those who have a history of pneumocystic pneumonia and a CD4 cell count of less than 200 cells per microliter, doctors may prescribe the antibiotic sulfamethoxazole and trimethoprim to prevent further bouts of pneumonia. Patients suffering from recurring thrush may be given the antifungal drug fluconazole for prolonged periods. For people with CD4 cell counts of less than 100 cells per microliter, doctors may prescribe clarithromycin or azithromycin to prevent Mycobacterium avium infections.

The AIDS quilt travels on display to promote public awareness of acquired immunodeficiency syndrome (AIDS). The quilt project, initiated in 1986 by the NAMES Project organization, consists of thousands of panels. Each panel is individually designed and is dedicated to the memory of someone who has died of AIDS.

A person diagnosed with HIV infection, he faces many challenges, including choosing the best course of treatment, paying for health care, and providing for the needs of children in the family while ill. In addition to these practical considerations, people with HIV infection must cope with the emotional toll associated with the diagnosis of a potentially fatal illness. The social stigma that continues to surround a diagnosis of AIDS because of the disease's prevalence among gay men or drug users causes many people to avoid telling family or friends about their illness. People with AIDS often feel incredibly lonely as they try to cope with a devastating illness on their own. Loneliness, anxiety, fear, anger, and other emotions often require as much attention as the medical illnesses common to HIV infection.

Since the AIDS epidemic began in the United States in 1981, grassroots organizations have been created to meet the medical and emotional needs of people who have AIDS and also to protect their civil rights. The Gay Men's Health Crisis, founded in 1982, was the first nonprofit organization to provide medical, education, and advocacy services for people with AIDS. The Los Angeles Shanti Group was established in 1983 to provide emotional support and medical guidance to people with AIDS and other life-threatening illnesses. Activist organizations such as the AIDS Coalition to Unleash Power (ACT UP), founded in 1986, have been created to initiate faster change in public policies and to speed up the course of AIDS clinical research. American Foundation for AIDS Research (AMFAR), created in 1985, is the nation's leading nonprofit organization dedicated to the support of AIDS research and the advocacy of fair and compassionate AIDS-related public policies. In Canada, the AIDS Committee of Toronto (ACT) was established in 1983 by community activists intent on fighting for the civil rights of people infected with HIV. As the AIDS epidemic grew, ACT expanded its mission to help people disabled by the disease and to spread health information to halt the spread of the disease. AIDS Vancouver (AV), also layed the groundwork, in 1983, that became the principal education, prevention, and support service organization for that city.

Counselling Centres and churches provide individual or group counselling to help people with HIV infection or AIDS share their feelings, problems, and coping mechanisms with others. Family counselling can address the emotions of other family members who are disturbed by the diagnosis of HIV infection in another family member. Grief counselling also helps people who have lost friends or family members to AIDS.

In the United States and Canada, government-funded and privately funded organizations help people cope with disease. For instance, local, city-funded clinics provide AIDS testing as well as counselling to prepare people for a test result that indicates HIV infection. Health experts at clinics explain the medical progression of the illness, arrange medical appointments with health care specialists, and help people choose appropriate treatment options. State-appointed social workers and community nonprofit organizations help people find federally funded programs that offset the high cost of medical care and child care.

The United States Congress has passed legislation to help HIV-infected individuals. In 1990 the American peoples with Disabilities Act (ADA) were enacted, protecting people with disabling diseases, including AIDS, from discrimination in activities such as applying for jobs or buying a house. The Ryan White Comprehensive AIDS Resources Emergency Act was established in 1990 and reauthorized in 1996. This program provides medical and dental care, counselling, transportation, and home and hospice care for low-income or uninsured people living with AIDS. The AIDS Drug Assistance Program (ADAP) is funded in large part by this act and administered by all 50 states. It pays for costly AIDS medications for people who do not have private insurance and who are not poor enough to be eligible for Medicaid.

A landmark United Nations (UN) report, issued in June 2000, documents the terrible effects that acquired immunodeficiency syndrome (AIDS) has had on millions of people around the world. This excerpt focuses on some of the successes that individual nations have achieved in stabilizing or halting the spread of the disease and what other countries can learn from those successes.

With a vaccine for AIDS years away and no cure on the horizon, experts believe that the most effective treatment for AIDS is to prevent the occurrence of HIV infection. Health officials focus public education programs on altering risky behaviours linked to HIV transmission, particularly unsafe sexual practices and needle-sharing by intravenous drug users. Safe-sex campaigns sponsored by health clinics, social Centres, schools, and churches encourage sexual abstinence or monogamy (sexual relations with only one partner). Education programs instruct about the proper way to use condoms to provide a protective barrier against transmission of HIV during sexual intercourse. Needle-exchange programs, which provide clean needles to drug users, enable intravenous drug abusers to avoid sharing HIV-contaminated needles. Needle-exchange programs have been widely criticized because they seem to condone illicit drug use. However, numerous US government-funded studies have indicated that such programs reduce HIV transmission without promoting greater drug use. To reduce the accidental transmission of HIV during medical procedures, both the United States and Canada have established strict guidelines for health care settings, including the use of protective clothing and proper instrument disposal.

In the United States, the effectiveness of public education programs that target people at risk for HIV infection was well demonstrated in the gay community of San Francisco, California, in the 1980s. In 1982 and 1983, 6,000 to 8,000 people in San Francisco became infected with HIV. The gay community rallied to promote condom use and advocate monogamy through extensive education programs and public health advertisements geared for gay men. These public education programs were credited with reducing the number of gay men in San Francisco who became HIV infected. By 1993 the number of new infections declined to 1,000, and by 1999, fewer than 500 people were infected each year.

Public education about AIDS has also proven effective in other countries. Uganda was one of the first African countries to report cases of HIV infection. The first cases of AIDS were reported there in 1982, and by the late 1980s Uganda had one of the highest rates of HIV infection in the world. The Ugandan government was one of the first countries to set up a partnership with WHO to create a national AIDS control program called the AIDS Information Centre (AIC). The AIC has established extensive education programs promoting condom use and other methods to prevent HIV from spreading further. The program has also worked with community organizations to change social behaviours that increase the risk of HIV infection. The AIC promotes its message using innovative drama, song, and dance programs, a particularly effective communication method for African communities. AIC established confidential HIV testing services that provide same-day results and community counselling programs. As a result of Uganda's quick response to the AIDS epidemic, the number of HIV infected people in that country has declined significantly since 1993, during a time when most other African nations faced a frightening increase in the incidence of HIV infection.

Public health officials have learned that education programs that teach and reinforce safe behaviours through a series of meetings are more effective than one-time exposure to public-health information provided in a class lecture, magazine article, advertisement, or pamphlet. Education programs tailored to reflect specific ethnic and cultural preferences prove even more effective. For example, the Canadian Aboriginal AIDS Network creates

HIV education programs that fight the common misperception among the indigenous peoples of Canada that AIDS is primarily a disease of white, affluent people. Among indigenous communities, the network promotes programs that use colloquial language to increase awareness about safe sex practices and needle use.

In the short time since the first cases of the AIDS epidemic were reported in 1981, scientists have identified the viral cause of the illness, the basic modes of transmission, accurate tests for the presence of infection, and effective drugs that slow or halt the progression of the disease. During that same period, governments and grassroots organizations around the world were spurred into action to meet the growing need for AIDS education, counselling, patients' rights, and clinical research. Despite these advances, critics observe that many governments were slow to respond to the crisis. For example, United States president Ronald Reagan did not discuss AIDS in public until 1987, more than six years after the start of the AIDS epidemic. By that time, 41,000 Americans had already died from the disease. AIDS advocates believe that the lack of federal support for AIDS research in these early years delayed the development of an effective vaccine or a cure for the disease.

Using computer technology to study the structure of HIV, scientists have determined that HIV originated around 1930 in rural areas of Central Africa, where the virus may have been present for many years in isolated communities. The virus probably did not spread because members of these rural communities had limited contact with people from other areas. But in the 1960s and 1970s, political upheaval, wars, drought, and famine forced many people from these rural areas to migrate to cities to find jobs. During this time, the incidence of sexually transmitted infections, including HIV infection, accelerated and quickly spread throughout Africa. As world travel became more prevalent, HIV infection developed into a worldwide epidemic. Studies of stored blood from the United States suggest that HIV infection was well established there by 1978.

In 1970, at about the same time that the HIV epidemic was taking hold in Africa, American molecular biologist David Baltimore and American virologist Howard Temin independently discovered the enzyme reverse transcriptase, which could be used to identify retroviruses. Over the next ten years, many retroviruses were identified in animals. But not until 1980, shortly before the first AIDS cases were recognized in the United States, did American virologist Robert Gallo identify the first human retroviruses, HTLV-I and HTLV-II (HTLV stands for human T cell lymphotropic virus).

Other studies demonstrated that these human retroviruses were more closely related to a retrovirus found in African chimpanzees than to each other. This discovery suggests that the human retroviruses may have evolved from retroviruses that originally infected chimpanzees. The chimpanzee retrovirus likely infected people and underwent mutations to form the human retrovirus. In 1999 scientists confirmed that HIV had been initially generated from chimpanzees to humans, as, on three separate occasions in Central Africa, probably beginning in the 1940s or 1950s.

In 1983 French biologist and cancer specialist Luc Montagnier and his research team isolated the human immunodeficiency virus (HIV), the virus that causes AIDS. Montagnier has since become a champion of AIDS prevention education and has devoted his career to developing an AIDS vaccine.

Beginning in June 1981 the CDC published reports on clusters of gay men in New York and California who had been diagnosed with pneumocystic pneumonia or Kaposi's sarcoma. These two rare illnesses had previously been observed only in people whose immune systems had been damaged by drugs or disease. These reports triggered concern that a disease of the immune system was spreading quickly in the homosexual community. Initially called gay-related immunodeficiency disease (GRID), the new illness soon was identified in population groups outside the gay community, including users of intravenous drugs, recipients of blood transfusions, and heterosexual partners of infected people. In 1982 the name for the new illness was changed to acquired immunodeficiency syndrome, or AIDS.

While the disease was making headlines for the speed with which it was spreading around the world, the cause of AIDS remained unidentified. Fear of AIDS and ignorance of its causes resulted in some outlandish theories. Some thought the disease was God's punishment for behaviours that they considered immoral. These early theories created a social stigma surrounding the disease that still lingers.

Scientists quickly identified the primary modes of transmission— sexual contact with an infected person, contact with infected blood products, and mother-to-child transmission. From these modes of transmission it was clear that the new illness was spread in a specific manner that matched the profile of a viral infection. In 1983 French cancer specialist Luc Montagnier and his colleagues isolated what appeared to be a new human retrovirus from AIDS patients. They named it lymphadenopathy virus (LAV). Eight months later Gallo and his colleagues isolated the same virus in AIDS patients, naming the virus HTLV-III. Eventually, scientists agreed to call the infectious agent human immunodeficiency virus (HIV). In 1985 a new AIDS-causing virus was discovered in West Africa. Named HIV-2, the new virus is closely related to the first

HIV, but it appears to be less harmful to cells of the immune system and reproduces more slowly than HIV-1.

Research leading to the development of the ELISA test was conducted simultaneously by teams led by Gallo in the United States and Montagnier in France. In 1985 the ELISA test to identify HIV in blood became available, followed by the development of the Western Blot test. These tests were first employed to screen blood for the presence of HIV before the blood was used in medical procedures. The tests were later used to identify HIV-infected people, many of whom did not know they were infected. These diagnostic tests also helped scientists study the course of HIV infection in populations.

The CDC presented its first definition of AIDS in 1982. The CDC recommended that physicians diagnose AIDS if a person has an illness known to be caused by immune deficiency, as long as there is no known cause for this immune deficiency (people who undergo radiation therapy or who take certain drugs may impair their immune systems). As more information became known about the course of HIV infection and the nature of the virus itself, this definition of AIDS was revised repeatedly to expand the list of illnesses considered diagnostic indicators of the disease. Early definitions were based on the opportunistic infections commonly found in HIV-infected men. As a result, many women who did not have symptoms covered in the official AIDS definition were denied disability benefits and AIDS-related drug therapies.

The current definition of AIDS was created in 1993 and includes 26 opportunistic infections and cancers, known as diagnostic indicators, that affect both men and women. The definition also emphasizes the importance of the level of CD4 cells in the blood.

Today doctors make the diagnosis of AIDS in anyone with a CD4 count below 200 cells per microliter of blood, regardless of the associated illnesses they may have.

Although new and effective AIDS drugs have brought hope to many HIV-infected persons, a number of social and ethical dilemmas still confront researchers and public-health officials. The latest combination drug therapies are far too expensive for infected persons in the developing world—particularly in sub-Saharan Africa, where the majority of AIDS deaths have occurred. In these regions, where the incidence of HIV infection continues to soar, the lack of access to drugs can be catastrophic. In 1998, responding to an international outcry, several pharmaceutical firms announced that they would slash the price of AIDS drugs in developing nations by as much as 75 percent. However, some countries argued that drug firms had failed to deliver on their promises of less expensive drugs. In South Africa government officials developed legislation that would enable the country to override the patent rights of drug firms by importing cheaper generic medicines made in India and Thailand to treat HIV infection. In 1998, 39 pharmaceutical companies sued the South African government on the grounds that the legislation violated international trade agreements. Pharmaceutical companies eventually dropped their legal efforts in April 2001, conceding that South Africa's legislation did comply with international trading laws. The end of the legal battle was expected to pave the way for other developing countries to gain access to more affordable AIDS drugs.

AIDS research in the developing world has raised ethical questions pertaining to the clinical testing of new therapies and potential vaccines. For example, controversy erupted over 1997 clinical trials that tested a shorter course of AZT therapy in HIV-infected pregnant women in developing countries. Earlier studies had shown that administering AZT to pregnant women for up to six months prior to birth could cut mother-to-child transmission of HIV by up to two-thirds. The treatment's $800 cost, however, made it too expensive for patients in developing nations.

The controversial 1997 clinical trials, which were conducted in Thailand and other regions in Asia and Africa, tested a shorter course of AZT treatment, costing only $50. Some pregnant women received AZT, while others received a placebo—a medically inactive substance often used in drug trials to help scientists determine the effectiveness of the drug under study. Ultimately the shorter course of AZT treatment proved to be successful and is now standard practice in a growing number of developing nations. However, at the time of the trials, critics charged that using a placebo on HIV-infected pregnant women—when AZT had already been shown to prevent mother-to-child transmission—was unethical and needlessly placed babies at fatal risk. Defenders of the studies countered that a placebo was necessary to accurately gauge the effectiveness of the AZT short-course treatment. Some critics speculated whether such a trial, while apparently acceptable in the developing nations of Asia and Africa, would ever have been viewed as ethical, or even permissible, in a developed nation like the United States.

Similar ethical questions surround the testing of AIDS vaccines in developing nations. Vaccines typically use weakened or killed HIV to spark antibody production. In some vaccines, these weakened or killed viruses have the potential to cause infection and disease. Critics questioned whether it is ethical to place all the risk on test subjects in developing regions such as sub-Saharan Africa, where a person infected by a vaccine would have little or no access to medical care. At the same time, with AIDS causing up to

5,500 deaths a day in Africa, others feel that developing nations must pursue any medical avenue for stemming the epidemic and protecting people from the virus.

For the struggling economies of some developing nations, AIDS has brought yet another burden: AIDS tends to kill young adults in the prime of their lives—the primary breadwinners and caregivers in families. According to figures released by the United Nations in 1999, AIDS has shortened the life expectancy in some African nations by an average of seven years. In Zimbabwe, life expectancy for adults declined from 61 years in 1993 to 38 in 2003, according to the World Health Organization (WHO). The next few decades may see average life expectance fall even lower in sub-Saharan Africa. As of 2003, 14 million children around the world had been orphaned by the AIDS epidemic. Those children who survive face a lack of income, a higher risk of malnutrition and disease, and the breakdown of family structure.

In Africa, the disease has had a heavy impact on urban professionals—educated, skilled workers who play a critical role in the labour force of industries such as agriculture, education, transportation, and government. The decline in the skilled workforce has already damaged economic growth in Africa, and economists warn of disastrous consequences in the future.

The grassroots AIDS organization AIDS Coalition to Unleash Power, commonly known as ACT UP, uses nonviolent civil disobedience to protest against government and societal indifference to the AIDS epidemic.

From the early days of the identification of AIDS, the disease has been powerfully linked to behaviours that are illegal (such as illicit drug use) or are considered immoral by many people (such as promiscuity and homosexuality). Consequently, a diagnosis of AIDS was a mark of disgrace, although medical research revealed that the disease follows well-defined modes of transmission that can affect any person. As the extent of the epidemic unfolded as misinformation about AIDS and how it is transmitted triggered widespread fear of contracting the disease. Some communities responded with hysteria that resulted in violence. In the United States in 1987, a Florida family with three HIV-positive sons who had become infected from blood transfusions were driven from their home when it was torched by an arsonist. In other communities, parents protested when HIV-infected children attended school. In many areas of the world, women in particular may face consequences if their HIV status is discovered. Reports indicate that many HIV-infected women are subject to domestic violence at the hands of their husbands—even if the husbands themselves are the source of infection. As a result, some women in developing nations fear being tested for HIV infection and cut themselves off from medical care and counselling.

In addition to social stigma, HIV-infected persons must grapple with more immediate concerns—daily struggles for basic medical care and other basic rights in the face of discrimination and fear because of their HIV status. In China, for example, the number of HIV-positive individuals is a comparatively small problem so far. Yet nurses and other medical personnel who fear infection commonly refuse to perform procedures on HIV-infected people. This sort of discrimination against HIV-infected individuals has long been a problem in the United States. In 1998 the United States Supreme Court heard the case of Sidney Abbott, a young woman in Maine who sued dentist Randon Bragdon after he refused to treat her when he learned of her HIV-positive status. Basing its ruling on the Americans with Disabilities Act, the

Supreme Court ruled in Bragdon v. Abbott that the woman's HIV infection constituted a disability, even though she suffered from no disease symptoms. AIDS advocates expect this decision to protect the rights of many people with AIDS in the United States.

Some developing nations, such as Uganda, have met the AIDS crisis head-on, attempting to educate citizens and change high-risk behaviours in the population. However, other nations have been slow to even acknowledge the disease. In India, for example, the nation's prime minister did not speak publicly about the dangers posed by the epidemic until 1999.

In developed nations, some of the stigma attached to a diagnosis of AIDS has lessened in recent years, in part due to the admissions by public figures and celebrities, especially in the United States, that they were HIV infected. The deaths from AIDS of actor Rock Hudson and tennis players Arthur Ashe, and the AIDS advocacy roles of basketball player Magic Johnson and Olympic diver Greg Louganis have personalized the disease and helped society come to terms with the enormity of the epidemic.

To some scientists, the AIDS epidemic signals a troubling trend in humanity's future. Along with other deadly microbial threats of recent years—most notably Ebola virus, which has caused sporadic epidemics in Africa, and hantavirus, which broke out in the American Southwest in the early 1990s—AIDS is viewed by some as yet another in a series of emerging diseases that demonstrate how vulnerable humans are to newly encountered microbes. With population and land development increasing, humans have encroached farther into rain forests and other formerly wild areas, unleashing previously unknown disease agents. Meanwhile, global travel has become faster, more convenient, and more accessible to many people. Some scientists are worried by these trends, fearing the potential for an as-yet-unknown pathogen to arise and spread quickly and lethally around the globe.

The social, ethical, and economic effects of the AIDS epidemic are still being played out, and no one is entirely certain what the consequences will be. Despite the many grim facts of the AIDS epidemic, however, humanity is armed with proven, effective weapons against the disease: knowledge, education, prevention, and the ever-growing store of information about the virus's actions.

Human Immunodeficiency Virus, infectious agent that causes acquired immunodeficiency syndrome (AIDS), a disease that leaves a person vulnerable to life-threatening infections. Scientists have identified two types of this virus. HIV-1 is the primary cause of AIDS worldwide. HIV-2 is found mostly in West Africa.

The human immunodeficiency virus (HIV), the cause of acquired immunodeficiency syndrome (AIDS), is genetically programmed to do one thing: highjack the reproductive machinery of a human cell, then trick it into churning out as many copies of the virus as it can before the cell dies. The current best hope for the treatment of AIDS requires that patients take a number of different drugs, each of which interferes with certain steps of the HIV infection process.

The human immunodeficiency virus (HIV) consists of a nucleoid core and the surrounding protein matrix, both enclosed in a lipid envelope. The nucleoid core contains the viral genetic material and the reverse transcriptase enzyme, which are used in viral replication. The transmembrane glycoprotein gp41 and the envelope glycoprotein gp120 are attached to the envelope; these proteins enable HIV to bind and fuse with a target host cell.

Human immunodeficiency viruses (HIV) is the cause of acquired immunodeficiency syndrome (AIDS). By infecting CD4 T-lymphocytes, a type of white blood cell, HIV weakens the immune system and leaves the infected individual open to deadly infections. The viruses gain access to a T-lymphocyte by attaching to CD4 proteins on the outer surface of the cell membrane.

In 1999 alone, 4 million people in sub-Saharan Africa became infected with the human immunodeficiency virus (HIV), the virus that causes acquired immunodeficiency syndrome (AIDS). In several African countries, at least half of males currently aged 15 will eventually die of AIDS. These and other shocking facts about the level of devastation that HIV/AIDS has inflicted and will inflict on the people and economies of Africa are documented in the Report on the Global HIV/AIDS Epidemic. The report, excerpted here, was published in June 2000 by the Joint United Nations Programme on HIV/AIDS, known as UNAIDS.

A landmark United Nations (UN) reports, issued in June 2000, the document of the terrible effects that acquired immunodeficiency syndrome (AIDS) has had on millions of people around the world. This excerpt focuses on some of the successes that individual nations have achieved in stabilizing or halting the spread of the disease and what other countries can learn from those successes.

HIV belongs to the retrovirus family of viruses, whose members share a unique method of replicating themselves when they infect living cells. Retroviruses store their genetic information in molecules of ribonucleic acid (RNA). However, unlike other RNA viruses, retroviruses use RNA as a template (a master pattern) for forming deoxyribonucleic acid (DNA), the genetic material that puts viral replication instructions into effect. This process, called reverse transcription, is the exact opposite of the normal flow of genetic information in living things, in which DNA serves as the template for RNA formation.

HIV consisted of a flexible outer membrane, called the envelope, that surrounds a protein case known as the capsid. The envelope is studded with glycoproteins, chemical receptors that enable the virus to lock onto target cells. Inside the capsid is lodged of two identical strands of RNA. These RNA strands make up the virus's genetic program and store all the instructions needed to replicate HIV once it has infected a host cell. HIV also contains molecules of an enzyme called reverse transcriptase. When HIV infects a cell, reverse transcriptase copies the genetic instructions in the virus's RNA and uses the instructions to build complementary strands of DNA.

HIV transmission occurs when a person is exposed to body fluids infected with the virus, such as blood, semen, vaginal secretions, and breast milk. The primary modes of HIV transmission are (1) sexual relations with an infected person, (2) sharing hypodermic needles or accidental pricking by a needle contaminated with infected blood; (3) transfer of the virus from an infected mother to her baby during pregnancy, childbirth, or through breast-feeding.

When HIV enters the body, it infects lymphocytes, which are a type of white blood cell in the immune system. HIV uses its glycoproteins to attach itself to receptors on the surface of a lymphocyte. The outer envelope of HIV then fuses with the lymphocyte, enabling the HIV capsid to enter the lymphocyte itself. HIV commandeers the genetic material of the lymphocyte, instructing the cell to replicate more viruses. The newly formed viruses break free from the host, destroying the cell in the process. The new viruses go on to infect and destroy other lymphocytes.

Over a period that may last from a few months to up to 15 years, HIV may destroy enough lymphocytes that the immune system becomes unable to function properly. An infected person develops multiple life-threatening illnesses from infections that normally do not cause illnesses in people with a healthy immune system. Some people who have HIV infection may not develop any of the clinical illnesses that define the full-blown disease of AIDS for ten years or more. Doctors prefer to use the term AIDS for cases where a person has reached the final, life-threatening stage of HIV infection.

No treatment is available that cures AIDS, but a number of drugs have been developed that suppress HIV replication, thereby preventing the destruction of the immune system. Known as antiretroviral therapy, these drugs target different stages in the life cycle of HIV. There are four main classes of drugs used against HIV: nucleoside analogues, non-nucleoside reverse transcriptase inhibitors, protease inhibitors, and fusion inhibitors. Nucleoside analogues and non-nucleoside reverse transcriptase inhibitors use different mechanisms to block the action of the enzyme reverse transcriptase. Protease inhibitors interfere with protease, an enzyme vital to the formation of new HIV. When these drugs block protease, defective HIV forms that is unable to infect new cells. In 2003 the US Food and Drug Administration approved the use of enfuvirtide, sold under the brand name Fuzeon. This drug belongs to a new class of drugs called fusion inhibitors, which prevent the binding or fusion of HIV to lymphocytes.

Ribonucleic Acid (RNA), genetic material of certain viruses (RNA viruses) and, in cellular organisms, the molecule that directs the middle steps of protein production. In RNA viruses, the RNA directs two processes—protein synthesis (production of the virus's protein coat) and replication (the process by which

RNA copies itself). In cellular organisms, another type of genetic material, called deoxyribonucleic acid (DNA), carries the information that determines protein structure. But DNA cannot act alone and relies upon RNA to transfer this crucial information during protein synthesis (production of the proteins needed by the cell for its activities and development).

Like DNA, RNA consists of a chain of chemical compounds called nucleotides. Each nucleotide is made up of a sugar molecule called ribose, a phosphate group, and one of four different nitrogen-containing compounds called bases. The four bases are adenine, guanine, uracil, and cytosine. These components are joined together in the same manner as in a deoxyribonucleic acid (DNA) molecule. RNA differs chemically from DNA in two ways: The RNA sugar molecule contains an oxygen atom not found in DNA, and RNA contains the base uracil in the place of the base thymine in DNA.

In cellular organisms, RNA is a single-stranded polynucleotide chain, a strand of many nucleotides linked together. There are three types of RNA. Ribosomal RNA (rRNA) is found in the cell's ribosomes, the specialized structures that are the sites of protein synthesis. Transfer RNA (tRNA) carries amino acids to the ribosomes for incorporation into a protein. Messenger RNA (mRNA) carries the genetic blueprint copied from the sequence of bases in a cell's DNA. This blueprint specifies the sequence of amino acids in a protein. All three types of RNA are formed as needed, using specific sections of the cell's DNA as templates.

Some RNA viruses have double-stranded RNA—that is, their RNA molecules consist of two parallel polynucleotide chains. The base of each RNA nucleotide in one chain pairs with a complementary base in the second chain—that is, adenine pairs with uracil, and guanine pairs with cytosine. For these viruses, the process of RNA replication in a host cell follows the same pattern as that of DNA replication, a method of replication called semi-conservative replication. In semi-conservative replication, each newly formed double-stranded RNA molecule contains one polynucleotide chain from the parent RNA molecule, and one complementary chain formed through the process of base pairing. The Colorado tick fever virus, which causes mild respiratory infections, is a double stranded RNA virus.

There are two types of single-stranded RNA viruses. After entering a host cell, one type, polio virus, becomes double-stranded by making an RNA strand complementary to its own. During replication, although the two strands separate, only the recently formed strand attracts nucleotides with complementary bases. Therefore, the polynucleotide chain that is produced as a result of replication is exactly the same as the original RNA chain.

The other type of single-stranded RNA viruses, called retroviruses, include the human immunodeficiency virus (HIV), which causes AIDS, and other viruses that cause tumours. After entering a host cell, a retrovirus makes a DNA strand complementary to its own RNA strand using the host's DNA nucleotides. This new DNA strand then replicates and forms a double helix that becomes incorporated into the host cell's chromosomes, where it is replicated along with the host DNA. While in a host cell, the RNA-derived viral DNA produces single-stranded RNA viruses that then leave the host cell and enter other cells, where the replication process is repeated.

In 1981, American biochemist Thomas Cech discovered that certain RNA molecules appear to act as enzymes, molecules that speed up, or catalyze, some reactions inside cells. Until this discovery biologists thought that all enzymes were proteins. Like other enzymes, these RNA catalysts, called ribozymes, show great specificity with respect to the reactions they speed up. The discovery of ribozymes added to the evidence that RNA, not DNA, was the earliest genetic material. Many scientists think that the earliest genetic molecule was simple in structure and capable of enzymatic activity. Furthermore, the molecule would necessarily exist in all organisms. The enzyme ribonuclease-P, which exists in all organisms, is made of protein and a form of RNA that has enzymatic activity. Based on this evidence, some scientists suspect that the RNA portion of ribonuclease-P may be the modern equivalent of the earliest genetic molecule, the molecule that first enabled replication to occur in primitive cells.

Deoxyribonucleic acid (DNA), one of the nucleic acids, stores genetic information within cells, while enzymes are protein molecules that cause cellular reactions. RNA is the go-between, translating genetic information to protein by means of small molecules called transfer RNA (tRNA). While studying the formation of tRNA in 1978, Altman discovered an enzyme called ribonuclease P (RNase P), composed of both RNA and a protein. He noted that RNase P caused the splicing of tRNA molecules and assumed that the protein portion of the enzyme had caused this reaction. He then noted that the protein component acting alone did not splice the transfer RNA molecule. After isolating the RNA component (called M1 RNA) and repeating the experiment, Altman demonstrated that the M1 RNA had acted alone to cause the reaction. Because this process violated an absolute of molecular biology (that only proteins function as catalysts), Altman's findings were initially greeted with skepticism and indifference. But Thomas Robert Cech, working independently of Altman, documented a cellular reaction in which RNA acted as a self-catalyst. Cech called this self-acting RNA a ribozyme.

These discoveries astounded the scientific community. It was now possible to suggest that RNA, not proteins, may have served as the regulator in primitive cells when life was first formed. Since DNA cannot form without a catalyst, and proteins cannot act as a catalyst without DNA, it now appears that RNA serves both functions. Altman and Cech had basically provided a new theory as to how life develops.

Individual viruses, or virus particles, also called virions, contain genetic material, or genomes, in one of several forms. Unlike cellular organisms, in which the genes always are made up of DNA, viral genes may consist of either DNA or RNA. Like cell DNA, almost all viral DNA is double-stranded, and it can have either a circular or a linear arrangement. Almost all viral RNA is single-stranded; it is usually linear, and it may be either segmented (with different genes on different RNA molecules) or nonsegmented (with all genes on a single piece of RNA).

Nucleic acids are complex molecules produced by living cells and are essential to all living organisms. These acids govern the body's development and specific characteristics by providing hereditary information and triggering the production of proteins within the body. This computer-generated model shows two strands of deoxyribonucleic acid (DNA) and the double-helical structure typical of this class of nucleic acids.

One of a cell's most important tasks is the synthesis of proteins, giant molecules that underlie most cellular functions. The hereditary material known as deoxyribonucleic acid (DNA), found within the nucleus of a cell, orchestrates a series of steps resulting in the manufacture of proteins tailored to meet the needs for a cell's development and growth.

A Gene, is the basic unit of heredity found in the cells of all living organisms, from bacteria to humans. Genes determine the physical characteristics that an organism inherits, such as the shape of a tree's leaf, the markings on a cat's fur, and the colour of a human hair.

Genes are composed of segments of deoxyribonucleic acid (DNA), a molecule that forms the long, threadlike structures called chromosomes. The information encoded within the DNA structure of a gene directs the manufacture of proteins, molecular workhorses that carry out all life-supporting activities within a cell.

Chromosomes within a cell occur in matched pairs. Each chromosome contains many genes, and each gene is located at a particular site on the chromosome, known as the locus. Like chromosomes, genes typically occur in pairs. A gene found on one chromosome in a pair usually has the same locus as another gene in the other chromosome of the pair, and these two genes are called alleles. Alleles are alternate forms of the same gene. For example, a pea plant has one gene that determines height, but that gene appears in more than one form—the gene that produces a short plant is an allele of the gene that produces a tall plant. The behaviour of alleles and how they influence inherited traits follow predictable patterns. Austrian monk Gregor Mendel first identified these patterns in the 1860

In organisms that use sexual reproduction, offspring inherit one-half of their genes from each parent and then mix the two sets of genes together. This produces new combinations of genes, so that each individual is unique but still possesses the same genes as its parents. As a result, sexual reproduction ensures that the basic characteristics of a particular species remain largely the same for generations. However, mutations, or alterations in DNA, occur constantly. They create variations in the genes that are inherited. Some mutations may be neutral, or silent, and do not affect the function of a protein. Occasionally a mutation may benefit or harm an organism and over the course of evolutionary time, these mutations serve the crucial role of providing organisms with previously nonexistent proteins. In this way, mutations are a driving force behind genetic diversity and the rise of new or more competitive species that are better able to adapt to changes, such as climate variations, depletion of food sources, or the emergence of new types of disease.

Geneticists are scientists who study the function and behaviour of genes. Since the 1970s geneticists have devised techniques, cumulatively known as genetic engineering, to alter or manipulate the DNA structure within genes. These techniques enable scientists to introduce one or more genes from one organism into a second organism. The second organism incorporates the new DNA into its own genetic material, thereby altering its own genetic characteristics by changing the types of proteins it can produce. In humans these techniques form the basis of gene therapy, a group of experimental procedures in which scientists try to substitute one or more healthy genes for defective ones in order to eliminate symptoms of disease.

Genetic engineering techniques have also enabled scientists to determine the chromosomal location and DNA structure of all the genes found within a variety of organisms. In April 2003 the Human Genome Project, a publicly funded consortium of academic scientists from around the world, identified the chromosomal locations and structure of the estimated 20,000 to 25,000 genes found within human cells. The genetic makeup of other organisms has also been identified, including that of the bacterium stems Escherichia coli, the yeast Saccharomyces cerevisiae, the roundworm Caenorhabditis elegans, and the fruit fly Drosophila melanogaster. Scientists hope to use this genetic information to develop life-saving drugs for a variety of diseases, to improve agricultural crop yields, and to learn more about plant and animal physiology and evolutionary history.

American neurologist Stanley B. Prusiner was awarded the 1997 Nobel Prize in physiology or medicine for his discovery of a class of infectious proteins called prions. Prions are implicated in several degenerative brain diseases of mammals, including bovine spongiform encephalopathy, commonly known as mad cow disease.

Prion, shortened term for proteinaceous infectious particle, a small protein linked to certain rare, fatal brain diseases in cows, sheep, humans, and other mammals. If the prion is an infectious agent, it is the first infectious agent identified that does not contain the nucleic acids deoxyribonucleic acid (DNA) or ribonucleic acid (RNA). While the prion's role in causing disease is still controversial, its discovery has opened the door to alternative ideas about how infectious diseases may be transmitted.

American neurologist Stanley B. Prusiner was awarded the 1997 Nobel Prize in physiology or medicine for his discovery of a class of infectious proteins called prions. Prions are implicated in several degenerative brain diseases of mammals, including bovine spongiform encephalopathy, commonly known as mad cow disease.

Discovered by American neurologist Stanley B. Prusiner, prions are proteins with an abnormal shape, believed to be caused by a mutation to the gene that encodes for the protein. Normal proteins are found on the surfaces of nerve cells in the brain, white blood cells, muscle cells, and cells of many other tissues. The role of the normal protein is not yet understood, but the mystery of its structure has been solved. A hundred times smaller than the smallest virus, the normal protein is composed of 208 amino acids twisted into three long telephone cordlike coils known as helices. A floppy tail of 97 amino acids extends from the end of one of the helices. The abnormal protein is built of the same amino acids. However, instead of the coil shape, the abnormal protein is folded like the flat pleats of a partly opened accordion.

In the mid-1980s American neurologist Stanley Prusiner first proposed the existence of infectious agents that contain no genetic material and are made entirely of protein. Prusiner suggested that these particles—which he called prions—were responsible for neurodegenerative diseases, such as bovine spongiform encephalopathy (BSE), or "mad cow disease," in cows and Creutzfeldt-Jakob disease (CJD) in humans. He described his research on prions in a 1995 Scientific American article. In 1997 Prusiner was the sole recipient of the Nobel Prize in physiology or medicine "for his discovery of Prions—a new biological principle of infection." The award was unusual because it went to a single recipient and because Prusiner's findings still lack a scientific consensus. Some scientists believe a slow-acting virus may cause the spongiform encephalopathy diseases.

Applied Behaviour analysis is used to develop educational and treatment techniques that can be tailored to each individual's requirements while still following a constant format, whether the patients are retarded or disturbed children in a school or residential setting, or adults in a psychiatric hospital or rehabilitation centre. Five essential steps characterize this approach: (1) deciding what the individual can do to ameliorate the problem; (2) devising a program to weaken undesirable Behaviour and strengthen desirable substitute Behaviour; (3) carrying out the treatment program according to behavioural principles; (4) keeping careful and objective records; and (5) altering the program if progress can thereby be improved.

Is consciousness determinative, or is it determined? English philosophers such as John Locke equated consciousness with physical sensations and the information they provide, whereas European philosophers such as Gottfried Wilhelm Leibniz and Immanuel Kant gave a more central and active role to consciousness.

The philosopher who most directly influenced subsequent exploration of the subject of consciousness was the 19th-century German educator Johann Friedrich Herbert, who wrote that ideas had quality and intensity and that they may inhibit or facilitate one another. Thus, ideas may pass from "states of reality" (consciousness) to "states of tendency" (unconsciousness), with the dividing line between the two states being described as the threshold of consciousness. This formulation of Herbert clearly presages the development, by the German psychologist and physiologist Gustav Theodor Fechner, of the psychophysical measurement of sensation thresholds, and the later development by Sigmund Freud of the concept of the unconscious.

The experimental analysis of consciousness dates from 1879, when the German psychologist Wilhelm Max Wundt started his research laboratory. For Wundt, the task of psychology was the study of the structure of consciousness, which extended well beyond sensations and included feelings, images, memory, attention, duration, and movement. Because early interest focussed on the content and dynamics of consciousness, it is not surprising that the central methodology of such studies was introspection; that is, subjects reported on the mental contents of their own consciousness. This introspective approach was developed most fully by the American psychologist Edward Bradford Titchener at Cornell University. Setting his task as that of describing the structure of the mind, Titchener attempted to detail, from introspective self-reports, the dimensions of the elements of consciousness. For example, taste was "dimensionalized" into four basic categories: sweet, sour, salt, and bitter. This approach was known as structuralism.

By the 1920s, however, a remarkable revolution had occurred in psychology that was to essentially remove considerations of consciousness from psychological research for some 50 years: Behaviourism captured the field of psychology. The main initiator of this movement was the American psychologist John Broadus Watson. In a 1913 article, Watson stated, "I believe that we can write a psychology and never use the terms consciousness, mental states, mind . . . imagery and the like." Psychologists then turned almost exclusively to Behaviour, as described in terms of stimulus and response, and consciousness was totally bypassed as a subject. A survey of eight leading introductory psychology texts published between 1930 and the 1950s found no mention of the topic of consciousness in five texts, and in two it was treated as a historical curiosity.

Beginning in the late 1950s, however, interest in the subject of consciousness returned, specifically in those subjects and techniques relating to altered states of consciousness: sleep and dreams, meditation, biofeedback, hypnosis, and drug-induced states. Much of the surge in sleep and dream research was directly fuelled by a discovery relevant to the nature of consciousness. A physiological indicator of the dream state was found: At roughly 90-minute intervals, the eyes of sleepers were observed to move rapidly, and at the same time the sleepers' brain waves would show a pattern resembling the waking state. When people were awakened during these periods of rapid eye movement, they almost always reported dreams, whereas if awakened at other times they did not. This and other research clearly indicated that sleep, once considered a passive state, was instead an active state of consciousness.

During the 1960s, an increased search for "higher levels" of consciousness through meditation resulted in a growing interest in the practices of Zen Buddhism and Yoga from Eastern cultures. A full flowering of this movement in the United States was seen in the development of training programs, such as Transcendental Meditation, that were self-directed procedures of physical relaxation and focussed attention. Biofeedback techniques also were developed to bring body systems involving factors such as blood pressure or temperature under voluntary control by providing feedback from the body, so that subjects could learn to control their responses. For example, researchers found that persons could control their brain-wave patterns to some extent, particularly the so-called alpha rhythms generally associated with a relaxed, meditative state. This finding was especially relevant to those interested in consciousness and meditation, and a number of "alpha training" programs emerged.

Another subject that led to increased interest in altered states of consciousness was hypnosis, which involves a transfer of conscious control from the subject to another person. Hypnotism has had a long and intricate history in medicine and folklore and has been intensively studied by psychologists. Much has become known about the hypnotic state, relative to individual suggestibility and personality traits; the subject has now largely been demythologized, and the limitations of the hypnotic state are fairly well known. Despite the increasing use of hypnosis, however, much remains to be learned about this unusual state of focussed attention.

Finally, many people in the 1960s experimented with the psychoactive drugs known as hallucinogens, which produce disorders of consciousness. The most prominent of these drugs are lysergic acid diethylamide, or LSD; mescaline and psilocybin; the latter two have long been associated with religious ceremonies in various cultures. LSD, because of its radical thought-modifying properties, was initially explored for its so-called mind-expanding potential and for its psychotomimetic effects (imitating psychoses). Little positive use, however, has been found for these drugs, and their use is highly restricted.

Scientists have long considered the nature of consciousness without producing a fully satisfactory definition. In the early 20th century American philosopher and psychologist William James suggested that consciousness is a mental process involving both attention to external stimuli and short-term memory. Later scientific explorations of consciousness mostly expanded upon James's work. In this article from a 1997 special issue of Scientific American, Nobel laureate Francis Crick, who helped determine the structure of DNA, and fellow biophysicist Christof Koch explain how experiments on vision might deepen our understanding of consciousness.

As the concept of a direct, simple linkage between environment and Behaviour became unsatisfactory in recent decades, the interest in altered states of consciousness may be taken as a visible sign of renewed interest in the topic of consciousness. That persons are active and intervening participants in their Behaviour has become increasingly clear. Environments, rewards, and punishments are not simply defined by their physical character. Memories are organized, not simply stored. An entirely new area called cognitive psychology has emerged that centres on these concerns. In the study of children, increased attention is being paid to how they understand, or perceive, the world at different ages. In the field of animal Behaviour, researchers increasingly emphasize the inherent characteristics resulting from the way a species has been shaped to respond adaptively to the environment. Humanistic psychologists, with a concern for self-actualization and growth, have emerged after a long period of silence. Throughout the development of clinical and industrial psychology, the conscious states of persons in terms of their current feelings and thoughts were of obvious importance. The role of consciousness, however, was often de-emphasised in favour of unconscious needs and motivations. Trends can be seen, however, toward a new emphasis on the nature of states of consciousness.

As accorded to states of consciousness, is that, no simple, agreed-upon definition of consciousness exists. Attempted definitions tend to be tautological (for example, consciousness defined as awareness) or merely descriptive (for example, consciousness described as sensations, thoughts, or feelings). Despite this problem of definition, the subject of consciousness has had a remarkable history. At one time the primary subject matter of psychology, consciousness as an area of study suffered an almost total demise, later reemerging to become a topic of current interest.

French thinker René Descartes applied rigorous scientific methods of deduction to his exploration of philosophical questions. Descartes is probably best known for his pioneering work in philosophical skepticism. Author Tom Sorell examines the concepts behind Descartes's work Meditationes de Prima Philosophia (1641; Meditations on First Philosophy), focussing on its unconventional use of logic and the reactions it aroused.

Most of the philosophical discussions of consciousness arose from the mind-body issues posed by the French philosopher and mathematician René Descartes in the 17th century. Descartes asked: Is the mind, or consciousness, independent of matter? Is consciousness extended (physical) or unextended (nonphysical)? Is consciousness determinative, or is it determined? English philosophers such as John Locke equated consciousness with physical sensations and the information they provide, whereas European philosophers such as Gottfried Wilhelm Leibniz and Immanuel Kant gave a more central and active role to consciousness.

The philosopher who most directly influenced subsequent exploration of the subject of consciousness was the 19th-century German educator Johann Friedrich Herbert, who wrote that ideas had quality and intensity and that they may inhibit or facilitate one another. Thus, ideas may pass from "states of reality" (consciousness) to "states of tendency" (unconsciousness), with the dividing line between the two states being described as the threshold of consciousness. This formulation of Herbert clearly presages the development, by the German psychologist and physiologist Gustav Theodor Fechner, of the psychophysical measurement of sensation thresholds, and the later development by Sigmund Freud of the concept of the unconscious.

The experimental analysis of consciousness dates from 1879, when the German psychologist Wilhelm Max Wundt started his research laboratory. For Wundt, the task of psychology was the study of the structure of consciousness, which extended well beyond sensations and included feelings, images, memory, attention, duration, and movement. Because early interest focussed on the content and dynamics of consciousness, it is not surprising that the central methodology of such studies was introspection; that is, subjects reported on the mental contents of their own consciousness. This introspective approach was developed most fully by the American psychologist Edward Bradford Titchener at Cornell University. Setting his task as that of describing the structure of the mind, Titchener attempted to detail, from introspective self-reports, the dimensions of the elements of consciousness. For example, taste was "dimensionalized" into four basic categories: sweet, sour, salt, and bitter. This approach was known as structuralism.

By the 1920s, however, a remarkable revolution had occurred in psychology that was to essentially remove considerations of consciousness from psychological research for some 50 years: Behaviourism captured the field of psychology. The main initiator of this movement was the American psychologist John Broadus Watson. In a 1913 article, Watson stated, "I believe that we can write a psychology and never use the terms consciousness, mental states, mind . . . imagery and the like." Psychologists then turned almost exclusively to Behaviour, as described in terms of stimulus and response, and consciousness was totally bypassed as a subject. A survey of eight leading introductory psychology texts published between 1930 and the 1950s found no mention of the topic of consciousness in five texts, and in two it was treated as a historical curiosity.

Beginning in the late 1950s, however, interest in the subject of consciousness returned, specifically in those subjects and techniques relating to altered states of consciousness: sleep and dreams, meditation, biofeedback, hypnosis, and drug-induced states. Much of the surge in sleep and dream research was directly fuelled by a discovery relevant to the nature of consciousness. A physiological indicator of the dream state was found: At roughly 90-minute intervals, the eyes of sleepers were observed to move rapidly, and at the same time the sleepers' brain waves would show a pattern resembling the waking state. When people were awakened during these periods of rapid eye movement, they almost always reported dreams, whereas if awakened at other times they did not. This and other research clearly indicated that sleep, once considered a passive state, was instead an active state of consciousness.

During the 1960s, an increased search for "higher levels" of consciousness through meditation resulted in a growing interest in the practices of Zen Buddhism and Yoga from Eastern cultures. A full flowering of this movement in the United States was seen in the development of training programs, such as Transcendental Meditation, that were self-directed procedures of physical relaxation and focussed attention. Biofeedback techniques also were developed to bring body systems involving factors such as blood pressure or temperature under voluntary control by providing feedback from the body, so that subjects could learn to control their responses. For example, researchers found that persons could control their brain-wave patterns to some extent, particularly the so-called alpha rhythms generally associated with a relaxed, meditative state. This finding was especially relevant to those interested in consciousness and meditation, and a number of "alpha training" programs emerged.

Another subject that led to increased interest in altered states of consciousness was hypnosis, which involves a transfer of conscious control from the subject to another person. Hypnotism has had a long and intricate history in medicine and folklore and has been intensively studied by psychologists. Much has become known about the hypnotic state, relative to individual suggestibility and personality traits; the subject has now largely been demythologized, and the limitations of the hypnotic state are fairly well known. Despite the increasing use of hypnosis, however, much remains to be learned about this unusual state of focussed attention.

Finally, many people in the 1960s experimented with the psychoactive drugs known as hallucinogens, which produce disorders of consciousness. The most prominent of these drugs are lysergic acid diethylamide, or LSD; mescaline and psilocybin; the latter two have long been associated with religious ceremonies in various cultures. LSD, because of its radical thought-modifying properties, was initially explored for its so-called mind-expanding potential and for its psychotomimetic effects (imitating psychoses). Little positive use, however, has been found for these drugs, and their use is highly restricted.

Scientists have long considered the nature of consciousness without producing a fully satisfactory definition. In the early 20th century American philosopher and psychologist William James suggested that consciousness is a mental process involving both attention to external stimuli and short-term memory. Later scientific explorations of consciousness mostly expanded upon James's work. In this article from a 1997 special issue of Scientific American, Nobel laureate Francis Crick, who helped determine the structure of DNA, and fellow biophysicist Christof Koch explain how experiments on vision might deepen our understanding of consciousness.

As the concept of a direct, simple linkage between environment and Behaviour became unsatisfactory in recent decades, the interest in altered states of consciousness may be taken as a visible sign of renewed interest in the topic of consciousness. That persons are active and intervening participants in their Behaviour has become increasingly clear. Environments, rewards, and punishments are not simply defined by their physical character. Memories are organized, not simply stored. An entirely new area called cognitive psychology has emerged that centres on these concerns. In the study of children, increased attention is being paid to how they understand, or perceive, the world at different ages. In the field of animal Behaviour, researchers increasingly emphasize the inherent characteristics resulting from the way a species has been shaped to respond adaptively to the environment. Humanistic psychologists, with a concern for self-actualization and growth, have emerged after a long period of silence. Throughout the development of clinical and industrial psychology, the conscious states of persons in terms of their current feelings and thoughts were of obvious importance. The role of consciousness, however, was often de-emphasised in favour of unconscious needs and motivations. Trends can be seen, however, toward a new emphasis on the nature of states of consciousness

Psychoactive Drugs, chemical substances that alter mood, Behaviour, perception, or mental functioning. Throughout history, many cultures have found ways to alter consciousness through the ingestion of substances. In current professional practice, psychoactive substances known as psychotropic drugs have been developed to treat patients with severe mental illness.

Psychoactive substances exert their effects by modifying biochemical or physiological processes in the brain. The message system of nerve cells, or neurons, relies on both electrical and chemical transmission. Neurons rarely touch each other; the microscopic gap between one neuron and the next, called the synapse, is bridged by chemicals called neuroregulators, or neurotransmitters. Psychoactive drugs act by altering neurotransmitter function. The drugs can be divided into six major pharmacological classes based on their desired behavioural or psychological effect: alcohol, sedative-hypnotics, narcotic analgesics, stimulant-euphoriants, hallucinogens, and psychotropic agents.

Psychotropic drugs have been in use since the early 1950s. Antipsychotic drugs decrease the symptoms of schizophrenia, allowing many schizophrenic patients to leave the hospital and rejoin community life. Antidepressant drugs help the majority of patients with severe depression recover from their disorder. Lithium salts eliminate or diminish the episodes of mania and depression experienced by manic-depressive patients.

Alfred Adler (1870-1937), Austrian psychologist and psychiatrist, born in Vienna, and educated at Vienna University. After leaving the university he studied and was associated with Sigmund Freud, the founder of psychoanalysis. In 1911 Adler left the orthodox psychoanalytic school to found a neo-Freudian school of psychoanalysis. After 1926 he was a visiting professor at Columbia University, and in 1935 he and his family moved to the United States.

In his analysis of individual development, Adler stressed the sense of inferiority, rather than sexual drives, as the motivating force in human life. According to Adler, conscious or subconscious feelings of inferiority (to which he gave the name inferiority complex), combined with compensatory defence mechanisms, are the basic causes of psychopathological Behaviour. The function of the psychoanalyst, furthermore, is to discover and rationalize such feelings and break down the compensatory, neurotic will for power that they engender in the patient. Adler's works include

The Theory and Practice of Individual Psychology (1918) and The Pattern of Life (1930).

Johann Friedrich Herbert (1776-1841) saying that, inferiority from which the philosophy stems from the analysis of experience. The system includes logic, metaphysics, and aesthetics as coordinate elements. He rejected all concepts of separate mental faculties, postulating instead that all mental phenomena result from interaction of elementary ideas. Herbert believed that educational methods and systems should be based on psychology and ethics: psychology to furnish necessary knowledge of the mind and ethics to be used as a basis for determining the social ends of education. Among his major works is A Textbook in Psychology (1816; trans. 1894).

In the philosophy expounded by Leibniz, the universe is composed of countless conscious centres of spiritual force or energy, known as monads. Each monad represents an individual microcosm, mirroring the universe in varying degrees of perfection and developing independently of all other monads. The universe that these monads constitute is the harmonious result of a divine plan. Humans, however, with their limited vision, cannot accept such evils as disease and death as part of a universal harmony. This Leibnizian universe, "the best of all possible worlds," is satirized as a utopia by the French author Voltaire in his novel Candide (1759).

Behaviourism was first developed in the early 20th century by the American psychologist John B. Watson. The dominant view of that time was that psychology is the study of inner experiences or feelings by subjective, introspective methods. Watson did not deny the existence of inner experiences, but he insisted that these experiences could not be studied because they were not observable.

He was greatly influenced by the pioneering investigations of the Russian physiologists Ivan P. Pavlov and Vladimir M. Bekhterev on conditioning of animals (classical conditioning). Watson proposed to make the study of psychology scientific by using only objective procedures such as laboratory experiments designed to establish statistically significant results. The behaviouristic view led him to formulate a stimulus-response theory of psychology. In this theory all complex forms of Behaviour—emotions, habits, and such— are seen as composed of simple muscular and glandular elements that can be observed and measured. He claimed that emotional reactions are learned in much the same way as other skills.

Watson's stimulus-response theory resulted in a tremendous increase in research activity on learning in animals and in humans, from infancy to early adulthood. Between 1920 and midcentury, Behaviourism dominated psychology in the United States and also had wide international influence. By the 1950s, the new behavioural movement had produced a mass of data on learning that led such American experimental psychologists as Edward C. Tolman, Clark L. Hull, and B. F. Skinner to formulate their own theories of learning and Behaviour based on laboratory experiments instead of introspective observations.

American psychologist B. F. Skinner became famous for his pioneering research on learning and Behaviour. During his 60-year career, Skinner discovered important principles of operant conditioning, a type of learning that involves reinforcement and punishment. A strict behaviorist, Skinner believed that operant conditioning could explain even the most complex of human behaviours.

Skinner's position, known as radical (or basic) Behaviourism, is similar to Watson's view that psychology is the study of the observable Behaviour of individuals interacting with their environment. Skinner, however, disagrees with Watson's position that inner processes, such as feelings, should be excluded from study. He maintains that these inner processes should be studied by the usual scientific methods, with particular emphasis on controlled experiments using individual animals and humans. His research with animals, focussing on the kind of learning—known as operant conditioning—that occurs as a consequence of stimuli, demonstrates that complex Behaviour such as language and problem solving can be studied scientifically. He postulated a type of psychological conditioning known as reinforcement.

Since 1950, behavioural psychologists have produced an impressive amount of basic research directed at understanding how various forms of Behaviour are developed and maintained. These studies have included the role of (1) the interactions preceding Behaviour, such as the attention span and perceptual processes; (2) changes in Behaviour itself, such as the formation of skills; (3) interactions following Behaviour, such as the effects of incentives or rewards and punishments; and (4) conditions prevailing over all the events, such as prolonged emotional stress and deprivations of the essentials of life.

Some of these studies were conducted with humans in rooms especially equipped with observational devices and also in natural settings, as in school or at home. Other studies used animals, particularly rats and pigeons, as subjects, in standard laboratory settings. Most studies with animals required simple responses. For example, the animal was trained to press a lever or peck a disk in order to receive something of value, such as food, or to avoid painful stimulation, such as a slight electric shock.

At the same time, psychologists have undertaken studies using behavioural principles on practical problems. This work has yielded a body of knowledge known as Behaviour modification, or applied Behaviour analysis. Applied behavioural research has been carried out in three main areas. The first focuses on the techniques of psychological treatment for troubled adults and children with Behaviour disorders. This area is known as Behaviour therapy. The second centres on improving teaching and training methods. Some studies have explored the teaching processes used in the educational system from preschool to college; others have focussed on training in business and industry and in the armed forces. Methods of programmed instruction have been developed. Many studies have dealt with the problems of improving teaching and training methods for handicapped children at home, in school, or in institutions. The third area of applied research is concerned with the long and short-term effects of drugs on Behaviour. In these studies, drugs usually are administered to animals in various dosages and combinations. Changes are then observed in the way in which these animals perform repetitious tasks, such as pressing a lever.

The initial influence of Behaviourism on psychology was to minimize the introspective study of the mental processes, emotions, and feelings and to substitute the study of the objective Behaviour of individuals in relation to their environment by means of experimental methods. This orientation suggested a way to relate human and animal research and to bring psychology into line with the natural sciences, such as physics, chemistry, and biology.

Present-day Behaviourism has extended its influence on psychology in three ways functional concept that emphasizes the meaningfulness of stimulating conditions to the individual. It has introduced a research method for the experimental study of a single individual. Finally, it has demonstrated that behavioural concepts and principles can be applied to many practical problems.

The term psychology comes from two Greek words: psyche, which means "soul," and logos, "the study of." These root words were first combined in the 16th century, at a time when the human soul, spirit, or mind was seen as distinct from the body.

Psychology overlaps with other sciences that investigate Behaviour and mental processes. Certain parts of the field share much with the biological sciences, especially physiology, the biological study of the functions of living organisms and their parts. Like physiologists, many psychologists study the inner workings of the body from a biological perspective. However, psychologists usually focus on the activity of the brain and nervous system.

The social sciences of sociology and anthropology, which study human societies and cultures, also intersect with psychology. For example, both psychology and sociology explore how people behave when they are in groups. However, psychologists try to understand Behaviour from the vantage point of the individual, whereas sociologists focus on how Behaviour is shaped by social forces and social institutions. Anthropologists investigate Behaviour as well, paying particular attention to the similarities and differences between human cultures around the world.

Psychology is closely connected with psychiatry, which is the branch of medicine specializing in mental illnesses. The study of mental illness is one of the largest areas of research in psychology. Psychiatrists and psychologists differ in their training. A person seeking to become a psychiatrist first obtains a medical degree and then engages in further formal medical education in psychiatry. Most psychologists have a doctoral graduate degree in psychology.

The study of psychology draws on two kinds of research: basic and applied. Basic researchers seek to test general theories and build a foundation of knowledge, while applied psychologists study people in real-world settings and use the results to solve practical human problems. There are five major areas of research: biopsychology, clinical psychology, cognitive psychology, developmental psychology, and social psychology. Both basic and applied research is conducted in each of these fields of psychology.

In 1860 German physicist Gustav Fechner theorized that if the human brain were divided into right and left halves, each side would have its own stream of consciousness. Modern medicine has actually allowed scientists to investigate this hypothesis. People who suffer from life-threatening epileptic seizures sometimes undergo a radical surgery that severs the corpus callosum, a bridge of nerve tissue that connects the right and left hemispheres of the brain. After the surgery, the two hemispheres can no longer communicate with each other.

Wilhelm Wundt (1832-1920), German psychologist, generally recognized as the founder of scientific psychology as an independent discipline. He was born in Neckarau (now part of Mannheim), and educated at the universities of Tübingen and Heidelberg and the Institute of Physiology in Berlin. After teaching physiology at the University of Heidelberg (1858-74), he taught inductive philosophy at the University of Zürich (1874-75). He was professor of philosophy at the University of Leipzig from 1875 to 1917. Wundt offered in 1862 the first academic course in psychology and established the first laboratory for experimental psychology in 1879. He founded the first psychological journal, Philosophische Studien (Studies in Philosophy), in 1881.

Wundt promoted what is known as structuralist or content psychology, emphasizing observations of the conscious mind rather than inference. Wundt also carried out extensive experimental research on perception, feeling, and apperception. His more than 500 published works include Principles of Physiological Psychology (2 volumes, 1873-74; trans. 1904) and the monumental work Elements of Folk Psychology (10 volumes, 1900-20; trans. 1916). He also wrote Logik (1880), Ethik (1886), and System der Philosophie (1889).

The human brain is the most highly organized form of matter known, and in complexity the brains of the other higher animals are not greatly inferior. For certain purposes it is expedient to regard the brain as being analogous to a machine. Even if it is so regarded, however, it is a machine of a totally different kind from those made by man. In trying to understand the workings of his own brain man meets his highest challenge. Nothing is given; there are no operating diagrams, no maker's instructions.

The first step in trying to understand the brain is to examine its structure in order to discover the components from which it is built and how they are related to one another. After that one can attempt to understand the mode of operation of the simplest components. These two modes of investigation—the morphological and the physiological—have now become complementary. In studying the nervous system with today's sensitive electrical devices, however, it is all too easy to find physiological events that cannot be correlated with any known anatomical structure. Conversely, the electron microscope reveals many structural details whose physiological significance is obscure or unknown.

At the close of the past century the Spanish anatomist Santiago Ramón y Cajal showed how all parts of the nervous system are built up of individual nerve cells of many different shapes and sizes. Like other cells, each nerve cell has a nucleus and a surrounding cytoplasm. Its outer surface consists of numerous fine branches—the dendrites—that receive nerve impulses from other nerve cells, and one relatively long branch—the axon—that transmits nerve impulses. Near its end the axon divides into branches that terminate at the dendrites or bodies of other nerve cells. The axon can be as short as a fraction of a millimetre or as long as a metre, depending on its place and function. It has many of the properties of an electric cable and is uniquely specialized to conduct the brief electrical waves called nerve impulses. In very thin axons these impulses travel at less than one metre per second; in others, for example in the large axons of the nerve cells that activate muscles, they travel as fast as 100 metres per second.

The electrical impulse that travels along the axon ceases abruptly when it comes to the point where the axon's terminal fibres make contact with another nerve cell. These junction points were given the name "synapses" by Sir Charles Sherrington, who laid the foundations of what is sometimes called synaptology. If the nerve impulse is to continue beyond the synapse, it must be regenerated afresh on the other side. As recently as 15 years ago some physiologists held that transmission at the synapse was predominantly, if not exclusively, an electrical phenomenon. Now, however, there is abundant evidence that transmission is effectuated by the release of specific chemical substances that trigger a regeneration of the impulse. In fact, the first strong evidence showing that a transmitter substance acts across the synapse was provided more than 40 years ago by Sir Henry Dale and Otto Loewi.

It has been estimated that the human central nervous system, which of course includes the spinal cord as well as the brain itself, consists of about 10 billion (10^{10}) nerve cells. With rare exceptions each nerve cell receives information directly in the form of impulses from many other nerve cells—often hundreds—and transmits information to a like number. Depending on its threshold of response, a given nerve cell may fire an impulse when stimulated by only a few incoming fibres or it may not fire until stimulated by many incoming fibres. It has long been known that this threshold can be raised or lowered by various factors. Moreover, it was conjectured some 60 years ago that some of the incoming fibres must inhibit the firing of the receiving cell rather than excite it. The conjecture was subsequently confirmed, and the mechanism of the inhibitory effect has now been clarified. This mechanism and its equally fundamental counterpart—nerve-cell excitation

The electron microscope has revealed structural details of synapses that fit in nicely with the view that a chemical transmitter is involved in nerve transmission. Enclosed in the synaptic knob are many vesicles, or tiny sacs, which appear to contain the transmitter substances that induce synaptic transmission. Between the synaptic knob and the synaptic membrane of the adjoining nerve cell is a remarkably uniform space of about 20 millimicrons that is termed the synaptic cleft. Many of the synaptic vesicles are concentrated adjacent to this cleft; it seems plausible that the transmitter substance is discharged from the nearest vesicles into the cleft, where it can act on the adjacent cell membrane. This hypothesis is supported by the discovery that the transmitter is released in packets of a few thousand molecules.

The study of synaptic transmission was revolutionized in 1951 by the introduction of delicate techniques for recording electrically from the interior of single nerve cells. This is done by inserting into the nerve cell an extremely fine glass pipette with a diameter of .5 micron—about a fifty-thousandth of an inch. The pipette is filled with an electrically conducting salt solution such as concentrated potassium chloride. If the pipette is carefully inserted and held rigidly in place, the cell membrane appears to seal quickly around the glass, thus preventing the flow of a short-circuiting current through the puncture in the cell membrane. Impaled in this fashion, nerve cells can function normally for hours. Although there is no way of observing the cells during the insertion of the pipette, the insertion can be guided by using as clues the electric signals that the pipette picks up when close to active nerve cells.

To study the large nerve cells called motoneurons, which lie in the spinal cord and whose function is to activate muscles. This was a fortunate choice: intracellular investigations with motoneurons have proved to be easier and more rewarding than those with any other kind of mammalian nerve cell.

Finding that when the nerve cell responds to the chemical synaptic transmitter, the response depends in part on characteristic features of ionic composition that are also concerned with the transmission of impulses in the cell and along its axon. When the nerve cell is at rest, its physiological makeup resembles that of most other cells in that the water solution inside the cell is quite different in composition from the solution in which the cell is bathed. The nerve cell is able to exploit this difference between external and internal composition and use it in quite different ways for generating an electrical impulse and for synaptic transmission.

The composition of the external solution is well established because the solution is essentially the same as blood from which cells and proteins have been removed. The composition of the internal solution is known only approximately. Indirect evidence indicates that the concentrations of sodium and chloride ions outside the cell are respectively some 10 and 14 times higher than the concentrations inside the cell. In contrast, the concentration of potassium ions inside the cell is about 30 times higher than the concentration outside.

How can one account for this remarkable state of affairs? Part of the explanation is that the inside of the cell is negatively charged with respect to the outside of the cell by about 70 millivolts. Since like charges repel each other, this internal negative charge tends to drive chloride ions (Cl-) outward through the cell membrane and, at the same time, to impede their inward movement. In fact, a potential difference of 70 millivolts is just sufficient to maintain the observed disparity in the concentration of chloride ions inside the cell and outside it; chloride ions diffuse inward and outward at equal rates. A drop of 70 millivolts across the membrane therefore defines the "equilibrium potential" for chloride ions.

To obtain a concentration of potassium ions (K+) that is 30 times higher inside the cell than outside would require that the interior of the cell membrane be about 90 millivolts negative with respect to the exterior. Since the actual interior is only 70 millivolts negative, it falls short of the equilibrium potential for potassium ions by 20 millivolts. Evidently the thirtyfold concentration can be achieved and maintained only if there is some auxiliary mechanism for "pumping" potassium ions into the cell at a rate equal to their spontaneous net outward diffusion.

The pumping mechanism has the still more difficult task of pumping sodium ions (Na+) out of the cell against a potential gradient of 130 millivolts. This figure is obtained by adding the 70 millivolts of internal negative charge to the equilibrium potential for sodium ions, which is 60 millivolts of internal positive charge. If it were not for this postulated pump, the concentration of sodium ions inside and outside the cell would be almost the reverse of what is observed.

In their classic studies of nerve-impulse transmission in the giant axon of the squid, A. L. Hodgkin, A. F. Huxley and Bernhard Katz of Britain demonstrated that the propagation of the impulse coincides with abrupt changes in the permeability of the axon membrane. When a nerve impulse has been triggered in some way, what can be described as a gate opens and lets sodium ions pour into the axon during the advance of the impulse, making the interior of the axon locally positive. The process is self-reinforcing in that the flow of some sodium ions through the membrane opens the gate further and makes it easier for others to follow. The sharp reversal of the internal polarity of the membrane constitutes the nerve impulse, which moves like a wave until it has travelled the length of the axon. In the wake of the impulse the sodium gate closes and a potassium gate opens, thereby restoring the normal polarity of the membrane within a millisecond or less.

With this understanding of the nerve impulse in hand, one is ready to follow the electrical events at the excitatory synapse. One might guess that if the nerve impulse results from an abrupt inflow of sodium ions and a rapid change in the electrical polarity of the axon's interior, something similar must happen at the body and dendrites of the nerve cell in order to generate the impulse in the first place. Indeed, the function of the excitatory synaptic terminals on the cell body and its dendrites is to depolarize the interior of the cell membrane essentially by permitting an inflow of sodium ions. When the depolarization reaches a threshold value, a nerve impulse is triggered.

As a simple instance of this phenomenon we have recorded the depolarization that occurs in a single motoneurons activated directly by the large nerve fibres that enter the spinal cord from special stretch-receptors known as annulospiral endings. These receptors in turn are located in the same muscle that is activated the motoneurons under study. Thus the whole system forms a typical reflex arc, such as the arc responsible for the patellar reflex, or "knee jerk."

To conduct the experiment we anaesthetize an animal (most often a cat) and free by dissection a muscle nerve that contains these large nerve fibres. By applying a mild electric shock to the exposed nerve one can produce a single impulse in each of the fibres; since the impulses travel to the spinal cord almost synchronously they are referred to collectively as a volley. The number of impulses contained in the volley can be reduced by reducing the stimulation applied to the nerve. The volley strength is measured at a point just outside the spinal cord and is displayed on an oscilloscope. About half a millisecond after detection of a volley there is a wavelike change in the voltage inside the motoneurons that has received the volley. The change is detected by a microelectrode inserted in the motoneurons and is displayed on another oscilloscope.

What we find is that the negative voltage inside the cell becomes progressively less negative as more of the fibres impinging on the cell are stimulated to fire. This observed depolarization is in fact a simple summation of the depolarisation produced by each individual synapse. When the depolarization of the interior of the motoneurons reaches a critical point, a "spike" suddenly appears on the second oscilloscope, showing that a nerve impulse has been generated. During the spike the voltage inside the cell changes from about 70 millivolts negative to as much as 30 millivolts positive. The spike regularly appears when the depolarization, or reduction of membrane potential, reaches a critical level, which is usually between 10 and 18 millivolts. The only effect of a further strengthening of the synaptic stimulus is to shorten the time needed for the motoneurons to reach the firing threshold. The depolarizing potentials produced in the cell membrane by excitatory synapses are called excitatory postsynaptic potentials, or EPSP's.

Through one barrel of a double-barrelled microelectrode one can apply a background current to change the resting potential of the interior of the cell membrane, either increasing it or decreasing it. When the potential is made more negative, the EPSP rises more steeply to an earlier peak. When the potential is made less negative, the EPSP rises more slowly to a lower peak. Finally, when the charge inside the cell is reversed so as to be positive with respect to the exterior, the excitatory synapses give rise to an EPSP that is actually the reverse of the normal one.

These observations support the hypothesis that excitatory synapses produce what amounts virtually to a short circuit in the synaptic membrane potential. When this occurs, the membrane no longer acts as a barrier to the passage of ions but lets them flow through in response to the differing electric potential on the two sides of the membrane. In other words, the ions are momentarily allowed to travel freely down their electrochemical gradients, which means that sodium ions flow into the cell and, to a lesser degree, potassium ions flow out. It is this net flow of positive ions that creates the excitatory postsynaptic potential. The flow of negative ions, such as the chloride ion, is apparently not involved. By artificially altering the potential inside the cell one can establish that there is no flow of ions, and therefore no EPSP, when the voltage drop across the membrane is zero.

How is the synaptic membrane converted from a strong ionic barrier into an ion-permeable state? It is currently accepted that the agency of conversion is the chemical transmitter substance contained in the vesicles inside the synaptic knob. When a nerve impulse reaches the synaptic knob, some of the vesicles are caused to eject the transmitter substance into the synaptic cleft. The molecules of the substance would take only a few microseconds to diffuse across the cleft and become attached to specific receptor sites on the surface membrane of the adjacent nerve cell.

Presumably the receptor sites are associated with fine channels in the membrane that are opened in some way by the attachment of the transmitter-substance molecules to the receptor sites. With the channels thus opened, sodium and potassium ions flow through the membrane thousands of times more readily than they normally do, thereby producing the intense ionic flux that depolarizes the cell membrane and produces the EPSP. In many synapses the current flows strongly for only about a millisecond before the transmitter substance is eliminated from the synaptic cleft, either by diffusion into the surrounding regions or as a result of being destroyed by enzymes. The latter process is known to occur when the transmitter substance is acetylcholine, which is destroyed by the enzyme acetylcholinesterase.

The substantiation of this general picture of synaptic transmission requires the solution of many fundamental problems. Since we do not know the specific transmitter substance for the vast majority of synapses in the nervous system we do not know if there are many different substances or only a few. The only one identified with reasonable certainty in the mammalian central nervous system is acetylcholine. We know practically nothing about the mechanism by which a presynaptic nerve impulse causes the transmitter substance to be injected into the synaptic cleft. Nor do we know how the synaptic vesicles not immediately adjacent to the synaptic cleft are moved up to the firing line to replace the emptied vesicles. It is conjectured that the vesicles contain the enzyme systems needed to recharge themselves. The entire process must be swift and efficient: the total amount of transmitter substance in synaptic terminals is enough for only a few minutes of synaptic activity at normal operating rates. There are also knotty problems to be solved on the other side of the synaptic cleft. What, for example, is the nature of the receptor sites? How are the ionic channels in the membrane opened up?

Let us turn now to the second type of synapse that has been identified in the nervous system. These are the synapses that can inhibit the firing of a nerve cell even though it may be receiving a volley of excitatory impulses. When inhibitory synapses are examined in the electron microscope, they look very much like excitatory synapses. Microelectrode recordings of the activity of single motoneurons and other nerve cells have now shown that the inhibitory postsynaptic potential (IPSP) is virtually a mirror image of the EPSP. Moreover, individual inhibitory synapses, like excitatory synapses, have a cumulative effect. The chief difference is simply that the IPSP makes the cell's internal voltage more negative than it is normally, which is in a direction opposite to that needed for generating a spike discharge.

By driving the internal voltage of a nerve cell in the negative direction inhibitory synapses oppose the action of excitatory synapses, which of course drive it in the positive direction. Hence if the potential inside a resting cell is 70 millivolts negative, a strong volley of inhibitory impulses can drive the potential to 75 or 80 millivolts negative. One can easily see that if the potential is made more negative in this way the excitatory synapses find it more difficult to raise the internal voltage to the threshold point for the generation of a spike. Thus the nerve cell responds to the algebraic sum of the internal voltage changes produced by excitatory and inhibitory synapses.

If, as in the experiment described earlier, the internal membrane potential is altered by the flow of an electric current through one barrel of a double-barrelled microelectrode, one can observe the effect of such changes on the inhibitory postsynaptic potential. When the internal potential is made less negative, the inhibitory postsynaptic potential is deepened. Conversely, when the potential is made more negative, the IPSP diminishes; it finally reverses when the internal potential is driven below minus 80 millivolts.

One can therefore conclude that inhibitory synapses share with excitatory synapses the ability to change the ionic permeability of the synaptic membrane. The difference is that inhibitory synapses enable ions to flow freely down an electrochemical gradient that has an equilibrium point at minus 80 millivolts rather than at zero, as is the case for excitatory synapses. This effect could be achieved by the outward flow of positively charged ions such as potassium or the inward flow of negatively charged ions such as chloride, or by a combination of negative and positive ionic flows such that the interior reaches equilibrium at minus 80 millivolts.

In an effort to discover the permeability changes associated with the inhibitory potential my colleagues and I have altered the concentration of ions normally found in motoneurons and have introduced a variety of other ions that are not normally present. This can be done by impaling nerve cells with micropipettes that are filled with a salt solution containing the ion to be injected. The actual injection is achieved by passing a brief current through the micropipette.

If the concentration of chloride ions within the cell is in this way increased as much as three times, the inhibitory postsynaptic potential reverses and acts as a depolarizing current; that is, it resembles an excitatory potential. On the other hand, if the cell is heavily injected with sulfate ions, which are also negatively charged, there is no such reversal. This simple test shows that under the influence of the inhibitory transmitter substance, which is still unidentified, the subsynaptic membrane becomes permeable momentarily to chloride ions but not to sulfate ions. During the generation of the IPSP the outflow of chloride ions is so rapid that it more than outweighs the flow of other ions that generate the normal inhibitory potential.

The effect of injecting motoneurons with more than 30 kinds of negatively charged ion. With one exception the hydrated ions (ions bound to water) to which the cell membrane is permeable under the influence of the inhibitory transmitter substance are smaller than the hydrated ions to which the membrane is impermeable. The exception is the formate ion (HCO_2-), which may have an ellipsoidal shape and so be able to pass through membrane pores that block smaller spherical ions.

Apart from the formate ion all the ions to which the membrane is permeable have a diameter not greater than 1.14 times the diameter of the potassium ion; that is, they are less than 2.9 angstrom units in diameter. Comparable investigations in other laboratories have found the same permeability effects, including the exceptional behaviour of the formate ion, in fishes, toads and snails. It may well be that the ionic mechanism responsible for synaptic inhibition is the same throughout the animal kingdom.

The significance of these and other studies is that they strongly indicate that the inhibitory transmitter substance opens the membrane to the flow of potassium ions but not to sodium ions. It is known that the sodium ion is somewhat larger than any of the negatively charged ions, including the formate ion, that are able to pass through the membrane during synaptic inhibition. It is not possible, however, to test the effectiveness of potassium ions by injecting excess amounts into the cell because the excess is immediately diluted by an osmotic flow of water into the cell.

The concentration of potassium ions inside the nerve cell is about 30 times greater than the concentration outside, and to maintain this large difference in concentration without the help of a metabolic pump the inside of the membrane would have to be charged 90 millivolts negative with respect to the exterior. This implies that if the membrane were suddenly made porous to potassium ions, the resulting outflow of ions would make the inside potential of the membrane even more negative than it is in the resting state, and that is just what happens during synaptic inhibition. The membrane must not simultaneously become porous to sodium ions, because they exist in much higher concentration outside the cell than inside and their rapid inflow would more than compensate for the potassium outflow. In fact, the fundamental difference between synaptic excitation and synaptic inhibition is that the membrane freely passes sodium ions in response to the former and largely excludes the passage of sodium ions in response to the latter.

This fine discrimination between ions that are not very different in size must be explained by any hypothesis of synaptic action. It is most unlikely that the channels through the membrane are created afresh and accurately maintained for a thousandth of a second every time a burst of transmitter substance is released into the synaptic cleft. It is more likely that channels of at least two different sizes are built directly into the membrane structure. In some way the excitatory transmitter substance would selectively unplug the larger channels and permit the free inflow of sodium ions. Potassium ions would simultaneously flow out and thus would tend to counteract the large potential change that would be produced by the massive sodium inflow. The inhibitory transmitter substance would selectively unplug the smaller channels that are large enough to pass potassium and chloride ions but not sodium ions.

To explain certain types of inhibition other features must be added to this hypothesis of synaptic transmission. In the simple hypothesis chloride and potassium ions can flow freely through pores of all inhibitory synapses. It has been shown, however, that the inhibition of the contraction of heart muscle by the vagus nerve is due almost exclusively to potassium-ion flow. On the other hand, in the muscles of crustaceans and in nerve cells in the snail's brain synaptic inhibition is due largely to the flow of chloride ions. This selective permeability could be explained if there were fixed charges along the walls of the channels. If such charges were negative, they would repel negatively charged ions and prevent their passage; if they were positive, they would similarly prevent the passage of positively charged ions. One can now suggest that the channels opened by the excitatory transmitter are negatively charged and so do not permit the passage of the negatively charged chloride ion, even though it is small enough to move through the channel freely.

One might wonder if a given nerve cell can have excitatory synaptic action at some of its axon terminals and inhibitory action at others. The answer is no. Two different kinds of nerve cell are needed, one for each type of transmission and synaptic transmitter substance. This can readily be demonstrated by the effect of strychnine and tetanus toxin in the spinal cord; they specifically prevent inhibitory synaptic action and leave excitatory action unaltered. As a result the synaptic excitation of nerve cells is uncontrolled and convulsions result. The special types of cell responsible for inhibitory synaptic action are now being recognized in many parts of the central nervous system.

This account of communication between nerve cells is necessarily oversimplified, yet it shows that some significant advances are being made at the level of individual components of the nervous system. By selecting the most favourable situations we have been able to throw light on some details of nerve-cell behaviour. We can be encouraged by these limited successes. But the task of understanding in a comprehensive way how the human brain operates staggers its own imagination

In general, each neuron uses only a single compound as its neurotransmitter. However, some neurons outside the central nervous system are able to release both an amine and a peptide neurotransmitter.

Neurotransmitters are manufactured from precursor compounds like amino acids, glucose, and the dietary amine-called choline. Neurons modify the structure of these precursor compounds in a series of reactions with enzymes. Neurotransmitters that come from amino acids include serotonin, which is derived from tryptophan; dopamine and norepinephrine, which are derived from tyrosine; and glycine, which is derived from threonine. Among the neurotransmitters made from glucose are glutamate, aspartate, and GABA. Choline serves as the precursor for acetylcholine.

In the nervous system, a message-carrying impulse travels from one end of a nerve cell to the other by means of an electrical impulse. When it reaches the terminal end of a nerve cell, the impulse triggers tiny sacs called presynaptic vessicles to release their contents, chemical messengers called neurotransmitters. The neurotransmitters float across the synapse, or gap between adjacent nerve cells. When they reach the neighbouring nerve cell, the neurotransmitters fit into specialized receptor sites much as a key fits into a lock, causing that nerve cell to "fire," or generate an electric message-carrying impulse. As the message continues through the nervous system, the presynaptic cell absorbs the excess neurotransmitters, and repackages them in presynaptic vessicles in a process called neurotransmitter.

Neurotransmitters are released into a microscopic gap, called a synapse, that separates the transmitting neuron from the cell receiving the chemical signal. The cell that generates the signal is called the presynaptic cell, while the receiving cell is termed the postsynaptic cell.

After their release into the synapse, neurotransmitters combine chemically with highly specific protein molecules, termed receptors, that are embedded in the surface membranes of the postsynaptic cell. When this combination occurs, the voltage, or electrical force, of the postsynaptic cell is either increased (excited) or decreased (inhibited).

When a neuron is in its resting state, its voltage is about -70 millivolts. An excitatory neurotransmitter alters the membrane of the postsynaptic neuron, making it possible for ions (electrically charged molecules) to move back and forth across the neuron's membranes. This flow of ions makes the neuron's voltage rise toward zero. If enough excitatory receptors have been activated, the postsynaptic neuron responds by firing, generating a nerve impulse that causes its own neurotransmitter to be released into the next synapse. An inhibitory neurotransmitter causes different ions to pass back and forth across the postsynaptic neuron's membrane, lowering the nerve cell's voltage to -80 or -90 millivolts. The drop in voltage makes it less likely that the postsynaptic cell will fire.

If the postsynaptic cell is a muscle cell rather than a neuron, an excitatory neurotransmitter will cause the muscle to contract. If the postsynaptic cell is a gland cell, an excitatory neurotransmitter will cause the cell to secrete its contents.

While most neurotransmitters interact with their receptors to create new electrical nerve impulses that energize or inhibit the adjoining cell, some neurotransmitter interactions do not generate or suppress nerve impulses. Instead, they interact with a second type of receptor that changes the internal chemistry of the postsynaptic cell by either causing or blocking the formation of chemicals called second messenger molecules. These second messengers regulate the postsynaptic cell's biochemical processes and enable it to conduct the maintenance necessary to continue synthesizing neurotransmitters and conducting nerve impulses. Examples of second messengers, which are formed and entirely contained within the postsynaptic cell, include cyclic adenosine monophosphate, diacylglycerol, and inositol phosphates.

Once neurotransmitters have been secreted into synapses and have passed on their chemical signals, the presynaptic neuron clears the synapse of neurotransmitter molecules. For example, acetylcholine is broken down by the enzyme acetylcholinesterase into choline and acetate. Neurotransmitters like dopamine, serotonin, and GABA are removed by a physical process called reuptake. In reuptake, a protein in the presynaptic membrane acts as a sort of sponge, causing the neurotransmitters to reenter the presynaptic neuron, where they can be broken down by enzymes or repackaged for reuse.

Neurotransmitters are known to be involved in a number of disorders, including Alzheimer's disease. Victims of Alzheimer's disease suffer from loss of intellectual capacity, disintegration of personality, mental confusion, hallucinations, and aggressive—even violent—behaviour. These symptoms are the result of progressive degeneration in many types of neurons in the brain. Forgetfulness, one of the earliest symptoms of Alzheimer's disease, is partly caused by the destruction of neurons that normally release the neurotransmitter acetylcholine. Medications that increase brain levels of acetylcholine have helped restore short-term memory and reduce mood swings in some Alzheimer's patients.

Neurotransmitters also play a role in Parkinson disease, which slowly attacks the nervous system, causing symptoms that worsen over time. Fatigue, mental confusion, a masklike facial expression, stooping posture, shuffling gait, and problems with eating and speaking are among the difficulties suffered by Parkinson victims. These symptoms have been partly linked to the deterioration and eventual death of neurons that run from the base of the brain to the basal ganglia, a collection of nerve cells that manufacture the neurotransmitter dopamine. The reasons why such neurons die are yet to be understood, but the related symptoms can be alleviated. L-dopa, or levodopa, widely used to treat Parkinson disease, acts as a supplementary precursor for dopamine. It causes the surviving neurons in the basal ganglia to increase their production of dopamine, thereby compensating to some extent for the disabled neurons.

Many other effective drugs have been shown to act by influencing neurotransmitter behaviour. Some drugs work by interfering with the interactions between neurotransmitters and intestinal receptors. For example, belladonna decreases intestinal cramps in such disorders as irritable bowel syndrome by blocking acetylcholine from combining with receptors. This process reduces nerve signals to the bowel wall, which prevents painful spasms.

Other drugs block the reuptake process. One well-known example is the drug fluoxetine (Prozac), which blocks the reuptake of serotonin. Serotonin then remains in the synapse for a longer time, and its ability to act as a signal is prolonged, which contributes to the relief of depression and the control of obsessive-compulsive behaviour.

In general, each neuron uses only a single compound as its neurotransmitter. However, some neurons outside the central nervous system are able to release both an amine and a peptide neurotransmitter.

Neurotransmitters are manufactured from precursor compounds like amino acids, glucose, and the dietary amine-called choline. Neurons modify the structure of these precursor compounds in a series of reactions with enzymes. Neurotransmitters that come from amino acids include serotonin, which is derived from tryptophan; dopamine and norepinephrine, which are derived from tyrosine; and glycine, which is derived from threonine. Among the neurotransmitters made from glucose are glutamate, aspartate, and GABA. Choline serves as the precursor for acetylcholine.

In the nervous system, a message-carrying impulse travels from one end of a nerve cell to the other by means of an electrical impulse. When it reaches the terminal end of a nerve cell, the impulse triggers tiny sacs called presynaptic vessicles to release their contents, chemical messengers called neurotransmitters. The neurotransmitters float across the synapse, or gap between adjacent nerve cells. When they reach the neighbouring nerve cell, the neurotransmitters fit into specialized receptor sites much as a key fits into a lock, causing that nerve cell to "fire," or generate an electric message-carrying impulse. As the message continues through the nervous system, the presynaptic cell absorbs the excess neurotransmitters, and repackages them in presynaptic vessicles in a process called neurotransmitter reuptake.

Neurotransmitters are released into a microscopic gap, called a synapse, that separates the transmitting neuron from the cell receiving the chemical signal. The cell that generates the signal is called the presynaptic cell, while the receiving cell is termed the postsynaptic cell.

After their release into the synapse, neurotransmitters combine chemically with highly specific protein molecules, termed receptors, that are embedded in the surface membranes of the postsynaptic cell. When this combination occurs, the voltage, or electrical force, of the postsynaptic cell is either increased (excited) or decreased (inhibited).

When a neuron is in its resting state, its voltage is about -70 millivolts. An excitatory neurotransmitter alters the membrane of the postsynaptic neuron, making it possible for ions (electrically charged molecules) to move back and forth across the neuron's membranes. This flow of ions makes the neuron's voltage rise toward zero. If enough excitatory receptors have been activated, the postsynaptic neuron responds by firing, generating a nerve impulse that causes its own neurotransmitter to be released into the next synapse. An inhibitory neurotransmitter causes different ions to pass back and forth across the postsynaptic neuron's membrane, lowering the nerve cell's voltage to -80 or -90 millivolts. The drop in voltage makes it less likely that the postsynaptic cell will fire.

If the postsynaptic cell is a muscle cell rather than a neuron, an excitatory neurotransmitter will cause the muscle to contract. If the postsynaptic cell is a gland cell, an excitatory neurotransmitter will cause the cell to secrete its contents.

While most neurotransmitters interact with their receptors to create new electrical nerve impulses that energize or inhibit the adjoining cell, some neurotransmitter interactions do not generate or suppress nerve impulses. Instead, they interact with a second type of receptor that changes the internal chemistry of the postsynaptic cell by either causing or blocking the formation of chemicals called second messenger molecules. These second messengers regulate the postsynaptic cell's biochemical processes and enable it to conduct the maintenance necessary to continue synthesizing neurotransmitters and conducting nerve impulses. Examples of second messengers, which are formed and entirely contained within the postsynaptic cell, include cyclic adenosine monophosphate, diacylglycerol, and inositol phosphates.

Once neurotransmitters have been secreted into synapses and have passed on their chemical signals, the presynaptic neuron clears the synapse of neurotransmitter molecules. For example, acetylcholine is broken down by the enzyme acetylcholinesterase into choline and acetate. Neurotransmitters like dopamine, serotonin, and GABA are removed by a physical process called reuptake. In reuptake, a protein in the presynaptic membrane acts as a sort of sponge, causing the neurotransmitters to reenter the presynaptic neuron, where they can be broken down by enzymes or repackaged for reuse.

Neurotransmitters are known to be involved in a number of disorders, including Alzheimer's disease. Victims of Alzheimer's disease suffer from loss of intellectual capacity, disintegration of personality, mental confusion, hallucinations, and aggressive—even violent—behaviour. These symptoms are the result of progressive degeneration in many types of neurons in the brain. Forgetfulness, one of the earliest symptoms of Alzheimer's disease, is partly caused by the destruction of neurons that normally release the neurotransmitter acetylcholine. Medications that increase brain levels of acetylcholine have helped restore short-term memory and reduce mood swings in some Alzheimer's patients.

Neurotransmitters also play a role in Parkinson disease, which slowly attacks the nervous system, causing symptoms that worsen over time. Fatigue, mental confusion, a masklike facial expression, stooping posture, shuffling gait, and problems with eating and speaking are among the difficulties suffered by Parkinson victims. These symptoms have been partly linked to the deterioration and eventual death of neurons that run from the base of the brain to the basal ganglia, a collection of nerve cells that manufacture the neurotransmitter dopamine. The reasons why such neurons die are yet to be understood, but the related symptoms can be alleviated. L-dopa, or levodopa, widely used to treat Parkinson disease, acts as a supplementary precursor for dopamine. It causes the surviving neurons in the basal ganglia to increase their production of dopamine, thereby compensating to some extent for the disabled neurons.

Many other effective drugs have been shown to act by influencing neurotransmitter behaviour. Some drugs work by interfering with the interactions between neurotransmitters and intestinal receptors. For example, belladonna decreases intestinal cramps in such disorders as irritable bowel syndrome by blocking acetylcholine from combining with receptors. This process reduces nerve signals to the bowel wall, which prevents painful spasms.

Other drugs block the reuptake process. One well-known example is the drug fluoxetine (Prozac), which blocks the reuptake of serotonin. Serotonin then remains in the synapse for a longer time, and its ability to act as a signal is prolonged, which contributes to the relief of depression and the control of obsessive-compulsive behaviour.

Some evidence suggests that schizophrenia may result from an imbalance of chemicals in the brain called neurotransmitters. These chemicals enable neurons (brain cells) to communicate with each other. Some scientists suggest that schizophrenia results from excess activity of the neurotransmitter dopamine in certain parts of the brain or from an abnormal sensitivity to dopamine. Support for this hypothesis comes from antipsychotic drugs, which reduce psychotic symptoms in schizophrenia by blocking brain receptors for dopamine. In addition, amphetamines, which increase dopamine activity, intensify psychotic symptoms in people with schizophrenia. Despite these findings, many experts believe that excess dopamine activity alone cannot account for schizophrenia. Other neurotransmitters, such as serotonin and norepinephrine, may play important roles as well.

Other mechanisms reduce pain sensation by blocking, or inhibiting, the transmission of the pain message to the brain. To alter the pain sensation, the brain and spinal cord release specialized neurotransmitters called endorphins and enkephalins.

These chemicals interfere with pain impulse transmission by occupying the nerve cell receptors required to send the impulse across the synapse. By making the pain impulse travel less efficiently, endorphins and enkephalins can significantly lessen the perception of pain. In extreme circumstances, they can even make severe injuries nearly painless. If an athlete is injured during the height of competition, or a soldier injured during combat, they may not realize they have been injured until after the stressful situation has ended. This happens because the brain produces abnormally high levels of endorphins or enkephalins in periods of intense stress or excitement.

Concentrated chemical substances, or hormones, which control 10 to 12 functions in the body, have been obtained as extracts from the anterior pituitary glands of cattle, sheep, and swine. Eight hormones have been isolated, purified, and identified; all of them are peptides, that is, they are composed of amino acids. Growth hormone (GH), or the somatotropic hormone (STH), is essential for normal skeletal growth and is neutralized during adolescence by the gonadal sex hormones. Thyroid-stimulating hormone (TSH) controls the normal functioning of the thyroid gland; and the adrenocorticotropic hormone (ACTH) controls the activity of the cortex of the adrenal glands and takes part in the stress reaction. Prolactin, also called lactogenic, luteotropic, or mammotropic hormone, initiates milk secretion in the mammary gland after the mammary tissues have been prepared during pregnancy by the secretion of other pituitary and sex hormones. The two gonadotropic hormones are follicle-stimulating hormone (FSH) and luteinizing hormone (LH). Follicle-stimulating hormone stimulates the formation of the Graafian follicle in the female ovary and the development of spermatozoa in the male. The luteinizing hormone stimulates the formation of ovarian hormones after ovulation and initiates lactation in the female; in the male, it stimulates the tissues of the testes to elaborate testosterone. In 1975 scientists identified the pituitary peptide endorphin, which acts in experimental animals as a natural pain reliever in times of stress. Endorphin and ACTH are made as parts of a single large protein, which subsequently splits. This may be the body's mechanism for coordinating the physiological activities of two stress-induced hormones. The same large prohormone that contains ACTH and endorphin also contains short peptides called melanocyte-stimulating hormones. These substances are analogous to the hormone that regulates pigmentation in fish and amphibians, but in humans they have no known function.

Many people learn to control their pain with strategies that do not rely on drugs or surgery. Some people control the normally involuntary components of pain message transmission using a behaviour modification technique-called biofeedback. Acupuncture is widely used for pain relief. Many scientists now believe that this ancient medical procedure may trigger the release of endorphins and enkephalins, the body's own pain-inhibiting neurotransmitters. Others suspect that the pain-relieving attributes of acupuncture are due, in part, to a patient's expectation of relief. Although it is not completely understood, physicians and pain specialists have found that when a person suffering from pain expects that a particular procedure—in this case acupuncture—will make their pain subside, it actually does.

In cases where no treatment effectively relieves pain, doctors may recommend a surgical procedure in which pain-transmitting nerves in the brain or spinal cord are severed. Only a small fraction of pain sufferers need such surgical treatment. Another pain-relieving procedure involves placing electrical stimulators on the skin, nerves, spinal cord, or brain to reduce pain sensation.

Some injuries take a long time to heal, and even then, pain does not always completely subside. People suffering from this condition, known as chronic pain, may continue to experience debilitating pain for years, without having any apparent tissue damage. This may be the result of permanent damage to the nervous system. There is new evidence that the nerves in the spinal cord and brain can alter their connections after severe pain—that is, even after healing, the nervous system never returns to normal. Pain that subsides and then returns periodically, such as headaches or low back pain, also falls under the category of chronic pain. In their search for pain relief, many chronic pain sufferers become dependent on strong painkilling medicines, and they often fall into an endless cycle of pain, depression, and inactivity.

The complexity of human pain often requires a combination of pain therapies to achieve relief. Pain management specialists are usually medical doctors with specialized training in neurology, psychiatry, or surgery who have restricted their practice to the analysis and treatment of pain. Psychologists are usually important members of a pain management team. Many people are turning to alternative healthcare practitioners, such as those that specialize in acupuncture or chiropractic, for pain relief. Often, pain management specialists and practitioners of alternative pain therapies join forces in multi disciplinary pain clinics.

The complexity of human pain often requires a combination of pain therapies to achieve relief. Pain management specialists are usually medical doctors with specialized training in neurology, psychiatry, or surgery who have restricted their practice to the analysis and treatment of pain. Psychologists are usually important members of a pain management team. Many people are turning to alternative healthcare practitioners, such as those that specialize in acupuncture or chiropractic, for pain relief. Often, pain management specialists and practitioners of alternative pain therapies join forces in multidisciplinary pain clinics.

Acetaminophen, nonprescription drug used for the relief of minor pain, such as headaches and structural muscle aches, and for the reduction of fever. Like the other common analgesic drugs aspirin and ibuprofen, acetaminophen relieves pain by inhibiting the synthesis of prostaglandins in the body. It does not reduce inflammation as do those other two analgesics, but it also does not irritate the stomach lining, as aspirin tends to do for some users. A large overdose of acetaminophen may cause severe liver damage.

Aspirin, synthetic chemical compound, acetylsalicylic acid. It is made from salicylic acid, found in the bark of the willow tree, which was used by the ancient Greeks and Native Americans, among others, to counter fever and pain. Salicylic acid is bitter, however, and irritates the stomach. The German chemist Felix Hoffman synthesized the acetyl derivative of salicylic acid in 1893 in response to the urging of his father, who took salicylic acid for rheumatism. Aspirin is currently the first-choice drug for fever, mild to moderate pain, and inflammation due to arthritis or injury. It is a more effective analgesic than codeine. Aspirin causes insignificant gastrointestinal bleeding that can over time, however, cause iron deficiency; gastric ulcers may also occur with long-term use. Complications can be avoided by using enteric-coated aspirin, which does not dissolve until reaching the intestine. Aspirin should not be given to children who have chicken pox or influenza, because it increases the risk of contracting the rare and frequently fatal Reye's syndrome, a disease of the brain and some abdominal organs.

Aspirin is thought to act by interfering with synthesis of prostaglandins, which are implicated in inflammation and fever.

Studies of aspirin's anticlotting activities suggest that half an aspirin tablet per day may reduce the risk of heart attack and stroke in some persons.

Ibuprofen, drug used to reduce inflammation, fever, and the sensation of pain. In prescription form, ibuprofen is usually taken to relieve the more severe symptoms associated with arthritis. The nonprescription form available over the counter is taken for low-intensity pain, inflammation, or fever.

Ibuprofen works by inhibiting the action of prostaglandins (chemicals that cause inflammation and contribute to the brain's perception of pain). Ibuprofen reduces fever by blocking prostaglandin synthesis in the hypothalamus, a structure in the brain that regulates body temperature. Ibuprofen also acts as an anticoagulant, suppressing the formation of blood clots.

In adults, the dosage of ibuprofen commonly prescribed for arthritis is 1200 to 3200 mg per day, usually divided into 3 or 4 doses. For mild to moderate pain in nonprescription uses, the dosage is generally 400 mg taken every 4 to 6 hours as necessary. Because ibuprofen can cause stomach upset, pills should be swallowed with a full glass of water, and may be taken with food. Ibuprofen is not recommended for use by pregnant women.

Prolonged use of ibuprofen can result in ulcers and internal bleeding because it blocks the production of the stomach lining's protective mucous barrier.

Ibuprofen prevents the body from excreting salt and water properly, and it should be used with caution by people who suffer from kidney disease, liver disease, or high blood pressure. The anticoagulant effect of ibuprofen can also result in excessive bleeding when taken prior to tooth extraction or minor surgery. When taken in excessive amounts, ibuprofen can produce a potentially fatal overdose syndrome, which usually involves vomiting, diarrhea, rapid breathing, or rapid heartbeat. Alcoholic beverages should be avoided while taking this medication.

The opium poppy's green, unripe seed capsule, revealed when the flower petals drop, contains a milky sap that is the source of opium. To collect the sap, slits are made along the circumference of the seed capsules, enabling the milky sap to ooze out and dry. It is then scraped from the capsules, pressed into cakes, and dried to form the rubbery, yellow-brown opium. Natural derivatives of opium include morphine and codeine, used extensively in medicine as sedatives and pain killers. Heroin is a synthetic derivative of morphine. Morphine and codeine are habit forming. Heroin, which is especially addictive, is illegal in the United States.

Opium, narcotic drug produced from the drying resin of unripe capsules of the opium poppy, Papaver somniferum. Opium is grown mainly in Myanmar (formerly Burma) and Afghanistan. The legitimate world demand for opium amounts to about 680 metric tons a year, but many times that amount is distributed illegally.

In its commercial form, opium is a chestnut-coloured globular mass, sticky and rather soft, but hardening from within as it ages. It is processed into the alkaloid morphine which has long served as the chief painkiller in medical practice, although synthetic substitutes such as meperidine (trade name Demerol) are now available. Heroin, a derivative of morphine, is about three times more potent. Codeine is another important opium alkaloid.

The molecules of opiates have painkilling properties similar to those of compounds called endorphins or enkephalins produced in the body. Being of similar structure, the opiate molecules occupy many of the same nerve-receptor sites and bring on the same analgesic effect as the body's natural painkillers. Opiates first produce a feeling of pleasure and euphoria, but with their continued use the body demands larger amounts to reach the same sense of well-being. Withdrawal is extremely uncomfortable, and addicts typically continue taking the drug to avoid pain rather than to attain the initial state of euphoria. Malnutrition, respiratory complications, and low blood pressure are some of the illnesses associated with addiction.

As long ago as 100 ad, opium had been used as a folk medicine, taken with a beverage or swallowed as a solid. Only toward the middle of the 17th century, when opium smoking was introduced into China, did any serious addiction problems arise. In the 18th century opium addiction was so serious there that the Chinese made many attempts to prohibit opium cultivation and opium trade with Western countries. At the same time opium made its way to Europe and North America, where addiction grew out of its prevalent use as a painkiller.

With the invention of the hypodermic syringe during the American Civil War, the injection of morphine became indispensable in treating patients who had to undergo some of the newly developed surgical operations. Physicians of that time hoped that injecting morphine directly into the blood stream would avoid the addictive effects of smoking or eating opium, but instead it proved more addictive. With the discovery of heroin in 1898 came a similar hope, but this more potent drug created a much stronger dependency than opium or morphine.

Today opium is sold on the street as a powder or dark brown solid and is smoked, eaten, or injected. Heroin addicts in the United

States number around 2 million people. Although the synthetic narcotic methadone has been used to offer addicts some relief from opiates, it is itself addictive. Complete recovery from opiate addiction requires years of social and psychological rehabilitation

Narcotics, term originally applied to all compounds that produce insensibility to external stimuli through depression of the central nervous system, but now applied primarily to the drugs known as opiates—compounds extracted from the opium poppy and their chemical derivatives. Also classed as narcotics are the opioids, chemical compounds that are wholly synthesized, but which resemble the opiates in their actions.

The most important attribute of narcotics is their capacity to decrease pain, not only by decreasing the perception of pain, but also by altering the reaction to it. Although they do have sedative properties when used in large doses, they are not used primarily for sedation.

The major constituent of opium and the prototype of all narcotic analgesics is morphine, which was isolated and chemically analyzed by the German apothecary F. W. A. Sterner between 1805 and 1817. Other narcotics used in the US are meperidine (trade name Demerol), codeine, and propoxyphene (trade name Darvon). Heroin, synthesized from morphine, is a potent analgesic, but its use is forbidden in the US Some of the newer synthetic compounds are 1000 to 10,000 times more potent than morphine.

In addition to their painkilling properties, the narcotic analgesics cause a profound feeling of well-being (euphoria). It is this feeling that is in part responsible for the psychological drive of certain persons to obtain and self-administer these drugs. When taken chronically in large doses, the narcotics have the capacity to induce tolerance (whereby a larger and larger dose is required by the body to achieve the same effect), and ultimately psychological and physical dependence, or addiction. In this respect they are similar to the barbiturates and to alcohol. These properties make the medical use of narcotics extremely difficult and have led to strict regulation of the prescription and dispensing of this class of drugs. Even so, they are widely abused.

The mode of action of the narcotic analgesics is still not fully understood. Recent research has determined that specific regions of the brain and spinal cord have an affinity for binding opiates, and the binding sites in the brain are in the same general areas where pain centres are believed to be. This research has also succeeded in isolating compounds, called enkephalins, that are produced in the body to reduce pain; the compounds consist of five amino acids. Apparently they can depress neurons throughout the central nervous system. They belong to a group of larger compounds called endorphins, consisting of many amino acids, that have also been isolated in the body and that are produced by the pituitary gland. Administration of endorphins, including the enkephalins, results in effects similar to those produced by opiates.

The discovery of a class of compounds that are specific antagonists to the action of the opiates has made it possible to treat opiate over the dosage quickly and efficiently. The standard drug for this use is naloxone. Some of the antagonists also have opiate like properties, and this has led to the introduction of a new class of analgesics, the mixed agonists-antagonists. It is hoped that these drugs will produce analgesia without euphoria, reducing their potential for abuse. The three drugs of this class approved so far in the US—pentazocine, butorphanol, and nalbuphine— are as analgesic as morphine for many uses and induce little or no euphoria. All appear to have a lower abuse potential than morphine or propoxyphene.

Chromosome, are the microscopic structure within cells that carries the molecule deoxyribonucleic acid (DNA)—the hereditary material that influences the development and characteristics of each organism. In bacteria and bacteria-like organisms called archaebacteria, chromosomes consist of simple circles of DNA floating freely in the organism. In all other life forms, collectively called eukaryotes, chromosomes reside within a well-defined nucleus. In eukaryotes, chromosomes are highly complex structures in which the shape of the DNA molecules is linear, rather than circular.

Chromosomes consist chiefly of proteins and DNA. Tiny chemical subunits called nucleotide bases form the structure of DNA. A sequence of bases along a DNA strand that codes for the production of a protein is known as a gene. Genes occupy precise locations on the chromosome.

Each cell contains enough DNA to form a thread extending about 2 m (about 7 ft). Proteins called histones play a key role in packaging DNA within chromosomes. Sections of the DNA molecule wind around clusters of histones to form units called nucleosomes, which resemble spools encircled with thread. Another type of protein, called nonhistone chromosomal protein, further compresses nucleosomes into a compact, narrow coil. Chromosomes become most condensed when a cell is preparing to divide.

The chromosome structure ensures that even when the DNA is highly confined, it is free to carry out transcription, or the production of messenger ribonucleic acid (mRNA). The messenger ribonucleic acid is the molecule that carries the DNA instructions that determine the types of proteins a cell will reproduce to the sites where proteins are constructed. In addition, chromosomes permit DNA to replicate, or reproduce itself, so that as a cell divides to produce two cells, each of these new cells will contain all of the necessary genetic information.

Scientists are learning how DNA loosens its connection with histones in order to replicate itself and participate in the synthesis of mRNA. Evidence suggests that enzymes interact with the tails of histones, which protrude from the nucleosomes. These interactions may temporarily disrupt the nucleosome structure so that the DNA is free to interact with the enzymes that help to generate either mRNA or new copies of DNA.

The chromosomes of nearly all eukaryotic life forms contain two important structures: centromeres and telomeres. During cell division, the centromere—visible through a microscope as a knotlike structure—connects to an apparatus called the spindle. The spindle contains fibres that move the centromeres around, causing the rest of each chromosome to follow. This process ensures that each chromosome moves to its proper place during mitosis, when a cell divides to give rise to two cells, and during meiosis, the process of cell division that gives rise to eggs or sperm.

Telomeres are specialized sequences of DNA that are found at the tips of chromosomes. Telomeres serve as a kind of cap that prevents the ends of chromosomes from attaching to the ends of other chromosomes. Scientists suspect that telomeres may influence the activity of nearby genes and may play a role in determining the life span of a cell.

In the cells of most organisms that reproduce sexually, chromosomes occur in pairs: One chromosome is inherited from the female parent, and one is inherited from the male parent. The two chromosomes of each pair contain genes that correspond to the same inherited characteristics. Each pair of chromosomes is different from every other pair of chromosomes in the same cell.

The number of chromosome pairs in an organism varies depending on the species. The number of chromosomes characteristic of a particular organism is known as the diploid number. Dogs, for example, have 38 pairs of chromosomes and a diploid number of 76, while tomato plants have 12 pairs of chromosomes and a diploid number of 24.

Sex cells (eggs or sperm) contain only half the number of chromosomes found in the other cells of an organism. This reduced number of chromosomes in the sex cells is known as the haploid number. During fertilization, an egg and sperm unite to form a cell known as a zygote, the first cell of the offspring. The zygote contains the diploid number of chromosomes characteristic of the species.

Most organisms have complete sets of matching chromosomal pairs, known as autosomes. In mammals, birds, and some other organisms, one pair of chromosomes is not identical. Known as the sex chromosomes, this pair plays a dominant role in determining the sex of an organism. Females have two copies of the X chromosome, while males have one Y chromosome and one X chromosome. Both males and females inherit one sex chromosome from the mother (always an X chromosome) and one sex chromosome from the father (an X in female offspring and a Y in male offspring). The presence of the Y chromosome determines that a zygote will develop into a male.

The Y chromosome is about one-third the size of the X chromosome and contains only a fraction of the number of genes. At one point in evolutionary history, the X and Y chromosomes were equal in size and gene number, but the two chromosomes gradually diverged over the course of 300 million years. These unmatched sex chromosomes produce a pattern of gene inheritance known as sex-linked inheritance, which differs from genes found on autosomes. In males, which carry an X and a Y chromosome, some genes found on the X chromosome may be missing on the Y chromosome. As a result, the organism will usually develop the trait associated with the gene on the X chromosome. In fruit flies, for instance, the gene for eye colour is located on the X chromosome. A male fruit fly will inherit the eye colour found on the X chromosome, since no gene for eye colour is found on the Y chromosome.

A karyotype, like the ones shown here, is a photographic image that depicts all of the chromosomes in an individual cell. Laboratory workers use computers to rearrange the images so that the chromosomes are lined up in pairs, typically beginning with the autosomes—chromosomes 1 through 22—and ending with the sex chromosomes—normally XX or XY. A complete karyotype helps doctors determine if a person has extra chromosomes, missing chromosomes, or chromosomes that have attached to one another in unusual ways.

Humans have 23 pairs of chromosomes, with a diploid number of 46. Scientists number these chromosome pairs according to their size—the largest is chromosome 1 and the smallest is chromosome 23. In human chromosomes, errors may occur that give rise to embryos with more or less genetic material, sometimes resulting in developmental disabilities or health problems. In a process called nondisjunction, paired members of chromosomes fail to separate from one another during meiosis. Nondisjunction can lead to a condition known as Down syndrome, in which a person inherits three copies of chromosome 21. Another condition that may result from nondisjunction is Turner syndrome, a disorder in which a female inherits only a single X chromosome.

Genetic errors occur if part of a chromosome is either missing or duplicated. Chromosomes sometimes undergo changes called translocation, in which part of one chromosome breaks off and attaches to another chromosome. A translocation involving chromosomes 9 and 22 is linked to a type of leukemia called chronic myelogenic leukemia. On the sex chromosomes, problems arise in men when an abnormal gene is present on the X chromosome. With no healthy gene found on the Y chromosome to override the abnormal gene, disease may result. For example, men who inherit a mutated gene that causes hemophilia from their mother on the X chromosome will develop this bleeding disorder since they are missing a normal version of the gene on their Y chromosome.

Scientists called cytogeneticists look at a person's chromosomes in the laboratory to determine whether the individual has the usual number of chromosomes and whether these chromosomes have missing or extra segments. To examine chromosomes, cytogeneticists grow samples of a person's blood cells in the laboratory and expose the cells to a chemical called colchicine, which disrupts the spindle apparatus that is normally present in dividing cells. This disruption immobilizes the chromosomes during cell division, when they are most condensed and visible. Chromosomes are then stained with various dyes, which produce a pattern of vertical bands. Cytogeneticists take photographs of the banded chromosomes through a microscope to create images called karyotypes, in which the members of each chromosome pair are arranged next to each other for easy comparison. The analysis of karyotypes reveals whether a person has extra or missing chromosomes, as well as whether large segments of chromosomes are absent, rearranged, or duplicated.

Experiments involving artificial chromosomes—chromosomes that are synthesized in the laboratory—are providing new insights into the structure and function of chromosomes. The first artificial chromosomes, produced in the 1980s, were chromosomes of yeast cells. The first artificial human chromosomes were created in 1997.

Researchers have successfully identified all the genes located on chromosomes 5, 16, 19, 21, and 22. This research has revealed a number of disease-causing genes associated with these chromosomes. For instance, genes found on chromosome 5 have been linked to a colorectal cancer, basal cell carcinoma (a form of skin cancer), and a type of dwarfism. Chromosome 16 contains genes implicated in adult polycystic renal disease, which affects 5 million people worldwide. Identifying disease-causing genes and their chromosome locations will help researchers devise new diagnostic tools to determine a person's risk for disease as well as new therapies to replace or repair faulty genes.

Heredity, process of transmitting biological traits from parent to offspring through genes, the basic units of heredity. Heredity also refers to the inherited characteristics of an individual, including traits such as height, eye colour, and blood type.

This karyotype of a human male shows the 23 pairs of chromosomes that are typically present in human cells. The chromosome pairs labelled 1 through 22 are called autosomes, and have a similar appearance in males and females. The 23rd pair, shown on the bottom right, represents the sex chromosomes. Females have two identical-looking sex chromosomes that are both labelled X, whereas males have a single X chromosome and a smaller chromosome labelled Y.

Heredity accounts for why offspring look like their parents: when two dogs mate, for example, they have puppies, not kittens. If the parents are both Chihuahuas, the puppies will also be Chihuahuas, not great Danes or Labrador retrievers. The puppies may be a little taller or shorter, a little lighter or a lot heavier than their parents are. Their faces may look a little different, or they may have different talents and temperaments. In all the important characteristics, however—the number of limbs, arrangement of organs, general size, fur type—they will share the traits of their parents. The principles of heredity hold true not only for a puppy but also for a virus, a roundworm, a pansy, or a human.

Genetics is the study of how heredity works and, in particular, of genes. A gene is a section of a long deoxyribonucleic acid (DNA) molecule, and it carries information for the construction of a protein or part of a protein. Through the diversity of proteins they code for, genes influence or determine such traits as eye colour, the ability of a bacterium to eat a certain sugar, or the number of peas in a pod. A virus has as few as a dozen genes. A simple roundworm has 5000 to 8000 genes, while a corn plant has 60,000. The construction of a human requires an estimated 50,000 genes.

If the DNA in a single human cell could be unravelled, it would form a single thread about five feet long and about 50 trillionths of an inch thick. To prevent this fine string of DNA from becoming knotted like a big tangle of yarn, parts of the strand are wrapped around proteins like a thread is wound around spools. These units of wrapped DNA are called nucleosomes, and they coil and fold into structures called chromosomes. Humans have 23 pairs of chromosomes. In each pair, one chromosome comes from the mother and the other from the father. Twenty-two of the pairs are the same in both men and women, and these are called autosomes. The twenty-third pair consists of the sex chromosomes, so called because they are the primary factor in determining the gender of a child. The sex chromosomes are known as the X and Y chromosomes.

Females have two X chromosomes, and males have one X and one Y chromosomes. The Y chromosome is about one-third the size of the X chromosome. A sperm, the reproductive cell produced by the male, can carry either one X or one Y chromosome. An egg, the reproductive cell produced by the female, can carry only the X chromosome. When a sperm with an X chromosome unites with an egg, the result is a child with two X-chromosomes-a female. When a sperm with a Y chromosome unites with an egg, however, the result is a child with one X and one Y chromosome—a male. Thus, the father determines the gender of the child.

The single-celled amoeba demonstrates a simple method of asexual reproduction; it divides in half by a process called fission, producing two smaller daughter cells. After a period of feeding and growth, these two daughter cells will themselves divide in half.

Throughout the entire world of life, evolution has brought about only two types of reproduction—asexual and sexual. Asexual reproduction does not require a mate and is less complicated than sexual reproduction. It is used by simple life forms, such as bacteria, complex one-celled organisms, such as amoebas and diatoms, and certain explicable worms, such as flatworms, fungi and several plants.

In asexual reproduction, one parent transmits all of its genetic information to the offspring, and the offspring is therefore identical to the parent. Asexual reproduction typically is a rapid and reliable method of reproduction. It is limited, however, because the genetic uniformity in the offspring makes them all equally susceptible to a change in the environment. If a new disease, a new predator, or a climate change is lethal to one individual, it is lethal to all genetically identical organisms. Such changes can effectively wipe out entire populations of genetically identical organisms. Sexual reproduction results in offspring with diverse traits, and is the predominant form of reproduction among plants, animals, and most other organisms.

In contrast to asexual reproduction, sexual reproduction requires two parents. Each parent creates sex cells, or gametes that contain half the parent's genetic information. Human sex cells—sperm and eggs—contain 23 single, unpaired chromosomes rather than the 23 paired chromosomes found in all other body cells, or somatic cells. When egg and sperm unite in the process called fertilization, they form one cell that contains 23 pairs of chromosomes, the normal number for human body cells? The cell develops into a child that has a mixture of genetic information from both parents. As a result, the child is similar to each of the parents but not identical to either of them.

If these same parents have a second child, it is the product of fertilization of a different sperm and a different egg. Therefore the second child is unique, because each sperm and egg contains a unique set of chromosomes. Scientists estimate that each person is capable of producing 223 or 8,388,608 unique sex cells. The total number of unique children possible from one couple is a phenomenal 223 ´ 223 or 246. This genetic diversity that results from sexual reproduction enables populations to withstand changing environments through evolution.

With the exception of the X and Y chromosomes, genes come in twos on the paired chromosomes, but the genes are not necessarily identical. The hair colour gene from the father may carry information for black hair, but its partner on the chromosome from the mother may specify red hair. These different forms of genes that carry information for specific traits are called alleles. A person's hair colour depends on several alleles interacting in complex ways to determine the actual trait of the offspring.

The pattern of inheritance describes how alleles work together to produce traits. Understanding inheritance patterns enables geneticists to predict the probability that a child will inherit a certain trait. A variety of inheritance patterns influence the diverse traits found not only in humans, but in other animals, plants, fungi, and bacteria.

Some genes that cause genetic diseases interact in a dominant-recessive pattern. In these cases, two copies of the recessive gene are required for the disease to occur. A person who has just one copy of the recessive gene is termed a carrier, since he or she carries the gene but is not affected by it. In the illustration above, the dominant gene is represented in green, and the recessive in blue. For the couple on the left, the father has one copy of the dominant gene and one copy of the recessive gene. The mother has two copies of the dominant gene. Each parent can contribute just one gene to the child. The four children shown on the lower left represent the probabilities (not the actual children) for the combinations that can result from their parents. The children on the far left received the recessive gene from their father and the dominant gene from their mother, and are therefore carriers. For any child born to these parents, there is a 50 percent chance that the child will be a carrier. Since none of the children can inherit two copies of the recessive gene, none of the children will develop the disease. When both parents are carriers, however, as shown by the couple on the right, there is a 25 percent chance that any child born has the disease, a 50 percent chance that a child is a carrier, and a 25 percent chance that a child does not have the disease and is not a carrier.

The dominant-recessive pattern of inheritance, a relatively simple pattern, involves paired alleles that influence one trait. In this pattern, one of the two alleles contains information for a certain characteristic—the lavender colour of sweet pea flowers, for example—while the second allele directs the production of an alternate characteristic—the white flower colour. In sweet peas, if these two alleles occur together, the allele for lavender flowers is expressed, and the flowers are lavender. The allele for lavender is therefore called the dominant allele. The allele for white is known as the recessive allele. Lavender flowers also occur when two alleles for lavender colour are paired. Only when two alleles for the recessive characteristic are paired do white flowers appear. This genetic rule applies regardless of the organism or the trait. In the dominant recessive pattern, the recessive trait shows up only when two recessive alleles are paired.

In humans, several hundred genetic diseases and disorders follow the dominant-recessive pattern. These conditions result when a mutation, or a change in a normal allele, is found in a sperm or egg, and the mutation causes disease when the child inherits a pair of mutated alleles. If a child inherits one dominant allele and one recessive allele he or she typically does not have the disease. Such individuals are termed carriers, since although healthy, they carry the recessive allele. A carrier can pass either the dominant or recessive allele to their child. If both parents are carriers, these alleles can be passed along in four ways. The child can receive a normal allele from each parent, in which case it does not develop the disease. It can receive a mutated allele from the mother and a normal allele from the father, or a normal allele from the mother and a mutated allele from the father. In both of these cases, the child will be a carrier. The child develops the disease only if he or she receives a mutated allele from each parent. When both parents are carriers, there is a 25 percent chance that a child will be disease-free, a 25 percent chance that it will have the disease, and a 50 percent chance that it will be a carrier. Examples of genetic diseases that follow the dominant-recessive pattern include sickle-cell anaemia, beta-thalassemia, cystic fibrosis, and severe combined immunodeficiency disease.

A significant number of human traits, such as eye colour, skin colour, height, weight, and muscle strength are typically regulated by more than one allele in a pattern known as polygenic inheritance. Several thousand alleles, for example, may combine to determine a person's potential for pole-vaulting, and several hundred may play a role in establishing a person's normal weight. Certain diseases may result from mutations in one or more alleles involved in polygenic inheritance. Researchers have identified nearly a dozen mutated alleles that are associated with diabetes mellitus, and a similar number are linked to asthma. Heart disease may be linked to two or three times that number. Some types of cancer may be correlated with more than 100 different genes. Polygenic inheritance is quite complex, and the ways in which multiple genes interact to produce traits are not fully understood.

X-Y linked, or sex-linked, inheritance results from the size differences between the X and Y chromosomes. The longer X chromosome carries an estimated 250 genes, which are responsible for critical biochemical functions such as normal blood clotting. The shorter Y chromosome carries 6 genes, which are responsible for other traits, such as producing significant amounts of testosterone, the male sex hormone.

X-Y linked conditions typically occur in a male when the single X chromosome carries a mutated allele, one that prevents normal blood clotting, for example. A male does not have a second X chromosome with a normal allele to override the mutation. As a result, the male in this case will have hemophilia, a disease in which blood does not clot normally. If one of the female's X chromosomes carries the mutated allele, however, her second X chromosome is usually normal. The normal allele is the dominant allele, so the female does not have hemophilia. Thus, females are typically carriers of X-Y linked diseases but do not develop them unless they receive a mutated allele from each parent, an unusual event. Among the genetic disorders typically carried by females but inherited by males are hemophilia, colour blindness, and Duchenne's muscular dystrophy.

In most organisms, the chromosomes located in the cell nucleus contain the vast majority of the DNA. But another structure in the cell, called a mitochondrion, also holds a chromosome. The DNA on this chromosome is referred to as mitochondrial DNA. While both sperm and egg contain mitochondria, only the egg's mitochondria are transmitted to the offspring. The sperm's mitochondria are contained in the sperm's tail, which never penetrates the egg.

Mutations in mitochondrial DNA have been implicated in a number of genetic diseases. These diseases include diabetes mellitus, deafness, heart disease, Alzheimer's disease, Parkinson disease, and Leber's hereditary optic neuropathy, a condition of complete or partial blindness resulting from degeneration of the optic nerve. Mitochondrial medicine is a relatively new specialty that seeks to explain the disorders and the patterns of inheritance associated with mitochondrial DNA.

Since mitochondrial DNA is inherited only from the mother—a type of inheritance known as maternal inheritance—scientists can trace these genes from one generation to the next, a simpler task than tracing genes that might come from either the mother or the father. The study of mitochondrial DNA has been employed to study human evolution. Recently scientists extracted mitochondrial DNA from Neanderthal bones believed to be between 30,000 and 100,000 years old. They compared these ancient genes with those of hundreds of people around the world. As a result, they determined that Neanderthal are a different species than humans and not their ancestors, as was formerly believed.

Alleles differ in the degree to which they determine traits. If a person inherits the alleles for Type A blood, for example, they have Type A blood from birth to death. Traits associated with some alleles, however, show up only under certain circumstances. For example, a specific allele might place a person at risk for developing diabetes mellitus, but only if they suffer a particular viral infection. Alleles that influence depression may make an individual more likely to become depressed, but only if they encounter life experiences that enhance the allele's effects. Researchers increasingly find evidence that many alleles are associated only with a tendency toward particular traits. The expression of these alleles can vary during a person's lifetime. Some alleles appear to be involved in an interplay with the environment: triggers such as toxins, light, certain nutrients, or stress may "turn on" an allele, resulting in expression of the trait.

Psychologists and biologists have long debated whether interaction with the environment—a person's family and culture, for instance—is more important than genes in shaping disease, character, and behaviour. It is becoming more obvious that environment and genes have different degrees of influence, depending on the trait. Some traits such as eye colour appear to depend on only a genetic component with little or no environmental input. However, others such as muscle strength or musical achievement seem to require contributions from both genes and the environment. If a person is born with the alleles for great athletic or musical potential, for example, those talents will not develop without practice. A child may be born with the alleles for potentially high academic intelligence, but lack of stimulation and limited exposure to new experiences in early childhood may keep the child from realizing that potential. Lack of nutrition during childhood can turn a person with the potential to be six feet tall into someone who barely clears five feet. Current research indicates that expression of alleles in certain individuals may also depend on their unique internal environment—their nervous system, hormone balance, or other aspects of their biochemistry.

Gregor Mendel developed the principles of heredity by studying the variation and heredity of seven pairs of inherited characteristics in pea plants. Although the significance of his work was not recognized during his lifetime, it became the basis for the present day field of genetics.

Current knowledge of heredity is the result of more than 2000 years of contemplation of how inheritance works. The ancient Babylonians knew that pollen from a male date palm tree must be applied to the carpels of a female flower to obtain fruit, but they did not know about the reproductive cells in humans. The Greek scientist and philosopher Aristotle believed that inheritance was passed through the blood. This concept was embraced for centuries and persists today in such terminology as bloodlines, half bloods, and blue bloods.

The past few centuries have witnessed tremendous advances in understanding the role of reproductive cells in heredity. In 1651 the British scientist William Harvey proposed the idea, based on his experiments with embryos of different organisms, that all animals develop from eggs. In 1677 a different view was advocated by the Dutch naturalist Anton van Leeuwenhoek, who was the first to observe human sperm under the microscope. Leeuwenhoek believed that sperm contained a child in miniature, which grew larger inside the female's body. Two centuries of experiment and debate followed. Then in 1879, with the use of improved microscopes, German zoologists Herman Fol and Oscar Hertwig observed the union of egg and sperm in animals. This observation crystallized our understanding of the roles of male and female sex cells in reproduction.

Exactly how traits are transmitted to offspring from the sperm and egg was a topic of vigorous discussion in the 19th century. In 1866, the Austrian monk Gregor Mendel published his groundbreaking studies on inheritance in peas. At the time of his work, chromosomes, genes, and DNA were unknown. Even so, Mendel discovered a variety of genetic rules, including the concept of dominant and recessive genes. Mendel hypothesized that plants contain two factors for each plant trait, such as height, seed shape, and flower colour, and that each plant received one factor from each parent. His work anticipated the discoveries that chromosomes are the factors that transmit heredity and that parents contribute one of each member of a pair of chromosomes to their offspring.

Known as the father of modern genetics, Gregor Mendel developed the principles of heredity by studying the variation and heredity of seven pairs of inherited characteristics in pea plants. Although the significance of his work was not recognized during his lifetime, it became the basis for the present day field of genetics.

Gregor Mendel (1822-1884), Austrian monk, whose experimental work became the basis of modern hereditary theory.

Mendel was born on July 22, 1822, to a peasant family in Heinzendorf (now Hynice, Czech Republic). He entered the Augustinian monastery at Brünn (now Brno, Czech Republic), which was known as a centre of learning and scientific endeavour. He later became a substitute teacher at the technical school in Brünn. There Mendel became actively engaged in investigating variation, heredity, and evolution in plants at the monastery's experimental garden. Between 1856 and 1863 he cultivated and tested at least 28,000 pea plants, carefully analyzing seven pairs of seed and plant characteristics. His tedious experiments resulted in the enunciation of two generalizations that later became known as the laws of heredity. His observations also led him to coin two terms still used in present-day genetics: dominance, for a trait that shows up in an offspring; and recessiveness, for a trait masked by a dominant gene.

Mendel's Laws, principles of hereditary transmission of physical characteristics. They were formulated in 1865 by the Augustinian monk Gregor Johann Mendel. Experimenting with seven contrasting characteristics of pure-breeding garden peas, Mendel discovered that by crossing tall and dwarf parents, for example, he got hybrid offspring that resembled the tall parent rather than being a medium-height blend. To explain this he conceived of hereditary units, now called genes, which often expressed dominant or recessive characteristics. Formulating his first principle (the law of segregation), Mendel stated that genes normally occur in pairs in the ordinary body cells, but segregate in the formation of sex cells (eggs or sperm), each member of the pair becoming part of the separate sex cell. When egg and sperm unite, forming a gene pair, the dominant gene (tallness) masks the recessive gene (shortness?).

To corroborate the existence of such hereditary units, Mendel went on to interbreed the first generation of hybrid tall peas and found that the second generation turned out in a ratio of three tall to each short offspring. He then correctly conceived that the genes paired into AA, Aa, and aa ("A" representing dominant and "a" representing recessive). Continuing the breeding experiments, he found that the self-pollinated AA bred true to produce pure tall plants, that the aa plant produced pure dwarf plants, and that the Aa, or hybrid, tall plants produced the same three-to-one ratio of offspring. From this Mendel could see that hereditary units did not blend, as his predecessors believed, but remained unchanged from one generation to another. He thus formulated his second principle (the law of independent assortment), in which the expression of a gene for any single characteristic is usually not influenced by the expression of another characteristic. Mendel's laws became the theoretical basis for modern genetics and heredity.

Mendel published his important work on heredity in 1866. Despite, or perhaps because of, its descriptions of large numbers of experimental plants, which allowed him to express his results numerically and subject them to statistical analysis, this work made virtually no impression for the next 34 years. Only in 1900 was his work recognized more or less independently by three investigators, one of whom was the Dutch botanist Hugo Marie de Vries, and not until the late 1920s and the early '30s was its full significance realized, particularly in relation to evolutionary theory. As a result of years of research in population genetics, investigators were able to demonstrate that Darwinian evolution can be described in terms of the change in gene frequency of Mendelian pairs of characteristics in a population over successive generations.

Mendel's later experiments with the hawkweed Hieracium proved inconclusive, and because of the pressure of other duties he ceased his experiments on heredity by the 1870s. He died in Brünn on January 6, 1884.

Mendel's work was initially ignored, however, while other theories of heredity were advanced. French naturalist Jean-Baptiste Lamarck proposed that characteristics acquired during an individual's lifetime are passed to offspring. This idea was embraced by many 19th-century scientists, including the British naturalist Charles Darwin. Darwin and others believed that particles in the body, called gemmules, reside in the limbs and organs. The gemmules become imprinted with any changes acquired by the body, such as development of a strong heart through exercise. The gemmules then move to the reproductive cells and transfer information about the body's alterations to these cells. The reproductive cells transmit the acquired traits to the offspring through particles called pangenes. Darwin's theory of heredity, known as pangenesis, attempted to account for both the process of heredity and the variety of traits seen among offspring.

The deoxyribonucleic acid (DNA) molecule is the genetic blueprint for each cell and ultimately the blueprint that determines every characteristic of a living organism. In 1953 American biochemist

James Watson, left, and British biophysicist Francis Crick, right, described the structure of the DNA molecule as a double helix, somewhat like a spiral staircase with many individual steps. Their work was aided by X-ray diffraction pictures of the DNA molecule taken by British biophysicist Maurice Wilkins and British physical chemist Rosalind Franklin. In 1962 Crick, Watson, and Wilkins received the Nobel Prize for their pioneering work on the structure of the DNA molecule.

In 1889 the German biologist August Weismann published his opposition to this view. His experiments with reproduction in jellyfish and similar animals led him to believe that variations in offspring result from the union of a substance from the parents. He referred to this substance as germ plasm. Other scientists observed the movement of chromosomes in cell division and suggested that chromosomes transmit the hereditary information from parent to offspring. About the same time, Aristotle's belief that blood transmitted inheritance was disproved by the British scientist Francis Galton. To do this, Galton transfused blood from black rabbits into white rabbits. If traits were indeed transmitted through blood, those white rabbits should have produced black offspring, but their offspring were, in fact, white.

In 1900 several biologists independently theorized that the union of sperm and egg, which resulted in a combination of the male and female chromosomes, corresponds to Mendel's description of inheritance through factors. With the rediscovery of Mendel's principles, genetics studies accelerated. In the early decades of the 19th century, the work of the American geneticist Thomas Hunt Morgan spearheaded these investigations. Working with fruit flies, Morgan proved that Mendel's factors, or genes (shortened from the word pangenes), are transmitted from parent to offspring through the action of chromosomes. Morgan also found that genes for many traits are arranged in a linear fashion on each chromosome. He created the first chromosome maps, which laid the groundwork for modern genetics.

During the first few decades of the 20th century, researchers established that chromosomes are composed of DNA and protein. At that time, it was widely held that proteins contained the genetic information. In 1928, however, the British scientist Frederick Griffith carried out experiments that ruled out proteins as the genetic material. In 1944, the American geneticist Oswald T. Avery and his colleagues clearly demonstrated that DNA carried the genetic information in bacteria. Avery's work was not generally accepted until 1952, when American scientists Alfred Hershey and Martha Chase showed that the hereditary material of the T2 virus, a virus that infects bacteria, is also DNA. The work of Avery, Hershey, and Chase led scientists to the understanding that DNA is the heredity molecule for all organisms. Related experiments were carried out in the early 1940s by the American biologist George Beadle and the American geneticist Edward Tatum. Their investigations with the fungus Neurospora demonstrated that mutations in genes result in defective enzymes, the specialized proteins that speed up biochemical reactions. Thus, the link between genes and proteins was established.

United States biochemist Marshall Nirenberg won the 1968 Nobel Prize in physiology or medicine. His independent investigation into the genetic code revealed how different combinations of bases within amino acids instruct cells to build protein.

While many researchers accepted the role of DNA in inheritance, they did not understand how it could transmit genetic information from one generation to the next. In 1953, American biochemist James Watson and British biophysicist Francis Crick proposed the now-famous double-helix model of DNA. They offered compelling evidence that DNA consists of two parallel strands twisted like a spiral staircase. The "banisters" of this staircase are formed from sugar and phosphate molecules. Other molecules, called bases, form the "stairs." Watson and Crick demonstrated that one "stair" consists of a base pair, which is either an adenine bonded to a thymine or a cytosine bonded to a guanine. Hundreds of thousands of these paired bases run the length of a DNA molecule. The Watson-Crick model suggested that during cell division, the bond between the base pairs is broken, causing the strands of the double helix to separate. Each of the two strands serves as a template to construct a second strand of DNA, and two new DNA molecules are formed. The two DNA molecules are exactly the same, and one goes to each new cell, resulting in cells with the same hereditary information. The dramatic discovery of DNA architecture stimulated a quest to uncover its precise role in determining heredity.

Drawing on the work of Beadle and Tatum, and using the Watson-Crick model of DNA, scientists determined that DNA must be a code that directs the construction of proteins. Proteins are built of small molecules called amino acids, which link together to form the protein. The amino acids must be lined up in a particular order, like letters in a correctly spelled word, for the protein to form correctly. Scientists inferred that DNA instructs the cell to link amino acids in the proper order. They further determined that a unique sequence of three bases on DNA, a triplet, is a code for one amino acid, and that unique triplets code for each of the twenty amino acids. In 1961 American biochemist Marshall W. Nirenberg and his colleagues began to unravel the code. Using an artificial mixture of amino acids and ribonucleic acid (RNA), a molecule similar to DNA, they showed that the base adenine repeated three times in a row is the code for the amino acid phenylalanine.

By 1967 scientists had translated the genetic code for all twenty amino acids. They had also confirmed that one gene, a section of DNA, is a code for one protein or part of a protein. Within 15 years, researchers had developed the capability of inserting genes from one organism into another, a breakthrough that ushered in the field of biotechnology. In the not-too-distant future, scientists may perfect the technology for inserting or removing genes from an egg, sperm, or embryo. This development may drastically alter the traditional principles of heredity, opening the door to a new array of rules governing the transmission of traits from parent to offspring.

Gene, representing the basic unit of heredity found in the cells of all living organisms, from bacteria to humans. Genes determine the physical characteristics that an organism inherits, such as the shape of a tree's leaf, the markings on a cat's fur, and the colour of a human hair.

Genes are composed of segments of deoxyribonucleic acid (DNA), a molecule that forms the long, threadlike structures called chromosomes. The information encoded within the DNA structure of a gene directs the manufacture of proteins, molecular workhorses that carry out all life-supporting activities within a cell.

Chromosomes within a cell occur in matched pairs. Each chromosome contains many genes, and each gene is located at a particular site on the chromosome, known as the locus. Like chromosomes, genes typically occur in pairs. A gene found on one chromosome in a pair usually has the same locus as another gene in the other chromosome of the pair, and these two genes are called alleles. Alleles are alternate forms of the same gene. For example, a pea plant has one gene that determines height, but that gene appears in more than one form—the gene that produces a short plant is an allele of the gene that produces a tall plant. The behaviour of alleles and how they influence inherited traits follow predictable patterns. Austrian monk Gregor Mendel first identified these patterns in the 1860s

In organisms that use sexual reproduction, offspring inherit one-half of their genes from each parent and then mix the two sets of genes together. This produces new combinations of genes, so that each individual is unique but still possesses the same genes as its parents. As a result, sexual reproduction ensures that the basic characteristics of a particular species remain largely the same for generations. However, mutations, or alterations in DNA, occur constantly. They create variations in the genes that are inherited. Some mutations may be neutral, or silent, and do not affect the function of a protein. Occasionally a mutation may benefit or harm an organism and over the course of evolutionary time, these mutations serve the crucial role of providing organisms with previously nonexistent proteins. In this way, mutations are a driving force behind genetic diversity and the rise of new or more competitive species that are better able to adapt to changes, such as climate variations, depletion of food sources, or the emergence of new types of disease.

Geneticists are scientists who study the function and behaviour of genes. Since the 1970s geneticists have devised techniques, cumulatively known as genetic engineering, to alter or manipulate the DNA structure within genes. These techniques enable scientists to introduce one or more genes from one organism into a second organism. The second organism incorporates the new DNA into its own genetic material, thereby altering its own genetic characteristics by changing the types of proteins it can produce. In humans these techniques form the basis of gene therapy, a group of experimental procedures in which scientists try to substitute one or more healthy genes for defective ones in order to eliminate symptoms of disease.

Genetic engineering techniques have also enabled scientists to determine the chromosomal location and DNA structure of all the genes found within a variety of organisms. In April 2003 the Human Genome Project, a publicly funded consortium of academic scientists from around the world, identified the chromosomal locations and structure of the estimated 20,000 to 25,000 genes found within human cells. The genetic makeup of other organisms has also been identified, including that of the bacterium Escherichia coli, the yeast Saccharomyces cerevisiae, the roundworm Caenorhabditis elegans, and the fruit fly Drosophila melanogaster. Scientists hope to use this genetic information to develop life-saving drugs for a variety of diseases, to improve agricultural crop yields, and to learn more about plant and animal physiology and evolutionary history.

Plasmid, small, usually ring-shaped molecule of deoxyribonucleic acid (DNA), which is the hereditary material in all living cells. Plasmids are present in almost all bacteria and may also be found in some yeasts and other fungi, protozoa, and even some plants and animals. They are separate from chromosomes, the primary structures that contain DNA in cells. Plasmids are important tools used in genetic engineering—the deliberate manipulation of an organism's genetic material—and they are also key to scientists' understanding of how bacteria cause human disease.

Plasmids carry hereditary information in the form of genes, the basic units of inheritance. Plasmids generally carry fewer genes than do chromosomes, and the genes that they carry are useful, but not essential, to the survival of the cell. For example, some Plasmids help bacteria make use of unusual food sources, such as camphor or petroleum. Fertility Plasmids carry genes that a bacterial cell must have in order to transfer DNA to another bacterium. Resistance Plasmids enable bacteria to degrade or inactivate antibiotics used to halt bacterial growth, or to survive in the presence of heavy metals by converting the metals into less toxic forms. Other Plasmids enable bacteria to produce chemicals that are toxic to other organisms, including insects, humans, and other bacteria.

Bacteria cells typically are surrounded by a rigid, protective cell wall. The cell membrane, also called the plasma membrane, regulates passage of materials into and out of the cytoplasm, the semifluids that fills the cell. The DNA, located in the nucleoid region, contains the genetic information for the cell. Ribosomes carry out protein synthesis. Many bacteria contain a pilus (plural pili), a structure that extends out of the cell to transfer DNA to another bacterium. The flagellum, found in numerous species, is used for the locomotion. Some bacteria contain a plasmid, a small loop of DNA with extra genes. Others have a capsule, a sticky substance external to the cell wall that protects bacteria from attack by white blood cells. Mesosomes were formerly thought to structures with unknown functions, but now are know to be artifacts created when cells are prepared for viewing with electron microscopes.

Most bacteria have only one chromosome under normal circumstances, but may contain 1 to 100 or more copies of a given plasmid. Plasmids replicate independently of cell division, and when a cell containing Plasmids divides, the Plasmids distribute randomly among the two resulting daughter cells. In this way, each daughter cell receives approximately, but not always exactly, the same number of Plasmids.

Genetic engineering enables scientists to produce clones of cells or organisms that contain the same genes. (1) Scientists use restriction enzymes to isolate a segment of deoxyribonucleic acid (DNA) that contains a gene of interest—for example, the gene regulating insulin production. (2) A plasmid removed from a bacterium and treated with the same restriction enzyme binds with the DNA fragment to form a interbred plasma. (3) The interbred Plasmids is re-inserted back into the bacterium, where it replicates as part of the cell's DNA. (4) A large number of identical daughter cells (clones) can be cultured and their gene products extracted for human use.

Plasmids are important tools that are used in genetic engineering. The structure of DNA is the same in all living cells, so DNA from almost any organism can be combined with Plasmids. DNA Plasmids thus serves as a convenient vehicles for transferring genes from one organism to another.

In 1977 scientists successfully manipulated bacteria to produce a human protein. That same year American molecular biologist Walter Gilbert found a way to accelerate dramatically the labourious task of sequencing the chemicals that make up a strand of genetic material. He shared the 1980 Nobel Prize in chemistry for this achievement. In a 1980 Scientific American article, Gilbert and American molecular biologist Lydia Villa-Komaroff describes basic biotechnology techniques and their laboratory's success in producing rat insulin with genetically engineered bacteria. Human insulin was first produced in the lab using recombinant (genetically engineered) bacteria in 1978, and five years later recombinant human insulin, used to treat diabetes mellitus, became the first biopharmaceutical on the market.

Using enzymes known as restriction endonucleases and DNA ligase, which act, respectively, like molecular scissors and glue, scientists cut and paste pieces of DNA from different sources together to create molecules known as recombinant DNA. A recombinant Plasmids made by such techniques can then be introduced into a bacterial cell to produce bacteria with useful characteristics.

The ability to combine human and bacterial DNA has given rise to a number of medical advances. The first commercial use of a recombinant Plasmids came in 1982, when scientists created a genetically engineered bacterium able to produce human insulin. Insulin is a hormone that helps regulate blood sugar and is needed by many people with diabetes. To create the insulin-producing bacterium, scientists inserted the gene that directs the production of human insulin into a plasmid, and then introduced the plasmid into bacterial cells. As the bacteria grew and multiplied in the laboratory, they produced large quantities of human insulin that could be collected and packaged for use by diabetics. Previously, insulin for diabetics had been harvested from slaughtered cattle. Insulin produced by recombinant bacteria is cheaper and of better quality than insulin from cattle. In addition, it is virtually identical to the hormone produced in the human body and does not cause allergic reactions.

Other useful medical substances now manufactured with the aid of recombinant Plasmids include human growth hormone, an immune system protein known as interferon, blood-clotting proteins, and proteins that are used in making vaccines. Not all applications of recombinant Plasmids are medical. Scientists have produced bacteria that can remove mercury and other harmful chemicals from the soil or water in a process known as bioremediation. Other bacteria that contain recombinant Plasmids make insecticides that may be safer than traditional synthetic insecticides.

Bacterial Plasmids are also used to transfer foreign genes to plants. Genetic engineering of plants often involves a Plasmids known as a tumour inducing, or Ti, Plasmids found in Agrobacterium tumefaciens, the bacterium that causes crown gall disease in plants. Typically, when Agrobacterium tumefaciens bacteria enter a plant through a wound, they transfer the Ti Plasmids into nearby plant cells. The presence of this Plasmids drastically changes the growth of the plant cells, resulting in the formation of a large tumour on the plant. Scientists manipulate this natural process by removing the Ti Plasmids from Agrobacterium tumefaciens cells to replace the plasmids' tumour-causing genes with genes that code for desirable characteristics. These recombinant Plasmids are then introduced into plant cells to produce, for example, crop plants that are resistant to certain diseases, insect pests, or herbicides. These techniques may someday be used to improve the nutritional value of food plants.

Overuse of antibiotics in recent years has enabled the development of strains of bacteria that are resistant to antibiotics. Resistance Plasmids, which may be transferred from bacterium to bacterium, are responsible for antibiotic resistance. This scanning electron micrograph shows disease-causing Streptococcus bacteria, commonly found in the human mouth, throat, respiratory tract, bloodstream, and wounds.

Plasmids also help scientists understand how bacteria cause human disease. Some bacteria carry Plasmids known as virulence Plasmids that make them harmful to humans. Without a virulence Plasmids, these bacteria are harmless, but when they carry such a Plasmids, to which they can cause disease. For example, the bacterium Clostridium tetani causes tetanus only if it carries a virulence Plasmids containing the gene for the tetanus toxin. Certain strains of Staphylococcus aureus cause food poisoning and certain strains of Escherichia coli cause diarrhea only because they contain virulence Plasmids.

Resistance Plasmids are currently a topic of intense research because of the growing problem with disease-causing bacteria that are resistant to penicillin and other commonly used antibiotics. Scientists have learned that bacteria can readily transfer resistance Plasmids to other bacteria. When a bacterial cell acquires two different antibiotic resistance Plasmids, the antibiotic resistance genes carried on the two Plasmids are sometimes assembled onto a single Plasmids. This new Plasmids may then be transferred to other bacteria, where it may acquire additional antibiotic resistance genes. This process may be repeated several times, giving rise to a Plasmids that will make bacteria resistant to a number of different antibiotics. Infections caused by such bacteria are extremely difficult to treat.

Inappropriate use of antibiotics contributes to the spread of antibiotic resistant bacteria. When physicians prescribe drugs unnecessarily or when patients fail to take the full course of antibiotics prescribed because they are feeling better, resistant bacterial strains are more likely to survive. Scientists are studying how resistance Plasmids are maintained and transferred in populations of bacteria in hope of learning how to stop the spread of antibiotic resistance.

Chromosomal disorders are caused by the presence of an extra or missing whole or partial chromosome. In some cases, whole chromosomes or pieces of chromosomes are attached to one another in abnormal ways, which cause a person or their offspring to have an incorrect amount of chromosomal material. Chromosomal disorders are sometimes caused by an error in a type of cell division called meiosis, which occurs during the formation of eggs and sperm. Chromosomal disorders disrupt the biological functions of many genes. They produce multiple problems in the affected individual, often including mild or severe mental retardation. More than 600 chromosomal syndromes have been identified.

Down syndrome is the most common chromosomal disorder, affecting about 1 in 800 newborns. People with Down syndrome characteristically have three copies of the autosomal chromosome known as number 21 instead of the normal pair of number 21 chromosomes. For this reason, Down syndrome is commonly called trisomy 21. People with Down syndrome usually have mild to severe learning disabilities and physical symptoms that include a small skull, an extra fold of skin at the inner corner of each eye, and a flattened bridge of the nose. They also may have heart defects and other serious health problems.

Some chromosomal disorders involve the sex chromosomes. In many instances, an extra or missing sex chromosome is less life threatening than an extra or missing autosome. A person with Klinefelter syndrome, which affects about 1 in 500 males, has two X chromosomes and one Y chromosome. Males with Klinefelter syndrome are typically tall, and they may have small testes and slight breast development. They also may have minor problems with learning and are usually infertile.

Another chromosomal disorder that affects the sex chromosomes is Turner syndrome, which affects 1 in 2,500 females. In this disorder, a female has one functioning X chromosome instead of two. Females with this condition are typically short, with a thick, webbed neck. They may have mild problems with learning, and they usually are infertile because they lack normal ovaries.

Multifactorial disorders are caused by several genes as well as the influence of a person's environment, such as diet or lifestyle. An example of a multifactorial disorder is a category of birth defects called neural tube defects. In a neural tube defect, a fetus's neural tube—the structure that develops into the spinal cord and brain—is damaged. The two most common types of neural tube defects are anencephaly and spina bifida. Anencephaly is a fatal condition in which a baby is born with only a partial brain or no brain at all. About 1,000 to 2,000 babies with anencephaly are born each year in the United States. Spina bifida results when a neural tube defect causes an opening in the spine. In the United States, about one infant in every 2,000 live births is born with spina bifida. These infants need surgery to close the opening in the spine, and they may develop problems with walking or with bowel or bladder control. Geneticists believe that certain genes may play a role in damage to the neural tube, but the mother's diet during pregnancy also plays a role. A woman's risk of giving birth to an infant with a neural tube defect significantly decreases if she consumes adequate amounts of folic acid, a vitamin in the B complex, during the first three months of pregnancy and one month before conception.

Some common diseases that run in families but do not display an obvious pattern of inheritance are also thought to be multifactorial. Two examples are coronary heart disease and diabetes mellitus. In both cases, genes may cause a person to be predisposed to develop the disease, but lifestyle choices can help to prevent the disease from developing or from worsening after it occurs.

Thousands of inherited diseases caused by altered genes and chromosomal abnormalities affect humans. These disorders cause problems such as physical deformities, metabolic dysfunction, and developmental problems. Medical surveys indicate that roughly 1 percent of newborns in the United States have a single-gene defect. As many as 1 baby in 200 is born with a chromosomal abnormality serious enough to produce physical defects or mental retardation.

Genetic causes include single-gene defects such as Fragile X syndrome and chromosomal disorders such as Down syndrome. Scientists in 1992 identified Fragile X syndrome as the most common inherited cause of mental retardation, responsible for up to 10 percent of cases. People with this condition inherit a defective gene that results in a weak spot on the X chromosome, a sex chromosome. The weak part of the chromosome is susceptible to breaking. Fragile X syndrome is more likely to cause retardation in males then females.

Chromosomal disorders, which occur in about 7 out of every 1000 infants, involve an abnormal number of chromosomes or changes in the structure of a chromosome. Down syndrome occurs when people inherit all or part of an extra copy of a pair of chromosomes known together as chromosome 21. Although regarded as genetic disorders, chromosomal disorders are not necessarily inherited. Both parents may have normal genes, with the defect resulting from a random error when chromosomes reproduce.

Other genetic causes of mental retardation are inborn errors of metabolism. They involve inheritance of a defective gene unable to produce enzymes or proteins needed for critical cell functions. Scientists have identified more than 300 gene disorders involving inborn errors of metabolism. Many can result in mental retardation, including phenylketonuria (PKU), Tay-Sachs disease, galactosemia, homocystinuria, maple syrup urine disease, and biotinidase deficiency.

Another common cause of mental retardation, congenital hypothyroidism, occurs in about 1 in every 4000 births. Infants with this disorder are unable to produce enough thyroxine, a hormone secreted by the thyroid gland. Mental retardation and stunted growth result unless they receive thyroid replacement therapy.

A number of other disorders may include characteristics of autism. In fragile X syndrome, which results from a defective X chromosome, people may show poor eye contact, limited speech, hand flapping, and hyperactivity. People with Asperger's disorder may show some symptoms of autism such as difficulties in social interactions, poor eye contact, repetitive body movements, and an insistence on routines and rituals. However, they have normal language development and do not have mental retardation. Rett's disorder involves repetitive hand movements, social withdrawal, and impaired language development. The disorder appears before the age of four and affects only girls. Some experts regard these disorders as mild forms of autism rather than as separate disorders.

One of the most common fatal genetic disorders in the United States, cystic fibrosis occurs in about one in every 3,900 babies. About 1,000 new cases are diagnosed each year, usually before a child reaches three years of age. Approximately 30,000 American children and young adults have cystic fibrosis. The disease affects white people more often than black people: One in every 3,300 white babies is born with cystic fibrosis, but only one in every 15,300 black babies is born with the disease.

Cystic fibrosis is caused by a defect in the gene responsible for manufacturing cystic fibrosis transmembrane conductance regulators (CFTR), a protein that controls the flow of chloride ions into and out of certain cells. In healthy people, CFTR forms a channel in the plasma membrane through which chloride ions enter and leave the cells lining the lungs, pancreas, sweat glands, and small intestine. In people with cystic fibrosis, malfunctioning (or absent) CFTR prevents chloride from entering or leaving cells, resulting in production of a thick, sticky mucus that clogs ducts or tubes in these organs. In the lungs, this mucus blocks airways and impedes natural infection-fighting mechanisms, eventually turning the body's immune system against its own lung tissue. A similar blockage prevents crucial digestive enzymes produced in the pancreas from reaching the intestines, impairing the ability to break down certain foods. In healthy people most of the chloride in sweat is reabsorbed, but in people with cystic fibrosis, sweat glands cannot take up chloride ions, enabling excessive amounts of salt to escape in the sweat.

Cystic fibrosis is an autosomal recessive genetic disorder. This means that to have the disease, a child must inherit two copies of the defective gene, one from each parent. Many people carry a single cystic fibrosis gene, although they do not experience any significant health problems as a result; in the general population, approximately 1 in 31 Americans carries the gene. The disease can only occur in babies with two carrier parents. When both parents are carriers, they have a 25 percent chance with every pregnancy of passing two copies of the defective gene to their child. Prospective parents may elect to undergo genetic testing to determine if one or both of them carry the defective gene.

Researchers identified the gene responsible for cystic fibrosis in 1989. Since that time more than 200 different defects in the cystic fibrosis gene have been described, many of which produce cystic fibrosis in varying degrees of severity. Researchers also learned that two different gene defects—one from each parent—can combine to produce varying effects.

Depending on the disease's severity, symptoms may be apparent soon after birth, or they may escape detection for months or years. In nearly 20 percent of all cases, the first symptom is meconium ileus, intestinal blockage in newborns. In other babies, the first evidence of cystic fibrosis is bulky stool, poor weight gain, flabby muscle tone, or slow growth, all products of low levels of digestive enzymes in the intestines. About half of all children with cystic fibrosis first see the doctor for coughing, wheezing, or respiratory tract infections. Teenagers with cystic fibrosis may grow slowly and enter puberty later than their peers. Cystic fibrosis often causes impaired reproductive function. About 98 percent of adult men who have cystic fibrosis produce little or no sperm, and females have decreased fertility and are more likely to experience complications during pregnancy and childbirth. Cystic fibrosis patients of all ages are prone to dehydration because they lose so much salt in their sweat. Infections, particularly in the lungs, plague people with cystic fibrosis throughout their lives. These chronic infections destroy lung tissue, a complication that ultimately takes the lives of most people with cystic fibrosis.

The earlier a diagnosis is made the better so that early treatment can slow the progression of lung damage caused by infection. Prenatal tests are available to determine if a baby will be born with cystic fibrosis. In newborns, blood tests indicating high levels of digestive enzymes suggest cystic fibrosis, but a certain diagnosis requires a sweat test to determine the amount of salt in the sweat.

Sweat tests provide a valid diagnosis in babies over 24 hours old, and this test is also used to confirm diagnosis in older children and adults.

Cystic fibrosis remains incurable; existing treatments aim to relieve discomfort and delay the devastating and inevitable effects of the disease. Meconium ileus, the intestinal obstruction occurring in newborns, may require surgery. Patients with pancreatic blockages must take pancreatic enzymes with meals. Even with such enzymes, people with cystic fibrosis must consume adequate amounts of protein, vitamins, and higher-than-normal amounts of fat to ensure growth. Those with respiratory infections are treated with antibiotics, often in aerosol form. When inhaled, these medicated vapours fight infection and relieve constriction of the airways. Using a procedure called chest physical therapy or postural drainage, caregivers of people with cystic fibrosis repeatedly and vigorously pound on the patient's back and chest to dislodge mucus obstructing the airways. Increasingly, cystic fibrosis patients with severe, irreparable lung damage turn to lung transplantation surgery. Although complications with transplantation surgery may pose problems for some patients, lung or combination heart and lung transplants provide nearly 80 percent of cystic fibrosis patients with severe lung damage an entirely new lease on life.

Although no cure has yet been found, cystic fibrosis presents one of the most promising areas of research in modern medicine. Scientists are investigating the use of gene therapy to introduce healthy copies of the CFTR gene into the cells of patients with cystic fibrosis. Scientists hope that once inside the cells, healthy copies of the gene will manufacture functional CFTR protein, permitting the flow of chloride into and out of cells in affected organs and restoring healthy function. Just one of many new treatment strategies under investigation, such research provides the cystic fibrosis community—scientists, patients, and families—with hope that more-effective treatments and possibly a cure may soon be discovered.

Down syndrome occurs in about 1 out of every 800 births worldwide. In the United States each year, about 1,600 babies are born with this condition. Down syndrome results when a person inherits all or part of an extra copy of chromosome 21. This can occur in a variety of ways, the causes of which are unknown. The most common chromosomal abnormality that produces Down syndrome (accounting for about 95 percent of all cases) is Trisomy 21, a defect in which an extra, third copy of chromosome 21 is present in every cell in the body. The risk of Trisomy 21 is directly related to the age of the mother. The number of Down syndrome births is relatively low for 18-year-old mothers—about 1 in 2,100 births. In the later childbearing years the risk increases significantly—from 1 in 1,000 births for 30-year-old women to 1 in 100 births for 40-year-old women.

Two other chromosomal abnormalities cause Down syndrome and occur in about 2 to 3 percent of all cases. The first, translocation, takes place when a child inherits a small, extra piece of the 21st chromosome that is attached to another chromosome. If, in addition to the translocation, two normal 21st chromosomes are also present, the person will have some of the features of Down syndrome. If there is only one normal 21st chromosome, the person will not display symptoms but the children may inherit Down syndrome. Mosaic Down syndrome results from a second type of chromosomal abnormality in which only some cells in the body have an extra chromosome.

There is no cure for Down syndrome. However, prenatal tests are available to identify fetuses with the disorder. The American

College of Obstetricians and Gynecologists recommends that the so-called triple-screen blood test be offered to all pregnant women. This test measures the levels of three chemicals in the blood of the pregnant woman to indicate the baby's risk of Down syndrome. If the risk is high, amniocentesis, a procedure for removing a sample of the amniotic fluid surrounding the fetus, is administered to confirm the findings from the blood tests. Fetal cells are present in the amniotic fluid and can be checked for the presence of the chromosomal disorder.

People with Down syndrome are subject to a variety of medical conditions. Heart abnormalities that may require surgery are present in about half of all Down syndrome cases. Thyroid problems (underproduction or overproduction of thyroid hormones) affect 10 to 20 percent of people with Down syndrome, but these problems respond well to treatment. The risk of acute leukemia is somewhat increased, although treatment is successful in the majority of cases.

There have been dramatic increases in the survival rates of people with Down syndrome since the 1970s. As the risks of medical problems specific to Down syndrome have become known, doctors are now able to recognize those problems earlier, and develop more effective treatments. Today, 44 percent of people with Down syndrome survive to age 60, and this life expectancy is slowly approaching that of people without Down syndrome.

Although people with Down syndrome have a range of learning disabilities, physicians, educators, and parents now recognize that these people's achievements may be most influenced by what is expected of them. This so-called environmental expectation is perhaps the most important factor in determining the educational and vocational potential of people with Down syndrome. On the other hand, intelligence-quotient test scores, once considered an authoritative indicator of educational potential, are now seen to be of questionable value.

Educational and vocational opportunities have also advanced. In the recent past, children with Down syndrome were relegated to institutions, receiving minimal social interaction or educational opportunities. Today, children with Down syndrome usually remain with their families and are enrolled in public schools. Often they attend regular classes and learn skills such as reading and writing alongside children without Down syndrome. Adults with Down syndrome are employed in a range of fields. Some may live in supervised group homes, while others live independently.

Primary immune deficiencies caused by genetic factors have been studied extensively, and a number of genes responsible for these defects have been identified. Some genes have been found on the X chromosome, the sex chromosome inherited from the mother. These X-linked diseases include x-linked agammaglobulinemia, Wiskott-Aldrich Syndrome, and some forms of SCID.

Klinefelter's Syndrome, genetic disease affecting 1 in 850 males. It occurs when a male inherits an extra X, or female, sex chromosome that interferes with the development of male characteristics. Klinefelter's syndrome is characterized by enlarged breasts (gynecomastia), little or no facial and body hair, a small penis and testes, reduced sex drive, and the inability to produce sperm. Although a child with the condition is not developmentally disabled, he may learn to speak later than other children and have difficulty learning to read and write. The disorder was first described by American endocrinologist Harry F. Klinefelter in 1942.

Both men and women normally have 23 pairs of chromosomes. One of these pairs is the sex chromosome. A female normally inherits an X chromosome from each parent so that her chromosomal complement is XX. A male inherits an X chromosome from his mother and a Y chromosome from his father so that his chromosomal complement is XY. It is the presence of the Y chromosome that determines maleness. A male with Klinefelter's syndrome inherits an extra X chromosome, giving him an abnormal chromosomal complement of XXY. In some cases, more than one extra X chromosome is inherited. The cause of Klinefelter's syndrome is unknown, although to occur more often in boys born to older mothers.

In most cases, a boy with Klinefelter's syndrome has a normal physical appearance until he reaches puberty. Diagnosis of the disorder may be delayed until physical symptoms develop, or until the adult male is tested for infertility. Diagnosis of the disorder is made by performing a chromosomal analysis in which body cells are studied in the laboratory to identify any chromosomal irregularities.

There is no treatment for Klinefelter's syndrome, although regular injections of the male sex hormone testosterone may increase muscle size and strength, stimulate the growth of facial and body hair, and produce a normal sex drive in some cases. Enlarged breasts may be reduced surgically. Reversing infertility associated with Klinefelter's syndrome may not be possible. Some men with the disorder may produce a small number of sperm, and they may benefit from modern fertility techniques in which a single sperm is injected into an egg to achieve fertilization

Turner syndrome is caused by a partially or completely missing sex chromosome. Chromosomes are gene-carrying structures found within the nuclei of cells. In the human body, all cells except for sperm and egg cells contain 46 chromosomes arranged in 23 pairs. Of these, 22 of the pairs each consist of chromosomes that are almost identical, while the 23rd pair contains special chromosomes that determine the sex of the individual. The sex chromosome pair in healthy males contains an X and a Y chromosome, while the sex chromosome pair in females contains two X chromosomes. In a female born with Turner syndrome, part or all of one X chromosome in her sex chromosome pair is absent. Scientists do not know what causes this chromosomal abnormality—it apparently occurs randomly and is not linked to factors known to increase the risk of a birth defect, such as a pregnant woman's exposure to drugs, radiation, or disease-causing viruses or bacteria.

Chromosomal disorders are caused by the presence of an extra or missing whole or partial chromosome. In some cases, whole chromosomes or pieces of chromosomes are attached to one another in abnormal ways, which cause a person or their offspring to have an incorrect amount of chromosomal material. Chromosomal disorders are sometimes caused by an error in a type of cell division called meiosis, which occurs during the formation of eggs and sperm. Chromosomal disorders disrupt the biological functions of many genes. They produce multiple problems in the affected individual, often including mild or severe mental retardation. More than 600 chromosomal syndromes have been identified.

Twenty percent, or more malformed fetuses are spontaneously aborted; the rest result in a newborn with a birth defect. Although each single type of birth defect is rare, taken together they make up almost 5 percent of all live births and cause about 20 percent of infant deaths in the period immediately after birth. About one in ten developmental disorders is hereditary and arises from an abnormality in a single gene. Another 5 percent of birth defects arise from physical abnormalities in the chromosome.

Some genes that cause genetic diseases interact in a dominant-recessive pattern. In these cases, two copies of the recessive gene are required for the disease to occur. A person who has just one copy of the recessive gene is termed a carrier, since he or she carries the gene but is not affected by it. In the illustration above, the dominant gene is represented in green, and the recessive in blue. For the couple on the left, the father has one copy of the dominant gene and one copy of the recessive gene. The mother has two copies of the dominant gene. Each parent can contribute just one gene to the child. The four children shown on the lower left represent the probabilities (not the actual children) for the combinations that can result from their parents. The children on the far left received the recessive gene from their father and the dominant gene from their mother, and are therefore carriers. For any child born to these parents, there is a 50 percent chance that the child will be a carrier. Since none of the children can inherit two copies of the recessive gene, none of the children will develop the disease. When both parents are carriers, however, as shown by the couple on the right, there is a 25 percent chance that any child born has the disease, a 50 percent chance that a child is a carrier, and a 25 percent chance that a child does not have the disease and is not a carrier.

A mutation in the gene responsible for producing oxygen-carrying haemoglobin in the blood causes a disease known as sickle-cell anaemia. In this disease the structure of haemoglobin in the human bloodstream is severely altered. The mutation changes the structure of red blood cells to a slender sickle shape.

Some genetic disorders have symptoms that are manifest at birth. These disorders may result from mutations in a single gene or from more general chromosomal abnormalities. Many diseases and conditions are inherited in a recessive manner: Neither parent may have the defect even though they both carry the causative gene. When both parents have a dominant gene A and a recessive gene a, their offspring may inherit one of four different combinations: AA, Aa, aA, or aa. If the recessive gene a is defective, the statistical probability is that one in four of the offspring will bear the defective trait. In other congenital disorders the presence of only one copy of the recessive gene is sufficient to cause the condition

Genetic disorders may result from defects in genes or from chromosomal abnormalities. Prenatal tests, performed early in a woman's pregnancy, can identify a fetus with a genetic abnormality. Prenatal diagnosis using amniocentesis or chorionic villus sampling pose a slight risk to the fetus, and health professionals generally recommend these tests only if the mother or father has a family history of a genetic disorder or an increased risk of having a child with a chromosomal abnormality.

Physical anthropologists studying human genetics use sophisticated laboratory techniques to analyze human chromosomes and DNA (deoxyribonucleic acid), the structures through which people inherit traits from their parents. With these techniques, researchers have identified human populations that have genetic predispositions to specific diseases, such as types of cancer. This knowledge has promoted increased focus on the use of preventive measures among people with higher risk for disease.

Sometimes mutations are caused by transposition, in which long stretches of DNA (containing one or more genes) move from one chromosome to another. These jumping genes, called transposons, that can disrupt transcription and change the type of amino acids inserted into a protein. Transposons rearrange and interrupt genes in a way that generally improves the genetic variation of a species.

While mutations can occur spontaneously, some can be caused by exposure to physical or chemical agents in the environment called mutagens. Common environmental mutagens include ultraviolet rays from the sun and various chemicals, such as asbestos, cigarette smoke, and nitrous acid. High-energy radiation, such as medical X rays, can cause DNA strands to break, leading to the deletion of potentially important genetic information.

Lewis Edward devoted his entire academic career to the study of the fruit fly's genetic makeup. By studying mutations in the fruit fly and identifying which genes caused the mutations, he made two far-reaching discoveries about genes. The first was that a particular group of genes, called homeotic genes, controls the development of all the regions of the fly's body. These genes direct each cell to its proper location along the developing embryo's body. His second discovery was the principal of colinearity, or the linear sequence of the homeotic genes. He found that the homeotic genes are arranged on the chromosome in a linear order that exactly corresponds to the order of the body regions that each gene controls. This finding, which was subsequently found to hold true for other animals as well, won him the Nobel Prize.

Born in Lexington, Kentucky, and educated at the State College of Kentucky, Morgan studied embryology at Johns Hopkins University, where he received his PhD in 1891. As professor of experimental zoology at Columbia University from 1904 to 1928, he was at first critical of Mendelian theory, which had not been physically demonstrated. Performing breeding experiments and cytological analyses on the vinegar fly, Drosophila melanogaster, Morgan and his graduate students Alfred Henry Sturtevant, Calvin Blackman Bridges, and Hermann Joseph Muller revealed that chromosomes behave very similarly to the ways in which Mendel believed genes segregate and become randomly assorted. Discovering also that genes for many character traits are arranged in a linear fashion on each chromosome, Morgan and his coworkers created linear chromosome maps in which each gene is assigned to a specific position. This work resulted in The Mechanism of Mendelian Heredity (1915), an influential book that was an important step in the development of modern genetics.

Morgan continued his experimental work, demonstrating in Theory of the Gene (1926) that genes are held together in different linkage groups, and that alleles (pairs of genes affecting the same trait) interchange, or cross over, in the same linkage group. In 1933 Morgan won the Nobel Prize for physiology or medicine.

Nettie Stevens (1861-1912), American biologist and geneticist whose research helped prove that chromosomes determine the sex of an organism. Researchers had previously believed that gender was influenced by food and temperature conditions during the early stages of an organism's development.

The Soviet government made development of science a national priority and showered top scientists with honours. Although day-to-day supervision was less oppressive than in the arts, there were countless episodes of arbitrary suppression of ideas. In the most notorious, the Ukrainian agronomist Trofim Lysenko rejected the chromosome theory of heredity generally accepted by modern genetics. Claiming his theories corresponded to Marxism, he convinced Stalin in 1948 to outlaw population genetics and several related fields of biological research; the decision was not reversed until the mid-1960s. Concern with freedom of inquiry and expression drew some scientists into the political realm. The best example is Andrey Sakharov, the nuclear physicist who became the most famous member of the hard-pressed liberal opposition in the 1970s. Sakharov was awarded the 1975 Nobel Peace Prize for his efforts, though the government would not allow him to go to Norway to accept the prize.

Kennedy's Telegram to Khrushchev After First Manned Space Mission On April 12, 1961, the White House made public President John F. Kennedy's telegram to the Soviets, congratulating them on the first successful manned space mission. Cosmonaut Yuri Gagarin's orbit of the earth spurred American scientists and engineers to step up efforts to send United States astronauts into space.

The core of basic science was the Academy of Sciences, originally founded in 1725 and relocated from Leningrad to Moscow in 1934. It contained 250 research institutes and 60,500 full-time researchers in 1987, predominantly in the natural sciences. Several hundred scholars (330 in 1988) had the privileged status of "academician" and about twice as many had the status of "corresponding members" of the academy. In addition, all of the union republics but the RSFSR had their own paradigms of science. About 90 percent of research was carried on outside the academy system. Most of this was of an applied character and much of it was related to weapons systems and done in secret facilities in the defence-production ministries.

The launch of the artificial satellite Sputnik 1 by the Union of Soviet Socialist Republics (USSR) in 1957 marked the beginning of the space race. The satellite fell out of orbit three months after launch, but it had an electrifying effect—enhancing the international image of the USSR and creating the illusion of technological inferiority in the United States. In the aftermath, according to this 1978 National Aeronautics and Space Administration (NASA) report by historians Edward Clinton Ezell and Linda Neuman Ezell, tentative efforts to promote international cooperation in space gave way to competition.

Soviet scientists won lofty reputations in many fields. They were at the cutting edge of world science in mathematics and in several branches of physical science, notably theoretical and nuclear physics, chemistry, and astronomy. The physical chemist and physicist Nikolay Semenov was the first Soviet citizen to win a Nobel Prize, in 1956. Nobel Prizes were subsequently awarded in 1958 to the physicists Pavel Cherenkov, Ilya Frank, and Igor Tamm, for their discovery of the Cherenkov effect; in 1962 to the physicist Lev Landau, for his pioneer work in cryogenics, or low-temperature physics, such that, in1964 the physicists in Nikolay Basov and Aleksandr Prokhorov, development the laser (light amplification) and the maser (microwave amplification); and in 1978 to the physicist Peter Kapitza, for his research in magnetism and low-temperature physics.

Soviet technology was most impressive in the areas of nuclear weaponry and space exploration, where the arms race with the West prodded policy makers to set aside the needed resources. By virtue of a crash program directed by Igor Kurchatov, the Soviet Union was the second country to explode an atomic bomb, in 1949, four years after the United States. The Soviet Union detonated a hydrogen device in 1953, only ten months after the United States. In October 1957 it put the first artificial satellite, Sputnik 1, into earth orbit, and in April 1961 a Russian cosmonaut, Yuri Gagarin, became the first man in space. Though disappointed that the United States beat them to the moon, the

Soviets kept up a strong space program until economic problems led to cutbacks in the 1980s.

When new research is published, it often acts as a springboard for further work. Its impact can then be gauged by seeing how often the published research appears as a cited work. Major scientific breakthroughs are cited thousands of times a year, but at the other extreme, obscure pieces of research may be cited rarely or not at all. However, citation is not always a reliable guide to the value of scientific work. Sometimes a piece of research will go largely unnoticed, only to be rediscovered in subsequent years. Such was the case for the work on genes done by American geneticist Barbara McClintock during the 1940s. McClintock discovered a new phenomenon in corn cells known as transposable genes, sometimes referred to as jumping genes. McClintock observed that a gene could move from one chromosome to another, where it would break the second chromosome at a particular site, insert itself there, and influence the function of an adjacent gene. Her work was largely ignored until the 1960s when scientists found that transposable genes were a primary means for transferring genetic material in bacteria and more complex organisms. McClintock was awarded the 1983 Nobel Prize in physiology or medicine for her work in transposable genes, more than 35 years after performing the research.

After sperm are produced, they move out of the testes and into the epididymis, a long tube coiled against the testes, where the sperm are stored and mature. The vas deferens transports the sperm from the epididymis through the prostate, after which the vas deferens becomes the ejaculatory duct. Here, fluids from the prostate and seminal vesicles (small sacs that hold semen) combine with the sperm to form semen, a thick, yellowish-white fluid. The average discharge of semen, called ejaculate, contains approximately 300 million sperm.

There are two periods of marked sexual differentiation in human life. The first occurs prenatally and the second occurs at puberty. Although adult women and men may differ greatly in genital appearance and secondary sexual characteristics, they are almost identical during prenatal development. When an egg and a sperm unite during fertilization, they each bring to the new cell half the number of chromosomes (threadlike structures that contains genetic material) presented in other cells. From fertilization through about the first six weeks of development, male and female embryos differ only in the pair of sex chromosomes they have in each cell—two X chromosomes (XX) in females and one X and one Y chromosome (XY) in males. At this stage, both male and female embryos have undifferentiated gonads (ovaries or testes), two sets of ducts (one set capable of developing into male internal organs and the other into female organs), and undifferentiated external genital folds and swellings.

About six weeks after conception, if a Y chromosome is present in the embryo's cells (as it is in normal males), a gene on the chromosome directs the undifferentiated gonads to become testes. If the Y chromosome is not present (as in normal females), the undifferentiated gonads will become ovaries.

If the gonads become testes, they begin to produce androgens (male hormones, primarily testosterone) by about eight weeks after conception. These androgens stimulate development of the one set of the genital ducts into the epididymis, vas deferens, and ejaculatory duct. The presence of androgens also stimulates development of the penis and the scrotum. The testes later descend into the scrotum. Males also produce a substance that inhibits the development of the second set of ducts into female organs. In the absence of such hormonal stimulation, female structures develop.

Prenatal hormones also play a role in the sexual differentiation of the brain. For example, prenatal hormones direct the development of sex differences in some cells and the neural pathways in the hypothalamus (the part of the brain that controls the endocrine system). Beginning at puberty, based on prenatal sexual differentiation, the hypothalamus directs either the cyclic secretion of sex hormones that controls the female menstrual cycle or the relatively continuous production of male sex hormones. Other brain differences may be related to differences in sexual and aggressive behaviour or in cognitive and perceptual characteristics. Most of the research on sexual differentiation of the brain has been performed with animals or with biassed human samples, and there is much debate about the nature and behavioural relevance of these differences in humans.

In animals, the sex of an individual is generally determined at the time of fertilization by the sperm cell. If a sperm cell carrying an X chromosome fertilizes the egg, the offspring will be female (XX); if a sperm cell carrying a Y chromosome fertilizes the egg, the offspring will be male (XY). The term primary sexual characteristics denotes the kind of gamete the gonad produces: The ovary produces egg cells in the female, and the testis produces sperm cells in the male. The term secondary sexual characteristics denotes all other sexual distinctions that play indirect roles in uniting sperm and eggs. Secondary sexual characteristics include everything from the specialized male and female features of the genital tract, to the brilliant plumage of male birds or facial hair of humans, to behavioural features such as courtship.

Generally, the more highly evolved the species, the more elaborate are its secondary sexual characteristics. At the time the eggs of starfish ripen, the male merely releases great quantities of sperm cells into the ocean water, and a tiny but sufficient number of them find and penetrate distant eggs. Frogs and toads are drawn to mates by calls, and they spawn in water; the male makes cloacal contact with the female and releases sperm externally, simultaneously with the eggs. Terrestrial animals, especially mammals, which do not have an environment of water through which sperm can propel itself, rely on herding and flocking, courtship, competition among males, and more specialized genitalia including an erectile penis, fallopian tubes, and a uterus in which eggs are fertilized and develop internally.

In mammals, the hormones that influence sexual differentiation and development are androgens (mainly testosterone), which stimulate later development of the ovary. In the sexually undifferentiated embryo, testosterone stimulates the development of the Wolffian duct system, the forerunner of the male genital tract. Later, testosterone, along with gonadotropins released by the pituitary gland, stimulates spermatogenesis. The Müllerian duct system, the forerunner of the female genital tract in the female embryo, probably differentiates spontaneously without hormonal stimuli. After female sex is well defined, estradiol, produced in the ovaries and the placenta, plays a major role in the development and the functioning of the female reproductive tract.

Within the cytoplasm of all prokaryotes is deoxyribonucleic acid (DNA), a complex molecule in the form of a double helix, a shape similar to a spiral staircase. The DNA is about 1,000 times the length of the cell, and to fit inside, it repeatedly twists and folds to form a compact structure called a chromosome. The chromosome in prokaryotes is circular, and is located in a region of the cell called the nucleoid. Often, smaller chromosomes called Plasmids are located in the cytoplasm. The DNA is divided into units called genes, just like a long train is divided into separate cars. Depending on the species, the DNA contains several hundred or even thousands of genes. Typically, one gene contains coded instructions for building all or part of a single protein. Enzymes, which are specialized proteins, determine virtually all the biochemical reactions that support and sustain the cell.

The manufacture of ribosomes requires that the components of ribosomes—ribonucleic acid (RNA) and protein—be synthesized and brought together for assembly. The ribosomes of eukaryotic cells contain four strands of RNA and from 70 to 80 proteins. Using genes that reside on regions of chromosomes located in the nucleolus, three of the four ribosomal RNA strands are synthesized in the centre of the nucleolus. The fourth RNA strand is synthesized outside of the nucleolus, using genes at a different location. The fourth strand is then transported into the nucleolus to participate in ribosome assembly.

The genetic information for ribosomal proteins, found in the nucleus, is copied, or transcribed, into special chemical messengers called messenger RNA (mRNA), a different type of RNA than ribosomal RNA. The mRNA travels out of the nucleus into the cell's cytoplasm where its information is transferred, or translated, into the ribosomal proteins. The newly created proteins enter the nucleolus and bind with the four ribosomal RNA strands to create two ribosomal structures: the large and small subunits. These two subunits leave the nucleus and enter the cytoplasm. When protein synthesis is initiated, the two subunits merge to form the completed ribosome.

The nucleolus creates the two subunits for a single ribosome in about one hour. Thousands of subunits are manufactured by each nucleolus simultaneously, however, since several hundred to several thousand copies of the ribosomal RNA genes are present in the nucleolus. Before a cell divides, the nucleolus assembles about ten million ribosomal subunits, necessary for the large-scale protein production that occurs in cell division.

The nuclear envelope is attached to a network of membrane-enclosed tubules that extends throughout the cell called the endoplasmic reticulum. The nuclear envelope is perforated by many holes, called nuclear pores, that permit the movement of selected molecules between the nucleus and the rest of the cell, while blocking the passage of other molecules.

The nucleus contains the nucleolus, which manufactures protein-producing structures called ribosomes. Genetic information in the form of deoxyribonucleic acid (DNA) is stored in threadlike, tangled structures called chromatin within the nucleus. During the process of cell division known as mitosis, in which the nucleus divides, the chromatin condense into several distinct structures called chromosomes. Each time the cell divides, the heredity information carried in the chromosomes is passed to the two newly formed cells.

The DNA in the nucleus also contains the instructions for regulating the amount and types of proteins made by the cell. These instructions are copied, or transcribed, into a type of ribonucleic acid (RNA) called messenger RNA (mRNA). The mRNA is transported from the nucleus to ribosomes, where proteins are assembled.

DNA Fingerprinting, method of identification that compares fragments of deoxyribonucleic acid (DNA) It is sometimes called

DNA typing. DNA is the genetic material found within the cell nuclei of all living things. In mammals the strands of DNA are grouped into structures called chromosomes. With the exception of identical twins, the complete DNA of each individual is unique.

A DNA fingerprint is constructed by first extracting a DNA sample from body tissue or fluid such as hair, blood, or saliva. The sample is then segmented using enzymes, and the segments are arranged by size using a process called electrophoresis. The segments are marked with probes and exposed on X-ray film, where they form a characteristic pattern of black bars—the DNA fingerprint. If the DNA fingerprints produced from two different samples match, the two samples probably came from the same person.

DNA fingerprinting was first developed as an identification technique in 1985. Originally used to detect the presence of genetic diseases, DNA fingerprinting soon came to be used in criminal investigations and forensic science. The first criminal conviction based on DNA evidence in the United States occurred in 1988. In criminal investigations, DNA fingerprints derived from evidence collected at the crime scene are compared to the DNA fingerprints of suspects. The DNA evidence can implicate or exonerate a suspect.

Generally, courts have accepted the reliability of DNA testing and admitted DNA test results into evidence. However, DNA fingerprinting is controversial in a number of areas: the accuracy of the results, the cost of testing, and the possible misuse of the technique.

The accuracy of DNA fingerprinting has been challenged for several reasons. First, because DNA segments rather than complete DNA strands are "fingerprinted," a DNA fingerprint may not be unique; large-scale research to confirm the uniqueness of DNA fingerprinting test results has not been conducted. In addition, DNA fingerprinting is often performed in private laboratories that may not follow uniform testing standards and quality controls. Also, since human beings must interpret the test, human error could lead to false results. DNA fingerprinting is expensive. Suspects who are unable to provide their own DNA experts may not be able to adequately defend themselves against charges based on DNA evidence.

In the United States, the Federal Bureau of Investigation (FBI) has created a national database of genetic information called the National DNA Index System. The database contains DNA obtained from convicted criminals and from evidence found at crime scenes. Some experts fear that this database might be used for unauthorized purposes, such as identifying individuals with stigmatizing illnesses such as acquired immunodeficiency syndrome (AIDS).

DNA Fingerprinting, method of identification that compares fragments of deoxyribonucleic acid (DNA) It is sometimes called DNA typing. DNA is the genetic material found within the cell nuclei of all living things. In mammals the strands of DNA are grouped into structures called chromosomes. With the exception of identical twins, the complete DNA of each individual is unique.

A DNA fingerprint is constructed by first extracting a DNA sample from body tissue or fluid such as hair, blood, or saliva. The sample is then segmented using enzymes, and the segments are arranged by size using a process called electrophoresis. The segments are marked with probes and exposed on X-ray film, where they form a characteristic pattern of black bars—the DNA fingerprint. If the DNA fingerprints produced from two different samples match, the two samples probably came from the same person.

DNA fingerprinting was first developed as an identification technique in 1985. Originally used to detect the presence of genetic diseases, DNA fingerprinting soon came to be used in criminal investigations and forensic science. The first criminal conviction based on DNA evidence in the United States occurred in 1988. In criminal investigations, DNA fingerprints derived from evidence collected at the crime scene are compared to the DNA fingerprints of suspects. The DNA evidence can implicate or exonerate a suspect.

Generally, courts have accepted the reliability of DNA testing and admitted DNA test results into evidence. However, DNA fingerprinting is controversial in a number of areas: the accuracy of the results, the cost of testing, and the possible misuse of the technique.

The accuracy of DNA fingerprinting has been challenged for several reasons. First, because DNA segments rather than complete DNA strands are "fingerprinted," a DNA fingerprint may not be unique; large-scale research to confirm the uniqueness of DNA fingerprinting test results has not been conducted. In addition, DNA fingerprinting is often performed in private laboratories that may not follow uniform testing standards and quality controls. Also, since human beings must interpret the test, human error could lead to false results. DNA fingerprinting is expensive. Suspects who are unable to provide their own DNA experts may not be able to adequately defend themselves against charges based on DNA evidence.

In the United States, the Federal Bureau of Investigation (FBI) has created a national database of genetic information called the National DNA Index System. The database contains DNA obtained from convicted criminals and from evidence found at crime scenes. Some experts fear that this database might be used for unauthorized purposes, such as identifying individuals with stigmatizing illnesses such as acquired immunodeficiency syndrome (AIDS).

Ribonucleic Acid (RNA), genetic material of certain viruses (RNA viruses) and, in cellular organisms, the molecule that directs the middle steps of protein production. In RNA viruses, the RNA directs two processes—protein synthesis (production of the virus's protein coat) and replication (the process by which RNA copies itself). In cellular organisms, another type of genetic material, called deoxyribonucleic acid (DNA), carries the information that determines protein structure. But DNA cannot act alone and relies upon RNA to transfer this crucial information during protein synthesis (production of the proteins needed by the cell for its activities and development).

Like DNA, RNA consists of a chain of chemical compounds called nucleotides. Each nucleotide is made up of a sugar molecule called ribose, a phosphate group, and one of four different nitrogen-containing compounds called bases. The four bases are adenine, guanine, uracil, and cytosine. These components are joined together in the same manner as in a deoxyribonucleic acid (DNA) molecule. RNA differs chemically from DNA in two ways: The RNA sugar molecule contains an oxygen atom not found in DNA, and RNA contains the base uracil in the place of the base thymine in DNA.

In cellular organisms, RNA is a single-stranded polynucleotide chain, a strand of many nucleotides linked together. There are three types of RNA. Ribosomal RNA (rRNA) is found in the cell's ribosomes, the specialized structures that are the sites of protein synthesis. Transfer RNA (tRNA) carries amino acids to the ribosomes for incorporation into a protein. Messenger RNA (mRNA) carries the genetic blueprint copied from the sequence of bases in a cell's DNA. This blueprint specifies the sequence of amino acids in a protein. All three types of RNA are formed as needed, using specific sections of the cell's DNA as templates.

Some RNA viruses have double-stranded RNA—that is, their RNA molecules consist of two parallel polynucleotide chains. The base of each RNA nucleotide in one chain pairs with a complementary base in the second chain—that is, adenine pairs with uracil, and guanine pairs with cytosine. For these viruses, the process of RNA replication in a host cell follows the same pattern as that of DNA replication, a method of replication called semi-conservative replication. In semi-conservative replication, each newly formed double-stranded RNA molecule contains one polynucleotide chain from the parent RNA molecule, and one complementary chain formed through the process of base pairing. The Colorado tick fever virus, which causes mild respiratory infections, is a double stranded RNA virus.

There are two types of single-stranded RNA viruses. After entering a host cell, one type, polio virus, becomes double-stranded by making an RNA strand complementary to its own. During replication, although the two strands separate, only the recently formed strand attracts nucleotides with complementary bases. Therefore, the polynucleotide chain that is produced as a result of replication is exactly the same as the original RNA chain.

The other type of single-stranded RNA viruses, called retroviruses, include the human immunodeficiency virus (HIV), which causes AIDS, and other viruses that cause tumours. After entering a host cell, a retrovirus makes a DNA strand complementary to its own RNA strand using the host's DNA nucleotides. This new DNA strand then replicates and forms a double helix that becomes incorporated into the host cell's chromosomes, where it is replicated along with the host DNA. While in a host cell, the RNA-derived viral DNA produces single-stranded RNA viruses that then leave the host cell and enter other cells, where the replication process is repeated.

In 1981, American biochemist Thomas Cech discovered that certain RNA molecules appear to act as enzymes, molecules that speed up, or catalyze, some reactions inside cells. Until this discovery biologists thought that all enzymes were proteins. Like other enzymes, these RNA catalysts, called ribozymes, show great specificity with respect to the reactions they speed up. The discovery of ribozymes added to the evidence that RNA, not DNA, was the earliest genetic material. Many scientists think that the earliest genetic molecule was simple in structure and capable of enzymatic activity. Furthermore, the molecule would necessarily exist in all organisms. The enzyme ribonuclease-P, which exists in all organisms, is made of protein and a form of RNA that has enzymatic activity. Based on this evidence, some scientists suspect that the RNA portion of ribonuclease-P may be the modern equivalent of the earliest genetic molecule, the molecule that first enabled replication to occur in primitive cells.

Nucleic acids are complex molecules produced by living cells and are essential to all living organisms. These acids govern the body's development and specific characteristics by providing hereditary information and triggering the production of proteins within the body. This computer-generated model shows two strands of deoxyribonucleic acid (DNA) and the double-helical structure typical of this class of nucleic acids.

Nucleic Acids, extremely complex molecules produced by living cells and viruses. Their name comes from their initial isolation from the nuclei of living cells. Certain nucleic acids, however, are found not in the cell nucleus but in cell cytoplasm. Nucleic acids have at least two functions: to pass on hereditary characteristics from one generation to the next, and to trigger the manufacture of specific proteins. How nucleic acids accomplish these functions is the object of some of the most intense and promising research currently under way. The nucleic acids are the fundamental substances of living things, believed by researchers to have first been formed about 3 billion years ago, when the most elementary forms of life began on earth. The origin of the so-called genetic code they carry has been accepted by researchers as being very close in time to the origin of life itself. Biochemists have succeeded in deciphering the code, that is, determining how the sequence of nucleic acids dictates the structure of proteins.

The two classes of nucleic acids are the deoxyribonucleic acids (DNA) and the ribonucleic acids (RNA). The backbones of both DNA and RNA molecules are shaped like helical strands. Their molecular weights are in the millions. To the backbones are connected a great number of smaller molecules (side groups) of four different types. The sequence of these molecules on the strand determines the code of the particular nucleic acid. This code, in turn, signals the cell how to reproduce either a duplicate of itself or the proteins it requires for survival.

All living cells contain the genetic material DNA. The cells of bacteria may have but one strand of DNA, but such a strand contains all the information needed by the cell in order to reproduce an identical offspring. The cells of mammals contain scores of DNA strands grouped together in chromosomes. In short, the structure of a DNA molecule or combination of DNA molecules determines the shape, form, and function of the offspring. Some viruses, called retroviruses, contain only RNA rather than DNA, but viruses in themselves are generally not considered true living organisms.

The pioneering research that revealed the general structure of DNA was performed by the British biophysicists Francis Crick and Maurice Wilkins and by the American biochemist James Dewey Watson. Using an X-ray diffraction picture of the DNA molecule obtained by Wilkins in 1951, Crick and Watson were able to construct a model of the DNA molecule that was completed in 1953. For their work, the three scientists received the 1962 Nobel Prize in physiology or medicine. The American biochemist Arthur Kornberg synthesized DNA from "off-the-shelf" substances, for which he was awarded, with the American biochemist Severo Ochoa (for research on RNA), the 1959 Nobel Prize in physiology or medicine. The DNA that he synthesized, although structurally similar to natural DNA, was not biologically active. In 1967, however, Kornberg and a team of researchers at Stanford University succeeded in producing biologically active DNA from relatively simple chemicals.

Certain kinds of RNA have a slightly different function from that of DNA. They take part in the actual synthesis of the proteins a cell produces. This is of particular interest to virologists because many viruses reproduce by "forcing" the host cells to manufacture more viruses. The virus injects its own RNA into the host cell, and the host cell obeys the code of the invading RNA rather than that of its own. Thus the cell produces proteins that are, in fact, viruses instead of the proteins required for cell function. The host cell is destroyed, and the newly formed viruses are free to inject their RNA into other host cells.

The structure of two types of RNA and their function in protein production have been determined, one type by a team of Cornell University and US Department of Agriculture investigators led by Robert W. Holey of Cornell, and the other type by James T. Madison and George A. Everett of the Department of Agriculture. Important research into the interpretation of the genetic code and its role in protein synthesis was also performed by the Indian-born American chemist Har Gobind Khorana at the University of Wisconsin Enzyme Institute and the American biochemist Marshall W. Nirenberg of the National Heart Institute. In 1970 Khorana achieved the first complete synthesis of a gene and repeated his feat in 1973. Since then, one type of RNA has been synthesized. Also, in the early 1980s, American biochemists Thomas Robert Cech and Sidney Altman independently proved that certain types of RNA, called ribozymes, can function as true catalysts

Poliomyelitis, infectious viral disease that sometimes results in paralysis. The infection chiefly affects children and young adults and is caused by any one of three related viruses called polio viruses. In more than 95 percent of cases, the infection may pass without creating severe or even noticeable illness because the body's immune system neutralizes the invading virus and protects against future infection. In a small percentage of cases the virus penetrates to the central nervous system, infecting cells that control muscle function. Such infection can result in permanent paralysis of limbs. In its most perilous form, the infection attacks the brain, creating complications that sometimes result in death.

The term poliomyelitis derives from Greek words referring to inflammation (its) of the gray (polios) matter of the spinal cord (myelos). The shortened term polio is commonly used by the public and medical professionals, and the disease has also been referred to as infantile paralysis.

While still a health threat in many parts of the world, polio also represents one of the greatest medical success stories of the 20th century. The number of polio cases found worldwide today constitutes a 90 percent reduction from the number of cases reported in the late 1980s. Most health experts credit this achievement to a mass vaccination program called the Global Polio Eradication Initiative that WHO initiated in 1988 to eradicate polio worldwide by the year 2005.

In the United States and Canada, polio has been effectively eliminated, with fewer than ten cases reported in each country per year. This statistic contrasts strikingly with those from the first half of the 20th century, when epidemic polio was one of the most dreaded and feared diseases in North America. The first large-scale outbreak in the United States occurred in 1916, when over 37,000 cases were reported in 26 states, resulting in 6,000 deaths. Each year thereafter the number of polio cases in the United States averaged about 38,000 per year, including about 21,000 paralytic cases each year. In Canada the epidemic peaked in 1953, resulting in one of the highest national polio rates ever recorded in the world.

Fearing infection during epidemics in the first half of the 20th century, some people avoided beaches, public pools, theatres, fairs—any place of public gathering. Occasionally schools were closed until epidemics subsided. In response to the public's fear of this disease, in 1938 President Franklin Delano Roosevelt (who had himself lost the use of both legs to polio) founded the National Foundation for Infantile Paralysis. Now known as the March of Dimes Birth Defects Foundation, the organization raised millions of dollars for polio research and the support of victims.

The discovery in the 1950s of vaccines that protect against poliovirus infection eventually led to successful polio vaccination programs in North America, Latin America, and Europe. By the early 1990s, WHO declared the western hemisphere free of polio. But the struggle to eradicate polio continues in many developing nations. Furthermore, health officials stress that vaccination programs must be maintained in areas considered polio free. They warn that the virus could easily become dangerous again in populations of children who have not acquired immunity, the body's ability to resist infection from the polio virus. This danger was chillingly demonstrated in 1979 when an outbreak of paralytic polio erupted among unvaccinated members of an Amish sect in Pennsylvania and Maryland.

The three types of poliovirus belong to the virus family known as picornaviruses. This name derives from a combination of the words pico, meaning "small," and RNA, indicating that the viruses contain a core of the genetic material known as ribonucleic acid, or RNA. Three types of poliovirus have been identified: Type 1 (also known as Brunhilde), Type 2 (Lansing), and Type 3 (Leon). Type 1 is the most common form and the one most closely associated with polio's more severe, paralytic progression. A person who develops immunity from exposure to one poliovirus type will not have immunity against the other polio viruses.

Poliovirus typically enters the body through the mouth and multiplies in the tonsils and lymph nodes of the upper respiratory tract. Infection proceeds from the mouth into the gastrointestinal tract through the stomach to the intestines. The virus multiplies in the intestines and is shed from the body in faeces, often resulting in further infections. For example, a parent can become infected by an infant during diaper changes, or improper waste disposal can lead to contamination of a water supply. These infections, in turn, will spread the virus more widely.

Large quantities of poliovirus multiply in intestinal tissue known as Weyer's patches, where cells of the body's lymphatic system are concentrated. Passage of the virus into the body's lymphatic system stimulates the production of antibodies. These specialized immune-system defenders, in time, will destroy the viral intruder. From the lymphatic system, the virus typically invades the bloodstream.

Retrovirus, of any virus belonging to the family Retroviridae, whose members share a unique method of replicating (copying) themselves when they infect living cells. Retroviruses store their genetic information in molecules of ribonucleic acid (RNA). However, unlike other RNA viruses, retroviruses use RNA as a template (master pattern) for forming deoxyribonucleic acid (DNA), the genetic material that puts viral replication instructions into effect. This process, called reverse transcription, is the exact opposite of the normal flow of genetic information in living things in which DNA serves as the template for RNA formation.

Retroviruses affect a wide range of animals, although the best-known types are those that target vertebrates. Some retroviruses are harmless, but many can cause malignant transformation—a genetic change that makes healthy cells cancerous. Disease-forming retroviruses can cause diseases such as leukemia (cancer of the blood) in mammals and malignant tumours and other disorders in birds. From a human perspective, by far the most significant retroviruses are a small group called lentiviruses, which include human immunodeficiency virus (HIV), the virus that causes acquired immunodeficiency syndrome (AIDS).

Deoxyribonucleic Acid (DNA), genetic material of all cellular organisms and most viruses. DNA carries the information needed to direct protein synthesis and replication. Protein synthesis is the production of the proteins needed by the cell or virus for its activities and development. Replication is the process by which DNA copies itself for each descendant cell or virus, passing on the information needed for protein synthesis. In most cellular organisms, DNA is organized on chromosomes located in the nucleus of the cell.

The deoxyribonucleic acid (DNA) molecule is the genetic blueprint for each cell and ultimately the blueprint that determines every characteristic of a living organism. In 1953 American biochemist James Watson, left, and British biophysicist Francis Crick, right, described the structure of the DNA molecule as a double helix, somewhat like a spiral staircase with many individual steps. Their work was aided by X-ray diffraction pictures of the DNA molecule taken by British biophysicist Maurice Wilkins and British physical chemist Rosalind Franklin. In 1962 Crick, Watson, and Wilkins received the Nobel Prize for their pioneering work on the structure of the DNA molecule.

A molecule of DNA consists of two chains, strands composed of a large number of chemical compounds, called nucleotides, linked together to form a chain. These chains are arranged like a ladder that has been twisted into the shape of a winding staircase, called a double helix. Each nucleotide consists of three units: a sugar molecule called deoxyribose, a phosphate group, and one of four different nitrogen-containing compounds called bases. The four bases are adenine (A), guanine (G), thymine (T), and cytosine ©. The deoxyribose molecule occupies the centre position in the nucleotide, flanked by a phosphate group on one side and a base on the other. The phosphate group of each nucleotide is also linked to the deoxyribose of the adjacent nucleotide in the chain. These linked deoxyribose-phosphate subunits form the parallel side rails of the ladder. The bases face inward toward each other, forming the rungs of the ladder.

The nucleotides in one DNA strand have a specific association with the corresponding nucleotides in the other DNA strand. Because of the chemical affinity of the bases, nucleotides containing adenine are always paired with nucleotides containing thymine, and nucleotides containing cytosine are always paired with nucleotides containing guanine. The complementary bases are joined to each other by weak chemical bonds called hydrogen bonds.

In 1953 American biochemist James D. Watson and British biophysicist Francis Crick published the first description of the structure of DNA. Their model proved to be so important for the understanding of protein synthesis, DNA replication, and mutation that they were awarded the 1962 Nobel Prize for physiology or medicine for their work.

One of a cell's most important tasks is the synthesis of proteins, giant molecules that underlie most cellular functions. The hereditary material known as deoxyribonucleic acid (DNA), found within the nucleus of a cell, orchestrates a series of steps resulting in the manufacture of proteins tailored to meet the needs for a cell's development and growth.

DNA carries the instructions for the production of proteins. A protein is composed of smaller molecules called amino acids, and the structure and function of the protein is determined by the sequence of its amino acids. The sequence of amino acids, in turn, is determined by the sequence of nucleotide bases in the DNA. A sequence of three nucleotide bases, called a triplet, is the genetic code word, or codon, that specifies a particular amino acid. For instance, the triplet GAS (guanine, adenine, and cytosine) is the codon for the amino acid leucine, and the triplet CAG (cytosine, adenine, and guanine) is the codon for the amino acid valine. A protein consisting of 100 amino acids is thus encoded by a DNA segment consisting of 300 nucleotides. Of the two polynucleotide chains that form a DNA molecule, only one strand contains the information needed for the production of a given amino acid sequence. The other strand aids in replication.

Protein synthesis begins with the separation of a DNA molecule into two strands. In a process called transcription, a section of one strand acts as a template, or pattern, to produce a new strand called messenger RNA (mRNA). The mRNA leaves the cell nucleus and attaches to the ribosomes, specialized cellular structures that are the sites of protein synthesis. Amino acids are carried to the ribosomes by another type of RNA, called transfer RNA (tRNA). In a process called translation, the amino acids are linked together in a particular sequence, dictated by the mRNA, to form a protein.

A gene is a sequence of DNA nucleotides that specify the order of amino acids in a protein via an intermediary mRNA molecule. Substituting one DNA nucleotide with another containing a different base causes all descendant cells or viruses to have the altered nucleotide base sequence. As a result of the substitution, the sequence of amino acids in the resulting protein may also be changed. Such a change in a DNA molecule is called a mutation. Most mutations are the result of errors in the replication process. Exposure of a cell or virus to radiation or to certain chemicals increases the likelihood of mutations.

In most cellular organisms, replication of a DNA molecule takes place in the cell nucleus and occurs just before the cell divides. Replication begins with the separation of the two polynucleotide chains, each of which then acts as a template for the assembly of a new complementary chain. As the old chains separate, each nucleotide in the two chains attracts a complementary nucleotide that has been formed earlier by the cell. The nucleotides are joined to one another by hydrogen bonds to form the rungs of a new DNA molecule. As the complementary nucleotides are fitted into place, an enzyme called DNA polymerase links them together by bonding the phosphate group of one nucleotide to the sugar molecule of the adjacent nucleotide, forming the side rail of the new DNA molecule. This process continues until a new polynucleotide chain has been formed alongside the old one, forming a new double-helix molecule.

Several tools and procedures facilitate are used by scientists for the study and manipulation of DNA. Specialized enzymes, called restriction enzymes, found in bacteria act like molecular scissors to cut the phosphate backbones of DNA molecules at specific base sequences. Strands of DNA that have been cut with restriction enzymes are left with single-stranded tails that are called sticky ends, because they can easily realign with tails from certain other DNA fragments. Scientists take advantage of restriction enzymes and the sticky ends generated by these enzymes to carry out recombinant DNA technology, or genetic engineering. This technology involves removing a specific gene from one organism and inserting the gene into another organism.

Another tool for working with DNA is a procedure called polymerase chain reaction (PCR). This procedure uses the enzyme DNA polymerase to make copies of DNA strands in a process that mimics the way in which DNA replicates naturally within cells. Scientists use PCR to obtain vast numbers of copies of a given segment of DNA.

DNA fingerprinting, also called DNA typing, makes it possible to compare samples of DNA from various sources in a manner that is analogous to the comparison of fingerprints. In this procedure, scientists use restriction enzymes to cleave a sample of DNA into an assortment of fragments. Solutions containing these fragments are placed at the surface of a gel to which an electric current is applied. The electric current causes the DNA fragments to move through the gel. Because smaller fragments move more quickly than larger ones, this process, called electrophoresis, separates the fragments according to their size. The fragments are then marked with probes and exposed on X-ray film, where they form the DNA fingerprint—a pattern of characteristic black bars that is unique for each type of DNA.

A procedure called DNA sequencing makes it possible to determine the precise order, or sequence, of nucleotide bases within a fragment of DNA. Most versions of DNA sequencing use a technique called primer extension, developed by British molecular biologist Frederick Sanger. In primer extension, specific pieces of DNA are replicated and modified, so that each DNA segment ends in a fluorescent form of one of the four nucleotide bases. Modern DNA sequencers, pioneered by American molecular biologist Leroy Hood, incorporate both lasers and computers. Scientists have completely sequenced the genetic material of several microorganisms, including the bacterium Escherichia coli. In 1998, scientists achieved the milestone of sequencing the complete genome of a multicellular organism—a roundworm identified as Caenorhabditis elegans. The Human Genome Project, a collaboration of international research has been correlated to determine the sequence of all of the three billion nucleotide base pairs that make up the human genetic material.

An instrument called an atomic force microscope enables scientists to manipulate the three-dimensional structure of DNA molecules. This microscope involves laser beams that act like tweezers—attaching to the ends of a DNA molecule and pulling on them. By manipulating these laser beams, scientists can stretch, or uncoil, fragments of DNA. This work is helping reveal how DNA changes its three-dimensional shape as it interacts with enzymes.

In the late 20th century scientists devised methods of altering the genetic makeup of food crops. Humans have modified crops for thousands of years to increase yield and resistance to pests, but changes on the molecular level have caused some people to wonder if science has gone too far. Recent studies suggest that some genetically altered crops may pose health risks and other dangers. Proponents of genetically modified food, however, point to increased yields and health benefits.

Research into DNA has had a significant impact on medicine. Through recombinant DNA technology, scientists can modify microorganisms so that they become so-called factories that produce large quantities of medically useful drugs. This technology is used to produce insulin, which is a drug used by diabetics, and interferon, which is used by some cancer patients. Studies of human DNA are revealing genes that are associated with specific diseases, such as cystic fibrosis and breast cancer. This information is helping physicians to diagnose various diseases, and it may lead to new treatments. For example, physicians are using a technology called chimeraplasty, which involves a synthetic molecule containing both DNA and RNA strands, in an effort to develop a treatment for a form of hemophilia.

Forensic science uses techniques developed in DNA research to identify individuals who have committed crimes. DNA from semen, skin, or blood taken from the crime scene can be compared with the DNA of a suspect, and the results can be used in court as evidence.

In a landmark intersection of science and fiction, cloning leapt from the world's imagination to its front page in February 1997. It arrived in the innocent form of a sheep named Dolly: the first exact genetic duplicate of an adult mammal due to genetic engineering. Scottish scientists had created Dolly from deoxyribonucleic acid (DNA)—the basic unit of heredity—taken from a single adult sheep cell. The accomplishment threw open the door to profound ethical as well as scientific controversy over the potential uses and abuses of cloning. "However the debate is resolved," wrote Los Angeles Times science reporter Thomas H. Maugh II, "the genie is irretrievably out of the bottle."

DNA has helped taxonomists determine evolutionary relationships among animals, plants, and other life forms. Closely related species have more similar DNA than do species that are distantly related. One surprising finding to emerge from DNA studies is that vultures of the Americas are more closely related to storks than to the vultures of Europe, Asia, or Africa.

Techniques of DNA manipulation are used in farming, in the form of genetic engineering and biotechnology. Strains of crop plants to which genes have been transferred may produce higher yields and may be more resistant to insects. Cattle have been similarly treated to increase milk and beef production, as have hogs, to yield more meat with less fat.

Despite the many benefits offered by DNA technology, some critics argue that its development should be monitored closely. One fear raised by such critics is that DNA fingerprinting could provide a means for employers to discriminate against members of various ethnic groups. Critics also fear that studies of people's DNA could permit insurance companies to deny health insurance to those people at risk for developing certain diseases. The potential use of DNA technology to alter the genes of embryos is a particularly controversial issue.

The use of DNA technology in agriculture has also sparked controversy. Some people question the safety, desirability, and ecological impact of genetically altered crop plants. In addition, animal rights groups have protested against the genetic engineering of farm animals.

Despite these and other areas of disagreement, many people agree that DNA technology offers a mixture of benefits and potential hazards. Many experts also agree that an informed public can scrutinize and help to assure that DNA technology is used wisely.

Drugs in the class known as nitrosoureas interfere with DNA repair. They are primarily used in treating brain cancer. Another group of chemotherapy drugs, referred to as antimetabolites, interferes with cell replication by preventing the cell from assembling the building blocks of DNA and ribonucleic acid (RNA), the molecule that directs protein synthesis. Antimetabolites are used to treat breast cancer, ovarian cancer, and cancers of the gastrointestinal tract.

Mitotic inhibitors constitute another class of chemotherapeutic agents. As their name implies, these drugs interfere with mitosis, the part of the cell cycle when the cell actually divides. These agents are used to treat lung cancer, breast cancer, and testicular cancer. Other groupings of cancer drugs, known as antitumor antibiotics, treat a variety of cancers, including leukemias. These drugs work by inhibiting the synthesis of RNA.

In his early work beginning in the mid-1950s, Brenner Sydney studied how deoxyribonucleic acid (DNA), the genetic material of living things, instructs cells to make proteins. Working with French biologist and future Nobel laureate François Jacob and other scientists, in 1961 Brenner identified messenger ribonucleic acid (mRNA), a molecule that acts as an intermediary between DNA and protein production. In that same year Brenner and British biophysicist Francis Crick, who won a Nobel Prize in 1962, identified codons, as groups of three nucleotides (the structural building blocks of DNA and RNA). Brenner and Crick showed that codons provide instructions for the creation of all 20 amino acids that form the foundation of proteins.

The story of how cells evolved remains an open and actively investigated question in science. The combined expertise of physicists, geologists, chemists, and evolutionary biologists has been required to shed light on the evolution of cells from the nonliving matter of early Earth. The planet formed about 4.5 billion years ago, and for millions of years, violent volcanic eruptions blasted substances such as carbon dioxide, nitrogen, water, and other small molecules into the air. These small molecules, bombarded by ultraviolet radiation and lightning from intense storms, collided to form the stable chemical bonds of larger molecules, such as amino acids and nucleotides—the building blocks of proteins and nucleic acids. Experiments indicate that these larger molecules form spontaneously under laboratory conditions that simulate the probable early environment of Earth.

Scientists speculate that rain may have carried these molecules into lakes to create a primordial soup—a breeding ground for the assembly of proteins, the nucleic acid RNA, and lipids. Some scientists postulate that these more complex molecules formed in hydrothermal vents rather than in lakes. Other scientists propose that these key substances may have reached Earth on meteorites from outer space. Regardless of the origin or environment, however, scientists do agree that proteins, nucleic acids, and lipids provided the raw materials for the first cells. In the laboratory, scientists have observed lipid molecules joining to form spheres that resemble a cell's plasma membrane. As a result of these observations, scientists postulate that millions of years of molecular collisions resulted in lipid spheres enclosing RNA, the simplest molecule capable of self-replication. These primitive aggregations would have been the ancestors of the first prokaryotic cells.

Fossil studies indicate that cyanobacteria, bacteria capable of photosynthesis, were among the earliest bacteria to evolve, an estimated 3.4 billion to 3.5 billion years ago. In the environment of the early Earth, there was no oxygen, and cyanobacteria probably used fermentation to produce ATP. Over the eons, cyanobacteria performed photosynthesis, which produces oxygen as a byproduct; the result was the gradual accumulation of oxygen in the atmosphere. The presence of oxygen set the stage for the evolution of bacteria that used oxygen in aerobic respiration, a more efficient ATP-producing process than fermentation. Some molecular studies of the evolution of genes in archaebacteria suggest that these organisms may have evolved in the hot waters of hydrothermal vents or hot springs slightly earlier than cyanobacteria, around 3.5 billion years ago. Like cyanobacteria, archaebacteria probably relied on fermentation to synthesize ATP.

Eukaryotic cells may have evolved from primitive prokaryotes about 2 billion years ago. One hypothesis suggests that some prokaryotic cells lost their cell walls, permitting the cell's plasma membrane to expand and fold. These folds, ultimately, may have given rise to separate compartments within the cell—the forerunners of the nucleus and other organelles now found in eukaryotic cells. Another key hypothesis is known as endosymbiosis. Molecular studies of the bacteria-like DNA and ribosomes in mitochondria and Chloroplasts indicate that mitochondrion and chloroplast ancestors were once free-living bacteria. Scientists propose that these free-living bacteria were engulfed and maintained by other prokaryotic cells for their ability to produce ATP efficiently and to provide a steady supply of glucose. Over generations, eukaryotic cells complete with mitochondria—the ancestors of animals—or with both mitochondria and chloroplasts—the ancestors of plants

Outside of a host cell, a virus is an inert particle. Once inside a cell, a virus can replicate many times, creating thousands of viruses that leave the cell to find host cells of their own. Viruses that cause disease do so by destroying or damaging cells as they leave them.

Like all viruses, human immunodeficiency virus (HIV) is comprised of only genetic material, a few proteins, and a protective envelope. Its genetic material, carried by single-stranded RNA molecules, contains all the information necessary to make more viruses. HIV cannot reproduce itself outside of a cell, but when

HIV invades a living cell, it turns the cell into a factory for making more HIV.HIV penetrates the cell membrane and releases its contents into the host cell.

Ribonucleic Acid (RNA), genetic material of certain viruses (RNA viruses) and, in cellular organisms, the molecule that directs the middle steps of protein production. In RNA viruses, the RNA directs two processes—protein synthesis (production of the virus's protein coat) and replication (the process by which RNA copies itself). In cellular organisms, another type of genetic material, called deoxyribonucleic acid (DNA), carries the information that determines protein structure. But DNA cannot act alone and relies upon RNA to transfer this crucial information during protein synthesis (production of the proteins needed by the cell for its activities and development).

Like DNA, RNA consists of a chain of chemical compounds called nucleotides. Each nucleotide is made up of a sugar molecule called ribose, a phosphate group, and one of four different nitrogen-containing compounds called bases. The four bases are adenine, guanine, uracil, and cytosine. These components are joined together in the same manner as in a deoxyribonucleic acid (DNA) molecule. RNA differs chemically from DNA in two ways: The RNA sugar molecule contains an oxygen atom not found in DNA, and RNA contains the base uracil in the place of the base thymine in DNA.

In cellular organisms, RNA is a single-stranded polynucleotide chain, a strand of many nucleotides linked together. There are three types of RNA. Ribosomal RNA (rRNA) is found in the cell's ribosomes, the specialized structures that are the sites of protein synthesis. Transfer RNA (tRNA) carries amino acids to the ribosomes for incorporation into a protein. Messenger RNA (mRNA) carries the genetic blueprint copied from the sequence of bases in a cell's DNA. This blueprint specifies the sequence of amino acids in a protein. All three types of RNA are formed as needed, using specific sections of the cell's DNA as templates.

Some RNA viruses have double-stranded RNA—that is, their RNA molecules consist of two parallel polynucleotide chains. The base of each RNA nucleotide in one chain pairs with a complementary base in the second chain—that is, adenine pairs with uracil, and guanine pairs with cytosine. For these viruses, the process of RNA replication in a host cell follows the same pattern as that of DNA replication, a method of replication called semi-conservative replication. In semi-conservative replication, each newly formed double-stranded RNA molecule contains one polynucleotide chain from the parent RNA molecule, and one complementary chain formed through the process of base pairing. The Colorado tick fever virus, which causes mild respiratory infections, of a double stranded RNA virus.

There are two types of single-stranded RNA viruses. After entering a host cell, one type, is a polio virus, becomes double-stranded by making an RNA strand complementary to its own. During replication, although the two strands separate, only the recently formed strand attracts nucleotides with complementary bases. Therefore, the polynucleotide chain that is produced as a result of replication is exactly the same as the original RNA chain.

The other type of single-stranded RNA virus, called retroviruses, include the human immunodeficiency virus (HIV), which causes AIDS, and other viruses that cause tumours. After entering a host cell, a retrovirus makes a DNA strand complementary to its own RNA strand using the host's DNA nucleotides. This new DNA strand then replicates and forms a double helix that becomes incorporated into the host cell's chromosomes, where it is replicated along with the host DNA. While in a host cell, the RNA-derived viral DNA produces single-stranded RNA viruses that then leave the host cell and enter other cells, where the replication process is repeated.

In 1981, American biochemist Thomas Cech discovered that certain RNA molecules appear to act as enzymes, molecules that speed up, or catalyze, some reactions inside cells. Until this discovery biologist thought that all enzymes were proteins. Like other enzymes, these RNA catalysts, called ribozymes, show great specificity with respect to the reactions they speed up. The discovery of ribozymes added to the evidence that RNA, not DNA, was the earliest genetic material. Many scientists think that the earliest genetic molecule was simple in structure and capable of enzymatic activity. Furthermore, the molecule would necessarily exist in all organisms. The enzyme ribonuclease-P, which exists in all organisms, is made of protein and a form of RNA that has enzymatic activity. Based on this evidence, some scientists suspect that the RNA portion of ribonuclease-P may be the modern equivalent of the earliest genetic molecule, the molecule that first enabled replication to occur in primitive cells.

Deoxyribonucleic acid (DNA), one of the nucleic acids, stores genetic information within cells, while enzymes are protein molecules that cause cellular reactions. RNA is the go-between, translating genetic information to protein by means of small molecules called transfer RNA (tRNA). While studying the formation of tRNA in 1978, Altman discovered an enzyme called ribonuclease P (RNase P), composed of both RNA and a protein. He noted that RNase P caused the splicing of tRNA molecules and assumed that the protein portion of the enzyme had caused this reaction. He then noted that the protein component acting alone did not splice the transfer RNA molecule. After isolating the RNA component (called M1 RNA) and repeating the experiment, Altman demonstrated that the M1 RNA had acted alone to cause the reaction. Because this process violated an absolute of molecular biology (that only proteins function as catalysts), Altman's findings were initially greeted with skepticism and indifference. But Thomas Robert Cech, working independently of Altman, documented a cellular reaction in which RNA acted as a self-catalyst. Cech called this self-acting RNA a ribozyme.

These discoveries astounded the scientific community. It was now possible to suggest that RNA, not proteins, may have served as the regulator in primitive cells when life was first formed. Since DNA cannot form without a catalyst, and proteins cannot act as a catalyst without DNA, it now appears that RNA serves both functions. Altman and Cech had basically provided a new theory as to how life develops.

Individual viruses, or virus particles, also called virions, contain genetic material, or genomes, in one of several forms. Unlike cellular organisms, in which the genes always are made up of DNA, viral genes may consist of either DNA or RNA. Like cell DNA, almost all viral DNA is double-stranded, and it can have either a circular or a linear arrangement. Almost all viral RNA is single-stranded; it is usually linear, and it may be either segmented (with different genes on different RNA molecules) or nonsegmented (with all genes on a single piece of RNA).

Nucleic acids are complex molecules produced by living cells and are essential to all living organisms. These acids govern the body's development and specific characteristics by providing hereditary information and triggering the production of proteins within the body. This computer-generated model shows two strands of deoxyribonucleic acid (DNA) and the double-helical structure typical of this class of nucleic acids.

One of a cell's most important tasks is the synthesis of proteins, giant molecules that underlie most cellular functions. The hereditary material known as deoxyribonucleic acid (DNA), found within the nucleus of a cell, orchestrates a series of steps resulting in the manufacture of proteins tailored to meet the needs for a cell's development and growth.

A Gene, is the basic unit of heredity found in the cells of all living organisms, from bacteria to humans. Genes determine the physical characteristics that an organism inherits, such as the shape of a tree's leaf, the markings on a cat's fur, and the colour of a human hair.

Genes are composed of segments of deoxyribonucleic acid (DNA), a molecule that forms the long, threadlike structures called chromosomes. The information encoded within the DNA structure of a gene directs the manufacture of proteins, molecular workhorses that carry out all life-supporting activities within a cell.

Chromosomes within a cell occur in matched pairs. Each chromosome contains many genes, and each gene is located at a particular site on the chromosome, known as the locus. Like chromosomes, genes typically occur in pairs. A gene found on one chromosome in a pair usually has the same locus as another gene in the other chromosome of the pair, and these two genes are called alleles. Alleles are alternate forms of the same gene. For example, a pea plant has one gene that determines height, but that gene appears in more than one form—the gene that produces a short plant is an allele of the gene that produces a tall plant.

The behaviour of alleles and how they influence inherited traits follow predictable patterns. Austrian monk Gregor Mendel first identified these patterns in the 1860

In organisms that use sexual reproduction, offspring inherit one-half of their genes from each parent and then mix the two sets of genes together. This produces new combinations of genes, so that each individual is unique but still possesses the same genes as its parents. As a result, sexual reproduction ensures that the basic characteristics of a particular species remain largely the same for generations. However, mutations, or alterations in DNA, occur constantly. They create variations in the genes that are inherited. Some mutations may be neutral, or silent, and do not affect the function of a protein. Occasionally a mutation may benefit or harm an organism and over the course of evolutionary time, these mutations serve the crucial role of providing organisms with previously nonexistent proteins. In this way, mutations are a driving force behind genetic diversity and the rise of new or more competitive species that are better able to adapt to changes, such as climate variations, depletion of food sources, or the emergence of new types of disease.

Geneticists are scientists who study the function and behaviour of genes. Since the 1970s geneticists have devised techniques, cumulatively known as genetic engineering, to alter or manipulate the DNA structure within genes. These techniques enable scientists to introduce one or more genes from one organism into a second organism. The second organism incorporates the new DNA into its own genetic material, thereby altering its own genetic characteristics by changing the types of proteins it can produce. In humans these techniques form the basis of gene therapy, a group of experimental procedures in which scientists try to substitute one or more healthy genes for defective ones in order to eliminate symptoms of disease.

Genetic engineering techniques have also enabled scientists to determine the chromosomal location and DNA structure of all the genes found within a variety of organisms. In April 2003 the Human Genome Project, a publicly funded consortium of academic scientists from around the world, identified the chromosomal locations and structure of the estimated 20,000 to 25,000 genes found within human cells. The genetic makeup of other organisms has also been identified, including that of the bacterium stems Escherichia coli, the yeast Saccharomyces cerevisiae, the roundworm Caenorhabditis elegans, and the fruit fly Drosophila melanogaster. Scientists hope to use this genetic information to develop life saving drugs for a variety of diseases, to improve agricultural crop yields, and to learn more about plant and animal physiology and evolutionary history.

American neurologist Stanley B. Prusiner was awarded the 1997 Nobel Prize in physiology or medicine for his discovery of a class of infectious proteins called prions. Prions are implicated in several degenerative brain diseases of mammals, including bovine spongiform encephalopathy, commonly known as mad cow disease.

Prion, shortened term for proteinaceous infectious particle, a small protein linked to certain rare, fatal brain diseases in cows, sheep, humans, and other mammals. If the prion is an infectious agent, it is the first infectious agent identified that does not contain the nucleic acids deoxyribonucleic acid (DNA) or ribonucleic acid (RNA). While the prion's role in causing disease is still controversial, its discovery has opened the door to alternative ideas about how infectious diseases may be transmitted.

American neurologist Stanley B. Prusiner was awarded the 1997 Nobel Prize in physiology or medicine for his discovery of a class of infectious proteins called prions. Prions are implicated in several degenerative brain diseases of mammals, including bovine spongiform encephalopathy, commonly known as mad cow disease.

Discovered by American neurologist Stanley B. Prusiner, prions are proteins with an abnormal shape, believed to be caused by a mutation to the gene that encodes for the protein. Normal proteins are found on the surfaces of nerve cells in the brain, white blood cells, muscle cells, and cells of many other tissues. The role of the normal protein is not yet understood, but the mystery of its structure has been solved. A hundred times smaller than the smallest virus, the normal protein is composed of 208 amino acids twisted into three long telephone cordlike coils known as helices. A floppy tail of 97 amino acids extends from the end of one of the helices. The abnormal protein is built of the same amino acids. However, instead of the coil shape, the abnormal protein is folded like the flat pleats of a partly opened accordion.

In the mid-1980s American neurologist Stanley Prusiner first proposed the existence of infectious agents that contain no genetic material and are made entirely of protein. Prusiner suggested that these particles—which he called prions—were responsible for neurodegenerative diseases, such as bovine spongiform encephalopathy (BSE), or "mad cow disease," in cows and Creutzfeldt-Jakob disease (CJD) in humans. He described his research on prions in a 1995 Scientific American article. In 1997 Prusiner was the sole recipient of the Nobel Prize in physiology or medicine "for his discovery of Prions—a new biological principle of infection." The award was unusual because it went to a single recipient and because Prusiner's findings still lack a scientific consensus. Some scientists believe a slow-acting virus may cause the spongiform encephalopathy diseases.

Some scientists think that the abnormal protein causes disease when it contacts the normal protein and triggers part of it to switch from the coiled to the pleated form. A chain reaction follows, resulting in a cluster of tangled, nonfunctional proteins called plaques. These plaques are found in the brains of animals that die from prion-related diseases. The plaques destroy the brain cells, resulting in one of the diseases collectively known as transmissible spongiform encephalopathies (TSEs).

TSEs cause inflammation and characteristic spongelike holes in the delicate membranes surrounding brain cells. This physical damage results in loss of coordination, dementia, and, eventually, death. Perhaps the best-known TSE is bovine spongiform encephalopathy (BSE), more popularly known as mad cow disease. BSE made headlines in 1996 when about a million cattle in the United Kingdom became infected with the disease. Most scientists believe the infection originally spread when cows contracted BSE after eating animal feed containing sheep's brains and other sheep byproducts infected with scrapie, a fatal spongiform disease affecting sheep and goats. Later, the epidemic spread when brains and other tissues from infected cattle were used in protein supplements distributed to cattle throughout Britain. By 2003, ingestion of the infected cow meat had caused about 150 people in Britain and Europe to develop an unusual form of Creutzfeldt-Jakob disease known as variant Creutzfeldt-Jakob disease (vCJD). Other TSEs include kuru, a rare disease contracted by natives of New Guinea who ate the infected brains of their dead relatives during ritual cannibalism, however.

www.ingramcontent.com/pod-product-compliance
Lightning Source LLC
Chambersburg PA
CBHW020426130626
46549CB00001B/1